Origins of Southern Radicalism

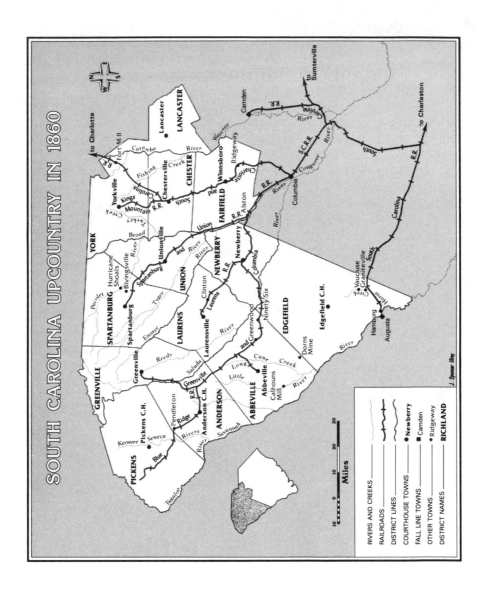

SOUTH CAROLINA UPCOUNTRY IN 1860

Legend:
- RIVERS AND CREEKS
- RAILROADS
- DISTRICT LINES
- COURTHOUSE TOWNS — ●Newberry
- FALL LINE TOWNS — ■Camden
- OTHER TOWNS — ●Ridgeway
- DISTRICT NAMES — **RICHLAND**

Miles
10 0 10 20 30

J. Spencer Ubey

Districts: LANCASTER, CHESTER, YORK, FAIRFIELD, SPARTANBURG, UNION, NEWBERRY, GREENVILLE, LAURENS, EDGEFIELD, PICKENS, ANDERSON, ABBEVILLE, RICHLAND

Towns: Lancaster, Fort Mill, Chesterville, Winnsboro, Ridgeway, Yorkville, Kings Mountain, Unionville, Spartanburg, Newberry, Clinton, Laurens, Columbia, Ninety Six, Greenwood, Edgefield C.H., Dorns Mine, Abbeville, Calhouns Mill, Pickens C.H., Anderson C.H., Pendleton, Seneca, Keowee, Blue Ridge, Greenville, Graniteville, Vaucluse, Hamburg, Augusta, Camden

Rivers/Creeks: Catawba River, Fishing Creek, Carolina River, Kings Creek, Turkey Creek, Broad River, Bivingsville, Hurricane Shoals, Pacolet, Tyger, Enoree, Reedy, Saluda, Little River, Long Cane Creek, Savannah River, Tugaloo, Keowee River, Wateree River, Congaree River, Alston, Columbia, Cane Creek, Turkey Creek, Horse Creek

Railroads: to Charlotte, to Sumterville, to Charleston, R.R., S.C.R.R., South Carolina R.R.

ORIGINS OF SOUTHERN RADICALISM

The South Carolina Upcountry, 1800–1860

LACY K. FORD, JR.

OXFORD UNIVERSITY PRESS

New York   Oxford

Oxford University Press

Oxford   New York   Toronto
Delhi   Bombay   Calcutta   Madras   Karachi
Petaling Jaya   Singapore   Hong Kong   Tokyo
Nairobi   Dar es Salaam   Cape Town
Melbourne   Auckland

and associated companies in
Berlin   Ibadan

Copyright © 1988 by Lacy K. Ford, Jr.

First published in 1988 by Oxford University Press, Inc.,
200 Madison Avenue, New York, New York 10016

First issued as an Oxford University Press paperback, 1991

Oxford is a registered trademark of Oxford University Press

Library of Congress Cataloging-in-Publication Data
Ford, Lacy K., Jr.
Origins of Southern radicalism: The South Carolina upcountry.
1800–1860 / Lacy K. Ford, Jr.
p.   cm.   Bibliography: p.   Includes index.
ISBN 0-19-504422-3
1. South Carolina—Politics and government—1775–1865.
2. Radicalism—South Carolina—History—19th century.
3. Secession. I. Title.
F273.F68 1988
975.7'03—dc19   88–4221

ISBN 0-19-506961-7 (pbk)

1 3 5 7 9 8 6 4 2

Printed in the United States of America
on acid-free paper

For Mother and Daddy

Preface

No discussion of the coming of the American Civil War, no attempt to explain how the promising young republic almost destroyed itself in fratricidal carnage, can avoid addressing the pivotal question of why the plain folk of the Old South, the white majority, willingly joined the region's planter elite to fight a long and bloody war seemingly waged in defense of slavery. Why did the fire-eater's vision of a perfect slaveholders' republic triumph among the great mass of common whites in the South, whites who had long displayed a rooted recalcitrance against being driven toward visions? Centuries ago, that most enduring of republican theorists, Niccolò Machiavelli, reminded his prince that success in the effort to conquer and control a province depended less on the putative "*virtu* of the conquerer" than on the actual "circumstances of the vanquished."[1] If Machiavelli was right, and I think he was, then any meaningful interpretation of sectional conflict in antebellum America must explain not only the logic and strategy of the radicals who led the South out of the Union but also the circumstances and values of the society and polity which eventually heeded the fire-eaters' call and rallied behind the secession cause.

But ferreting out the circumstances and values of those who ultimately supported secession is no easy task. With South Carolina poised on the brink of secession in December 1860, Abraham Lincoln's future Attorney General, the former Whig Edward Bates of Missouri, tried to plumb the depths of the Palmetto state's unyielding radicalism. A Virginian by birth, Bates was not without resources for the endeavor: his wife, Julia Coalter, was the daughter of a South Carolina native and the sister-in-law of two prominent South Carolinians, former United States Senator William C. Preston and Chancellor William Harper. But desite his Palmetto connections, Bates found it easier to ridicule South Carolina than to explain her actions. The secession campaign, he concluded, was simply "the last expiring struggle of her [South Carolina's] pride," and yet another indication that the state lacked "the good sense and courage to stop in her mad

---

[1]Niccolò Machiavelli, *The Prince*, trans. Robert M. Adams (New York: W. W. Norton, 1977), p. 14.

career.'' What most fascinated (and frustrated) Bates about South Carolina, however, was not so much the state's fiery radicalism as its penchant for concealing its internal divisions, such as they were, from the eyes of the world. On the eve of secession, Bates commented on this most striking aspect of the South Carolina style at some length:

> The People of S[outh] C[arolina], however widely they may differ in fact, have a politic desire to present an undivided front to outsiders, and to appear before the world as all of one mind. This feature of their character (the desire to keep up *appearances* whatever the *facts* may be) is not shewn for the first time in their *present* revolutionary struggle. As long ago as 1790, the Convention which formed their constitution deliberately *burned its records,* to conceal from posterity the differences of opinion which existed among them.[2]

Like Edward Bates, many historians have found it easier to see the folly of South Carolina's "mad career" than to explain how the state managed to present an essentially united front on a question as inherently controversial and explosive as secession. In an effort to put Machiavelli's age-old advice to good use, this study attempts to explain why the white majority of the Old South ultimately supported the secession movement by examining the nature of white society and polity in one important Southern subregion, the South Carolina Upcountry, which was the cradle of upland cotton culture in the South and produced that quintessential Southern statesman and pro-slavery advocate, John C. Calhoun. During the first six decades of the nineteenth century, the South Carolina Upcountry evolved from an isolated subsistence region that served as a stronghold of Jeffersonian Republicanism in 1800 into a mature cotton-producing region with a burgeoning commercial sector that served as a hotbed of Southern radicalism by 1860. An analysis of this evolution, I believe, will not only render the frightening logic of Southern radicals more understandable but will also explain why so many common whites of the Old South ultimately found the appeal of these radicals so compelling.

For the purpose of this study, I have defined the Upcountry as the thirteen-district area lying north and west of the state's fall line. A crudely triangular region, the Upcountry is bounded on the east by the fall line, on the southwest by the Savannah River (which also served as the South Carolina-Georgia border), and to the north by the state's boundary with North Carolina. The Blue Ridge Mountains dip teasingly into the far northwest corner of the region, but well over 90 percent of the surface area of the Upcountry is part of the broad, arcing Southern Piedmont that sweeps from Virginia through the two Carolinas and across much of Georgia. Along the fall line, the narrow belt of sandhills that stretches across the middle of South Carolina spills over into the Upcountry, especially in border districts such as Lancaster and Edgefield, but no true sandhills district was included in this study. In addition to the Savannah River and its

---

[2]Howard K. Beale, ed., *The Diary of Edward Bates, 1859–1866* (Washington, D.C.: Government Printing Office, 1933), especially p. 168.

tributaries which flow along the Upcountry's lower border, the region is also
served by the rivers of the vast Santee system. These long, finger-like rivers,
which flow into the Santee below Columbia, extend far into the Upcountry. Near
the eastern edge of the region, the Catawba-Wateree River flows from the North
Carolina border to the fall line at Camden, and then joins the Congaree southeast
of Columbia to form the Santee. Two major Upcountry rivers, the Broad and the
Saluda, traverse the heart of the region before combining near Columbia to form
the Congaree. The Broad River runs north to south from the North Carolina
border to Columbia, but its major tributaries, the Pacolet, the Tyger, and the
Enoree rivers rise in the high hill country and run west to east through the center
of the Upcountry. The Saluda River, which rises in the Blue Ridge Mountains,
also meanders through the middle of the Upcountry before merging with the
Broad just above Columbia. All of these rivers and a number of their more
important tributaries appear on the map of the Upcountry included in this
volume.[3]

Finally, as a way of defining the entirely man-made boundaries of this book,
I should note that this is a study of white society, politics, and political culture in
the South Carolina Upcountry. The Old South's peculiar institution, chattel
slavery for blacks, looms large in the book because of its enormous impact on the
Upcountry economy and on the politics and ideology of the region's white
inhabitants. The nature of everyday life in the slave quarters, the spread of
Christianity among slaves, the growth of self-conscious slave communities, and
even the complex dynamics of actual relationships between masters and slaves
(as opposed to the white descriptions of those relationships used in pro-slavery
arguments), though important subjects in their own right, lie, for the most part,
beyond the scope of this study. But they are not being ignored. In addition to the
pathbreaking works by Eugene Genovese, Lawrence Levine, Herbert Gutman,
John Blassingame, and Albert Raboteau on these subjects, Charles Joyner, John
Scott Strickland, Cheryll Cody, and others are now producing important and
original works on slave life, work, community, and religion in South Carolina
that will soon admirably fill any voids created by the very different focus of this
study.[4]

[3]For an excellent treatment of the geography of the region, see Charles F. Kovacik and John J.
Winberry, *South Carolina: A Geography* (Boulder: Westview Press, 1987), pp. 1–48.

[4]For a survey of the major works mentioned in the paragraph above, see Charles B. Dew, "The
Slavery Experience," in John B. Boles and Evelyn Thomas Nolen, eds., *Interpreting Southern
History: Historiographical Essays in Honor of Sanford W. Higginbotham* (Baton Rouge: Louisiana
State University Press, 1987), pp. 120–161; for examples of the important recent work on slaves in
South Carolina, see Charles Joyner, *Down by the Riverside: A South Carolina Slave Community*
(Urbana: University of Illinois Press, 1984); John Scott Strickland, "Across Space and Time:
Conversion, Community, and Cultural Change Among South Carolina Slaves" (Ph.D. dissertation,
University of North Carolina at Chapel Hill, 1985); Cheryll Ann Cody, "There Was No 'Absalom'
on the Ball Plantations: Slave Naming Practices in the South Carolina Low Country, 1720–1865,"
American Historical Review 92 (June, 1987):563–596; and Philip D. Morgan, "The Ownership of
Property by Slaves in the Mid-Nineteenth Century Low Country," *Journal of Southern History* 49
(August, 1983):399–420.

*   *   *

Modern economic forecasters view the per capita indebtedness of a society as a critical index of its economic prosperity. Unlike those of us reared on the biblical wisdom of using the years of plenty to save for the years of famine, these forecasters deem high per capita indebtedness a good thing, a signal of strong public confidence in future prosperity. If the forecasters are right, if the aged wisdom is indeed flawed, then perhaps the indebtedness I have incurred while working on this book is a very good thing, a sign of a strong collective faith in the future of historical research and writing. In any case, I find comfort in the fact that most of my obligations are debts of gratitude which can be repaid through acknowledgment and reciprocity rather than with cold cash. I realize that these brief acknowledgments do not fully satisfy my obligations, but I do hope they reveal the depths of my gratitude to the many people whom I can never fully repay.

I am grateful to the staffs of the Baker Library at the Harvard School of Business Administration, the manuscripts division of the Perkins Library at Duke University, and the Southern Historical Collection at the University of North Carolina at Chapel Hill. At the University of South Carolina, members of the fine staff of the South Caroliniana Library went out of their way to make that repository's rich resources available to me and allowed me to make the library virtually a second home during my work on this project. Like every other scholar who labors in the vineyard of South Carolina history, and most of those who work in Southern history, I owe an enormous debt to Allen H. Stokes, the Director of the South Caroliniana Library. Allen went above and beyond the highest professional standards to help me make the best possible use of the library's holdings. In addition to his unsurpassed talents as a manuscript librarian, Allen's gifts as historian and critic saved me from many foolish errors, and, more important, his calm advice, warm encouragement, and unfailing friendship have steadied me since my undergraduate years.

During my years at the University of South Carolina, both as a student and as a faculty member, a number of people in the Department of History have been generous with their time and knowledge. Among my fellow graduate students, Barbara Bellows, John Hildreth, Mary Morgan, Mary Watson Edmonds, and Steve Wise all shared parts of their own work with me. George D. Terry placed his exhaustive knowledge of primary sources at my disposal and offered a number of helpful suggestions. More recently, James Dunlap, Rebecca Starr, and Thomas Sims provided valuable research help, and James Hill has proven an imaginative and diligent research assistant. During their respective terms as department chairman, George C. Rogers, Jr., and Thomas L. Connelly provided much-needed encouragement and assistance. Walter B. Edgar and his staff at the Institute for Southern Studies helped provide a stimulating atmosphere for intellectual sparring with visiting scholars such as Irving Bartlett, Stephanie McCurry, and Larry McDonnell. Shirley Cook and Alexander Moore of The Papers of John C. Calhoun have always greeted a frequent intruder with helpful advice.

Robert M. Weir shared his remarkable grasp of ideology and political culture in South Carolina with me and offered useful comments on several chapters. Clyde N. Wilson, who first took an interest in my education when I walked into his survey course as a headstrong undergraduate, has doubtless read and reread more drafts of this manuscript than he cares to recall, but he has remained a tireless critic, supporter, and friend. John G. Sproat has devoted more time, energy, and effort to my development as a scholar than a student or colleague has any right to expect, and he has always been a sharp critic of style and content. I hope this final product serves as a modest reward for his efforts. Directing this study in dissertation form must have strained even Tom Terrill's reservoir of ministerial virtues, but Tom has given unselfishly of his time, talent, and friendship to make this a better book. Moreover, he never lost faith in the author, even during the project's lowest moments, and for that I will always be grateful.

Grants from the University of South Carolina's Venture Fund and its Research and Productive Scholarship program helped provide valuable research, computer, and logistical assistance. J. Spencer Ulrey drew the splendid maps. Peggy Clark of the Henry Laurens Papers spent many nights and weekends at the word processor in order to see this book through to completion. She deciphered my scrawling hand without complaint, provided valuable editorial assistance, and worked through seemingly endless revisions with incredible patience, understanding, and good cheer.

Nor is my indebtedness entirely local in nature. Leon Litwack revived my interest in Southern history in one of my first graduate seminars and has provided valuable guidance and helpful criticism through the years. A semester's work with Eric Foner heightened my awareness of the relationship between politics, ideology, and social change, and his continued encouragement and criticism have made this a better book. James L. Roark spent many hours sharing his knowledge of Southern planters with me and remains a source of warm support and keen criticism. Orville Vernon Burton educated me about the vagaries of Edgefield district. Dan Hammond interrupted his own economic research to advise me about banking, credit, currency, capital formation, and regional economic development. John Scott Strickland also took time out from his own important work to offer valuable suggestions and to help solve methodological problems during the research stage of this project. Eugene D. Genovese read a draft of my first chapter and helped clarify my ideas about the spread of evangelical Christianity.

Reid Mitchell and Charles Sellers read an earlier draft of this manuscript and shared their extensive knowledge of the Jacksonian era with me. James Oakes's comments helped me place my argument within the larger Southern perspective. David Weiman's criticisms helped me tighten my economic arguments. Steven Hahn, whose pioneering work on Southern yeomen stimulated my thinking, read the entire manuscript and offered many useful suggestions and much helpful criticism. Bertram Wyatt-Brown's thorough commentary helped me tighten and clarify arguments at crucial points. Few ideas pass Michael O'Brien's sharp scrutiny unscathed, and mine were certainly not exceptions, but his vast knowledge of intellectual life in the Old South and his unforgiving editorial eye helped improve this volume. And J. Mills Thornton III, whose bold and original ideas have done much to advance our understanding of the Old South, provided a meticulous and penetrating commentary on my manuscript which improved the final product immeasurably.

A travel and research grant from the American Philosophical Society helped me collect additional material during the summer of 1986. This book benefited a great deal from that research. An Independent Study and Research Fellowship from the National Endowment for the Humanities (log number: FA-26636) allowed me a research leave during the 1986–87 academic year in order to complete this study. Without that support the book would have taken much longer to finish. I am also grateful to Sheldon Meyer, Rachel Toor, and Stephanie Sakson-Ford of Oxford University Press for their encouragement and editorial assistance.

Unquestionably the most rewarding aspect of researching and writing this book has been the opportunity to work with friends and colleagues such as Peter Coclanis and David Carlton. On the surface, either a personal or an intellectual alliance between the sluggish repose of rural South Carolina and the ethnic urbanity of Chicago's bustling West Side would seem altogether unlikely. Yet I owe no greater personal or intellectual debt to anyone than to Peter Coclanis. Peter's work on the expansion of early modern capitalism into the American South and on the rise of plantation agriculture in the South Carolina Lowcountry has done much to help place the South Carolina economy in a larger perspective and has influenced my thinking a great deal. Moreover, Peter spent many hours helping me analyze data and refine ideas, especially on economic issues. Peter read drafts of my chapters and offered a long list of valuable comments and criticisms. Peter also shared many of the day-to-day tribulations of research and writing alongside a temperamental friend with unfailing humor, ready encouragement, endless patience, and steadfast loyalty. No one could ask more of anyone than that.

I can scarcely remember working on the history of nineteenth-century South Carolina without the help and guidance of David Carlton. We have shared research, exchanged ideas, debated issues, and refined arguments for so long and so often that David often seems to be as much an intellectual alter ego as a friend and colleague. David's enthusiasm for history and his affection and concern for his native state have served as models of professional dedication, and his own work on industrialization in South Carolina is a shining example to all who follow. David has read and commented on the entire manuscript and has done much to remedy its shortcomings. Yet even so profuse an acknowledgment as this does not adequately state my intellectual debt to David. As colleague and critic, but more importantly as friend, David deserves much credit for anything that is valuable in this study.

Having acknowledged the importance of so many people to the completion of this book, I must hasten to add that none of them are responsible for any of its faults. Those can all be blamed squarely on a stubborn author who does not

always make the most of good advice. The final, and most important, acknowledgment must go to my family, which has sustained me throughout the project.
A completed monograph must seem like a small repayment for the trouble they
have endured. I can only say that it is my own work, done with independence of
mind and my own hands, and that is the kind of work that I think they can all be
proud of. I dedicate this book to my parents, Lacy K. Ford, Sr., and Martha
Brandon Ford, who taught me those first and longest lasting lessons about the
unbought Grace of life. I am the first professional historian in the family, but I
am hardly the first family member to recognize that the most important responsibilities are those filled with an urgency born of ancient obligation. I owe that,
and much more, to my parents.

Columbia   L.K.F.
March 1988

Contents

List of Abbreviations

Baker   Baker Library, Harvard Graduate School of Business Administration, Cambridge, Massachusetts

DU   Manuscripts Division, Perkins Library, Duke University, Durham, North Carolina

LC   Library of Congress, Washington, D.C.

SCDAH   South Carolina Department of Archives and History, Columbia, S.C.

SCL   South Caroliniana Library, University of South Carolina, Columbia, South Carolina

SCHS   South Carolina Historical Society, Charleston, South Carolina

SHC   Southern Historical Collection, University of North Carolina at Chapel Hill

Origins of Southern Radicalism

I

ECONOMY AND SOCIETY

During the halcyon years of the Age of Exploration, Christopher Columbus purportedly declared that "the best thing in the world is gold . . . it can even send souls to heaven." Three hundred and fifty years later, when James Henry Hammond rose to defend his native South before the United States Senate, the eloquent South Carolinian claimed only sovereignty, not divinity, for cotton. "No, you dare not make war on cotton. No power on earth dares to make war upon it," Hammond declared. "Cotton is King."[1] Tendentious as their claims appear at first glance, probably neither Columbus nor Hammond was guilty of anything more than slight metaphoric exaggeration. The mercantilist lust for gold bullion certainly saved no souls, and probably damned more than a few, but the precious metal provided the foundation for an unparalleled expansion of world commerce and international trade during the sixteenth and eighteenth centuries. Later, in the late eighteenth and early nineteenth century, the cotton trade became the mainstay of the burgeoning industrial revolution in Great Britain and the catalyst for a smaller industrial boom in the northern United States. "The traditional view which has seen the history of the British Industrial Revolution primarily in terms of cotton is correct," argues Eric Hobsbawm. "If cotton flourished, the economy flourished, if it slumped so did the economy."[2]

After the invention of the cotton gin made it possible to clean large quantities of short-staple cotton quickly and cheaply, the American South rapidly became the world's largest cotton supplier. Over 80 percent of all cotton consumed by the growing British textile industry came from the South. Demand for Southern cotton surged and sagged with the cyclical fluctuations of the British Industrial Revolution, but beneath the spectacular fits and starts, the underlying need for

[1]Andre Gunder Frank, "Economic Dependence, Class Structure, and Underdevelopment Policy," in *Dependence and Underdevelopment: Latin America's Political Economy,* eds. James Cockroft, Andre Gunder Frank, and Dale L. Johnson (New York: Doubleday, 1972), p. 20; James Henry Hammond, "Speech on the Admission of Kansas, under the Lecompton Constitution," in *Selections from the Letters and Speeches of the Hon. James H. Hammond,* with introduction by Clyde N. Wilson (Spartanburg, S.C.: The Reprint Company, 1978), p. 317.

[2]Eric Hobsbawm, *The Age of Revolution 1789–1848* (London: Weidenfield and Nicholson, 1962), pp. 51–61.

the fiber increased throughout the first half of the nineteenth century. This growing orientation toward production of cotton for the international market sparked a peculiar dual revolution in the South, roughly paralleling the twin upheavals that staggered Great Britain and the European continent between 1789 and 1850. While the industrial revolution transformed the British economy and most of Europe struggled to control the spirit of democracy alive among some of its people, staple agriculture was sweeping across the lower South, spreading slavery with its triumph, and simultaneously fostering the development of a full-fledged ideological defense of the Southern experiment in slave-labor republicanism.[3] Yet, to most outside observers, the South's dual revolution seemed to proceed backwards, or at least in the wrong direction. As other parts of the transatlantic world were moving toward industrialization and taking a few halting steps toward more inclusive definitions of citizenship, the American South was rapidly intensifying its involvement in staple agriculture, thus fortifying the link between white independence and black slavery with the strong glue of cotton profits, while attempting to convince an increasingly skeptical, if not hostile, world that slavery was a proper and, in fact, desirable basis for a republican social order.[4]

The South appeared to be investing both its wealth and its honor in a doomed crusade, heroic in its proportions if not in its aims, to thwart the steady march of progress and defy world opinion. Certainly James Henry Hammond and other Southern pro-slavery spokesmen seemed to relish standing defiantly astride the course of secular trends. Yet these Southern champions cannot be dismissed as vainglorious *provocateurs* or guilt-ridden would-be martyrs; they believed that the South argued from a position of strength, not weakness. If the South abstained from cotton production for three years, Hammond argued, "England will topple headlong and carry the whole civilized world with her, save the South."[5] The source of the South's economic strength, Hammond believed, was its staple agriculture. Northerners, Hammond conceded, were "a brave and

---

[3]See Hobsbawm, *Age of Revolution*, pp. 1–42; Gavin Wright, "An Econometric Study of Cotton Production and Trade, 1830–1860," *The Review of Economics and Statistics* 53 (May, 1971):111–120; Peter Temin, "The Causes of Cotton Price Fluctuations in the 1830's," *The Review of Economics and Statistics* 49 (November, 1967):463–470.

[4]An excellent discussion on the compatibility of slavery and republican ideology is found in Edmund Morgan, *American Slavery, American Freedom: The Ordeal of Colonial Virginia* (New York: Norton, 1975). Morgan's interpretation is carried into the nineteenth century by Robert E. Shalhope, "Thomas Jefferson's Republicanism and Antebellum Southern Thought," *Journal of Southern History* 12 (November, 1976):529–557. The most thorough and convincing account to date of the relationship between slavery and white independence is J. Mills Thornton III, *Politics and Power in a Slave Society: Alabama, 1800–1860* (Baton Rouge: Louisiana State University Press, 1978), especially pp. xviii–xxi.

[5]David Brion Davis, "Slavery and the Idea of Progress," *The Bulletin of the Center for the Study of Southern Culture and Religion* 3 (June, 1979):1–9; Howard Temperly, "Capitalism, Slavery, and Ideology," *Past and Present* 75 (May, 1977):94–118; Eric Foner, "Politics, Ideology, and the Origins of the American Civil War," in *A Nation Divided: Essays on the Civil War and Reconstruction*, ed. George M. Fredrickson (Minneapolis: Burgess Publishing, 1975), pp. 15–34; Hammond, "Speech on the Admission of Kansas," p. 317.

energetic race, full of intellect,'' but they were economically a vulnerable people because they produced ''no great staple that the South does not produce; while we [Southerners] produce two or three . . . that she [North] can never produce.'' No great nation, Hammond argued, could afford to be satisfied with mere subsistence. Independence and republican virtue, not to mention national power, could be enhanced by national plenitude. ''The strength of a nation depends . . . upon its wealth, and the wealth of a nation like that of a man is to be estimated by its surplus production,'' Hammond declared. Therefore, Southern cotton, the United States' largest surplus, buoyed the national economy, filling the coffers of Northern ''financiers, cotton lords, and merchant princes'' as well as of Southern planters. Pulling at the roots of Southern wealth, Hammond warned, would ultimately deprive the North of its own best source of economic nourishment.[6]

Intuitively, Hammond had developed a ''staple theory of value,'' which ascribed economic primacy to commodities rather than to the power of capital to generate new markets and develop new products to fill them. Placing cotton at the center of his economic universe, Hammond saw Great Britain and the North as part of a system of commercial and industrial satellites revolving around a staple-producing metropole—the South. Unfortunately for his section, the South Carolina planter's economic model inverted the real pattern of economic dependence developing in the transatlantic world and, as a result, greatly exaggerated the industrial world's vulnerability to disruptions in the Southern cotton supply.

Misguided as Hammond's ideas now seem, they were compatible at the time with a number of widely shared assumptions about republican political economy. To nineteenth-century republican theorists, the crucial role in economic development belonged to independent producers, men who controlled productive property as well as labor. The proliferation of non-producers weakened the economy by burdening producers with a class of parasites, while the alienation of producers from productive property sapped aggregate economic initiative by reducing men to a state of indifferent dependence. By adopting a system of slave labor and staple agriculture, the South, Hammond believed, had solved the riddle of how to increase wealth while at the same time protecting the independent producer. Widespread ownership of productive land insured the capacity for self-sufficiency, while at the same time cotton allowed the region to increase its wealth through staple production. Cotton and slavery were the powers that permitted the South to enjoy the best of two worlds, defending the inherited equation of personal independence with ownership of productive property on the one hand, while responding to the call of wealth and progress on the other.

With the benefit of hindsight, scholars have readily identified the fallacies in Hammond's argument, and have suggested that cotton and slavery, in fact,

---

[6]Hammond, ''Speech on the Admission of Kansas,'' pp. 313–317. For a thorough discussion of the links between independence, virtue, and wealth, see Drew R. McCoy, *The Elusive Republic: Political Economy in Jeffersonian America* (Chapel Hill: University of North Carolina Press, 1980), pp. 13–75.

retarded Southern economic development. Yet as short-staple cotton spread across the South during the periodic cotton booms of the nineteenth century, only a handful of visionaries could see the staple as a potential source of dependence and stagnation. Instead, most Southerners agreed with planter Joseph Jenkins of South Carolina, who saw cotton as the basis of all "wealth, independence, individual happiness, and respectability." Cotton was the main chance in the antebellum South, and Southerners pursued it furiously.[7]

[7]Joseph E. Jenkins, "Address Delivered before the Agricultural Society of St. Johns, Colleton," *Southern Agriculturalist* 11 (August, 1838):393–410.

1

Cotton and Evangelical Christianity

At the close of the American Revolution, the Upcountry was a backwater region isolated from the main currents of South Carolina society which ran through the mercantile center of Charleston and the plantation society of the coastal parishes. The interior, or backcountry, an untamed region which had experienced deadly Indian raids as late as 1763, supported only a coarse frontier society that was still more frontier than society. In 1783, the backcountry was sparsely populated, almost exclusively white, and essentially unchurched. Inhabitants of the backcountry clustered in scattered pockets of settlement that served as nodes of social and community organization, but taken together these nodes hardly comprised an identifiable or articulate society. Moreover, the backcountry remained on the fringe of the state's export-oriented economy despite the rise of a small but prominent class of aspiring planters and land speculators eager to establish commercial agriculture in the region. Lacking economic purpose and institutional moorings, backcountry society had not yet cohered.[1]

During the next half-century, this bare-bones backcountry society developed muscle and sinew. This development was nourished largely by short-staple cotton and evangelical Christianity. The emergence of short-staple cotton as an important cash crop provided the Upcountry with an economic purpose and a viable material base for its society. Initiated by a major religious awakening in the region and sustained by continuing revival efforts, the spread of evangelical Christianity knitted communities out of scattered rural households whose previous sense of common identity rested almost entirely on kinship ties. Evangelical churches soon emerged as institutional centers of community life and touchstones of community identity. Though they worked independently, the

[1]Peter A. Coclanis, *The Shadow of a Dream: Economic Life and Death in the South Carolina Low Country, 1670–1920* (New York: Oxford University Press, forthcoming); George C. Rogers, Jr., *Charleston in the Age of the Pinckneys* (Norman: University of Oklahoma Press, 1966), pp. 3–115; Rachel Klein, "The Rise of the Planters in the South Carolina Backcountry, 1767–1808" (Ph.D. dissertation, Yale University, 1979), pp. 9–86; Robert L. Meriwether, *The Expansion of South Carolina, 1729–1765* (Kingsport, Tenn.: Southern Publishers, 1940).

combined impact of the cotton boom and the evangelical awakening shaped a vital and coherent society in the Upcountry. This society was sustained by the cotton economy and steadied by the values, communities, and institutions spawned by evangelical Christianity. To fully understand exactly how Upcountry society was forged and what kind of society it was once fully formed, it is necessary to take a closer look at the emergence of the cotton economy and the expansion of evangelical Christianity in the region.

As early as the 1720s and throughout the rest of the eighteenth century, South Carolina's economic fortunes rose and fell with those of staple agriculture. First rice, then indigo, and finally long-staple or sea-island cotton emerged as important cash crops for planters in tidewater South Carolina. By the eve of the American Revolution, export staples had generated a broadly, if unevenly, shared prosperity in the South Carolina Lowcountry and created the economic basis for South Carolina's unique social and political harmony.[2] But the prosperity of eighteenth-century South Carolina rested on staple crops which were not easily adaptable to the soil and climate of the state's vast backcountry. Rice and sea-island cotton flourished only near the coast, along the great tidal rivers, or in the expansive Lowcountry swamps. Indigo, a crop better suited for the interior, initially brought substantial profits to backcountry planters, but after the Revolution new foreign competition and the loss of the lucrative British bounty pushed the South Carolina indigo industry to the brink of collapse. As indigo declined, more and more backcountry farmers turned to tobacco as a cash crop. Upcountry and middle-district legislators abandoned their otherwise tenacious commitment to strict economy in state spending long enough to support the creation of state licensed and financed tobacco weighing and inspection stations in the backcountry. Tobacco growing remained the ruling economic passion among backcountry planters and farmers until shortly after 1800, but over the long term tobacco proved a poor provider. Low yields, poor quality leaves, and strong competition from other tobacco growing regions eventually killed all dreams of a full-fledged Piedmont tobacco bonanza.[3]

[2]Peter A. Coclanis, "Rice Prices in the 1720s and the Evolution of the South Carolina Economy," *Journal of Southern History* 48 (November, 1982):531–544; David L. Coon, "The Development of Market Agriculture in South Carolina, 1670–1785" (Ph.D. dissertation, University of Illinois, 1972), pp. 164–268; Robert M. Weir, *Colonial South Carolina: A History* (Millwood, N.Y.: KTO Press, 1983), pp. 141–172; Alice Hanson Jones, *Wealth of a Nation to Be: The American Colonies on the Eve of the Revolution* (New York: Columbia University Press, 1980), p. 357; Robert M. Weir, "'The Harmony We Were Famous For': An Interpretation of Pre-Revolutionary South Carolina Politics," *William and Mary Quarterly* 26 (October, 1969):473–501.

[3]G. Terry Sharrar, "The Indigo Bonanza in South Carolina, 1740–1790," *Technology and Culture* 12 (July, 1971):447–455; Peter A. Coclanis, "The Rise and Fall of the South Carolina Low Country: An Essay in Economic Interpretation," *Southern Studies* 24 (Summer, 1985):143–166; Patrick Brady, "Political and Civil Life in South Carolina, 1787–1833" (Ph.D. dissertation, University of California at Santa Barbara, 1971), pp. 74–97; Marjorie S. Mendenhall, "A History of Agriculture in South Carolina, 1790–1860" (Ph.D. dissertation, University of North Carolina at Chapel Hill, 1940), pp. 93–132.

To make matters worse, traditional markets for surplus Upcountry foodstuffs softened just as Upcountry experiments with export staples foundered. In the first years after the Revolution, wheat grown in the Catawba-Wateree River basin and corn raised in all parts of the Upcountry found buyers in the city of Charleston or Lowcountry plantation areas, but by the early 1790s an oversupply of Upcountry grain glutted the Charleston market.[4] In 1793, Congressman Robert Goodloe Harper, a Charleston lawyer and land speculator with vast Upcountry holdings, lamented that the Upcountry "is far removed from navigation, has very little to export, and must therefore supply its own wants."[5] On the whole, late eighteenth-century efforts to extend the staple-based prosperity of the Lowcountry parishes into the backcountry failed miserably. Forays into indigo and tobacco production were accompanied by reckless land speculation on a grand scale, but ultimately both staple production and land speculation produced more bankruptcies than fortunes. Lacking a consistently profitable export staple and without a ready market for their surplus foodstuffs, Piedmont farmers of the early 1790s seemed confined to a subsistence economy which offered little upward mobility and little hope for improved living standards.[6]

Short-staple cotton soon changed all that. By 1800, the British textile revolution and the invention of the cotton gin opened new market possibilities for Upcountry farmers. During the first two decades of the nineteenth century, short-staple cotton production spread into the South Carolina interior with remarkable speed. Upcountry soils proved as receptive to cotton as they had been forbidding to other staples. Cotton flourished in varying degrees in every part of the Upcountry except the tiny alpine region in the far northwestern corner of the state. The fertile Savannah River valley and other portions of the lower Piedmont quickly emerged as the heartland of the South's first short-staple cotton boom. Cotton output increased dramatically during the first boom. In 1793, the entire state produced only 94,000 pounds of cotton, and the bulk of that crop was the delicate and luxurious long-staple cotton grown primarily on the sea-islands, but by 1811 the Upcountry alone exported over 30 million pounds of short-staple cotton.[7]

With the emergence of short-staple cotton as a profitable cash crop, staple agriculture escaped its narrow tidewater confines to bring flush times to the Upcountry. During the heady years of the first upland cotton boom, substantial landholders parlayed bumper cotton crops and high prices into large fortunes.

[4]Mendenhall, "A History of Agriculture in South Carolina," pp. 93–132.

[5]Robert Goodloe Harper [Appius], "An Address to the People of South Carolina" (Charleston, 1794), pp. 31–34.

[6]Klein, "The Rise of the Planters," pp. 231–236; Lacy K. Ford, "Self-Sufficiency, Cotton, and Economic Development in the South Carolina Upcountry, 1800–1860," *Journal of Economic History* 45 (June, 1985):261–267.

[7]Mendenhall, "A History of Agriculture in South Carolina," pp. 105–108; James Simons, *A Rallying Point for All True Friends to Their Country* (Charleston, 1800), pp. 9–19; J. L. Watkins, *King Cotton* (New York: J. L. Watkins, 1908), pp. 69–93; Mark D. Kaplanoff, "Making the South Solid: Politics and the Structure of Society in South Carolina, 1790–1815" (Ph.D. dissertation, University of Cambridge, 1979), pp. 9–13.

Near the fall line, Richland district planter Wade Hampton I, a Virginia native "brought up to labor in the field . . . almost entirely without the advantage of even a common school education," earned $75,000 on his first cotton crop in 1799. By 1810, Hampton had increased his annual cotton earnings to $150,000. When Wade Hampton I died in 1835 he was one of the richest men in the entire South, controlling a personal fortune that rivaled that of even the wealthiest Lowcountry rice baron.[8] In the Piedmont, entrepreneur John Springs began growing cotton on his extensive landholdings along the Catawba River in York district shortly after 1800 and quickly amassed a second fortune based on cotton and slaves that surpassed his first fortune in land. During the first cotton boom, Springs made annual slave-buying trips which took him as far south as Savannah and as far north as Baltimore in search of prime hands to work his expanding cotton fields. John Springs increased his slave holdings from fewer than ten in 1800 to forty-four by 1820, and by 1826 the value of Springs's assets exceeded $100,000.[9]

Scions of other established Upcountry families were also enthusiastic participants in the cotton bonanza. Patrick Calhoun, a land surveyor, politician, and Revolutionary leader who many South Carolinians considered "the patriarch of the upper country," owned over 1200 acres of land and nearly thirty slaves when he died in 1796.[10] Calhoun's death left the management of his substantial holdings in Abbeville district to his wife, Martha Caldwell Calhoun, and his sons William, James, John Caldwell, and Patrick. The eldest son, William, was only twenty when his father died, but after a brief stint as a clerk in a Charleston mercantile house he married an Upcountry heiress, Catherine DeGraffenreid, in 1805 and quickly established himself as a successful cotton planter in his native Abbeville. Labeled "Cotton Billy" by admiring neighbors, William Calhoun steadily increased his slaveholdings from eighteen in 1810 to thirty-one in 1820 and, finally, to seventy-six by the time of his death in 1840. From his early cotton profits William Calhoun helped pay for the education of family protégé George McDuffie, a poor young clerk of uncommon drive and ability, and contributed to Martha Calhoun's support of John C. Calhoun's expensive educa-

[8]"The Diary of Edward Hooker, 1805–1808," *American Historical Association Annual Report, 1896* (Washington, D.C.: Government Printing Office, 1897), vol. 1, p. 846; Whitemarsh B. Seabrook, *A Memoir on the Origin, Cultivation, and Use of Cotton* (Charleston, 1844), pp. 6–17; Ronald E. Bridwell, "The South's Wealthiest Planter: Wade Hampton I of South Carolina, 1754–1833" (Ph.D. dissertation, University of South Carolina, 1980), pp. 397–504.

[9]Katherine Wooten Springs, *The Squires of Springfield* (Charlotte, N.C.: William Lofton, 1965), pp. 16–33; John Springs to Mary Springs, September 23, 1806, John Springs to Mary Springs, September 5, 1807, John Springs to Mary Springs, June 8, 1808, John Springs to Mary Springs, October 2, 1820, Springs Family Papers, SHC; Inventory and Will of John Springs, January 1, 1853, Davidson Family Papers, SHC.

[10]Mary Katherine Davis, "The Featherbed Aristocracy: Abbeville District in the 1790s," *South Carolina Historical Magazine* 80 (April, 1979):136–155; Robert Mills, *Statistics of South Carolina* (Charleston, S.C.: Hurlbut and Lloyd, 1826), p. 355; Margaret L. Coit, *John C. Calhoun: American Portrait* (Boston: Houghton Mifflin, 1950), pp. 1–13.

tion at Yale and Litchfield.[11] James Calhoun, Patrick's second son, briefly operated a mercantile firm in Augusta, where he discovered McDuffie, before setting himself up as an Upcountry planter. By 1820 James Calhoun owned twenty-eight slaves. As a young man, John C. Calhoun, Patrick's third son, practiced law at Abbeville courthouse and maintained one of the family's old plantations in the Long Canes section of Abbeville district, near his brother-in-law Moses Waddel's log academy at Willington. Later, while serving as Vice President during Andrew Jackson's first term, Calhoun established a permanent home in the Upcountry on a hilly five-hundred-acre plantation along the Seneca River in Pickens district. Around 1830 Calhoun changed the name of the plantation from "Clergy Hall" to "Fort Hill" and by 1840 he housed sixty-nine slaves there. The youngest of the four Calhoun brothers, Patrick, also married a DeGraffenreid and prospered as an Abbeville planter who owned forty-two slaves by 1820.[12]

Even before the first cotton boom, the Springs and Calhoun families, and others like them, were comfortably situated and reasonably wealthy, at least by prevailing Upcountry standards. John Springs and the Calhoun brothers were second-generation Upcountrymen, not pioneers but the sons of pioneers. Using their own considerable energy, they built successful cotton plantations and new personal fortunes on the substantial foundations laid by an earlier generation of Upcountrymen. Other successful cotton planters put down Upcountry roots as adults as the cotton boom lured old and respected family names inland from the Lowcountry. Edward G. Palmer, son of a wealthy St. Stephens parish rice planter, married the daughter of a prominent Fairfield district planter-physician while studying law in Columbia. Palmer moved to Fairfield in 1823, chose a planting career over the practice of law, and invested heavily in land and slaves. By 1826, Palmer owned over 1700 acres and more than 100 slaves at his "Valencia" plantation near Ridgeway.[13] Other Lowcountry interlopers brought names which carried more stigma than respect. In 1811, Francis Fincher Gist, son of the hated Tory William Gist, left Charleston and settled permanently in Union district. Gist arrived with eight slaves and purchased 400 acres along the

[11]Coit, *John C. Calhoun*, pp. 12–31; Charles M. Wiltse, *John C. Calhoun, Nationalist* (Indianapolis: Bobbs-Merrill, 1944), pp. 1–31; Edwin L. Green, *George McDuffie* (Columbia, S.C.: The State Co., 1936), pp. 8–11; Robert L. Meriwether, ed., *The Papers of John C. Calhoun* (Columbia, S.C.: University of South Carolina Press, 1959), vol. 1, pp. 431–434; George F. Townes to Henry H. Townes, February 4, 1834, SCL; South Carolina Manuscript Census, 1810, South Carolina Manuscript Census, 1820, South Carolina Manuscript Census, 1840, SCDAH; Estate Appraisal (copy), Calhoun Family Papers, SCL.

[12]Green, *George McDuffie*, pp. 8–11; South Carolina Manuscript Census, 1820, SCDAH; Wiltse, *John C. Calhoun, Nationalist*, pp. 32–45; Clyde N. Wilson and W. Edwin Hemphill, eds., *The Papers of John C. Calhoun* (Columbia, S.C.: University of South Carolina Press, 1977), vol. 10, xvi–xviii; South Carolina Manuscript Census, 1840, SCDAH; Meriwether, ed., *The Papers of John C. Calhoun*, vol. 1, pp. 431–434; South Carolina Manuscript Census, 1820, SCDAH.

[13]Chalmers G. Davidson, *The Last Foray: The South Carolina Planters of 1860* (Columbia: University of South Carolina Press, 1971), p. 215; Fitz Hugh McMaster, *History of Fairfield County, South Carolina* (Columbia, S.C.: State Commercial Printing Co., 1946), pp. 41–42.

Tyger River. When he died in 1819, at age forty, Gist left a thriving 1400-acre plantation, "Rose Hill," and thirty-three slaves. Francis Gist's illegitimate son William, who later evolved into a rabid secessionist, marketed cotton crops in excess of 200 bales from "Rose Hill."[14]

Few Upcountry planters carried names as prominent as Calhoun, Hampton, and Springs, or so notorious as Gist, but cotton growers in every district enjoyed remarkable success during the first boom. Peter Moragne of Abbeville district increased his slave holdings from thirteen in 1800 to forty-three in 1820. In 1800 Laurens farmer John Eichelberger owned ten slaves; by 1820 he had become a successful cotton planter with thirty-three slaves. Like William and James Calhoun, Austin Peay pursued a mercantile career before becoming a cotton planter. Peay, whose father thought him "too frivolous" to become a successful farmer, worked as a Camden merchant until he acquired enough capital to establish "Flint Hill," a cotton plantation near the Wateree River in Fairfield district. Peay owned no slaves in 1800, but by 1810 he was master of over seventy-five. At his death in 1841, Peay owned ten plantations in four different districts and held 323 slaves. Also in Fairfield district, James Pearson increased his holdings from thirteen to thirty-six slaves between 1800 and 1810. Waddy Thompson, Sr., a planter, lawyer, and one-time solicitor from Greenville district, increased his slave holdings on his Saluda River plantation from ten in 1800 to fifty-nine in 1820. Even in the far Upcountry district of Pendleton, Samuel Maverick, whose son later earned a measure of fame for his practice of leaving his cattle unbranded, enlarged his slaveholdings from ten in 1810 to thirty-two in 1820. Not every cotton grower became wealthy during the first boom, but planter success stories were certainly common enough during the early 1800s to convince scores of ambitious Upcountrymen that wealth was merely a few good cotton crops away.[15]

If the first cotton boom bred prodigious ambition among planters and would-be planters, it also opened new market opportunities for Upcountry yeomen. Requiring no large capital outlays and subject to no particular economies of scale in production, short-staple cotton seemed the ideal cash crop for small farmers.[16]

[14]Daniel J. Bell, "Interpretive Booklets for Local Historical Sites: Rose Hill State Park, Union, South Carolina as a Model" (M.A. thesis, University of South Carolina, 1983), pp. 10–17, 98–105. Although it is primarily a study of the Rose Hill plantation, Bell's study is an excellent source of information on the Gist family.

[15]South Carolina Manuscript Census, 1800, South Carolina Manuscript Census, 1810, South Carolina Manuscript Census, 1820, SCDAH; N. Louise Bailey, Mary L. Morgan, and Carolyn R. Taylor, eds., *Biographical Directory of the South Carolina Senate, 1776–1985* (Columbia, S.C.: University of South Carolina Press, 1986), vol. 2, pp. 1247–1249; N. Louise Bailey, ed., *Biographical Directory of the South Carolina House of Representatives* (Columbia, S.C.: University of South Carolina Press, 1984), vol. 4, pp. 561–562; Irvin and Kathryn Sexton, *Samuel A. Maverick* (San Antonio: The Naylor Co., 1964); Caroll Ainsworth McElligott, "Maverick South Carolinian," *Carologue* (May–June, 1986):1–9.

[16]Gavin Wright, *The Political Economy of the Cotton South: Households, Markets, and Wealth in the Nineteenth Century* (New York: W. W. Norton, 1978), pp. 74–87. Wright's general conclusions regarding economies of scale under slavery have been challenged by Robert Fogel and Stanley

According to Charleston's David Ramsay, short-staple cotton placed "new and strong inducements to industry" in the hands of yeoman farmers because it could be grown "profitably by individuals or white families without slaves." Moreover, Ramsay continued, "it appears . . . that the clear profits on one crop planted in cotton . . . will purchase the fee simple of the land. Two, three, or four will in like manner pay for the negroes who make it." The Charlestonian estimated that cotton "trebled the price of land suitable to its growth" and doubled the annual income of its growers between 1800 and 1808. Ramsay marveled at the moral as well as economic stimulation that the cotton boom supplied to the Upcountry. "In estimating the value of cotton," he insisted, "its capacity to incite industry among the lower classes of people, and to fill the country with an independent virtuous yeomanry is of the highest importance."[17] In 1802, Governor John Drayton noted that the "inhabitants" of "the upper country" had "turned their attention towards the raising of cotton, with good prospects of success." Because good Upcountry cotton land usually sold for less than six dollars per acre, "men possessing any capital whatever, may settle themselves independently upon lands which descend to their posterity, together with every improvement made thereon by their industrious labor."[18] Another prominent South Carolinian, Federal Judge William Johnson, agreed with Ramsay and Drayton, explaining that before the short-staple cotton boom "the whole interior . . . was languishing, and its inhabitants emigrating, for want of some object to engage their attention and employ their industry." As a result of the boom, Johnson declared, "individuals who were depressed in poverty and sunk in idleness have suddenly risen to wealth and respectability. Our debts have been paid off, our capital increased, and our lands trebled in value."[19] Cannon Edwards, a farmer from the Fisher Hill section of Union district, gleefully reported in 1816 that he and his brother, both former clerks in Charleston mercantile firms, had planted fifteen acres of cotton from which they expected to earn "more than can be obtained by a salary in a Counting-House." Edwards and his brother also preferred the relative independence of farming to the routine of merchandising, noting that farmers "are not so much confined to hours,

Engerman. For a sampling of the debate, see Robert W. Fogel and Stanley L. Engerman, "Explaining the Relative Efficiency of Slave Agriculture in the Antebellum South," *American Economic Review* 67 (June, 1977):275–296; Gavin Wright, "The Efficiency of Slavery: Another Interpretation," *American Economic Review* 69 (March, 1979):219–226; Robert W. Fogel and Stanley L. Engerman, "Explaining the Relative Efficiency of Slave Agriculture in the Antebellum South: A Reply," *American Economic Review* 70 (September, 1980):672–690.

[17]David Ramsay, *The History of South Carolina*. 2 vols. (Charleston, S.C., 1809), vol. 2, pp. 120–121, 139–191, 230–246.

[18]John Drayton, *A View of South Carolina* (Charleston, S.C.: W. P. Young, 1802), pp. 110–113.

[19]*The Federal Cases, Comprising Cases Argued and Determined in the Circuit and District Courts of the United States* (St. Paul, Minn., 1894–97), vol. 29, p. 1072; Donald G. Morgan, *Justice William Johnson: The First Dissenter* (Columbia, S.C.: University of South Carolina Press, 1954), especially pp. 41–109.

nor . . . much confined to the house."[20] Concurring with these contemporary
observers, historian Marjorie Mendenhall credited the cotton boom with "rescu-
ing the small farmer from the doldrums into which many had come since their
acquisition of a loghouse and a few score acres."[21]

The cotton boom not only provided yeomen farmers in the Upcountry with a
valuable source of cash income; it also created opportunities for slaveless farmers
to acquire slave property. In 1800, before the full impact of the cotton boom was
realized, only 25 percent of all white families (5,144 out of 20,025) in the
Upcountry belonged to the ranks of slaveholders. Yet by 1820, just under 40
percent of all white families (9,449 out of 24,066) in the region owned slaves.
The impact of the cotton boom on the incidence of slaveholding was most
dramatic in the lower Piedmont, where the absolute number of slaveholders rose
from 3,280 in 1800, to 5,138 in 1810, and finally to 6,117 by 1820. The
proportion of white families owning slaves in the lower Piedmont also increased
from just over 28 percent in 1800 to nearly 45 percent in 1820. In the richest
short-staple cotton-growing districts the increases in both the number and the
percentage of slaveholders were even more striking. In 1800, one third (603) of
all white families in Abbeville held slaves, but by 1820, 1,148 of Abbeville's
2,444 free families, or about 47 percent, owned slaves. In Fairfield the number
of slaveholders increased from 384 in 1800 to 839 in 1820, while the percentage
of white families owning slaves rose from 28 to 49 during the same period. In
Laurens district, only one white household in five (397 out of 1930) contained a
slaveholder in 1800, but twenty years later over 40 percent (939 of 2,230) of all
household heads owned slaves. Thus the first cotton boom helped create over
4,000 new masters in the South Carolina Upcountry, adding hundreds to the
slaveholding ranks in virtually every district.[22]

Yet the Upcountry had not evolved into a full-blown plantation society by
1820 despite the almost phenomenal success of some first-generation cotton
planters. To be sure, the first cotton boom spawned some rich planters, but most
Upcountry masters owned relatively few slaves. Of the more than 9,000
slaveholders in the Upcountry in 1820, over 60 percent owned no more than five
slaves and over 70 percent owned fewer than ten slaves. Over 35 percent of all
slaveholders owned only one or two slaves. At the other end of the slaveholding
spectrum, the number of masters who owned twenty or more slaves increased
from just over 100 in 1800 to more than 600 in 1820, thus broadening and
enlarging the region's planter elite substantially. Yet only 6 percent of all
slaveholders and under 3 percent of all free household heads owned as many as
twenty slaves, and only 64 individuals in the entire Upcountry owned fifty or

[20]D. Cannon Edwards to Moultrie [?], June 4, 1816, John Ewing Colhoun Papers, SHC.

[21]Mendenhall, "A History of Agriculture in South Carolina," p. 108.

[22]Data compiled and statistics calculated from the South Carolina Manuscript Census, 1800, the
South Carolina Manuscript Census, 1810, and the South Carolina Manuscript Census, 1820,
SCDAH.

more slaves in 1820.[23] The cotton boom had indeed widened traditional avenues of upward social mobility, and those contemporary observers who viewed short-staple cotton as a great economic blessing for common whites were, at least for the short run, quite perceptive.

To be sure, not all of the new slaveholders were sturdy yeomen who acquired slaves through their own pluck and industry. Many of the new slaveholders inherited their slaves or received them as gifts from slaveholding parents. All of Patrick Calhoun's sons eventually inherited a number of slaves from their father's estate. In Union district, planter William Sims divided his slaves among his nine children long before he died in 1853. John Springs deeded a significant number of slaves to each of his sons and daughters while still a vigorous planter himself.[24] Other Upcountry farmers acquired slaves by marrying into slaveholding families. James Madison, a farmer and clerk of court in Union district, viewed propitious marriages as an important avenue of upward mobility during the first boom. "I can assure you that here are some of the greatest openings for a speculating Genius that you could imagine," Madison wrote to relatives in Virginia during 1803, "provided he would not be against taking a handsome young widow with or without Children as he might chose."[25] Long after the first cotton boom ended, the inviting dowries of Upcountry heiresses continued to attract many suitors. Despite his energy, intellectual prowess, and polemical talent, James Henry Hammond, the son of a school master, orchestrated his rise to prominence through a marriage to Catherine Fitzsimmons, daughter of a wealthy Charleston merchant.[26] John Springs whimsically noted in November 1838 that three local Baptist ministers had found brides in his neighborhood during the three preceding months. The young Baptist clergymen, Springs observed, always married "the handsomest and Richest" young women of York district.[27] Zelotus Holmes, a New Yorker who came to South Carolina to study at Columbia Theological Seminary, supplied various Presbyterian pulpits in the Upcountry after his graduation. In 1844 Holmes married the daughter of Dr. James Nickels, a prominent Laurens planter-physician. Holmes described his new father-in-law, who owned nearly forty slaves, as a "rustic plain old republican Planter." Shortly after his fortunate marriage Holmes settled in Lau-

[23]Ibid.

[24]Coit, *John C. Calhoun*, pp. 1–66; Davis, "The Featherbed Aristocracy," pp. 136–155; A Just and True Inventory and Appraisement of the Personal Estate of Patrick Calhoun, Box 19, Abbeville County Probate Records, microfilm, SCDAH; Edwin Thomas Sims, "Joseph Starke Sims: A Nineteenth Century Upcountry Planter, Politician, and Business Entrepreneur of South Carolina" (M.A. thesis, University of South Carolina, 1983), pp. 1–11, 19–42; List of property deeded by John Springs, January 1, 1831, Springs Family Papers, SHC; Springs, *The Squires of Springfield*, pp. 21–54.

[25]James Madison to Richard Bibb, October 12, 1803, Richard Bibb Papers, DU.

[26]Drew Gilpin Faust, *James Henry Hammond and the Old South: A Design for Mastery* (Baton Rouge: Louisiana State University Press, 1982) in an excellent biography of Hammond, see especially pp. 56–65.

[27]John Springs to Andrew Baxter Springs, November 13, 1838, Springs Family Papers, SHC.

rens, became a slaveholder through Nickels's generosity, and vigorously championed slavery in the face of strenuous objections from his antislavery relatives in the North.[28]

As the incidence of slaveholding increased and the average size of slaveholdings expanded, slave ownership became a widely recognized symbol of social respectability. Social climbers and young men-on-the-make aspired to become slaveholders, whether through marriage, inheritance, or cotton profits. Slaves became a symbol as well as a source of prosperity. But if the South Carolina Upcountry, or at least certain parts of it, was evolving into more and more of a slaveholding society, it was short-staple cotton which paid the bills and precipitated the evolution. Cotton profits paid for land and slaves; cotton put cash in hands of small farmers who used it to pay taxes and buy horses, plows, salt, and other items important to their livelihood. Cotton profits were the source of the Upcountry's new-found prosperity.

Cotton prosperity was flush but fragile. As early as 1807 commercial disruptions resulting from the Napoleonic Wars threatened the international cotton trade. Lowcountry planter George Izard voiced sentiments popular in the Upcountry when he fumed, "Curse that Bonaparte. He may frighten or fight or do anything he pleases . . . but, damn him, why lower the price of cotton?"[29] Jefferson's trade embargo and the subsequent war with Great Britain produced a prolonged interruption in the cotton boom, yet both the embargo and the war were supported whole-heartedly by the Upcountry at the expense of its short-run self-interest. When the war ended in 1815, the cotton boom revived. Short-staple prices, which had fallen below ten cents per pound during the war, soared to nearly thirty cents by 1818. But the heady prosperity of the immediate postwar years, financed by easy credit and abundant paper currency, collapsed in 1819 when the Bank of the United States reduced the supply of paper money in an effort to slow spiraling inflation and end the widespread land speculation which had characterized the postwar boom. The subsequent run on banks reached panic proportions, forcing those institutions to call in their loans. The Bank of England responded to the panic by restricting the flow of specie to the United States, and these restrictions quickly triggered a sharp decline in cotton prices at London, Liverpool, and the major American ports. In the Charleston market the average price of cotton in 1819 was nearly twelve cents per pound less than it had been in 1818. Between 1819 and 1822, the supply of paper currency in circulation in South Carolina declined by 50 percent, and cotton prices fell to half their 1818 levels. The South Carolina economy was trapped in the vortex of rapid deflation.[30]

---

[28]Zelotus Holmes to a relative, December 13, 1842, Zelotus Holmes to his cousin, July 20, 1844, Zelotus Holmes to his aunt, May 10, 1847, Zelotus Holmes to his aunt, January 2, 1856, Zelotus L. Holmes Papers, SCL. In the postbellum era, Zelotus Holmes's son, J. Nickles Holmes, became a leader of the Pentecostal movement in the South.

[29]George Izard to Henry Izard, February 13, 1807, Izard Papers, SCL.

[30]John Harold Wolfe, *Jeffersonian Democracy in South Carolina* (Chapel Hill: University of North Carolina Press, 1940), pp. 213–286; Kaplanoff, "Making the South Solid," pp. 9–13; Alfred

For many cotton growers the damaging effects of falling staple prices were mitigated by a corresponding fall in the price of most other commodities. But for Upcountry farmers who had contracted substantial debts during the flush times of the cotton boom, the collapse of the cotton market and the general deflation brought dire consequences. Following the Panic of 1819, deflation doubled the real dollar value of outstanding debts within five years. Many Upcountry debtors were unable to meet their payment schedules. Bankruptcies and foreclosures multiplied. South Carolina newspapers ran long columns featuring property for sale.[31] Large numbers of slaves and large amounts of real property changed hands under the sheriff's hammer. Early in 1823, William A. A. Belton, a large planter from Fairfield district, offered to sell some or all of his more than forty slaves. Belton explained that his slaves, who he described as "a first rate set of hands," were on the market "not . . . for any faults in themselves . . . but merely to relieve their owner from his pecuniary embarrassments."[32]

Deflation slowed markedly in 1822, when the Bank of England resumed specie payments, but the continued geographic expansion of cotton production and slower growth in world demand for the staple kept cotton prices low through 1829. Thus, between 1822 and 1829, with income from cotton still low and going lower while other commodity prices either stabilized or increased, the depression in the Upcountry deepened.[33] In 1827, John Ewing Colhoun, a prosperous Abbeville planter and brother-in-law of John C. Calhoun, reported that "times are so dreadful that there is no possibility of selling any kind of property." Capital was so scarce, Colhoun added, that there was not "enough in the Dist[trict] of Abbeville to purchase what is under execution." In 1818, Ezekial Noble raised nearly fifty bales of cotton and a "sufficiency of corn" on his Abbeville plantation, but by 1827 Noble's family was forced to sell many of their possessions, including "even the beds from under them," to pay off old debts until they were left with only "a fine house . . . and nothing in it."[34] The first cotton boom was over.

Before the first boom ended, however, Upcountry leaders had moved to shore up the region's position in the cotton economy. Their efforts, which centered on internal improvements, received valuable assistance from Charleston

---

Glaze Smith, Jr., *Economic Readjustment of an Old Cotton State: South Carolina, 1820–1860* (Columbia, S.C.: University of South Carolina Press, 1958), pp. 1–18; William W. Freehling, *Prelude to Civil War: The Nullification Controversy in South Carolina, 1816–1836* (New York: Harper and Row, 1965), pp. 25–48; Bray Hammond, *Banks and Politics in America: From the Revolution to the Civil War* (Princeton: Princeton University Press, 1957), pp. 251–285.

[31]Camden *Southern Chronicle*, January 23 and March 12, 1823, December 8, 1824, March 19, 1825; Camden *Journal*, July 22 and August 26, 1826, October 11, 1828; Charleston *Courier*, November 15, 1824.

[32]Camden *Southern Chronicle*, January 8, 1823.

[33]Freehling, *Prelude to Civil War*, pp. 26–27.

[34]John Ewing Colhoun to James Edward Calhoun, May 4, 1827, James Edward Calhoun Papers, SCL; Alexander Noble to Joseph Noble, December 4, 1818, Noble Family Papers, SCL.

merchants and politicians eager to expand the port city's hinterland.[35] The diffi-
culty of transporting crops to market down the swift-running, shoal-infested
Piedmont rivers or along rutted country roads had concerned Upcountry landholders long before cotton emerged as a major cash crop. In 1786, Upcountry
leaders supported a Lowcountry initiative to improve transportation between
Charleston and the fall line through the construction of a canal connecting the
Santee and the Cooper rivers.[36] A year later, Patrick Calhoun, Andrew Pickens,
Sr., and Leroy Hammond, all Savannah River valley planters, petitioned the
legislature in support of a canal between the Edisto and Ashley rivers which they
claimed would "improve communication between the northwestern parts of this
State and the city of Charleston."[37] By 1795, the state legislature had chartered
four inland navigation companies and had deeded tracts of ungranted public land
to each company as an indirect subsidy. With the important exception of the
Santee-Cooper Canal Company, none of the inland navigation companies
effected any lasting improvements. As the companies failed to provide better
transportation, public criticism of the private companies and the "unrepublican
monopolies" granted by their charters mounted.[38]

In 1817, Andrew Pickens, Jr., the first governor from above the fall line,
proposed a new approach to the question of internal improvements. Instead of
granting monopolies and indirect subsidies to private companies, Pickens recommended the use of money from the state treasury to fund a system of state-
controlled roads and canals. Following the favorable report of a civil engineer
hired to study the project, the South Carolina legislature created a state Board of
Internal Improvements and appropriated $1,000,000 in 1818 for an extensive
system of canals and roads designed to link the Upcountry with fall-line markets
and to facilitate travel from the fall line to Charleston. Most of the money was
earmarked for the construction of eight canals along major Piedmont rivers.
Canals at Wateree, Rocky Mount, Landsford, and Fishing Creek were to make
the Catawba-Wateree navigable from Camden to the North Carolina line. The
Broad River was to be opened for 110 miles above Columbia by the Columbia
and Lockhart canals, while the Saluda and Dreher canals were to make the
Saluda River navigable through Laurens and Abbeville districts, 140 miles northwest of Columbia.[39]

In an era when total annual state expenditures were normally around
$250,000 and when yearly state spending on education never exceeded $60,000,

---

[35]Smith, *Economic Readjustment,* pp. 135–142; the best account of these internal improvement
projects is Daniel W. Hollis, "Costly Delusion: Inland Navigation in the South Carolina Piedmont,"
Proceedings of the South Carolina Historical Association (1968):29–44.

[36]*State Gazette of South Carolina,* April 19, 1787.

[37]Klein, "The Rise of the Planters," pp. 284–285.

[38]Carl Epting, "Inland Navigation in South Carolina and Traffic on the Columbia Canal,"
Proceedings of the South Carolina Historical Association (1936):18–23; Klein, "The Rise of the
Planters," pp. 283–288; Chester District Grand Jury Presentments, 1816, SCDAH.

[39]*Camden Gazette,* November 29, 1817; *Camden Gazette and Mercantile Advertiser,* December
23, 1819; David Kohn, ed., *Internal Improvements in South Carolina, 1817–1828* (Washington,
D.C., 1938), pp. 69–93; Hollis, "Costly Delusion," pp. 29–31.

such lavish spending on internal improvements provoked quick criticism. A few opponents of the appropriation simply opposed government promotion of private economic interests, in this case, those of Upcountry planters and fall-line merchants.[40] But most of the criticism came from those who resented the state's promoting other interests more vigorously than their own. Spokesmen from the Pee Dee area, frustrated at the comparatively small share of the new appropriations designated for their region, charged that huge amounts of money were being spent on the Broad and Saluda rivers because they flowed "in the magical vicinity of Columbia." And Camden interests questioned whether the potential volume of cotton traffic on the Saluda and Broad justified such expensive improvements on those rivers.[41]

Criticism of the Upcountry canal projects as wasteful and extravagant reached new heights in 1822 when construction on the canals was reported behind schedule and over budget. Sensitive to charges of corruption and profligacy, and aware that the projects were a "disappointment," the state legislature demanded a full-scale investigation of its entire public works program. The lengthy report of the legislative committee on internal improvements candidly admitted that the program had been poorly managed, but also concluded that, after a reorganization of the project's management, the improvements should be completed. The committee requested a supplemental appropriation of $200,000 toward that end.[42]

Accepting the committee's recommendations, the legislature abolished the Board of Internal Improvements and consolidated its functions under a Superintendent of Public Works. It hired Abram Blanding, formerly a member of the defunct Board and a respected lawyer-engineer, to fill the position of superintendent, and displayed its determination to salvage previous investments by appropriating the additional $200,000 requested for the completion of the canals.[43] Camden's "Agricola" quickly charged that only "great Planters and great Merchants" would benefit from the canals since small farmers used wagons to market their crops, but canal promoters replied that improved transportation would save a poor Upcountry family enough each year on the cost of salt alone to pay its annual tax bill.[44] Between 1823 and 1827 the legislature appropriated several hundred thousand more dollars for the canals. With seven of the eight canals still unfinished by 1827, however, a new torrent of public criticism appeared. A Fairfield district grand jury complained that the canals "directly benefit but a very small number" while "the whole are being taxed for the benefit of the few." The Camden Journal dismissed the entire canal program as

[40]Hollis, "Costly Delusion," pp. 29–34; Smith, Economic Readjustment, pp. 144–145.

[41]Pee Dee Gazette, quoted in Camden Gazette, August 16, 1821, July 3, 1822; Camden Gazette and Mercantile Advertiser, December 7, 1820; Southern Chronicle and Camden Gazette, August 28, 1822.

[42]Reports and Resolutions of the General Assembly of South Carolina, 1822 (Columbia, S.C., 1823), pp. 95–100.

[43]Hollis, "Costly Delusion," pp. 34–36.

[44]Southern Chronicle (Camden), June 18, 1823.

"blundering speculations, false calculations, delusive theories, and vain expenditures."[45]

The legislature's generous support for internal improvements persisted in the face of withering fire from critics because of old-fashioned pork-barrel politics. The internal improvement projects proved an excellent source of public favors for politicians in a state where patronage was ordinarily hard to come by. Valuable construction contracts were awarded to former legislators and to friends of those still in office. One opponent of state funding, William J. Grayson, later explained that the project "took like wildfire" because every district had its own pet project, and each legislator was allowed to "get what he wanted." One scheme supported another, Grayson maintained, as "Mr. A. voted for Mr. B's canal and B voted for A's road."[46] Legislators defended themselves against charges of spoilsmanship. "Not an individual concerned has been guilty of corruption," insisted the Committee on Internal Improvements.[47] But criticism of the internal improvements program intensified despite such denials. When the legislature convened in November 1828, cotton prices were down to eight cents a pound, and a strong political faction led by the state's tight-fisted Comptroller General Alexander Speer, an Abbeville native, pushed hard for drastic reduction in state spending. This economy-minded legislature cut Superintendent Blanding's salary by over 25 percent, prompting his resignation, and refused to fund any new contracts related to the state's internal improvements program. Existing contracts were honored, and many of the roads and canals were completed, but South Carolina's spending binge was halted.[48]

Between 1818 and 1828, the state of South Carolina spent nearly $2,000,000 on internal improvements, and nearly 1.2 million went directly into Piedmont canals, but Upcountry farmers who yearned for easy and reliable access to fall-line markets remained frustrated. Once completed, the Piedmont canal system seldom worked well. Faulty design and damaging freshets left it in constant need of repair. By 1840 most of the canals had fallen into disuse. The state tried to lease the canals to private operators but found few takers. Even the Columbia Canal, built near the confluence of the Saluda and Broad rivers at a cost of over $250,000 and once the pride of the canal system, was abandoned by the state after a flood on the Broad in 1840 severely damaged it. The fast waters of the Upcountry rivers had proved far more difficult to tame than the state's commercial promoters had imagined. Indeed, these rivers defied conquest until the financial resources of the Duke family and the engineering genius of William States Lee harnessed the Catawba for the production of electric power over three-

[45]Fairfield District Grand Jury Presentments, November, 1827, SCDAH; *Camden Journal,* March 15, 1828.

[46]Robert D. Bass, ed., "The Autobiography of William J. Grayson" (Ph.D. dissertation, University of South Carolina, 1933), pp. 237–238.

[47]*Reports and Resolutions of the General Assembly of South Carolina, 1827* (Columbia, S.C., 1828), p. 65.

[48]Hollis, "Costly Delusion," pp. 37–39; *Camden Journal,* January 3, 1829; William W. Freehling, *Prelude to Civil War,* pp. 105–106, 120–121.

quarters of a century later. Yet the costly failure of the canal project not only failed to dampen the enthusiasm of Upcountry boosters for internal improvements but actually heightened interest in new technology that could provide the region with better access to major cotton markets.[49]

As interest in internal improvements attests, the cotton boom not only breathed new life into a moribund Upcountry economy but it also redefined the fundamental economic interests and aspirations of many Upcountry whites. The heady prosperity of the cotton boom generated a sense of economic optimism and a faith in the main chance which prevailed in the region for at least a generation. The cotton boom also brought thousands of Upcountry households into the slaveholding ranks, creating a stronger economic self-interest in slavery in the region and lessening its contrast with the slave-rich Lowcountry. Deepening involvement in the cotton economy also revived and enhanced Upcountry interest in closer ties to outside markets. The cotton boom had brought opportunity and wealth to the Upcountry and helped end the region's isolation. The boom's impact on Upcountry households is nicely illustrated by the example of the Spratt family of York district. Thomas Spratt, an Ulsterman, arrived in the 1760s to become York's first permanent white settler, but he owned only seven slaves when he died in 1807. His son, James Spratt, became one of "the first to plant cotton on a vast and extensive acreage" and increased his slaveholdings from only four when he started planting cotton in the early 1800s to twenty-five by 1830. In later years, James Spratt's son, Thomas Dryden Spratt, wryly observed, "My father's generation . . . by exploiting the fertility of the virgin soil and the fecundity of the virgin slave produced a wealth and established a culture."[50] Yet for all short-staple cotton had done to shape Upcountry society, Thomas D. Spratt exaggerated its claim. Cotton had not "established a culture" by itself.

Concurrent with the cotton boom, evangelical Christianity emerged from its scattered Baptist and Presbyterian enclaves to spread into almost every Upcountry neighborhood. This religious awakening in the Upcountry was part of a larger evangelical movement which began in Kentucky and Virginia around 1800, reached South Carolina by 1802, and lasted for most of a decade. Collectively this religious upheaval became known as the Great Revival, or, with less definite chronological boundaries, the Second Great Awakening. In the South Carolina

---

[49]Kohn, *Internal Improvements,* p. 517; Hollis, "Costly Delusion," pp. 39–43; Smith, *Economic Readjustment,* pp. 150–158; Epting, "Inland Navigation in South Carolina," pp. 18–23; David L. Carlton, "The Columbia Canal and Reconstruction: A Case Study," especially pp. 3–5, unpublished manuscript, SCL; Ulrich Bonnell Phillips, *A History of Transportation in the Eastern Cotton Belt to 1860* (New York: Columbia University Press, 1908), pp. 46–132; George B. Tindall, *The Emergence of the New South, 1913–1945* (Baton Rouge: Louisiana State University Press, 1967), pp. 72–73.

[50]Thomas Dryden Spratt's "Recollections of His Family," [c. 1875], Spratt Family Papers, SCL; Manuscript Census of South Carolina, 1800; Manuscript Census of South Carolina, 1810; Manuscript Census of South Carolina, 1830, SCDAH.

Upcountry, the Great Revival brought the message of evangelical Christianity to the ears of an overwhelming majority of residents, whether slave or free, and converted a significant minority of these hearers of the gospel into Christian communicants. By 1810 evangelical churches not only exerted a powerful moral influence on the region but also served as centers of community life in many parts of the Upcountry.[51]

During the eighteenth century, organized religion had flourished only sporadically in the South Carolina backcountry. Probably a majority of the region's settlers shared some type of Calvinist or dissenting heritage, since the two most numerous groups of Upcountry immigrants were Scotch-Irish Presbyterians and New Light Baptists who had moved into South Carolina down the Great Piedmont Road. Once in the Upcountry, however, the sparseness of the population, the danger and difficulty of travel, and the more pressing demands of subsistence and survival militated against successful church organization. In 1766, Patrick Calhoun and several of his neighbors in the Long Canes section of Abbeville asked the Provincial Assembly to provide a church in the Upcountry because "many people had never seen a church or heard a sermon." By 1769, Calhoun succeeded in organizing Hopewell Presbyterian Church, where he became a ruling elder, but the handful of Presbyterian and Baptist churches in the Upcountry ministered to only a tiny fraction of the population.[52]

Moreover, efforts by Lowcountry Anglicans to proselytize the backcountry met with indifference and even hostility. Anglican missionary Charles Woodmason's celebrated tour of the backcountry in the 1760s was a disaster. His meeting with Upcountry Baptist leader Philip Mulkey, pastor of Fairforest Church, ended in mutual disdain and distrust. Worse still, his visit to the Waxhaw region, near the birthplace of Andrew Jackson, resulted in a dramatic confrontation with angry Presbyterians and "lawless Ruffians" who insulted the Anglican cleric "with Impugnity." These Upcountry dissenters bluntly informed Woodmason that "they wanted no D- - - -d Black Gown Sons of Bitches among them" and threatened to lay the Anglican "behind the fire" if he

[51]John B. Boles, *The Great Revival, 1787–1805* (Lexington: University Press of Kentucky, 1972), especially pp. 70–89; Donald G. Mathews, *Religion in the Old South* (Chicago: University of Chicago Press, 1977), pp. 39–80; Kaplanoff, "Making the South Solid," pp. 76–94; George Howe, *History of the Presbyterian Church in South Carolina*. 2 vols. (Columbia, S.C.: Walker, Evans, Cogswell, 1883), vol. 2, pp. 106–120; Albert D. Betts, *History of South Carolina Methodism* (Columbia, S.C.: Advocate Press, 1952), pp. 159–167; Leah Townsend, *South Carolina Baptists* (Florence, S.C.: Florence Printing Company, 1935), pp. 296–305; Albert M. Shipps, *The History of Methodism in South Carolina* (Nashville: Southern Methodist Publishing House, 1883), especially pp. 270–396; Donald G. Mathews, "The Second Great Awakening as an Organizing Process, 1780–1830," *American Quarterly* 21 (Spring, 1969):23–43.

[52]Kaplanoff, "Making the South Solid," pp. 76–77; David T. Morgan, Jr., "The Great Awakening in South Carolina," *South Atlantic Quarterly* 70 (Autumn, 1971):595–606; Weir, *Colonial South Carolina*, pp. 205–227; Klein, "The Rise of the Planters," pp. 42–51; Rachel Klein, "Ordering the Backcountry: The South Carolina Regulation," *William and Mary Quarterly* 38 (October, 1981):661–680; Margaret Watson, *Greenwood County Sketches* (Greenwood, S.C.: Attic Press, 1970), p. 5.

refused to heed their warning. Neither the established Anglican church nor the formal liturgy of the Anglican service carried much appeal among the plain, independent, and relatively unlettered settlers of the backcountry.[53]

The halting advance of evangelical Christianity in South Carolina after the American Revolution is more difficult to explain. Despite the formal organization of the Methodist denomination in 1784 and the persistent efforts of Baptists and Presbyterians to enlarge their influence, only 8 percent of all white adults in the Upcountry were church members in 1799.[54] Baptists and Presbyterians were doubtless plagued by lingering doctrinal doubts over exactly how evangelical their essentially Calvinist denominations should be. The Calvinist doctrine of predestination, which holds that salvation is available only to those selected in advance for that opportunity by God, was threatened, at least to some extent, by the evangelical impulse, which tended to offer salvation more freely. Both Baptists and Presbyterians rejected the Arminian teaching of the Methodists that salvation was open to anyone who accepted God's free grace. To be sure, Upcountry Baptists and Presbyterians were much less rigorously Calvinist in

[53]Richard J. Hooker, ed., *The Carolina Backcountry on the Eve of the Revolution: The Journal and Other Writings of Charles Woodmason, Anglican Itinerant* (Chapel Hill: University of North Carolina Press, 1953), pp. 16–17, 112; Floyd Mulkey, "Reverend Philip Mulkey, Pioneer Baptist Preacher in Upper South Carolina," *Proceedings of the South Carolina Historical Association* (1945):3–12; Durwood T. Stokes, "The Presbyterian Clergy in South Carolina and the American Revolution," *South Carolina Historical Magazine* 71 (October, 1970):270–282; Durwood T. Stokes, "The Baptist and Methodist Clergy in South Carolina and the American Revolution," *South Carolina Historical Magazine* 73 (April, 1972):87–96; S. Charles Bolton, *Southern Anglicanism: The Church of England in Colonial South Carolina* (Westport, Conn.: Greenwood Press, 1982), especially pp. 37–85.

[54]Estimates of church membership in the Upcountry were constructed using the following sources: *Minutes of the Annual Conferences of the Methodist Episcopal Church for the Years 1773–1828* (New York, 1840); David Benedict, *A General History of the Baptist Denomination in America.* 2 vols. (Boston, 1813), vol. 2, pp. 528–531; Betts, *South Carolina Methodism,* pp. 53–110; Townsend, *South Carolina Baptists,* especially pp. 122–270. In using these sources, I have systematically excluded churches not located in the Upcountry. Membership records for Upcountry Presbyterian churches are too scattered to provide a reliable estimate. Thus I have followed Donald G. Mathews's assumption that Presbyterian membership was roughly 40 percent of the combined Methodist and Baptist membership; see Mathews, *Religion in the Old South,* p. 7. Based on impressionistic evidence, this assumption seems plausible though given the strength of Presbyterianism in certain parts of the Upcountry, this assumption may slightly understate the number of Presbyterians in the region. Only the Methodists reported membership by race. I have used scattered information on black-white ratios in Baptist churches from Townsend, *South Carolina Baptists,* to estimate that about 86 percent of all Upcountry Baptists were white during this era, and I have assumed that whites constituted roughly the same proportion of Upcountry Presbyterians. Using these assumptions, I have estimated that roughly 4500 white adults were members of evangelical churches in 1799. Over 1700 were Baptists, nearly 1500 were Methodists, and about 1300 were Presbyterians. These calculations parallel those made in Kaplanoff, "Making the South Solid," pp. 336–337. A study of evangelical efforts to convert blacks and of the important role blacks played in the evangelical movement lies beyond the scope of this volume but important new work is now underway on those subjects. For example, see John Scott Strickland, "Across Space and Time: Conversion, Community, and Cultural Change among South Carolina Slaves" (Ph.D. dissertation, University of North Carolina at Chapel Hill, 1985).

practice than their formal theology implied. But even as the competition with the Methodists for new members intensified, Baptists and Presbyterians continued to examine candidates for membership carefully. Occasionally, Baptists and Presbyterians declined to accept candidates, despite outward piety, because they were not satisfied with the evidence of true spiritual regeneration. Such selectivity about new members, no matter how irregularly applied, hampered evangelical efforts.[55]

Yet the nominal Calvinism of Upcountry Baptists and Presbyterians probably did less to slow the spread of evangelicalism than did the avowed antislavery sentiments common among the evangelical clergy. The Methodists, whose evangelical efforts proceeded without the slightest twinge of Calvinist doubt, were the most outspoken critics of slavery, and thus their denomination encountered the most serious opposition from slaveholders. In 1784, the first Methodist General Conference listed slaveholding as an offense punishable by expulsion from the church. Vociferous protests from individual congregations forced a suspension of this rule the very next year, but in 1795 Methodist ministers in the Upcountry signed a covenant which required them to free any slaves they owned unless state laws concerning manumission prohibited such action. In 1800 the Methodist General Conference ordered its ministers to divest themselves of all slave property. Mindful of these Methodist positions, Upcountry slaveholders viewed the Bible-toting, slaveless bachelors who rode the Methodist circuits with considerable suspicion.[56]

Antislavery sentiment was less pervasive among Presbyterian ministers than among Methodists but it was no less controversial when it did appear. In 1796, an outspoken opponent of slavery, James Gilleland, was ordained by the South Carolina Presbytery for a pastorate in Anderson district only after he agreed to refrain from preaching on the subject. The following year Gilleland appealed his restriction to the full Synod, but that body emphatically upheld the Presbytery's earlier ruling and advised Gilleland to "content himself with using his utmost endeavours in private to open the way for emancipation." Finally, in 1804, a frustrated Gilleland left Anderson for Ohio, where he became an active abolitionist.[57] At least two other Presbyterian ministers, William Williamson of Fairforest

[55]Mathews, *Religion in the Old South*, pp. 31–34; Boles, *The Great Revival*, pp. 125–164; Townsend, *South Carolina Baptists*, pp. 262–270, 286–291; Flint Hill Baptist Church Records, June 11, 1796, SCL; Poplar Springs Baptist Church Minutes, June, 1797, SCL; Brushy Creek Baptist Church Records, May 15, 1802, SCL; Fishing Creek Presbyterian Church Records, June 15, 1800, SCL.

[56]James D. Essig, *The Bonds of Wickedness: American Evangelicals Against Slavery, 1770–1808* (Philadelphia: Temple University Press, 1982), especially pp. 97–157; Donald G. Mathews, *Slavery and Methodism: A Chapter in American Morality, 1780–1845* (Princeton: Princeton University Press, 1965), pp. 3–29; Betts, *South Carolina Methodism*, pp. 53–100; Abel M. Chreitzberg, *Early Methodism in the Carolinas* (Nashville: Publishing House of the Methodist Episcopal Church, South, 1897), especially pp. 48–89.

[57]Howe, *Presbyterian Church in South Carolina*, vol. 1, pp. 534–635, 687–688; Margaret B. DesChamps, "Antislavery Presbyterians in the Carolina Piedmont," *Proceedings of the South Carolina Historical Society* (1954):6–13.

and Robert Wilson of Long Canes left South Carolina for Ohio by 1805 because of their opposition to slavery. Williamson, a slaveholder, freed his slaves before leaving. Wilson's successor at Long Canes, Daniel Gray, privately likened slavery in the Upcountry to the "fleshpots of Egypt" and vowed to follow his friends to Ohio. He soon muted his public opposition to slavery, however, and remained in South Carolina until he died in 1816.[58]

Antislavery leanings appeared far less frequently among Baptist ministers than among their Methodist and Presbyterian counterparts. Leah Townsend's study of the economic status of South Carolina's Baptists revealed that 40 percent of the state's Baptist ministers held slaves in 1790, while only about 30 percent of the laity were slaveowners.[59] Yet since a number of antislavery Presbyterian ministers were also slaveowners, self-interest alone is not an adequate explanation for the weakness of antislavery sentiment among Baptist clergymen. A probable explanation can be derived from the fact that the Baptists did not require formal theological education of the clergy, and thus their ministers were usually less learned than Presbyterian pastors and thus far less familiar with the antislavery movement growing throughout the transatlantic intellectual community.[60] During the 1790s, Upcountry Baptist associations consistently upheld the rights of slaveholders whose conduct as masters was consistent with other standards of Christian behavior, without any apparent objections from Baptist ministers. In 1793, the Buffalo Baptist Church in Union district asked the Bethel Association: "Where a master, and a negro servant, are both members in a gospel church, is the master justifiable in correcting the servant with stripes for disobedience?"[61] The Association answered in the affirmative. Two years later, it reluctantly acquiesced in the selling of slaves and allowed slave members to remarry if their spouses were sold to new masters who lived a great distance away. Pendleton district Baptists censured slave members who failed to report runaways. The only serious question regarding the compatibility of slavery and evangelical values arose in 1798, when Cedar Springs Baptist Church in Spartanburg district considered "whether or not it is agreeable to the gospel to hold Negroes in Slavery." After considerable discussion of the issue, the Cedar Springs church forwarded the query to the Bethel Association, which promptly buried the question in committee. Slaveholders continued as members of Cedar Springs, and in 1803 the church ordained David Golightly, a substantial local slaveholder, as minister.[62]

[58]Howe, *Presbyterian Church in South Carolina*, pp. 123, 129–30, 146, 166, 281–285, 316; DesChamps, "Antislavery Presbyterians," pp. 8–10.

[59]Townsend, *South Carolina Baptists*, pp. 280–281.

[60]David Brion Davis, *The Problem of Slavery in the Age of Revolution, 1770–1823* (Ithaca: Cornell University Press, 1965), pp. 286–296; Winthrop D. Jordan, *White over Black: American Attitudes Toward the Negro, 1550–1812* (Chapel Hill: University of North Carolina Press, 1968), pp. 343–374; Essig, *Bonds of Wickedness*, pp. 1–72; James A. Rogers, *Richard Furman: Life and Legacy* (Macon, Ga.: Mercer University Press, 1985), pp. 117–134.

[61]*Minutes of the Bethel Baptist Association, 1793*, p. 2; Townsend, *South Carolina Baptists*, p. 258.

[62]Townsend, *South Carolina Baptists*, pp. 257–258; Ellen Batson Watson, *A History of the Bethel Baptist Association* (Spartanburg, S.C.: B.F. Long Printing, 1967), pp. 3–31.

Antislavery views, no matter how doggedly held by a portion of the clergy, never attracted much of a lay following. Even before the cotton boom triggered a sharp rise in the number and proportion of Upcountry whites who owned slaves, uncompromising congregations forced antislavery ministers to either silence their opposition or move on. As early as 1797 the powerful Methodist Bishop Francis Asbury, a determined antislavery advocate, conceded that some accommodation on the subject of slavery was necessary because "it is of great consequence to us [evangelicals] to have proper access to the masters and slaves."[63] Once the cotton boom began and the ranks of the slaveholders grew, antislavery pastors faced congregations even more determined to preserve slavery. By 1803, Bishop Asbury, while remaining a trenchant critic of slavery in private, decided that antislavery activity must be abandoned if Methodism was to flourish in South Carolina. "I am called upon to suffer *for Christ's sake, not for slavery,*" a dejected Asbury explained.[64] At his suggestion, the Methodist General Conference of 1804 dropped all strictures against slavery and slaveholding from the denomination's book of discipline. Abandoning their futile and counter-productive criticism of slavery, Upcountry Methodists joined Baptists and Presbyterians in a renewed effort to Christianize the slaves and to instill an evangelical sense of moral stewardship in the minds of Upcountry masters.[65] As evangelical leaders muted their objections to slavery, whatever social stigma evangelicalism had acquired because of its antislavery potential dissipated and the evangelical message found a more receptive audience in the Upcountry.

Beginning with the first of the great revivals in 1802, and proceeding for the rest of the decade, evangelical Christianity captured the attention of Upcountry people as never before. Between 1799 and 1810, church membership grew from 8 percent of the adult white population to over 23 percent.[66] Baptist leader Richard Furman boasted that for every actual communicant (church member) there were six others who accepted evangelical teachings but remained outside of the church.[67] Doubtless Furman's claim was an exaggeration born of pious enthusiasm, but he was right to point out that church membership figures understated the scope of evangelical influence on Upcountry society. The forum in which the evangelicals enjoyed so much success during the decade was the

[63]Francis Asbury to George Roberts, February 11, 1797, in Elmer T. Clark, ed., *The Journal and Letters of Francis Asbury* (Nashville: Abingdon Press, 1958), vol. 3, p. 160.

[64]Francis Asbury to George Roberts, January 5, 1803, in Clark, ed., *The Journal and Letters of Francis Asbury,* vol. 3, p. 258.

[65]Asbury's entry of April 10, 1804, in Clark, ed., *The Journal and Letters of Francis Asbury,* vol. 2, p. 430; Mathews, *Slavery and Methodism,* pp. 23–87; Rogers, *Richard Furman,* pp. 221–230; James Oscar Farmer, Jr., *The Metaphysical Confederacy: James Henley Thornwell and the Synthesis of Southern Values* (Macon, Ga.: Mercer University Press, 1986), especially pp. 195–233; Eugene D. Genovese, *"Slavery Ordained of God": The Southern Slaveholders' View of Biblical History and Modern Politics* (Gettysburg, Pa.: Gettysburg College, 1985); Mathews, *Religion in the Old South,* pp. 167–184.

[66]Estimates made using the same sources and methods outlined in footnote 46. By 1810, nearly 14,000 white adults in the Upcountry were members of evangelical churches. Over 6000 were Baptists; Methodists numbered about 4000, as did Presbyterians.

[67]Benedict, *General History of the Baptist Denomination,* vol. 2, p. 172.

interdenominational outdoor revival, or camp meeting. Often lasting five to seven days, camp meetings were characterized by huge crowds, the mingling of denominations, sermons from a variety of preachers, intense revivalistic appeals and emotional responses, and unprecedented success in winning converts. From the outset, the emotionalism and casual theology of the camp meeting movement troubled some conservative evangelical leaders, but at its peak the camp meeting movement won dozens of souls daily for the evangelical cause.[68]

Following the patterns of earlier revivals in other states, the first recorded Upcountry camp meeting began in late May 1802 on the old Waxhaw militia ground in Lancaster district. The revival was organized by local Presbyterians but was also attended by over 3000 Carolinians who heard Baptist and Methodist as well as Presbyterian sermons. The Waxhaw camp meeting went on five days and featured more than twenty ministers. Rows of tents housed the congregated masses. Wagons scattered around the meeting ground served as rostrums. One observer estimated that over one hundred persons were converted during the course of the meeting, and that at least twenty persons "fell" on the first day. One group of skeptics who raced horses to the camp ground and then drank and cursed for much of the day was allegedly converted by nightfall. One "sinner" who vowed that "nothing but his bottle should ever bring him down" ended the first day on his knees wailing repentence.[69] Richard Furman, pastor of the First Baptist Church in Charleston, heard of the Waxhaw revival while on a visit to his boyhood home in the High Hills of Santee. Furman traveled to Lancaster to see the meeting firsthand. "Many seemed to be seriously concerned for the salvation of the souls," he reported approvingly, "and the preaching or exhortation of the ministers in general were well calculated to inspire right sentiments and make right impressions." Furman viewed the powerful emotions and the bodily man-ifestations of those emotions that characterized the revival with some concern but could not bring himself to entirely disapprove:

> Several persons suffered, at this meeting, those bodily affections which have been experienced in Kentucky, North Carolina, and at other places where the extraordinary revivals in religion . . . have taken place. Some of them fell instantaneously, as though struck with lightning, and continued insensible for a length of time; others were more mildly affected and soon recovered their bodily strength with a proper command of their mental powers. . . . In a few cases there were indications . . . of enthusiasm and even affectation, but in others a strong evidence of supernatural power and gracious influence.

On balance, Furman concluded, "these general meetings have a great tendency to excite the attention and engage it to religion. Were there no other argument in

---

[68]Dickson D. Bruce, Jr., *And They All Sang Hallelujah: Plain-Folk Camp-Meeting Religion, 1800–1845* (Knoxville: University of Tennessee Press, 1974); Boles, *The Great Revival,* pp. 69–110.

[69]"Testimony of Reverend Jonathan McGready, May 28, 1802," in Howe, *Presbyterian Church in South Carolina,* vol. 2, pp. 107–109.

their favor, this alone would carry great weight with a reflecting mind, but there are many more which may be urged."[70]

From Waxhaw, the revival spirit quickly spread into nearby York district, where the elders of the Bethesda Presbyterian Church organized a large camp meeting in June 1802. Attended by over a thousand people, the meeting attracted listeners from over forty miles away. The Holy Spirit, one Bethesda member recalled, "passed through that vast assembly like some mighty whirlwind. The people were moved as the trees of the wood are moved by the wind." Converts were won "from almost every age, character, class, and condition." Largely as a result of this camp meeting, the Bethesda congregation grew from about 60 persons in 1802 to over 300 by 1805, as "religion required an ascendency which it had not previously held" in the Bethesda area.[71]

In July 1802 the camp meeting movement reached Spartanburg district. Again local Presbyterians organized the meeting, but all evangelical denominations participated and over five thousand people attended. As evening approached on the third day of services, the meeting turned into what one participant called "one of the most sublime, awfully interesting and glorious scenes which could possibly be exhibited on this side of eternity." The emotions and physical enthusiasms of the revival reached a fever pitch.

> The penetrating sighs and excruciating struggles of those under exercise, the grateful exultations of those brought to a sense of their guilty condition . . . were sufficient to bow the stubborn neck of infidelity. . . . Some are more easily and gently wrought than others . . . different stages from mild swoon to convulsive spasms may be seen.[72]

Another Upcountryman who attended revivals during the Second Great Awakening remembered that converts "would suddenly fall to the ground and become strangely convulsed with what was called the jerks: the head and neck, and sometimes the body also, moving backwards and forwards with spasmodic violence."[73]

Between 1802 and 1805 over a dozen of these huge camp meetings and scores of smaller revivals were held in the Upcountry. James Jenkins, a Meth-

[70]"A Letter from Dr. Furman of Charleston to Dr. Rippon of London," in Benedict, *A General History of the Baptist Denomination*, vol. 2, pp. 167–171; Furman's letter was later printed in Howe, *Presbyterian Church in South Carolina*, vol. 2, pp. 109–113; see also Rogers, *Richard Furman*, pp. 101–115.

[71]"A History of Bethesda Presbyterian Church," pp. 79–87 in Bethesda Presbyterian Church Records, SCL.

[72]Townsend, *South Carolina Baptists*, pp. 298–299; "Ebenezer H. Cummings to a Friend in Augusta, July 7, 1802," *Georgia Analytical Repository* (1802):94–95; the Cummings letter is also printed in Catherine Cleveland, *The Great Revival in the West, 1797–1805* (Chicago: University of Chicago Press, 1916), appendix III, pp. 165–172.

[73]William Capers, "An Autobiography," in William M. Wightman, *Life of William Capers* (Nashville: Southern Methodist Publishing House, 1858), pp. 53–54.

odist itinerant and revival leader, was so impressed by their success that he informed Bishop Asbury that "Hell is trembling and Satan's kingdom failing."[74] During 1802 Big Creek Baptist Church in Anderson district added 124 new members. Between 1802 and 1804, Fairforest Baptist added 216 new members while Bethel Baptist of Spartanburg added 247.[75] As late as 1809 a series of revivals in Edgefield added nearly one thousand new members to church rolls in that district. Regular Baptist leader Edmund Botsford, pastor of the First Baptist Church of Georgetown, praised the Edgefield revivals as meetings marked "with deepest solemnity" and "not attended with any noise or falling down."[76]

Each evangelical denomination moved quickly, though in its own way, to institutionalize the revival movement. The demonstrative emotionalism, physical enthusiasm, and lack of rigorous doctrinal instruction that accompanied the camp meeting movement continued to trouble some evangelicals, especially Baptists and Presbyterians. Edmund Botsford claimed that "the greater part of the back-country people have incorrect Ideas on the nature of a gospel church" because of the inadequate and sometimes contradictory instruction given at camp meetings. Richard Furman acknowledged that "there are some incidental evils which attend them [camp meetings] that must give pain to anyone who feels a just regard for religion." In particular, Furman criticized "the too free intercourse between the sexes" and the antics of converts "of enthusiastic disposition." The church historian of Bethesda Presbyterian noted that "the irregularities and excesses" of the early revivals allowed "good and judicious men" to reach different conclusions about their usefulness. In 1804, the Presbyterian General Assembly issued a pastoral letter expressing its disapproval of the "corporeal phenonena" which accompanied camp meetings.[77]

Moreover, the Arminian doctrines of "free grace" and universal salvation promulgated by Methodist revivalists at the camp meetings troubled Baptist and Presbyterian leaders whose Calvinism had been diluted but not destroyed by the extraordinary success of the revivals. Baptists were especially concerned about preserving the integrity of the sacrament of the Lord's Supper. Baptists traditionally practiced "close communion," which allowed only true believers, defined as Baptist church members, to share the sacrament. When individual Baptist churches asked for permission to commune with Presbyterians and Methodists at camp meetings, the ruling Baptist associations steadfastly refused to grant approval. The combination of anxiety over excessive physical enthusiasm and concern for doctrinal purity led some Baptists and Presbyterians to infor-

[74]James Jenkins, *Experiences, Labours and Sufferings of the Rev. James Jenkins of the South Carolina Conference* (Columbia, S.C.: State Printing Co., 1842), pp. 115–116.

[75]Townsend, *South Carolina Baptists*, p. 301.

[76]Edmund Botsford to [?], November 1, 1809, Edmund Botsford Papers, SCL.

[77]Ibid.; "A Letter from Dr. Furman" in Benedict, *A General History of the Baptist Denominations,* pp. 167–171; see also Richard Furman to William Rogers, April 22, 1802, Richard Furman Papers, SCL; Bethesda Presbyterian Church Records, pp. 83–84, SCL; Howe, *Presbyterian Church in South Carolina,* p. 119.

mally withdraw from the camp meeting movement by the end of 1805.[78]

In an effort to remain aggressively evangelical and keep the revival spirit alive and yet maintain a semblance of propriety and doctrinal orthodoxy, Baptists and Presbyterians instituted a different revival form, the protracted meeting. Protracted meetings were usually sponsored by an individual church and often held indoors. Some visitors pitched tents on or near the church grounds, but most either lived in the area or stayed in private homes as guests. Due to the different logistical arrangements, protracted meetings normally attracted smaller crowds and were easier to control than camp meetings, thus allowing the host church to monitor revival teachings and congregational behavior more closely. Though open to all, protracted meetings were certainly more denominationally oriented than camp meetings, and the shift of Baptist and Presbyterians to protracted meetings marked a renewed emphasis on the winning of new members for specific churches as well as for the kingdom of the Lord.[79] Evangelism in the broadest sense was sacrificed, to some extent, to the more narrow aim of strengthening evangelical churches.

Despite their modest scope, however, protracted meetings were nevertheless effective evangelical tools. Rosannah P. Rogers, daughter of a prominent Union district planter, reported that a Baptist protracted meeting near Newberry in 1831 produced "a great revival" and fifty-one conversions.[80] In 1838, Elizabeth Cunningham of Laurens attended a protracted meeting at a local Presbyterian church which lasted for nearly two weeks. The meeting, Cunningham claimed, drew "large assemblies of people," produced "a great revival of religion in our Church," and added forty converts to the church roll.[81] It is clear that Baptists and Presbyterians, despite their refusal to abandon their Calvinist beliefs, remained active in the evangelical movement long after they withdrew from camp meetings. Yet Elizabeth Cunningham's comment on the Laurens revival of 1838 subtly revealed the new focus of revivalism among Presbyterians and Baptists; the protracted meeting in Laurens, successful as it was, produced a revival "in our Church." Church building now enjoyed nearly as much emphasis as soul saving in evangelical crusades.

Once Baptist and Presbyterian leaders decided that their denominations would no longer sponsor camp meetings, the Methodists moved quickly to capitalize on their rivals' withdrawal. At the height of the Great Revival, Methodist minister James Jenkins complained that, "for want of someone to nurse our converts," the fruits of the Methodist revivalist's labors were often reaped by

[78] "A Letter of Dr. Furman" in Benedict, *A General History of the Baptist Denomination,* vol. 2, pp. 167–171; Townsend, *South Carolina Baptists,* pp. 297–299; A. V. Huff, Jr., "A History of South Carolina United Methodism" in Morgan David Arant, Jr., and Nancy McCracken Arant, eds., *United Methodist Ministers in South Carolina* (Columbia, S.C.: South Carolina Conference of United Methodist Churches, 1984), pp. 351–439.

[79] Boles, *The Great Revival,* pp. 90–100; Bethesda Presbyterian Church Records, pp. 85–87, SCL; James Littlejohn to Robert Y. Russell, October 6, 1821, Robert Y. Russell Letters, DU; Henry H. Townes and Lucretia Townes to George F. Townes, June 6, 1832, Townes Family Papers, SCL.

[80] Rosannah P. Rogers to David S. Rogers, October 29, 1831, W. W. Renwick Papers, DU.

[81] Elizabeth Cunningham to Benjamin C. Yancey, October 18, 1838, Benjamin Cudworth Yancey Papers, SHC.

Baptists and Presbyterians.[82] The decision of the latter two denominations not to sponsor any more camp meetings made it easier for the Methodists to consolidate their gains. By 1804 the Methodist Conference moved to strengthen local churches by establishing one permanent camp ground in each circuit. Annual revivals, sponsored and managed by local Methodists, were to be held on these grounds in the hope of winning new converts for local Methodist congregations. These Methodist camp meetings remained inclusive, since all evangelicals were encouraged to participate and the Arminian message of open salvation was preached. But just as the protracted meetings institutionalized the evangelical impulse for the Baptists and Presbyterians, the more routinized camp meetings harnessed and institutionalized that impulse among Methodists.[83]

By 1820, the identification of camp meetings with the Methodist denomination had grown quite strong, and the meetings remained a very effective evangelical technique. In 1821, the Reverend James E. Glenn, an Abbeville Methodist, claimed that a nearby camp meeting left the people "very much afflicted in Every part of this Country." A year later, Glenn reported a "memorable" camp meeting in Abbeville, where "eighty souls" were "converted to God."[84] By 1842, an aging James Jenkins feared that Methodist camp meetings had become so routinized that they had lost their original spiritual purity and evangelical vigor. Jenkins acknowledged that the "tents are better" and the meetings conducted "with more regularity and order," but he also claimed that there was "too much smoking of tobacco, and light, frothy and trifling conversation" and not enough "singing and praying." Jenkins also criticized the "extravagance in dress" that characterized latter-day camp meetings, complaining, "Many, I have no doubt, live much better and dress much finer at camp-meetings than they do at home."[85] Order and respectability, however, apparently lay in the eyes of the beholder; after preaching at a Methodist camp meeting in Newberry in 1848, Baptist revivalist William Hill decried the "laughing, squealing, and clapping of hands and whooping" which still occurred during the services.[86]

As Donald G. Mathews has pointed out, by the 1820s evangelical Christianity no longer concentrated solely on the salvation of lost souls, but instead devoted a healthy portion of its resources to the maturation and refinement of church institutions, which more often than not were designed to nurture souls already saved.[87] The regularization of the revival process and the increasing

---

[82]Jenkins, *Experiences*, p. 118.

[83]Betts, *South Carolina Methodism*, pp. 101–109, 159–167; Jenkins, *Experiences*, pp. 111–122; Jesse Lee, *A Short History of the Methodists in the United States of America* (Baltimore, 1810), pp. 280–281; Capers "An Autobiography," pp. 51–228; Huff, "A History of South Carolina United Methodism," pp. 365–376.

[84]James E. Glenn to John Wesley Young, October 22, 1821, and James E. Glenn to John Wesley Young, August 26, 1822, John Wesley Young Papers, DU.

[85]Jenkins, *Experiences*, pp. 149–150.

[86]Entry of October 29, 1848, William P. Hill Diary, SHC.

[87]Mathews, "The Second Great Awakening as an Organizing Process," pp. 23–43; see also William Warren Sweet, *Religion in the Development of American Culture, 1765–1840* (New York: Scribner, 1952).

denominational control over all forms of revival were simply part of this process of institutional maturation and of the concomitant emphasis on denominational distinctions within the evangelical movement. Yet without the fruits of the Great Revival the rise of the institutional church and denominationalism among Upcountry evangelicals would have been neither possible nor necessary. The Great Revival brought thousands of new converts and their families into the church and triggered the creation of scores of new churches, giving evangelicalism popularity, social respectability, and moral influence in Upcountry communities that it had never before enjoyed. Each evangelical denomination worked hard to consolidate and enhance its gains, and out of their efforts grew the evangelical institutions that would wield significant influence in the region by the late antebellum years.[88]

If the Great Revival, or Second Great Awakening, laid the foundation for later evangelical development in the Upcountry, the awakening itself, and especially its timing, remains largely unexplained, and perhaps inexplicable, in secular terms. Why did evangelical Christianity, virtually inert for so long, suddenly spread so rapidly through the Upcountry? The camp meetings provided an easily accessible public forum for evangelical teaching, but why did the evangelical message suddenly develop so much popular appeal? Some historians have linked the religious awakening of this era to a heightened sense of guilt over the material success spawned by the cotton boom, which began just a few years before the Great Revival reached South Carolina. According to this interpretation, as the simple subsistence economy, where virtue was imposed by harsh circumstances, gave way to a burgeoning market economy, where cotton, slaves, and credit brought new prosperity, men and women confronted their own greed and ambition, their own appetite for worldly comfort and pleasure. Confronting one's own sinfulness is always difficult, but it was all the more so for these Upcountry men and women because they were unwilling to give up the new material comforts and pleasures that were the tangible manifestations of their wickedness. Evangelical Christianity offered a solution. One accepted that he or she had fallen short of the glory of God, cried the expected *mea culpa,* asked for forgiveness, and accepted Grace. That done, the newly saved evangelicals could proceed to acquire more earthly wealth, provided that it was gained and marshaled in a spirit of Christian stewardship.[89]

---

[88]Boles, *The Great Revival,* pp. 193–203; Mathews, *Religion in the Old South,* pp. 81–135; Eugene D. Genovese and Elizabeth Fox-Genovese, "The Religious Ideals of Southern Slave Society," *Georgia Historical Quarterly* 70 (Spring, 1986):1–16; Anne C. Loveland, *Southern Evangelicals and the Social Order, 1800–1860* (Baton Rouge: Louisiana State University Press, 1980). For an argument stressing the persistence of more traditional ethical codes as powerful counterweights to evangelicalism, see Bertram Wyatt-Brown, *Southern Honor: Ethics and Behavior in the Old South* (New York: Oxford University Press, 1982), especially pp. 101–105.

[89]For an example of this argument applied to South Carolina, see Kaplanoff, "Making the South Solid," pp. 82–91; James Oakes, *The Ruling Race: A History of American Slaveholders* (New York: Alfred A. Knopf, 1982), pp. 97–104 emphasizes the evangelical suspicion of wealth and materialism. See also Mathews, *Religion in the Old South,* pp. 136–184.

For all the apparent plausibility of this interpretation, however, the evidence offers only very limited support for it. Material success undoubtedly created discomfiture in the minds of at least some Upcountry whites who had been exposed to evangelical teaching. After attending a Methodist camp meeting in 1806, William Capers, the son of a prosperous Camden planter, felt uncomfortable about enjoying "the pleasures of the gay world" at a formal ball where "elegance and fashion" prevailed. Capers later converted to Methodism, gave up his "breastpin and ruffles," and rose to the rank of Bishop. Yet Capers felt little anxiety about his wealth and finery until after his appearance at a camp meeting, and even then he admitted "no extraordinary guilt" regarding his worldly possessions.[90] On the whole, few Upcountry whites seemed unduly troubled by whatever worldly success they enjoyed during the first cotton boom. If anything, they appeared more likely to associate prosperity with Providential blessing than with personal wickedness.[91]

But if the Great Revival did not appear solely to assuage consciences rendered guilty by the cotton boom, it did appear just in time to provide another important social function. Between 1790 and 1800, the white population of the Upcountry grew by nearly 50 percent. In certain Upcountry districts, the population increased even more dramatically. The white population of Greenville district rose by over 80 percent between 1790 and 1800, and the white population of Pendleton doubled during the same decade. Thus during the first decade of the nineteenth century, large numbers of recent arrivals were making new homes in the Upcountry. But a good number of these settlers did not call the Upcountry home for long. Almost as soon as the cotton boom began, some Upcountry families headed further south in search of better cotton growing lands. Between 1800 and 1810, nearly a quarter of the original white population of the Upcountry left the region. Due to continued in-migration and a healthy birth rate, the white population of the Upcountry increased slightly during the decade, but Upcountry society was clearly in a state of flux during the early years of the nineteenth century.[92]

This state of social flux can hardly be said to have caused the Great Revival, or even to fully explain its timing, but the highly mobile nature of the Upcountry population during the early 1800s undoubtedly helped create a social context

[90]Capers, "An Autobiography," pp. 51–83.

[91]Boles, *The Great Revival,* pp. 166–171; Survey of records and minute books from Bush River Baptist Church, Newberry, Sandy Level Baptist Church, Fairfield, Brushy Creek Baptist Church, Greenville, Clear Springs Baptist Church, Greenville, Mountain Creek Baptist Church, Greenville, Bethabara Baptist Church, Laurens, Poplar Springs Baptist Church, Laurens, Big Creek Baptist Church, Anderson, Padgett's Creek Baptist Church, Union, Flint Hill Baptist Church, York, Bethesda Presbyterian Church, York, Bethel Presbyterian Church, York, Fairview Presbyterian Church, Greenville, Fishing Creek Presbyterian Church, Chester, Cedar Springs Presbyterian (later Associate Reformed Presbyterian) Church, Abbeville, SCL. No records from Methodist churches in the Upcountry were available at the South Caroliniana Library.

[92]Calculations made from Julian J. Petty, *The Growth and Distribution of Population in South Carolina* (Columbia, S.C.: South Carolina State Council for Defense, 1943), pp. 68–74, appendix F; Kaplanoff, "Making the South Solid," pp. 28–49.

favorable to a religious awakening. In an era when people were moving about frequently in search of a home, evangelical Christianity offered social as well as moral moorings both to those who had just arrived and to those left behind. While the cotton boom preferred economic opportunity, evangelicalism and church membership offered spiritual sustenance, moral guide-posts, and a sense of belonging to a community that extended beyond one's own household. In this sense, the Second Great Awakening in the South Carolina Upcountry fueled a process of community creation, rather than community purification and regeneration.

Analysis of the changing composition of Upcountry congregations during the early nineteenth century confirms that the religious awakening of that era was, in part, a process of community organization. The evangelical denominations included a broad cross-section of the region's population: wealthy planters, small slaveholders, non-slaveholders, and slaves. On balance, however, the preponderance of evangelicals were neither planters nor poor whites, but were instead the small slaveholders and substantial yeomen who comprised the "middling sort" of Upcountry society.[93] Yet as the cotton boom spread through the region, the composite economic position of evangelical congregations improved significantly. In 1800, only 27 percent of the adult white male members of Brushy Creek Baptist Church in Greenville district owned slaves, and among slaveowners the size of the average holding was 3.5. By 1810, 60 percent of Brushy Creek's adult white male members owned slaves, and the average size of their holdings had grown to 5.1.[94] At Fairview Presbyterian, also in Greenville district, the percentage of adult white male members owning slaves rose from 23 in 1790 to 57 in 1810. In Greenville district as a whole, only 17 percent of all households owned slaves in 1800, and only 25 percent owned slaves in 1810.[95] In York district, only 28 percent of Flint Hill Baptist's adult male members owned slaves in 1800, but by 1810 exactly 50 percent were slaveholders. During the same decade, the size of the average slaveholding for Flint Hill members increased from 4.2 to 7.6.[96]

Church leaders tended to be men of more substantial means than the typical member, but they were still men of the "middling sort." At Bethesda Presbyterian, a church located in a fertile cotton growing area near the Catawba River, 45 percent of all ruling elders owned slaves in 1790, but nearly 70 percent owned slaves in 1810 and over 80 percent held slaves by 1820. The average number of slaves held by members of the Bethesda session grew from 1.8 in

[93]See church records cited in footnote 87.

[94]Calculation made from information gathered from Brushy Creek Baptist Church Records, SCL, and South Carolina Manuscript Census, 1800, and South Carolina Manuscript Census, 1810, SCDAH.

[95]Fairview Presbyterian Church Records, SCL, and South Carolina Manuscript Census, 1790, South Carolina Manuscript Census, 1800, South Carolina Manuscript Census, 1810, SCDAH.

[96]Flint Hill Baptist Church Records, SCL, and the manuscript census data cited in footnote 91.

1790, to 3.4 in 1800, to 5.5 in 1810, and to 8.0 by 1820.[97] During this era of rapid church expansion, the evangelical denominations drew heavily from the ranks of Upcountry families who were moving up, at least modestly, with the cotton boom.

Moreover, a disproportionate share of the new converts won by the evangelicals between 1800 and 1820 came from upwardly mobile, and relatively young, Upcountry families. At Brushy Creek Baptist, Flint Hill Baptist, and Fairview Presbyterian, over three-quarters of all adult males who joined the church between 1800 and 1820 were heads of households, and a solid majority of them were between the ages of 26 and 45. At Brushy Creek Baptist married couples usually joined the church together, and this practice was common at other evangelical churches as well. Fifty percent of the adult white males who joined Brushy Creek Baptist during the Great Revival and remained long enough to be enumerated in the 1810 census owned no slaves in 1800 but had become slaveholders by 1810. Over 90 percent of the Brushy Creek converts who held slaves in 1800 had increased their holdings by 1810. A similar pattern prevailed at Flint Hill Baptist, where a majority of white males converted during the early revivals increased their slave holdings between 1800 and 1810.[98] These young white males and their families, enjoying a modicum of upward mobility in the early 1800s, were the backbone of the evangelical congregations during the Second Great Awakening. To these young families trying to find their place in a kinetic society, church affiliation served as an expression of membership in the community, a symbol of respectability, and a source of fellowship. For the many sincere evangelicals, the sense of community gained through church membership no doubt paled by comparison with the promise of salvation and eternal life, but the sense of belonging and the enjoyment of the church's earthly fellowship were still matters of some importance.

Also important was the moral guidance offered by evangelical Christianity to a society scarcely one generation removed from the frontier. Evangelical morality was taught in the churches and enforced by church courts, but in the final analysis the only power evangelicals held over those who violated church teachings was their ability to exclude violators from the fellowship of the church. If church fellowship was valued, church courts could be a potent disciplinary force; if fellowship was not valued, church courts had little means of correcting allegedly wayward behavior.[99]

[97]Bethesda Presbyterian Church Records, SCL, South Carolina Manuscript Census, 1820, SCDAH, and the manuscript census records cited in footnote 91.

[98]Calculation made from the Brushy Creek Baptist Records and the Flint Hill Baptist Church Records, SCL, and the South Carolina Manuscript Census, 1800, and South Carolina Manuscript Census, 1810, SCDAH. I would like to thank James Hill of the University of South Carolina for his help in compiling this data.

[99]Howe, *Presbyterian Church in South Carolina*, pp. 712–714; W. D. Blanks, "Corrective Church Discipline in the Presbyterian Churches of the Nineteenth Century South," *Journal of Presbyterian History* 44 (June, 1966):89–105.

Church courts stayed active between 1800 and 1820, ordinarily enforcing evangelical morality with a careful balance between rigor and compassion. By far the greatest number of cases which came before church courts during these years dealt with personal immorality and vice. Offenses usually centered around drunkenness, dancing, or gambling, though charges involving fornication, adultery, and bastardy were not uncommon. Drinkers, dancers, and gamblers were ordinarily censured or rebuked rather than expelled for their first offense. Even those who had been expelled were usually restored to full fellowship if they asked for forgiveness and promised to repent.[100] By August 1806 the Poplar Springs Baptist Church in Laurens district expelled Elizabeth Simmons for a second time on charges of excessive drinking, but Sister Simmons was restored to full fellowship in October 1807. Brushy Creek Baptist censured Archibald Fowler for drunkenness and other sins in June 1802, but restored him the following July after Fowler admitted his guilt. By 1804, however, Fowler was again charged with drunkenness. Fowler admitted his guilt, and Brushy Creek, after a considerable delay, excommunicated him.[101]

Even fornication and adultery were readily forgiven by church courts when the offenders expressed repentance. Cedar Springs Presbyterian Church in Abbeville district received William Stewart into full fellowship in 1802 after he gave "public satisfaction for the sin of fornication," and later that year the same church restored John and Mary Douglas to fellowship after they gave "satisfaction for the sin of adultery."[102] In 1815, the Fishing Creek Presbyterian Church of Chester district baptized the infant child of Sarah Latta, who was not married, and admitted Sarah to membership following "a profession of her repentence in respect to the crime of fornication . . . and of her faith in the Divine Redeemer."[103] The spirit of forgiveness, the purposeful leniency, which prevailed in church courts on these matters was calculated to enhance the influence of evangelical morality through the nurture of backsliders and the expansion of the evangelical flock. If evangelical morality was to conquer the region, it would be through the power of persuasion rather than punishment.

The influence of church discipline was even more circumscribed in the realm of economic activity. Since the expansion of the market economy associated with the first cotton boom proceeded concurrently with the expansion of evangelicalism fostered by the Great Revival, churches faced a number of questions concerning the compatibility of evangelical values and market values. In practice, most evangelical churches used their disciplinary power to encourage honesty and fairness in economic activity and to discourage cheating, reckless profiteering, and violations of the Sabbath. In 1799, Brushy Creek Baptist rebuked Abraham Carney for grinding corn on the Sabbath. Four years later Big Creek Baptist Church in Anderson district expressed its disapproval of "starting to

[100]Generalizations based on study of church records listed in footnote 87.

[101]Poplar Springs Baptist Church Records, August, 1806, October, 1807, April, 1812, SCL; Brushy Creek Baptist Church Book, June 19, 1802, July 17, 1802, December 15, 1805, SCL.

[102]Cedar Springs Presbyterian Church Session Book, May 6, 1802, June 20, 1802, SCL.

[103]Fishing Creek Presbyterian Church Minutes, September 30, 1815, SCL.

market" or "rolling hogshead" on the Sabbath. Brushy Creek Baptist also found Archibald Fowler guilty of extortion when he intimidated a woman into selling him three chairs for one dollar. In 1803, the Friendship Baptist Church of Spartanburg disciplined a member for fraudulent horse trading.[104]

Evangelical church courts were also uncompromising in their support of legal contracts and private property rights. In 1801, Cedar Springs Presbyterian rebuked James Robinson for keeping a bolt of cloth which he found along the road to Abbeville village but which did not belong to him. Big Creek Baptist rebuked Adam Williamson in 1804 for presenting "a stray hound dog" which followed him home one day as his own, and that same year Cedar Springs Presbyterian rebuked Andrew White for incorporating unmarked hogs into his own marked flock. Between 1799 and 1804, the Enoree Baptist Church in Greenville district disciplined members who failed to pay legal debts, and Cedar Springs Presbyterian rebuked members who refused to fulfill contractual obligations. In these instances, the evangelical insistence on Christian conduct in matters of trade and property actually raised the standards of trust, discipline, and reliability on which public confidence in the marketplace depended.[105]

Churches occasionally found it more difficult to square evangelical values with market impulses in cases involving extortion, profiteering, and price-gouging. As early as 1786 the Turkey Creek Baptist Church of Abbeville district resolved unanimously "that no member . . . shall sell corn for more than two shillings per bushel nor wheat for more than three shillings per bushel." But in 1799, Baptists in Pendleton district dismissed charges brought against Josiah Burgess for selling his gain at extraordinary prices because "owing to the Various Sircumstances [sic] which often attend contracts Respecting that article" it was considered impossible to fix a regular price on grain.[106]

The most serious controversy over price-gouging emerged from Anderson district during a severe drought in 1807. Benjamin Bowen of Big Creek Baptist accused some of his fellow members with taking advantage of conditions by charging exorbitant prices for corn. The church court at Big Creek could not reach a decision on Bowen's complaint and referred it to a higher ecclesiastical authority, the Saluda Baptist Association. When Bowen refused "to take gospels steps" with the accused, he was declared "out of fellowship" by the Big Creek church.[107] In the meantime, the Big Creek congregation pledged to accept the Saluda Association's decision. At its August 1807 meeting the Saluda Baptist

[104]Brushy Creek Baptist Church Book, July 16, 1799, SCL; Big Creek Baptist Church Minutes, December 3, 1803, SCL; Brushy Creek Baptist Church Book, March 20, 1802, SCL; Townsend, *South Carolina Baptists*, pp. 134–135.

[105]Cedar Springs Presbyterian Church Session Book, July 16, 1801, SCL; Big Creek Baptist Church Minutes, December 3 and 31, 1803, February 4, March 3 and 31, 1804, SCL; Townsend, *South Carolina Baptists*, p. 215; Cedar Springs Presbyterian Church Session Book, August 13, 1801, SCL.

[106]Townsend, *South Carolina Baptists*, pp. 186–187, 233–234.

[107]Big Creek Baptist Church Minutes, August 1, September 5, October 31, 1807, January 2 and May 30, 1808, SCL.

Association considered the query from Big Creek: "Shall we hold members in fellowship who sell corn at one dollar per bushel?" The Association refused to debate the query formally, but advised Big Creek that while the church had no authority to "make the price of a bushel of corn an article of faith," it did have the power to discipline members "who grind the face of the poor, or oppress the widow or the fatherless in the sale of corn or otherwise."[108] Thus by the height of the cotton boom evangelicals refused to interfere with market price fluctuations by setting a "just" price, but at the same time they insisted that Christian stewardship and charity must not be sacrificed on the altar of greed. In a circular letter issued following its decision on the query from Big Creek, the Saluda Baptist Association stated its general position forcefully. Evangelical doctrine, the Association declared, held "that everything lawful be done to promote our own and our neighbor's estate, and all dishonesty, stealing, robbery, extortion . . . be detested."[109] Evangelicalism moved to meliorate the wrongs and excesses attendant to the market economy, but not to displace the market as the principal arbiter of economic transactions.

Even if evangelicals had wanted to contest the growing dominance of the marketplace more directly, they probably lacked the leverage necessary for a successful challenge. A substantial majority of free adults in the Upcountry were not church members and thus were beyond the authority of church courts altogether. Disputes among members of different congregations within the same denomination were difficult for church courts to adjudicate, and disputes among evangelicals of different denominations were even more difficult to handle. And even though members were sometimes censured for taking their disputes to civil authorities, church courts could not prevent members from doing just that. "In this country, no ecclesiastical body has any power to enforce its decisions by temporal sanctions," explained equity chancellor and Presbyterian lay leader Job Johnston, "Such decisions are in this sense advisory—that they are addressed to the conscience of those who have voluntarily subjected themselves to their spiritual sway." The decisions of church courts, Johnston continued, "can have no influence beyond the tribunal from which they emanate." In civil matters, Johnston concluded, "it is the civil court, and not the ecclesiastical, which is to decide."[110] Evangelical churches enjoyed considerable moral influence over the minds of the faithful, but their influence on society as a whole was far too limited and segmented to support the imposition of a moral economy based on evangelical values. Many souls were rendered unto God, but by and large debt cases and contract disputes were taken to the civil courts of the state of South Carolina, and prices were determined by the marketplace.

[108]T. J. Garrett, *A History of the Saluda Baptist Association* (Richmond: B. F. Johnson Publishing Co., 1896), pp. 18–19.

[109]"A Circular Letter," in *Minutes of the Saluda Baptist Association, 1807,* p. 11.

[110]Harmon v. Dreher, 1 Speer, Eq. 87; John Caldwell et al., to Job Johnston, May 28, 1835, and Statement by Job Johnston to session of Cannon's Creek Church [c. 1835]; Job Johnston Papers, DU, offer evidence of Johnston's interest in the fine points of evangelical theology.

The expansion of evangelical Christianity during the early nineteenth century helped move the Upcountry from frontier to society. It helped build communities where only settlements had existed earlier, and it brought a humane and dignified moral code into the human wilderness of the backcountry. It encouraged self-discipline in a world where civil authority was often too remote to restrain license. In many ways, evangelical Christianity fit the Upcountry well. It was voluntary and intensely personal. It depended little on church hierarchy. The Upcountry was a region dominated by independent households whose heads were suspicious of outside authority and jealous of their own autonomy. But the power of evangelical Christianity to mold Upcountry society in its own image was clearly limited. In order to expand beyond its original enclaves, evangelicalism had to drop its objections to slavery. Once evangelicalism began to expand, it subordinated its economic authority to that of the marketplace. By 1820, or even by 1830, the Upcountry was influenced by evangelical values but hardly dominated by them. Indeed, it was not until after the Civil War that the peculiar combination of religiosity and genuine piety which turned evangelical Christianity into the Southern civil religion and manufactured the so-called Bible-belt gained full sway in the region.

During the early 1830s, the short-staple cotton economy showed signs of recovery. World demand for cotton once again grew rapidly, and cotton prices rebounded.[111] With the recovery, the "El Dorado" mentality of the earlier boom returned, albeit fleetingly. "Cotton is up to 20," Union district planter Robert Gage exclaimed in 1836, "and of course everybody is as rich as Rothschild and can buy what he pleases." Moreover, the rapid appreciation of slave property during the recovery prompted Abbeville planter Henry Townes to advise his brother in Greenville against selling any slaves because "they are yet the best stock a man can own." On Christmas, 1836, Robert Gage wryly observed that "Money, Money is all the cry—money here [Union] would almost get a man's wife if she would bring enough to buy a negro."[112]

The return of cotton prosperity was short-lived, however, as the calamitous Panic of 1837 and the severe aftershocks of 1839 and 1841 knocked the cotton economy into a tailspin which lasted until the late 1840s.[113] "It is likely to be the most distressing times for the people generally I have ever witnessed," lamented Spartanburg attorney James Edward Henry during the winter of 1840, "There is no money in the Country, everybody are in debt and the end is not yet in

---

[111]Smith, *Economic Readjustment of an Old Cotton State,* pp. 52–54; Gavin Wright, "An Econometric Study of Cotton Production and Trade, 1830–1860," *Review of Economics and Statistics* 53 (May, 1971):111–120.

[112]Robert I. Gage to James M. Gage, April 3, 1836, and Robert I. Gage to James M. Gage, December 25, 1836, James M. Gage Papers, SHC; H. H. Townes to George F. Townes, November 21, 1836, Townes Family Papers, SCL.

[113]Smith, *Economic Readjustment of an Old Cotton State,* pp. 19–44; Gavin Wright, *Political Economy of the Cotton South,* pp. 10–42.

sight."[114] By November 1842, cotton sold for less than five cents per pound in Columbia, and John Springs feared that even worse times lay ahead. "We have been peculiarly blessed with a succession of good crop years and an abundant supply of Provisions," Springs reasoned, "but let there come a bad season or unproductive crop . . . and then we may cry hard times in earnest. Distress will then pervade the country."[115]

The long agricultural depression of the 1840s worked special hardships on older cotton regions, like those in South Carolina, where soil exhaustion and erosion were serious problems. The cotton plant itself was not naturally destructive of the soil, but the type of cultivation practiced by most growers, especially the habit of shallow soil preparation and their indifference to proper drainage, led to rapid erosion and soil exhaustion.[116] "The successful cotton planter sits down in the choicest of his lands, slaughters the forest, and murders the soil," complained Fairfield planter William Ellison in 1828.[117] By 1841, James Henry Hammond claimed that higher yields on the fresh cotton lands in the old Southwest enabled Alabama planters to enjoy profits when the price of cotton was as low as six cents per pound, while South Carolina growers lost money whenever the price fell below eight cents.[118] Thus as yields on their older cotton land declined, Upcountry growers displayed a voracious appetite for the virgin lands of the cotton frontier. When his own lands were exhausted, the typical Upcountry planter, according to William Ellison, "buys all that he can from his neighbors . . . and continues the work of destruction until he has created a desert of old fields around him, and when he thinks he can be no better, sells his lands for what he can get . . . and marches off to a new country to recommense the same process."[119] The hard times of the 1840s exacerbated this long-standing tendency of Upcountry farmers to emigrate to the old Southwest.

Americans have often been characterized as an unusually restless or unsettled people, but antebellum South Carolinians were extremists in their passion for mobility. Nearly one-half of all whites born in South Carolina after 1800 eventually left the state. These emigrants from South Carolina usually proceeded in steplike fashion across the deep South, often staying in Georgia for a decade or a generation and then moving further west. By 1850 more than 50,000 South

[114]James Edward Henry to Samuel F. Patterson, January 14, 1840, Samuel F. Patterson Papers, DU.

[115]John Springs to Andrew Baxter Springs, November 10, 1842, Springs Family Papers, SHC.

[116]Mendenhall, "A History of Agriculture in South Carolina," pp. 166–227; Arthur R. Hall, *The Story of Soil Conservation in the South Carolina Piedmont, 1800–1860* (Washington, D.C.: United States Department of Agriculture, 1940).

[117]*South Carolina State Gazette and Columbia Advertiser,* September 27, 1828.

[118]James Henry Hammond, "Anniversary Oration of the State Agricultural Society, November 25, 1841," in *The Proceedings of the Agricultural Convention of the State of South Carolina* (Columbia, S.C.: Summer and Carroll, 1846), pp. 179–181.

[119]*South Carolina State Gazette and Columbia Advertiser,* September 27, 1828.

[120]See Table 1.1; Tommy W. Rogers, "The Population Exodus from South Carolina, 1850–1860," *The South Carolina Historical Magazine* 68 (January, 1967):14–22; Petty, *Growth and Distribution of Population in South Carolina,* pp. 68–84.

Carolina natives lived in Georgia, more than 45,000 lived in Alabama, and some 26,000 lived in Mississippi. South Carolina natives accounted for over 30 percent of all in-migrants living in these three deep South states. Hardest hit by the exodus were the short-staple cotton growing areas of the Palmetto state. From the earliest days of the cotton boom, the steady outmigration of Upcountry whites kept the growth of the white population well below the normal rate of natural increase. From 1800 to 1830, the average increase in the white population of the Upcountry was less than 10 percent per decade. Between 1830 and 1850, the Upcountry's white population actually declined by just over 1 percent per decade. Out-migration took its heaviest toll on the cotton-oriented lower Piedmont, where six of seven districts lost white population between 1830 and 1850. The white population of the lower Piedmont declined by 6 percent during the 1830s and by 7.3 percent during the 1840s. By contrast, most upper Piedmont districts showed modest increases in white population during these same decades, but these small gains were well below the natural rate of increase. A steady stream of upper Piedmont whites flowed into the Southwest between 1830 and 1850, while during those same years whites abandoned the lower Piedmont for the cotton frontier in unprecedented numbers.[120]

The relative importance of the push of hard times and soil exhaustion in the Upcountry versus the pull of cheap land and quick profits in the Southwest on prospective emigrants can never be measured precisely. Doubtless some Upcountry farmers were driven to the Southwest by the press of circumstances in South Carolina; others were lured to the cotton frontier by rumors of flush times there. As early as 1819, John H. Sims, a native of Union district and cousin of prominent Upcountry planter William Sims, offered a glowing report on prospects in Mississippi. The Natchez area, Sims insisted, "is the Richest section of country I ever Saw . . . the cotton generally as high as I can reach and set on my horse." Sims also praised the Mississippi hill country as a region where "any person May go, and make a choice of a cite, settle down, and Go to work. This is the Best Poor Man's Country I have ever seen," Sims told his cousin, "If you was to See this Country you never would be satisfied where you are."[121] Fairfield's William Ellison also recognized the pull of the cotton frontier. "The abundance and fancied cheapness of Western lands," Ellison admitted, "produce a disposition to emigrate."[122] During a visit to Alabama in 1833, Greenville natives George F. Townes and Samuel A. Townes judged that "in an ordinary crop year" an able Alabama planter could make three times as much cotton per acre as a Greenville district planter.[123] But these and other accounts praising the old Southwest as a land of milk and honey often fell on receptive ears due to hard times in the Upcountry. In 1845 John Springs's worst fears of "hard times in earnest" were realized when a severe drought caused the wide-

[121]John H. Sims to William Sims, October 9, 1819, William Sims Papers, DU.

[122]*South Carolina State Gazette and Columbia Advertiser,* September 28, 1828.

[123]George F. Townes and Samuel A. Townes to Rachel Townes, December 7, 1833, Townes Family Papers, SCL.

Table 1.1 Population Growth in the Upcountry, 1830–1850
(Percent Gain or Loss by District)

	1830–1840			1840–1850		
	White	Black	Total	White	Black	Total
Lower Piedmont						
Abbeville	−6.6	16.4	4.3	−8.6	26.8	10.1
Chester	−0.5	8.6	3.3	−19.1	27.7	1.6
Edgefield	0.5	14.7	7.7	8.2	29.0	19.5
Fairfield	−21.8	6.2	−6.4	−6.8	14.0	6.1
Laurens	−7.3	23.5	3.4	−9.6	31.2	8.4
Newberry	−8.0	19.0	5.2	−11.8	27.2	9.8
Union	−1.6	16.5	5.6	−11.1	24.7	4 8
Upper Piedmont						
Anderson	0.3	28.7	7.7	8.8	37.2	16.1
Greenville	9.8	5.1	8.3	7.0	26.9	13.0
Lancaster	−9.7	3.5	−4.4	5.2	18.1	10.9
Pickens	0.7	−6.7	−0.8	13.9	42.4	17.7
Spartanburg	11.0	14.9	11.9	2.1	40.8	11.5
York	3.6	2.9	3.3	1.3	17.3	5.7
Lower Piedmont	−6.0	14.6	3.5	−7.3	26.0	9.7
Upper Piedmont	4.0	8.4	5.4	5.7	27.9	12.4
Upcountry	−1.4	12.8	4.2	−1.0	26.5	10.8

Source: Julian J. Petty, *The Distribution of Wealth and Population in South Carolina*
(Columbia, S.C.: State Council for Defense, 1943), Appendix F.

spread failure of subsistence crops and created a serious shortage of food and
feed grain in the region. A "Corn Panic" gripped much of the Upcountry during
the fall of 1845, and by November failed farmers were leaving the region in
droves. John Springs witnessed a caravan of "130 souls" preparing to leave
Yorkville in early November and predicted that many more would emigrate
before spring. In nearby Lancaster district, planter George M. Witherspoon, who
worked with Springs in an effort to import enough corn to relieve the crisis, also
lamented that "many of our citizens have left the County in consequence of the
failure of the provision crop."[124]

For the South as a whole, the large-scale exodus of whites from the South
Carolina Upcountry produced more good than harm. Migration to the cotton
frontier offered struggling farmers new opportunity; farmers who stayed behind
had room to expand without pushing displaced landowners into a state of propertyless dependence. Moreover, recent econometric studies have indicated that
migrants who left the Upcountry for the Southwest moved into a region of
expanding opportunity and rapidly rising incomes. In fact, most of the South's

[124]John Springs to Andrew Baxter Springs, November 19, 1845, John Springs to Andrew Baxter
Springs, November 5, 1845, George M. Witherspoon to John Springs, December 8, 1845, Springs
Family Papers, SHC.

impressive economic growth between 1840 and 1860 can be attributed to the massive shift of population to the more productive lands of the old Southwest.[125] Upcountry families who remained behind hardly flourished at the expense of those who chose to leave. Some individuals found disappointment, misfortune, failure, and even tragedy on the cotton frontier, but on the whole, the road to the Southwest was the principle avenue of opportunity in the Old South.

In an even larger sense, the role that bountiful western land played in both sustaining the cotton economy and shaping the character of Southern society can hardly be exaggerated. The westward movement of the population infused the Old South with a dynamism which it would otherwise have lacked. The much criticized indifference of most Southern farmers toward soil conservation resulted not from laziness or ignorance of sound agricultural practices but rather from the realization that labor, not land, was the scarce factor in nineteenth-century cotton production, as in most American agriculture of the period. Cotton growers tried to maximize output per hand instead of yield per acre.[126] This strategy explains much of the slaveholders' seemingly unquenchable thirst for fresh land and reveals the strong influence which the existence of slavery had on economic decisions in Southern society. Fresh land on the frontier provided cotton growers with a place to go; slavery provided Southern slaveholders with a mobile base of social and economic power unavailable to European landlords. Southern planters naturally developed bonds of attachment to their community and usually enjoyed considerable influence in their locales, but their slave property provided them with a source of wealth and independence that transcended any particular tract of land. Slavery prevented Southern planters from becoming quasi-feudal seigneurs bound to their rural manors and allowed them to follow cotton and the main chance from the banks of the Catawba to beyond the Sabine.[127] And every planter who chose to move westward found himself in the

[125]Richard A. Easterlin, "Regional Income Trends, 1840–1950," in Seymour Harris, ed., *American Economic History* (New York: McGraw-Hill, 1961), pp. 525–547; Robert E. Gallman, "Gross National Product in the United States, 1834–1909," in *Output, Employment, and Productivity in the United States After 1800*, Studies in Income and Wealth, Vol. 30 (New York: Columbia University Press, 1966), p. 26; Stanley L. Engerman, "The Effects of Slavery upon the Southern Economy: A Review of the Recent Debate," *Explorations in Entrepreneurial History* 4 (Winter, 1967):71–97; Stanley L. Engerman, "Some Factors in Southern Backwardness in the Nineteenth Century," in John F. Kain and John R. Meyer, eds., *Essays in Regional Economics* (Cambridge: Harvard University Press, 1971), pp. 274–307; Harold D. Woodman, "Economic History and Economic Theory: The New Economic History in America," *Journal of Interdisciplinary History* 3 (Autumn, 1972):323–350. The position of Gallman and Easterlin has been challenged by Gerald Gunderson, "Southern Antebellum Income Reconsidered," *Explorations in Economic History* 10 (Winter, 1973):151–176; and reasserted by Robert E. Gallman, "Slavery and Southern Economic Growth," *Southern Economic Journal* 45 (April, 1979):1007–1022.

[126]Gavin Wright, *Old South, New South: Revolutions in the Southern Economy Since the Civil War* (New York: Basic Books, 1986), pp. 17–50.

[127] The argument that the Old South was essentially a seigneurial society has been made by Raimondo Luraghi, *The Rise and Fall of the Plantation South* (New York: New Viewpoints, 1978), pp. 64–83. For a provocative recent study emphasizing the entrepreneurial bent of Southern planters, see James Oakes, *The Ruling Race*, especially pp. 153–191.

company of a score of yeomen eager to learn the secrets of success in the "school of hard knocks" that was the cotton frontier. In the South Carolina Upcountry, the love of mobility so pervaded the world views of planter and yeoman alike that one observer bluntly noted that "no man expects to die in his father's house."[128]

Yet while the South as a whole benefited from the steady westward flow of population, the section's gain was South Carolina's loss, and that loss eventually emerged as a major concern of the Palmetto State's political and economic leaders. As a rule, these leaders recognized that, in the short run, outmigration enhanced possibilities for those who remained; but they also viewed the shift of comparative advantage in cotton production away from South Carolina and the resulting loss of human capital as a serious long-run problem. Emigration, opined Lancaster's George Witherspoon during the corn panic of 1845, "will for the time being benefit those who remain by lessening consumption to some extent, but in the end it is feared the State will suffer a great loss."[129] The prolonged agricultural depression, highlighted by the wholesale exodus of whites, which followed the Panic of 1837 spurred concerned South Carolina leaders into action. Spearheaded by the newly formed State Agricultural Society of South Carolina, a well-organized agricultural reform and economic diversification movement emerged during the early 1840s. Politicians, entrepreneurs, and agricultural reformers collaborated in an effort to diagnose and treat the state's economic ills.[130]

The state legislature joined in the effort in 1842 when it commissioned Edmund Ruffin of Virginia, a noted agricultural reformer, to conduct agricultural and geological surveys of the state. Ruffin's report ultimately confirmed what some South Carolina leaders had long suspected. Cotton, the prime mover of the state's economy, was also a major contributor to its decline. Over the years, Ruffin's report concluded, emphasis on cotton production had worn out the soil, undermined subsistence farming, and retarded economic diversification. Ruffin's recommended cure was simple, but painful. South Carolina should wean itself from excessive dependence on cotton by diversifying its agricultural output and expanding its industrial activity. This reform program would purchase long-term economic revitalization with short-run sacrifices.[131]

Economic leaders and politicians of many persuasions quickly threw their support behind the reform crusade. New farming techniques were introduced. Boosterism flourished. A plethora of railroad-building schemes crystallized; in-

---

[128]Dr. S. H. Dickson, "An Address to the Charleston Horticultural Society, 1832," *Southern Agriculturalist* 5 (1932): 449–456.

[129]George M. Witherspoon to John Springs, December 8, 1845, Springs Family Papers, SHC.

[130]Smith, *Economic Readjustment of an Old Cotton State*, pp. 45–111; Drew Gilpin Faust, "The Rhetoric and Ritual of Agriculture in Antebellum South Carolina," *Journal of Southern History* 45 (November, 1979):541–568.

[131]Edmund Ruffin, *Report on the Commencement and Progress of the Agricultural Survey of South Carolina for 1843* (Columbia, S.C.: A. H. Pemberton, 1843).

vestment in manufacturing increased. Simpson Bobo, an aggressive entrepreneur with iron and grist mill interests at Hurricane Shoals, touted railroad development as the solution to the transportation problems which he blamed for the "perpetual cramp on trade in the Upcountry." Railroads, Bobo claimed, "would stimulate labor and industry, cause the farmers to improve their lands, [and] draw an increased amount of capital and labor in the country."[132] Following the lead of the State Agricultural Society, local agricultural societies sprang up to promote the familiar reform litany of crop rotation and diversification, proper drainage, and careful fertilization. "In the cultivation of cotton we have found the means of accomplishing two highly important but diametrically opposite results," reformer O. R. Broyles told the Anderson district agricultural society, "the sudden accumulation of great pecuniary profits and an almost total destruction of our lands." Broyles conceded that earlier admonitions for agricultural reform had been "about as effective as if addressed by a planter to his hog in the hope of convincing him that his proboscis or snout was unsuited to the business of rooting up potatoes" but warned that the hard times of the early 1840s made reform a "necessity."[133]

The long-term impact of the reform crusade is difficult to assess. When the Upcountry economy finally pulled out of its long slump in the late 1840s, the vocal reform movement quieted to a whisper. In 1849, Upcountry farmers produced 75 percent more cotton than they had a decade earlier and were as deeply enmeshed in the cotton trade as ever. But in that same year the Upcountry was largely self-sufficient in foodstuffs and a network of railroads which would eventually revolutionize transportation and trigger a commercial boom in the region was already under construction.[134] If the reform movement failed to lessen the Upcountry's involvement in the cotton economy, it succeeded in planting seeds of economic diversification that reached partial fruition during the 1850s. Still, many planters, middling slaveholders, and yeoman farmers stood willing to commit more resources to cotton if the price lines from Liverpool promised profits. Yet whether heeded or not, the advice of the reformers lingered in the minds of Upcountry farmers. If nothing else, the chorus of influential voices preaching the evils of cotton monoculture reminded the Upcountry subjects of King Cotton of their declining position relative to farmers in newer cotton areas and of the common vulnerability of all cotton growers to the recurring booms and busts of the international cotton trade.[135]

[132]Simpson Bobo to James H. Saye, November 22, 1848, James H. Saye Papers, DU.

[133]Draft of Address to Agricultural Society, c. 1845, Oze Reed Broyles Papers, DU.

[134]Lacy K. Ford, "Rednecks and Merchants: Economic Development and Social Tensions in the South Carolina Upcountry, 1850–1900," *Journal of American History* 71 (September, 1984):294–318.

[135]On the place of the South in the world economy, see Eugene D. Genovese and Elizabeth Fox-Genovese, "The Slave Economies in Political Perspective," *Journal of American History* 66 (June, 1979):7–23; and Immanuel Wallerstein, "American Slavery and the Capitalist World Economy," *American Journal of Sociology* 81 (March, 1976):1119–1213.

2

Planters and Plain Folk

By 1850, the Southern cotton culture had spread from the eastern cotton belt, which included the South Carolina Upcountry, southwest into Alabama, Mississippi, Louisiana, and to the Texas border. The gray sandy and red clay loam soils of the South Carolina Piedmont were no longer the South's most fertile cotton lands, but the Upcountry still produced about 5 percent of the South's cotton—more than North Carolina, Florida, and Texas combined and as much as the entire state of Louisiana. Despite having lost pride of place in the cotton economy to the newer growing regions of Alabama and Mississippi, the Upcountry remained an integral part of the cotton South.[1] Moreover, throughout the antebellum era, the South Carolina Upcountry occupied something of a middle ground between plantation black-belt and family-farm hill country. As a general rule, the expansion of cotton culture transformed the small-farm backcountry of one generation into the plantation-dominated black-belt of the next. Parts of the South Carolina Upcountry evolved in precisely this fashion. The gradual, almost systematic, expansion of cotton production between 1800 and 1850 turned backcountry districts where the population was over 80 percent white in 1800 into plantation districts which were well over 50 percent black a half-century later. But the expansion of plantation agriculture into the Upcountry proceeded unevenly and failed altogether in some places; thus the Upcountry remained in perpetual transition, no longer truly backcountry but never entirely a plantation region.[2]

In 1849, the Upcountry produced over 56 percent of all the cotton grown in South Carolina even though it contained only 36 percent of the state's large black population. Moreover, the Upcountry as a whole had a significant white majority in a state where 60 percent of the population was black. By contrast, Georgia's upper Piedmont was over 75 percent white and raised less than 10 percent of that state's cotton. But the South Carolina Upcountry was decidedly less dominated by plantation agriculture than the Delta region of western Mississippi. The Delta

[1]J. D. B. DeBow, *Statistical View of the United States . . . Being a Compendium of the Seventh Census* (Washington: Beverly Tucker, 1854), pp. 194–337.

[2]See Table 2.1; the standard account of the expansion of plantation agriculture is Ulrich Bonnell Phillips, "The Origins and Growth of the Southern Black Belts," *American Historical Review* 11 (July, 1906):798–816.

Table 2.1 Racial Composition of the Upcountry Population, 1800–1850

	Whites as a Percentage of the Total Population					
	1800	*1810*	*1820*	*1830*	*1840*	*1850*
Lower Piedmont						
Abbeville	77.8	68.0	58.3	52.8	47.3	39.3
Chester	85.8	75.9	67.3	57.9	55.8	44.4
Edgefield	72.0	62.3	51.2	49.0	45.8	41.4
Fairfield	80.3	65.7	54.6	45.0	37.7	33.1
Laurens	84.9	77.7	72.1	65.0	58.3	48.6
Newberry	80.9	70.5	53.2	51.1	44.8	36.0
Union	82.8	73.5	69.3	59.5	55.6	47.0
Upper Piedmont						
Anderson	—	—	—	74.0	69.0	64.6
Greenville	87.1	81.8	75.8	69.1	70.1	65.9
Lancaster	81.5	68.0	67.0	59.5	56.2	51.4
Pendleton	88.6	84.6	81.9	—	—	—
Pickens	—	—	—	79.2	80.5	77.6
Spartanburg	87.5	83.6	80.4	76.3	75.1	69.4
York	82.1	68.0	68.6	62.1	62.3	58.2
Totals						
Lower Piedmont	79.7	69.6	61.2	53.8	48.8	41.3
Upper Piedmont	86.3	79.6	76.5	70.7	70.0	65.7
Upcountry	82.4	73.5	67.2	60.4	57.0	51.0

Source: Julian J. Petty, *The Distribution of Wealth and Population in South Carolina* (Columbia, S.C.: State Council for Defense, 1943), Appendix F.

was over 70 percent black and raised 70 percent of Mississippi's cotton crop, which was 60 percent larger than South Carolina's by 1850. Another indication of the South Carolina Upcountry's anomalous position among Southern regions was the incidence of slaveholding in the area. Roughly half of all farm operators in the Upcountry owned slaves. In the hillcountry of north-central Alabama and Georgia's upper Piedmont less than 30 percent of all farm operators were slaveholders, while over 70 percent of all farmers in the vast southeastern black-belt owned slaves.[3]

[3]DeBow, *Statistical View of the United States*, pp. 194–337; Steven Hahn, *The Roots of Southern Populism: Yeoman Farmers and the Transformation of the Georgia Upcountry, 1850–1890* (New York: Oxford University Press, 1983), pp. 15–49; Herbert Weaver, *Mississippi Farmers, 1850–1860* (Nashville: Vanderbilt University Press, 1945), pp. 90–94; Michael Wayne, *The Reshaping of Plantation Society: The Natchez District, 1860–1880* (Baton Rouge: Louisiana State University Press, 1983), pp. 5–28; William L. Barney, *The Secessionist Impulse: Alabama and Mississippi in 1860* (Princeton: Princeton University Press, 1974), pp. 134–135; James D. Foust, "The Yeoman Farmer in the Westward Expansion of United States Cotton Production" (Ph.D. dissertation, University of North Carolina at Chapel Hill, 1967), pp. 115–135. Figures on the incidence of slaveholding among Upcountry farmers calculated from a sample of farms drawn from the Manuscript Census of South Carolina, 1850, Abbeville, Anderson, and York Districts, Schedules I, II, and IV, SCDAH. For a description of the sample see Statistical Methods and Samples at the back of this volume.

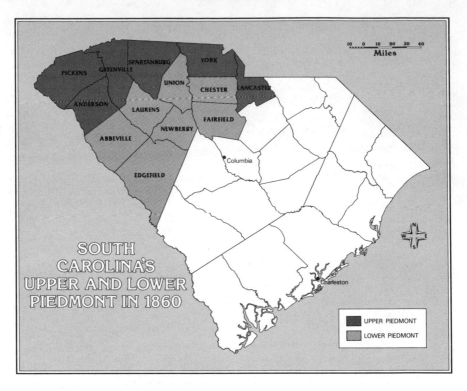

A closer look at the South Carolina Upcountry reveals that much of its apparent peculiarity can be explained by an important variation within the region itself. The Piedmont plateau of South Carolina was composed of two subregions which shared many environmental and geological characteristics, and a common political heritage, but which differed significantly in their suitability for plantation agriculture. By 1850 the most obvious difference in the two subregions involved racial demography. The lower Piedmont, which consisted of the seven Upcountry districts lying just above the fall line, was only 46 percent white. Characterized by a plantation economy similar to that of cotton-growing districts below the fall line, the lower Piedmont districts of Edgefield, Abbeville, Fairfield, and Newberry developed black majorities as early as 1840. Further into the interior, Chester, Union, and Laurens districts lay predominantly in the lower Piedmont but did not acquire black majorities until 1845. The other Upcountry subregion, the upper Piedmont, consisted of six districts: Anderson, Pickens, Greenville, Spartanburg, York, and Lancaster. All of these districts rested in the gently rolling red clay hills along South Carolina's borders with Georgia and North Carolina. By 1850 these districts were still nearly two-thirds white, and while plantations were not uncommon in the upper Piedmont, the area remained dominated by small and medium-sized farms.[4]

[4]See Table 2.1. Julian J. Petty, *The Growth and Distribution of Population in South Carolina* (Columbia, S.C.: State Council for Defense, 1943), Appendix F.

Table 2.2 Cotton Production in Regional Perspective, 1850

Area	Cotton-Corn Ratio	Area	Cotton-Corn Ratio
Georgia		*Tennessee*	
Upper Piedmont		Middle	
Jackson	1.6	Davidson	0.3
Carroll	1.6	Maury	2.0
Lower Piedmont		West	
Hancock	10.6	Fayette	11.7
Warren	9.3	Haywood	8.5
Jefferson	11.8		
Alabama		*Mississippi*	
Hill Country		Pine Belt	
Blount	0.4	Marion	4.3
Walker	1.2	Perry	2.6
Black Belt		Delta & Black Belt	
Dallas	11.1	Adams	20.6
Lowndes	10.2	Jefferson	15.4
Marengo	12.9	Issaquena	23.8
Perry	7.8	Yazoo	15.8

Source: Seventh Census of the United States, 1850 (Washington, 1853), pp. 334–351. The cotton-corn ratio is calculated by dividing pounds of cotton by bushels of corn.

By any measure, the lower Piedmont was much more deeply involved in the cotton economy than the upper Piedmont. In 1849 every district in the lower Piedmont produced at least 14,000 bales of cotton (and two districts produced over 25,000 bales each), while no district in the upper Piedmont produced as many as 10,000 bales (and two districts raised less than 2500 bales each). The cotton-corn ratio of the lower Piedmont was nearly three times that of the upper Piedmont. The grip of plantation agriculture on the local economy was also decidedly stronger in the lower Piedmont than in the upper Piedmont. On the eve of the Civil War, over half of all farms in the lower Piedmont contained more than 100 improved acres, and almost one in five farm operators owned at least twenty slaves. In the upper Piedmont, however, over 60 percent of all farms in every district except York contained no more than 100 improved acres, and nearly one-third of all farms in the area contained no more than fifty improved acres. Less than one in twenty farm operators in the upper Piedmont was a planter.[5]

The Upcountry as a whole remained overwhelmingly agricultural in 1850. Just under 75 percent of all household heads were farmers, although some who were identified as farmers by census takers were tenants or farm laborers rather than farm owners. About 9 percent of all household heads were laborers of various sorts. Roughly half of these laborers were primarily agricultural laborers, while the other half worked at saw and grinding mills, in small textile operations,

[5]See Tables 2.2, 2.3, and 2.4. United States Bureau of the Census, *Seventh Census of the United States, 1850* (Washington, D.C., 1853), pp. 334–351; United States Bureau of the Census, *Eighth Census of the United States, Agriculture, 1860* (Washington, D.C., 1864), pp. 214, 237.

Table 2.3 Cotton Production and Specialization in 1850

	Bales of Cotton	Bushels of Corn	Cotton-Corn Ratio
Lower Piedmont			
Abbeville	27,192	1,054,233	10.3
Chester	17,810	573,070	12.4
Edgefield	25,880	1,155,489	9.0
Fairfield	18,122	529,461	13.6
Laurens	15,842	895,291	7.1
Newberry	19,894	664,058	12.0
Union	14,156	665,078	8.6
Upper Piedmont			
Anderson	6,670	820,549	3.3
Greenville	2,452	637,784	1.5
Lancaster	8,661	352,218	9.8
Pickens	1,357	634,011	0.9
Spartanburg	6,671	873,654	3.1
York	9,986	690,447	5.8
Totals			
Lower Piedmont	138,896	5,526,680	10.1
Upper Piedmont	35,797	4,008,663	3.6
Upcountry	174,693	9,535,343	7.3
South Carolina	300,901	16,264,919	7.4

Source: United States Bureau of the Census, *Seventh Census of the United States, 1850* (Washington, 1853), pp. 334–351.

as construction laborers, or in other day-labor jobs. The Upcountry also supported small classes of merchants, professionals, and artisans whose members earned their keep largely by handling trade and providing services for local agriculture. Over 65 percent of all household heads in the Upcountry owned real property and about 38 percent were slaveholders. The incidence of land and slave ownership was significantly higher among farm operators than among the general population. More than 80 percent of all farmers were landed proprietors and nearly half owned at least one slave. In sum, the Upcountry in 1850 was a region dominated by landholding farmers. Three out of every five household heads were independent farmers, and more than one in three household heads was also a slaveholding farmer.[6]

Yet even though the vast majority of household heads in the Upcountry owned property, the distribution of wealth in the region was very uneven. The richest 10 percent of all households controlled nearly 55 percent of the total wealth in the region, while the poorest 30 percent of all households owned virtually nothing.[7] As Gavin Wright has pointed out, the use of slave labor

[6]See Table 2.5. The source of this information is a sample of Upcountry households drawn from the Manuscript Census of South Carolina, 1850, Laurens, Spartanburg, and York Districts, Schedule I, II, and IV. For description of this sample, see Statistical Methods and Samples.

[7]See Table 2.6.

Table 2.4 Distribution of Farms by Improved Acreage–1860
(in Percentage of Total Farms in District)

	Improved Acreage			
	0–50	*51–100*	*101–500*	*over 500*
Lower Piedmont				
Abbeville	14.6	23.3	53.8	8.3
Chester	14.5	19.5	53.9	12.1
Edgefield	22.6	22.3	44.9	10.2
Fairfield	4.3	12.5	62.1	21.1
Laurens	7.5	19.1	62.1	11.3
Newberry	22.8	22.4	50.6	4.2
Union	27.6	25.3	41.6	5.5
Upper Piedmont				
Anderson	32.5	32.8	33.4	1.3
Greenville	33.2	39.2	26.1	1.5
Lancaster	40.7	27.9	27.8	3.6
Pickens	35.5	33.1	30.1	1.3
Spartanburg	37.5	28.7	32.9	0.9
York	19.5	23.9	53.9	2.7

Source: Eighth Census of the United States, Agriculture, 1850 (Washington, 1864),
p. 214.

allowed Southern farmers to expand the scope of their operations beyond the limits imposed by the supply of family and wage labor in areas where slavery was not allowed. To a large extent, slavery removed the constraint on farm size normally imposed by labor scarcity. Thus the average size of Southern farms was substantially larger than that of Northern farms and agricultural wealth tended to be more unevenly distributed in the South than in the North.[8] The South Carolina Upcountry was no exception to these patterns. But while wealth in the South Carolina Upcountry was more unevenly distributed than wealth in the rural North, the Upcountry's wealth distribution compared favorably with that of the more unbanized areas of the Northeast. Although the distribution of all forms of wealth in the Upcountry was highly uneven and skewed very much in favor of the wealthiest one-fifth of all households, the existing inequalities were not uncommon by the standards of antebellum America.[9]

Given the system of political economy which prevailed in the Upcountry during the late antebellum era, and the ideology which flourished in close combination

[8]Gavin Wright, *The Political Economy of the Cotton South: Households, Markets, and Wealth in the Nineteenth Century* (New York: W. W. Norton, 1978), pp. 44–55; Heywood Flesig, "Slavery, the Supply of Agricultural Labor, and the Industrialization of the South," *Journal of Economic History* 36 (September, 1976):572–597.

[9]See Table 2.7; see also Wright, *The Political Economy of the Cotton South*, p. 26; for a more general comparison, see Edward Pessen, "How Different from Each Other Were the Antebellum North and South?," *American Historical Review* 85 (December, 1980):1119–1149.

Table 2.5 Occupation of Upcountry
Household Heads, 1850

Farmer	74.7%
Laborer	9.1%
Artisans and Mechanics	8.8%
Merchants and Professionals	3.9%
Overseers	1.2%
Other	2.3%

Source: Manuscript Census of 1850, South Carolina, Laurens, Spartanburg and York Districts, Schedule I.

with that system, the widespread ownership of productive property among households in the region effectively calmed any gnawing popular anxiety over the uneven distribution of wealth. Like other South Carolinians, Upcountrymen clung tenaciously to an inherited "country-republican" ideology in which personal independence formed the very foundation of liberty. According to the tenets of "country-republicanism," men lacked true independence if their ability to control the affairs of their household, including its economic affairs, was denied or even circumscribed in any meaningful way. Thus personal independence, the very essence of freedom for citizens of the antebellum Upcountry, was secure only when it rested on a proper economic foundation. The surest guarantee of personal independence, most South Carolinians believed, was a system of political economy based on widespread ownership of productive property. Control of productive property freed men from dependence upon others for subsistence and allowed the producer to enjoy the fruits of his own labor and that of his family. Without productive property men became dependent upon others for their livelihood and as a result were rendered vulnerable to manipulation by

Table 2.6 Distribution of Wealth
among Heads of Households, 1850.
The South Carolina Upcountry

Rank	Share
Top Decile	54.7%
Second Decile	21.2
Third Decile	13.8
Fourth Decile	5.4
Fifth Decile	3.0
Sixth Decile	1.3
Seventh Decile	0.6
Eighth Decile	0.0
Ninth Decile	0.0
Tenth Decile	0.0
	100.0

Source: Manuscript Census of South Carolina, 1850, Laurens, Spartanburg, and York Districts, Schedules I and II.

Table 2.7 Upcountry Wealth Distribution in
Comparative Perspective. Free Males over 20

Area	Year	Gini Coefficient
South Carolina Upcountry	1850	.805
Laurens	1850	.776
Spartanburg	1850	.834
York	1850	.775
Massachusetts	1860	.822
New York	1860	.811
Pennsylvania	1860	.728
Ohio	1860	.780
Wisconsin	1860	.752
United States	1860	.832
United States	1921	.690
United States	1962	.760

Note: All Gini coefficients shown herein are for the free population
only.

Sources: Lee Soltow, *Men and Wealth in the United States* (New
Haven: Yale University Press, 1975); Randolph Cambell and
Richard Lowe, *Wealth and Power in Antebellum Texas* (College
Station: Texas A & M Press, 1977); Manuscript Census of 1850,
South Carolina, Schedules I and II.

scheming demagogues and exploitation by ruthless capitalists. Such men lacked
the independence requisite for republican citizenship. The actual political economy of the Upcountry bore rather strong resemblance to the ideal political economy of "country-republican" theory. The bulk of the free population were freeholders who controlled widely varying amounts of wealth but who usually met at
least the minimum economic standard for personal independence. The overwhelming portion of the dependent population, black slaves, were considered
subordinate and outside of the political equation altogether. Thus the Upcountry
economy, composed of a constellation of independent producers both large and
small, provided the proper material base for a flourishing republican social
order.[10]

[10]The recent proliferation of studies examining the influence of republican ideology on the course
of American history in the late eighteenth and early nineteenth century has left even the most
industrious historiographer straining to keep pace. Two excellent summaries of this explosion of
scholarship are Robert E. Shalhope, "Toward a Republican Synthesis," *William and Mary Quarterly* 29 (January, 1972):49–80, and Robert E. Shalhope, "Republicanism and Early American
Historiography," *William and Mary Quarterly* 39 (April, 1982):334–356. Sean Wilentz, "On Class
and Politics in Jacksonian America," *Reviews in American History* 10 (December, 1982):45–63
charts the growing influence of the concept of republicanism on our understanding of the Jacksonian
era. To date, the most trenchant critic of the recent emphasis on republicanism has been Joyce
Oldham Appleby. See especially Joyce O. Appleby, *Capitalism as a New Social Order: The Republican Vision of the 1790s* (New York: New York University Press, 1984), and Joyce O. Appleby,
"Republicanism in Old and New Contexts," *William and Mary Quarterly* 43 (January, 1986):20–

Yet while the economic reform movement of the 1840s failed to convince Upcountry farmers to wean themselves from their reliance on cotton, it did force many Upcountry whites to confront the possible tension between their ideological devotion to personal independence and their economic interest in commercial agriculture. At least in theory, production for the market encouraged specialization rather than self-sufficiency and involved the producer in an increasingly complex network of economic relationships which threatened to undermine his independence. Unless properly leveraged, participation in the market economy portended an end to the splendid isolation of self-sufficiency which did so much to preserve personal independence.[11] In particular, the reformers of the 1840s saw the neglect and abandonment of subsistence farming as a serious threat to personal independence. Though subsistence crops should be the first priority of every farmer, cotton profits tempted Upcountry farmers to sell their republican birthright for small bundles of cash. At the second annual meeting of the State Agricultural Society in 1840, former South Carolina governor George McDuffie, a leading planter from Abbeville, emphasized the importance of subsistence production. "It should be . . . an inviolable rule in the economy of every plantation," McDuffie contended, "to produce an abundant supply of every species of grain, and every species of livestock, required for its own consumption."[12] Appalled at the indifference toward self-sufficiency which he discovered during his agricultural survey in 1842, reformer Edmund Ruffin admonished every planter "to promptly render himself independent in reference to those articles which can be produced on his plantation."[13] Agricultural reformers believed that

34. Lance Banning, "Jeffersonian Ideology Revisited: Liberal and Classical Ideas in the New American Republic," *William and Mary Quarterly* 43 (January, 1986):3–19, offers a conciliatory but effective rebuttal of Appleby's objections. On the special popularity of classical republican ideas in eighteenth-century South Carolina, see Robert M. Weir, "'The Harmony We Were Famous For': An Interpretation of Pre-Revolutionary South Carolina Politics," *William and Mary Quarterly* 26 (October, 1969):473–501. The term "country-republicanism" is my own. It is used primarily to emphasize the strength of Revolutionary era political ideals in the political culture of nineteenth-century South Carolina rather than to deny the emergence of Smithian liberalism as an intellectual force in the state. It is also used as a convenient means of avoiding confusion between the South Carolina brand of republicanism, which emphasized black slavery as the basis for white liberty, and the free-labor ideology of the Republican party of the 1850s analyzed in Eric Foner, *Free Soil, Free Labor, Free Men: The Ideology of the Republican Party before the Civil War* (New York: Oxford University Press, 1971).

[11]On the traditional republican tension between personal independence and commercial activity, see J. G. A. Pocock, "Virtue and Commerce in the Eighteenth Century," *Journal of Interdisciplinary History* 3 (Summer, 1972):119–134; and Drew R. McCoy, *The Elusive Republic: Political Economy in Jeffersonian America* (Chapel Hill: University of North Carolina Press, 1980), especially pp. 76–104.

[12]George McDuffie, "Anniversary Oration of the State Agricultural Society of South Carolina, 26 November, 1840," in *The Proceedings of the Agricultural Convention of the State of South Carolina* (Columbia, S.C.: Summer and Carroll, 1846), p. 98, hereinafter this volume will be cited as *Proceedings of the Agricultural Convention*.

[13]Edmund Ruffin, *Report on the Commencement and Progress of the Agricultural Survey of South Carolina for 1843* (Columbia, S.C.: A. H. Pemberton, 1843), p. 73.

not only was it foolhardy to concentrate on cotton production when prices for the staple were low, but also that personal independence was endangered if subsistence crops were neglected. "What signifies money if a Man can make all he needs?" John Springs asked rhetorically, as reform rhetoric transformed the drudgery of subsistence farming into a moral duty of republican citizens.[14] Distinguished jurist John Belton O'Neall of Newberry best summed up reform sentiment when he stated:

> True independence is to be found in the abundance resulting from your own farms. Raise, my countrymen, everywhere in South Carolina, your own hogs, sheep, cattle, horses, and mules, clothe your own households by domestic wheel and loom . . . supply your own tables with flour, potatoes, butter, and cheese, of your own crops . . . and you can bid defiance to all the tariffs in the world.[15]

Agricultural reformers knew from personal experience that self-sufficiency was more difficult to achieve than the glowing rhetoric of their speeches suggested. Even in the best years some farmers found it difficult to feed their families. When there was too much or too little rain, or when the quality of the seed supply was poor, even more farmers failed to achieve self-sufficiency. The difficulty of maintaining self-sufficiency in the face of nature's depredations was emphasized by the serious food crisis that followed the devastating drought of 1845. By late summer of that year a serious grain shortage developed. Zelotus Holmes reported from Spartanburg district that hundreds of acres of corn would not yield a single ear. "There will perhaps on an average be sufficient [corn] to bread the country," Holmes surmised, "but stock of all sorts must suffer if not perish." In Chester district, Elizabeth Cowan, the wife of a small farmer, complained that the drought "nearly burnt up everything that was planted." As early as August, members of the Townes family conceded that they "could not make a supply of provisions" on their Greenville plantation.[16]

In eastern York district, an unusual number of farmers drove their wagons to the Springfield plantation that summer with the hope of buying or bartering corn from the owner, John Springs. Springs, who prided himself on the practice of diversified agriculture and had once boasted that he had "never yet bought the first Barrel of Flour or pound of Pork" since setting up housekeeping, responded to his neighbors' plight with the measured generosity that had earned him respect and influence in the community. He sold corn for one dollar per bushel to those who could afford to pay but limited their purchases to the amount needed to last until more grain could be imported. To widows and destitute farmers, Springs

[14]John Springs to Andrew Baxter Springs, December 27, 1842, Springs Family Papers, SHC.

[15]John Belton O'Neall, "An Address Delivered before the State Agricultural Society, at Their Meeting in Greenville, 11 September, 1844," in *Proceedings of the Agricultural Convention*, p. 219.

[16]Zelotus Holmes to his Aunt, August 12, 1845, Zelotus L. Holmes Papers, SCL; Elizabeth Cowan to William and Martha Cowan, May 22, 1845, Nancy Cowan Papers, DU; Henry H. Townes to Rachel Townes, August 12, 1845, Townes Family Papers, SCL.

gave enough corn to last until the fall harvest. When John Springs left Springfield for a July vacation in Saratoga, he turned the management of the plantation
over to his son, Andrew Baxter Springs, but left clear instructions about his
obligations to the community. "I am under no responsibility to furnish any
individual with corn," the elder Springs explained, "but I do plan to divide out
what I have among the poor people for they will suffer without help."[17] As the
steady stream of supplicants flowed into Springfield throughout the summer the
younger Springs found his duties trying. In late August one widow traveled nine
miles by wagon and crossed the Catawba by ferry just to ask for corn at the
Springs plantation. The woman presented her condition as "destitute and lamen-
table in the extreme" and asked for corn for her children. "Of course *she* was
not to be assisted," Baxter Springs observed sarcastically, "and thus is a poor
fellow daily bedeviled, having nothing to relieve the monotony of his solitude
save the bewailings of the Widow and the cries of half-starved children on the
one hand, and the *soft harpings* of moping, lazy, 'no corn making' sons of
Bitches on the other."[18] Scores of other Upcountry planters and farmers helped
their needy neighbors through the crisis of 1845–46, but the situation nonetheless added credence to the reformers' complaints about the neglect of subsistence
agriculture.

But despite the suffering and anxiety it produced, and for all the urgency it
lent to the reform agenda, the food crisis of 1845 was an exception to a more
general pattern of self-sufficiency. In 1842 John Springs observed that all Upcountry farmers "who manage well" ordinarily produced an "abundance" of
corn, flour, and pork, as well as "other necessaries."[19] Indeed, even as the
reformers preached the gospel of self-sufficiency with full voice, most Upcountry farmers claimed that they usually produced a surplus of foodstuffs which they
found difficult to market. The Milton Agricultural Society, which embraced
parts of Laurens and Newberry districts, reported, "We raise among ourselves
nearly all the hogs, and all the cattle, that we need for consumption," and that
"every farmer raises all the grain which he consumes, and usually markets a
surplus of wheat and flour." Markets for grain surpluses in the Upcountry,
however, were spotty. The Fishing Creek Agricultural Society, composed of
farmers in southeastern and northwestern Chester, spoke bluntly about the lack
of demand for Upcountry food crops. "Cotton is our only market produce," the
Society reported, "We make our own breadstuffs and would frequently spare
large quantities of corn and wheat, but have no regular market for them." Other
reports from various parts of the Upcountry also suggest that the reformers'
concern about the neglect of subsistence crops were overblown.[20]

---

[17]John Springs to Andrew Baxter Springs, June 13, 1842, John Springs to Andrew Baxter
Springs, September 8, 1845, Springs Family Papers, SHC.

[18]Andrew Baxter Springs to John Springs, August 27, 1845, Springs Family Papers, SHC.

[19]John Springs to Andrew Baxter Springs, June 13, 1842, SHC.

[20]"Report of the Committee appointed by the Milton Agricultural Society," in Ruffin, *Report on
the Agricultural Survey, an Appendix,* pp. 8–10; "Report of the Fishing Creek Agricultural Society," in Ruffin, *Report on the Agricultural Survey, an Appendix,* pp. 5–8; Elizabeth Cowan to her
brother and sister, September 11, 1847, Nancy Cowan Papers, DU.

Table 2.8 Percentage of Upcountry Farms
Achieving Self-Sufficiency in 1850

	Farm Size (Improved Acres)			
	1–49	50–99	100–199	200 or more
Grain	53.6	82.5	89.6	91.9
Meat	42.2	71.4	74.6	63.4
Total Farms =	752			

Source: Manuscript Census of South Carolina, 1850, Abbeville, Anderson and York
Districts, Schedules I, II, and IV.

Quantitative analysis of food production on Upcountry farms generally supports the claims of the local agricultural societies that a general pattern of self-sufficiency prevailed. Nearly 75 percent of all Upcountry farms were self-sufficient in basic subsistence crops in 1849. But the incidence of self-sufficiency in subsistence crops varied sharply with farm size. Over 87 percent of all Upcountry farms with fifty or more improved acres were self-sufficient in grain, but only about half of all farms with fewer than fifty acres raised enough grain to meet their own subsistence requirements. Thus while a general pattern of self-sufficiency in food crops prevailed in the Upcountry in 1850, a substantial minority failed to achieve self-sufficiency in grain, and two out of three farms which failed to produce enough grain to meet their own needs were farms with less than fifty improved acres. Upcountry farmers were less successful in producing enough meat to fulfill the requirements of their households. Since antebellum fence laws required that crops be fenced and allowed livestock to roam free on the "open range," Upcountry farmers usually turned their herds out to forage for most of the year. Farmers with corn to spare often fattened their hogs on feed for a few weeks before slaughter, but poorer farmers often used virtually no grain at all in keeping their herds. Even with the help of open-range grazing, however, only 60 percent of all Upcountry farms achieved self-sufficiency in meat in 1850. Again, large farms were more likely to achieve self-sufficiency than small ones. Over 70 percent of all farms with fifty or more improved acres were self-sufficient in meat in 1850, but only 42 percent of farms with fewer than fifty acres produced enough meat to satisfy basic subsistence requirements. Of course, analysis of census data fails to tell the complete story about meat supplies in the Upcountry. Hunting and fishing were part-time vocations and favorite avocations of many rural Upcountrymen, who undoubtedly supplemented meat from their herds with wild game and fish. Other Upcountry families who fell short of self-sufficiency simply tightened their belts a bit in order to live on what they did produce.[21]

[21]See Table 2.8. Conclusions based on analysis of a sample of Upcountry farms drawn from the Manuscript Census of South Carolina, 1850, Abbeville, Anderson, and York Districts, Schedules I, II, IV, SCDAH. For a full discussion of the sample, see Statistical Methods and Samples at the end of this volume. The test for self-sufficiency used in these calculations was that devised by Robert Gallman, "Self-Sufficiency in the Cotton Economy of the Antebellum South," *Agricultural History*

On the whole, Upcountry farmers were very successful with subsistence crops and at least reasonably successful in raising livestock, but a significant minority were not self-sufficient in either meat or grain. This minority either purchased food in the local market or depended on the charity of their neighbors. Townsmen and other non-agricultural people in the region also purchased food in local markets, where activity was sporadic but sometimes brisk. Yet as farmers who produced surplus food regularly complained, the general self-sufficiency of the Upcountry severely limited the local market for foodstuffs. The existence of local market activity did not result from an aggregate shortfall in food production as agricultural reformers seemed to fear. Yet even the fact that one-fourth of all Upcountry farmers failed to achieve self-sufficiency in food crops alarmed reformers. In a society where dependence and degradation were so closely linked, self-styled stewards of republican virtue saw anything less than complete self-sufficiency as a sign of weakness and decline. "It seems next to impossible," Edmund Ruffin maintained, "that there can exist any thriving agricultural class which, as a regular system, buys, instead of raising, the necessary and most important articles of food."[22] To agricultural reformers, traffic in the Upcountry food market loomed as an ominous symbol of declension. Yet the pleas of the reformers fell largely on deaf ears among Upcountry farmers, who knew from experience that demand for their surplus food production was limited and irregular.

The ideal, or ethic, of self-sufficiency, espoused with such vigor by reformers, was almost universally shared by Upcountry farmers, and, despite the lamentations of the reformers, a healthy majority of Upcountry farmers enjoyed self-sufficiency in basic foodstuffs. But the shared ideal of self-sufficiency, an ethic which was at least partially political in origin, did not reflect any lingering commitment to a hermetic subsistence economy. For Upcountrymen, it was the capacity for self-sufficiency, and the resulting ability to protect one's household and property from hostile outside forces, that mattered. Isolation from market forces through immersion in a subsistence economy was an unnecessarily radical approach to the problem of maintaining personal independence. The ethic of self-sufficiency was less spartan, and therefore more popular, because it required only that farmers leverage their involvement in market agriculture by maintaining a sufficiency in subsistence production. Economic independence rested not on isolation from market activity but rather on the control of property which made self-sufficiency possible. If recklessly pursued, market involvement might endanger property ownership, but when properly leveraged production for the market posed no particular threat to economic independence.[23]

---

44 (January, 1970):5–23. See also James D. Applewhaite, "Some Aspects of Society in Rural South Carolina in 1850," *North Carolina Historical Review* 29 (January, 1952):39–63.

[22]Ruffin, *Report on the Agricultural Survey*, p. 73.

[23]On the strength of the ideal of independence in antebellum Southern society, see J. Mills Thornton III, *Politics and Power in a Slave Society: Alabama, 1800–1860* (Baton Rouge: Louisiana State University Press, 1978), especially pp. 54–58; Steven Hahn, *The Roots of Southern Populism*, especially pp. 86–133; William J. Cooper, Jr., *Liberty and Slavery: Southern Politics to 1860* (New York: Alfred A. Knopf, 1983).

Scholars have long argued that a "dual-economy" flourished in the ante-bellum South.[24] Focusing primarily on the differences between planters cultivating staple crops for the transatlantic market and plain dirt farmers concentrating on subsistence crops, the dual-economy hypothesis posited the co-existence of two distinct economic sectors distinguished from each other chiefly by their dramatically different market orientations. The "modern," commercial, market-oriented sector consisted of plantations and large farms raising staple crops. The traditional sector of the Southern economy consisted primarily of family farms and other households which produced enough meat and grain for their own subsistence and remained isolated from regular market activity. Useful as the concept of the dual-economy may be in suggesting that different groups within the Southern economy had dramatically different market orientations, it nevertheless suggests a crude economic bipolarity which simply did not exist in the South Carolina Upcountry. Instead, most Upcountry households, including those headed by yeoman farmers, were involved in a variety of small economic networks. To be sure, most of these networks were primarily local in nature, but a few involved participation in a much broader market economy.

Through the antebellum era, the household remained the principal unit of production as well as consumption in the Upcountry, and the heads of these productive households were the independent producers who served as the primary actors in the region's economy. For the petty producers who dominated the region numerically, the household normally consisted of a male head of the family, his wife and children, and perhaps one or two slaves. For the large producers, who accounted for the bulk of the region's total output, the concept of the household was enlarged to include not only the slaveholder and his family but also dozens of slave laborers. Even though their relative wealth and the scope of their market activity varied widely, both large and small producers shared a common status as independent freeholders. Moreover, both were involved in production for the market, albeit on a different scale, as well as in production for household consumption.[25]

---

[24]The standard statement of the dual-economy argument as applied to the Old South is Morton Rothstein, "The Antebellum South as a Dual Economy: A Tentative Hypothesis," *Agricultural History* 41 (October, 1967):373–382; see also Douglas North, *The Economic Growth of the United States, 1790–1860* (Englewood Cliffs, N.J.: Prentice-Hall, 1961), pp. 101–155. On the theoretical foundations of the dual-economy concept, see Walt W. Rostow, *The Stages of Economic Growth: A Non-Communist Manifesto* (Cambridge: Cambridge University Press, 1962); Albert O. Hirschman, *The Strategy of Economic Development* (New Haven: Yale University Press, 1957); Dale W. Jorgenson, "The Development of Dual Economy," *Economic Journal* 71 (June, 1961):309–334.

[25]Elizabeth Fox-Genovese, "Antebellum Southern Households: A New Perspective on a Familiar Question," *Review* 7 (Fall, 1983):215–253. For a comparative perspective, see Christopher Clark, "The Household Economy, Market Exchange, and the Rise of Capitalism in the Connecticut Valley, 1800–1860," *Journal of Social History* 8 (Winter, 1979):169–190; James H. Henretta, "Families and Farms: *Mentalité* in Pre-industrial America," *William and Mary Quarterly* 35 (January, 1978):3–33; Winifred Rothenberg, "The Market and Massachusetts Farmers, 1750–1855," *Journal of Economic History* 41 (June, 1981):283–314; Rona S. Weiss, "The Market and Massachusetts Farmers, 1750–1850: Comment," *Journal of Economic History* 43 (June, 1983):475–478; Winifred B. Rothenberg, "The Market and Massachusetts Farmers: A Reply," *Journal of Economic History,* 43 (June,

Planters were the Upcountry producers who were most heavily involved in production for the market, who had the strongest ties to supralocal markets, and who generally developed the broadest range of commercial interests. The principal market commodity grown by planters was, of course, cotton. Over 90 percent of all Upcountry planters raised cotton, and most of the tiny minority who did not were one-time cotton nabobs enjoying semi-retirement after having made a small fortune growing the royal fiber. Planters supervised the production of nearly 75 percent of all cotton grown in the Upcountry, and in the cotton-rich districts of the lower Piedmont, planters controlled nearly 60 percent of all farm wealth. John Bauskett, an Edgefield planter who owned over 100 slaves, raised 140 bales of cotton in 1838 but referred to his yield as "a sorry crop." Another prominent Edgefield planter, Francis W. Pickens, owned more than 250 slaves scattered across several plantations. In 1842, the 165 slaves housed on Pickens's "Edgewood" plantation produced over 140 bales of cotton. John Springs's plantation housed 34 slaves and produced over 75 bales of cotton in 1837, while Springs's son, Richard Austin Springs, housed just over 20 slaves on his "Springsteen" plantation on the west bank of the Catawba River and made 30 bales of cotton in 1839. In Abbeville district, planter-physician Henry Townes received over $2,200 for the 50 bales of cotton he raised in 1846, and chortled that his earnings were "pretty good you will say for a poor doctor." Some planters managed considerably more modest operations. Typical of these lesser planters was Mabra Madden of Laurens. Madden owned 22 slaves by 1840 but produced no more than 10 bales of cotton a year during the following decade.[26]

Yet even though cotton accounted for over 40 percent of total output on most Upcountry plantations, nearly 85 percent of all plantations were self-sufficient in basic food crops. As Gallman and Anderson have pointed out in their study of slave labor on Southern plantations, efficiency-minded planters were able to use their slaves to work corn and other subsistence crops during those portions of the growing season when the cotton required very little work.[27] The fixed costs of maintaining slaves were high, but the marginal costs of extracting additional increments of labor were relatively low. Thus planters had every incentive to keep slaves busy at all times. Francis Pickens planted a certain number of acres

1983):479–480; Harriet Friedman, "Household Production and the National Economy: Concepts for the Analysis of Agrarian Functions," *The Journal of Peasant Studies* 7 (January, 1980):158–164; Bettye Hobbs Pruitt, "Self-Sufficiency and the Agricultural Economy of Eighteenth Century Massachusetts," *William and Mary Quarterly* 41 (July, 1984):335–364.

[26]See Tables 2.9 and 2.10. Calculations based on a sample of farms drawn from the Manuscript Census of South Carolina, 1850, Abbeville, Anderson, and York Districts, Schedules I, II, and IV, SCDAH; John Bauskett to Ann B. Waddlington, September 25, 1838, Thomas Ellison Keitt Papers, DU; Entry for 1842, Francis W. Pickens Plantation Record Book, DU; John Springs to Andrew Baxter Springs, December 12, 1837, and Richard Austin Springs to John Springs, October 18, 1839, Springs Family Papers, SHC; Henry H. Townes to William Augustus Townes, July 20, 1847, Townes Family Papers, SCL; Receipts of October 13, 1846, October 23, 1848, October 16, 1849, Mabra Madden Papers, SCL.

[27]See Table 2.10; Ralph V. Anderson and Robert E. Gallman, "Slaves as Fixed Capital: Slave Labor and Southern Economic Development," *Journal of American History* 64 (June, 1977):24–46.

Table 2.9 Distribution of Production and Wealth on Upcountry Farms, 1850
(in percent)

	Type of Farm Operator				
	Non-slaveholding Yeomen (0 slaves)	Slaveholding Yeomen (1–5 slaves)	Middling Slaveholders (6–19 slaves)	Planters (20 or more slaves)	Tenants
Farms	31.1	22.6	23.6	9.6	13.2
Slaves	0	8.6	37.4	53.3	0.8
Cotton	11.0	10.9	28.7	44.9	4.6
Corn	20.8	16.9	31.1	27.7	3.5
Swine	25.2	18.8	28.5	24.7	3.0
Improved Acreage	22.8	17.0	28.7	31.3	NA
Cash value	14.6	16.0	29.4	39.9	NA
Total Farms = 752					

Source: Manuscript Census of South Carolina, 1850, Abbeville, Anderson, and York Districts, Schedules I, II, and IV.

of cotton and a certain number of acres of corn per field hand. John Springs expected to produce 200 bushels of corn as well as three or four bales of cotton for each full hand he owned. Of course, some planters were forced to supplement their homegrown supplies with purchased grain, at least on occasion. Fairfield planter William Smith bought 100 bushels of wheat in 1833 when his own crop failed, and Smith's brother, John Winsmith, purchased twenty barrels of flour to augment his own production in 1843. And the drought of 1845 forced the usually

Table 2.10 Production and Value on Upcountry Farms, 1850

	Type of Farm Operator				
Mean Output	Non-slaveholding Yeomen	Slaveholding Yeomen (1–5 slaves)	Middling Slaveholders (6–19 slaves)	Planters (20 or more slaves)	Tenants
Cotton (lbs.)	1160.0	1760.0	4480.0	17,240.0	760.0
Corn (bushels)	325.8	389.0	688.3	1500.8	143.2
Swine	20.2	21.5	29.5	62.8	10.5
Mean Value					
Improved Acres	73.0	80.0	129.5	345.5	NA
Cash Value of Farms	$962.8	$1542.1	$2718.7	$9007.2	NA
% Growing					
Cotton	71.7	81.6	87.2	96.3	67.0
% Self-Sufficient					
Grain	66.0	79.4	80.9	84.6	43.4
Meat	64.0	66.3	55.0	45.0	28.3
Cotton-Corn Ratio	3.6	4.5	6.5	11.5	5.3

Source: Manuscript Census of South Carolina, Abbeville, Anderson, and York Districts, Schedules I, II, and IV.

self-reliant Andrew Whyte, a York district planter, to buy twenty-five bushels of corn from John Springs.[28] Under normal circumstances, however, Upcountry planters raised all the corn and wheat they needed and more. In the winter of 1847, Henry Townes reported that he had made "an abundance of wheat . . . corn, oats, barley, peas, [and] potatoes"; the following summer Townes gloated that his plantation yielded "about two years supply of corn. . . ." Also in the late 1840s, Francis Pickens estimated that his "Edgewood" plantation produced nearly 2000 bushels more corn each year than it consumed.[29]

Upcountry planters were decidedly less successful in producing enough meat to satisfy the subsistence requirements of the slave quarters. Partly because of the relatively high proportion of improved to unimproved, or "open-range" acreage in plantation areas, and partly because slave labor offered no particular economies to livestock raising under the open-range system, only 45 percent of all planters were self-sufficient in meat.[30] In 1846, Abbeville planter-lawyer Armistead Burt allotted each of his forty-eight adult slaves two and one half pounds of bacon per week, but Burt did not keep enough hogs to raise more than a fraction of his own supply. Francis Pickens always bought one-third to one-half of the pork used on his plantations. Henry Townes, justifiably proud of his self-sufficincy in grain, raised only half as much pork as needed on his plantation in 1847.[31] Pork was usually plentiful in local markets. Planters purchased some pork from Upcountry herdsmen like G. A. Taylor of Pickens, who sometimes sold as many as forty hogs a year, but most of the pork available in Upcountry markets was provided by out-of-state drovers who passed through the Upcountry regularly on drives to Charleston and Augusta. Upcountry planters frequently bought hogs from these drovers in late November or early December, fed them for three or four weeks, and then slaughtered the animals on cold, crisp days in late December and early January.[32] Planters also joined beef clubs, combinations

[28]Entry for 1840, Francis W. Pickens Plantation Journal, DU; John Springs to Andrew Baxter Springs, December 27, 1842, Springs Family Papers, SHC; William Smith to Elihu P. Smith, June 17, 1833, and John Winsmith to Elihu P. Smith, June 26, 1843, Elihu Penquite Smith Papers, SCL; Andrew Whyte to John Springs, March 25, 1846, Springs Family Papers, SHC.

[29]Henry H. Townes to William Augustus Townes, January 16, 1847, and Henry H. Townes to William Augustus Townes, July 20, 1847, Townes Family Papers, SCL; Entry for 1847, Francis W. Pickens Plantation Journal, DU.

[30]On the nature of open range grazing in the nineteenth century South, see J. Crawford King, "The Closing of the Southern Range: An Exploratory Essay," *Journal of Southern History* 48 (February, 1982):53–70; Forrest McDonald and Grady McWhiney, "The Antebellum Southern Herdsmen: A Reinterpretation," *Journal of Southern History* 41 (May, 1975):147–166; and Steven Hahn, "Common Right and Commonwealth: The Stock-Law Struggle and the Roots of Southern Populism," in J. Morgan Kousser and James M. McPherson, eds., *Region, Race, and Reconstruction* (New York: Oxford University Press, 1982), pp. 51–88.

[31]C. D. Palmer to Armistead Burt, April 4, 1846, Armistead Burt Papers, DU; Entries for 1841, 1842, 1844, Francis W. Pickens Plantation Record Book, DU; Henry H. Townes to William A. Townes, January 16, 1847, Townes Family Papers, SCL.

[32]G. A. Taylor to J. J. Norton, May 10, 1853, Joseph J. Norton Papers, SCL; Mrs. Hosea J. Dean to Hosea J. Dean, December 1, 1843, Simpson, Young, Dean, and Coleman Papers, SCL; Entry of December 27, 1855, John D. Ashmore Plantation Journal, SHC; Henry H. Townes to Samuel Townes, November 29, 1848, Townes Family Papers, SCL.

of six or eight planters from the same neighborhood who killed beef cattle periodically and divided the meat, which spoiled easily, among themselves for quick consumption. Beef normally went to the big house rather than the slave quarters.[33] Enormously successful with staple crops, and generally self-sufficient in subsistence crops, planters often turned to the local market for pork, a mainstay of the plantation diet.

At the same time, production of staple crops drew Upcountry planters into a number of economic networks which extended well beyond the borders of their region. Planters marketed their crops through factors and commission merchants in the port of Charleston, and, to a lesser extent, in the fall-line towns of Columbia, Camden, Hamburg, and even Cheraw. They purchased agricultural supplies and household goods from mercantile houses in these same trading centers. Wade Hampton I of Richland district, perhaps South Carolina's largest producer of short-staple cotton, used factors in New York, Philadelphia, and New Orleans as well as Charleston, and his son, Wade Hampton II, developed working relationships with cotton merchants and businessmen in Liverpool. In the Upcountry, however, most planters dealt exclusively with South Carolina factors. Some preferred to cultivate a close relationship with one particular factorage house. William Kincaid, a wealthy planter from Jenkinsville, sold his large cotton crops through Ker Boyce, whose King Street factorage house was one of Charleston's most successful during the 1820s. During the 1830s, Kincaid shifted his business to another Charleston firm where his new son-in-law was employed. Elihu P. Smith, a wealthy planter-merchant from southeast Spartanburg, traded almost exclusively through the Charleston branch of the Baltimore-based firm of Alexander Brown and Company. Other planters spread their business among a number of different firms in an effort to enlarge their network of business contacts and safeguard themselves against the failure of any one firm. Throughout his long career as a planter, John Springs rarely placed all of his business in the hands of a single factorage house, and John S. Bratton, owner of a small plantation in lower York, sold his substantial cotton crops through several competing Charleston factors.[34]

Transportation problems often made the long-distance trade between Upcountry planters and coastal or fall-line factors and merchants anything but easy. By the early 1840s, the completion of the South Carolina Railroad from Charleston to Hamburg, Columbia, and Camden facilitated the passage of goods

[33]Henry H. Townes to George F. Townes, August 4, 1831, Townes Family Papers, SCL; John Springs to Andrew Baxter Springs, December 27, 1842, Springs Family Papers, SHC.

[34]John Stoney to Wade Hampton, September 28, 1831, and Joseph Drury to Wade Hampton, December 30, 1831, Hampton Family Papers, SCL; Ronald Edward Bridwell, "The South's Wealthiest Planter: Wade Hampton I of South Carolina, 1754–1835" (Ph.D. dissertation, University of South Carolina, 1980), pp. 379–504; Boyce and Henry to William Kincaid, June 12, 1830, and William Anderson to Edward K. Anderson, November 23, 1837, Kincaid-Anderson Papers, SCL; Alexander Brown and Co. to Elihu P. Smith, December 25, 1833, and November 9, 1844, Elihu Penquite Smith Papers, SCL; Receipt of November 23, 1843, McDowall and Cooper to Andrew Baxter Springs, August 21, 1851, John Springs to Andrew Baxter Springs, January 30, 1851, Springs Family Papers, SHC; Bratton and Rainey Ledger Book, 1843–1847, Bratton Family Papers, SCL.

from the fall line to the coast. But until the railroad network was extended into the Upcountry during the 1850s, planters living above the fall line continued to face difficult journeys downriver by boat or barge and overland by wagon just to reach trans-shipment points at the head of the railroad line. Union district planters William Sims and James Dawkins and Fairfield's William Kincaid moved their cotton down the Broad River by boat to Columbia before sending it on to Charleston. And before the South Carolina Railroad reached Camden in 1842, John Springs shipped his cotton by wagon to Cheraw, a fall-line town on the Pee Dee River, and from there by packet to Charleston. Late in 1839, however, fifty bales of Springs's cotton were stranded in Cheraw because of low water on the Pee Dee River; as a result, Springs found it difficult to meet some of his financial obligations. After 1842, the Springs family diverted most of its cotton to Camden where it was transferred to the railroad for shipment to Charleston. Laurens planter Thomas Foster Jones complained mightily about the difficulty of transporting his cotton by wagon for over seventy miles to the Hamburg market, a journey which included the slow crossing of the swift-running Saluda River at Chappell's Ferry. Even John C. Calhoun was momentarily distracted from national affairs in March 1837 by the difficulty of finding a boatman willing to negotiate the treacherous Portman Shoals in the Seneca River in order to haul cotton from Fort Hill to Hamburg.[35]

The distance and difficulty of communication between planter and factor enlarged the factor's role in making crucial marketing decisions. As a rule, planters depended heavily on factors for information about prices and advice about when to sell. Often planters simply provided their factors with general guidelines regarding the disposal of his crop, leaving the precise timing of the sale to the discretion of the factor. Planters ordinarily sold the bulk of their cotton in the late fall or winter, but those who could afford to do so often held at least a portion of their crop off the market until spring when there was less cotton being offered for sale. At times, planters held their cotton off the market for weeks or even months due to low prices. In December 1840, Thomas F. Jones stored 114 bales of cotton on the advice of his factor, James Gadsden, despite being hardpressed by creditors.[36]

[35]Samuel M. Derrick, *Centennial History of the South Carolina Railroad* (Columbia, S.C.: The State Co., 1930), pp. 99–127; Donald A. Grinde, Jr., "Building the South Carolina Railroad," *South Carolina Historical Magazine* 77 (April, 1976):84–96; William Smith to William Sims, September 9, 1819, Boyce, Johnston, and Henry to William Sims, July 13, 1825, William Sims Papers, DU; Carwile and Co. to William Kincaid, April 29, 1830, Kincaid-Anderson Papers, SCL; R. Caldwell and J. Caldwell to James Dawkins, January 28, 1843, James Dawkins Papers, SHC; John Springs to Andrew Baxter Springs, January 9, 1837, John Springs to Andrew Baxter Springs, October 23, 1839, John Springs to Andrew Baxter Springs, October 10, 1842, Springs Family Papers, SHC; Thomas F. Jones to the *Southern Agriculturalist*, n.d., Jones, Watts, Davis Papers, SCL; John C. Calhoun to James Edward Colhoun, March 27, 1837, in Clyde N. Wilson, ed., *The Papers of John C. Calhoun* (Columbia, S.C.: University of South Carolina Press, 1981), vol. 13, p. 499.

[36]Harold D. Woodman, *King Cotton and His Retainers: Financing and Marketing the Cotton Crop of the South, 1800–1925* (Lexington: University of Kentucky Press, 1968), especially pp. 3–71; Thomas F. Jones to James Gadsden, December 1, 1840, Jones, Watts, Davis Papers, SCL.

The lines of credit extended to Upcountry planters by distant factors and commission houses were crucial to the region's economy, since there were no banks in the Upcountry prior to 1850. For paper currency, planters were forced to rely on bills issued by banks outside the region. Since bills issued by faraway banks were usually scarce, even the wealthiest Upcountry planter often found himself strapped for cash. The shortage of bank bills encouraged Upcountry planters to use promissory notes as circulating currency. Commission houses or banks in Charleston would accept a promissory note drawn on an Upcountry planter at a discount in anticipation of being paid the full value of the note from the planter's cotton proceeds. When a planter delayed the sale of his cotton, as Thomas F. Jones did in 1840, he had to seek accommodation from merchants and other individuals who held his notes.[37]

The shortage of paper currency and the ready availability of credit through distant banks, commission houses, and mercantile firms encouraged Upcountry planters to buy plantation supplies in large quantities either in Charleston or in towns along the fall line. The planter became, in effect, a central purchasing agent for his plantation, buying on his own authority virtually everything he needed for his family, his slaves, and his extensive agricultural operations. Since the marketing and financing of his cotton crop had already involved him in a long-distance trade with business houses in Columbia, Charleston, and beyond, the Upcountry planter worked through the same channels when purchasing plantation supplies. The long-distance nature of the planter's commercial activity had a profound impact on the Upcountry economy. Since planters traded primarily with merchants outside of the Upcountry, interior merchants suffered and inland towns failed to develop as rapidly as they might have if plantation commerce had depended heavily on local merchants. Recent studies indicate that Southern per capita income was growing at a healthy rate during the late antebellum era, and, as Robert Gallman has pointed out, new evidence suggests that planters spent no more of their income on luxury items than did wealthy elites elsewhere. Yet because planters controlled such a large percentage of Upcountry income and spent so much of it outside the region, Upcountry towns remained stagnant even though aggregate demand was neither inadequate nor skewed in the direction of luxury goods.[38]

The business and entrepreneurial interests of Upcountry planters were not limited to the cotton and plantation-supply trade. Not only were planters in-

[37]Alfred G. Smith, Jr., *Economic Readjustment of an Old Cotton State: South Carolina, 1820–1860* (Columbia, S.C.: University of South Carolina Press, 1958), pp. 193–217; J. Mauldin Lesesne, *The Bank of the State of South Carolina: A General and Political History* (Columbia, S.C.: University of South Carolina Press, 1970), pp. 52–135; John Cunningham, *Suggestions on the Causes of the Present Scarcity of Money* (Charleston: James, Williams, and Gitsinger, 1854); J. D. Allen, *The Banking System: A Speech* (Columbia, S.C.: R. W. Gibbes, 1857).

[38]Woodman, *King Cotton*, pp. 187–195; Robert Gallman, "Slavery and Southern Economic Growth," *Southern Economic Journal* 14 (April, 1979):1007–1022; William Parker, "Slavery and Southern Economic Development: An Hypothesis and Some Evidence," *Agricultural History* 44 (January, 1970):115–125; Stanley Engerman, "The Effects of Slavery upon the Southern Economy: A Review of the Recent Debate," *Explorations in Entrepreneurial History* 4 (Winter, 1967):71–97.

volved in a steady traffic in land and slaves but they were also involved in a number of railroad, banking, and manufacturing projects. John Garlington of Laurens, a planter-merchant who married the daughter of one-time United States Senator John Hunter, diversified his investments. In addition to plantations in South Carolina, Florida, and Alabama, Garlington invested heavily in both the Southwestern Railroad and the Southwestern Railroad Bank. Thomas F. Jones, though already plagued by debts, borrowed heavily in 1840 to invest in the Southwestern Railroad. Spartanburg's Elihu P. Smith owned over two thousand dollars' worth of bank stock, and even small planters such as Laurens's Mabra Madden invested in railroads. The leading capitalist among Upcountry planters was almost certainly John Springs. By 1845, Springs owned stock in three Charleston banks, in fall-line banks in Hamburg, Columbia, Camden, and Cheraw, and in out-of-state banks in North Carolina, Georgia, and New York. Springs's $80,000 worth of stock in the Bank of Hamburg made him that institution's second largest stockholder, and his total holdings of bank stock totaled well over $200,000. Springs also held over $50,000 worth of United States government bonds and invested heavily in railroads and manufactures.[39]

Indeed, a number of Upcountry planters found manufacturing investments alluring even though the planter elite possessed little expertise in the actual management of factory operations. As early as 1829, John Ewing Colhoun, brother-in-law of John C. Calhoun, established a woolen factory at his mill seat in Pendleton district. Some of Colhoun's products were exhibited at the Franklin Institute in Philadelphia and received acclaim for their quality.[40] At about the same time, Edgefield planter Christian Breithaupt erected a small textile factory and a village for the operatives at Vaucluse in Edgefield's Horse Creek Valley. After the original factory building was destroyed by fire, Breithaupt quickly reorganized the company and attracted a number of prominent investors, including George McDuffie, Abbeville planter Richard Cunningham, and Charleston banker Mitchell King. In 1837, George McDuffie and Edgefield planter John Bauskett bought the company for $33,000; shortly thereafter Bauskett purchased McDuffie's share and by 1840 the Vaucluse mill produced $60,000 worth of cotton goods.[41] John Springs and retired planter Joel Smith of Abbeville were both charter subscribers to William Gregg's Graniteville Manufacturing Com-

[39]*Cyclopedia of Eminent and Representative Men of the Carolinas of the Nineteenth Century* (Madison: Brant and Fuller, 1892), vol. 1, pp. 416–418; E. H. Edwards to Thomas F. Jones, November 23, 1840, Jones, Watts, Davis Papers, SCL; Christopher G. Memminger to Elihu P. Smith, January 15, 1833, Elihu Penquite Smith Papers, SCL; Mabra Madden to W. D. Watts, John Garlington, and J. D. Wright, October 29, 1847, Mabra Madden Papers, SCL; List of Debts and Assets, December 31, 1844, and List of Stockholders of the Bank of Hamburg, June 26, 1852, Springs Family Papers, SHC.

[40]Ernest McPherson Lander, Jr., *The Textile Industry in Antebellum South Carolina* (Baton Rouge: Louisiana State University Press, 1969), pp. 22–23; John Ewing Colhoun to James Edward Calhoun, June 28, 1824, John Ewing Colhoun Papers, SHC.

[41]Lander, *The Textile Industry,* pp. 35–49; George McDuffie to John Bauskett, February 3, 1838, George McDuffie Papers, SCL; John Bauskett to Thomas Bauskett, April 19, 1839, Thomas Ellison Keitt Papers, DU.

pany. Smith's initial investment of $40,000 was matched only by Charleston banker Ker Boyce and Hamburg banker Hiram Hutchinson, while Springs's original investment of $15,000 made him the company's fifth largest stock-holder.[42] And John C. Calhoun, who worried that the growth of a Southern textile industry would breed a strong tariff party in the region, invested in a Georgia gold mine whose mechanical operations fascinated him.[43]

To be sure, many Upcountry planters made no substantial non-agricultural investments prior to 1850, and many of the projects financed by planter capital were hardly spectacular successes. The proposed Southwestern Railroad was never completed; John Ewing Colhoun's mill closed in 1848, and John C. Calhoun received relatively little profit from his gold mine. James Henry Hammond, usually a promoter of economic diversification, once admitted that he held railroad stock essentially for its value as a sort of cash substitute rather than for high dividends.[44] But enough Upcountry planters showed a willingness to invest in banks, railroads, and industry to suggest that the planter elite had more than a passing interest in economic development. Even though Upcountry planters continued to speak with scores of different and sometimes contradictory voices regarding exactly what kind of economic system provided the best foundation for a republican society, the traditional Jeffersonian fears about economic development gradually yielded to a growing, but still largely inchoate, Whiggish faith in material progress. Thus the sustained economic boom of the early 1850s found many Upcountry planters both willing and able to become active participants in the dynamic period of economic expansion which Eric Hobsbawm has so aptly labeled the "Age of Capital."[45]

Yet while Upcountry planters were developing broad entrepreneurial interests, they were also becoming deeply enmeshed in a variety of local economic activities which placed them at the center of economic life in their beat, community or crossroads settlement. Many planters operated milling concerns that provided valuable services to nearby farmers. Almost without exception, Upcountry grinding mills were individually owned, and most of them were designed

[42]Hiram Hutchinson to John Springs, October 20, 1846, Springs Family Papers, SHC; Broadus Mitchell, William Gregg, *Factory Master of the Old South* (Chapel Hill: University of North Carolina Press, 1928), pp. 33–59, 278–279.

[43]Farish Carter to John C. Calhoun, November 14, 1836, in Wilson, ed., *The Papers of John C. Calhoun,* vol. 13, pp. 300–301.

[44]Smith, *Economic Readjustment of an Old Cotton State,* pp. 161–174; Lander, *The Textile Industry,* p. 48; Matthew McDonald to John C. Calhoun, March 7, 1843, in Clyde N. Wilson, ed., *The Papers of John C. Calhoun* (Columbia, S.C.: University of South Carolina Press, 1987), vol. 17, p. 116; James Henry Hammond to Marcellus C. M. Hammond, February 20, 1849, and entry of May 14, 1836, Hammond Plantation Diary, in James Henry Hammond Papers, SCL.

[45]On this point, see also McCoy, *The Elusive Republic,* pp. 76–104; Thornton, *Politics and Power in a Slave Society,* pp. 20–58; Charles G. Sellers, Jr., "Who Were the Southern Whigs?," *American Historical Review* 59 (January, 1954):335–346; Daniel Walker Howe, *The Political Culture of the American Whigs* (Chicago: University of Chicago Press, 1979), especially pp. 96–122; Eric J. Hobsbawm, *The Age of Capital, 1848–1875* (London: Weidenfeld and Nicolson, 1975), pp. 29–47.

not only to grind grain for use on the owner's plantation but also as small businesses which ground wheat and corn for neighborhood farmers at a nominal fee. William Kincaid's grinding mills near Jenkinsville ground wheat and corn for farmers throughout western Fairfield. James Edward Calhoun, another brother-in-law of John C. Calhoun, maintained both saw and grist mills equipped with state-of-the-art machinery at his "Millwood" plantation in Abbeville. In southwest Laurens, farmers trekked regularly to one of John Garlington's fine grinding mills along Rabun creek. In the upper Piedmont, where water power was abundant, a few grinding mills developed into major commercial operations. Vardry McBee of Greenville, a planter and small-scale textile entrepreneur, ran two flour mills on the Reedy River which were patronized by farmers from all over the upper Piedmont and parts of western North Carolina.[46]

In addition to their grist and saw mill operations, Upcountry planters also provided ginning services for their neighbors. Planters usually charged only a nominal fee and sometimes provided the service for free. James Henry Hammond felt that ginning the cotton of nearby farmers increased his stature in the community and helped establish his credentials as a benevolent local patriarch. John Bratton ginned cotton for farmers in southern York, while Elihu P. Smith accepted cotton as payment on accounts at his store and then ginned and marketed the staple.[47] In an economy where so much cotton was grown and yet the cost of a gin was higher than most farmers could afford, the ginning of the cotton was one of the most important services planters offered to their communities. Moreover, prior to the arrival of railroads in the region, Upcountry planters often marketed the cotton crops of small growers in their neighborhood. Union's William Sims hauled cotton downriver for other farmers in his district and sold it at Columbia and Charleston. John Springs often arranged for the transportation and sale of cotton grown by small farmers in York district. Once Upcountry railroads were completed in the 1850s, however, the role played by planters in the marketing of yeoman crops diminished considerably.[48]

[46]In February, 1838, the Kincaid family announced the opening of two new grinding mills, one for corn and one for wheat, that were "inferior to none in the State." See Kincaid-Anderson Papers, SCL; F. de Sales Dundas, *The Calhoun Settlement, District of Abbeville, South Carolina* (Staunton, Va., 1949), pp. 10–18; Ernest McPherson Lander, Jr., *The Calhoun Family and Thomas Green Clemson: The Decline of a Southern Patriarchy* (Columbia, S.C.: University of South Carolina Press, 1983), p. 12; *Eminent Men of the Carolinas,* vol. 1, pp. 416–418; "Sketch of Vardry McBee's Life," *DeBow's Review* 13 (1852):314–318; William L. Sherrill, *Annals of Lincoln County, North Carolina* (Baltimore: Regional Publishing, 1972), pp. 298–30; Greenville *News,* September 26, 1962, section A, p. 3.

[47]Drew Gilpin Faust, *James Henry Hammond and the Old South: A Design for Mastery* (Baton Rouge: Louisiana State University Press, 1982), pp. 130–134; on Hammond's relations with his neighbors, see entries for December 13, 1831, February 13, 1845, and December 12, 1846, James Henry Hammond Plantation Diary, SCL; Receipt of March 24, 1833, Elihu P. Smith Papers, SCL; Bratton Family Papers, SCL.

[48]Boyce and Johnston to William Sims, June 12, 1819, William Smith to William Sims, September 9, 1819, Samuel M. Gowdy to William Sims, January 15, 1823, William Sims Papers, DU; John Springs to Andrew Baxter Springs, October 21, 1836, Springs Family Papers, SHC; Lacy K. Ford, "Yeoman Farmers in the South Carolina Upcountry: Changing Production Patterns in the Late Antebellum Era," *Agricultural History* 60 (Fall, 1986):17–37.

Despite the economic importance of plantations to the local economy, relations between planters and their yeomen neighbors were occasionally anything but friendly. In 1847, Laurens planter Jonathan Davis complained that even though he kept his own fences in good repair his crops were often damaged by roaming stock belonging to John Gary, a neighboring yeoman.[49] Five years later, James Henry Hammond became embroiled in a bitter dispute with a neighbor who refused to pay ten cents a year for the right to use a stream that crossed Hammond's Silver Bluff plantation. Hammond levied the token annual fee simply to assert his private property rights, but his neighbor claimed that custom guaranteed free use of the watercourse. Confronted with his neighbor's flat refusal to pay, Hammond privately conceded that local opinion prevented anyone with his political ambitions from pressing the matter any further.[50] Though an aggravation to both parties, the dispute was relatively minor, and one needlessly provoked by Hammond's bluster and overweening pretension. Hammond, a *parvenu* who married wealth, never seemed satisfied with his position as a member of the planter gentry unless his new status was recognized by others.[51] The majority of Upcountry planters, more sensitive to the demands of the prevailing social protocol than Hammond, knew better than to expect any figurative tugging of the forelock from their yeoman neighbors.

Not all disputes between planters and their less fortunate neighbors were as contrived and avoidable as that involving Hammond. In 1853, Andrew Baxter Springs discovered that a family of poor whites named Nivens were providing his slaves with corn whiskey in return for food stolen from Springs's corn crib and smokehouse. Springs described the Nivens clan as "a large and most lazy and worthless family" but he could not bring charges against them because he had no evidence except that provided by slave informants.[52] John Springs urged his son to put an end to the illicit traffic by selling one of the slaves involved to Mississippi (as an example to the others) and by keeping his meat and corn under lock and key. Speaking with the wizened voice of experience, the elder Springs advised his son against any effort to prosecute the Nivenses. Such prosecutions, John Springs recalled, were "most unpleasant . . . unthankful, unpopular, and unprofitable." While some in the community credited the plaintiff with "ferreting out villainy," Springs mused, many others "charge you with seeking undue advantages and taking advantages of the neighbors and grinding the Poor."[53] Springs knew that in order to maintain the political support of the yeoman majority, planters could exercise their legal and economic power only within parameters loosely defined by community mores and opinion.

[49]Jonathan H. Davis to John Gary, December 3, 1837, Jones, Watts, Davis Papers, SCL.

[50]Entry of September 8, 1842, Hammond Plantation Diary, James Henry Hammond Papers, SCL; Entry of September 10, 1842, Hammond Diary, James Henry Hammond Papers, LC (on microfilm at SCL).

[51]Drew Gilpin Faust, *James Henry Hammond and the Old South*, see pp. 133–134 for a complete account of the incident discussed in this paragraph. See also Carol R. Bleser, *The Hammonds of Redcliffe* (New York: Oxford University Press, 1981), pp. 3–18.

[52]Andrew Baxter Springs to John Springs, August 8, 1853, Springs Family Papers, SHC.

[53]John Springs to Andrew Baxter Springs, August 15, 1853, Springs Family Papers, SHC.

For the most part, Upcountry planters developed a social style befitting a self-made gentry in an aggressively republican society. Prominent planter-politician George McDuffie, known for his "great industry, energy, and attention to business," wore "plain, farmer-like garb" and was credited with exerting "a very favorable influence on the farmers and planters . . . of the whole [Abbeville] district." When not holding public office, McDuffie, a widower, usually spent six days a week living in a cabin on his plantation with his overseer. One friend claimed that, while on the plantation, McDuffie worked "like a negro from the break of day until dark" and did not "change a particle of his dress until Sunday morning like any common day laborer."[54] To be sure, few Upcountry planters went to such extremes to preserve the common touch, but most led lives remarkably free of aristocratic pretensions or elitist hauteur. John C. Calhoun, and all of his brothers and sisters, were characterized by one of their Abbeville neighbors as a family of "warm and unpretending cordiality."[55] And Zelotus Holmes, an *arriviste* blessed with astute powers of observation, defended the planter elite from Northern charges that it constituted an unrepublican aristocracy. Upcountry society, Holmes allowed, was "not so refined" and "more secluded from City intercourse" than that of his native Buffalo, New York; nevertheless, Holmes continued, the Upcountry was a place of "intelligence and taste—and some display." But despite its obvious wealth and pride, the planter elite remained essentially republican in its posture. "Call it what you please," Holmes admonished his Northern relatives, "I am as true a republican at heart as any man and as warm a Brother. . . ."[56]

Upcountry planters moved with aplomb in many circles. A day in the life of a planter might involve studying a letter from his factor analyzing the cotton market in Liverpool, reading essays on the advantages of crop rotation and marling, and attending a public meeting to encourage subscription to some new railroad project. Yet the same day might also find the planter ginning a few hundred pounds of cotton for a yeoman farmer, arguing with a disgruntled neighbor over customary land use rights, and "sharing" a few bushels of corn with a tobacco-chewing widow and her children. Planters were the leading entrepreneurs of the Upcountry and their plantations were the hubs of local economic activity, especially in the lower Piedmont. They were involved in both a complex and risky international trade and a variety of highly localized activities where there was often nothing more, or less, to worry about than a band of angry neighbors.[57]

[54]Henry H. Townes to George F. Townes, June 14, 1833, Samuel A. Townes to George F. Townes, June 6, 1833, Townes Family Papers, SCL.

[55]Entry of March 8, 1836, Mary Elizabeth Moragne Diary, SCL. This diary is also available in published form, see Delle M. Craven, ed., *The Neglected Thread: A Journal from the Calhoun Community, 1836–1842* (Columbia, S.C.: University of South Carolina Press, 1951). Quotation is taken from p. 3.

[56]Zelotus L. Holmes to his Aunt, November 6, 1843, Zelotus L. Holmes Papers, SCL.

[57]In addition to the examples discussed in the preceding paragraphs, see John Gage to James M. Gage, November 15, 1835, James M. Gage Papers, SHC; Andrew Baxter Springs to John Springs,

A wealthy Richland district slaveholder, William Taylor, once referred to his fellow planters as "lovers of independence and prosperity."[58] Perhaps no single phrase ever captured so completely the planter ethos; but it was an ethos with its share of internal contradictions even when so succinctly stated. Prosperity and independence may well have been mutually reinforcing during the early cotton boom, but when the staple bonanza was interrupted, as it was in the late 1830s, the dangers inherent in the cotton economy became all too apparent. For years planters served as economic brokers who provided important links between largely isolated backcountry communities and the larger market economy. Operating in both local and international markets, planters recognized that the local economies of their communities were becoming more and more vulnerable to cyclical fluctuations in the international economy. The same prosperity which nurtured independence by enlarging the material base of individual autonomy also fostered networks of dependence which accompanied commercial expansion and economic specialization. The vital self-sufficiency of the independent freeholder could fall victim to economic efficiency and a more highly articulated division of labor. Nor was beguiling prosperity the only potential threat to personal independence; independence also seemed capable of destroying itself. Independence freed the individual producer from traditional fetters and spurred him to shoulder the wheel of progress resolutely. But to the extent that such freedom represented the emancipation of self-interest from traditional restraints, it caused considerable anxiety among republican theorists. An expanding material foundation for personal independence was a good thing, but the uncontrolled pursuit of individual aggrandizement could lead to the neglect of civic duty, or, worse, to the elevation of special interests over those of the community. The planter-led agricultural reform crusades were part of a struggle to insure that neither independence nor prosperity was seriously jeopardized by the excesses of the other. In sounding these warnings, planters, the entrepreneurs and venture capitalists of the Upcountry, assumed their more truncated identity as independent producers and urged their fellow planters and yeoman neighbors to adhere to thoroughly republican notions of political economy. Such reform-minded planters seldom practiced all that they preached. In 1843, F. W. Davie, a prominent Chester district planter, formally proposed that all South Carolina planters reduce their cotton acreage by one-third and increase the number of acres devoted to subsistence crops by the same proportion. A select committee of the reform-minded State Agricultural Society studied the proposal, but after praising the public-spiritedness of the author the committee rejected the plan as hopelessly

---

May 25, 1847, Springs Family Papers, SHC. For a colorful description of the fondness of many Southern white women for chewing tobacco, see George Ward Nichols, *The Story of the Great March* (New York: Harper and Brothers, 1865), pp. 155–159.

[58]William Taylor, "Anniversary Address: Delivered before the State Agricultural Society of South Carolina, November 30, 1843," in *Proceedings of the Agricultural Convention*, pp. 203–211.

impractical. "The habits of planters," the select committee reported, "are those of separate action: they combine less than any other class of men."[59]

Planters left behind impressive documentation of their ideas and activities, and, on the whole, they have been richly rewarded for their efforts by historians. Yet over 85 percent of all Upcountry farm operators were not planters. Indeed, over 80 percent of rural whites and over 45 percent of all slaves in the Upcountry lived on small or medium-sized farms rather than on plantations. Roughly 20 percent of these farms were operated by slaveholders who owned more than five but less than twenty slaves. These "middling slaveholders" controlled just over one-fourth of all farm wealth in the Upcountry and produced slightly more than one-fourth of all cotton grown in the region. In the lower Piedmont, middling slaveholders owned about one-fifth of all slaves, but in the upper Piedmont, where there were fewer plantations, middling slaveholders owned about one-half of all slaves.[60]

Nearly 90 percent of all middling slaveholders grew cotton, and while their cotton crops were not as large as those of most planters, they produced substantially more cotton per farm than did yeomen. In the lower Piedmont, farmers who owned at least ten but less than twenty slaves raised an average of seventeen bales of cotton per farm in 1850, and farmers who owned more than five but less than ten slaves raised an average of eleven bales per farm that same year. In the Upcountry as a whole, middling slaveholders usually worked farms with more than 100 improved acres, and over 80 percent were self-sufficient in grain despite their deep involvement in the cotton economy. Like planters, middling slaveholders purchased some of their pork in the marketplace, since only 55 percent were self-sufficient in meat.[61]

Representative of these middling slaveholders was Marshall Sharp, an Abbeville district farmer who owned twelve slaves and a 150-acre farm valued at $3000 in 1850. Sharp produced sixteen bales of cotton in 1849 and was self-sufficient in both grain and meat, raising 1000 bushels of corn, 350 bushels of oats, and keeping a herd of sixty swine on his unimproved land. Sharp also kept ten beef cattle, eight milk cows, six horses, and three mules. Sharp's counterparts in the upper Piedmont were only slightly less prosperous. York district farmer William McNeel kept nine slaves on his 100 improved acres, where he

[59]"Report on the Reduction of the Cotton Crop: A Reply to Col. F. W. Davie," in *Proceedings of the Agricultural Convention*, pp. 322–327.

[60]The rich historiography concerning the planter elite of the Old South began with the early work of U. B. Phillips and has continued through the recent work of Eugene D. Genovese, who has brought a valuable comparative perspective and a new level of conceptual rigor to the scholarly debate. For examples, see Ulrich B. Phillips, *Life and Labor in the Old South* (Boston: Little, Brown, 1929); Eugene D. Genovese, *The World the Slaveholders Made: Two Essays in Interpretation* (New York: Pantheon, 1969). Percentages calculated from the sample of Upcountry households taken from the Manuscript Census of South Carolina, 1850, Laurens, Spartanburg, and York Districts, Schedules I, II, and IV, and the sample of Upcountry farms drawn from the Manuscript Census of South Carolina, 1850, Abbeville, Anderson, and York Districts, Schedules I, II, and IV, SCDAH.

[61]See Table 2.9.

raised ten bales of cotton, 400 bushels of corn, and 300 bushels of oats in 1849. McNeel kept twenty-six head of swine, fifteen beef cattle, seven milk cows, seven horses, and two mules. His farm was valued at just over $2400. Another York district farmer, William Cowan, who owned seven slaves, raised eleven bales of cotton and 1000 bushels of corn and kept thirty-eight swine in 1849. A year earlier, William Cowan's son, Washington Cowan, had boasted that the family "made a fine crop . . . corn to sell and fodder and hay and oats also and we have sold 18 new bales [of cotton]."[62]

A few middling slaveholders even developed larger entrepreneurial interests. Thomas Taylor, a Greenville district farmer who owned fifteen slaves and a 400-acre farm valued at $2500 in 1850, also owned a small but profitable sawmill. In 1850, the sawmill was actually operated by Alfred Taylor, the twenty-four-year-old son of Thomas Taylor. The Taylor sawmill represented a capital investment of only $500 and produced about $1200 worth of lumber products in 1849.[63] On the whole, however, middling slaveholders made relatively few non-agricultural investments, especially when compared to those made by planters, but they were large producers of market commodities. However important self-sufficiency was to these middling slaveholders, and however limited their entrepreneurial efforts were, their economic interests were tied to the fate of the market economy.

The majority of white farmers in the Upcountry were yeomen.[64] Non-slaveholding farmers and slaveholding farmers who owned fewer than six slaves operated over 55 percent of all farms in the region. Despite their numerical preponderance, however, the yeoman majority worked just over one-third of all the improved acreage in the Upcountry and controlled only one-third of all farm wealth in the region. Yeoman farmers produced nearly 38 percent of all corn but only 20 percent of all cotton grown in the Upcountry. Slaveholding yeomen operated nearly 23 percent of all Upcountry farms and produced 10 percent of the

[62]Manuscript Census of South Carolina, 1850, Abbeville, Anderson, and York Districts, Schedules I, II, and IV, SCDAH; Washington Cowan to John Cowan, March 4, 1849, Nancy Cowan Papers, DU.

[63]Manuscript Census of South Carolina, 1850, Greenville District, Schedules I, II, IV, and V, SCDAH; for more information on the Taylor family business, see Alfred Taylor Books, SHC.

[64]The pioneering work on Southern yeomen was that of the so-called "Owsley school." For examples, see Frank L. Owsley and Harriet C. Owsley, "The Economic Basis of Society in the Late Antebellum South," *Journal of Southern History* 6 (February, 1940):24–45; Frank L. Owsley, *Plain Folk of the Old South* (Baton Rouge: Louisiana State University Press, 1949); Herbert Weaver, *Mississippi Farmers*; Blanche Henry Clark, *The Tennessee Yeomen* (Nashville: Vanderbilt University Press, 1942). The questions about method and interpretation raised by Fabian Linden in "Economic Democracy in the Slave South: An Appraisal of Some Recent Views," *Journal of Negro History* 31 (April, 1946):140–189 seemed to stifle rather than encourage further scholarly examination of Southern yeomen. The relative historiographical neglect of Southern yeomen in the quarter-century following the appearance of Owsley's book was ably documented in Ira Berlin, "White Majority: A Review Essay," *Social History* 5 (May, 1977):653–660. Since the publication of Berlin's essay, a spate of recent work has appeared to suggest that the long era of yeoman neglect may be over. Foremost among these recent studies is Steven Hahn's pathbreaking account of yeoman farmers in Georgia's upper Piedmont, *Roots of Southern Populism*, which suggests that yeomen played a crucial role in shaping antebellum Southern society.

cotton raised in the region; slaveless yeomen operated just over 33 percent of all Upcountry farms and also raised only 10 percent of the region's cotton. But if yeoman farmers produced a comparatively small, though certainly significant, percentage of the Upcountry cotton crop, the vast majority of Upcountry yeomen were hardly outside the cotton economy. Over 75 percent of all yeoman farmers in the Upcountry grew at least one bale of cotton in 1849, and the average cotton output on yeoman-operated farms was well over three bales per farm. More than 70 percent of all non-slaveholding yeomen raised cotton. On the average, these slaveless farmers produced nearly three bales of cotton per farm. In York district, slaveless yeoman John Walker produced two bales of cotton on a fifty-acre farm valued at less than $400 in 1849. Walker's neighbor, James McSwain, also a non-slaveholder, raised four bales of cotton on his sixty-acre farm that same year. Participation in the cotton economy was even more pervasive among slaveholding yeomen. In 1849, over 80 percent of all small slaveholders grew some cotton. The average cotton output on farms operated by slaveholding yeomen was well over four bales per farm. Abbeville's Samuel Wideman raised six bales of cotton on his sixty-acre farm with the help of his three slaves in 1849; that same year, York's A. A. McKenzie, owner of four slaves, produced five bales of cotton on a farm with sixty-five improved acres. Moreover, a healthy majority of yeoman farmers were self-sufficient in food despite their involvement in the cotton economy. In 1849, two-thirds of all Upcountry yeomen were self-sufficient in grain, and over 60 percent were self-sufficient in meat.[65]

The apparent success of most yeomen in achieving self-sufficiency in basic foodstuffs while at the same time producing at least some cotton for the market belies the existence of a sharp dichotomy between commercial and subsistence agriculture as posited by the conventional "dual-economy" hypothesis. By and large, Upcountry yeomen were not forced to make an all-or-nothing choice between commercial agriculture and subsistence farming, or between traditional mores and market values. Instead, Upcountry yeomen made a set of crop-mix decisions each year, balancing their need for a sure and steady food supply with their desire for cotton profits, a cash income, and a higher standard of living. However valuable agricultural production statistics are in helping shape interpretations of yeoman behavior, these statistics reveal considerably less than

[65]See Tables 2.9 and 2.10. For comparisons, see Gavin Wright, "'Economic Democracy' and the Concentration of Agricultural Wealth in the Cotton South," *Agricultural History* 44 (January, 1970):63–94; Randolph B. Campbell, "Planters and Plain Folk: Harrison County, Texas, as a Test Case, 1850–1860," *Journal of Southern History* 40 (August, 1974):369–398; Donald Schaefer, "Yeoman Farmers and Economic Democracy: A Study of Wealth and Economic Mobility in the Western Tobacco Region, 1850–1860," *Explorations in Economic History* 15 (October, 1978):421–437; for an older, but still useful study, see James C. Bonner, "Profile of a Late Antebellum Community," *American Historical Review* 49 (July, 1948):663–680. Eugene D. Genovese, "Yeoman Farmers in a Slaveholders' Democracy," *Agricultural History* 49 (April, 1975):331–342 offers some provocative hypotheses about the position of the yeoman farmer in antebellum Southern society. For further elaboration of these ideas, see Elizabeth Fox-Genovese and Eugene D. Genovese, *Fruits of Merchant Capital: Slavery and Bourgeois Property in the Rise and Expansion of Capitalism* (New York: Oxford University Press, 1983), pp. 249–264.

historians would like to know about the actual motivations and ambitions of yeoman farmers. Nevertheless, judging from their production habits, most Upcountry yeomen seem to have practiced what Gavin Wright has aptly described as "safety-first" farming.[66] Though hardly isolated from market incentives, yeoman farmers were motivated by concerns other than the desire to extract every last dollar of profit from their farms. Foremost among the typical yeoman's aims was the protection of his property, the basis of his independence, from attachment, levy, and sale. Above all, yeomen wanted to preserve their position as landowners. As a result, they were as concerned about avoiding unnecessary economic risks as they were with earning cash profits. Given the economic and ideological premium placed on the ownership of productive property in antebellum society, such risk aversion in defense of property titles was quite rational behavior.

Unlike planters and middling slaveholders, small farmers operated under tight land and labor constraints, especially in the short term. If a yeoman committed too much of his improved land to cotton and either produced a poor crop or was forced to sell at low prices, he risked having neither enough home-grown food on hand to meet the needs of his household nor enough cash to purchase food on the open market. Farmers who practiced the "safety-first" method avoided this dilemma by first allocating enough acreage to subsistence crops to guarantee self-sufficiency and then planting staples on whatever land was not needed for the production of food. The logic behind "safety-first" farming was simple enough. A farmer who raised only cotton and purchased his food supplies out of cotton profits faced three major uncertainties in his budgetary calculations: his own cotton yields, the market price of cotton, and the market price of food. But a farmer who followed "safety-first" logic braved only the uncertainty of his subsistence crop yields. Thus the estimation of exactly how much land should be devoted to subsistence crops in order to insure an ample "margin of safety" against a failure to achieve self-sufficiency demanded some educated guesswork. Yet any farmer with even a few years' experience in making such estimates would doubtless begin to display considerable accuracy. And the guesswork involved in cotton specialization was decidedly more complex.[67]

The application of "safety-first" logic to crop-mix decisions allowed a healthy majority of Upcountry yeomen to achieve self-sufficiency without forgo-

[66]Gavin Wright, *The Political Economy of the Cotton South*, pp. 55–88; Gavin Wright, "Cotton, Corn, and Risk in the Nineteenth Century," *Journal of Economic History* 35 (September, 1975):526–551. The argument of Wright and Kunreuther was challenged by Robert McGuire and Robert Higgs, "Cotton, Corn, and Risk: Another View," *Explorations in Economic History* 14 (April, 1977):167–182; see also Gavin Wright and Howard Kunreuther, "Cotton, Corn, and Risk in the Nineteenth Century: A Reply," *Explorations in Economic History* 14 (April, 1977):183–185. On a related point, see Michael Merrill, "Cash Is Good to Eat: Self-Sufficiency and Exchange in the Rural Economy of the United States," *Radical History Review* 3 (Winter, 1977):42–71.

[67]Howard Kunreuther and Gavin Wright, "Safety-First, Gambling, and the Subsistence Farmer," in James A. Roumasset et al., eds., *Risk, Uncertainty, and Agricultural Development* (New York: Agricultural Development Council, 1979):213–230.

ing entirely the benefits of participation in the cotton economy. Yeoman farmers wanted to make money on cotton, but most preferred to leverage their involvement in the market with the security of self-sufficiency in subsistence crops. The particular blend of subsistence and commercial agriculture dictated by "safety-first" logic allowed yeomen to protect their homesteads while enjoying a small share of the cotton bounty. Yeomen who practiced "safety-first" agriculture protected their republican birthright of personal independence but also mounted a controlled pursuit of the main chance. Despite their substantial involvement in the cotton economy, however, a majority of yeomen still adhered to the traditional republican belief that "a proper sense of independence" could be maintained only by people who "rely upon the resources of their own soil for their bread."[68] This cautionary aspect of the republican creed not only tempered yeoman farmers' enthusiasm for the main chance but also shaped, at least in part, their response to the wholesale expansion of commercial agriculture which occurred during the second half of the nineteenth century.[69]

The co-existence of market involvement with the ethic of self-sufficiency disguised sharply contrasting patterns of yeomen behavior within the Upcountry itself. In particular, the production patterns of yeoman farmers in the white-majority hill country differed significantly from those of yeomen living in the black-belt areas of the lower Piedmont. In the upper Piedmont, an area situated largely on the geographic margins of the antebellum cotton economy, the familiar pattern of "safety-first" agriculture prevailed. In Anderson district, where 88 percent of all farm operators were yeomen, two-thirds of all non-slaveholding farmers and nearly four-fifths of all slaveholding yeomen participated in the cotton economy. But yeomen in Anderson raised relatively small amounts of cotton, producing an average of just over two bales per farm in 1849, and over 70 percent of all Anderson yeomen achieved self-sufficiency in grain. Slaveless farmers in Anderson produced almost as much cotton per farm as small slaveholders, but non-slaveholders raised only three-fourths as much grain per farm as slaveholding yeomen. As a result, nearly one-third of all slaveless yeomen failed to achieve self-sufficiency in grain while only 20 percent of all small slaveholders failed to produce enough grain to satisfy the needs of their households. Moreover, cotton accounted for only 15 percent of total output on farms operated by yeomen in Anderson district. In York, an upper Piedmont district somewhat better suited for cotton production than Anderson, cotton accounted for roughly 20 percent of all agricultural output on yeoman-operated farms. On plantations and larger farms, cotton often accounted for 40 to 50

[68]Joel R. Poinsett, "An Agricultural Address," in *Proceedings of the Agricultural Convention,* p. 242.

[69]Lacy K. Ford, "Rednecks and Merchants: Economic Development and Social Tensions in the South Carolina Upcountry, 1865–1900," *Journal of American History* 71 (September, 1984):294–318; Steven Hahn, "The 'Unmaking' of the Southern Yeomanry: The Transformation of the Georgia Upcountry, 1860–1890," in Steven Hahn and Jonathan Prude, ed., *The Countryside in the Age of Capitalist Transformation: Essays in the Social History of Rural America* (Chapel Hill: University of North Carolina Press, 1985), pp. 179–204.

percent of total output. For yeomen in the upper Piedmont, involvement in the cotton economy was clearly cautious and measured.[70]

Representative of upper Piedmont yeomen was John Crocker, a non-slavcholder from Spartanburg district, who raised two bales of cotton on a small farm valued at $400 in 1849. In Anderson, Gabriel Cox, also a non-slaveholder, raised four bales of cotton and 600 bushels of corn on seventy-five improved acres in 1849. Cox also kept nineteen swine and was self-sufficient in both meat and grain. Anderson's David Duncan, owner of three slaves, also raised four bales of cotton and a sufficiency of food on his sixty improved acres. But not all upper Piedmont yeoman fared as well as Crocker, Cox, and Duncan. Thomas Beatty, a slaveless yeoman from Anderson district, worked thirty-five improved acres in 1849. Beatty produced one bale of cotton but his subsistence crop yields were not sufficient to meet his household needs. In Anderson district, most of the slaveless yeomen who failed to achieve self-sufficiency were simply the poorest of all Upcountry farmers. Like Thomas Beatty, these hardscrabble farmers worked plots of forty acres or less and failed to achieve self-sufficiency because they could not rather than because they did not want to. Their hard lot reveals just how difficult survival was for some families in the red hills of the backwoods South.[71]

In the lower Piedmont, a different production pattern prevailed among yeomen. Nearly 90 percent of all lower Piedmont yeomen, including 89 percent of all non-slaveholders, grew cotton, and the average cotton output on yeoman-operated farms in the lower Piedmont was nearly double that of yeoman-operated farms in the upper Piedmont. Slaveless yeomen in the lower Piedmont district of Abbeville grew over 40 percent more cotton per farm than did their counterparts in Anderson, and cotton production among small slaveholders in Abbeville outstripped that of small slaveholders in Anderson by an even wider margin. Abbeville's William Riley, a non-slaveholder, produced five bales of cotton on a twenty-nine-acre farm valued at $400 in 1859; James Criswell, also a slaveless yeoman from Abbeville, produced eleven bales of cotton on sixty improved acres that same year. Moreover, yeoman farmers in the lower Piedmont devoted a substantially larger percentage of their productive efforts to cotton than did upper Piedmont yeomen. In Abbeville, cotton accounted for roughly 33 percent of total output on farms operated by yeomen, a share nearly twice as high as that of Anderson yeomen. But if lower Piedmont yeomen were more heavily involved in the cotton economy than upper Piedmont yeomen, they were also much less likely to be self-sufficient. Abbeville yeomen produced less than two-thirds as much corn per farm as yeomen in Anderson. Only slightly more than half of all

[70]See Tables 2.11 and 2.12; for comparisons, see David F. Weiman, "Petty Commodity Production in the Cotton South: Upcountry Farmers in the Georgia Cotton Economy" (Ph.D. dissertation, Stanford University, 1984), especially pp. 143–253; John C. Inscoe, "Mountain Masters: Slaveholding in Western North Carolina," *North Carolina Historical Review* 61 (April, 1984): 143–173.

[71]Manuscript Census of South Carolina, 1850, Anderson and Spartanburg Districts, Schedules I, II, and IV, SCDAH.

Table 2.11 Yeoman Farmers in the Upper and Lower Piedmont, 1850

	Non-slaveholding Yeomen		Slaveholding Yeomen	
	Mean Value	Share of Total	Mean Value	Share of Total
Anderson District				
Cotton (lbs.)	880.0	52.4%	920.0	18.2%
Corn (bushels)	335.2	46.2	456.9	16.8
Swine	19.9	45.8	20.8	17.9
Improved acres	67.4	52.2	87.6	20.4
Cash Value of Farms	$1159.9	45.7	$1303.4	23.9
Abbeville District				
Cotton (lbs.)	1320.0	5.0%	2400.0	7.2%
Corn (bushels)	197.2	7.0	321.7	9.3
Swine	16.3	17.0	35.9	14.8
Improved acres	41.1	12.1	60.9	9.3
Cash Value of Farms	$880.2	6.4	$1607.9	9.5

Source: Manuscript Census of South Carolina, 1850, Abbeville and Anderson Districts, Schedules I, II, and IV.

non-slaveholding yeomen in Abbeville were self-sufficient in grain. Slaveholding yeomen in Abbeville fared slightly better, with two-thirds achieving self-sufficiency. To some extent at least, the lower Piedmont yeoman's greater emphasis on cotton production came at the expense of self-sufficiency.[72]

Nor did the contrast between upper Piedmont yeomen and lower Piedmont yeomen end with different rates of self-sufficiency and different levels of cotton production. Yeoman farmers in the upper Piedmont controlled a far larger share of their area's wealth, produced a larger percentage of its crops, and owned a larger share of its livestock than did yeomen in the lower Piedmont. In 1850, yeomen in Anderson owned over 65 percent of all improved farm land in the district, raised over 70 percent of the cotton and nearly two-thirds of the corn, and owned over 60 percent of all swine. Indeed, yeomen in Anderson controlled nearly 70 percent of the district's total farm wealth. By contrast, yeoman farmers possessed a much smaller share of total wealth in the plantation economy of the lower Piedmont. In 1850, yeomen operated nearly 40 percent of all farms in Abbeville district, but controlled less than 16 percent of its farm wealth. Abbeville yeomen produced only 11 percent of the district's cotton and only 14 percent of its corn. But even though lower Piedmont yeomen owned a smaller share of their region's wealth than their counterparts in the upper Piedmont, they were generally no worse off in absolute terms. The average wealth of yeoman farmers was roughly the same in both regions. Hill-country yeomen were not any

[72]See Tables 2.11 and 2.12; Manuscript Census of South Carolina, 1850, Abbeville District, Schedules I, II, and IV, SCDAH. For comparisons, see J. William Harris, *Plain Folk and Gentry in a Slave Society: White Liberty and Black Slavery in Augusta's Hinterlands* (Middletown, Conn.: Wesleyan University Press, 1985), especially pp. 15–40; and John Solomon Otto, "Slaveholding General Farmers in a 'Cotton' County," *Agricultural History* 55 (April, 1981):167–178.

Table 2.12 Cotton and Self-Sufficiency in the Upper and
Lower Piedmont, 1850

	Non-slaveholding Yeomen	Slaveholding Yeomen
Anderson District		
% Growing Cotton	66.3	78.7
% Self-Sufficient (Grain)	68.5	79.0
Cotton-Corn Ratio	2.7	2.0
Abbeville District		
% Growing Cotton	88.7	90.0
% Self-Sufficient (Grain)	51.5	68.0
Cotton-Corn Ratio	6.6	7.5

Source: Manuscript Census of South Carolina, 1850, Abbeville and Anderson Districts, Schedules I, II, IV.

richer than yeomen in the black belt; they simply owned a larger share of a smaller economic pie.[73]

Nevertheless, the position of yeoman farmers in the two sections of the Piedmont relative to the larger cotton economy differed significantly. Lower Piedmont yeoman displayed a stronger cotton orientation than upper Piedmont yeomen and were either less able or less anxious to achieve self-sufficiency than their fellow yeomen in the hill country. Living in the heart of the antebellum cotton belt, lower Piedmont yeomen doubtless owned land better suited for cotton production and enjoyed better access to ginning and marketing services than did most upper Piedmont yeomen. As a result, yeomen in the black belt stood much better chance of reaping quick cash bonanzas than did their hill-country counterparts. At the same time, however, lower Piedmont yeomen were more dependent on the market for necessities and seemingly somewhat more vulnerable to the ups and downs of the larger market economy. Upper Piedmont yeomen, or at least the majority of them, also participated in the market economy, but theirs was a limited, and very carefully leveraged, market involvement. Their apparent devotion to the ethic of self-sufficiency, and the widespread practice of "safety-first" farming, shielded upper Piedmont yeomen from many of the vicissitudes of the market economy while allowing them to enjoy some measure of its benefits. Yet whether deeply enmeshed in the cotton economy as in the lower Piedmont, or working largely outside its vortex as in the upper Piedmont, yeomen maintained relatively similar standards of material well-being.[74]

[73]See Tables 2.11 and 2.12.

[74]On contrasts between hill-country and black-belt yeomen in other parts of the South, see Hahn, *Roots of Southern Populism*, pp. 15–49; Steven H. Hahn, "The Yeomanry in the Non-Plantation South: Upper Piedmont Georgia, 1850–1860," in Orville V. Burton and Robert C. McMath, eds., *Class, Conflict, and Consensus: Antebellum Southern Community Studies* (Westport, Conn.: Green-

To an extent not possible in the black belt, yeoman farmers in the upper Piedmont, operating on the geographic fringe of the cotton economy, shaped the local economy to their own needs rather than to those of planters. Such was the case in the yeomen-dominated community around Tolleson's store in the eastern portion of Spartanburg district.[75] The Tolleson community was overwhelmingly agricultural in 1850. Of the 63 voters at Tolleson's precinct who could be located in the manuscript census, 57 were farmers. Of the six who were not farm operators, one was a carpenter, one a blacksmith, one a farm laborer, and one a retired overseer. Two listed no occupation. Two farm operators doubled as local merchants. Apparently there were no planters living in the immediate vicinity. The largest slaveholder in the Tolleson community, Samuel Littlejohn, age fifty-four, owned sixteen slaves and ran a 250-acre farm valued at $6000. The community's largest cotton producer, merchant-farmer B. F. Bates, raised twenty-four bales of cotton and owned six slaves. Only eight of the 57 farm operators in the Tolleson area owned more than five slaves; 28 of the remaining 49 were yeomen and 21 were tenants or squatters.[76]

For the most part, yeoman farmers in the Tolleson community struggled to manage a modest existence. Slaveless yeomen ordinarily worked farms of eighty improved acres valued at just over $700. Roughly three-fourths of the Tolleson yeomen achieved self-sufficiency in food.[77] Yet despite their ownership of productive property and their general success with subsistence crops, yeomen households in the Tolleson community were hardly islands unto themselves. These hill-country yeomen often depended on local artisans for needed services and on neighboring farmers for timely labor. James F. Sloan, a poll manager at Tolleson's precinct and a substantial yeoman, regularly participated in log-rollings, rail-splittings, wheat-thrashings, corn-shuckings, and even quiltings in the Tolleson community.[78]

---

wood Press, 1982), pp. 29–56; Weiman, "Petty Commodity Production in the Cotton South," pp. 254–365; John Mitchell Allman, "Yeoman Regions in the Antebellum Deep South: Settlement and Economy in Northern Alabama, 1815–1860" (Ph.D. dissertation, University of Maryland, 1979), pp. 221–320; William Barney, "Towards the Civil War: The Dynamics of Change in a Black-Belt County," in Burton and McMath, eds., Class, Conflict, and Consensus, pp. 146–172.

[75]The yeoman-dominated community surrounding Tolleson's store, which also served as a polling place, was reconstructed using a list of eligible voters compiled by the poll managers for the Tolleson precinct and found in the James F. Sloan Papers, SCL. In the Sloan Papers, the voter list is dated circa 1845, but James Sloan was a poll manager at Tolleson's in the middle of the 1850s. If the list does, in fact, date from 1845 it would have been an old list handed down to Sloan by his predecessors. It is also possible that the list dates from around 1855 rather than 1845. Names from the list were matched with names on the Manuscript Census of South Carolina, 1850, Spartanburg District, Schedules I, II, and IV. Since the census was taken either five years after or five years before the list was compiled, the matching process proved difficult. Of the 120 or so names on the voting list only 63 could be unambiguously identified in the manuscript census. All voters found in the census were heads of households.

[76]Manuscript Census of South Carolina, 1850, Spartanburg District, Schedules I, II, and IV; List of Voters, [c. 1845], Sloan Family Papers, SCL.

[77]Ibid.

[78]Entries of May 7, 1856, December 27, 1856, March 21, 1857, July 21, 1857, October 29, 1857, April 10, 1858, August 8, 1858, James F. Sloan Journals, SCL.

Sloan's own life was a story of modest upward mobility. Born in Laurens district in 1819, Sloan was the son of Daniel Sloan, a Scotch-Irish Presbyterian and yeoman farmer. The younger Sloan married at the age of twenty-one and began his adult life as a tenant farmer. Sloan also worked for a year as an overseer before saving enough money to buy his own farm in Spartanburg district in 1843. Sloan's first wife died just ten months after they set up housekeeping in Spartanburg. At age twenty-four, Sloan was a widower left with the care of three young children. Two years later, Sloan remarried, taking Doreas Lee, member of a Tolleson area family, as his second bride.[79]

By the late 1850s, Sloan worked sixty improved acres valued at $1000. A hard-working, attentive farmer who never owned a slave, Sloan carefully calculated ways to make the most of his limited resources. During the growing season Sloan pushed himself and other members of his family hard. He had little use for anyone habitually fond of idleness. Sloan regularly planted corn, wheat, oats, and cotton and always kept sizable herds of swine and sheep.[80] During the 1850s, Sloan's farm was self-sufficient in meat and grain, and, together with members of his family, Sloan made some of the clothes and shoes used by members of the household. But Sloan's quest for self-sufficiency involved him in a local economic network that included many of his neighbors. Sloan raised his own cattle, but his hides were cured into leather at a tanyard run by W. H. Bagwell, a substantial farmer who owned eleven slaves. Sloan used the leather to make and repair shoes for his family, but he often received help from Samuel Thornton, a neighborhood shoemaker. Sloan had his wheat and corn ground into flour and meal at a grist mill run by James Brown, a sixty-year-old farmer with real estate valued at $2000. Sloan also purchased cotton seed from Brown. Sloan's substantial cotton crops, which ranged from four to six bales a year, were ginned at M. C. Lee's.[81] Sloan bought most of his farm supplies and other necessities which he could not raise or make at B. F. Bates's general store. For a number of years Sloan maintained a close personal and working relationship with Bates, and he earned small amounts of extra cash by hauling crops and other commodities for the merchant. In 1859, however, Sloan became convinced that he had been "rather slighted" by Bates during a drinking session at the store. Whether Sloan believed that he had been short-changed by the merchant in a business transaction or whether he interpreted some of Bates's remarks as a personal insult remains unclear, but the incident aroused Sloan's prickly spirit of independence. "I hope to maintain my integrity," Sloan vowed, "and that is

[79]John W. Rumble, "A Carolina Country Squire in the Old South and the New: The Papers of James F. Sloan," *South Atlantic Quarterly* 81 (Summer, 1982):323–337; Sloan's example provides an instructive comparison with that of a North Carolina yeoman; see Arthur C. Menius III, "James Bennitt: Portrait of an Antebellum Yeoman," *North Carolina Historical Review* 58 (Autumn, 1981):305–326.

[80]Manuscript Census of South Carolina, 1850, Spartanburg District, Schedules I, II, and IV, SCDAH; Survey of James F. Sloan Journals, 1854–1861, SCL.

[81]Entries of January 14, 1855, July 30, 1857, October 20, 1857, February 26, 1858, June 14, 1858, August 10, 1859, September 22, 1859, October 28, 1859, November 17, 1859, James F. Sloan Journals, 1854–1861, SCL.

never to take ardent spirits with him any more at his store.''[82] Sloan's normal farming routine produced economic involvement with a local tanner, a shoe-maker, a grist mill operator, a cotton gin owner, and a prosperous crossroads merchant; also, his occasional need for extra labor and the reciprocal labor needs of his neighbors involved Sloan in a variety of cooperative harvesting and con-struction projects each year. Like most other Upcountry yeomen, Sloan dis-covered that the pursuit of economic independence necessarily involved eco-nomic interaction with others in the surrounding community.

Important at this local economic network was to Sloan, however, his eco-nomic activities were not confined to it. Every year, Sloan devoted more of his resources and more of his productive energy to the production and marketing of cotton than any other single endeavor. Even in a hill-country community such as Tolleson, a healthy majority of all farmers were actively involved in the cotton economy. Sixty percent of all yeomen and two-thirds of all tenant farmers in the Tolleson community raised cotton. Moreover, exactly half of the yeomen who did not grow cotton were either old, semi-retired farmers or small, part-time farmers with other occupations or other sources of income. Abraham Lancaster, age seventy-two, raised only subsistence crops on his seventy-acre farm in 1849, and James Bryant, age eighty, raised 150 bushels of corn but no cotton on his fifteen improved acres. Lucas Cannon, age seventy-five, raised no cotton on his 300-acre farm valued at $2700 in 1849. Jeremy Lindsay, age twenty-seven, also raised no cotton on his $40 farm of less than ten acres, but Lindsay earned his living as a carpenter rather than as a farmer. Among the majority of Tolleson yeomen who did grow cotton, the average output was three bales per farm. Eighty percent of all Tolleson yeomen who grew cotton produced at least two bales. Jeremiah Lee, a non-slaveholder, raised four bales of cotton on his fifty-acre farm in 1849, and Fulton Brown raised three bales of cotton on a farm with eighty-six improved acres that same year.[83]

Throughout the 1850s, James F. Sloan's cotton crops always accounted for over 30 percent of his total farm output. A careful farmer generally, Sloan was especially solicitous of his cotton crop. He never failed to note the appearance of the first cotton blooms, a source of special delight, in his journal. In late spring, Sloan and his family often worked late into the night harrowing cotton fields. During the fall picking season, Sloan and the family worked steadily. Sloan hauled his own cotton to market. Every winter, sometime during January or February, Sloan set out on the two- or even three-day trip to Columbia by wagon. Once in Columbia, Sloan sold his cotton, bought supplies, and conversed with other farmers. These trips often kept Sloan away from his home for more than a week. Sloan monitored cotton prices as closely as he could, given the relative isolation of rural Spartanburg from major markets, and tried to hold his cotton off the market when prices were low.[84] Nor was Sloan's market involvement un-

[82]Entry of August 18, 1859, James F. Sloan Journals, SCL.

[83]Manuscript Census of South Carolina, 1850, Spartanburg District, Schedules I, II, and IV, SCDAH; List of Voters, [c. 1845], Sloan Family Papers, SCL.

[84]Entries of May 3, 1855, September 15, 1856, September 25, 1856, October 21, 1856, January

usual for upper Piedmont yeomen. In 1851, Edward Lipscomb, a slaveless yeoman living in a community adjoining the Tolleson community, complained that he had made "only" five bales of cotton and called his yield the "sorriest I ever saw." In a letter to his brother in Alabama, the profit-minded Lipscomb discussed his cotton crop and various commodity prices in some detail before matter-of-factly reporting, "Mother has gone insane."[85] In York district, A. A. McKenzie, a slaveholding yeoman from the Zeno community, not only marketed a substantial cotton crop but also operated a profitable grinding mill on a branch of Crowders Creek. McKenzie's mill, valued at $2500, both served the local community and shipped flour to the Charleston market. Although he possessed a net worth of less than $7000, McKenzie was described by a credit reporter as a "man of independent circumstances" who "owes no man anything."[86] Men like Sloan and McKenzie embodied the republican ideal and provided the raw material from which the legend of the sturdy yeoman was made.

Except for a few mountaineer enclaves deep in the northwest corner of the region, no Upcountry community, including yeoman-dominated communities in the upper Piedmont, existed in genuine isolation from the market economy. Indeed, the very concept of self-sufficiency as it has been applied in this and other recent studies of yeoman farmers is a severely truncated one. Measures of self-sufficiency currently used by Southern historians deal almost exclusively with self-sufficiency in food for the household and in grain for livestock but rarely apply to household production of clothes or agricultural supplies.[87] Of course, even largely self-contained peasant economies often imported a few special commodities, such as salt, and thus were not truly hermetic, but in many subsistence-oriented economies, including that of the South Carolina Upcountry during the late eighteenth and early nineteenth century, household manufactures played a dominant role in the clothing of most rural families.[88] In 1800, most

---

1, 1857, February 24, 1857, June 26, 1857, February 3, 1858, February 12, 1858, November 30, 1858, May 10, 1859, James F. Sloan Journals, 1854–1861, SCL.

[85]Edward Lipscomb to Smith Lipscomb, December 31, 1852, Lipscomb Family Papers, SHC; Manuscript Census of South Carolina, 1850, Spartanburg District, Schedules I, II, and IV, SCDAH; on the proximity of Lipscomb to Sloan's community, see entry of August 15, 1859, James F. Sloan Journals, SCL.

[86]R. G. Dun and Company, Credit Ledger, South Carolina, XIV, 124, Baker; Manuscript Census of South Carolina, 1850, York District, Schedules I, II, and IV, SCDAH.

[87]See Sam Bowers Hilliard, *Hog Meat and Hoecake: Food Supply in the Old South, 1840–1860* (Carbondale: Southern Illinois University Press, 1972); Roger L. Ransom and Richard Sutch, *One Kind of Freedom: The Economic Consequences of Emancipation* (Cambridge: Cambridge University Press, 1977), pp. 244–253; Gallman, "Self-Sufficiency in the Cotton Economy," pp. 5–23.

[88]Jan De Vries, "Peasant Demand Patterns and Economic Development: Friesland, 1550–1750," in William N. Parker and Eric L. Jones, eds., *European Peasants and Their Markets: Essays in Agrarian Economic History* (Princeton: Princeton University Press, 1975), pp. 205–268; Jan De Vries, *The Dutch Rural Economy in the Golden Age, 1500–1700* (New Haven: Yale University Press, 1974), pp. 1–21; Stephen Hymer and Stephen Resnick, "A Model of an Agrarian Economy with Nonagricultural Activities," *American Historical Review* 59 (September, 1969):493–506; Robert Mills, *Statistics of South Carolina* (Charleston, S.C.: Hurlbut and Lloyd, 1826), pp. 348–782.

Upcountry families were clothed almost exclusively in homespun cloth and other homemade goods. When Irish immigrant Michael Gaffney made his way into the Upcountry in December 1800, after brief sojourns in New York City and Charleston, it was the prevalence of homespun and the almost total self-reliance of farm households that first captured his attention. Upcountrymen, Gaffney observed, "dress generally in a hunting shirt and trousers of coarse cotton yarn. Every farmer or planter is his own shoemaker, tanner, tailor, carpenter, brazier, and, in fact, everything else." Farm women and their daughters, Gaffney explained, had to pick cotton from the seed, and then "spin it, weave it, and make it ready for your back."[89] In 1808, a northern visitor to Columbia noted that when "country people" came to town for court week, "both men and women, almost without exception, dressed in course homespun cotton of a mixed color."[90] Even as late as the 1820s, when Robert Mills conducted his remarkable survey of South Carolina, most Upcountry families were still clothed largely in homespun cloth. "None but domestic manufactures thrive here," an observer reported from Newberry district, "[but] almost every family manufactures their own clothing." Mills also discovered that in the hill-country district of Pendleton "every family manufactures cotton cloth for their own use."[91]

By mid-century, however, household manufacturing played a much smaller role in the clothing of Upcountry families. By 1840, the per capita value of household manufactures in the Upcountry had fallen to less than one-third of its 1810 level. In the lower Piedmont, per capita output of household goods fell from $5.84 in 1810 to $2.16 in 1840 and, finally, to $1.93 by 1850. In the yeoman-dominated upper Piedmont the decline was even more pronounced. Upper Piedmont households produced manufactures valued at $10 per capita in 1810, but per capita output in the hill country had fallen to $2.56 by 1840 and to $2.26 by 1850.[92] In Spartanburg district, per capita output of domestic manufactures declined from $15 in 1810 to less than $1.50 by 1850. Nor was the decline of household manufacturing simply the result of a switch to market goods by planters and middling slaveholders, since in 1850 the per capita output of domestic goods was only slightly higher among yeoman households than among households headed by planters and other substantial slaveholders. In 1850, per capita output of household manufactures by yeoman families was only $1.60, a figure only nominally higher than the district average for all families. Moreover, nearly one-fourth of all slaveless farm families in Spartanburg did no household manufacturing at all in 1850.[93] By the late antebellum years, homespun was still an

[89]December, 1800, Michael Gaffney Journal, SHC; also printed in Ronald G. Killian and Bobby G. Moss, *The Journal of Michael Gaffney* (Greenville, S.C.: A Press, 1981), p. 25.

[90]"The Diary of Edward Hooker, 1805–1808," *American Historical Association Annual Report, 1896* (Washington, D.C.: Government Printing Office, 1897), vol. 1, p. 862.

[91]Mills, *Statistics of South Carolina,* pp. 645–646, 677.

[92]See Table 2.13; Rolla Milton Tryon, *Household Manufactures in the United States, 1640–1860: A Study in Industrial History* (Chicago: University of Chicago Press, 1917), especially pp. 177, 329–330.

[93]Based on calculations from a sample of farms in Spartanburg and Laurens Districts. See Manuscript Census of South Carolina, 1850, Laurens and Spartanburg Districts, Schedules I, II, and IV, SCDAH.

Table 2.13 Household Manufactures in the South
Carolina Upcountry

	Per Capita Value of Output		
	1810	*1840*	*1850*
Lower Piedmont			
Abbeville	$4.18	$0.72	$2.22
Chester	8.12	2.96	1.24
Edgefield	8.32	3.80	2.41
Fairfield	2.97	0.82	0.76
Laurens	5.65	2.67	2.34
Newberry	5.53	1.55	1.75
Union	4.49	2.21	2.11
Upper Piedmont			
Anderson	—	$4.35	$4.06
Greenville	No report	1.71	1.42
Lancaster	$7.32	2.66	1.78
Pendleton	7.61	—	—
Pickens	—	3.53	4.06
Spartanburg	14.99	3.22	1.48
York	10.26	1.44	0.94
Totals			
Lower Piedmont	$5.84	$2.16	$1.93
Upper Piedmont	10.00	2.56	2.26
Upcountry	7.25	2.33	2.06

Note: In 1826, the district of Pendleton was divided into two new
districts, Anderson and Pickens.

Source: Rolla Milton Tryon, *Household Manufactures in the United
States, 1640–1860: A Study in Industrial History* (Chicago: University of Chicago Press, 1917), pp. 177, 329–330.

important component of yeoman garb in the Upcountry, but it was no longer the
sole source of clothing for most yeoman families.

By 1850, most yeoman farmers in the South Carolina Upcountry were at least
nominally involved in the market economy. The vast majority of yeomen produced some cotton for the market and depended on cotton proceeds for the
greater part of their cash income. Moreover, most yeomen bought some cloth or
clothing from local or fall-line merchants, and some even depended on the
market for meat and grain.[94] Thus the necessity of providing for subsistence
needs and the desire to market a surplus involved Upcountry yeomen in an active
local economy that both facilitated self-sufficiency and provided the specialized
services needed for participation in the larger market economy. Nor did the
subsistence and market aspects of these local economies stand in sharp dichotomy. Family subsistence strategies depended not only on household production
but also on active trade in the local economy. And when yeomen needed extra
labor, they usually turned to their neighbors for help, knowing full well that

[94]For examples, see John Kirby Mercantile Ledger, 1831, Kirby Family Papers, DU.

reciprocity was expected. By mid-century, household self-sufficiency in any literal sense was a thing of the past.

Yet even as they participated in a variety of market activities, Upcountry yeomen remained committed to an ideal of independence sustained by an economy of free, productive households. These independent households, buoyed by the control of productive property, were often aggressively involved in production for the market, but they rarely allowed the market economy to penetrate the household itself by forcing members of the household into the labor market. Any division of labor within the household was usually designed to enhance the household's self-sufficiency and independence rather than to introduce specialization that could lead to participation in the labor market. Also, yeomen involvement in a local economy where special services were provided and their cooperation with neighbors in community projects were efforts to sustain and enhance rather than encumber the independence of the individual household. The fear that gnawed at the mind of the yeoman farmers was not some vague fear of market activity as such, but fear of the dependence and marginalization that could be their fate if their productive property were lost through reckless market involvement. The yeoman farmer feared the fall from independent producer to dependent proletarian, a status he equated with enslavement.[95] To preserve their independence, and to build a future for their families, yeoman farmers searched for a leveraged market involvement which could provide insulation from the ravages of a market gone sour while permitting controlled pursuit of the main chance. Mary Moragne, the literary-minded daughter of prominent Abbeville planter Isaac Moragne, captured the essence of the common whites' love of independence succinctly and with sympathy. "They are," she confided to her diary, "so republican—so proud."[96]

For another group of Upcountry farm operators, tenant farmers, independence proved an elusive goal. Tenants controlled productive property, at least temporarily, but it was property rented from landowners, usually on a year-to-year basis. As renters, however, tenant farmers enjoyed more autonomy than farm laborers. Within contractual boundaries, tenants controlled the rented property for the duration of the tenancy, and enjoyed full property rights in the crops they grew during that period. Laborers, whether paid in cash or by a share of the crop, were wage-hands who had no property rights in the output.[97]

[95]The planter elite recognized the widespread fear of dependency among the yeomanry, see Hiram Hutchinson to John Springs, April 22, 1846, Springs Family Papers, SHC; see also Thornton, *Politics and Power in a Slave Society*, pp. 25, 54–58; Hahn, *Roots of Southern Populism*, pp. 86–116; Harris, *Plain Folk and Gentry in a Slave Society*, pp. 15–20, 125–131. For a perceptive survey of the recent literature on yeoman farmers which also emphasizes this point, see Harry L. Watson, "Conflict and Collaboration: Yeomen, Slaveholders, and Politics in the Antebellum South," *Social History* 10 (October, 1985):273–298.

[96]Entry for May 8, 1839, Mary Elizabeth Moragne Diary, SCL; see also Craven, ed., *The Neglected Threat*, p. 124.

[97]The study of tenancy in the antebellum South is still a relatively undeveloped field. The best introduction to the subject is Majorie S. Mendenhall, "The Rise of Southern Tenancy," *Yale Review*

Landlord-tenant agreements in the Upcountry varied widely on such matters as length of tenure, amount of rent, and method of payment. While life and other long-term tenancies were not unknown, most tenancy agreements were for only one year. Some tenants made cash, or fixed in-kind payments to their landlords, but others paid a share of the crop as rent. The ordinary rental rate for share-tenants varied between one-third and one-fourth of the crop. Occasionally, tenants were allowed to work whatever land they could clear and clean for no charge, and in some cases landowners conceded to local custom or opinion and permitted certain tenants to occupy a tract of land for a lifetime without paying rent. The law also provided the tenant with a few important rights. Legal precedents protected the renter from premature eviction. Once a tenant had planted his crops, he could not be removed from his plot until the end of the year, even if the length of the renter's tenure had not been specified in the original tenancy agreement. Moreover, landlords who wished to terminate an arrangement were required to give tenants at least three months' notice. This provision assured that tenants who were forced to move would have ample time to find a new landlord.[98] Thus, while the "independence" of tenant farmers was clearly more tenuous and circumscribed than that of freeholders, law, custom, and kinship provided renters with a measure of autonomy.

In 1850, between 12 and 20 percent of all Upcountry farm operators were tenants.[99] Although there is little statistical data available on the size of tenant

27 (September, 1937):110–129; for more recent work, see Hahn, *Roots of Southern Populism,* pp. 22–23, 64–69; Harris, *Plain Folk and Gentry in a Slave Society,* pp. 78–90; on the legal status of tenants in antebellum South Carolina, see Fowke v. Beck, 1 Spears 291 (1843); McLaurin v. McCall, 3 Strobhart 21 (1847).

[98]Legal agreement between John Watson and Rachel Townes, November 7, 1837, Townes Family Papers, SCL; Entry of February 21, 1838, John McLees Journal, SCL; Floyd v. Floyd, 4 Richardson 23 (1850); Fowke v. Beck, 1 Spears 291 (1843).

[99]Sample of Manuscript Census of South Carolina, 1850, Abbeville, Anderson, and York Districts, Schedules I, II, and IV, SCDAH. The census takers in the Upcountry in 1850 did not systematically identify tenant farmers, so it is not possible to identify exactly what percentage of farm operators were tenants. However, census takers did adopt certain conventions in recording information on the agricultural schedule which can be used to identify probable tenants. I have classified as tenants all propertyless farm operators for whom no cash value of farms and, in some cases, no improved acreage was recorded by the census takers, as well as all those farm operators who were explicitly identified as tenants or renters on either the population or the agricultural schedules. I have excluded from my calculations the handful of "renters" who were actually quite wealthy and were renting an entire plantation or large farm. In a few districts, the census takers apparently failed to record tenant farmers at all. This appears to have been the case in York district, where no tenants were found among the farm operators sampled in 1850. Ten years later, just over 14 percent of all farm operators in York were tenants. Thus it is likely that the actual percentage of tenant farmers in the Upcountry was closer to the upper bound of my estimate (20 percent) than to the lower bound (12 percent). On identifying tenants, see Frederick A. Bode and Donald E. Ginter, "A Critique of Landholding Variables in the 1860 Census and the Parker-Gallman Sample," *Journal of Interdisciplinary History* 15 (Autumn, 1984):277–295; John T. Houkek and Charles F. Heller, Jr., "Searching for Nineteenth Century Farm Tenants: An Evaluation of Methods," *Historical Methods* 19 (Spring, 1986):55–61.

Table 2.14   Tenant Farmers in the Upper and
Lower Piedmont, 1850

	Anderson District	Abbeville District
% of Total Farms	20.0	18.0
% Growing Cotton	50.0	87.5
% Self-Sufficient		
Grain	52.6	34.0
Meat	24.6	34.0
Mean Output per Farm		
Cotton (lbs.)	400.0	1480.0
Corn (bushels)	154.2	132.8
Swine (head)	10.0	11.2

Source: Manuscript Census of South Carolina, 1850, Abbeville and
Anderson Districts, Schedules I, II, and IV.

farms, the existing evidence suggests that tenant plots rarely exceeded forty
improved acres and were often a good deal smaller. In the upper Piedmont, just
over half of all tenant farmers were self-sufficient in grain, and the average
tenant farm produced less than half as much corn as the average yeoman-operated farm. In Anderson, half of all tenant farmers grew cotton, and while the
average cotton output for tenants was only one bale per farm, over half of all
tenants who grew cotton raised at least two bales. Tenants in the lower Piedmont
were more heavily involved with cotton but much less likely to achieve self-
sufficiency than upper Piedmont tenants. Over 87 percent of all tenants in Abbeville district grew cotton, and the average cotton output by tenant farmers was
over two and one-half bales. Over 90 percent of all Abbeville tenants who grew
cotton produced at least two bales. Only one-third of all lower Piedmont tenants
were self-sufficient in grain.

The production patterns of tenant farmers, and the rather high incidence of
cotton production among them, are easily explained. Since plots farmed by
Upcountry tenants were very small, self-sufficiency was difficult for tenants to
achieve even if they devoted all their resources to subsistence production. Thus
tenants, a disproportionate number of whom were young men just establishing
their own households, often gambled on cotton production with the hope of
moving up the agricultural ladder to the status of freeholder. This gambling
strategy was more likely to pay in the lower Piedmont because cotton yields per
acre tended to be higher there, and, as a result, tenants in the lower Piedmont
were more cotton-oriented.[100]

Even in the upper Piedmont, however, tenant farmers tended to grow cotton.
In the community around Tolleson's precinct in Spartanburg district, two-thirds
of all tenants raised cotton, and the average output for cotton-growing tenants

[100]See Table 2.14; Gavin Wright, *The Political Economy of the Cotton South*, pp. 158–184.

was nearly two and one-half bales per farm. In fact, tenants in the Tolleson community grew almost as much cotton per farm as the area's yeoman farmers. But Tolleson tenants raised only half as much corn per farm and owned only half as many swine per household as area yeomen. Tenant farmer William F. Lee, age twenty-eight, raised three bales of cotton and 125 bushels of corn in 1840. Lee probably rented land from his father, a fifty-year-old yeoman who owned 100 improved acres valued at $1200. The younger Lee kept only four swine, but the father owned twenty-six. Arthur Rakestraw, a thirty-four-year-old tenant, raised two bales of cotton and was self-sufficient in grain in 1849, growing 250 bushels of corn; another tenant, Matt Gossett, raised five bales of cotton that same year. Their general emphasis on cotton production rather than subsistence crops suggests that many Tolleson area tenant farmers saw cotton profits as the key to upward mobility. Moreover, one-third of all household heads in the Tolleson area were tenant farmers. This proportion was unusually high by Upcountry standards, but well over half of all landless farmers in the Tolleson area shared surnames with nearby landowners. Doubtless kinship ties, as well as cotton profits, helped mitigate the hardship and insecurity which most tenant farmers faced.[101]

On the whole, tenant farmers lived difficult lives, and some struggled for survival. The Fishing Creek Agricultural Society lamented that tenants in York and Chester districts were too often "poor people who can neither buy nor move away."[102] In addition to their relative poverty, tenants were also subject to the whims of capricious landlords. In March of 1848, John Floyd, a tenant farmer in Newberry district, was ordered off his rented property shortly after he had completed spring planting. When Floyd refused to leave, his landlord and uncle, Washington Floyd, plowed up all his crops and replanted the land in cotton, and then seized a few of John's livestock. Over a year later, John Floyd won a court decision granting him full damages and ordering Washington Floyd to rent the property to his former tenant for at least one more year, but the decision came too late to help John Floyd find food during the winter of 1848–1849.[103] In York district, an angry landlord plowed up the small cotton patch of a tenant, Ruth Givens, who had testified against him in court. Givens, an elderly, illiterate widow, waited for over a year before a South Carolina court awarded her $35 in damages.[104] Clearly neither kinship nor age could protect tenant farmers from angry landlords. The law was a valuable ally, but it was also a slow and clumsy one. Yet if Upcountry tenants were usually poorer and more vulnerable than freeholders, they nevertheless enjoyed a degree of autonomy denied wage laborers. Tenant farmers not only controlled their own labor time but also enjoyed the

[101]Manuscript Census of South Carolina, 1850, Spartanburg District, Schedules I, II, and IV, SCDAH; List of Voters, [c. 1845], James F. Sloan Papers, SCL. Calculations based on the reconstruction of the Tolleson community described above in footnote 66.

[102]"Report of the Fishing Creek Agricultural Society," in *Proceedings of the State Agricultural Convention*, pp. 5–8.

[103]Floyd v. Floyd, 4 Richardson 23 (1850).

[104]Givens v. Mullinox, 4 Richardson 590 (1851).

use of productive property. In a society where personal independence was revered, even the limited and precarious autonomy of the tenant farmer was better than no independence at all.

Upcountry planters bought the bulk of their supplies from mercantile firms in Charleston or along the fall line, but Upcountry merchants and storekeepers enjoyed the patronage of most of the region's yeomen and tenants, and played an important secondary role in furnishing plantation supplies. Prior to the construction of railroads in the Upcountry, interior merchants were seldom involved in the marketing of cotton, although a number of storekeepers, whether concentrated in courthouse towns or isolated at rural crossroads, enjoyed a profitable trade in general merchandise. Town merchants and crossroads storekeepers furnished essentially the same goods and services to their largely rural clientele, but they were businessmen with rather different outlooks and ambitions.[105]

Merchants operating at country crossroads often had little or no direct competition, since the nearest rival store was usually at least several miles away. These crossroads merchants also knew that they were unlikely to attract customers from outside their beat and concentrated instead on turning their stores into centers of social, as well as business, activity for their community. Crossroads stores frequently served as post offices, polling places, points of distribution for weekly newspapers, and gossip stands, with the storeowner having a hand in all the activities. William McFadden, a crossroads merchant widely recognized as "proverbial for honesty," ran a business which enjoyed the profitable "exclusive custom" of a large section of eastern York. McFadden procured his regular trade through a liberal extension of credit, although he suffered occasionally when his customers failed to pay their debts. At the other end of York district, John McGill of Clark's Fork ran a profitable country store on more conservative principles. McGill was a "plain, close" merchant who was cautious in extending credit. But McGill's frugality inspired a jealous brother to open a rival store on nearby Crowders Creek with plans to make credit a weapon in sibling rivalry.[106]

Other crossroads stores were operated by planters who hoped to make a little extra money while giving their sons some practical business experience. In 1845, planters T. C. Jeter and F. C. Jeter opened a country store near Fish Dam in Union district. They soon turned the business over to younger members of their family, who managed the store successfully for a number of years. The Bratton and Rainey general store at Brattonsville in southern York opened in the 1840s with the backing of the two families' extensive holdings in land and slaves. Bratton and Rainey did a healthy business throughout the decade selling agri-

[105]Lewis E. Atherton, *The Southern Country Store, 1800–1860* (Baton Rouge: Louisiana State University Press, 1979); Woodman, *King Cotton*, pp. 76–97; Bratton and Rainey Account and Ledger Books, SCL; John Kirby Mercantile Ledger, 1831, Kirby Family Papers, DU; Receipts of March 30, 1847, March 31, 1848, Elihu P. Smith Papers, SCL.

[106]R. G. Dun and Company, Credit Reporting Ledgers of the Mercantile Agency, South Carolina, XIV, 125, 131, 135, Baker.

cultural supplies and dry goods to the prosperous agricultural community near Fishing Creek, but both the Bratton and Rainey families continued to earn by far the largest percentage of their income from their cotton crops.[107]

If most crossroads merchants were small-time traders satisfied with a regular country business or planters dabbling in mercantile activity as a convenient sideline, a few country merchants rose from modest beginnings to become prominent Upcountry entrepreneurs. One such man was Gabriel Cannon of Spartanburg district. After serving for a few years as a superintendent of the Cowpens Furnace and Iron Foundry in the "old Iron District," Cannon opened a general store a few miles south of the North Carolina border at New Prospect in the early 1830s. Gradually developing a large clientele among local yeomen and tenants, he became one of the most powerful economic and political leaders in northern Spartanburg, a region dominated by small farms. In 1848, Cannon formed a partnership with a nearby grist-mill operator, Joseph Finger, and the two men established a textile mill at Fingerville. The Fingerville cotton mill was small, employing only thirteen hands and housing only 396 spindles in 1860, but it operated successfully until the outbreak of the Civil War. Cannon established a second general store at the mill and during the 1850s became a leading promoter of the Spartanburg and Union Railroad, of which he later became president. By 1860, Cannon was not only a wealthy and prominent businessman but also the leader of the most powerful faction in Spartanburg politics. In his later years, Cannon moved to Spartanburg courthouse where he became president of the town's first bank and served as a director of two railroads.[108]

The spread of short-staple cotton throughout the Upcountry and the corresponding intensification of the "long-distance" trade with Charleston and the fall-line towns stunted the growth of Upcountry towns during the first half of the nineteenth century. As late as 1848, most Upcountry towns were still somnolent courthouse villages which came to life once or twice a month on sales day or during court week. The number of mercantile firms in Upcountry towns remained virtually constant throughout the 1840s, with the older, established firms doing the largest trade.[109] In fact, there was so little growth in Upcountry towns prior to the arrival of the railroads that Benjamin Perry's description of Greenville courthouse in 1823 was still applicable in 1850:

> I remember the first day I reached Greenville. I saw two drunken black-guards throwing stones at each other on the Public Square, cursing and abusing

[107]R. G. Dun and Company, Credit Ledgers, South Carolina, XIV, 100, 125, Baker; Bratton and Rainey Account and Ledger Books, SCL.

[108]R. G. Dun and Company, Credit Ledgers, South Carolina, XIII, 10, 14, Baker; Gabriel Cannon to Elihu P. Smith, June 5, 1849, Elihu Penquite Smith Papers, SCL; J. B. O. Landrum, *A History of Spartanburg County* (Atlanta: Franklin Printing, 1900), pp. 437–439.

[109]Systematic study of the towns of Anderson, Laurensville, and Yorkville indicates that the number of firms operating in the towns remained virtually constant during the 1840s, until the anticipation of railroad development led to the creation of a number of new firms at the end of the decade. See R. G. Dun and Company, Credit Ledgers, South Carolina, II, XI, XIV, Baker; Lacy K. Ford, "Self-Sufficiency, Cotton, and Economic Development in the South Carolina Upcountry, 1800–1860," *Journal of Economic History* 45 (June, 1985):261–267.

each other with gross epithets for several hours. It was customary for the young men of the village and the old ones to meet in the piazzas of the Stores . . . and play cards all the morning or evening, drinking in the meantime toddy, which was very often placed in front of them on the table at which they were playing. I have seen thus situated Chancellor Thomson, Judge Earle, Col. Toney, Captain Cleveland, Warren R. Davis and others. There was very little business of any character to occupy the people and scarcely any of them thought of spending their time in reading.[110]

Unlike crossroads merchants, who operated in isolated areas where the nearest competitor was often miles away, town merchants were literally surrounded by rivals. General mercantile, hardware, and dry goods firms clustered around the courthouse or post office and struggled to attract an ever larger share of the area's rural trade. Advertisements in local weekly newspapers helped town firms attract customers, but a good reputation among friends, relatives, and political allies probably helped more. George Ratchford, a Yorkville merchant operating on capital of only $2000, developed a large clientele through his association with A. S. Wallace, a popular farmer-politician from Turkey Creek. Ratchford accommodated Wallace supporters with credit regardless of the risk involved and allowed his store to be used as an informal caucus site by Wallace and his followers. Ratchford also parlayed his open fondness for whiskey and women into a competitive advantage for his store. York farmers frequently drove to Ratchford's store from many miles away just to check up on one of York's most notorious rakes.[111]

Ratchford's method of building a clientele was unusual. Upcountry merchants were more likely to attract customers with caution, sobriety, and solid financial backing. In fact, the overwhelming majority of the most successful mercantile firms in Upcountry towns were either owned or backed by planters worth over $20,000 in land and slaves. Leading Unionville merchant John Young and successful Laurensville merchants John Garlington, Samuel Fleming, and S. R. Todd, all of whom were related by marriage, were wealthy planters as well as owners of profitable mercantile firms. The prominent Yorkville mercantile house of Richard Springs and R. A. Moore was backed by $20,000 of planter-entrepreneur John Springs's capital. Similarly, the highly successful Spartanburg firm of Joseph Foster and D. C. Judd received a long line of credit from New York wholesale firms because it was backed by over $100,000 worth of land and slaves.[112] Not all Upcountry mercantile firms were backed by planter capital, but most of those that were not were small firms carrying only a limited

---

[110]B. F. Perry, "Reminiscences of the County of Greenville," in the Greenville *Enterprise*, September 27, 1871; the passage is also quoted in Lillian Kibler, *Benjamin F. Perry: South Carolina Unionist* (Durham, N.C.: Duke University Press, 1946), p. 41.

[111]R. G. Dun and Company, Credit Ledgers, South Carolina, XIV, 126, 136, Baker.

[112]*Eminent Men of the Carolinas,* pp. 390–393; Katherine Wooten Springs, *The Squires of Springfield* (Charlotte, N.C.: William Lofton, 1965), pp. 82–85; R. G. Dun and Company, Credit Ledgers, South Carolina, XI, 98, 113, XIV, 78, 125, XII, 8, Baker.

stock of goods. Solid financial backing was essential for larger firms, which needed credit from wholesale houses in Charleston or the North in order to finance the purchase of large quantities of goods. Along with their heavy involvement in plantation agriculture, merchants in the Upcountry towns were also vocal and energetic champions of town development. Most of the clamor and an important share of the capital which supported the building of railroads and the establishment of banks in the Upcountry during the 1850s were raised by town merchants eager to see their respective villages grow and prosper.[113]

No less than planters and farmers, Upcountry merchants suffered from the uncertainly and confusion surrounding currency and credit in the region. Most merchants sold to farmers on credit, with the expectation that the debts would be paid with bank bills after the year's cotton crop was sold. Since there was no crop-lien law in antebellum South Carolina, merchants found the legal process of collecting neglected debts both costly and time-consuming. More important, strict usury laws limiting the interest or discount rate to 7 percent per annum restricted the use of credit and borrowed capital. Upcountry planters seeking credit from Lowcountry banks frequently found the banks unwilling to issue their own notes, but eager to provide a special note known as an "inland bill of exchange." These bills, which were simply drafts drawn on out-of-state banks, could be legally discounted at the "ordinary rate of exchange between merchants" even if that rate was higher than the 7 percent allowed by the usury law. Naturally, attempts to define the "ordinary rate of exchange" sparked considerable controversy in South Carolina banks, stores, and courtrooms throughout the antebellum period, but the rate usually fluctuated between 9 and 12.5 percent.[114]

The scarcity of currency and the high cost of credit underscored a fundamental weakness of the South Carolina cotton economy: it was largely dependent on outside sources for operating capital. The cotton trade was financed primarily through the Bank of England and the Bank of the United States, and secondarily through scores of lesser banks operating in the shadow of the two financial giants. With bills from the major banks, cotton buyers purchased the staple from planters and farmers, who then settled their debts with merchants, who then paid their wholesale suppliers. As long as cotton profits were high, the currency relatively stable, and credit readily available, the system worked well enough; but if demand for cotton slackened or the supply of currency and credit was interrupted, a vicious circle of failure followed. If banks could not buy, cotton

[113]Survey of R. G. Dun and Company, Credit Ledgers, South Carolina, II, X, XI, XIII, and XIV, Baker; *Proceedings of the Stockholders Meeting of the Greenville and Columbia Railroad Company, May 1 and 2, 1848* (Columbia, S.C., 1848), pp. 1–30; Woodman, *King Cotton,* pp. 87–95, 319–344.

[114]William Gregg, *Letter of William Gregg to Thornton Coleman* (Charleston: Walker Evans, and Co., 1858), pp. 3–15; *South Carolina Statutes at Large* (Columbia, S.C.: A. S. Johnston, 1839), vol. 6, p. 409; Quarles v. Brannon and Quarles, 5 Strobhart 151 (1850); Thompson v. Nesbit, 2 Richardson 73 (1845); Garlington v. Coleman, 2 Spears 238 (1843); Harp v. Chandler and Neel, 1 Strobhart 461 (1847); The Planters' Bank of Fairfield v. The Bivingsville Cotton Manufacturing Co., 11 Richardson 677 (1857).

growers could not sell. If cotton growers could not sell, they could not pay their debts to mercantile firms, who in turn could not pay their wholesale suppliers. Any bottleneck in the money supply could bring the Upcountry economy to its knees in a matter of months, even if there was plenty of cotton on hand to sell and plenty of textile operations willing, but unable, to buy.[115]

The panic and economic collapse of 1837, and the ensuing agricultural depression, were precipitated by just such a bottleneck. When a variety of complex economic and political pressures prompted the Bank of England to refuse to redeem some American paper bills and ultimately forced the Pennsylvania-chartered remnant of the Bank of the United States to suspend specie payment, smaller banks in all parts of the country followed suit; credit dried up, and confidence in paper currency was shattered. Every bank in South Carolina, including the state-controlled Bank of the State of South Carolina, suspended specie payment, refused to extend credit, and began calling on its debtors to meet their obligations. Since there was no money or credit to finance the cotton trade, prices dropped rapidly and soon the entire South Carolina economy was in shambles.[116]

Like other Jacksonian Americans, South Carolinians responded to the panic and its aftermath with an outpouring of hostility directed at banks. Some citizens demanded that banks be abolished outright; others demanded drastic reform of existing banking laws in order to prevent future panics.[117] United States Senator John C. Calhoun, the most popular and most powerful figure in South Carolina politics, led the political attack on entrenched economic power and privilege. Calhoun knew that reform of the credit system was a "delicate" matter, but the economic paralysis which gripped his native region in 1837 convinced the "Fort Hill" planter that the time had come for carefully planned but nonetheless radical reform of the existing banking and monetary systems.[118] Calhoun viewed government involvement in the banking industry as a threat "to the permanency of our free republican institutions," and argued that neither credit nor currency could serve the people fairly and equitably without a complete and final separation of government from the banks. In a speech to the Senate on October 3, 1837,

[115]Bray Hammond, *Banks and Politics in America: From the Revolution to the Civil War* (Princeton: Princeton University Press, 1957), pp. 451–458; Woodman, *King Cotton,* pp. 167–168.

[116]Hammond, *Banks and Politics,* pp. 429–549; Smith, *Economic Readjustment of an Old Cotton State,* pp. 202–209; Lesesne, *Bank of the State of South Carolina,* pp. 39–43. For a view which places less emphasis on the role of banks in precipitating this economic crisis, see Peter Temin, *The Jacksonian Economy* (New York: W. W. Norton, 1969).

[117]James Roger Sharp, *The Jacksonians versus the Banks: Politics in the States after the Panic of 1837* (New York: Columbia University Press, 1970), especially pp. 321–329; William G. Shade, *Banks or No Banks* (Detroit: Wayne State University Press, 1972); Lesesne, *Bank of the State of South Carolina,* pp. 52–70.

[118]John C. Calhoun, "Speech on the Bill Authorizing an Issue of Treasury Notes," September 18, 1837, in Wilson, ed., *The Papers of John C. Calhoun,* vol. 13, p. 548.

Calhoun explained the evil inherent in allowing a powerful combination of banks and government to control the money supply:

> The currency of a country is to the community what the blood is to the human system. It constitutes a small part, but it circulates through every portion, and is indispensable to all the functions of life . . . if the currency be increased or decreased, the other portion of the capital remaining the same, according to the well-known laws of currency, property would rise or fall with the increase or decrease. . . . With this law so well established, place the money power in the hands of a single individual or combination of individuals, and, by expanding or contracting the currency, they may raise or sink prices at pleasure; and by purchasing when at greatest depression, and selling at the greatest elevation, may command the whole property and industry of the community, and control its fiscal operations. The banking system concentrates and places this power in the hands of those who control it . . . Never was an engine invented better calculated to place the destiny of the many in the hands of the few, or less favorable to that equality and independence which lie at the bottom of all free institutions.[119]

But Calhoun's crusade to effect a permanent separation of government and banking and to limit the power of banks to create money was not born, like that of some hard-money Democrats, out of a distrust of credit and paper currency, or by a fear of the increase in commercial activity fostered by easy credit and soft money. Instead, Calhoun was motivated by a desire to provide independent producers with a safe and plentiful supply of currency that could not easily be manipulated by special or privileged interests. To achieve his goal, Calhoun proposed that the government retain sole control of the creation of paper currency, and that the value of paper money rest on that "which regulates the value of everything else," the law of supply and demand.[120]

Nor was Calhoun unusually wary of the widespread use of credit. "I am not the enemy, but the friend of credit," he explained. "I hold credit to possess, in many respects, a vast superiority over the metals themselves." The question, Calhoun contended, is "not between credit and no credit as some would have us believe, but in what form credit can best perform the functions of a safe and sound currency." The removal of the heavy hand of government from the credit system would wrest power away from a privileged few stock-jobbers and financiers and restore it to the people. "The credit of an individual is his property," Calhoun argued, "and belongs to him as much as his land and houses, to use it as

---

[119]John C. Calhoun, "Speech on His Amendment to Separate the Government and the Banks," October 3, 1837, in Wilson, ed., *The Papers of John C. Calhoun,* vol. 13, pp. 592–616, quotation taken from pp. 601–602.

[120]John C. Calhoun, Speech on the Bill Authorizing an Issue of Treasury Notes," September 18, 1837, in Wilson, ed., *The Papers of John C. Calhoun,* vol. 13, p. 565.

he pleases, with the single restriction, which is imposed on all our rights, that they not be used so as to injure others.''[121]

Calhoun's attack on the existing banking and monetary systems was quintessentially ''country-republican'' in purpose, and was certainly a controlled expression of the popular anger toward banks which boiled throughout South Carolina. Yet many of Calhoun's usual allies thought his ideas on the subject of credit and currency radical and far-fetched.[122] Even George McDuffie, a long-time ally and protégé of the Calhoun family, politely advised Calhoun against pressing his attack too far. McDuffie worried that any dramatic change in the banking system would seriously injure South Carolina farmers, who had long since grown deeply involved in the world of commercial agriculture. Writing from his ''Cherry Hill'' home in Abbeville in late October 1837, McDuffie outlined the dangers of excess in the war against banks:

> We must regulate and restrain the banks as far as we can, but I cannot believe either in the wisdom or practicality of any measure which looks to their destruction. . . . The banking system as it now exists has not been the creation of a day. In a slow progress of a half century, it has 'grown with our growth and strengthened with our strength,' gradually accommodating itself to the wants of society, and stimulating *industry* and *enterprise*. It has thus become inseparably connected with every interest in the community, and however you may suppose it to be diluted, it is the actual blood which invigorates our social system. Now weak and insufficient as this blood may be, I should think it extremely hazardous to open the veins of the body politic by way of invigorating the patient. I solemnly believe it would expire under the operation, or more probably, would use what strength it has left to resist it.

Neither political tirades against banks nor jeremiads lamenting the rise of indebtedness and extravagence, McDuffie warned, could roll back decades of market expansion in South Carolina.[123]

Yet whatever their differences on the specifics of bank reform, Calhoun and McDuffie both applauded South Carolina's furious response to the banking crisis as the sign of healthy republican vigilance among the citizenry. The popular agitation of the money question proved once again that South Carolinians were aware that independence required political maintenance, as well as a proper economic base, if it was to endure. To some out-of-state observers, South Carolina's tendency to adopt animated, even belligerent, political postures revealed a fetish for independence that had evolved into a dangerous preoccupation.

[121]John C. Calhoun, ''Speech on His Amendment to Separate the Government and the Banks,'' October 3, 1837, in Wilson, ed., *The Papers of John C. Calhoun,* vol. 13, pp. 606, 613–616.

[122]Charles M. Wiltse, *John C. Calhoun, Nullifier* (Indianapolis: Bobbs-Merrill, 1949), pp. 346–392; John Stanford Coussons, ''Thirty Years with Calhoun, Rhett, and the Charleston *Mercury*: A Chapter in South Carolina Politics'' (Ph.D. dissertation, Louisiana State University, 1971), pp. 77–122.

[123]George McDuffie to John C. Calhoun, October 29, 1837, in Wilson, ed., *The Papers of John C. Calhoun,* vol. 13, pp. 631–635.

Those familiar with the republican ethos dominant in South Carolina recognized that such political forwardness was the collective expression of a *mentalité* which flourished in planter dens and by yeoman firesides throughout the state. In South Carolina, every man became Hotspur when his own independence was threatened.[124]

[124]James Banner, "The Problem of South Carolina," in Stanley Elkins and Eric McKitrick, eds., *The Hofstadter Aegis: A Memorial* (New York: Alfred A. Knopf, 1974), pp. 60–93; Robert M. Weir, "The South Carolinian as Extremist," *South Atlantic Quarterly* 74 (December, 1975):86–103.

II

POLITICS AND POWER

3

"To Die like Freemen Rather than Live like Slaves": The Problem of South Carolina Reconsidered

Writing to his nephew, J. Calvin Hemphill, the editor of the Charleston *News and Courier,* in the early 1890s, James Hemphill, a prominent Upcountry lawyer-planter, passed along a sarcastic bit of folk wisdom deploring the violent political convulsions which seemed to grip South Carolina periodically during the nineteenth century. "An old-fashioned, sensible farmer here," the Chester native recounted, "says that South Carolina has a crazy fit every thirty years, and instances Nullification—1832, Secession—1861, and Tillmanism, 1891." Doubtless, James Hemphill, a man with a considerable reputation for wry humor and political conservatism, was himself the author of the statement which he attributed to an anonymous farmer-sage. He hoped his influential relative would publish the observation in the *News and Courier,* but wished to avoid, for political reasons, becoming the target of the public outrage the remark was sure to provoke. In 1892, James Hemphill's son, John J. Hemphill, was embroiled in a bitter campaign to defend his seat in Congress from the challenge of Thomas Jefferson Strait, the candidate backed by the increasingly powerful Farmers' Alliance and Ben Tillman. Doubtless the prospect that his son's ten-year Congressional career might be ended by a group of yeomen insurgents determined to wrest control of the Democratic party away from the "Conservative Regime" colored Hemphill's view of nullification and secession, but the Hemphill family, with the exception of James's renegade half-brother John, had long opposed political radicalism in South Carolina. "The idea of nullification," James Hemphill opined in retrospect, "is so absurd that to my mind it is utterly inconceivable." The Chester lawyer dismissed the idea "that we [South Carolinians] were the most down-trodden, wretched, oppressed people in the world" as "all imagination and exaggeration."[1]

[1]James Hemphill to J. Calvin Hemphill, July 7, 1892, Hemphill Family Papers, DU; Lacy K. Ford, "Rednecks and Merchants: Economic Development and Social Tensions in the South Carolina

Whatever James Hemphill's special personal grievances were, his belief that South Carolina experienced occasional fits of political insanity during the nineteenth century was shared by more than a few of his contemporaries. James Louis Petigru, the famous Unionist and political satirist, repeatedly suggested that South Carolinians had "gone mad" in their desire to break up the Union, and observed, just a few days prior to the election of Lincoln, that:

> My own countrymen here in South Carolina are distempered to a degree that
> makes them to a calm and impartial observer real objects of pity. They believe
> anything that flatters their delusions or their vanity; and at the same time are
> credulous to every whisper of suspicion about insurgents or incendiaries.[2]

The belief that the Palmetto state is subject to periodic convulsions of craziness has remained a popular axiom among the state's political observers and pundits well into the twentieth century. Yet perhaps more important than the prominence of Hemphill's judgment among that collection of bromides which embellishes the political culture of South Carolina is the fact that so many modern historians have viewed South Carolina's singular political course as the sign of a pervasive political paranoia and irrationality among her citizens.[3]

That political irrationality was especially acute in antebellum South Carolina, where politics was allegedly dominated by a powerful but anxious planter elite, has become virtually axiomatic among historians of the sectional conflict. According to the conventional wisdom, the South Carolina gentry, powerful and cohesive but concerned over abolitionist sentiment in the North and frightened about the possibility of slave insurrection at home, directed the state into a series of belligerent political stands which eventually isolated South Carolina from the mainstream of American politics and helped earn the state a well-deserved reputation as a breeding ground for reactionary radicalism. In a provocative essay addressing the uniqueness of South Carolina's hot-blooded politics, James M. Banner has argued:

> Historians agree that the political culture of South Carolina differed from
> that of any other state. No other southern state appeared quite so dedicated to the
> preservation of slavery and its distinctive way of life. None other responded so

Upcountry, 1865–1900," *Journal of American History* 71 (September, 1984):294–318; William J. Cooper, Jr., *The Conservative Regime: South Carolina, 1877–1890* (Baltimore: Johns Hopkins University Press, 1968), pp. 143–206.

[2]James Louis Petigru to Edward Everett, October 28, 1860, in James Petigru Carson, *Life, Letters, and Speeches of James Louis Petigru: The Union Man of South Carolina* (Washington, D.C.: W. H. Lowdermilk, 1920), pp. 359–360.

[3]William Watts Ball, *The State That Forgot: South Carolina's Surrender to Democracy* (Indianapolis: Bobbs-Merrill, 1932), pp. 138–289; David Duncan Wallace, *South Carolina: A Short History, 1520–1948* (Chapel Hill: University of North Carolina Press, 1951); William W. Freehling, *Prelude to Civil War: The Nullification Controversy in South Carolina, 1816–1836* (New York: Harper and Row, 1965), especially pp. 340–360; and Steven A. Channing, *Crisis of Fear: Secession in South Carolina* (New York: Simon and Schuster, 1970), especially pp. 17–57.

dramatically to threats from the North. South Carolina nullified alone and seceded first. . . . Nowhere else did the "fire-eaters" gain such an early ascendancy and maintain such a lasting hold.[4]

The problem, Banner insisted, was not in recognizing the obvious—that the political system of South Carolina was unique—but in explaining why. For Banner, the explanation for South Carolina's uniqueness lay in the peculiar economic and demographic characteristics of the state, as well as in the singular political system which emerged from those special social and economic circumstances. By the 1830s, almost every part of the state, except the alpine region in the northwestern corner of the Upcountry and the isolated pine barrens of the Pee Dee region, was involved in staple agriculture. With no vast hill country, mountain region, or wiregrass area to slow or limit the spread of commercial agriculture, and particularly the cultivation of short-staple cotton, over its terrain, South Carolina claimed a higher ratio of slaves to free people and a higher incidence of slaveholding than any other Southern state. Moreover, by 1850, the slave population in South Carolina was more evenly distributed territorially than anywhere else in the South, except perhaps Louisiana.[5]

Because of the pervasiveness of plantation agriculture and the density of the slave population in South Carolina, Banner argued, planters dominated the state's politics to an unusual degree. Unchallenged by a yeomanry with a strong demographic base, the planter "aristocracy" in South Carolina constructed and controlled a political structure designed to establish and preserve the primacy of the planter class and its interests. The better to serve their own ends, South Carolina planters concentrated power, including the election of many local office-holders, in the state legislature, where the plantation-dominated Lowcountry wielded more than its fair share of power. The legislature, in turn, thwarted all popular or democratic reform measures by refusing to relinquish any of its traditional powers and prerogatives. Particularly important, in Banner's view, was the legislature's refusal to permit direct popular election of either the governor or the state's presidential electors. By concentrating so much power in its own hands and by holding the number of popular elections in the state to a minimum, the planter-controlled state legislature prevented the Jacksonian two-party system, with all the partisan energy of Jacksonian democracy, which did so much to shape and animate political dialogue in other Southern states, from establishing itself in South Carolina. Thus, according to Banner, South Carolina developed a uniquely "aristocratic" political culture, committed to the militant defense of planter interests, and standing defiantly outside the mainstream of Jacksonian democracy.[6]

[4]James M. Banner, "The Problem of South Carolina," in Stanley Elkins and Eric McKitrick, eds., *The Hofstadter Aegis: A Memorial* (New York: Alfred A. Knopf, 1974), pp. 60–93. Quotation appears on p. 60.

[5]Ibid., p. 67.

[6]Ralph A. Wooster, *The People in Power: Courthouse and Statehouse in the Lower South, 1850–1860* (Knoxville: University of Tennessee Press, 1969), especially pp. 3–8, 97–100; Banner, "The Problem of South Carolina," pp. 75–83; Freehling, *Prelude to Civil War,* pp. 7–24.

This conventional wisdom about politics and power in antebellum South Carolina carries considerable weight. South Carolina was the only state to formally nullify a federal law, and the Nullifiers received only modest support from small bands of sympathizers in other states. South Carolina pushed farther and faster toward secession in 1850 than did any other state and seceded more quickly and with greater unanimity than did the rest of the South in 1860. South Carolina was also the only state that refused to allow the popular election of its governor and presidential electors until after the Civil War, and the only state in which a durable two-party system failed to dominate politics between the mid-1830s and the mid-1850s.[7]

At the same time, however, the conventional wisdom offers a view of the political culture of antebellum South Carolina that ignores important contradictory evidence and presents an incomplete, and perhaps misleading, picture of the dynamics of politics and power in the state during the three decades prior to the Civil War. South Carolina, after all, became the first state in the Union to adopt universal white manhood suffrage when it did so in 1810. Moreover, elections in South Carolina were contested in vigorous, democratic, and often bitter, grassroots campaigns. Certainly no student of South Carolina politics could argue that wire-pulling by political managers in the backrooms of Columbia hotels and guest houses played a larger role in the shaping of the state's political destiny than did the personal interaction between candidates and voters at the scores of barbecues and hundreds of stump meetings that accompanied virtually every political campaign in the state.[8]

If the style of Palmetto politics cannot be labeled "aristocratic" or "deferential" without a careful consideration of stump meetings and the district-wide canvass, neither can South Carolina politicians be characterized solely as spokesmen for planter interests without an examination of the remarkably coherent, and broadly shared, values which undergirded the political structure of South Carolina and did so much to influence its political actions. Indeed, a reexamination of politics and power in antebellum South Carolina suggests that, however well deserved her reputation as a Hotspur state may be, South Carolina's politics was not dominated by an anachronistic oligarchy which somehow forged a reactionary defense of planter interests without interference from democratic forces. Nor did a frightened, guilt-ridden, planter elite dragoon the cowed masses into an erratic, and ultimately suicidal, course of resistance inspired by overblown or imaginary grievances.

[7]Richard P. McCormick, *The Second American Party System: Party Formation in the Jacksonian Era* (Chapel Hill: University of North Carolina Press, 1966), especially pp. 7, 175–254; William J. Cooper, Jr., *Liberty and Slavery: Southern Politics to 1860* (New York: Alfred A. Knopf, 1983), pp. 170–191.

[8]Fletcher M. Green, *Constitutional Development in the South Atlantic States, 1776–1860: A Study in the Evolution of Democracy* (Chapel Hill: University of North Carolina Press, 1930), pp. 105–124, 248–251; Fletcher M. Green, "Cycles of American Democracy," *Mississippi Valley Historical Review* 48 (June, 1961):3–23.

*   *   *

Prior to the nullification crisis, there was little evidence to suggest that South Carolina was not part of the national political mainstream, or at the very least, typical of the other states along the South Atlantic seaboard. During the early national period South Carolina was the home of a vocal, active, and powerful wing of the Federalist party. In South Carolina, the Federalists were strongest in the rice and sea island cotton-growing parishes of the Lowcountry and in the city of Charleston. As George C. Rogers has noted, the membership lists of the Federalist party read like a directory of prominent Lowcountry families of the Revolutionary era. While committed to the protection of slavery and the defense of Southern political power, South Carolina's Federalists were very much like their counterparts in Virginia, New York, and even New England. Cautious by nature and conservative in interest, they feared the excesses of democracy more than the potential dangers of concentrated financial power. As a result, they supported national policies designed to increase involvement in transatlantic commerce and to keep that flourishing trade under the protection of the British mercantile umbrella. At the state level, South Carolina Federalists pointed with pride to the relatively sanguine and harmonious history of local government during the mid-eighteenth century and sought to preserve the Lowcountry gentry's political dominance in Columbia. Naturally, both the power and the policies of South Carolina Federalists inspired opposition, particularly from planters and farmers in the Upcountry. Not only did the inhabitants of the inland districts chafe under parish domination of state government but they also feared the centralizing tendencies of Federalist policy at the national level. Upcountry Republicans, under the leadership of ambitious landowners who were capitalizing on the first short-staple cotton bonanza of the early 1800s, hewed closely to plain Jeffersonian republicanism. Eager to defend the interests of independent agricultural producers, whether large or small, Upcountry Republicans campaigned against the perceived shift of power away from freeholders and toward the government and commercial or financial centers, while seeking to increase the representation of the Upcountry in the state legislature.[9]

[9]On the characteristics of the Federalist party throughout the young Republic, see David Hackett Fisher, *The Revolution of American Conservatism: The Federalist Party in the Era of Jeffersonian Democracy* (New York: Harper and Row, 1965); Shaw Livermore, *The Twilight of Federalism: The Disintegration of the Federalist Party, 1815–1830* (Princeton, N.J.: Princeton University Press, 1962), especially pp. 1–46; Linda K. Kerber, *Federalists in Dissent: Imagery and Ideology in Jeffersonian America* (Ithaca: Cornell University Press, 1970); and James Broussard, *The Southern Federalists, 1800–1816* (Baton Rouge: Louisiana State University Press, 1978). On South Carolina Federalists, see Ulrich B. Phillips, "The South Carolina Federalists, Part I and Part II," *American Historical Review* 14 (April and July, 1909):529–543, 731–790; George C. Rogers, Jr., *Evolution of a Federalist: William Loughton Smith of Charleston* (Columbia, S.C.: University of South Carolina Press, 1962); and Mark D. Kaplanoff, "Making the South Solid: Politics and the Structure of Society in South Carolina, 1790–1815" (Ph.D. dissertation, University of Cambridge, 1979), pp. 137–230. On South Carolina Republicans, see John Harold Wolfe, *Jeffersonian Democracy in South Carolina* (Chapel Hill: University of North Carolina Press, 1940), especially pp. 135–286.

In the struggle between Federalists and Republicans in South Carolina, time, energy, and numbers were clearly on the side of the Republicans. The population and wealth of the overwhelmingly Republican Upcountry was increasing rapidly. By the early 1800s, prominent Upcountry planters began to wield political power and influence that could match, if not surpass, that of the long-established Lowcountry gentry. At the same time, the Federalist party suffered not only from the political embarrassment of the unpopular Alien and Sedition Acts but also from the thinning of its leadership ranks by age, death, and defection.[10] Despite the fact that it was battling against increasingly long odds, Federalism in South Carolina did not yield without a struggle. In 1800, Charles Pinckney, a renegade from a leading Federalist family who cast his lot with the Republicans, described, in a letter to Thomas Jefferson, how South Carolina Federalists used their extensive patronage and economic power to intimidate Republican candidates and voters:

> I never before this knew the full extent of the federal interest connected with the British and the aid of the Banks and the federal Treasury and all their officers— they have endeavoured to shake Republicanism in South Carolina to its foundations—but we have resisted it firmly and I trust successfully—our country interest out of the reach of banks and custom houses and federal officers is I think as pure as ever. . . .[11]

By 1808, the once dominant Federalist party had clearly been overwhelmed by superior Republican numbers. The commercial and maritime complications arising from the Napoleonic Wars brought the long-smoldering Upcountry resentment of Great Britain to a white heat, and Jefferson's embargo of 1808, together with the end of the slave trade in the same year, permanently broke the power of the Federalist mercantile elite in the Lowcountry and forced the cosmopolitan British merchants out of Charleston. With its commercial lifeblood drained, the Federalist party in South Carolina disintegrated. A number of old Federalists joined the now dominant Republicans, seeking both to influence Republican policy and to find new political careers under the popular Jeffersonian banner. Others, perhaps the majority, simply abandoned public life altogether and retired to the enjoyment of their wealth and leisure; still others retrenched themselves in isolated Federalist enclaves throughout the tidewater, where they could continue to wield influence in state politics through the disproportionate power of the Lowcountry parishes in the state legislature.[12]

---

[10]Kaplanoff, "Making the South Solid," pp. 179–230; Ronald E. Bridwell, "The South's Wealthiest Planter: Wade Hampton I of South Carolina, 1754–1835" (Ph.D. dissertation, University of South Carolina, 1980); Anna King Gregorie, *Thomas Sumter* (Columbia, S.C.: R. L. Bryan and Company, 1931), pp. 224–282; Rogers, *Evolution of a Federalist*, pp. 342–400.

[11]Charles Pinckney to Thomas Jefferson, October 16, 1800, in the *American Historical Review* 4 (October, 1898):113–116.

[12]George C. Rogers, Jr., "South Carolina Federalists and the Origins of the Nullification Movement," *South Carolina Historical Magazine* 71 (January, 1970):17–32; William A. Schaper, "Sectionalism and Representation in South Carolina," in the *Annual Report of the American Historical*

The tenacity of the Federalist party left its mark on the subsequent political system in South Carolina in a variety of ways. First, the Federalists' use of patronage and of concentrated financial power to preserve and enhance their own political position reminded rising young Upcountry Republicans of the danger that a strong central government allied with powerful financial institutions would threaten personal independence in the new Republic, just as the alliance of the Court faction and the Bank of England had, they believed, corrupted government and undermined liberty in Walpolean Britain.[13] Second, Federalist power lingered long enough to help establish South Carolina College, a state-supported institution where a common education in the classics and a common network of friendships and rivalries helped draw prominent South Carolinians from all parts of the state toward common purposes. Henry William DeSaussure, a prominent Federalist and the leading architect of the proposal to establish a state college, made no effort to disguise his motives. "We of the lower country," he recounted, "well knew that the power of the State was thence forward to be in the upper country, and we desired our future rulers to be educated men."[14] The legislature passed a bill establishing the school in 1801 and the college opened its doors in 1805. Years later, James Louis Petigru, probably the last champion of Federalist values in antebellum South Carolina, referred to South Carolina College as "the last will and testament of the expiring Federalist party."[15]

If the purposes of the college's founders were to provide a common training ground for South Carolina politicians and to promote harmony among the leaders of different sections of the state, their aims were largely fulfilled. Between 1824 and 1865, twelve of the twenty-one men who served as governor of the state were graduates of South Carolina College, and James D. Blanding's *Catalogue,* compiled in 1854, listed 37 state senators and 157 state representatives, slightly over 40 percent of all antebellum state legislators, as alumni of South Carolina College.[16] Moreover, James Henley Thornwell, the brilliant Presbyterian theologian and one-time president of the college, believed that the school played an important role in bringing internal political harmony to the state. "The compro-

Association For the Year 1900 (Washington, D.C.: Government Printing Office, 1901), pp. 245–460; Kaplanoff, "Making the South Solid," pp. 231–277.

[13]On this point, see Wolfe, *Jeffersonian Democracy in South Carolina,* pp. 135–165; Kenneth S. Greenberg, "The Second American Revolution: South Carolina Politics, Society, and Secession, 1776–1860" (Ph.D. dissertation, University of Wisconsin, 1976); Lance Banning, *The Jeffersonian Persuasion: Evolution of a Party Ideology* (Ithaca, N.Y.: Cornell University Press, 1978), especially pp. 179–207; Peter G. Dickson, *The Financial Revolution in England, 1688–1756* (London: St. Martin's Press, 1967); Quentin Skinner, "The Principles and Practice of Opposition: The Case of Bolingbroke versus Walpole," in Neil McKendrick, ed., *Historical Perspectives: Studies in English Thought and Society* (London: Europa Publications, 1974), pp. 93–128.

[14]Quoted in John Belton O'Neall, *Biographical Sketches of the Bench and Bar of South Carolina* (Charleston, S.C.: S. G. Courtney, 1859), vol. 1, p. 245; see also Daniel Walker Hollis, *South Carolina College* (Columbia, S.C.: University of South Carolina Press, 1951), pp. 3–21.

[15]Hollis, *South Carolina College,* pp. 22–35; Carson, *James Louis Petigru,* p. 304.

[16]Hollis, *South Carolina College,* pp. 255–270.

mises of our present Constitution did something, but the South Carolina College has been the great healer," Thornwell argued in 1855. "It is in this fusion [of friendships among students at South Carolina College] which has made our Commonwealth united in the political agitation of the times."[17]

Finally, the Federalist party left its signature on subsequent political developments in South Carolina by surviving long enough to influence the Compromise of 1808, the last of the antebellum constitutional compromises. The Compromise of 1808 ended, at least temporarily, forty years of bickering between the parishes and the backcountry over the issue of representation. Political leaders of the backcountry, led by prominent planters such as Wade Hampton I and Thomas Sumter, agitated for reapportionment of the state legislature during the early 1800s. In 1807, a bill to reapportion the legislature exclusively on the basis of white population was defeated by a narrow margin, with the parishes voting as a bloc against the measure. With the threat of civil stife looming large, leaders of both sections hammered out a compromise designed to placate the restive Upcountry, and in 1808 that compromise passed as an amendment to the constitution of 1790.[18]

The Compromise of 1808 provided that each election district, including each parish, would have one state senator. This guaranteed that the city of Charleston, which included St. Philip's and St. Michael's parishes, would have two senators. Thus the state's legal "lower division" would have 22 senators, while the state's legal "upper division" would have 23 senators. The state house of representatives was to be apportioned according to a formula which weighed white population and taxable property equally.[19] In 1810, the House had 54 members from the lower division and 70 from the upper division. By the time of the nullification crisis, the upper division's dominance of the house of representatives had increased, as it had 77 representatives compared with 47 for the lower division, while the sectional division of power in the state senate remained essentially the same as in 1810. On the whole, the Compromise of 1808 established a *de facto* balance of power between the Upcountry and the Lowcountry. The Lowcountry, with the help of senators from black-majority districts along the fall line, controlled the senate, while the Upcountry enjoyed a comfortable majority in the house of representatives.[20]

---

[17]Untitled address given by James H. Thornwell, December, 1855, James Henley Thornwell Papers, SCL; see also Daniel W. Hollis, "James H. Thornwell and the South Carolina College," *Proceedings of the South Carolina Historical Association* (1953), pp. 17–36.

[18]Schaper, "Sectionalism and Representation in South Carolina," pp. 419–437; Wolfe, *Jeffersonian Democracy in South Carolina*, pp. 218–220; Wallace, *South Carolina: A Short History*, pp. 356–360.

[19]Thomas Cooper, *Statutes at Large of South Carolina* (Columbia, S.C.: A. S. Johnston, 1836), vol. 1, pp. 193–195.

[20]At the constitutional convention of 1790, a compromise was arranged to form a "dual government" in South Carolina. The state was divided into two separate legal divisions, each having its own treasurer. The Lower Division was comprised of the judicial districts of Georgetown, Charleston, and Beaufort and was headquartered in Charleston. The Upper Division was comprised of the Cheraw, Camden, Orangeburg, Ninety-Six, Pinckney, and Washington judicial districts, and its headquarters

Despite the concession made to the Upcountry, the Lowcountry wielded disproportionate influence in the legislature. By basing representation on wealth as well as on white population, the compromise guaranteed the Lowcountry, with its dense slave population, a strong voice in the house of representatives. For example, in 1830 there was one representative for every 144 voters in the tidewater parishes, while each representative from the districts represented almost 380 voters. Georgetown, with its large rice plantations, had 306 voters and three representatives, but Greenville, a hill-country district dominated by small farmers, had 1,630 voters and was still allotted only three seats in the House. Moreover, the Compromise of 1808 not only allowed the Lowcountry, with its small white population, to retain a disproportionate share of power in the state legislature, but it also allowed the black-majority areas of the state to preserve their political power. In 1810, 26 senators and 62 representatives were from black-majority areas, while 19 senators and 62 representatives hailed from election districts with white majorities. By 1830, the expansion of the black-belt gave these areas an advantage over the white-majority districts of 33 to 12 in the Senate and 81 to 43 in the House.[21]

Nevertheless, the Compromise of 1808 gave the Upcountry increased power in the legislature and allowed for that power to increase further as its white population grew and its wealth increased. Prior to 1808, there was no formula for apportioning representation in South Carolina and no provision mandating reapportionment at regular intervals. Both matters were left entirely to the discretion or whim of the legislature itself. The compromise not only created a formula upon which representation was to be based, but also called for reapportionment once every ten years. Thus, as the population and wealth of the Upcountry increased in proportion to that of the Lowcountry, as leaders of both sections believed that it would, the power of the Upcountry in state government would also increase. For the short run, at least, the people of each section seemed pleased with the new arrangement. The Lowcountry had succeeded in tying representation to property and thus secured the base of its political power. The Upcountry had finally succeeded in gaining an equal voice in state affairs, even if an equal voice was not as much as it deserved, and in establishing a constitutional mechanism which would, in all likelihood, serve automatically to increase the power of the region over the next several decades.[22]

---

were located in Columbia. Thus the Upper Division contained not only the thirteen election districts lying north and west of the fall line which I have defined as the "Upcountry" in this study but also the so-called "middle districts" of Barnwell, Claremont (Sumter), Clarendon, Kershaw, Lexington, Orangeburg, Richland, and Saint Mathews and the Pee Dee districts of Chesterfield, Darlington, and Marlboro. See Schaper, "Sectionalism and Representation in South Carolina," pp. 354–383.

[21]Figures calculated from Chauncey S. Boucher, "Sectionalism, Representation, and the Electoral Question in Antebellum South Carolina," *Washington University Studies* 4 (October, 1916):3–62; and Schaper, "Sectionalism and Representation in South Carolina," p. 437.

[22]John C. Calhoun to Alton H. Pemberton, November 19, 1838, and John Calhoun to Armistead Burt, December 24, 1838, in Clyde N. Wilson, ed., *The Papers of John C. Calhoun* (Columbia, S.C.: University of South Carolina Press, 1981), vol. 14, pp. 472–475, 498–500.

Some forty years later, in his "Discourse on the Constitution of the United States," John C. Calhoun pointed to the balance of power between Upcountry and Lowcountry in the South Carolina legislature as an example of how government by "concurrent majority" could work to promote peace and harmony. Since each section could exercise virtual veto power over any proposal before the legislature, the vital interests of each were protected and tensions between them reduced. Few, if any, of the architects of the Compromise of 1808 envisioned that their work would eventually be touted as a model for resolving conflicts in a large and diverse republic. They did, however, explicitly endorse a balance of power between Upcountry and Lowcountry not only as an effective way of reducing friction between the two regions but also as a means of checking power in a comparatively small state. Because South Carolina was so small, the danger that a minority might be unable to find enough allies to prevent a dominant faction from developing into a perpetual, and potentially oppressive, majority was magnified. The Compromise of 1808, perhaps the most important legacy of Federalism in South Carolina, guaranteed the vital interests of the Lowcountry at least a modicum of protection against any future aggression by the Upcountry majority.[23]

Immediately after reapportionment was approved, Upcountry legislative leaders pushed for the elimination of all property requirements for voting. In 1809, Abbeville representative John C. Calhoun chaired a special legislative committee which drafted a constitutional amendment providing for white manhood suffrage in South Carolina. The amendment passed the legislature by the necessary two-thirds majority in that same year and was officially ratified when it passed a new General Assembly by a two-thirds majority in December 1810. By the time this amendment actually became part of the state constitution, its principal architect, Calhoun, had parlayed his reputation as a champion of white manhood suffrage into election to the United States Congress at the age of twenty-seven, after serving only one term in the South Carolina legislature.[24]

Upcountry politics had developed a rough-and-tumble democratic style long before the suffrage was opened to all white men. As early as the 1790s, political campaigns in the region were marked by fierce competition and an intensely personal style. When Alexander Moore, a Revolutionary veteran, ran for a seat in the state legislature in 1790, the active support of his old military commander, Edward Lacey, proved indispensable. Lacey, a militia colonel who led Whig partisans from the York and Chester area at the pivotal Revolutionary battle of Kings Mountain, stationed himself near a polling place in Chester on election

[23]John C. Calhoun, "A Discourse on the Constitution and Government of the United States," in Richard K. Cralle, ed., *The Works of John C. Calhoun* (4 vols. New York: D. Appleton, 1853), vol. 1, pp. 400–406.

[24]Robert L. Meriwether, ed., *The Papers of John C. Calhoun* (Columbia, S.C.: University of South Carolina Press, 1959), vol. 1, p. 40; John C. Calhoun to Floride Colhoun, September 28, 1810, in Meriwether, ed., *The Papers of John C. Calhoun,* vol. 1, pp. 57–58; Margaret L. Coit, *John C. Calhoun: American Portrait* (Boston: Houghton Mifflin, 1950), pp. 52–66; Charles M. Wiltse, *John C. Calhoun: Nationalist, 1782–1828* (Indianapolis: Bobbs-Merrill, 1944), pp. 42–52.

day and spoke with approaching voters on Moore's behalf. Known as "a man of pleasant address and personal popularity," Lacey used his considerable electioneering skills to persuade many citizens to cast their vote for his friend Moore. But when his power of persuasion failed, Lacey often threatened to physically "whip any man that didn't vote for Alec Moore." Since Lacey's "bravery and vigor" were well known, few voters cared to defy him. With Lacey's help, Moore carried the precinct easily and won a place in the legislature.[25]

While popular local Revolutionary heroes were not always involved, lively political theatrics were an integral part of almost all election campaigns in the Upcountry during the early nineteenth century. The typical canvass was a highly competitive contest that saw each candidate court voters assiduously during face-to-face meetings. In 1806, the three-way battle for Congress in South Carolina's Eighth District, comprised of Pendleton and Greenville districts, developed into precisely such a contest. All three candidates, Elias Earle, Lemuel Alston, and Dr. William Hunter, were members of the local gentry even though the Eighth had the smallest slave population (12.6 percent) of any Congressional district in South Carolina. Earle, the forty-four-year-old incumbent, lived in Greenville district but also owned large tracts of land in Pendleton. A planter and iron-master, Earle owned over thirty slaves. But if Earle was rich by Upcountry standards, Alston was even richer. A native of North Carolina, Alston owned over 11,000 acres and nearly fifty slaves in Greenville district. His elegant plantation home on the Reedy River, "Prospect Hill," was considered one of the finest in the Upcountry. The third candidate, Dr. William Hunter, was the son of a well-known Pendleton district farmer, but he was also the son-in-law of Robert Anderson, a Revolutionary hero and a prominent Upcountry politican who served as a presidential elector for Thomas Jefferson in 1800. Hunter owned only eighteen slaves, but Anderson owned more than thirty slaves and over 6000 acres in Pendleton district.[26]

Each candidate took his cause to the voters during court sessions and on sales days, at militia musters and special barbecues, and even on church grounds. When Edward Hooker, the young New England lawyer, toured the area in September 1806, he was both surprised by the intensity of the campaign and dismayed by its tone. The people, Hooker complained, reflected "simplicity itself out-simplified," and the candidates played all too readily to the peoples' fancy. Any hint of Federalist leanings or aristocratic preferences meant certain defeat for a candidate. Firm support for slavery was also required. Rumors circulated intimating that Alston was "too rich" to represent the district prop-

[25]Maurice Moore, *Reminiscences of York* (Greenville, S.C.: A Press, 1981), pp. 24–28.

[26]"The Diary of Edward Hooker, 1805–1808," *American Historical Association Annual Report, 1896* (Washington, D.C., 1897), vol. I, pp. 893–903; N. Louise Bailey, Mary L. Morgan, and Carolyn R. Taylor, ed., *Biographical Directory of the South Carolina Senate, 1776–1985* (3 vols. Columbia, S.C.: University of South Carolina Press, 1986), pp. 59–60, 447–449; Richard W. Simpson, *History of Old Pendleton District* (Anderson, S.C.: Oulla Printing & Binding, 1913), pp. 180–184; Stanley B. Parsons, William W. Beach, Dan Hermann, *United States Congressional Districts, 1788–1841* (Westport, Conn.: Greenwood Press, 1978), pp. 123–124.

erly, that Earle did not respect religion enough to satisfy Christian voters, and that Hunter must be kept at home because of his talent as a physician. All three candidates met the people with relaxed conviviality. On September 21, Alston, who was accused of placing a Bible just inside the front door of his elegant home in an effort to impress evangelical guests with his piety, attended church services in Pendleton. Hooker, who was also at the service, believed that Alston had come "to worship the people" rather than God. Once the service was over, Alston, a "perfect master of the [political] art," met the congregation as they left the church. He greeted every man in the crowd, "taking care to call by name as many as possible," and putting himself "on terms of old acquaintance" with each one. Alston's whole demeanor, Hooker observed, "was marked with such easy civility as to gain the good will of all." Elias Earle also took his campaign onto church grounds; but rather than attending the worship service, he invited all interested men to rest and drink with him under the nearest shade trees until the services were completed.[27]

The frenzy of the campaign reached its peak on a public day in Greenville just two weeks before the election. Hundreds of people filled the streets of the tiny Upcountry town as Alston, Earle, and Hunter electioneered "with all their might," talking and even debating with prospective voters, many of whom believed, in Hooker's words, that "the national welfare was at stake and would be determined by the issue of this backwoods election." Hunter apparently refrained from "treating" voters, but Alston invited men into a bar where liquor was supplied generously on his account. But, as Hooker noted with sarcasm, it was Earle "*who loved the people more than any of them*" because he put his "grog bench in the middle of the street and presided over the whiskey jugs himself."[28]

For his trouble, the incumbent Earle not only lost his seat to the challenger Alston but actually finished third. Alston won the election by garnering nearly 40 percent of the vote, Hunter finished second with just over 30 percent, and Earle finished last with just under 30 percent. Nearly 53 percent of all white males in the district voted, and since suffrage was restricted at the time by property requirements, it is probable that roughly 80 percent of all eligible voters participated in the election. In a district where voters were Republicans virtually to a man, the election appears to have been decided largely by personal popularity and character rather than by national issues or party affiliation, but the campaign nevertheless revealed the feverishly democratic nature of the Upcountry's political culture.[29]

Except in rare instances, would-be candidates refrained from openly declaring for office during the early portion of an election year, preferring to wait, with a proper and studied disinterestedness, for the expected "draft" to emerge from supporters. This "bringing out" of a candidate usually involved having a hand-

[27]"The Diary of Edward Hooker," pp. 896–898.
[28]Ibid., pp. 900–901.
[29]Charleston *Courier,* December 8, 1806.

ful of local squires endorse one of their friends through the local newspaper or some other appropriate public forum and subsequently circulate their candidate's name, reputation, and views throughout the area. Once this was done, the candidate could begin active campaigning, which he usually did only after pleading reluctance to undertake such an effort. The candidate then justified his exertions by pointing to the draft or "bringing out" process as evidence of popular demand for his candidacy. To ignore such public sentiment, the candidate declared, was to neglect one's civic duty. After entering the field, candidates toured their districts meeting voters. A few candidates refused to ask citizens openly for their votes, fearing that they might be "condemned for violating the public conscience," but all candidates appeared "at all places of public assembly in order to make the acquaintance of voters," and most of them did not hesitate to solicit votes.[30] Candidates tried to assume familiarity with the voters and employ the common touch. Even John C. Calhoun, known more for his powerful political logic than for his campaign style, was praised by his rivals as a man who "remembers people [and] has great tact."[31] Any action or utterance which even faintly suggested elitism or hauteur usually meant political death. If there were excesses in these campaigns, they were excesses inspired by the fiercely democratic nature of the process—a touch of vulgarity, a certain pandering to popular appetites at the expense of decorum and propriety. Some Upcountry politicians lamented these excesses in private, but in public few dared to let their rivals appear more vigorous in the courting of popular favor.[32]

Frequently, when a candidate found little enthusiasm for his candidacy during the campaign, he would withdraw from the race before the election in order to avoid the stigma of defeat. Such withdrawals ratified the sentiments of sales day, militia musters, and public barbecues without waiting for the final judgment of the ballot box. During John C. Calhoun's first campaign for Congress in 1810, the incumbent, Joseph Calhoun, John C. Calhoun's older cousin, pulled out of the race well before election week. As the younger Calhoun's political skill and popularity became apparent on the stump, the elder Calhoun withdrew and left the field to his cousin and John A. Elmore, a planter and state legislator from Laurens district. In the October election, Calhoun won an overwhelming victory.[33] Two years later, in the first election held after the electorate was expanded to include all white men, a talented young Abbeville attorney, Benjamin Cudworth Yancey, challenged Calhoun for his seat. During weeks of campaigning at militia musters and public barbecues, an increasingly frustrated Yancey learned that the one-term Congressman was a formidable and popular foe. Seeing no

[30]For example, see John B. Carwile, *Reminiscences of Newberry County* (Charleston, S.C.: Walker, Evans, Cogswell, 1890), pp. 38–40.

[31]Introduction [c. 1832] to Benjamin F. Perry Diary, vol. I, SHC.

[32]For examples, see James D. Cooke to Stephen D. Miller, January 10, 1830, Stephen D. Miller Papers, DU; J. M. H. Adams to William Moultrie Reid, September 4, 1832, William Moultrie Reid Papers, DU; John Springs to Andrew Baxter Springs, January 3, 1843, Springs Family Papers, SHC; Greenville *Republican,* October 7, 1826.

[33]Coit, *John C. Calhoun,* pp. 62–63; Wiltse, *Calhoun: Nationalist,* p. 51.

chance of victory, Yancey withdrew from the race, leaving Calhoun unopposed.[34] The practice of using the campaigns themselves as informal referenda continued throughout the antebellum era. In 1836, F. W. Davie, a prominent planter and experienced politician from Chester district, wanted to run for Congress against William Clowney, a staunch Nullifier from Union district. Davie tested public sentiment in the spring, but quickly discovered that Clowney enjoyed such popularity that "nothing could be done with him." Davie grudgingly admitted, "I would not carry him [Clowney] light as he may be," and dropped out of the race.[35]

The Upcountry's intensively competitive politics centered around an informal, but direct and intimate, style of democracy. It was an open process through which free men bestowed political preferment and responsibility on the most capable or most popular within their own ranks. Moreover, the political culture of the Upcountry was characterized not only by a boisterous democratic style but also by high levels of voter participation. In elections held between 1800 and 1810, when men were still required to own a fifty-acre freehold or its equivalent in order to vote, voter turnout fluctuated between 44 and 50 percent of all adult white males. Based on the best available estimates, these participation rates suggest that roughly 75 percent of eligible voters exercised that right in the typical election of the era. After the constitutional amendment of 1810 opened the suffrage to all white men, large numbers of new voters entered the electoral process. In the last election held before the property requirement was eliminated, 47 percent of all adult white males voted. In the first elections held after the adoption of white manhood suffrage, 63 percent of all white men in the Upcountry voted. Six years later, in the election of 1818, nearly 78 percent of all white men voted, and voter participation rates in the Upcountry averaged better than 70 percent throughout the 1820s.[36]

The highly competitive nature of Upcountry politics not only generated large voter turnouts but also helped produce high rates of turnover among officeholders. During the first twenty-five years after the adoption of white manhood suffrage, the proportion of incumbents returned to the state legislature in any given election year never exceeded 50 percent. Indeed, the highest persistence rate among legislators was 48 percent in 1814, a year when many possible candidates and many voters were involved in military service and when those who voted were doubtless inclined toward legislative stability because of wartime dangers. Between 1810 and 1836, the median persistence rate was only 40 percent, and in 1818, a year of an unusually large voter turnout, only 20 percent of all incumbents were returned to the General Assembly. Of course not

---

[34]Ralph Brown Draughton, Jr., "The Political Transformation of William Lowndes Yancey, 1814–1848" (M.A. thesis, University of North Carolina at Chapel Hill, 1963).

[35]F. W. Davie to Armistead Burt, May 7, 1836, Armistead Burt Papers, DU.

[36]Kaplanoff, "Making the South Solid," pp. 113–117; calculations based on figures provided by Philip F. Wild, "South Carolina Politics, 1816–1833" (Ph.D. dissertation, University of Pennsylvania, 1949), pp. 101–301.

all incumbents who failed to return to the legislature were defeated at the polls. Many legislators surrendered their seats voluntarily. Some simply tired of politics or the time, trouble, and expense of spending four weeks a year in Columbia. Others did not stand for reelection due to the press of family problems and business matters back home. Some moved out of South Carolina. At least a few ran for other political offices or were elected to a judgeship. Still, a substantial number of incumbents were defeated at the ballot box or withdrew their names from consideration because they faced defeat. Upcountry politicians who failed to stay in touch with the voters did not usually remain in office very long.[37]

After 1810, Upcountry politics was a vigorous exercise in white man's democracy. Candidates wooed voters, praising republican values and denouncing aristocracy. Voters responded with high levels of participation. Incumbents held few advantages, and turnover rates among elected officials were extremely high. While most, though not all candidates were members of the gentry, political competition was so keen that no popular cause failed to find a champion. It was a raw-bonded democracy, lacking in organizational sophistication, but nonetheless effective. In a region where disparities in wealth were substantial, power at the polls made the rhetoric of republican equality ring true in the ears of common whites. Political democracy among white men gave enduring strength to what one visitor to South Carolina called "the grand fabric of republicanism."[38]

By 1815, the Jeffersonian Republicans in South Carolina had vanquished their opposition, but, like their counterparts throughout the nation, they soon found that victory created a consensus that was too large and unwieldy to be sustained. Without a common enemy to despise, intense internal bickering quickly divided the large and hegemonic Jeffersonian coalition into several factions, all of which paid rhetorical homage to the democratic-republican ethos of Jeffersonianism despite their differences over exactly what formula would yield the purist Jeffersonian dispensation. During the 1820s, the principal political conflict at the national level was the internecine contest between two groups of the Republicans: the "New" or "National" Republicans, who looked to Madison for their political ideas and who were led in the political arena by President Monroe and members of his Administration; and the hard-core, strict constructionist Old

[37]Turn-over rates calculated from data avilable in Bailey et al., ed., *Biographical Directory of the South Carolina Senate*, vol. 3, pp. 1803–1887; and Walter B. Edgar, ed., *Biographical Directory of the South Carolina House of Representatives* (Columbia, S.C.: University of South Carolina Press, 1974), vol. 1, pp. 254–385. Representatives were elected for two-year terms and senators for four-year terms. Thus every house seat but only half of all senate seats were contested in any given election. In calculating persistence rates, I included all house seats but only the one-half of all senate seats which were decided in each election. Property requirements for office-holding established by the South Carolina Constitution of 1790 remained in effect until after the Civil War. House members were required to own property worth 150 pounds sterling, while senators were required to own property valued at 300 pounds sterling.

[38]Raymond A. Mohl, "'The Grand Fabric of Republicanism': A Scotsman Describes South Carolina," *South Carolina Historical Magazine* 71 (July, 1970):170–188.

Republicans, who embraced the pastoral republicanism of John Taylor of Caroline and whose political spokesmen were men such as Nathaniel Macon, John Randolph of Roanoke, and, to a lesser extent, William Crawford of Georgia. The Old Republicans were particularly vehement in their charge that the Nationals were introducing too much latitude into the original Republican creed with their advocacy of increased commerce, tolerance of loose constructions of the Constitution, and acquiescence in the Missouri Compromise. Fearing that the mainstream of the party, led by Monroe's Secretary of War, John C. Calhoun, was drifting toward permanent apostasy, the Old Republicans were determined to regain control of the party and to return the nation to the pure republicanism which had triumphed in 1800.[39]

In South Carolina, factional strife in the 1820s mirrored the larger national conflict. A strict-constructionist faction, known simply as the Radicals, opposed a national Republican faction which supported qualified nationalism and identified closely with the Monroe Administration. The Radicals, who assumed the ideological mantle of the Old Republicans after the War of 1812, were led by William Smith of York, a colorful and vituperative politician who saw himself as the leader of a crusade to preserve states-rights republicanism. Energetic and combative by nature, Smith was elected to the United States Senate in 1816 and proved a worthy foe for the national Republican faction led by Calhoun, William Lowndes, and Langdon Cheves. The Radicals and the Nationals were the dominant political factions in South Carolina during the 1820s, and both factions drew the bulk of their following from the Upcountry. Calhoun's faction was particularly strong in the upper Savannah River valley, heartland of the early cotton boom, where his forces were led by men such as George McDuffie of Abbeville and Eldred Simkins of Edgefield. Moreover, the commercial orientation and qualified nationalism of the Calhounites allowed them to pick up grudging support from old Federalist areas of the Lowcountry and rather enthusiastic support from the Charleston legal and mercantile community. Smith's faction was strongest in that part of the Upcountry east of the Broad River, and in the Pee Dee region. Stephen Miller of Camden and David Rogerson Williams of Darlington supported Smith, who also found allies in parts of Pendleton, Greenville, Spartanburg, Union, and Laurens, where the Old Republican creed of minimal government and low taxes remained popular among hill-country yeomen.[40]

[39]For summaries of these developments at the national level, see Norman K. Risjord, *The Old Republicans: Southern Conservatives in the Age of Jefferson* (New York: Columbia University Press, 1965); Richard H. Brown, "The Missouri Crisis, Slavery, and the Politics of Jacksonianism," *South Atlantic Quarterly* 65 (Winter, 1966):55–72. For an excellent study of an awkward and factious Republican coalition in another state, see Michael Wallace, "Changing Concepts of Party in the United States: New York, 1815–1828," *American Historical Review* 74 (December, 1968):453–491. On South Carolina, see Wolfe, *Jeffersonian Democracy in South Carolina*, pp. 166–286; and Archie Vernon Huff, *Langdon Cheves of South Carolina* (Columbia, S.C.: University of South Carolina Press, 1977), pp. 47–127.

[40]Caroline P. Smith, "South Carolina Radical: The Political Career of William Smith to 1826" (M.A. thesis, Auburn University, 1971); Wild, "South Carolina Politics, 1816–1833," pp. 107–243; Freehling, *Prelude to Civil War*, pp. 89–122; Edwin L. Green, *George McDuffie* (Columbia,

Apart from the intense personal rivalries which inevitably arose between leaders of competing political factions in a small and intimate state, a tendency exacerbated in this situation by William Smith's penchant for feuding, the struggle between the Radicals and the Nationals was essentially one between fierce and persistent localism on the one hand and a nationalism justified as necessary to provide for the common defense on the other. The feuding factions learned different lessons from the War of 1812 and its aftermath. Calhoun and the nationals learned from the war itself that the young republic remained in peril because it had not yet become enough of a nation; its transportation system was poor, its military weak, and its finances in disarray.[41] The Nationals accepted a low tariff in 1816 in the interest of raising revenue to improve the national defense, and Calhoun and his followers also justified federally financed internal improvements on the grounds that they would make the republic easier to defend. In a speech on internal improvements delivered in February 1817, Calhoun acknowledged, "If we were only to consider the pecuniary advantages of a good system of roads and canals, it might indeed admit of some doubt whether they ought not to be left wholly to individual exertions." But the lack of a national system of roads and canals, Calhoun argued, bore much of the blame for "the tardiness and the consequential inefficiency of our military movements" during the War of 1812. Moreover, transportation problems stymied commercial intercourse during the war and thus made it difficult to raise the money needed to pay for the war effort. Without a regular commercial traffic, Calhoun contended, "we will be unable to raise the necessary supplies" and "the currency of the country must necessarily fall into the greatest disorder."[42] The Radicals learned less from the war than they did from what followed. To Smith and his followers, the cure for national weakness, which included taxes, tariffs, and an all-around invigoration of the federal government, seemed worse than the disease. Echoing traditional Old Republican arguments, Smith and other Radicals opposed the entire Nationalist program as a dangerous departure from the republican ideals of minimal federal power and strict economy in government. The tariff, for example, not only taxed agricultural producers for the benefit of manufacturers but also raised revenue which served as a source of federal largesse. A full treasury tempted both the government and the citizenry toward profligacy and corruption. If magistrates could not be trusted with more power than they were expected to use, Radicals maintained, the government could not be entrusted with money which it was not expected to spend.[43]

S.C.: The State Company, 1936), pp. 23–98; Harvey T. Cook, *The Life and Legacy of David Rogerson Williams* (New York, 1916).

[41]Wiltse, *Calhoun: Nationalist* pp. 103–154; W. R. Davie to William Gaston, February 14, 1815, and W. R. Davie to William Gaston, April 7, 1816, W. R. Davie Papers, SHC.

[42]"Speech on Internal Improvements," February 4, 1817, in Meriwether, ed., *The Papers of John C. Calhoun,* vol. I, pp. 398–407.

[43]William Smith, "To the Good People of South Carolina, No. IV," *National Intelligencer,* December 9, 1823; William Smith to Stephen D. Miller, January 13, 1827, Chesnut-Miller-Manning Papers, SCHS; Wild, "South Carolina Politics, 1816–1836," pp. 89–170.

As a senator from 1816 to 1822, William Smith spoke often and eloquently against the Nationalists within his own party and derived special enjoyment from his rival Calhoun's occasional disappointments. But in 1822 Calhoun's political lieutenants in South Carolina put the eager and talented Robert Y. Hayne in the field to contest Smith's bid for reelection. Hayne, a protégé of Langdon Cheves, was a talented young Charleston lawyer who had married the daughter of a wealthy rice planter and had risen to political prominence as a state legislator, speaker of the state house of representatives, and state attorney general. A National and supporter of Calhoun, yet a man with impeccable Lowcountry connections, Hayne was a formidable challenger to the incumbent. Hayne's operatives in the legislature publicized Smith's close ties to William H. Crawford, a rival of Calhoun and a presidential aspirant from Georgia, knowing that most South Carolinians had strong presidential hopes for the native-son Calhoun. Despite the efforts of leading Radicals in the legislature to downplay their candidate's loyalty to Crawford, Hayne's tactic worked and he defeated Smith by a vote of 91 to 74. Smith spent much of the next two years on the stump denouncing Calhoun and the South Carolina press as political tyrants, and, in 1824, Smith vowed to win a seat in the state legislature, to promote William H. Crawford for President, and to seek revenge against his political tormentor, Calhoun.[44]

The early jockeying for position in the presidential election of 1824 did not go well for Calhoun, partially due to opposition from the Radicals. A caucus of South Carolina political leaders announced that the nationalist William Lowndes, whose sympathies were virtually identical with those of Calhoun, was their preferred candidate for President. The caucus endorsement did little to help Lowndes, who had little or no chance of winning the presidency or even becoming a factor in the race, but it seriously damaged Calhoun's chances. The surprise endorsement was as much the handiwork of Radicals united in opposition to Calhoun as of the handful of loyal Lowndes enthusiasts. On the heels of his disappointment in South Carolina, Calhoun was overwhelmed in Pennsylvania by the increasingly vibrant campaign of the popular war hero Andrew Jackson. Lacking the whole-hearted backing of his home state and aware of the growing appeal of Jackson, Calhoun dropped out of the presidential race, and began a quest for the vice presidency.[45]

William Smith's joy over Calhoun's defeat was dampened by the recognition that the campaign of his old friend and ally, Crawford, was also floundering. Crawford's incapacitation following a stroke in late 1823 sent most of his already restive supporters in South Carolina scurrying into the Jackson camp. Several hundred citizens in Smith's home district of York publicly declared for Jackson in July of 1824, although Smith himself continued to stump for Crawford. In the

[44]Theodore D. Jervey, *Robert Y. Hayne and His Times* (New York: Macmillan, 1909), pp. 137–157; Smith, "South Carolina Radical: William Smith," pp. 175–184.

[45]Wiltse, *Calhoun: Nationalist*, pp. 272–284; Freehling, *Prelude to Civil War*, pp. 105–106; Jervey, *Robert Y. Hayne*, pp. 15–29.

fall election, Smith rode his personal popularity to a landslide victory in a race for one of York's seats in the state House, garnering over 73 percent of the vote. Moreover, Smith's friends Joseph Gist and John Wilson, Radicals and fellow Crawfordites, won election to Congress from the upper Piedmont. Buoyed by success in local elections, the Radicals were nevertheless outraged when the hated neo-Federalist John Quincy Adams, aided by Henry Clay, captured the presidency, and were annoyed that Calhoun had been elected Vice President.[46]

As soon as he arrived in Columbia to take his seat in the legislature, Smith began to press his advantage against the Calhounites. Since 1819, events had soured public opinion on the nationalism of Calhoun and his allies and, indeed, prompted reconsideration and retrenchment by many Calhounites. First, the debate over slavery in the territories and the Missouri Compromise alarmed the many South Carolinians who believed that Congress had no right to touch the question of slavery. Second, the Denmark Vesey insurrection conspiracy of 1822, though discovered easily with the aid of slaves who opposed the scheme and suppressed quickly and brutally by South Carolina whites, suggested that continued debate of the slavery issue in the national political arena might foment rebellion in the slave quarters. Finally, the new and higher protective tariffs approved by Congress in 1824 were perceived in South Carolina not only as a serious threat to the state's economy but also as a flagrant abuse of federal political power.[47] Smith sensed that the people were growing increasingly skeptical of nationalism, and with the aid of his political lieutenants, he seized the opportunity to attack Calhoun and the Nationalists. In 1824, Smith and Stephen Miller introduced a series of resolutions in the state legislature which set forth the traditional states' rights tenets of the Radicals in bold terms. The resolutions denied that Congress had constitutional authority "to adopt a general system of internal improvement as a national measure" and declared that protective tariffs were unconstitutional. The Smith-Miller resolutions asserted that any power not explicitly delegated to the national government by the Constitution remained in the hands of the several states. The battle against the resolutions was led by old Federalists Alfred Huger and William Crafts of Charleston as well as by Calhounite Eldred Simkins of Edgefield. After only brief debate, the resolutions passed the senate by a vote of 30 to 13 and were sent to the house for its approval. Chagrined at their poor showing in the senate, Calhounites in the House rallied against the resolutions, and with the legislature nearing adjournment, they succeeded in tabling the measures. Smith, however, was only stalled, not defeated. During the legislative session of 1825, he succeeded in getting the house to consider the Radical resolutions, and despite formidable opposition

[46]Smith, "South Carolina Radical: William Smith," pp. 202–203; Wild, "South Carolina Politics," pp. 18–220; Charleston *Courier,* October 23, 1824; Virgil Maxcy to William Gaston, July 2, 1823 and William Gaston to Daniel Webster, April 11, 1824, William Gaston Papers, SHC.

[47]Rogers, "South Carolina Federalists and the Origins of Nullification," pp. 17–32; Freehling, *Prelude to Civil War,* pp. 106–122; John Lofton, *Insurrection in South Carolina: The Federalist World of Denmark Vesey* (Yellow Springs, Ohio: Antioch Press, 1964).

from Calhounites and former Federalists, the resolutions passed by a two-to-one margin.[48]

By the end of 1825, Radicals in South Carolina had succeeded in passing resolutions which renounced the "qualified nationalism" of the so-called New Republicans and which served as an implied rebuke of Calhoun's leadership. They had succeeded, however, not by confronting Calhoun directly or making the new Vice President an issue in the debate, but by focusing on the questions of internal improvements and tariffs, issues on which there had always been some ambiguity in the Calhounite position. Despite Calhoun's early desire to "conquer space" and his support for a strong national defense, he had always vigorously opposed "local" or "piecemeal" internal improvement schemes, and after 1819 he objected to almost every attempt to use federal money for improvements on just those grounds. On the tariff question, Calhoun always emphasized the usefulness of low import duties in raising revenue more than their protective function. Aware that the tariff of 1824 was clearly protective, and therefore onerous to his state, Calhoun immediately began seeking political support for a downward adjustment of the new duties. Calhoun remained relatively quiet on the tariff issue during the election year of 1824 in order to keep his political options alive and to preserve a chance for political compromise on the tariff itself; but George McDuffie, Robert Y. Hayne, and James Hamilton, all Calhounites, had quickly distanced themselves from those Republicans who supported high duties. Still, the Radical victory in 1825 was important. It clearly signaled that South Carolinians, long convinced that some latitude could be given to the national government as long as that government was in the safe hands of Jeffersonian Republicans and the Virginia dynasty, were beginning to retreat from even the qualified and conditional nationalism of the Calhounites, just as other southern states were also beginning to shift their support away from the Nationalists and back to a rejuvenated band of strict-constructionist Old Republicans. Moreover, the Radical victory was clearly a defeat for Calhoun, even though it did him little lasting damage. Since his rise to national prominence in 1810, defeats for Calhoun in South Carolina were uncommon; after the loss to the Smithites in 1825, they were virtually unknown.[49]

In 1826, Smith, who had become a strong supporter of Andrew Jackson, was reelected to the United States Senate in a closely contested race against Nationalist Daniel Huger, a prominent neo-Federalist from Charleston. Smith interpreted his victory as a vindication of his lifelong struggle against the consolidation of power, the loose construction of the United States Constitution, and the political leadership of John C. Calhoun, and rushed to Washington eager to

    [48]Smith, "South Carolina Radical: William Smith," pp. 209–232; Wild, "South Carolina Politics," pp. 59–265.

    [49]"Second Speech of the Hon. George McDuffie in the House of Representatives Debate on the Tariff," May, 1830, [n.p.], SCL; Robert Y. Hayne, A Defense of the South (Charleston, S.C.: A. E. Miller, 1830), pp. 1–20; Freehling, Prelude to Civil War, p. 94; Charles M. Wiltse, John C. Calhoun: Sectionalist (Indianapolis: Bobbs-Merrill, 1951), pp. 50–59.

flaunt his recent success. Upon arriving in the capital, however, Smith found himself in a strange situation. Calhoun, Smith later admitted, "treated me with so much kindness and consideration that I could not hate him as I wished to do."[50] Moreover, Smith found that Calhoun was not only a strong supporter of Andrew Jackson, but also an unofficial yet highly regarded spokesman for Old Hickory's party. As William Freehling has pointed out, Smith loathed joining an opposition led or dominated by Calhoun, but as a champion of strict construction and states' rights he could hardly support John Quincy Adams. Left with a hard choice that was really no choice at all, Smith aligned himself with Jackson's backers in the Senate, undoubtedly wondering how the fruits of his victories in South Carolina could have turned bittersweet so quickly.[51]

The internecine Republican feud between Radicals and Calhounites (or National Republicans) during the early 1820s was antediluvian, developing quickly in the competitive void created by the demise of an antiquated Federalist party, yet preceding, without foreshadowing, the single most important political watershed of antebellum South Carolina, the nullification crisis. Politics in South Carolina prior to nullification was remarkably similar to politics in the other Southern states, as well as several Northern ones, during the so-called "Era of Good Feelings." Throughout virtually all the states outside of New England, the politics of the Monroe years consisted of factional squabbling among Republicans punctuated by the occasional efforts of a declining Federalist elite to regain influence.[52] South Carolina, despite its unique constitutional settlement in 1808, was no exception. Indeed, a superficial glance at South Carolina politics during the mid-1820s offers the observer little reason to believe that the state was about to veer off on a remarkable and controversial tangent that would not only place it in radical defiance of the national government but would also do much to isolate it from the other southern states. Instead, a far-sighted political sage in 1826 would have been far more likely to have predicted a continuation of politics-as-usual within South Carolina, with the Calhounites and Radicals effecting an uneasy but necessary reconciliation in order to oppose the highly self-conscious nationalism of John Quincy Adams, and with the ambitious but statesmanlike

[50]Benjamin F. Perry, *Reminiscences of Public Men* (Philadelphia: John D. Anvil, 1883), pp. 80–83.

[51]Freehling, *Prelude to Civil War,* pp. 118–120; Clyde N. Wilson and W. Edwin Hemphill, *The Papers of John C. Calhoun* (Columbia, S.C.: University of South Carolina Press, 1977), vol. 10, xxxvii–xli.

[52]See Cooper, *Liberty and Slavery,* pp. 120–169; Brown, "The Missouri Crisis"; Wallace, "Changing Concepts of Party"; Chase C. Mooney, *William H. Crawford, 1772–1834* (Lexington: University of Kentucky Press, 1974), pp. 213–301; C. Edward Skeen, "Calhoun, Crawford, and the Politics of Retrenchment," *South Carolina Historical Magazine* 73 (July, 1972):141–155; E. Wayne Cutler, "William H. Crawford: A Contextual Biography" (Ph.D. dissertation, University of Texas, 1971), pp. 98–201; Thomas P. Abernathy, *The South in the New Nation, 1789–1819* (Baton Rouge: Louisiana State University Press, 1961), pp. 403–443; Charles S. Sydnor, *The Development of Southern Sectionalism, 1819–1848* (Baton Rouge: Louisiana State University Press, 1948), pp. 104–176; Livermore, *Twilight of Federalism,* pp. 47–150.

Calhoun trying to rally the Palmetto state into the Jackson camp with the hope of emerging as Old Hickory's anointed successor. To be sure, the harmony of this fictive Jacksonian South Carolina would have been fragile indeed. At least some of the old tidewater Federalists, especially those in the Charleston mercantile community, would have rallied to Adams's defense and likely would have used every weapon at their disposal to repel Jackson's attack on the Bank of the United States. Moreover, the tenuous unity of the Democratic-Republicans undoubtedly would have been destroyed by the Bank War. Most of the old Radicals and more than a few Upcountry Calhounites were hard-money men who would eagerly have joined Old Hickory's crusade against the nation's financial monster, while virtually all of Calhoun's Lowcountry support, many Upcountry planters, and nearly all of his top political lieutenants would have opposed the outright termination of the National Bank. If this hypothetical scenario seems familiar, it is because it provides, allowing for the necessary adjustments for each state's idiosyncrasies, a basic outline of the history of Jacksonian politics in the other southern states.[53]

Yet South Carolina never joined the Jacksonian mainstream, at least as far as national party alignments and party structure delineated that mainstream. The hypothetical South Carolina of the 1830s briefly sketched in the preceding paragraph never emerged. Instead, however unlikely it may have seemed even as late as 1826, South Carolina proposed nullification as a constitutional remedy for high tariffs and other majoritarian abuses and stood toe-to-toe with the Jackson Administration in a high-stakes game of political brinksmanship. South Carolina's bit of derring-do produced a compromise on the tariff issue, but left the state isolated from the rest of the South throughout much of the pre-Civil War period. In a very real sense, the nullification crisis was the crucial force which deflected South Carolina off the normal Southern political course and onto its own peculiar, radical, and aberrant course. Yet the crucial question of why only South Carolina nullified a tariff law that was vehemently denounced in every southern state has never been fully answered. While any definitive explanation of why South Carolina nullified alone would require a detailed examination of politics in other states that lies beyond the scope of this study, it is possible to offer a tentative explanation of South Carolina's unique response to the Tariff of Abominations based on the existing body of knowledge.[54]

[53]Both the Unionists and the Nullifiers were badly divided over banking questions, and by the end of the 1830s those differences often became more important than agreement on the issue of nullification. Had not much of the old distrust and bitterness of the nullification campaign survived to make politicians reluctant to make common cause with their former enemies, and more important, to continue to influence voter preferences, the bank issue might have triggered a new and thorough bipolarization of politics in South Carolina, just as it did in most other states. The political realignment precipitated by the bank issue will be discussed at length in the next chapter. For a brief introduction to the question, see Wiltse, *Calhoun: Nullifier*, pp. 343–361.

[54]The response of other states to South Carolina's decisive course during the nullification crisis has been ably presented in a recent monograph; see Richard Ellis, *Union at Risk: Jacksonian Democracy, States' Rights, and the Nullification Crisis* (New York: Oxford University Press, 1987);

A striking confluence of idiosyncrasies pushed South Carolina toward radical protest against high tariffs during the late 1820s. The collective influence of a variety of factors, rather than the overwhelming influence of any single factor, provoked the nullification controversy in South Carolina. First, the Congress passed the despised "Tariff of Abominations" in 1828, at a time when South Carolina, and particularly the short-staple cotton-growing areas of the Upcountry, was struggling to recover from a severe economic slump. Falling cotton prices were a blow to the economies of other Southern states as well, but South Carolina was particularly hard hit because it was an old cotton state which also suffered from soil exhaustion and low crop yields. As a result, the economic slump of the 1820s hit South Carolina especially hard and accentuated a growing concern over the state's long-term economic well-being. As George McDuffie argued in his "forty-bale theory," the high tariffs imposed by the federal government seemed to be special and oppressive taxes placed on the already hard-pressed agricultural producers of South Carolina.[55]

Second, South Carolina was fertile ground for radicalism because of its strong and pervasive market orientation. Plantation agriculture dominated the Lowcountry and was common throughout the middle districts and lower Piedmont. Only in the hilly districts of the upper Piedmont was the market orientation of farmers less pronounced. Not only did South Carolina's pervasive market orientation make the real economic damage done by low cotton prices and high tariffs extensive, but it also magnified the growing concern about the political

---

also see E. Merton Coulter, "The Nullification Movement in Georgia," *Georgia Historical Quarterly* 5 (March, 1921):4–39; Paul H. Bergeron, "Tennessee's Response to the Nullification Crisis," *Journal of Southern History* 39 (February, 1973):23–44; Lucie Robertson Bridgeforth, "Mississippi's Response to Nullification, 1833," *Journal of Mississippi History* 45 (February, 1983):1–22; Edwin A. Miles, *Jacksonian Democracy in Mississippi* (Chapel Hill: University of North Carolina Press, 1960), pp. 62–69; J. Mills Thornton III, *Politics and Power in a Slave Society: Alabama, 1800–1860* (Baton Rouge: Louisiana State University Press, 1978), pp. 21–28; Harry L. Watson, *Jacksonian Politics and Community Conflict: The Emergence of the Second American Party System in Cumberland County, North Carolina* (Baton Rouge: Louisiana State University Press, 1981), pp. 153–154. For an overview, see William J. Cooper, Jr., *The South and the Politics of Slavery, 1828–1856* (Baton Rouge: Louisiana State University Press, 1978), pp. 45–48. The important question of why no other Southern state joined South Carolina in nullifying the tariff is not addressed directly in Freehling, *Prelude to Civil War*. Certainly the two factors which Freehling believes to be at the heart of the movement, fear of slave insurrections and concern over the depression in the short-staple cotton economy, were common throughout the deep South. Moreover, those who worried most about the potential for slave violence tended to be Unionists, not Nullifiers. For a thorough, well-documented refutation of the hypothesis that fear of slave insurrection was closely associated with support for nullification, see J. P. Ochenkowski, "The Origins of Nullification in South Carolina," *South Carolina Historical Magazine* 83 (April, 1982):121–153. See also Patrick Brady, "Political and Civic Life in South Carolina, 1787–1833" (Ph.D. dissertation, University of California at Santa Barbara, 1971).

[55]Alfred G. Smith, *Economic Readjustment of an Old Cotton State: South Carolina, 1820–1860* (Columbia, S.C.: University of South Carolina Press, 1958), especially pp. 49–60; Register of Debates, 21 Congress, I session, II, p. 819; Ralph Henry Fletcher, "George McDuffie: Orator and Politician" (M.A. thesis, University of South Carolina, 1986), pp. 72–164.

power of Northern mercantile and manufacturing interests. Lacking a large hill
country, where subsistence farmers could enjoy a degree of isolation from market vicissitudes, South Carolina was especially vulnerable to the kind of political
unrest which developed as a response to economic distress. At the same time, the
particular type of market activity in which South Carolina was engaged—staple
agriculture relying on slave labor—also strengthened the unity of interests in the
state after the expansion of slavery into nearly every area of the state.[56]

If the strong and extensive market orientation of South Carolina rendered her
especially susceptible to debilitating economic diseases, the state's singular political tradition did much to shape her response to all crises. As Robert M. Weir
has noted, South Carolina's politics during the Revolutionary era was strikingly
harmonious, based as it was on a broadly shared acceptance of the British
"country" ideology which praised the consensus ideal of disinterested statesmanship while scorning the competitive thrust of party politics.[57] The shared
tenets of the "country" ideology not only guided South Carolina into open
rebellion against Britain but also remained influential during the early national
period. As the series of compromises between Upcountry and Lowcountry ame-
liorated sectional tensions within the state, and as commercial agriculture grew
more pervasive, the political as well as the socioeconomic basis for internal
harmony grew stronger in the early 1800s, even though bitter factional disputes
born out of honest and important differences of opinion, such as the Radical-
National split, persisted. When Robert J. Turnbull, George McDuffie, Thomas
Cooper, and others began to pen political tracts portraying high tariffs as a threat
to basic republican values, South Carolinians responded vigorously, because
their political heritage was so rich and meaningful and because that tradition
continued to speak to their condition. South Carolina stood firm against the
British in the 1770s, and firm in defense of slavery at the Constitutional Convention in 1787, and she would stand firm against oppressive tariffs in 1832. Other
states, of course, shared South Carolina's commitment to republicanism and

[56]George McDuffie to Armistead Burt, February 19, 1833, George McDuffie Papers, SCL;
Richard A. Springs to Leroy Springs, July 6, 1832, Springs Family Papers, SHC; John Barrilon to
John T. Seibels, September 5, 1830, Seibels Family Papers, SCL; David Rogerson Williams to
Stephen D. Miller, September 25, 1828, David Rogerson Williams Papers, SCL; Thomas R.
Mitchell to Robert Witherspoon, December 11, 1831, Witherspoon Family Papers, SCL; for a
lengthy discussion of the degree of market orientation among South Carolina yeomen, see chapter 2
of this volume.

[57]Robert M. Weir, "'The Harmony We Were Famous For': An Interpretation of Pre-Revolution-
ary South Carolina Politics," *William and Mary Quarterly* 26 (October, 1969):473–501; Jack P.
Greene, "Changing Interpretations of Early American Politics," in Ray Allen Billington, ed., *The
Reinterpretation of Early American History: Essays in Honor of John E. Pomfret* (San Marino,
Calif.: Huntington Library, 1966); Jack P. Greene, "'Slavery or Independence': Some Reflections
on the Relationship among Liberty, Black Bondage, and Equality in Revolutionary South Carolina,"
South Carolina Historical Magazine 80 (July, 1979):193–214; Pauline Maier, "The Road Not
Taken: Nullification, John C. Calhoun, and the Revolutionary Tradition in South Carolina," *South
Carolina Historical Magazine* 82 (January, 1981):1–19.

slavery, but in no other state did a heritage of harmony from the Revolutionary era loom quite so large.[58]

Doubtless the large black population in South Carolina was important to the development of an unusual political unity among white South Carolinians. The demographics of the South Carolina Upcountry were more or less similar to those of the rest of the deep South, with some areas dominated by plantation agriculture and black majorities and other areas populated mainly by white small farmers. As a result, there is no reason to believe that fear of a slave insurrection was more acute in the Upcountry than in many other parts of the slave South. In parts of the Lowcountry, however, the size of the black majorities was overwhelming. In the coastal parishes around Georgetown, Charleston, and Beaufort, over 85 percent of the total population was black. In no other area of the South, except perhaps a few of the Louisiana sugar parishes, were whites so outnumbered by slaves. Indeed, the population distribution in a number of the Lowcountry parishes resembled that of the West Indies and other parts of the Caribbean slave empires far more than it did that of the Southern black belt. In these Lowcountry parishes, where a comparative handful of whites controlled a vast slave population, the threat of a slave insurrection was indeed ominous, and fears that a racial bloodbath along the lines of the Haitian revolution might occur in the American South were especially grave.[59]

Finally, South Carolina's uniquely radical response to the high tariffs of the 1820s was shaped by the towering political presence of John C. Calhoun. By 1830, Calhoun had been a national political figure as long as, or longer than, Alabama and Mississippi had been states. Although not yet fifty when he anonymously authored the famous "Exposition" outlining South Carolina's opposition to consolidated federal power and detailing the process of state interposition, Calhoun had already enjoyed a long and productive career as a congressman and cabinet officer, had heard and encouraged talk that he would make a fine President, and had been a consensus choice for Vice President in 1824.[60] As a political ally during the Monroe Administration, John Quincy Adams judged Calhoun "a man of fair and candid mind, of honorable principles, of clear and

---

[58]Robert J. Turnbull, *The Crisis* (Charleston: A. E. Miller, 1827); Dumas Malone, *The Public Life of Thomas Cooper* (New Haven: Yale University Press, 1926); Green, *George McDuffie*, pp. 76–119; Robert M. Weir, "The South Carolinian as Extremist," *South Atlantic Quarterly* 74 (December, 1975):86–103. See also Clyde N. Wilson's introduction to *The Papers of John C. Calhoun*, vol. 10, xiii–xlvi. On the influence of republican ideology on other Southern states, see, for examples, Thornton, *Politics and Power*, pp. 1–58; Marc W. Kruman, *Parties and Politics in North Carolina, 1836–1865* (Baton Rouge: Louisiana State University Press, 1983), especially pp. 3–28; Fred Siegel, "The Paternalist Thesis: Virginia as a Test Case," *Civil War History* 25 (September, 1979):246–261.

[59]Julian J. Petty, *The Growth and Distribution of Population in South Carolina* (Columbia, S.C.: State Council for Defense, 1943), pp. 226–229. The argument that racial anxieties were the single most important factor behind the nullification movement is skillfully made by Freehling, *Prelude to Civil War*, especially pp. 258–259.

[60]Coit, *Calhoun*, pp. 67–202.

quick understanding, of cool self-possession, of enlarged philosophical views, and of ardent patriotism.'' Years later, during the heat of the nullification crisis, Adams continued to respect Calhoun's ability despite their political and personal estrangement. "His insanity begins with his principles," Adams declared, "from which his deductions are ingeniously drawn."[61] Calhoun's political enemies in South Carolina also conceded him grudging respect. Unionist Benjamin F. Perry expressed "high regard" for Calhoun's character and deemed his manners "pleasant and very affable." Moreover, Perry maintained that Calhoun's "conversational powers" were "greater than those of any man living." Yet Calhoun's greatest gift, in Perry's view, was that of the "tact and management" necessary for "managing or governing men."[62] Another Unionist, Daniel Huger of Charleston, insisted that "when you speak of his moral principles you must not compare him with ordinary men but with Caesars."[63]

As his inability to defeat the Radicals in the 1820s demonstrated, Calhoun did not have dictatorial control over South Carolina politics, yet through his brilliance, his national prestige, and a large and carefully cultivated legion of political allies, the "Fort Hill" planter exercised an unusual degree of influence on the politics of his native state. Once Calhoun threw the full extent of his talent and energy behind the idea of state interposition, many otherwise hesitant South Carolinians mobilized to support nullification simply to give Calhoun more leverage in his struggle to check the growing power of the federal government. If Calhoun's prestige was on the line, many South Carolinians were determined that it should not be sabotaged by weak or half-hearted support at home. Although Andrew Jackson had a larger constituency in the region, no other Southern politician of the era had a local base that was as solid and unshakable as Calhoun's.[64]

Confident of his support in South Carolina, Calhoun was free to map a bold strategy of opposition to the tariff based on republican principles and his perception of long-term Southern interests, a strategy which made few concessions to the demands of partisan politics. If the strength and security of his political base in South Carolina gave Calhoun special latitude in shaping a response to the forces of consolidation, his reputation for intellect and integrity in Washington gave him the standing to present and defend a complicated constitutional innovation to a skeptical Congress. No other Southern politician could have commanded the nation's attention so completely, or presented the case for state interposition so forcefully as Calhoun. In a city where even his detractors granted him a grudging respect, the mere association of Calhoun's name with an idea gave that idea a respectability, even a legitimacy, that guaranteed it serious attention. It is, therefore, unlikely that South Carolina or any other state could have responded to the growing centralization of power in Washington with the doc-

[61]Allan Nevins, ed., *The Diary of John Quincy Adams, 1794–1845* (New York: Longmans, Green, 1929), pp. 265, 437.

[62]Introduction to Benjamin F. Perry Diary, [c. 1832], vol. I, SHC.

[63]Entry of September 7, 1839, Benjamin F. Perry Diary, vol. I, SHC.

[64]Wiltse, *Calhoun: Nullifier*, pp. 11–153; Cooper, *The Politics of Slavery*, pp. 103–118.

trine of nullification without a Calhoun to formulate and orchestrate such a response.[65]

In summary, the special vulnerability of South Carolina to the fluctuations of the world cotton economy and to competition from newer cotton regions, the high incidence of slaveholding in the state, the size of the black majority in the Lowcountry, the state's unique political heritage, and the presence of John C. Calhoun were each necessary, but insufficient, conditions for nullification. Each factor contributed in some way toward making nullification possible, but it was the collective force of them all operating together that made nullification a reality in South Carolina, and it was the absence of this particular confluence of forces in other states that made it unlikely that the rest of the South would join South Carolina in her open defiance of the federal government. Certainly South Carolina was not alone in her opposition to the tariff. Nor was South Carolina alone in her concern about the future of Southern economic interests, slavery, and the American experiment in republicanism. The most powerful and determined opponents of nullification, the loyal Jacksonians in the Old Southwest, were no less concerned about these matters than were the Nullifiers in South Carolina. Indeed, as Clyde N. Wilson had perceptively noted, the nullification controversy "almost reduces to a tactical dispute between two groups of Southerners, one wishing to continue to dominate the federal government by conventional politics and the other wanting to prepare for a possible future minority position," in which both sides were led by "Southern planters between whom there was no distinguishable difference in the firmness of their defense of slavery."[66] South Carolina did not nullify alone because her fears were unique, but because her circumstances were exceptional.

Nullification should be viewed not so much as a harbinger of future radicalism as the logical, though not inevitable, culmination of the continuing debate over how best to defend the republican principles inherited from the Founding Fathers against the centralizing and corrupting tendencies of the age. This debate raged in other states as well, but when juxtaposed on the circumstances of political and economic life in South Carolina it assumed a special urgency and volatility. It was from this vantage point, one looking backward to the Revolution, the Constitution, and the age of Jefferson, rather than forward to secession and Civil War, that South Carolinians made their decision to nullify.[67] No one

[65]Clyde N. Wilson, ed., *The Papers of John C. Calhoun* (Columbia: University of South Carolina Press, 1978), vol. 11, xiii–xxxix.

[66]See Wilson's introduction to *The Papers of John C. Calhoun*, vol. 11, xvi–xvii; for an account of how republican ideology also shaped Jackson's response to nullification, see Richard B. Latner, "The Nullification Crisis and Republican Subversion," *Journal of Southern History* 43 (February, 1977):19–38; and Robert V. Remini, *Andrew Jackson and the Course of American Diplomacy, 1833–1845* (New York: Harper and Row, 1984), pp. 8–44.

[67]Maier, "The Road Not Taken," pp. 1–19; J. William Harris, "Last of the Classical Republicans: An Interpretation of John C. Calhoun," *Civil War History* 30 (September, 1984):255–267; Mark D. Kaplanoff, "Charles Pinckney and the American Republican Tradition," in Michael O'Brien and David Moltke-Hansen, eds., *Intellectual Life in Antebellum Charleston* (Knoxville: University of Tennessee Press, 1986), pp. 85–122.

has explained the matter better than Thomas Sumter, the aging military hero of the American Revolution who lived through the nullification crisis. Living in active retirement as an Upcountry planter after a long career as a Jeffersonian congressman and senator, Sumter outlined his views in a long letter to his son during the summer of 1831:

> Contrary to your apprehension, you will see that few Carolinians will be found, even among my political enemies, if I still have any, who will not be ashamed to pretend to believe that I have knowingly turned my coat; that is, put off the republican character, which it cost me some toil to earn, and which I still wear with some pride. They all know, as their fathers or grandfathers knew, that, in this country, republicanism, in its true sense, was intended to mean, and did mean, that its possessors had both the right and the will to resist effectually unauthorized power, which in every shape means usurpation.
>
> If any of the present generation have forgotten this wholesome truth, let them . . . read carefully the Declaration of Independence, Debates on the Ratification of the Federal Constitution, the Constitution itself and its amendments, the Virginia and Kentucky Resolutions, adopted in the reign of terror, the proceedings of their own and other legislatures on the fraudulent tariff of 1828—and last, because latest, the able *Exposition* just offered to them by the second officer of the general Government.[68]

Nullification, Sumter contended, was merely the necessary, albeit drastic, remedy for the usurpation of power by the federal government. Sumter, who literally embodied South Carolina's revered political heritage, urged his fellow citizens to be ever vigilant in defense of their liberty. "It is a hard matter to enslave a free people," Sumter warned, "but such a people once enslaved, will hardly regain their liberty.[69]

The task of winning frustrated Radicals over to their cause was the principal challenge facing Upcountry Nullifiers during the late 1820s. Even after the election of 1828, three of the five congressmen representing Upcountry districts and a majority of state legislators from the region were Radicals.[70] These Upcountry Radicals saw most Calhounites as tainted by a nationalist past and doubted if politicians with such ideological heresy in their backgrounds could be trusted with the precious cause of states' rights in the present. Early in 1830, Radical James Black, an Abbeville native, reminded friends that it was Calhoun and his supporters who "in times past . . . have acted with too great liberality—to say the least of it" with regard to tariffs and internal improvements, and late in 1831 a public rally

[68]General Thomas Sumter to T. D. Sumter, August 23, 1831, Thomas Sumter Papers, SCL.

[69]General Thomas Sumter to [?], October 29, 1830, Thomas Sumter Papers, SCL.

[70]Wild, "South Carolina Politics, 1816–1836," pp. 418–477; Justin Bond Culler, "John Taylor: Neglected South Carolinian" (M.A. thesis, University of South Carolina, 1970), pp. 84–104; James D. Cooke to Stephen D. Miller, January 10, 1830, Stephen D. Miller Papers, DU; Columbia *Free Press and Hive,* March 10, April 3, July 21 and 30, October 8, 1831; Job Johnston to Stephen D. Miller, August 20, 1828, Chesnut-Miller-Manning Papers, SCHS.

in support of William Smith praised Radicals, Old Republicans, and strict constructionists as the true guardians of states' rights.[71] Congressman James Blair, a Radical who represented Lancaster district, openly attacked Calhoun as the "Father of the American System" and linked the Nullifiers to the old activist branch of the Republican party. Blair scoffed at the Nullifiers' claim that they were protectors of states' rights and praised Andrew Jackson as the true defender of the Constitution.[72]

Ironically, it was President Jackson's failure to act decisively against the tariff during his first term that gave the Nullifiers their strongest arguments against the Radicals. As long as John Quincy Adams was President, the Radicals could claim that relief from the tariff could be achieved through the regular electoral process. All that was required, the Radicals argued, was the election of a President who would use the powers of the executive, and especially the veto, to reestablish a strict construction of the Constitution. When Jackson equivocated on the tariff during his first term, Nullifiers demanded to know exactly how Radicals expected to force a return to strict construction and states' rights without resort to state interposition.[73] As early as 1828, Waddy Thompson, a Nullifier, told an Upcountry audience that the Radicals' willingness to depend on partisan politics to protect constitutional rights was nothing less than a policy of submission.[74] But in 1828, most Upcountry Radicals still doubted that a remedy as drastic as nullification was really necessary. "The backcountry are mostly for non-consumption opposition to the tariff," Fairfield planter Job Johnston observed, "they do not, as of yet, seem to relish the spirit of the people of the lower country on the subject of the tariff."[75] Public sentiment in the old Radical stronghold of Fairfield shifted decisively during the next three years. By August 1831, Fairfield Nullifier Edward Pearson reported that "the word nullification was electric" at a public meeting in a district once ruled by "Jackson mania."[76]

Ultimately the debate over nullification precipitated a wholesale realignment of political factions within South Carolina. By 1830, the old Radical faction was slowly, but surely, disintegrating. The issue of nullification forced most Radicals to choose between two of their most cherished principles: devotion to states' rights, and the absolute strict construction of the Constitution. For some Radicals, including the ambitious Stephen D. Miller, nullification was an acceptable tactical and constitutional innovation because it served to augment the power of individual states. Other Radicals, however, saw state interposition as a heresy

[71]James Black to Stephen D. Miller, February 15, 1830, Chesnut-Miller-Manning Papers, SCHS; Columbia *Free Press and Hive,* September 17, 1831.

[72]Columbia *Free Press and Hive,* July 20, 1831.

[73]John Springs to Leroy Springs, December 8, 1831, Springs Family Papers, SHC; Address of Robert Witherspoon to "Fellow Citizens," July 4, 1832, Witherspoon Family Papers, SCL; James H. Witherspoon to Stephen D. Miller, November 26, 1830, Chesnut-Miller-Manning Papers, SCHS.

[74]Entry of August 14, 1828, William Blanding Journal, DU.

[75]Job Johnston to Stephen D. Miller, August 20, 1828, Chesnut-Miller-Manning Papers, SCHS.

[76]J. Edward Pearson to Stephen D. Miller, August 8, 1831, Chesnut-Miller-Manning Papers, SCHS.

which encouraged imaginative readings of the Constitution, a document which they believed to be the best protector of states' rights. William Smith and his longtime ally from the Pee Dee, David R. Williams, gravitated toward the latter position, a move undoubtedly encouraged by a lingering reluctance to side with Calhoun when it was possible to oppose him.[77] Yet despite the protests of Smith and his loyal followers, by 1830 South Carolina could no longer afford the luxury of having two factions committed to states' rights and local autonomy. As Calhoun and the nullifiers emerged as champions of state sovereignty, the Radicals who refused to join the crusade found it increasingly difficult to hold their constituency. Smith, scarred by his years of battling Calhoun, moved to Alabama in 1831 after being narrowly defeated by his former ally, Miller, in the election for United States Senator in 1830; in addition, only months before Smith's departure, his longtime friend David R. Williams was killed in a freak accident on the Pee Dee River. With their best-known leaders gone, the old Radicals who opposed nullification gravitated toward Unionists such as James Blair of Lancaster and Benjamin F. Perry of Greenville.[78]

Fortunately for Calhoun, his gains among former Radicals more than offset the defection from his ranks of a number of strong nationalists, especially from the Lowcountry, who had supported his qualified nationalism of the early 1820s, but who now equated nullification with anarchy and disunion. Many of the defectors were Lowcountrymen of lingering Federalist sympathies who had joined Calhoun's faction in an effort to retain some influence on public policy. Such neo-Federalist defectors as William Drayton and Daniel Huger joined other old Federalist families such as the Elliotts and Pringles, who had always distanced themselves from the Calhounites, to form the core of the Unionist party in the Lowcountry. For the most part, these Lowcountry Unionists were conservatives—wealthy planters, prominent lawyers, bankers, scholars, and powerful Charleston merchants—and many of them were members of prominent old colonial families. As representatives of a refined, self-conscious, and perhaps effete, parish elite, these Unionists were conservative in the broadest sense of the term. They were cautious, cosmopolitan, and committed to maintaining a refuge for order and authority in South Carolina. They opposed nullification because it was radical in the sense of being new, untested, and controversial, because it contained a strain of fierce localism, because it threatened to disrupt normal channels of commercial and intellectual discourse, and because it appeared to threaten the most precious legacy of the Federalist era, the Union itself.[79]

[77]Cook, *David R. Williams*, pp. 280–87; Perry, *Reminiscences*, pp. 80–83; Culler, "John Taylor," pp. 105–114; Columbia *Telescope*, September 11, 1832.

[78]Freehling, *Prelude to Civil War*, pp. 213–217; Lillian Kibler, *Benjamin F. Perry: South Carolina Unionist* (Durham, N.C.: Duke University Press, 1946), pp. 87–158; Wild, "South Carolina Politics, 1816–1836," pp. 418–535; William Randolph Hill to Stephen D. Miller, June 6, 1832, Chesnut-Miller-Manning Papers, SCHS.

[79]Lacy Ford, "James Louis Petigru: The Last South Carolina Federalist," in O'Brien and Moltke-Hansen, eds., *Intellectual Life in Antebellum Charleston*, pp. 152–185; Lewis P. Jones, "William Elliott: South Carolina Non-conformist," *Journal of Southern History* 17 (August,

The rump of the old Radical faction constituted the bulk of the Union party in the Upcountry. These men were true Jacksonian Democrats of a type common outside of South Carolina. They supported states' rights, strict construction of the Constitution, minimal government, slavery, and Andrew Jackson. They opposed protective tariffs, national banks, federally financed internal improvements, John Quincy Adams, and nullification. The nationalism of these South Carolina Jacksonians, like that of their counterparts in the rest of the South, was a nationalism of spirit, an emotional attachment to the Union and to the glorious republican experiment that it represented. It was not a Hamiltonian nationalism, like that of John Quincy Adams, based on the consolidation of power, a strong central government, and a specific blueprint for national economic development. The leading Jacksonian Democrats in South Carolina were Ben Perry in the Upcountry, and Joel Poinsett and a young William Gilmore Simms in Charleston. Perry's brand of Jacksonian Democracy and his familiarity with the habits of the "mountaineers" of the hill country appealed to many former Radicals in the Upcountry. Poinsett, a veteran diplomat accustomed to representing the United States abroad, and Simms, a young man with political and literary ambitions who thrived on the enthusiasm of the Jacksonians, directed their Unionist appeals chiefly at waivering Jacksonians in the Upcountry while adding a democratic veneer to the conservative anti-nullifier broadsides of the increasingly decrepit tidewater Unionists.[80]

Calhoun and the Nullifiers, then, found themselves opposed by a Unionist party based on two distinctly different types of nationalism, one essentially conservative and cosmopolitan, born in the coastal parishes and trading centers in defense of wealth, tradition, and social standing, and the other essentially radical and provincial, born in the rough-and-tumble rural Upcountry frontier as part of the common man's attachment to the democracy of his own making. United almost solely in its opposition to Calhoun and Nullification, the Union party was a *mésalliance* of proto-Whigs and hard-money Democrats which lacked any firm basis for long-term unity. The dramatic political realignment sparked by nullification, therefore, resulted in a series of unnatural and uneasy alliances which existed nowhere else in the South. By 1832, political groupings in South Carolina, which had so closely paralleled those in other Southern states just a few years earlier, were peculiar to the Palmetto State, thoroughly idiosyn-

1951):361–381; Beverly R. Scafidel, "The Letters of William Elliott" (Ph.D. dissertation, University of South Carolina, 1978); Michael O'Brien, *A Character of Hugh Legare* (Knoxville: University of Tennessee Press, 1985), pp. 35–55, 169–185; Linda Rhea, *Hugh Swinton Legare: A Charleston Intellectual* (Chapel Hill: University of North Carolina Press, 1934).

[80]Major L. Wilson, "'Liberty and Union': An Analysis of Three Concepts Involved in the Nullification Controversy," *Journal of Southern History* 33 (August, 1967):331–355; Kibler, *B. F. Perry*, pp. 87–107; J. Fred Rippy, *Joel R. Poinsett: Versatile American* (Durham, N.C.: Duke University Press, 1946), pp. 134–148; Jon L. Wakelyn, *The Politics of a Literary Man: William Gilmore Simms* (Westport, Conn.: Greenwood Press, 1973), pp. 19–50; John McCardell, "Poetry and the Practical: William Gilmore Simms," in O'Brien and Moltke-Hansen, eds., *Intellectual Life in Antebellum Charleston*, pp. 186–210.

cratic, and clearly outside the national mainstream. Cut off at least temporarily from the emerging party alignments in the rest of Jacksonian America by the internal dynamics of the nullification campaign, South Carolinians experienced for the first time in the nineteenth century a sense of political isolation from the rest of the nation.[81]

Once the battle lines were drawn, each side faced the problem of how best to make its case to the voters, of how first to expand and then to consolidate its support. Prior to the nullification campaigns, political factions in South Carolina seldom ran coordinated tickets in all of the state's election districts. Instead, leaders of the various factions sought to bolster their support throughout the state by enlisting the aid of a handful of local notables in each district or parish. Usually men of wealth or popularity or both, these notables used their powers of persuasion and influence among the people of their beats or voting precincts to build support for the faction of their choice. At times, however, the search was not for followers but for leaders. Aware of public opinion in their community, local notables would combine to cajole or persuade a prominent politician to take up the cudgels for a certain cause. To a large extent, statewide factions were composed of competing clusters of local cliques or cabals which were led, but not necessarily controlled by, a neighborhood squire. The search for a safe majority, or political dominance, centered around efforts to work through ever-larger numbers of local notables to win the support of more and more local cliques. The practice of political negotiation and organization through this complex and ever-changing network of local cliques was a minor art form, requiring the skilled hand of a politician thoroughly familiar with local habits and sentiments and sensitive to the whims of the many delicate egos involved. Yet it was a political milieu in which Calhoun, his allies, and his opponents were all well-schooled.[82]

The nullification campaigns did not change the basic form of the canvass in South Carolina, but they did emphasize statewide organization and partisan mobilization in the state for the first time in at least a generation. As James Brewer Stewart has recently argued, the nullification crisis infused South Carolina politics with a new wave of democratic energy and a new level of organizational sophistication which began "to complete the traditional workings of personalized politics" and to override "the elite's distaste for partisanship."[83]

[81]Kenneth S. Greenberg, "Representation and the Isolation of South Carolina, 1776–1860," *Journal of American History* 64 (December, 1977):723–743; Banner, "The Problem of South Carolina," pp. 60–93.

[82]George McDuffie to David J. McCord, September 9, 1828, George McDuffie Papers, SCL; Henry H. Townes to George F. Townes, June 7, 1832, Townes Family Papers, SCL; Isaac D. Witherspoon to Stephen D. Miller, January 8, 1831, Chesnut-Miller-Manning Papers, SCHS; Columbia *Free Press and Hive*, July 21 and October 8, 1831; John C. Calhoun to William C. Preston, January 6, 1829, in Wilson, ed., *The Papers of John C. Calhoun*, vol. 10, pp. 545–551; Freehling, *Prelude to Civil War*, pp. 134–176.

[83]James Brewer Stewart, " 'A Great Talking and Eating Machine': Patriarchy, Mobilization and the Dynamics of Nullification in South Carolina," *Civil War History* 37 (September, 1981):197–220.

Throughout the state, both Nullifiers and Unionists sponsored large political barbecues at which they presented their arguments to the voters, and even routine militia musters were transformed into *de facto* stump meetings. These meetings were often volatile and occasionally degenerated into mob scenes marred by violence. In 1831, at a meeting in Union district, formerly a Radical stronghold, Unionists William Smith and James Blair were rudely shouted down by a newly forged Nullifier majority.[84] In Greenville district, at a regimental review muster held on Toney's Old Fields, Unionist B. F. Perry debated Nullifier Waddy Thompson in a rousing exchange which soured when Thompson accused Perry of lying. An irate Perry, who by his own admission "had scarcely ever fired a pistol," challenged Thompson to duel, but was persuaded by his friends to accept their adjustment of the matter. Later, Perry defended his actions, claiming that "if I permitted an insult to pass unnoticed it would provoke others."[85]

Historians have generally agreed that the Nullifiers had the bulk of the organizational and forensic talent in the state in their camp during the crisis. William Campbell Preston, Waddy Thompson, James Hamilton, Jr., George McDuffie, and a young James Henry Hammond were simply the most outstanding of scores of talented orators and polemicists who rallied to the Nullifier cause. Nullifiers organized and orchestrated an endless succession of public dinners, speeches, barbecues, and rallies which they used to take their case to the public. In July 1831, Nullification leaders met in Charleston and formed the States Rights and Free Trade Society and announced plans to organize support for nullification and to run a ticket of Nullifiers in every district or parish in the state. James B. Stewart estimated that this active organizational arm of the Nullification party sponsored at least 304 meetings, dinners, and celebrations throughout South Carolina during its first eighteen months of existence.[86] By December 1831, even staunch Unionists conceded that they were losing the organizational battle to the Nullifiers. Contrasting the two parties, Unionist Thomas R. Mitchell complained, "The disunion [Nullification] party is so well organized by means of their Jacobin clubs [States' Rights and Free Trade societies] through the State—its leaders are so indefatigable—so reckless in their means. . . . Our house is not organized. . . ."[87]

---

[84]Charleston *Mercury,* September 8, 1831; Pendleton *Messenger,* September 7, 1831.

[85]Quoted in Kibler, *B. F. Perry,* p. 109; see also entry of December 4, 1832, Benjamin F. Perry Diary, vol. I, SHC; Waddy Thompson to Benjamin F. Perry, March 6, 1842, Waddy Thompson Papers, SCL; Stephen Meats and Edwin T. Arnold, ed., *The Writings of Benjamin F. Perry: Essays, Public Letters and Speeches,* 3 vols. (Spartanburg, S.C.: The Reprint Company, 1980), vol. I, pp. 248–262.

[86]Stewart, "'A Great Talking and Eating Machine,'" pp. 216–217; John Springs to Leroy Springs, December 8, 1831, Springs Family Papers, SHC; John Barrilon to John T. Seibels, August 29, 1832, Seibels Family Papers, SCL; Samuel A. Townes to George F. Townes, July 5, 1832, and Henry H. Townes to George F. Townes, September 6, 1832, Townes Family Papers, SCL; William Randolph Hill to Stephen D. Miller, June 6, 1832, Chesnut-Miller-Manning Papers, SCHS.

[87]Thomas R. Mitchell to Robert Witherspoon, December 11, 1831, Witherspoon Family Papers, SCL.

In addition, James Hamilton, the governor of the state and a leading Nullifier, turned the mandatory inspection tour of militia units in 1832 into a traveling nullification rally. Hamilton traveled the state in a splendid military carriage drawn by two magnificent grey horses and trailed by slaves who carried his ceremonial sword and tended his horses. Upon arrival, Hamilton would emerge in full military regalia and faithfully review the local militia before large crowds of onlookers. Later, he would appear at a grand public dinner, where he was usually greeted by dozens of local Nullifiers wearing the ostentatious blue cockade that had become the symbol of their movement. After a hearty meal, Hamilton would deliver a fiery, passionate, yet plain-spoken speech praising nullification as the best method of defending republican "liberty and honor" and denouncing its opponents as cowardly, spineless "submissionists."[88]

The educational and mobilization campaigns orchestrated by the leading Nullifiers were of great importance in rallying the yeomanry to support a doctrine which was complicated and esoteric. Like almost everyone else in South Carolina, small farmers opposed the tariff and viewed it as a dangerous abuse of power by the federal government. Yet most yeomen at first heeded the Unionist line which equated nullification with disunion. B. F. Perry's assessment of the situation in Greenville in 1830 provides an indication of the problems the Nullifiers faced:

> Although the people of South Carolina have . . . grounds of complaint against the National government, we believe that they are attached to it by ties which can be severed [only] with difficulty. We know that the mass of citizens in Greenville, the hardy yeomanry of the mountains, the bone and sinew of government, are far, very far, from being in a revolutionary state. They feel, and are sensible of their wrongs; but they are disposed to exercise patience and forbearance.[89]

The Nullifiers were never able to attract much support from the "hardy yeomanry of the mountains," and Greenville and Spartanburg districts cast more votes against nullification than any other in the state, but the mobilization campaign spearheaded by the States' Rights societies convinced yeomen in other districts to support nullification enthusiastically. B. F. Whitner, a leading Nullifier charged with organizing Chester district, explained the effectiveness of the campaign to James H. Hammond:

> I have had repeated conversations with many of the plain but intelligent farmers . . . and I find the apprehension universal that the friends of the convention [Nullifiers] do not propose a peaceful remedy. But in every instance where I had an opportunity to explain and illustrate the right of the state to their exercise of sovereignty . . . I have found the people in favor of convention . . . I am glad to hear a great many of the yeomanry speak of attending the [pro-

[88]Carl Lewis Kell, "A Rhetorical History of James Hamilton, Jr.: The Nullification Era in South Carolina" (Ph.D. dissertation, University of Kansas, 1971), pp. 94–131.

[89]Greenville *Mountaineer,* July 9, 1830.

nullification] meeting in Columbia on the 20th . . . great good may yet result even in time for the approaching elections.[90]

By 1832, the mobilization campaign had gained so much momentum that William C. Preston of Richland could report:

In this quarter the public enthusiasm is more intense than my best hopes could have anticipated. Everybody is volunteering—old and young, the parent and his sons, rich and poor are found in the ranks shoulder to shoulder. . . . An equal enthusiasm, it is said, pervades Fairfield.[91]

The nullification campaign, with its openness, intensity, and drama breathed fresh life and fiery passion into the already highly personal face-to-face democracy of grassroots politics in the state. The techniques, indeed the theatrics, of political mobilization in South Carolina grew more sophisticated and were coordinated by statewide organizations for the first time. Involvement in politics was transformed from a matter of occasionally expressing a preference among local leaders into participation at huge rallies supporting one well-organized faction or the other. The grand spectacle and high public drama of the large campaign rallies undoubtedly left an indelible mark on that large body of South Carolinians who experienced intense political partisanship for the first time during the nullification era. One newspaper reporter from Portland, Maine, who visited Charleston during the nullification crisis, explained the excitement of the era to his readers with genuine amazement:

The Nullifiers are doing things in style. The Nullifiers are men of taste, men of little guns, big guns, swords and cutlasses, great spunk and fine speeches, pretty ladies and pretty dances.
Who would not be a Nullifier and live in such a land, fed on such chivalry and enjoy such a ball. . . .
Here is the Governor of the State in cap, plumes, and epaulettes, with his amiable lady, wearing the cockade of Carolina. There is ex-Governor Hamilton, Emperor of the South, far less humble than Napoleon when only trampling on the thrones of Europe. Here was a cluster of generals, colonels and captains, epauletted to the ears, with swords dangling between their feet, with spurs sticking into their heels. . . . Talk of nullification dying out, it is nonsense, when you work upon the passions and feelings of the people with such shows. Every man and child there will live and die a Nullifier. I was half a mind to become one myself.[92]

Nor was the festive atmosphere, the lavish entertainment, and the intensity of feeling peculiar to Nullifier rallies. Though boasting fewer colorful leaders, the

[90]B. F. Whitner to James Henry Hammond, September 11, 1830, James Henry Hammond Papers, LC (on microfilm at SCL).

[91]William C. Preston to James Henry Hammond, December 27, 1832, James Henry Hammond Papers, LC (microfilm at SCL).

[92]Portland (Maine) *Advertiser* reprinted in the Charleston *Mercury*, April 27, 1933.

Unionists also staged lavish parties designed to rally the faithful. One federal naval officer stationed in Charleston harbor during the crisis left a striking account of the campaign and his experience at a Unionist gala:

> The scene has been appalling, and God grant that it may never be our lot to witness another domestic strife of such fearful and bloody promise at any future period of our lives. Both parties were braced up for the battle, had buckled on their armour and flung away the scabbard, awaiting the signal for conflict. . . .
>
> We assisted at a grand fête Champêtre given at a Villa several miles from the city under the auspices of Mr. Poinsett. It was both Novel and agreeable. About a thousand persons were on the ground and shared in the entertainments. But I should scarcely have paper enough to describe all our doings at this place of dancing, dissipation, and disaffection, of Noise Novelties and Nullifiers, of racing, rice, and rout.[93]

Perhaps William John Grayson, a prominent member of the Beaufort gentry who reluctantly became a Nullifier despite his close personal ties to leading Unionists such as James L. Petigru, William Elliott, and Hugh S. Legaré, best described the fixation with electioneering and political rallying which gripped South Carolina during nullification. "The State," Grayson reminisced, "became for a time a great talking and eating machine. The appetites and lungs of the conflicting parties never failed, nor faultered, until the compromise . . . settled the controversy, composed the minds, and relieved the stomachs of the people.[94]

If the style of the nullification campaign revealed a political culture in South Carolina which allowed for furiously democratic grassroots campaigns and fostered large-scale political mobilization, the substance of the campaign revealed that the principles of "country-republicanism" still provided the ideological content of that political culture. The public debate between Nullifiers and Unionists in South Carolina was not primarily a debate over the tariff, slavery, or the personalities of Calhoun and Jackson. Instead, the debate over nullification revolved around competing concepts of how best to defend republican values of liberty and independence.[95] Calhoun and the Nullifiers argued that liberty and

---

[93]Levin M. Powell to Garrett J. Pendergast, March 10, 1833, quoted in Howard H. Wehmann, "Noise, Novelties, and Nullifiers: A U.S. Navy Officer's Impressions of the Nullification Controversy," *South Carolina Historical Magazine* 76 (January, 1975):21–24. Powell was a twenty-nine-year-old lieutenant serving on the sloop *Natchez,* which was stationed in Charleston harbor during the spring of 1833.

[94]Robert Duncan Bass, "The Autobiography of William John Grayson" (Ph.D. dissertation, University of South Carolina, 1934), pp. 68–169.

[95]The nullification campaign in South Carolina was not a debate over the tariff or a debate over slavery because a well-established consensus existed on both these questions. The tariff was oppressive and demanded strenuous opposition. Slavery was an essential form of labor and race control and had to be vigorously defended. The real debate was over how to oppose the tariff most effectively and over how best to defend slavery. Thus the nullification crisis was essentially a tactical dispute over means, not a philosophical dispute over aims. See, for example, Frederick Fraser to Mary Fraser, September 13, 1832, Frederic Fraser Papers, DU; Henry H. Townes to George F. Townes, December 2, 1832, Townes Family Papers, SCL; Address of Robert Witherspoon to "Fellow Citizens," July 4, 1832, Witherspoon Family Papers, SCL; Speech of John Simpson, c. 1833, John Simpson papers, DU; Address of George M. Witherspoon to "Fellow Citizens," c. 1833, George M. Witherspoon Papers, DU; Wilson, ed., *The Papers of John C. Calhoun,* vol. II, xxxiii–xxxix.

independence were best preserved through a unilateral assertion of state sovereignty, in the form of state interposition, which would suspend the operation of oppressive federal laws until each state of the Union, acting through state conventions, considered both the constitutionality and the political desirability of the law in question. If three-fourths of the states approved the law, state interposition would be overridden, but if the necessary number of states failed to give approval, the nullified law was permanently suspended.[96] By contrast, Unionists argued that the best defense of republican values lay in continued support of national politicians devoted to the purity of the Constitution and committed to a vigorous defense of Southern interests. Nullification, they charged, was not a legitimate constitutional remedy, but a radical, unconstitutional doctrine designed to precipitate disunion.[97]

Calhoun, no less than the Unionists, believed that the future of republican liberty was brighter with the Union than without it, but also believed that state interposition would strengthen the Union, though not the federal government, by improving the chances that conflicts of sections or interests could be compromised or resolved peacefully, instead of erupting into civil strife or triggering secession. "No government," Calhoun wrote in his personal draft of the South Carolina "Exposition," "based on the naked principle, that the majority ought to govern, however true the maxim in its proper sense, and under proper restrictions, ever preserved its liberty even for a generation. The history of all has been the same, violence, injustice, anarchy succeeded by the Government of one or a few, under which the people seek refuge from the more oppressive despotism of the many."[98] The Union, as Calhoun saw it, could only be a sanctuary for republican values as long as it was governed by republican principles. Nul-

[96]The purpose of nullification, in Calhoun's mind, was not to permanently thwart majority rule, but merely to force the settlement of important Constitutional issues by a direct appeal to the people of the individual states. Like all good republicans, Calhoun was aware of the dangers posed to republics by the excesses of democracy, or mob rule, but like most republicans of the Jeffersonian persuasion, he had great faith in the good judgment of the people. Calhoun saw one of the great virtues of nullification in the fact that it would place disputed issues directly in front of the people of the states. Calhoun explained his feelings on the matter to Duff Green. "In its tendency," Calhoun wrote, "I consider it [the tariff], by far the most dangerous question that has ever sprung up under our system; and mainly because its operation is so unequal among the parts. But I trust the good sense and virtue of the people, in which I put my trust, will find a remedy for this, as they have thus far, for all our political diseases." See John C. Calhoun to Duff Green, July 1, 1828, in Wilson, ed., *The Papers of John C. Calhoun*, vol. 10, p. 392.

[97]Carson, *James Louis Petigru*, pp. 91–114; Rippy, *Joel Poinsett*, p. 140; and Kibler, *B. F. Perry*, pp. 100–107. Kenneth M. Stampp, "The Concept of a Perpetual Union," *Journal of American History* 65 (June, 1978):5–33, argues that at the time of the nullification crisis the arguments for a perpetual union were far less sophisticated, and more reliant on emotion, than were the cases for nullification and peaceful secession.

[98]Draft of "The South Carolina Exposition," in Wilson, ed., *The Papers of John C. Calhoun*, vol. 10, p. 492. The "Exposition" was a document distinct from the "Protest," although they are often referred to as if they were a single document. Calhoun's rough draft of the "Exposition" was modified slightly by a special committee of the South Carolina House of Representatives constituted for the purpose of drafting a protest against the protective tariff. The "Protest" resolution was adopted by the House separately from the "Exposition." No draft of the "Protest" written in Calhoun's hand has survived.

lification was simply another mechanism to thwart the natural tendency of power to corrupt or aggrandize those who wield it.

The Unionists did not deny that high tariffs were oppressive or that they represented a threat to republican values. Nor did they deny that the tyranny of the many was as dangerous as the tyranny of the few. But they did refuse to concede that nullification was a safe and practical solution to the problem at hand. James Louis Petigru, the brilliant Charleston lawyer and leading Unionist spokesman, explained the Unionist position:

> There is no tariff party in South Carolina; we agree on every side that the tariff should be resisted by all constitutional means. So far there is no difference of opinion; but we are divided as to the character of the means that should be employed; and resistence by nullification is the fatal source of bitterness and discord. Even those who are in favor of nullification differ widely as to its character. It is recommended as constitutional and peaceful, when explained even by its advocates it assumes many different aspects, and furnishes an evil omen of interminable strife.[99]

The argument, then, between Nullifiers and Unionists, although terrifically bitter and divisive, was a disagreement over whether nullification was a proper remedy for the ills which plagued the American experiment in republicanism or whether it was a cure that was far worse than the disease.

Throughout the long and contentious campaign, leaders of both parties recruited followers from the local cliques and cabals scattered across every district. Calhoun was optimistic about the Nullifiers' chances from the very beginning. "As far as I can judge most of our leading men out[side] of Charleston have a correct conception of the subject," Calhoun told one of his top lieutenants. "This is gaining an important point. From them, truth will diffuse itself down among the people."[100] By 1832, the Nullifiers had clearly gained the momentum. During the late spring of 1832, Nullifier Henry Townes reported from Abbeville that "there are daily conversions to our doctrine" and that the Nullification party grappled only with "the shadow of opposition" because "the substance was long since annihilated."[101] Since the Calhounites had always been strong in Abbeville district, the Nullifiers' advantage there was hardly surprising. But encouraging reports from York, the home district of steadfast Unionist William Smith, revealed the significant gains made by the Nullifiers since 1828. William Randolph Hill, a Nullifier and grandson of Revolutionary hero William Hill, reported a successful pro-nullification rally in June, 1832, and observed, "Our cause is gaining." Hill added that he was confident that a majority of York district voters would support nullification by the time of the legislative elections in October.[102]

[99]Carson, *James Louis Petigru,* pp. 91–92.

[100]John C. Calhoun to William C. Preston, January 6, 1829, in Wilson, ed., *The Papers of John C. Calhoun,* vol. 10, pp. 545–546.

[101]Henry H. Townes to George F. Townes, June 6, 1832, Townes Family Papers, SCL.

[102]William Randolph Hill to Stephen D. Miller, June 6, 1832, Chesnut-Miller-Manning Papers, SCHS.

The Nullifiers' confidence was not misplaced. In the October elections, pro-nullification candidates forged a solid majority and routed the Unionists at the polls, winning over 60 percent of the vote in the state. In the Upcountry, where nearly two-thirds of the state's white population lived, the Nullifiers also won just over 60 percent of the vote and carried nine of the twelve election districts in the region. Outside of the Unionist strongholds in Greenville and Spartanburg districts, the Nullifiers polled nearly two-thirds of the vote in the Upcountry.[103] Moreover, J. P. Ochenkowski's recent analysis of the election returns shows that there was only a weak correlation between the percentage of votes cast in favor of nullification and the wealth, incidence of slaveholding, average size of slaveholdings, ratio of blacks to whites, or severity of economic distress in the various election districts. Party divisions had not been drawn along lines of planter against yeomen, slaveholder against non-slaveholder, Upcountryman and Lowcountryman, or commercial farmer against subsistence farmer. Since these social and economic factors do not appear to have been the major determinants of voting behavior, it seems likely that the crucial decisions were made on the basis of the ideological and tactical choices presented during the campaign, and that the Nullifiers had easily gotten the better of the exchange.[104]

Certainly the energetic mobilization efforts of both parties proved extraordinarily successful. Voter participation surged to an all-time high of 86 percent in the election of 1832. This huge turnout is all the more impressive because the election was close in only one Upcountry district, York, where the Nullifiers received 51 percent of the vote. In the other eleven districts, the winning party, whether Nullifier or Unionist, won at least 59 percent of the vote, and in seven of these districts the winning party's share of the vote was over 65 percent. In York, where the election was close, almost 95 percent of those eligible voted. In Laurens district, where the Nullifiers carried 60 percent of the vote, 99 percent of

[103]Chauncey Samuel Boucher, *The Nullification Controversy in South Carolina* (Chicago: University of Chicago Press, 1916), p. 203.

[104]Ochenkowski, "The Origins of Nullification in South Carolina," pp. 121–153. Ochenkowski unearthed valuable lists of tax returns from most of the parishes in the South Carolina Lowcountry. These tax lists allowed him to measure the impact of a variety of factors on voting behavior in the election of 1832. Ochenkowski's analysis shows that there was only a weak correlation (r = .3417) between the incidence of slaveholding and support for nullification in the Lowcountry. Moreover, the correlation between the size of the black majority and support for nullification was also weak (r = .3165). Also, based on an analysis of debt cases, Ochenkowski argues that, in the Upcountry, the Union party was strongest where economic distress was most acute, while Nullifiers were more successful in areas which were not hit as hard by economic woes. For another pointed critique of Freehling's analysis of voting patterns in the nullification election, see Paul H. Bergeron, "The Nullification Controversy Revisited," *Tennessee Historical Quarterly* 35 (Fall, 1976):263–275; see also Jane H. Pease and William Pease, "The Economics and Politics of Charleston's Nullification Crisis," *Journal of Southern History* 47 (November, 1981):335–362. For examples of how party lines were drawn at the local level, see William Joseph MacArthur, "Antebellum Politics in an Upcountry County: National, State, and Local Issues in Spartanburg County, South Carolina, 1850–1860" (M.A. thesis, University of South Carolina, 1966), pp. 1–18; James Wylie Gettys, "Mobilization for Secession in Greenville District" (M.A. thesis, University of South Carolina, 1967), pp. 3–15; and George C. Rogers, Jr., *A History of Georgetown County, South Carolina* (Columbia, S.C.: University of South Carolina Press, 1970), pp. 224–251.

all adult white males voted. These remarkably high levels of voter participation show that the issue of nullification captured the attention of the voters and that the campaign brought a new level of vigor to an already vigorous democracy in the Upcountry.[105]

Two months after the election, Calhoun, who had resigned the vice presidency, left South Carolina to return to Washington and assume his newly won seat in the United States Senate. He stopped overnight in Raleigh, North Carolina, where he explained the concept of nullification to a skeptical audience. Calhoun told his listeners that "the doctrine of nullification was perfectly understood in South Carolina from the Judge who presided on the Bench to the humblest tenant of a log-cabin in the Piney Woods."[106] Calhoun may have exaggerated only slightly. Pro-nullification broadsides were found among the papers of hardscrabble hill-country yeomen.[107] Almost nine out of ten eligible voters went to the polls. Even if they did not fully understand nullification, almost every white man in the Upcountry took the trouble to pass judgment on the issue.

Moreover, the rhetoric of the campaign revealed as much about South Carolina's political culture as did the high level of voter participation. The rhetoric and arguments of the campaign grew out of the state's deepest political instincts and passions and drew on the political language and political symbols with the most resonance in the hundreds of predominantly rural communities where the issue was ultimately decided. In this regard, the nullification campaign gave expression to the dearest hopes and deepest fears of South Carolinians. The voters' burning desire was to defend their liberty, the personal independence and virtue which allowed them to control their own persons, property, and family. Their gravest fear was that they would fall into slavery, that state of abject degradation which became the plight of those deprived of independence and basic political rights. South Carolina's familiarity with the day-to-day experience of the black chattels in their midst served only to intensify their fear of submission and dependence.[108] It was precisely this fear of political enslavement, of becoming the political vassals of a Northern majority, that spurred the Nullifiers to action. As planter John Springs, a leading York district Nullifier, explained in 1832, the tariff issue was for the South "completely a question of freedom or slavery, and when that is the issue there is no counting of cost, and it is not a time

[105]See Table 3.1. Calculations made from Boucher, *The Nullification Controversy*, p. 203, and *Fifth Census of the United States, 1830* (Washington, D.C.: Duff Green, 1832), pp. 94–95.

[106]William Gaston to Mrs. H. M. Manly, December 31, 1832, William Gaston Papers, SHC.

[107]Pro-nullification broadside, c. 1832, Lipscomb Papers, SHC.

[108]For examples, see Robert Y. Hayne, *An Oration Delivered in the Presbyterian Church in Columbia on July 4, 1831* (Columbia, S.C., 1831); Entry of November 29, 1832, Samuel Cram Jackson Diary, SHC; Unknown editor of the Spartanburg *Flag* to Taylor Bynum, July 20, 1832, Townes Family Papers, SHC; J. Edward Pearson to Stephen D. Miller, December 26, 1832, Chesnut-Miller-Manning Papers, SCHS; Columbia *Southern Times and State Gazette*, August 24, 1832, and January 11, 1833. On the persistence of these concerns, see "An Address Delivered before the Citizens of Spartanburg and Union," July 4, 1843, John Winsmith Papers, SCL; Speech to the Secession Convention, December, 1860, William King Easley Papers, SCL.

Table 3.1   Voter Participation in the Nullification Election—1832

District	Number of Votes Cast	Percent of Eligible Voters Participating	Percentage of Votes for Nullification
Abbeville	2612	86.3	64
Edgefield	2269	78.5	73
Fairfield	1850	89.8	94
Chester	1853	90.0	59
Greenville	1811	84.0	28
Lancaster	1053	83.6	41
Laurens	2469	99.8	60
Newberry	1294	69.9	89
Pendleton	3749	82.4	67
Spartanburg	2672	85.4	31
Union	1901	91.7	71
York	2178	94.4	51
Upcountry	25,711	86.0	60

Sources: Chauncey Boucher, *The Nullification Controversy in South Carolina,* p. 203; *Fifth Census of the United States, 1830* (Washington, D.C.: Duff Green, 1832), pp. 94–95.

to look back or dally by the wayside."[109] Even by mid-1833, when the compromise tariff had been adopted and further confrontation between South Carolina and the federal government was thus temporarily averted, the prominent Charleston Nullifier Henry L. Pinckney celebrated with a premonitory description of the horrible degradation which followed the loss of liberty:

> And what is slavery? The canker of the soul—the grave of genius and of every noble feeling—to be called a freeman, yet know that you are not free—to speak of your property, yet know that you are not free to enjoy its fruits—to speak of your rights, yet know that you have none worth naming, and that you dare speak of *them* only by the forebearance of a master—to relinquish your judgment and violate your conscience at the bidding of a tyrant—to look at the sun and be rebuked by his brightness—to look at the heavens, and see them blush for your degradation—to look at the mountain, and feel that you crawl, as a worm on the earth.[110]

The Unionists also drew heavily on the freeman's fear of being reduced to slavery, a fear deeply embedded in the rich "country-republican" tradition of South Carolina. Appealing for his fellow Upcountrymen not to support nullification, B. F. Perry spoke about liberty and slavery with a passion equal to that of his opponents:

> But will the people of South Carolina, professing an attachment to republican governments, volunteer their services in a cause so fatal to *liberty,* to

[109]John Springs to Leroy Springs, October 25, 1832, Springs Family Papers, SHC.

[110]Henry L. Pinckney, *An Oration Delivered in Charleston on July the Fourth* . . . (Charleston, S.C.: A. E. Miller, 1833), pp. 55–56.

honor, and to themselves? Are they willing . . . Are they ready to incur its guilt and meet a traitor's doom? If so, it behooves the Union Party to be prepared to defend themselves against a *brother's tyranny,* and to *die* like Freemen, rather than *live* like Slaves.[111]

All South Carolinians agreed that the purpose of politics was to protect the liberty of the citizens from its many enemies. They also endorsed the corollary assumption that the function of the politician was to identify those enemies, devise the appropriate strategy of resistance, and mobilize the people behind the cause. During the conflict over nullification, both parties believed that the very foundations of liberty and republican government were threatened and took their case to the voters in those terms. Calhoun and the Nullifiers identified the enemies as external ones: first in the form of high tariffs championed by special manufacturing interests in New England and approved by a numerical majority in Congress, and later embodied in the high-handed usurpation of power by the executive branch under the imperious Andrew Jackson. By 1832, the national government itself had become, in the eyes of the Nullifiers, the chief threat to liberty and the principal enemy of the people.[112] The Unionists simply were not prepared to go that far in their indictment of federal power, and instead continued to identify enemies, such as corrupt and demagogic politicians (Nullifiers), within the state as well as outside it. Only James L. Petigru, South Carolina's most dogged Federalist, scorned the hyperbolic rhetoric of the nullification campaign and expressed disenchantment with and alienation from South Carolina's strange and powerful political culture:

> I am devilishly puzzled to know whether my friends are mad or I beside myself. . . . That we are treated like slaves, that we are slaves in fact, that we are worse than slaves and made to go on all fours, are stories that seem to me very odd, and make me doubt whether I am not under some mental eclipse, since I can not see what is so plain to others. But I am not surprised that the people have been persuaded they are ill-used by government. Old Hooker says, "If any man will go about to persuade the people that they are badly governed, he will not fail to have plenty of followers." And I am inclined to think that the better the polity in which men live, the easier it is to persuade them they are cruelly oppressed.[113]

Either unable to grasp the basic axioms of South Carolina politics, or unwilling to accept its radical fear of power and profound suspicion of government, the maverick Petigru soon found himself in virtual political isolation, an isolation which testified as much to the power of the state's devotion to its republican

[111]Greenville *Mountaineer,* December 22, 1832.

[112]John C. Calhoun to F. W. Symmes, July 26, 1831, in Wilson, ed., *The Papers of John C. Calhoun,* vol. 11, pp. 413–440. For a comparative perspective, see Thornton, *Politics and Power,* pp. 50–58, 117–152; Watson, *Jacksonian Politics and Community Conflict,* pp. 151–197; Miles, *Jacksonian Democracy in Mississippi,* pp. 102–116.

[113]James Louis Petigru to William John Grayson, [c. 1830], in Carson, *James Louis Petigru,* pp. 79–80.

tradition as it did to Petigru's unyielding and anachronistic brand of high Federalism.[114]

Victorious at the polls, and able to muster a substantial majority of South Carolinians behind their cause, the Nullifiers found but little sympathy for their position in other Southern states, where the defense of Southern rights was still closely identified with the oversized persona of Andrew Jackson. Yet if few Southerners agreed with the logic of nullification or dared provoke a direct confrontation with the federal government, even fewer found the prospect of seeing a state coerced by federal power palatable. As a result, all sides worked toward a compromise. South Carolina nullified the tariff, and then Congress agreed to a graduated downward adjustment of the tariff. Having compromised the tariff to South Carolina's satisfaction, Congress passed a Force Bill denying the principle of nullification. South Carolina responded by nullifying the Force Bill. In the end, the confrontation ended in a stalemate which allowed both sides to claim victory. Calhoun and the Nullifiers had lowered the tariff, accomplishing the purpose of nullification while failing to establish the principle of state interposition. Jackson and the Congress had acted boldly to "save" the Union and, in all probability, had discredited the concept of nullification, not by proving it unconstitutional, but by fastening the stigma of political isolation on its supporters. With nullification behind him, Jackson was free to turn his full and considerable political powers against the Bank of the United States, while Calhoun turned his formidable skills toward salving the political wounds at home and monitoring Jackson's vigorous use and expansion of executive power in Washington.[115]

Despite the conciliatory aspects of the Compromise of 1833, the nullification crisis left a number of indelible marks, perhaps even scars, on South Carolina and its body politic. Undoubtedly, support of nullification isolated most of South Carolina's national politicians, and particularly Calhoun, from many of their natural allies. Just at the moment when loose political coalitions were beginning to form in response to Jackson's Bank War, South Carolina politicians were being pushed away from the mainstream by the momentum of nullification.[116]

[114]Ford, "James Louis Petigru," pp. 159–166; Alfred Huger to William Ravenel, June 24, 1865, William Ravenel Papers, SHC.

[115]Merrill D. Peterson, *Olive Branch and Sword: The Compromise of 1833* (Baton Rouge: Louisiana State University Press, 1982), especially pp. 85–127; Wiltse, *Calhoun: Nullifier*, pp. 169–195; Cooper, *The Politics of Slavery*, pp. 44–49; Richard B. Latner, *The Presidency of Andrew Jackson: White House Politics, 1829–1837* (Athens: University of Georgia Press, 1979), pp. 140–163; Major L. Wilson, *Space, Time, and Freedom: The Quest for Nationality and the Irrepressible Conflict, 1815–1861* (Westport, Conn.: Greenwood Press, 1974).

[116]See Latner, *The Presidency of Andrew Jackson*, pp. 164–192; Burton W. Folsom, "Party Formation and Development in Jacksonian America: The Old South," *Journal of American Studies* 7 (December, 1973):217–229; Clyde N. Wilson, ed., *The Papers of John C. Calhoun* (Columbia, S.C.: University of South Carolina Press, 1979), vol. 12, xxvi–xxxii. Both Thornton, *Politics and Power*, pp. 30–47, and Watson, *Jacksonian Politics and Community Conflict*, pp. 151–197, emphasize the importance of banking issues in precipitating and solidifying party divisions in Alabama and North Carolina, respectively.

At the state and local level, the legacies of nullification were even more profound. The bitter, often violent, political divisions of the nullification era continued to be important in local politics. For many South Carolinians, the nullification question became a political benchmark by which candidates for public office were judged for at least a decade, if not a generation. Districts and beats continued to be divided into Unionist and Nullifier factions, and the political pedigree earned in the nullification campaign remained an important, though not always a determining, factor in the election of most state legislators, sheriffs, and district tax collectors. The old labels, "Nullifier" and "Unionist," and the old allegiances yielded slowly in South Carolina during the 1830s, and the existing divisions made the state more difficult to organize into competing camps of Democrats and Whigs, even though those party labels gradually gained significance in South Carolina during the years of the Van Buren Administration.[117]

The nullification campaign also established a tradition of large-scale political mobilization which might be ignored somewhat when less compelling issues dominated political life, but which would never entirely disappear. Nullification took partisan politics to the hustings, literally to the stumps, muster fields, and "forks of the creek," even in the most remote or isolated areas of the state, and every major issue, every important election, in South Carolina politics would be contested on those grounds, and in those intimate forums, for the rest of the nineteenth century and perhaps beyond. It is this massive popular involvement of the "common man" in public life that historians have viewed as the most definitive characteristic of the movement known as "Jacksonian democracy." Ironically, the nullification crisis brought "Jacksonian democracy" to South Carolina at the same time that it placed the state and Old Hickory irreconcilably at odds with each other. Moreover, the nullification campaign not only brought "Jacksonian democracy" to South Carolina without Jackson but it also brought very high levels of voter participation to South Carolina politics eight years before the presidential election of 1840 inspired heavy turnouts of voters in the rest of the country.[118]

[117]On the continued importance of the Nullifier and Unionist labels, see James Hemphill to W. R. Hemphill, January 5, 1834, and James Hemphill to W. R. Hemphill, January 26, 1841, Hemphill Family Papers, DU; Henry Draft to William L. Miller, June 4, 1835, John Fox Papers, SCL; Entry of February 22, 1839, Benjamin F. Perry Diary, vol. 2, SHC; John Springs to Andrew Baxter Springs, January 21, 1843, Springs Family Papers, SHC; Speech of Joseph Starke Sims to "The Citizens of Union District," [c. December, 1838], Joseph Starke Sims Papers, DU; Kibler, *B. F. Perry*, pp. 159–176; Carson, *James Louis Petigru*, pp. 157–202; MacArthur, "Antebellum Politics in an Upcountry County," pp. 9–14.

[118]Sean Wilentz, "On Class and Politics in Jacksonian America," *Reviews in American History* 10 (December, 1982):45–63; Ronald P. Formisano, "Toward a Reorientation of Jacksonian Politics: A Review of the Literature, 1959–1975," *Journal of American History* 63 (June, 1976):42–65. The traditional view of the Jacksonian era as the "age of the common man" is skillfully presented in Marvin Meyers, *The Jacksonian Persuasion: Politics and Belief* (Stanford: Stanford University Press, 1957); and John William Ward, *Andrew Jackson: Symbol for an Age* (New York: Oxford University Press, 1955). The difficulty of defining "Jacksonian democracy" is discussed at length in Lee Benson, *The Concept of Jacksonian Democracy: New York as a Test Case* (Princeton, N.J.:

But "Jacksonian democracy" in South Carolina was "Jacksonian democracy" with important idiosyncracies, differences which placed South Carolina defiantly outside the national Jacksonian mainstream. The essence of Jacksonian politics was to identify a particular threat to the liberty and independence of the people, to make that threat into a pet political issue or "hobby," and to ride that hobby to partisan advantage in the next election. In Jacksonian America outside South Carolina, however, politicans were quick to identify enemies of republican values, such as special privilege, prerogative, and centers of concentrated economic power with their political opponents. The crusade in defense of republicanism was also a crusade to gain a numerical advantage for a particular party on election day. The common litany of enemies recited in the typical Jacksonian campaign speech outside South Carolina included concentrated wealth, centralized power, special privilege, and the opposition party. It was the party system which gave shape to that amorphous struggle between the defenders of republican values and their tireless enemies; it was the party system which gave Jacksonian democracy the internal dynamism necessary to sustain popular enthusiasm; and, ultimately, it was the party system which contained all conflicts and enthusiasms through an institutional structure which encouraged compromise in the interest of its own survival. In South Carolina, politicians identified threats to liberty not only with opposing factions but also with hostile political forces outside the state. The crusade in defense of republican values was designed first to establish political advantage within South Carolina, then to effect reconciliation or establish a consensus within the state without sacrificing the initial advantage, and finally to march as a solid phalanx into battle against the enemies of liberty. The difference between Jacksonian politics in South Carolina and elsewhere in the South lay chiefly in the perception of most South Carolinians that the forces working to undermine republican values were operating only in Washington, or at least beyond the borders of South Carolina, while other Southern states usually found a number of hostile forces at work within their own borders.[119]

The danger inherent in South Carolina's unique brand of politics was that, without the fetters of party to restrain it, the exuberant "friends and neighbors" democracy might spin wildly out of control, especially if South Carolina politicians, also freed from the constraints of party discipline, encouraged it to do so. Lacking the mitigating influence of party, South Carolina could mobilize in protest faster and make that protest more radical than any other state. South Carolina had all the energy of grassroots democracy but none of the chains of the

---

Princeton University Press, 1961). For the best introduction to the subject of massive popular participation in politics, see Ronald P. Formisano, "Deferential Participant Politics: The Early Republican's Political Culture, 1789–1840," *American Political Science Review* 68 (June, 1974):473–487; see also Richard P. McCormick, "New Perspectives on Jacksonian Politics," *American Historical Review* 65 (January, 1960):288–301.

[119]On the crucial role of parties in restraining radicalism, see Michael F. Holt, *The Political Crisis of the 1850s* (New York: John Wiley and Sons, 1978), pp. 1–38.

Jacksonian party system, a combination which proved to be a fine prescription for radicalism.[120] Unionist James Petigru explained the irony of his state's radicalism with strong disapproval:

> The majority of our folks are such citizens as Rome had in her worse days. No republic ever had worse as far as their duty to the United States is concerned. Here is one of the anomalies produced by our strange system: As citizens of the United States they are traitors, but as citizens of the State they are true men.[121]

Calhoun, of course, viewed South Carolina's political independence as virtue, and saw little to fear in his state's radical defense of republican values. "The danger of disunion is small," he remarked in 1834, "that of despotism great."[122]

[120]Weir, "South Carolinian as Extremist," pp. 86–103; Stewart, "'A Great Talking and Eating Machine,'" pp. 218–220.

[121]James Louis Petigru to Hugh S. Legare, July 15, 1833, in Carson, *James Louis Petigru*, pp. 123–124.

[122]John C. Calhoun, "Speech in Support of His Bill to Repeal the Force Act," April 9, 1834, in Wilson, ed., *The Papers of John C. Calhoun*, vol. 12, pp. 277–298. The quotation is taken from p. 297.

4

"Stand Now on My Own Bottom": Politics and Party in South Carolina in the Post-Nullification Era

The so-called Compromise of 1833 ended South Carolina's dramatic confrontation with the federal government. On the national level, the compromise left South Carolina isolated in a political world increasingly divided into two camps, one composed of the faithful followers of Old Hickory, and the other peopled by those opposed to the dictation of national policy by King Andrew and his court.[1] In South Carolina, the political strife generated by the nullification campaign lingered on. Two hostile, and sometimes armed, factions continued to battle each other long after the compromise tariff bill was accepted in Washington. A solid majority of South Carolinians were Nullifiers, and those who had championed state interposition believed that a united South Carolina, acting alone, could wield considerable power in national politics. The Nullifiers, with Calhoun at their head, sought to fashion a strategy for defending the minority interests of the South within a Union in which Southerners would soon be hopelessly outnumbered. At the same time, the sizable Unionist minority in South Carolina, themselves outnumbered within the state, retained strong ties to the Jackson Administration and hoped eventually to reintegrate South Carolina into the national mainstream. On the whole, the Unionists believed that the special interests of the South would be best defended by enlarging, or at least maintaining, Southern influence on the national parties. Undoubtedly Unionist leaders, from Petigru to Perry, hoped that their role in guiding South Carolina away from its defiant stance of 1832 and back into the national mainstream would win them the prominence and prestige necessary to diminish Calhoun's influence over South

---

[1]Charles M. Wiltse, *John C. Calhoun: Nullifier, 1829–1839* (Indianapolis: Bobbs-Merrill, 1949), pp. 143–204; Merrill D. Peterson, *Olive Branch and Sword: The Compromise of 1833* (Baton Rouge: Louisiana State University Press, 1982).

Carolina politics. Almost every Unionist leader bemoaned the baneful influence of Calhoun and attributed much of the state's radicalism to his leadership. South Carolina, according to James Louis Petigru, was "under an evil star" whose pernicious pull on the state's psyche could not be broken until "the wings of Calhoun's ambition" were clipped.[2]

Indeed, one of the most familiar quips about Palmetto politics during the 1830s and 1840s was that "when Calhoun took snuff, South Carolina sneezed." Like most clichés, this bit of political folklore both exaggerated and trivialized the nature and extent of Calhoun's influence in South Carolina. Calhoun never "ruled" the state in the manner of an autocratic feudal lord ruling his own personal fiefdom, but instead exercised strong leadership in South Carolina affairs based on the support and confidence he enjoyed among the state's citizens. This support and confidence was always crucial to Calhoun's success, and it was always temporary and conditional, never permanent and absolute. Calhoun worked hard to maintain the respect of his native state. South Carolina's continued support of his positions and policies had to be perpetually renegotiated and reaffirmed in the various forums provided by the political culture of South Carolina.[3]

From 1833 until 1850, South Carolina, under Calhoun's leadership, pursued an independent course in national politics, sometimes allied with the Democratic party and at other times looking to form temporary coalitions crossing normal party boundaries, but always looking for ways to protect Southern interests while preserving the American experiment in republican government. At the state level, Calhoun and his lieutenants were occupied with first restoring and then maintaining unity within the state so that it could speak with a single voice on national affairs. In order to establish and maintain unity within the Palmetto state, Calhounites not only had to reconcile Nullifiers and Unionists but they also had to douse a series of political brushfires of varying intensity ignited by Calhoun's opponents. Because of Calhoun's national prominence and his important role in the debate over national policy on a variety of matters, the South Carolina legislature involved itself to an unusual degree with the consideration of resolutions which outlined the state's position on national issues.

While devoting a good portion of its time to national questions, the legislature also grappled with problems created by South Carolina's long economic decline and worsened by the protracted agricultural slump of the late 1830s and early 1840s. Debates over the state's banking system and over schemes for

[2]Lillian A. Kibler, *Benjamin F. Perry: South Carolina Unionist* (Durham, N.C.: Duke University Press, 1946), pp. 137–158; J. Fred Rippy, *Joel R. Poinsett, Versatile American* (Durham, N.C.: Duke University Press, 1935), pp. 150–166; James Louis Petigru to William Drayton, March 26, 1834, and James Louis Petigru to Hugh Swinton Legaré, October 26, 1834, in James P. Carson, *Life, Letters, and Speeches of James Louis Petigru* (Washington, D.C.: W. H. Lowdermilk, 1920), pp. 130–131, 163.

[3]See Clyde N. Wilson, ed., *The Papers of John C. Calhoun* (Columbia, S.C.: University of South Carolina Press, 1981), vol. 14, pp. xviii–xxiv; Charles M. Wiltse, *John C. Calhoun: Sectionalist, 1840–1850* (Indianapolis: Bobbs-Merrill, 1951), pp. 50–59.

internal improvements involved state politicians in a series of rather acrimonious controversies which belied the image of a harmonious and cohesive polity which South Carolina tried to present to the rest of the nation. In fact, throughout the 1830s and 1840s, periodic outbreaks of bitter factional squabbling divided the state, even as the overwhelming majority of South Carolinians grew more and more alarmed at the rising tide of antislavery sentiment. The factional alignments generated by these controversies never hardened into a permanent two-party system, but they nevertheless kept the fury and fervor of political competition alive in South Carolina. Throughout each political seizure, however, South Carolinians remained motivated, as they had been during the nullification crisis, by the love of independence and the fear of power. Regardless of the particular issue which engaged the political energies of South Carolinians at any given moment, their vigil in defense of liberty continued.[4]

At the height of the nullification crisis, feelings ran high among both Nullifiers and Unionists. Abbeville Nullifier Henry Townes admitted the difficulty of keeping "the War Dogs chained" until after the nullification convention acted and Congress responded. By December 1832, Townes boasted that the Nullifiers of Abbeville "would rally as one man and spill every drop of blood tomorrow if their state called them" but worried that "the great mass of the nullifiers will be disappointed if nullification is carried out entirely by civil means."[5] Some visitors to the state agreed. Samuel Cram Jackson, a Congregational minister from Massachusetts who was touring South Carolina to escape the harsh New England winter, reported from Columbia in late January 1833 that, if "President Jackson was to enter this state, he would be assassinated without the least doubt." Even "the women would shoot him," Jackson added, "for they are as strong nullifiers as any, and in some cases, urge their husbands and sons to revolution."[6] The Unionists were fewer in number but no less devoted to their cause. In early December 1832, the Unionist majority in Greenville district was characterized as "very inflammable and ready to fight for the Union and against nullification." In Columbia, older Unionists threatened Nullifiers with the resistance of "our bayonet at every step." By early February 1833, the spirit of resistance ran so high among Upcountry Unionists that Benjamin F. Perry feared that the crisis would produce "a dreadful civil war" in the South.[7]

The Compromise of 1833 ended the battle over nullification in Washington, but it did little to lessen the hostility between Nullifiers and Unionists within

[4]For an example of a more or less typical legislative session, see *Journal of the Proceedings of the Senate and House of Representatives of the General Assembly of South Carolina, 1838* (Columbia, S.C.: A. H. Pemberton, 1839).

[5]Henry H. Townes to George F. Townes, August 2, 1832, and Henry H. Townes to George F. Townes, December 2, 1832, Townes Family Papers, SCL.

[6]Samuel C. Jackson to Elizabeth R. Jackson, January 28, 1833, Samuel Cram Jackson Papers, SCL.

[7]Entry of December 4, 1832, Benjamin F. Perry Diary, vol. 1, SHC; Samuel C. Jackson to William True, December 14, 1832, Samuel Cram Jackson Papers, SCL; entry of February 11, 1833, Benjamin F. Perry Diary, vol. 1, SHC.

South Carolina. Much of the continued tension between the two rival factions centered around the controversial test oath. The original Ordinance of Nullification, passed in November 1832, contained a clause requiring all civil and military officers of the state to swear an oath pledging to support and implement state interposition. When the Convention repealed the nullification ordinance in March 1833, the test oath was automatically repealed. Many ardent Nullifiers then urged that a new test oath be attached to the ordinance which nullified the Force Bill. The Convention was in a conciliatory mood, however, and decided to delegate special authority to enact a test oath to the state legislature, which was not scheduled to meet until the following November. When the legislature finally met, it decided, after considerable debate, to enact a simple military oath requiring new militia officers to pledge "faithful and true allegiance" to the state of South Carolina. Nullifiers considered the oath mild for two reasons. First, only new militia officers and not old militia leaders or civil authorities were required to take the oath. Second, the oath was vague on the issue of sovereignty, requiring only that militia officers swear allegiance to the state and not that they recognize allegiance to the state to be superior to allegiance to the federal government.[8]

Unionist leaders attending the legislative session in Columbia would have preferred the defeat of all test oaths, but, failing that, they were generally satisfied that the new test oath was not incompatible with loyalty to the federal government. Joel Poinsett, who had organized Unionist militia companies during the crisis of the previous winter, advised Unionist militia officers to take the new oath. James L. Petigru was indignant about this new affront to the Unionists, but after the usual grousing, he conceded that the oath was vague and recommended that it be quietly tolerated.[9]

Benjamin F. Perry's mountaineer constituency and other rank-and-file Unionists throughout the state, however, refused to accept the oath, and threatened full-scale rebellion if any attempt was made to enforce it. The majority of Unionists failed to see the eager hands of compromise at work in the passage of the new oath and feared that future judges might interpret the oath as a vow of absolute allegiance to the state. Hundreds of Unionist militiamen, concentrated heavily in the Upcountry districts of Greenville, Spartanburg, and Union, declined to take the oath, but remained organized as an illegal militia. Unionist leaders, who had seriously underestimated the militancy of their followers, found themselves faced with a rebellion within their own ranks that proved difficult to quell.[10] In Spartanburg district, Unionist leader James Edward Henry judged that

[8]Pendleton *Messenger*, March 12, 1834. For a thorough discussion of the test oath controversy, see William W. Freehling, *Prelude to Civil War: The Nullification Controversy in South Carolina, 1816–1836* (New York: Harper and Row, 1965), pp. 309–321.

[9]Simpson Bobo to Joel R. Poinsett, February 5, 1833, Joel R. Poinsett to Andrew Jackson, March 23, 1833, and Joel R. Poinsett to F. Tyrrell, March 25, 1833, in Grace E. Heilman and Bernard S. Levin, eds., *Calendar of Joel R. Poinsett Papers in the Henry D. Gilpin Collection* (Philadelphia: Historical Society of Pennsylvania, 1941), pp. 50–53; Petigru to William Drayton, March 26, 1834, in Carson, *James Louis Petigru,* p. 130.

[10]Greenville *Mountaineer,* February 8 and 22, 1834; George McDuffie to Waddy Thompson,

"the probabilities are greatly in favor of a revolution by an appeal to arms on the part of the Union Party in the up-country." Henry advised moderation, only to find himself "cried down by knaves" and branded "as a traitor to the cause which [he had] heretofore sustained." Most Unionist leaders in the Upcountry were "opposed to violence," but Henry feared that the militant spirit engendered among the rank-and-file would "never permanently subside until they have tasted blood—and felt some of the horrors of civil war."[11] At meetings in Greenville and Spartanburg in February 1834, Perry urged his fellow Unionists to seek legal redress before turning to armed resistance, and in March, Edward McCready, a militia lieutenant from Charleston, refused to take the oath and sued for his commission to be granted anyway, starting the legal battle against the test oath.[12]

Eventually the test oath case reached the state Court of Appeals in Columbia. The case pitted some of the best young legal minds in the state against each other. Brilliant young Beaufort attorney Robert Barnwell Rhett, probably with covert assistance from Governor Robert Y. Hayne, argued for the test oath on behalf of the Nullifiers, and Petigru, who had quickly risen to the top of the Charleston bar, Thomas S. Grimké, scion of Charleston's most distinguished legal family, and Abram Blanding, a prominent Columbia business lawyer, argued against the test oath for the Unionists. The legal arguments presented by both sides were inspired, but the Court's decision was nevertheless rendered along partisan lines. Unionist justices John Belton O'Neall and David Johnson found the oath in violation of the state constitution, while the lone Nullifier on the Court, William Harper, dissented. The decision was announced on June 2, 1834, and Nullifiers immediately defiled the ruling as "corrupt, slavish, and stupid" and demanded that Governor Hayne call the legislature into a special session for the purpose of impeaching the two Unionist judges. Hayne, after consultation with other leading Nullifiers, decided not to attempt punitive action against the Unionist judges, but worked in the 1834 elections to achieve the two-thirds' majority in the state legislature necessary to pass a constitutional amendment legalizing the test oath.[13]

January 24, 1834, Waddy Thompson Papers, LC; George F. Townes to John A. Townes, February 4, 1834, Townes Family Papers, SCL.

[11]James Edward Henry to Samuel F. Patterson, January 31, 1834, Samuel Finley Patterson Papers, DU.

[12]Kibler, *Perry*, p. 163; Wiltse, *Calhoun: Nullifier*, pp. 201–204; Freehling, *Prelude To Civil War*, pp. 317–319. The test-oath controversy aroused so much bitterness because it revealed the basic ideological division between Nullifiers and Unionists. Nullifiers believed that sovereignty inhered in the states, who had, in turn, delegated some authority to the federal government. Thus the principal allegiance of every citizen belonged to the state. According to this view, the oath pledging loyalty to the state had to transcend all other oaths, as a matter both of logic and of political necessity. Unionists, of course, disagreed.

[13]Robert Barnwell Rhett (Smith), *Argument Delivered in the Court of Appeals in the State of South Carolina, 3 April, 1834* (Charleston, S.C.: J. S. Burger, 1834); Thomas Smith Grimké, *Argument Delivered in the Court of Appeals in the State of South Carolina, 2 and 3 April, 1834* (Charleston, S.C.: J. S. Burger, 1834); Carson, *Petigru*, pp. 131–139; Theodore D. Jervey, *Robert Y. Hayne and His Times* (New York: Macmillan, 1909), pp. 373–381; James Hamilton, Jr., to Waddy Thompson, May 23, 1834, James Hamilton Papers, SHC.

Earlier in the spring of 1834, months before the Court struck down the test oath, both Unionists and Nullifiers had begun preparations for a tough election campaign. The Court's decision had raised the stakes. Although they expected a tough contest, the Nullifiers were confident that they would win control of the state legislature, and reasonably confident that they could win over two-thirds of the seats. Virtually assured of this prize, Nullifiers were also interested in winning congressional elections, and, in particular, in controlling the so-called "Western" congressional district, which included Pendleton, Calhoun's home district, and Greenville, home of Ben Perry and an important Unionist stronghold. In 1834, the Nullifier candidate was incumbent Warren R. Davis, a Greenville attorney and strong ally of Calhoun. Unionist notables in the district appealed to Perry to make the race against Davis, and the prominent Greenville Unionist yielded to the pressures of party loyalty and announced his candidacy.[14]

The test oath was the central issue of the campaign. In June, Perry began a summer of hard campaigning, making a house-to-house canvass in areas, such as the Pickens half of the Pendleton election district, where he was not well known. Perry warned the voters that they were "in danger of being . . . deprived of the liberty of Conscience and robbed of [their] rights as Freemen" unless they actively opposed the test oath which threatened to guarantee their "Slavery and Vassalage."[15] Aware of Perry's popularity among the mountaineers, Davis supporters organized "Whig Associations," composed largely of Nullifiers, who worked on Davis's behalf throughout the district, and courted followers of Pickens Unionist Joseph Grisham. Although Grisham had been unsuccessful in an earlier race against Davis, his supporters were miffed when Perry was chosen to carry the Union banner in 1834. Perry appealed to Grisham for aid, but while Grisham promised to do what he could, he also pleaded that he could not be expected "to quit [his] home now and ride about the country with no excuse but to promote [Perry's] election."[16]

Calhoun, apparently, took no active part in the canvass and spent little time rallying the faithful privately. Davis, Calhoun noted, had been "weakened by his long and frequent absences from his constituents," but Calhoun was confident that Davis could recover lost ground because "his manners are very popular."[17] Not all Nullifiers were as optimistic as Calhoun. Greenville native Henry Townes expected "a very close contest" between Davis and Perry and worried that a Perry victory "would have a bad effect at home and abroad."[18] But when

[14]Benjamin F. Perry, *Reminiscences of Public Men* (Philadelphia: John D. Avil, 1883), pp. 302–307; Kibler, *Perry,* pp. 163–169.

[15]Entries of July 25 and September 5, 1833, and October 26, 1834, Benjamin F. Perry Diary, vol. 1, SHC; Pendleton *Messenger,* August 27, 1834; Greenville *Mountaineer,* August 23, 1834; Kibler, *Perry,* p. 167.

[16]Pendleton *Messenger,* August 27, 1834; Joseph Grisham to B. F. Perry, quoted in Kibler, *Perry,* p. 165.

[17]John C. Calhoun to Duff Green, September 20, 1833, in Clyde N. Wilson, ed., *The Papers of John C. Calhoun* (Columbia, S.C.: University of South Carolina, 1979), vol. 12, pp. 362–363.

[18]Henry H. Townes to George F. Townes, September 21, 1834, Townes Family Papers, SCL.

the election returns were tallied in mid-October, Calhoun's reading of public opinion proved correct, although the election was extremely close. Davis polled 2,925 votes to 2,855 for Perry. Perry had carried the Unionist stronghold of Greenville by nearly 1,100 votes, but Davis carried Anderson by almost the same margin and edged Perry by 90 votes in Pickens.[19] Perry blamed his defeat on the half-hearted support he received from the Grisham faction in Pickens and on the "cursed Presbyterians" and other pious Christians who held Perry's duelling record against him.[20] The Nullifiers were delighted that a proven Unionist vote-getter such as Perry failed to win in the congressional district with the highest percentage of yeoman farmers in the state.

In the elections for seats in the state legislature the Nullifiers easily won the two-thirds' majority needed to add the controversial test oath amendment to the state constitution. With their position heartily endorsed by the electorate, leading Nullifiers, at Calhoun's behest, moved toward compromise. Fire-eating Nullifier James Hamilton approached his former law partner, James L. Petigru, and proposed to write the new amendment in language that could be accepted by Unionists. After hours of discussion Hamilton and Petigru agreed that "the allegiance required by the oath . . . is the allegiance which every citizen owes the State consistently with the Constitution of the United States."[21] Also, the Nullifiers agreed to postpone efforts at judicial reform and to table a proposed treason bill. In return Unionist leaders promised not to challenge the new test oath and to support ardent Nullifier George McDuffie as a "unification" candidate for governor.[22] The radical Hamilton promised Petigru that he would "work as hard now for peace as he ever did for nullification, at the risk of dividing his party forever." Even the usually skeptical Petigru allowed himself a moment of euphoria and proclaimed, "The spell of party is broken and Nullification in Car-

---

[19]Greenville *Mountaineer*, November 1, 1834. As mentioned in an earlier chapter, Pendleton district, which was created in 1789, was maintained as an election district until 1854. In 1827, however, the judicial district of Pendleton was divided into Anderson and Pickens districts, with courthouses in the towns of Anderson and Pickens. Officially, election results were reported for Pendleton only as a whole, but on occasion local newspaper editors would break the returns down and report for Anderson and Pickens individually. The unofficial returns for the Perry-Davis race were:

	Davis	Perry
Greenville	419	1,509
Pickens	776	688
Anderson	1,730	658
Total	2,925	2,855

[20]Kibler, *Perry*, pp. 168–169. During the newspaper wars of the nullification era, Perry, then editor of the *Mountaineer*, had fought a duel with Turner Bynum, editor of the pro-nullification Greenville *Sentinel*. Bynum was mortally wounded in the duel, which Perry later called "the most painful event in my life."

[21]James L. Petigru to Hugh Swinton Legaré, December 15, 1834, in Carson, *James Louis Petigru*, pp. 167–171.

[22]I. W. Hayne to James H. Hammond, December 8, 1834, Hammond Papers, LC (microfilm at SCL); Freehling, *Prelude to Civil War*, pp. 320–321.

olina is no more than a recollection. We have compromised and buried the tomahawk." Petigru was justifiably proud of his own role in the arrangement of a compromise but acknowledged that "Calhoun was the adviser of pacification."[23] Calhoun was also pleased with his handiwork and that of his lieutenants and supporters. On December 31, he explained the situation to one of his political allies in Pennsylvania:

> [W]e have made peace in our State and . . . we are a united people. I trust and believe the restoration of harmony is complete. It has been effected without the slightest surrender of principle in our party. The termination of the controversy is no less remarkable and honorable to the State, than the stand which she has made in favour of the Constitution and the liberty of the country.[24]

Once again, however, the truce arranged in Columbia was difficult to sell to the people in the hinterlands of the Upcountry. When Congressman Warren R. Davis died unexpectedly, at the age of forty-two, in Washington during the winter of 1835, Unionists in the "Western" district again drafted Perry to run in the special election that would be held to fill Davis's seat. The Nullifiers, anxious to retain the seat, selected the popular Waddy Thompson, a Greenville planter-lawyer and a gifted orator, as their candidate. Perry approached the campaign with realistic misgivings. "I shall be again brought into the field and again beaten," he confided to his journal.[25] Thompson, one of the staunchest and most popular Nullifiers in the Upcountry, worked the district hard during the spring, generally urging "peace and harmony" between the old factions. Thompson steadfastly refused to attack Perry, who was confined through most of the spring with a painful leg injury suffered in a carriage accident. Other Nullifiers, however, used the Pendleton *Messenger* to brand Perry a "Jackson-Van Buren man" and to remind voters of Perry's Unionism.[26]

After a series of delays, the special election was called in early September. This date came immediately after the annual militia encampment and reviews held during the last week in August, where Brigadier General Waddy Thompson was in constant, and highly visible, attendance. If the election had been postponed until mid-October, it would have been held during court week in Greenville and Perry might have gained an advantage. Perry suspected that the selection of the earlier date was made by Governor McDuffie in a calculated effort to aid Thompson.[27] Perry attended the militia musters anyway to woo

[23]Virginia Louise Glenn, "James Hamilton, Jr., of South Carolina: A Biography" (Ph.D. dissertation, University of North Carolina at Chapel Hill, 1964), pp. 174–215; Petigru to Legaré, December 15, 1834, in Carson, *James Louis Petigru,* p. 170.

[24]John C. Calhoun to Samuel D. Ingham, December 31, 1834, in Wilson, ed., *The Papers of John C. Calhoun,* vol. 12, pp. 377–378.

[25]Entry of February 8, 1835, Benjamin F. Perry Diary, vol. 1, SHC.

[26]Henry T. Thompson, *General Waddy Thompson* (Columbia, 1929), pp. 1–3; Greenville *Mountaineer,* March 28, July 11, August 1 and 8, 1835; Pendleton *Messenger,* July 11, 1835; Samuel A. Townes to George F. Townes, September 7, 1835, Townes Family Papers, SHC.

[27]For an excellent survey of the entire campaign, see Kibler, *Perry,* pp. 172–176.

potential voters. Despite his efforts, Perry lost the election to Thompson by more than 700 votes. Perry carried Greenville by 1000 votes, but lost Anderson by 1300 votes and Pickens by nearly 400.[28] Perry blamed the margin of his defeat on the fact that a "great many Union men left Greenville" during 1834, but other observers recognized that Thompson enjoyed much personal popularity and possessed "a smoothe hand to electioneer."[29]

Confident that Thompson's popularity and the Nullifier organization would carry the day, Calhoun again declined to play an active role in the campaign. Despite the best efforts of Thompson and Perry, however, the test-oath controversy had remained the central issue in the campaign and the vote divided largely along old factional lines. Calhoun, Thompson, and other leading Nullifiers were clearly anxious to begin putting the bitterness of the nullification years aside, and even Perry, the most militant Unionist leader, yearned for "old party distinctions" to "be dropped."[30] The Perry-Thompson contest proved to be the last campaign in which the test oath issue would be openly debated, but the influence of the nullification controversy on South Carolina politics lingered for many years.

Alienated from the Jackson Administration and the emerging Democratic party in national politics, but enjoying strong control of South Carolina, the Calhounites, by 1835, turned their attention toward making the best of both situations. In Washington, Calhoun and his small band of followers worked to slow what they perceived as the rapid accrual of power to the Jackson White House. Calhounites were especially concerned about the expansion of executive power, and thus Jackson's personal influence, through the broadening avenues of federal patronage. Well-versed in the Jeffersonian code of republican ethics, Calhoun feared that federal largesse, widely but unevenly distributed by partisan hands, would create a "mercenary majority" whose opinion would be controlled "by the will of the Executive."[31] Indeed, Calhoun publicly charged that the Jacksonians were united politically only by their desire to receive governmental favors. Addressing the Senate in 1835, Calhoun denounced the Jacksonians in bold terms:

> [T]he administration has not thought it proper to make this [pensions] or any other question of principle or policy a party question. A member may vote on any question of the kind for or against, and be still a good Jackson man. He may be for or against internal improvement—for or against the tariff—for or against this or that expenditure—for or against the bank, without forfeiting his party

[28]Greenville *Mountaineer*, September 12 and 19, 1835.

[29]Entries of February 8 and July 2, 1835, Benjamin F. Perry Diary, vol. 1, SHC; Edmund Webb to B. F. Perry, quoted in Kibler, *Perry*, p. 173.

[30]Greenville *Mountaineer*, July 12, 1834.

[31]John C. Calhoun to Samuel D. Ingham, January 9, 1835, in Wilson, ed., *The Papers of John C. Calhoun*, vol. 12, pp. 381–382.

character . . . the only cohesive principle which binds together the power party rallied under the name of General Jackson, is official patronage.[32]

Yet while the Calhounites were the harshest and most unrelenting critics of the Jackson Administration, they could hardly embrace the program, designed by Henry Clay and Daniel Webster, of the emerging Whig opposition. When Jackson removed government deposits from the Bank of the United States and its branches in 1833, his opponents, led by Clay and Webster, adopted the label "Whigs" and denounced Jackson for his high-handed abuse of executive power. Gradually, however, these so-called Whigs developed their own national agenda, one which called for a strong national bank, an extensive system of federally financed internal improvements, and a protective tariff. Calhoun and his followers made common cause with the Whigs in opposition to Jackson, but refused to endorse the profligate consolidationist program of Clay and Webster.[33] Determined to oppose Jackson's practice of executive usurpation yet unwilling to accept the Whigs' neo-Federalist design for national development, Calhoun pursued what Clyde N. Wilson has described as the course of a "free-lance states-man."[34] Calhoun himself explained the role in direct terms:

> Our situation is a peculiar one. We do not constitute the opposition; but a small independent party, condemning the general course of the administration, while we differ widely with the opposition in principle and policy. The danger in our position is absorption by one, or the other party, or partly by both, to guard against which, we are compelled . . . to bring forward our views . . . in order to be clearly distinguished from the contending parties.[35]

In order to be effective as a "free-lance statesman," however, Calhoun had to be sure of virtually unanimous support for his actions from within South Carolina. As a result, Calhoun urged his political lieutenants to promote reconciliation between Nullifiers and Unionists whenever possible. After years of political turmoil which sometimes had verged on armed conflict, many South Carolinians, from both the Nullifier and Unionist camps, could not easily put aside old differences, even when their most respected leaders urged them to do so. Moreover, certain leaders of the Unionist minority, such as Joel Poinsett, maintained close ties to Calhoun's opponents in Washington.[36]

---

[32]John C. Calhoun, "Remarks on the Executive Patronage Report in Exchange with Thomas H. Benton," February 13, 1835, in Wilson, ed., *The Papers of John C. Calhoun*, vol. 12, pp. 458–478, especially pp. 474–475.

[33]On the nature of the "Whig" opposition to Jackson, see Wiltse, *Calhoun: Nullifier*, pp. 223–236.

[34]See Wilson's introduction in *The Papers of John C. Calhoun*, vol. 12, pp. xxvii–xl.

[35]John C. Calhoun to Littleton W. Tazewell, March 27, 1834, in Wilson, ed., *The Papers of John C. Calhoun*, vol. 12, pp. 273–274.

[36]For example, see Rippy, *Poinsett*, pp. 160–166.

The Calhounites were especially anxious for South Carolina to present a united front against the rising tide of abolition. By 1835, abolitionists were flooding the Southern mail with antislavery literature and inundating Congress with antislavery petitions. Calhoun believed that the South should stop this escalating antislavery crusade at the threshold and moved quickly to rally South Carolina behind him. In September 1835, Calhoun attended a large meeting, organized by a number of leading local citizens, held at the Farmer's Hall in Pendleton village to discuss the threat of abolition. The meeting, attended by Nullifier and Unionist alike, produced a report and a series of resolutions denouncing abolitionist agitation and declaring that "interference" with the South's domestic institutions was tantamount to the "subversion of the constitutional compact on which the Union of the States rests."[37] Though there was no disagreement between Nullifiers and Unionists on the necessity of stopping the abolitionists, some leading Unionists opposed the aggressive anti-abolition strategy urged by Calhoun. B. F. Perry charged that the Nullifiers were now "aware that Slavery is the only thing that can produce a dissolution of the Union" and that the anti-abolition agitation was merely a thinly veiled plot, orchestrated by fire-eaters, to promote the cause of secession and Southern independence.[38]

The Calhounites were undeterred by such occasional opposition, and resolved to stop abolition petitions in the twenty-fourth Congress, which would meet in the winter of 1835 and 1836. Calhoun in the Senate, and his ally James Henry Hammond in the House, took the lead in the effort to have Congress refuse to receive abolition petitions on the grounds that Congress had no constitutional authority to abolish slavery. In February 1836, Hammond's efforts and Calhoun's strategy were unilaterally undermined in a surprise move by Congressman Henry L. Pinckney of Charleston, long a close associate of Calhoun and editor of the rabidly pro-Calhoun Charleston *Mercury* during the nullification crisis. Without consulting Calhoun, Pinckney introduced a series of resolutions in the House which called for all prayers for abolition to be tabled immediately upon reception, but which tacitly suggested that Congress had the power to abolish slavery in the District of Columbia by stating that Congress "ought not" to interfere with slavery in the federal district. Pinckney's motives in introducing the resolutions were obscure at the time and have baffled historians ever since. It was known that the Van Buren faction of the Democratic party favored a position similar to that of Pinckney's resolutions. Thus there was speculation that the Little Magician or his aides persuaded Pinckney to proceed, perhaps by promising their aid in attempting to locate a much-coveted navy yard in Charleston, or possibly by tempting Pinckney with the prospect of an influential position in a possible Van Buren Administration. Or Pinckney may simply have felt that his resolutions, which were the basis for what soon became known as the "gag

---

[37]Wiltse, *Calhoun: Nullifier*, pp. 268–280; Pendleton *Messenger*, September 11, 1835.
[38]Entry of August 8, 1835, Benjamin F. Perry Diary, vol. 1, SHC.

rule,'' offered a practical means of silencing the abolitionists by acquiring the cooperation of cautious Northern Democrats.[39]

Whatever Pinckney's motives, his resolutions were roundly denounced from almost every quarter in South Carolina. Francis W. Pickens, an Upcountry congressman from Edgefield and a cousin of Calhoun, was the only member of the South Carolina delegation who knew about Pinckney's resolutions in advance. Pickens urged the former editor to scuttle them. When Pinckney went ahead with his proposal, Pickens cursed him as "a traitor and a bastard." Pinckney's former newspaper, the *Mercury,* now edited by John A. Stuart, disowned its old master. Nullifier James Hamilton declared that Pinckney's course was "utterly inexplicable," and Calhoun's daughter, Anna Maria, noted that "all the Southerners" in Washington opposed Pinckney's actions. A few days later, James Henry Hammond told the House of Representatives that "a Union based on the principles of that [Pinckney's] resolution cannot stand."[40]

An angry Calhoun was concerned that Pinckney had yielded a crucial constitutional point to the enemies of slavery. Calhounites around Charleston were determined to use their formidable resources to defeat Pinckney in the next election. The only South Carolinians who applauded Pinckney were old Unionists who approved of anyone who opposed Calhoun. In the spring of 1836, Pinckney launched his reelection campaign not only with a spirited defense of his own actions but also with a repudiation of Calhoun and the Nullifiers. Appealing directly to former Unionists for support, Pinckney won the endorsement of the Charleston *Courier,* formerly a powerful Unionist organ. Calhounites first turned to Isaac E. Holmes, a leading Charleston Nullifier, to oppose Pinckney.[41] Calhoun, however, was eager to avoid further alienation of the former Unionists, and a few of his top lieutenants informed Charleston Unionists that the Calhounites would accept a compromise candidate. When Unionist leaders decided to push Hugh Swinton Legaré, a Charleston Unionist who had spent the past four years as *chargé d'affaires* in Brussels, for the seat, Calhounites agreed to throw their support to him, and persuaded Holmes to drop out of the race. The *Mercu-*

[39]Charleston *Mercury,* February 19 and 20, 1836,; John Stanford Coussins, "Thirty Years with Calhoun, Rhett, and the Charleston *Mercury:* A Chapter in South Carolina Politics" (Ph.D. dissertation, Louisiana State University, 1971), pp. 87–91; George C. Rogers, Jr., "Henry Laurens Pinckney—Thoughts on His Career," in James B. Meriwether, ed., *South Carolina Journals and Journalists* (Spartanburg: The Reprint Company, 1975), pp. 163–175. Henry Laurens Pinckney was the son of Charles Pinckney, who had been one of the delegates from South Carolina to the Constitutional Convention in Philadelphia, and the grandson of Henry Laurens.

[40]Francis W. Pickens to Patrick Noble, March 6, 1836, Noble Family Papers, SCL; Charleston *Mercury,* February 11, 1836; James Hamilton, Jr., to James H. Hammond, February 10, 1836, Hammond Papers, LC (microfilm at SCL); Anna Maria Calhoun to James Edward Colhoun, February 26, 1836, in Wilson, ed., *The Papers of John C. Calhoun,* vol. 13, p. 89; "Speech of James H. Hammond," *Register of Debates, 24th Congress, 1st Session,* cols. 2495–2497.

[41]Henry Laurens Pinckney, *An Address to Electors of Charleston District* (Charleston: Burger and Honour, 1836); Daniel E. Huger to James Chesnut, August 20, 1836, Williams-Chesnut-Manning Papers, SCL; James L. Petigru to Hugh S. Legaré, August 26, 1836, in Carson, *James Louis Petigru,* pp. 183–184.

ry, which had previously endorsed Holmes, began carrying the Legaré banner.[42] The *Courier,* however, stuck by its support of Pinckney. Petigru, Legaré's closest friend, lambasted his old allies at the *Courier* for thinking it "no shame to give as a reason for supporting Pinckney that it will mortify Calhoun."[43] Legaré, a lawyer with serious intellectual interests and a preference for aristocratic comforts, a man always viewed by many Charlestonians as effeminate and perhaps something of a dandy, was a poor campaigner. Petigru, who personally managed the Legaré campaign, warned the candidate that he should show "no whiskers, no rings, no chain, no foppery, nothing but civility and common sense till the election is over."[44] After a heated campaign, Legaré edged Pinckney by less than 100 votes, much to the delight of the Calhounites as well as many of Legaré's old Unionist friends.[45]

The Calhounite "purge" of the maverick Pinckney was widely noted in South Carolina political circles for a number of reasons. Pinckney was the first prominent Nullifier to break the old "party" discipline and defy Calhoun. His defeat served notice that those who opposed Calhoun could expect active opposition in subsequent elections. Yet, at the same time, the slim margin of Legaré's victory suggested that challenges to Calhoun's dominance had a chance to succeed. Moreover, Calhoun's support for the Unionist Legaré was another clear indication of his desire to encourage reconciliation between Unionists and Nullifiers. Calhoun's motives were still mistrusted and misunderstood by most Unionists, including many such as Legaré and Petigru who profited from Calhounite support in 1836, but the powerful senator proved willing to forget past differences when the present need was for harmony and cooperation.

Pinckney's "bolt" notwithstanding, most South Carolinians supported Calhoun's "free-lance" statesmanship in Washington. Indeed, Calhoun assured one important journalist, "I have no fear for the success of our party . . . throughout the State ¾ of the young men of talents are with us."[46] Calhoun's constant combat with Jackson convinced many South Carolinians that the state could never reconcile itself with the Democratic party. At the same time, the clear Federalist overtones of the Whig program made it difficult for most Calhounites to consider permanent alliance with the opposition. Of course, there was hope in a few of the old Federalist enclaves in the Lowcountry that Jackson, like Crom-

[42]Linda Rhea, *Hugh Swinton Legaré: A Charleston Intellectual* (Chapel Hill: University of North Carolina Press, 1934), pp. 130–177; Charleston *Mercury,* October 7, 1836.

[43]James L. Petigru to Hugh S. Legaré, September 6, 1836, in Carson, *James Louis Petigru,* pp. 184–185.

[44]Michael O'Brien, *A Character of Hugh Legaré* (Knoxville: University of Tennessee Press, 1985), especially pp. 222–224; James L. Petigru to Hugh S. Legaré, September 6, 1836, in Carson, *James Louis Petigru,* pp. 184–185.

[45]James L. Petigru to Jane Petigru North, October 27, 1836, in Carson, *James Louis Petigru,* pp. 185–186; Joel R. Poinsett to John Campbell, October 20, 1836, in Samuel G. Stoney, ed., "The Poinsett-Campbell Correspondence," *South Carolina Historical Magazine* 42 (October, 1941):149–168.

[46]John C. Calhoun to Duff Green, September 20, 1834, in Wilson, ed., *The Papers of John C. Calhoun,* vol. 12, pp. 362–364.

well, would carry the excesses of his personal rule so far that South Carolina would embrace the emerging Whig party. The Whigs, it was believed, could then effect a restoration, returning the neo-Federalist aristocracy to power.[47] On the other side of the South Carolina political spectrum, a handful of loyal Jacksonians, such as Perry, Poinsett, and Judge John Belton O'Neall of Newberry, continued to support the Administration, despite their growing reservations about Jackson's ability to separate personal vendetta from public policy. Poinsett even worked to help Van Buren, Jackson's hand-picked successor, secure the Democratic nomination for President in 1836.[48]

Among Calhounites, few political figures were as despised as Van Buren. Calhounites felt that Van Buren had used his considerable political wiles to corrupt the Jackson White House in much the same manner that Walpole had used his position to corrupt the House of Hanover. Van Buren, like Walpole, was seen as a "bad minister" who used patronage and executive influence to build a large, and essentially corrupt, "Court" faction which controlled the government. Calhoun himself was ever chary of his longtime rival, but was powerless to prevent Van Buren's nomination or election. In Calhoun's eyes, Van Buren was a skillful political manipulator, a man whose ability to control the party caucus or legislative cabal far outstripped his intellectual gifts or the intrinsic virtue of his policies. Yet Calhoun also realized that Van Buren's gifts were those of the master political wire-puller and the confident party whip, not of the charismatic Chief Executive. Van Buren in the White House was probably less to be feared than Van Buren as *de facto* chairman of the Kitchen Cabinet, and definitely less to be feared than Jackson, the Republic's most popular hero since Washington and a man who never doubted the rectitude of his own actions. Calhoun knew that while the vigorous use of executive patronage would continue, Van Buren, as President, would have to depend not on personal popularity, but on carefully cultivated support for his policies in order to be an effective leader.[49]

Moreover, shortly after Van Buren donned Jackson's outsized presidential toga in March 1837, the New Yorker's fledgling Administration was knocked off balance by the most serious financial panic to sweep the nation since 1819.

[47]Lacy Ford, "James Louis Petigru: The Last South Carolina Federalist," in Michael O'Brien and David Moltke-Hansen, eds., *Intellectual Life in Antebellum Charleston* (Knoxville: University of Tennessee Press, 1986), pp. 152–185.

[48]James Welch Patton, "John Belton O'Neall," *Proceedings of the South Carolina Historical Association* (1934):3–13; Joel R. Poinsett to John Campbell, October 20, 1836, in Stoney, ed., "The Poinsett-Campbell Correspondence," p. 155.

[49]On Calhoun's view of these matters, see Charles M. Wiltse, "John C. Calhoun: An Interpretation," *Proceedings of the South Carolina Historical Association* (1948):26–39. On the traditional fear of a powerful "Court" faction, see Robert M. Weir, "'The Harmony We Were Famous For': An Interpretation of Pre-Revolutionary South Carolina Politics," *William and Mary Quarterly* 26 (October, 1969):473–501; and Lance Banning, *The Jeffersonian Persuasion: Evolution of a Party Ideology* (Ithaca, N.Y.: Cornell University Press, 1978), especially pp. 126–160. On Walpole, see Quentin Skinner, "The Principles and Practice of Opposition: The Case of Bolingbroke versus Walpole," in Neil McKendrick, ed., *Historical Perspectives: Studies in English Thought and Society* (London: Europa Publications, 1974), pp. 93–128.

Although the Panic of 1837 was probably triggered by overseas events and the actions of the Bank of England rather than by domestic causes, many American business leaders blamed the nation's growing financial woes on the policies of Andrew Jackson. In the aftermath of Jackson's successful battle to deny a new charter to the Bank of the United States and his decision to deposit government funds in "pet" banks scattered throughout the country, both the number of banks and the volume of bank paper in circulation had increased dramatically. The consequent inflation fueled speculation, and by the summer of 1836 Jackson moved to curb speculation by issuing the Specie Circular, which declared that only gold and silver would be accepted by the government as payment for public lands. Whatever Jackson's intentions, the Specie Circular was widely interpreted as a sign that the federal government had lost confidence in paper money in particular and in the nation's banks in general. When the nation's financial system collapsed just months after Jackson left office, Old Hickory received much of the blame for precipitating the crisis. As a partial remedy for the country's new economic woes, Van Buren proposed the creation of a federal Treasury that would remain independent of all banks. This proposal, sometimes called the independent treasury plan, but more often referred to as the sub-treasury plan, was designed not only to separate the Treasury from the nation's chaotic banking system but also to sabotage Whig hopes for rechartering a National Bank. Calhoun favored a "divorce" between "the Government and the banking system," though he also felt that proper timing was essential if such a separation was to be achieved without destroying public confidence in the economy. In the fall of 1837, Calhoun believed the time was right, and on September 18, after long and careful study of Van Buren's proposal, Calhoun indicated his general support of the Administration's sub-treasury plan.[50]

Van Buren was, of course, delighted to have Calhoun's support. The new President was shrewd enough to know that he could not long stand against all of Jackson's old enemies, and hoped that he might woo Calhoun and his Southern support back into the Democratic fold. Calhoun was glad to make the break with the Whig opposition, calling alliance with the Democrats "more congenial to my feelings" and telling his daughter Anna Maria:

> It was impossible for me to go with the leaders of the nationals [Whigs]. We disagreed on almost all points except resistance to executive usurpation. . . . I stand now on my own bottom, with no influence acting on me but a rigid adherence to those great principles for which I have made so many sacrafices [sic].[51]

[50]Bray Hammond, *Banks and Politics in America* (Princeton, N.J.: Princeton University Press, 1957), pp. 407–499; Peter Temin, *The Jacksonian Economy* (New York: W. W. Norton, 1969), especially pp. 113–147; Wiltse, *Calhoun: Nullifier*, pp. 345–350; J. Roger Sharp, *The Jacksonians Versus the Banks: Politics in the States after the Panic of 1837* (New York: Columbia University Press, 1970); "Speech on the Bill Authorizing an Issue of Treasury Notes," September 18, 1837, in Wilson, ed., *The Papers of John C. Calhoun*, vol. 13, pp. 546–572.

[51]John C. Calhoun to Anna Maria Calhoun, September 8, 1837, in Wilson, ed., *The Papers of John C. Calhoun*, vol. 13, pp. 536–538.

* * *

Calhoun's decision, however, startled political observers everywhere. Whigs decried the treachery of their former ally while Democrats generally praised the return of the famous prodigal. Yet if Calhoun's move met with the expected partisan response in Washington, it shook the very foundation of his political base in South Carolina, where, as his biographer Charles M. Wiltse has observed, "Calhoun faced mutiny."[52]

Indeed, the initial political backlash triggered by Calhoun's support of the sub-treasury was the most serious rebellion among his supporters which the senator ever faced. Many prominent Nullifiers and Calhounites opposed the sub-treasury and criticized Calhoun's support of Van Buren. Longtime Calhoun allies such as Robert Y. Hayne, James Hamilton, Jr., Pierce M. Butler, John Springs, William C. Preston, and Waddy Thompson broke with Calhoun on the sub-treasury issue. Most of these men were pro-bank Calhounites who favored either a rechartering of the Bank of the United States or some similar measure designed to solidify the nation's banking system. Even George McDuffie, one of Calhoun's closest allies, warned the senator that he should avoid "any attempt to make an organization of political parties on this question."[53] James L. Petigru called the sub-treasury controversy "a divorce of Calhoun from his little party" and "a fatal breach between him [Calhoun] and his friends in Carolina."[54] Not only did Senator Preston oppose Calhoun and the sub-treasury bill, but so did seven of the nine congressmen from South Carolina. Only reliable loyalists Francis W. Pickens and Robert Barnwell Rhett supported Calhoun. Calhoun was probably surprised by the severity of the revolt in South Carolina, but he had known all along that there would be opposition and was prepared to meet it.[55]

Ultimately, the opposition to Calhoun's support of the sub-treasury and his political reunion with the Democrats resulted in an attempt to sustain organized opposition to Calhoun and his followers through the development of a Whig party in South Carolina. The appeal of the Whigs to many South Carolinians was natural. Because of Jackson's position on the tariff, local Whigs could brand the Democrats as the party of high tariffs, or downplay the tariff issue altogether. Other aspects of the so-called "American system," the backbone of the Whig

[52]Wiltse, *Calhoun: Nullifier*, p. 538.

[53]George McDuffie to John C. Calhoun, October 29, 1837, in Wilson, ed., *The Papers of John C. Calhoun*, vol. 13, pp. 631–634; George McDuffie to Waddy Thompson, October 23, 1837, Waddy Thompson Papers, SCL; Jervey, *Hayne*, pp. 430–460; Glenn, "Hamilton," pp. 240–267; Miles S. Richards, "Pierce Mason Butler: The South Carolina Years, 1830–1841," *South Carolina Historical Magazine* 87 (January, 1986):14–29; John Springs to Andrew Baxter Springs, July 11, 1838, Springs Family Papers, SHC; Ernest M. Lander, "The Calhoun-Preston Feud, 1836–1842," *South Carolina Historical Magazine* 59 (January, 1958):24–37.

[54]James L. Petigru to Jane P. North, September 17, 1837, in Carson, *James Louis Petigru*, pp. 190–191.

[55]John B. Edmunds, Jr., *Francis W. Pickens and the Politics of Destruction* (Chapel Hill: University of North Carolina Press, 1986), pp. 28–40; Laura A. White, *Robert Barnwell Rhett: Father of Secession* (Gloucester, Mass.: Peter Smith, 1965), pp. 32–50.

platform, had appeal to some South Carolinians. In a state which was steadily losing both people and dollars to the Southwest, internal improvements were viewed as vital to increased commerce. Improved transportation networks might do little to reduce the competitive advantage held by the cotton frontier relative to the Palmetto State, but many economic leaders believed that South Carolina, and especially Charleston, could profit from increased commerce with the West. Finally, support for a strong banking system was widespread in South Carolina, and many pro-bank politicians believed that a national bank should be the capstone of such a system. Upcountry planter John Springs attacked the sub-treasury plan as "another Administration experiment on the currency and the best interests of the community" and complained that Jackson and Van Buren had "already experimented the currency almost to Death." Springs, who later branded the Calhoun Democrats as the "Agrarian Loco Foco Party," joined Preston, Thompson, and Wade Hampton II in arguing that healthy banks and reliable paper currency helped sustain the heavy commercial involvement of many South Carolinians.[56] Bank notes and paper currency were, as George McDuffie argued, "the actual blood which envigorates our social system." In a larger sense, Whigs in South Carolina were those people who were convinced that expanding the material basis of individual autonomy was essential, in the long term, to the maintenance of personal independence, and that the power of government could be harnessed to encourage economic development.[57]

The Calhoun Democrats, by contrast, were now a coalition of loyal ex-Nullifiers and anti-bank Jacksonian Unionists. Most Calhounites had long accepted, somewhat uneasily, the encumbrance of commercial entanglements, and were not enemies of commerce. They did, however, fear that if the government put its power and resources at the disposal of the commercial classes of the country then the Republic would soon be subjected to the rule of a bloated plutocracy. "The whole Banking system is a fraud upon the world, and we *must never* sustain it," insisted Upcountry Congressman Francis Pickens. "The capitalists of the non-slaveholding states live by it. They resort to corporations by which the whole society may be moved as one man & become consolidated for political power and private gain."[58] In Union district, planter Joseph Starke Sims praised the independent Treasury as "entirely a Southern and republican measure" and denounced the national bank as "a source of power and corruption." If "General Jackson with all his power and popularity was almost forced to yield to the money power," Sims asked, "what could not Henry Clay do with

[56]John Springs to Andrew Baxter Springs, February 13, 1838, and John Springs to Andrew Baxter Springs, December 27, 1842, Springs Family Papers, SHC.

[57]For an overview of Whig ideology and programs, especially in the South, see Daniel Walker Howe, *The Political Culture of American Whigs* (Chicago: University of Chicago Press, 1979), especially pp. 238–262; Arthur C. Cole, *The Whig Party in the South* (Washington: American Historical Association, 1913); Thomas D. Brown, "The Southern Whigs and Economic Development," *Southern Studies* 20 (Spring, 1981): 20–38; McDuffie to Calhoun, October 29, 1837, in Wilson, ed., *The Papers of John C. Calhoun*, vol. 13, pp. 631–634.

[58]Francis W. Pickens to Richard Crallé, June 28, 1837, Francis W. Pickens Papers, DU.

a Bank of $50,000,000?''[59] Other Calhounites and most Unionist-Democrats believed that personal independence was best defended by limiting commercial involvement. They were suspicious of all banks, and opposed government-sponsored internal improvements. On the whole, South Carolina Democrats were not anti-commercial, but they were opposed to active government sponsorship and support of specific programs of economic development.[60]

Faced with a serious rebellion at home, Calhoun moved quickly and firmly to quell it. Calhoun urged his reliable organ, the Charleston *Mercury,* to support him actively, and quickly mobilized his friends and loyalists in an effort to rally public opinion on his behalf. The Whigs, led by Preston, won support from the old Unionist paper, the Charleston *Courier,* and from the Columbia *Telescope,* edited by Preston's kinsman A. S. Johnston. Old Unionists from the parish elite, such as Petigru, Cheves, and Legaré, also rallied to the Whig cause. With all this formidable talent in their camp in the fall of 1837, the Whigs thought that they could challenge Calhoun for the leadership of South Carolina. Then, poised for the battle, the Whigs hesitated, and lost. Preston advised his best campaigner, Waddy Thompson, not to take the stump, while Calhounites feverishly rallied support for the sub-treasury.[61] When the state legislature met in December, Calhoun was in Columbia, and resolutions endorsing the sub-treasury were introduced in both houses. James and Albert Rhett, brothers of Robert Barnwell Rhett, and B. T. Elmore led the fight in favor of the Treasury, while Petigru and Hamilton fought against it. The Calhounites had done their advance work well, and their resolutions passed by a margin of more than ten to one.[62] Petigru, now back in the familiar role of opposing Calhoun, commented upon the result with his usual sarcasm:

> The unanimity of the Legislature and of the people is unnatural. It is a forced and unsettled state of things. Mr. Calhoun's triumph is complete and even too great, for he has crushed his lieutenants.[63]

In a sense, Calhoun had crushed a rebellion led by some of his former lieutenants, alienating a few of them for life. At the same time, however, a young and energetic new cadre of Calhounite leaders had proven their mettle under fire. The key leaders in a Calhounite party without Preston, Thompson, Hamilton, and Pinckney were the Rhett family, the Elmore family, and a triumvirate of planters

[59]Speech of Joseph Starke Sims, December, 1838, Joseph Starke Sims Papers, DU.

[60]See John C. Calhoun to John Bauskett and others, November 3, 1837, in Wilson, ed., *The Papers of John C. Calhoun,* vol. 13, pp. 636–641; Francis W. Pickens to Patrick Noble, May 22, 1838, Noble Family Papers, SCL.

[61]Charleston *Courier,* November 15, 1837; Pendleton *Messenger,* November 3, 1837; William C. Preston to Waddy Thompson, [November] 1837, Preston Family Papers, SCL.

[62]Charleston *Mercury,* December 2 and 18, 1837; White, *Rhett,* p. 35; John C. Calhoun to Anna Maria Calhoun, December 24, 1837, in Wilson, ed., *The Papers of John C. Calhoun,* vol. 14, pp. 21–22.

[63]James L. Petigru to Hugh S. Legaré, December 17, 1837, in Carson, *James Louis Petigru,* p. 193.

from the rich Savannah River valley, James Henry Hammond of Barnwell, Francis Pickens of Edgefield, and Armistead Burt of Abbeville. This cadre of Calhounite leaders, and especially the so-called "Rhett-Elmore clique," performed magnificently in the fall of 1837 in winning what was merely the first of their many victories.[64]

In Washington, Nicholas Biddle commented that "Calhoun moved heaven and earth" to pass the sub-treasury bill, but by the fall of 1838 it still had not passed. Against the sentiments of the South Carolina legislature, Preston in the Senate, and Legaré and Thompson in the House, opposed the bill. Calhoun was piqued at these Whig leaders and vowed to work for their defeat.[65] "I think Preston and Thompson have done much mischief," Calhoun wrote to his brother-in-law, "more than they ever can repair, if they were to live 100 years."[66] Preston, elected by the legislature in 1836, had four years left on his term and thus was beyond Calhoun's reach. Thompson and Legaré, the most intransigent of the anti-sub-treasury congressmen, were not. In midsummer, Calhoun enlisted the aid of his former enemy Joel R. Poinsett, a national Democrat and Secretary of War under Van Buren, in his campaign against the Whigs. Calhoun urged Poinsett to encourage opposition to Legaré in the First Congressional District. Then Calhoun served public notice of his opposition to the "Preston faction" by refusing to appear at a barbecue in Columbia honoring Preston.[67] In the Fifth Congressional District, where Thompson was the incumbent, local Calhounite leaders persuaded Tandy Walker, a Greenville lawyer, to run as their candidate. Calhoun felt that "public sentiment" clearly favored the sub-treasury over the creation of a national bank, but feared that Thompson's personal popularity might carry the day against Walker, a relative unknown. Moreover, the ever-popular B. F. Perry threw his support behind Thompson. Perry was opposed to the Whig proposal for a national bank, but he also opposed the sub-treasury, largely because Calhoun favored it. Calhounites tried to counter Perry's influ-

[64]The "Rhett-Elmore" clique was led by Franklin H. Elmore and Robert Barnwell Rhett, both of whom were pro-Calhoun congressmen in 1837, and included Rhett's older brother James and his younger brother Albert, both members of the legislature, and another younger brother, Edmund Rhett, who later served as a director of the Bank of the State of South Carolina, and Elmore's younger brother, Benjamin T. Elmore, who also served in the state legislature. Albert Rhett, who served as Calhoun's floor leader in the legislature, was married to the Elmores' sister. The clique received journalistic support from John A. Stuart, editor of the Charleston *Mercury* who was married to a sister of the Rhetts. When Franklin Elmore became president of the Bank of the State of South Carolina in 1840, the clique grew even more powerful. See Lander, "The Calhoun-Preston Feud," pp. 28–29; Coussins, "Thirty Years with Calhoun, Rhett, and the Charleston *Mercury*," pp. 124–125.

[65]Wiltse, *Calhoun: Nullifier,* pp. 391–393.

[66]John C. Calhoun to James Edward Colhoun, April 24, 1838, in Wilson, ed., *The Papers of John C. Calhoun,* vol. 14, pp. 275–278.

[67]John C. Calhoun to Joel R. Poinsett, July 14, 1838, and John C. Calhoun to Joseph A. Black and others, July 24, 1838, in Wilson, ed., *The Papers of John C. Calhoun,* vol. 14, pp. 389–398; Joel R. Poinsett to Joseph Johnson, September 24, 1838, in Heilman and Levin, eds., *Calendar of Joel R. Poinsett Papers,* p. 74.

ence by approaching former Unionist leaders in Pickens, including Joseph Grisham, and winning these local notables over to their side.[68]

Aware that Thompson's personal charm and his campaign experience made him the favorite against any Calhounite, Calhoun decided to canvass the district personally on behalf of the sub-treasury. Appearing on the stump for the first time in more than fifteen years, the still handsome Calhoun, a lean and lanky Upcountry planter of Scotch-Irish extraction, toured Greenville, Pickens, and Anderson districts, speaking at great outdoor barbecues and militia musters, and making himself available to his fellow citizens for an exposition and exchange of views.[69] The return of Calhoun to the stump marked the campaign of 1838 as an important one, and indicated how strongly Calhoun opposed the creation of a viable Whig party in South Carolina. Here was arguably the nation's most famous active public figure, a former Vice President and Secretary of War, the author of nullification, and the powerful senator who debated Clay, Webster, and Benton, who opposed Jackson and Adams, now standing at barbecues at small country churches and courthouse towns in the Upcountry before many hundred sturdy yeomen and rugged backwoodsmen, speaking on matters he considered crucial to the future of the Republic. At most of these gatherings Calhoun was joined by Thompson, and the two antagonists joined in the informal debate that was the staple of stump meetings.[70]

The pattern for the campaign was established at a public barbecue held at Sandy Spring Church in Greenville District on August 28. Addressing a crowd of more than 1500, Calhoun denounced the connection between the government and the banks as "unequal, unjust, corrupting in its consequences, anti-republican, hostile to State rights, and subversive of our liberties." Calhoun blamed Alexander Hamilton and the Federalists for inaugurating the "unjust connexion" which was "contrary to the law and spirit of Republicanism." Finally, Calhoun concluded with an allegorical anecdote. Borrowing from Aesop's fables, Calhoun told the assembled farmers and mountaineers about the woodsman who humbly petitioned the Forest to grant him a small piece of timber to use as a helve for his axe. The Forest held a council and granted the request. The woodsman shaped and fitted his helve and soon felled the entire Forest. The axe, according to Calhoun, was the Bank. "Give to it a Charter," Calhoun warned, "and soon the tree of American Liberty will fall prostrate before it."[71]

[68]John C. Calhoun to Duff Green, August 10, 1838, in Wilson, ed., *The Papers of John C. Calhoun*, vol. 14, p. 402; Kibler, *Perry*, p. 219.

[69]For assessments of Calhoun's decision to return to the stump, see Clyde N. Wilson's introduction to *The Papers of John C. Calhoun*, vol. 14, pp. xviii–xxiv; and Wiltse, *Calhoun: Nullifier*, pp. 392–393.

[70]After one of the debates between Calhoun and Thompson, Thompson objected to some of Calhoun's remarks and asked Calhoun to withdraw them. Calhoun refused, but explained that they were not applied in the same context as Thompson had supposed, and the matter was dropped. See Waddy Thompson to John C. Calhoun, August 30, 1838, and John C. Calhoun to Waddy Thompson, September 2, 1838, in Wilson, ed., *The Papers of John C. Calhoun*, vol. 14, pp. 409–410, 416–418.

[71]John C. Calhoun, "Remarks at a Barbecue in Greenville District," August 28, 1838, in Wilson, ed., *The Papers of John C. Calhoun*, vol. 14, pp. 405–408.

Thompson responded by reminding the audience of Calhoun's earlier support of the Bank of the United States, and by blaming the existing financial chaos on Van Buren, the champion of the sub-treasury scheme. Throughout the campaign Thompson proved difficult to pin down on the banking issue. At various stump meetings, Thompson declared his opposition to the sub-treasury, to a national bank, and to Jackson's "pet" bank system, without ever saying exactly what he favored.[72] Thompson agreed with Calhoun's assessment that the majority of voters opposed a national bank, and therefore he appealed to the voters as a victim of Calhoun's "dictation and persecution" and not as a proponent of a national bank. Still a popular militia general, Thompson had made the most of the summer musters, and by September the Calhounites withdrew Walker, who was no match for Thompson on the stump, from the race, and coaxed Joseph N. Whitner, a popular Nullifier from Anderson, into the field. Once Whitner entered the race, Calhoun judged that Thompson was "giving ground daily." The election was held only three weeks after Whitner announced his candidacy, and, much to Calhoun's chagrin, Thompson carried the district by just over 1000 votes. Surprisingly, Whitner ran almost even with Thompson in the latter's native Greenville, but was swamped by the general in Anderson and Pickens districts. Whitner, however, carried Pendleton Courthouse, near Calhoun's home, by a margin of 263 to 30.[73]

Calhoun attributed Thompson's victory to the fact that the general "had gone around all the musters and told his own story without opposition, or contradiction" before the campaign even started and "resorted to all kind of artifice to mystify" the people regarding his stance on the issue of a national bank. Even the Greenville *Mountaineer*, a pro-Perry paper, agreed that "many people were not disposed to vote upon party principles" but instead voted on personalities, choosing the popular Thompson over the lesser known Whitner. Calhoun, though disappointed that Thompson had "for a time deluded the people," believed that the campaign had done much to educate the plain folk of the Upcountry on the sub-treasury issue and felt that if the Whigs could be flushed out into the open, they would be defeated.[74] In later years, even the victorious Thompson admitted that a substantial majority of his constituents supported the sub-treasury

[72]No verbatim accounts of Thompson speeches are extant, but the sketchy reports which are available indicate that Thompson always refused to state directly whether he preferred the sub-treasury or a national bank. Since, in practical terms, those were the options available, Calhoun tried to press the issue, but Thompson remained evasive. Thompson's friends and associates in Columbia openly favored a national bank, and it seems likely that, in private, Thompson did as well. Pendleton *Messenger*, October 5, 1838; John C. Calhoun to Duff Green, October 11, 1838, in Wilson, ed., *The Papers of John C. Calhoun*, vol. 14, pp. 434–435. For Thompson's own recollection of the campaign, see Waddy Thompson to Charles Lanman, October 14, 1858, Waddy Thompson Papers, SCL.

[73]John C. Calhoun to Robert Barnwell Rhett, September 13, 1838, in Wilson, ed., *The Papers of John C. Calhoun*, vol. 14, pp. 425–426; Pendleton *Messenger*, October 19, 1838. In Pendleton district, Thompson received 2,358 votes to Whitner's 1,361. Thompson also carried Anderson Courthouse, Whitner's home precinct, 281–102, and Pickens Courthouse by 366–238.

[74]John C. Calhoun to Duff Green, October 11, 1838, in Wilson, ed., *The Papers of John C. Calhoun*, vol. 14, pp. 434–435; Greenville *Mountaineer*, October 12, 1838.

plan endorsed by Calhoun and explained his own success as a purely personal triumph.[75] Still, Lowcountry Whig James Petigru hailed Thompson as "the true representative of the indignant spirit that throbs in the veins of those who despise all tyranny" and as a "solitary example of a man who thinks for himself" in bold defiance of "that sort of slavery which consists in absolute submission to party in anything and everything."[76]

In Charleston, the Democrats had more success. When Poinsett was unable to find a pro-sub-treasury Unionist to oppose Legaré, Isaac E. Holmes, the Nullifier, entered the race. Calhounite operatives worked skillfully to build opposition to Legaré within Charleston's conservative financial community, arguing that a national bank would inevitably damage state and local banks, and won the endorsement of Ker Boyce, the powerful president of the Bank of Charleston, for the sub-treasury. As the combined "troops of Calhoun and Poinsett" attacked Legaré, the Holmes campaign gained momentum. Hamilton and Petigru worked hard for Legaré, who remained an ineffectual campaigner. When the votes were counted, Holmes emerged as the easy winner, defeating Legaré in Charleston by 650 votes. Petigru complained that his friend Legaré had "delivered himself to them [Democrats] more like a supplicant than an adversary."[77] The pro-Calhoun *Mercury* gloated that "Mr. Petigru's little army of centurions without soldiers" had been defeated, and that Charleston was safely in Democratic hands. Moreover, Calhounite slates won election to the legislature in almost every district in the state, assuring that Calhoun Democrats would control that body for two more years.[78] With the exception of Thompson's reelection, the campaign of 1838 was a resounding success for Calhoun and the Democrats.

Miffed by their setbacks in 1838, but buoyed by Thompson's success in Calhoun's backyard, the South Carolina Whigs regrouped for a major challenge to the Calhoun Democrats in 1840. Determined to be better organized and to run more energetic campaigns, the Whigs planned to challenge Democrats in the congressional races and to run slates against Calhounites in races for the state legislature. The issues in the campaign of 1840 were pretty much the same as they had been in 1838, except for the fact that 1840 was a presidential year. In South Carolina, Whig leaders, on the whole, were open in their advocacy of a national bank. Democrats continued to champion the sub-treasury and missed few chances to brand the Whigs as the party of a national bank and "Hamiltonian" policies. Preston, a strong national bank advocate, had been boosting Clay for President since 1838, but gladly supported Harrison, a popular military chieftain from the Jackson mold, once "Tippecanoe" won the Whig nomination. Poinsett, of course, as a member of the Cabinet, wholeheartedly supported Van Buren. Though ever wary of Van Buren, Calhoun worked quietly but

[75]Undated manuscript [c. 1842], Waddy Thompson Papers, SCL.

[76]James Louis Petigru to Waddy Thompson, October 19, 1838, Waddy Thompson Papers, SCL.

[77]Pendleton *Messenger,* October 5, 1838; Charleston *Mercury,* October 6, 1838; Carson, *James Louis Petigru,* pp. 195–203; O'Brien, *A Character of Hugh Legaré,* pp. 226–241; James Louis Petigru to Waddy Thompson, October 19, 1838, Waddy Thompson Papers, SCL.

[78]Charleston *Mercury,* October 11, 1838; Carson, *James Louis Petigru,* pp. 195–202.

conscientiously for him and vigorously opposed Whig candidates at every level. Some Calhounites, such as George McDuffie, were explicit about their distrust of Van Buren, but supported all other Democrats. Both sides geared up for an all-out effort in the campaign; the Whigs were determined to break Calhoun's control of the state, and the Calhoun Democrats were anxious to crush the Whig opposition once and for all.[79]

Whiggery in South Carolina derived its support from some, though not all, of the expected places, and perhaps from a few unexpected ones. Around Charleston, and in the nearby parishes, remnants of the old Federalist elite gave strong support to the Whigs. Prominent old families such as the Draytons, the Grimkés, and the Pringles put wealth and tradition behind the Whig cause. Self-styled Charleston aristocrats and intellectuals such as Petigru, Legaré, and Thomas Bennett also tended to be Whigs.[80] In the Charleston financial and mercantile community, political divisions were complex. Most of the great Charleston bankers and merchants were initially alarmed at Calhoun's support of the sub-treasury. Indeed, James Hamilton, who became the first president of the Bank of Charleston when it was established in 1834, and Robert Y. Hayne, president of both a bank and a railroad company, had been leaders of the revolt of former Nullifiers against Calhoun in 1837. But Calhoun and his lieutenants worked hard to win the Charleston financial community over to their side. Reminding Charleston bankers that the old Charleston branch of the Bank of the United States had displayed a nasty habit of buying up notes of other banks and then demanding redemption in specie, Calhounites soon convinced many Charleston financial leaders that the sub-treasury was preferable to depredations by an omnipotent national bank. Leading Calhounites in state financial circles were Franklin Elmore, a longtime Calhoun supporter who had been elected president of the Bank of the State of South Carolina in 1838, Ker Boyce, a wealthy merchant who had succeeded Hamilton as president of the Bank of Charleston in 1837, and Henry W. Conner, another successful merchant and a director of the Bank of Charleston. With these prominent merchant-bankers on their side, Calhoun and the Democrats were able to calm fears that they were hostile to commerce or unconcerned about financial stability.[81]

In the Lowcountry, outside Charleston, Whigs found surprisingly little support. In Georgetown and Beaufort, almost all of the fabulously wealthy planters

[79]Lander, "The Calhoun-Preston Feud," pp. 24–37; George McDuffie to Armistead Burt, August 27, 1840, George McDuffie Papers, DU; James Seibels to John J. Seibels, September 21, 1840, Seibels Family Papers, SCL; Henry H. Townes to John A. Townes, July 13, 1840, Townes Family Papers, SCL; Benjamin T. Elmore to Armistead Burt, October 4, 1840, Armistead Burt Papers, DU.

[80]Carson, *James Louis Petigru,* pp. 195–211; Charleston *Courier,* November 11, 1840; Hugh Swinton Legaré to Waddy Thompson, August 13, 1838, Hugh Swinton Legaré Papers, SCL.

[81]On Ker Boyce's support for Calhoun, see the Pendleton *Messenger,* October 12, 1838. On Henry W. Conner, see John Amasa May and Joan Reynolds Faunt, *South Carolina Secedes* (Columbia, S.C.: University of South Carolina Press, 1960), pp. 131–132. On Elmore's support for Calhoun, see the Columbia *Southern Chronicle,* October 15, 1840. On the opposition of Hamilton and Hayne, see Glenn, "Hamilton," pp. 250–259, and Jervey, *Hayne,* pp. 461–488.

were Democrats. Indeed, the Allstons in Georgetown and the Rhetts (Smiths) in Beaufort led two of the most powerful Democratic organizations in the state. Although these areas were long-established plantation regions dominated by old wealth, vested interests, and staple agriculture, the leading planters in both districts were strong opponents of the Whig program. The proximity of the coast and easy access to Charleston limited enthusiasm for internal improvements, and parish agricultural production was financed largely through Charleston factors with solid British connections. For the great coastal planters, the Whig program to strengthen the American economic infrastructure was irrelevant, unnecessary, and expensive. Moreover, the criticism of slavery emanating from Whiggish areas of the North was downright alarming. By 1838, Robert F. W. Allston, a leading Georgetown rice planter and member of an old Federalist family, announced that his political creed was "based on the principles of Thomas Jefferson, as express'd during the discussion in Virginia in 1798."[82]

Beyond the Lowcountry, pockets of Whiggery were even more widely scattered. Richland district, and in particular the city of Columbia, was something of a Whig stronghold. It was the home district of the so-called "Preston cabal," a group of powerful and wealthy politicians loyal to William C. Preston. The core of Whig support around Columbia consisted of incredibly rich planter families such as the Prestons, the Hamptons, and the Taylors. Unlike their coastal counterparts, these super-rich planters had developed a wide range of entrepreneurial interests and invested heavily in banks, railroads, manufacturing, and southwestern lands. They supported the Whig program for economic development, which also received strong support from a Columbia mercantile community eager to expand its commercial connections.[83] Moving further inland, the Whig party attracted support from Upcountry planter-entrepreneurs such as John Springs of York and S. V. Cain of Abbeville, and from industrial developers such as Joseph Bivings of Spartanburg district. In general, the bulk of whatever strength the Whigs had in the Upcountry came from planters and inland merchants interested in developing better connections with coastal and fall-line markets. In Edgefield, Fairfield, Newberry, and the southern portions of Abbeville and Chester, which enjoyed relatively easy access to the fall-line markets of Augusta, Columbia, and Camden, planters and small farmers alike were overwhelmingly Democratic. Slightly deeper into the Upcountry, in northern Abbeville and southern Anderson, and in parts of Laurens, where large amounts of cotton were grown but where transportation to market was slow and difficult, the Whig party drew significant support from both planters and their yeoman neigh-

[82]George C. Rogers, Jr., *The History of Georgetown County, South Carolina* (Columbia, S.C.: University of South Carolina Press, 1970), pp. 361–366; Robert Duncan Bass, "The Autobiography of William John Grayson" (Ph.D. dissertation, University of South Carolina, 1933), pp. 163–167; Allston quotation from Rogers, *Georgetown County,* pp. 361–362.

[83]For example, see Columbia *Southern Chronicle,* October 8 and 15, November 5, and December 17, 1840.

bors.[84] Along the northern and western rim of the Upcountry, where specialization in commercial agriculture was less pervasive, the Whigs had little support. York, Spartanburg, and Union were overwhelmingly Democratic, and the Whig constituency in Greenville and Pickens was essentially limited to Waddy Thompson's personal following.[85]

In summary, the Whig party in South Carolina had pockets of strength among old Charleston Federalists and among inland planter-entrepreneur and mercantile interests, especially around Columbia. The great rice and long-staple cotton planters of the parishes, and the weight of the Charleston financial community, were behind Calhoun and the Democrats. In the Upcountry, the Whigs drew some support from planters, farmers, and merchants interested in improved transportation and better connections with large commercial centers. "Pure and simple" planters, that is, planters without significant non-plantation investments, yeoman farmers satisfied with their existing commercial connections, and subsistence farmers were Democrats almost to a man, especially in those areas of the Upcountry where the local notables were old-line members of the extensive Calhounite network. Of course the Whigs also tried to recruit local notables and their bands of followers, but enjoyed very limited success.

The political calculus outlined above suggests that the Whigs were badly outnumbered in South Carolina in 1840, and that their campaign was doomed to defeat from the beginning. In the summer of 1840, however, all things were still possible, and South Carolina saw its first contest waged along national party lines since 1812.[86] Incumbent Senator William Preston and his Columbia clique ran the Whig campaign, ably aided by Petigru in Charleston, and by Waddy Thompson, who declined to run for reelection to Congress in order to stump for Harrison, in the Upcountry. The Democrats depended on Calhounite leaders in the Upcountry, the Rhett-Elmore clique in the Lowcountry, and Administration spokesman Joel Poinsett in old Unionist enclaves.[87] As the usual canvassing, including barbecues, public dinners, militia musters, and traditional newspaper exchanges, proceeded, the Whigs saw their chances fade quickly. Outside of Richland, Charleston, and Pendleton, the Whigs found it difficult to field full

[84]Letter of John Springs, September 7, 1840, reprinted in Columbia *Southern Chronicle,* October 22, 1840; Katherine Wooten Springs, *The Squires of Springfield* (Charlotte, N.C.: William Loftin, 1965), pp. 81–82; Pendleton *Messenger,* August 21 and September 18, 1840.

[85]Yorkville *Compiler,* October 10 and 17, 1840; Greenville *Mountaineer,* October 16, 1840.

[86]The purpose here is to distinguish between planters whose business interests were essentially confined to staple agriculture and other "planter-entrepreneurs" whose basic source of wealth was land and slaves but who had substantial investments in mercantile firms, banks, railroads, manufacturing, and other non-agricultural concerns. For a comparison of these partisan alignments with those in one area of a neighboring state, see Harry L. Watson, *Jacksonian Politics and Community Conflict: The Emergence of the Second American Party System in Cumberland County, North Carolina* (Baton Rouge: Louisiana State University Press, 1981).

[87]Edmunds, *Francis W. Pickens,* pp. 61–70; White, *Rhett,* pp. 32–67; John S. Pressly to Joel R. Poinsett, June 22, 1840, in Heilman and Levin, eds., *Calendar of Joel R. Poinsett Papers,* pp. 109–110.

slates of candidates for the state legislature. In several congressional races, potential Whig candidates declined to run after making an informal canvass of their district. From the beginning of the campaign, the Democrats made Whig support of a national bank the central issue of the campaign. The Whigs responded by attacking the sub-treasury and appealing for popular support of the warrior-patriot Harrison. Touring the Upcountry, Calhoun "was surprised to learn there is so much Harrisonism in Abbeville," and in Pickens, the Unionist-turned-Democrat Joseph Grisham complained that in his neighborhood the Whig campaign was "little else than Hard Cider—and Log Cabin speeches."[88] While Democrats accused Whigs of ignoring the issues and appealing to voters with political theatrics rather than principles, the Whigs also complained about Democratic tactics. In Columbia, a Whig newspaper charged that "a band of the lowest ruffians . . . armed with bludgeon and blackjack, and preceded by a Democratic band of music" paraded through the streets taunting Whigs. The Whigs responded to "this band of Jacobins" by organizing a Tippecanoe Club whose purpose was to protect Whig voters.[89]

Since the legislature elected the presidential electors in South Carolina, the campaign revolved around legislative and congressional races. In the Upcountry, W. W. Starke, the pro-bank Whig editor of the Hamburg *Journal,* entered the race against Francis Pickens in the Sixth District (Edgefield and Abbeville), but dropped out in September when he realized that his cause was hopeless. In the Fourth District, composed of York, Chester, Union, and Spartanburg districts, early canvassing revealed that the Whigs would probably get no more than one-quarter of the vote in any district, so Democrat James Rogers of Union ran unopposed.[90] In the two other Upcountry congressional districts, however, the Whigs succeeded in making serious contests. In the Seventh District, consisting of Laurens, Newberry, and Fairfield, where the incumbent chose not to run, a Whig candidate, James H. Irby, a planter-lawyer from Laurens, ran against two Democrats, Patrick C. Caldwell of Newberry and Samuel G. Barkley of Fairfield. Despite the divided Democratic vote, Caldwell won the election over Irby, outpolling his Whig opponent 2,040 to 1,812, while Barkley trailed with 1,100 votes. Caldwell, a staunch Calhounite, won by carrying his native Newberry by a margin of more than three to one and by running well among Laurens Democrats who refused to support the Whig native son. Irby carried Laurens and received over 500 votes from Whig minorities in Fairfield and Newberry. Barkley won virtually all the Democratic votes in Fairfield but had little support elsewhere.

[88]Pendleton *Messenger,* September 18, 1840; John C. Calhoun to Andrew Pickens Calhoun, August 5, 1840, in Clyde N. Wilson, ed., *The Papers of John C. Calhoun* (Columbia, S.C.: University of South Carolina Press, 1983), vol. 15, pp. 322–323; Joseph Grisham to Joel R. Poinsett, July 15, 1840, in Heilman and Levin, eds., *Calendar of Joel R. Poinsett Papers,* p. 12.

[89]Columbia *Southern Chronicle,* October 15, 1840.

[90]Pendleton *Messenger,* October 30, 1840; Columbia *South Carolinian,* October 22, 1840; Edgefield *Advertiser,* September 3 and October 15, 1840; Yorkville *Compiler,* October 17, 1840; Greenville *Mountaineer,* October 16, 1840.

Yet even though Caldwell was elected by a rather small margin, the total Democratic strength in the Seventh District gave them a 1,200-vote majority over the Whigs.[91]

In the Fifth District, which included Greenville and Pendleton, the Whigs were stronger. William Butler of Greenville, brother of former governor Pierce M. Butler and brother-in-law of Whig incumbent Waddy Thompson, ran as the Whig candidate and enjoyed vigorous support on the stump from the popular Thompson.   J. W. Norris, a Pickens area planter, and Joseph Powell, a relative unknown from Greenville, ran as Democrats. Norris, who enjoyed solid support among Calhounites, attacked the Whigs for their support of a national bank and defended the sub-treasury but was careful not to identify himself with Van Buren. Powell, a former Unionist who had little use for the Calhounites, was a chronic debtor who hated all banks. B. F. Perry, a loyal supporter of Van Buren, rallied his followers in active opposition to the Whigs.[92] With Perry's help, Norris carried Greenville district by nearly 375 votes, but Butler, Thompson's hand-picked successor, beat Norris soundly in both Anderson and Pickens and won the election by 137 votes. The decisive factor in the race, however, was the candidacy of Powell, which siphoned just over 540 Democratic votes away from Norris and cost the Democrats the election. The pro-Calhoun Pendleton *Messenger* rightly interpreted the results as an endorsement of Democratic principles and a repudiation of the national bank even though Butler, a Whig, won the seat.[93]

Whigs fared no better in races for the state legislature. In the Upcountry, Whigs won seven of the eight seats in the legislature from Pendleton, but were soundly defeated in every other district. The Whig ticket in Edgefield was defeated nearly four to one. In Spartanburg, leading Democrats polled over 1700 votes while the top Whig vote-getter received only 739, and in Greenville and

---

[91]Columbia *South Carolinian*, October 22, 1840; Greenville *Mountaineer*, October 23, 1840. The actual returns, by district, were as follows:

	Caldwell (D)	Barkley (D)	Irby (W)
Newberry	1065	71	275
Laurens	878	8	1289
Fairfield	97	1021	248
	2040	1100	1812

[92]Pendleton *Messenger*, August 15, 1840; Greenville *Mountaineer*, September 4 and 11, 1840; entries of June 28, July 12, and September 2, 1840, Benjamin F. Perry Diary, vol. 2, SHC.

[93]Pendleton *Messenger*, October 16, 1840; Greenville *Mountaineer*, October 16, 1840. The returns from the Fifth District were:

	Butler (W)	Norris (D)	Powell (D)
Greenville	603	975	354
Anderson	1122	882	181
Pickens	993	714	8
	2718	2571	543

York, Democrats swept to victory virtually unopposed.[94] In Preston's home district of Richland, the Whig ticket for the legislature edged the Democrats by twenty-five votes in an election tarnished by charges of fraud, corruption, and vote-buying on both sides. Eventually the dispute was settled in favor of Whigs by a heavily Democratic legislature which felt no need to press its advantage.[95] In the state as a whole, the Whigs won only fifteen out of 169 seats in the state legislature. A few legislators who declined to run under a party label may have held Whiggish sympathies, but there were certainly no more than ten of these "closet Whigs" in the General Assembly. In 1842, most of this handful of Whig legislators were defeated, and Butler, the lone Whig congressman, was beaten by Richard D. Simpson, a pro-Calhoun Democrat.[96]

The election of 1840 was, on the whole, an overwhelming victory for the Democrats. They won eight of nine congressional districts and enjoyed almost absolute dominance of the state legislature. The disappointment of the election of Harrison was more than offset by the total rout of the Whigs in South Carolina. The victory at the polls was also a great personal victory for Calhoun. His decision to reaffiliate with the national Democratic party, even if that affiliation was clearly conditional, had been a calculated gamble. Calhoun knew that the move invited a rebellion at home. To stop the insurgency, Calhoun had moved quickly to cultivate support for Democratic positions, especially the party's opposition to a national bank. Defections from Calhoun's ranks by scores of former Nullifiers who supported the Whig position on banks and internal improvements were more than offset by his gains among anti-bank Unionists such as James Edward Henry of Spartanburg. A loyal Jacksonian Democrat and leader of Spartanburg's Unionist majority during the nullification crisis, Henry welcomed Calhoun's return to the Democratic fold even though he knew his own role as a leader would likely diminish. Henry also recognized what many Whig leaders did not: that Calhoun's views were extremely popular among Upcountry voters. "The Sub-Treasury . . . has an almost unanimous support by the Legislature and a large majority of the People in its favor," Henry reported as early as 1839. He also recognized that Calhoun's decision to rejoin the Democratic party had, on the whole, strengthened his popularity and standing in South Carolina. "[T]he truth is," Henry declared, "South Carolina and Mr. Calhoun are the same."[97]

[94]Pendleton *Messenger*, October 16, 1840; Greenville *Mountaineer*, October 16, 1840; Yorkville *Compiler*, October 17, 1840.

[95]The Richland Democratic party challenged the seating of the Whig delegation when the state legislature met in late 1840. A legislative committee studied the charges and ordered that new elections be held in mid-December. The Democrats, knowing that they controlled the legislature, decided against running a ticket in the new elections, giving the seats to the Whigs. Columbia *Southern Chronicle*, December 3 and 10, 1840.

[96]Pendleton *Messenger*, October 30, 1840 and March 3, 1842; Greenville *Mountaineer*, March 3, 1843.

[97]James Edward Henry to Samuel Finley Patterson, January 8, 1839, Samuel Finley Patterson Papers, DU.

Calhoun's victory, however, was a battlefield victory, won in the hard trench combat of the stump meeting, and not the triumph of "dictation" or unilateral decree. Calhoun, through a far-reaching network of friends, acquaintances, supporters, and political operatives, worked hard and long to win popular support for his policies, and won the endorsement he was looking for at the polls in October 1840. Indeed, James Louis Petigru, who spent most of his life "on the cold sack of opposition" to Calhoun, conceded early on what most of Calhoun's critics, as well as many future historians, were always loathe to admit: that, in South Carolina, "the people actually do govern, as they did in the days of Jefferson," and the Calhoun Democrats had the people's support.[98]

The Whig challenge to Calhoun was the last concerted effort to establish a viable two-party system within South Carolina during Calhoun's lifetime, and was itself something of an ironic tribute to Calhoun's leadership. Calhoun was a large Olympian political figure who cast a broad shadow across his native state. South Carolina was full of proud and talented men with political ambition. Yet with Calhoun around, there was little room at the top. The frustrations for other would-be leaders were enormous. Whig leaders such as Preston, Thompson, and Petigru were motivated not only by the desire to establish an opposition party in South Carolina but also by the desire to create a bright political future for themselves at the head of such a party, and to make more room at the top of South Carolina politics for people other than Calhoun. Thus the charge that the Whigs were a party of "centurions without soldiers" contained a kernel of truth. Despite the efforts of many talented leaders, the Whig insurgency ended as just another failed revolution in antebellum South Carolina politics. In South Carolina, the Whig party was not stillborn; instead, it was suffocated in its infancy by the hand of John C. Calhoun.[99]

In a larger sense, however, the Whigs failed to flourish in South Carolina simply because the majority of South Carolinians rejected the party's basic ideological assumptions. Taking their cue from a commercial elite comprised of merchants and planter-entrepreneurs, the Whigs wanted to use the power of government positively to foster entrepreneurship and promote economic development. Whigs such as John Springs believed that "no government on Earth has [ever] succeeded" without a national bank and supported government subsidies for internal improvement projects. They denounced the Democratic "Loco Foco Party" for waging a mindless war against the financial stability and economic vitality of the country.[100] In contrast, the Democrats preferred to use the power

[98]James Louis Petigru to Hugh S. Legaré, March 31, 1835, in Carson, *James Louis Petigru,* pp. 173–176.

[99]On the problem of the Whig party at the national level, see Lynn L. Marshall, "The Strange Still-birth of the Whig Party," *American Historical Review* 72 (January, 1967):445–468; on Southern Whiggery, see Thomas Brown, "Southern Whigs and the Politics of Statesmanship, 1833–1841," *Journal of Southern History* 46 (August, 1980):361–380.

[100]John Springs to Andrew Baxter Springs, February 6, 1843, John Springs to Andrew Baxter Springs, April 1, 1844, John Springs to Andrew Baxter Springs, April 20, 1844, and John Springs, "To Voters of York District" [c. June, 1844], Springs Family Papers, SHC.

of government negatively to defend the liberty of independent producers against outside power. Upcountry Democrats, like Anderson planter O. R. Broyles, denounced the Whigs as a "monied aristocracy" whose platform threatened "every vestige of liberty and equality now amongst us."[101]

South Carolina Democrats were especially successful in linking the Whig economic program with the despised "Hamiltonian" system of the Republic's early years while identifying the Democrats with the treasured Jeffersonian heritage. Democrat Joseph Starke Sims claimed that the Whigs were like the original Federalists, who stood "for an Aristocracy in disguise." Democrats, on the other hand, were supposedly descendants of Jeffersonian Republicans, who were "for a democracy with a written constitution defining all powers granted."[102] Calhoun branded the Whig platform as a revival of "the prostrate system of federalism" under which power would pass from the people "into the hands of one of the most corrupt and exacting moneyed oligarchies of which history has left any record" and excoriated the Whig party as "neither more nor less than old federalism, tainted with anti mason and abolition, and turned demagouge [sic] of the lowest order."[103] The Democrats, Calhoun told supporters, offered policies which could "bring back the government to where it was when it started, free from all the Federal consolidation measures of the Hamilton school, and take a fresh start, such as Jefferson would give were he alive and at the helm."[104]

Yet however sharp their rhetorical assaults on the "moneyed aristocracy," South Carolina Democrats were, on the whole, hardly anti-commercial. In addition to the independent petty producers who simply wanted the government off their backs and out of their pocketbooks and who feared all concentrations of power, the Democratic party also included a significant entrepreneurial wing which feared that government promotion of entrepreneurial activity would simply enhance the power and privilege of certain select elites (usually those already well-established) at the expense of rival entrepreneurs who were long on drive and ability but short on political clout and connections. Once the Whig party became identified with the idea of a national bank it was almost inevitable that Ker Boyce and other powerful directors of the Bank of Charleston would gravitate toward the Democratic fold. South Carolina Democrats did not frown on entrepreneurship or commercial activity but merely on active government sponsorship of entrepreneurial activity and the development of an unhealthy coziness between the government and well-placed commercial elites. Whig fears that the Democrats were a wildly agrarian, "Loco-Foco" party were not without

---

[101]Address of O. R. Broyles [c. 1845], Oze Reed Broyles Papers, DU.

[102][J. Starke Sims], "To the Citizens of Union District" [c. December, 1838], Joseph Starke Sims Papers, DU.

[103]"Speech on the Report of the Secretary of the Treasury," June 21, 1841, and John C. Calhoun to Armistead Burt, August 20, 1840, in Wilson, ed., *The Papers of John C. Calhoun,* vol. 15, pp. 577–591, 334–335.

[104]John C. Calhoun to James Hampson, January 1, 1840, in Wilson, ed., *The Papers of John C. Calhoun,* vol. 15, pp. 29–30.

grounds; a substantial number of Democrats held precisely those views, but such fears were nevertheless overblown. Taken as a whole, South Carolina Democrats were not anti-capitalist; they simply opposed a potentially dangerous alliance between the government and the capitalists. Ironically, the very ideal of minimal government, or the negative state, which Calhoun envisioned primarily as a means of protecting the independent producer and his property from the oppressive exactions of a capricious state, served, in the long run, as a bulwark of economic liberalism, which emphasized the role of free and boundless competition among entrepreneurs as the motive force needed to drive economic development, that fondest of Whiggish dreams.[105]

For all his popularity and influence in South Carolina, Calhoun remained an enigma whose carefully calculated actions baffled his supporters as well as his rivals. Such was the case during the 1840s. While engaged in an open struggle to crush the Whig party in South Carolina, he was also seeking to use that struggle, and the fruits of the Calhounite victory, to effect a final reconciliation between Nullifiers and Unionists. During the campaign of 1840, a group of Calhounite operatives, the so-called "Rhett-Elmore clique," acting with the tacit consent of Calhoun, endorsed John Peter Richardson of the Sumter area, a Unionist who had thrown his support to the Democrats and the subtreasury by 1838, for governor. Old-line Calhounites, including Calhoun's staunch congressional ally, James Henry Hammond, were shocked, since they had expected the honor to be bestowed upon a deserving Calhoun loyalist. Yet while Rhett and Elmore were quietly rounding up Calhounite support for Richardson, another Calhoun supporter, Francis Pickens, was encouraging Hammond to announce his own candidacy. Pickens was angry with R. B. Rhett and Franklin Elmore because of their lukewarm support of his bid to become Speaker of the House of Representatives in 1839 and was determined not to support their choice for governor. Hammond, a man of both talent and overweening ambition, had risen rapidly through the Calhounite ranks during the 1830s, and was eager to be rewarded for his service. Since Calhoun was publicly silent on the subject, Hammond interpreted Pickens's encouragement as the indirect blessing of Calhoun. When Pickens finally told Hammond that he did not have Calhoun's ear on the subject, Hammond grew bitter and decided that both Pickens and Calhoun were "acting treacherously" toward him. The Preston Whigs tried to aggravate the division among

---

[105]For a systematic analysis of Calhoun's views on these issues, see Lacy K. Ford, "Republican Ideology in a Slave Society: The Political Economy of John C. Calhoun," *Journal of Southern History* (forthcoming). On the growing influence of economic liberalism in nineteenth-century America, see Joyce O. Appleby, *Capitalism and a New Social Order: The Republican Vision of the 1790s* (New York: New York University Press, 1984); Joyce O. Appleby, "What Is Still American in the Political Philosophy of Thomas Jefferson?," *William and Mary Quarterly* 39 (April, 1982):287–309; and Robert Kelley, *The Transatlantic Persuasion: The Liberal-Democratic Mind in the Age of Gladstone* (New York: Alfred A. Knopf, 1969). On the spread of economic liberalism in the South, see James Oakes, "From Republicanism to Liberalism: Ideological Change and the Crisis of the Old South," *American Quarterly* 37 (Fall, 1985):551–571.

Calhounites by hinting at support for Hammond. Hammond wanted Whig support but knew that open courtship of it would sabotage his chances, so he accused Rhett and Elmore of circulating false rumors about Preston's support for him in order to damage his candidacy. Calhoun was not pleased with the internecine strife which had developed over the spoils of office, but he refused to intervene. When the legislature met in December, the efforts of Rhett and Elmore were rewarded when Richardson defeated Hammond 104 to 47. Hammond was later pacified when Albert Rhett indirectly informed him that Calhoun intended to support him for governor in 1842.[106]

Hammond was elected governor in 1842 with Calhoun's aid, but Calhoun's efforts to unify the state continued to mystify his supporters, this time at the expense of Robert Barnwell Rhett's senatorial ambitions. In 1842, William Preston, who had been a "dead man" in the Senate since the Whig defeat in 1840, retired from politics. At the same time, Calhoun, whose presidential ambitions had been rekindled by his return to the Democratic party, followed the advice of Pickens and Rhett and retired from the Senate in order to ready himself for the presidential campaign of 1844. For one of the open seats, Calhoun supported George McDuffie, a veteran Calhounite. For the other seat, two Calhounites, Robert Barnwell Rhett and Francis Pickens, and two former Unionists, W. F. Davie and Daniel Huger, vied for support. When Rhett and Huger emerged as the frontrunners after one ballot, resentment of the Rhett-Elmore clique surfaced, and most of Davie's support went to Huger. Still eager to unify the state behind his presidential candidacy, Calhoun urged Pickens to throw his support to Huger as a conciliatory gesture. With the added support of Pickens's followers, Huger defeated Rhett on the third ballot, 82 to 71. Thus, Huger, a former Unionist and longtime critic of Calhoun, was elected to the United States Senate by Calhounite votes, while Rhett, Nullifier, Democrat, and one of Calhoun's top lieutenants, tasted defeat. Still, despite the frustrated ambitions of Hammond, Pickens, and Rhett, Calhoun's efforts at uniting South Carolina behind him were generally successful, and the South Carolina legislature unanimously nominated him for President in their last act of 1842.[107] "If we are not

---

[106]James Henry Hammond to Francis W. Pickens, January 18, 1840, James P. Carroll to Francis W. Pickens, March 8, 1840, James Henry Hammond to Francis W. Pickens, April 29, 1840, Francis W. Pickens Papers, DU; Louis T. Wigfall to Armistead Burt, February 22, 1840, Armistead Burt Papers, DU; John C. Calhoun to James H. Hammond, January 25, 1840, James H. Hammond to John C. Calhoun, February 9, 1840, John C. Calhoun to James H. Hammond, February 23, 1840, James H. Hammond to John C. Calhoun, March 10, 1840, John C. Calhoun to James H. Hammond, April 2, 1840, James H. Hammond to John C. Calhoun, April 29, 1840, James H. Hammond to John C. Calhoun, May 4, 1840, John C. Calhoun to James H. Hammond, May 16, 1840, in Wilson, ed., *The Papers of John C. Calhoun,* vol. 15, pp. 61–62, 94–95, 116–118, 131–138, 172–174, 188–194, 197–200, 228–231; Drew Gilpin Faust, *James Henry Hammond and the Old South: A Design for Mastery* (Baton Rouge: Louisiana State University Press, 1982), pp. 204–223; Edmunds, *Francis W. Pickens,* pp. 54–56; Lander, "The Calhoun-Preston Feud," pp. 49–61; Lord, "Young Louis Wigfall," pp. 96–112.

[107]John P. Richardson to Robert Barnwell Rhett, January 21, 1842, Franklin H. Elmore to Robert Barnwell Rhett, January 4, 1843, Robert Barnwell Rhett Papers, SHC; Albert Rhett to Armistead

Priest ridden, we are terribly Calhoun ridden," John Springs complained at the end of the legislative session, "and he that clamors the loudest now in his [Calhoun's] favor is the greatest Patriot."[108]

From the time of Calhoun's first victory in the state legislature on the sub-treasury issue in 1837 until Hammond was elected governor in 1842, the center of Calhounite strength in Charleston and the Lowcountry had been the Rhett-Elmore clique. The clique functioned well because of the persuasive skills of Albert and James Rhett in the state legislature and, after 1839, because of the power of Franklin Elmore as president of the Bank of the State of South Carolina. Gradually, as Elmore mastered the intricacies of bank administration, the highly personal, even consanguinal, nature of the clique's influence was replaced by the institutional leverage of the Bank, and the power of the so-called "Bank faction" in state politics. Indeed, by 1843, circumstances had pretty well broken the power of the Rhett and Elmore clans. Robert Barnwell Rhett had been defeated in his bid for the Senate in 1842. In 1843, James Rhett was defeated in a race for Congress by Isaac Holmes. Benjamin T. Elmore, Franklin's brother, had died unexpectedly in 1841, and in 1843, Albert Rhett, Calhoun's top legislative whip, died suddenly at the age of thirty-three. With its ranks thinned by death and its remaining leaders embarrassed by defeat, the Rhett-Elmore clique's role in the Calhounite organization was assumed by Elmore's bank and its political supporters. Soon the BSSC, under Elmore's leadership, became the target of much political criticism.[109]

The Bank of the State of South Carolina was chartered in 1812 with an overwhelming majority of Upcountry legislators voting in favor of the charter. At least initially, Upcountry populists viewed the BSSC as the democratic alternative to powerful private banks in Charleston which financed the city's heavy commercial traffic but which generally refused to make agricultural loans. Upcountry Republicans expected the BSSC, a "people's" institution, to be more responsive to the needs of planters and farmers than banks owned and controlled by Lowcountry plutocrats. The BSSC functioned with remarkable success for the next thirty years. By 1840, it had a capital stock of over $4,000,000, and it served the state in a variety of ways. The BSSC issued notes, provided loans to private investors, and extended long-term agricultural credit to the state's farmers and planters. At the same time, the BSSC also functioned as the financial arm of state government, selling state bonds and paying interest on them when instructed to do so, using its stock as collateral for state investment in various railroad and banking projects, using its own profits to pay off portions of the state

Burt, December 23, 1842, Armistead Burt Papers, DU; Wiltse, *Calhoun: Sectionalist*, pp. 99–102; Faust, *James Henry Hammond and the Old South*, pp. 224–236; Edmunds, *Francis W. Pickens*, pp. 62–70; White, *Rhett*, pp. 55–60.

[108]John Springs to Andrew Baxter Springs, December 27, 1842, Springs Family Papers, SHC.

[109]John Stuart to Robert Barnwell Rhett, January 9, 1843, John Stuart to Robert Barnwell Rhett, November 11, 1844, Robert Barnwell Rhett Papers, SHC; James Henry Hammond to Francis W. Pickens, December 24, 1839, Francis W. Pickens Papers, DU; Charleston *Mercury*, February 14, 1840; White, *Rhett*, pp. 58–59.

debt, and safeguarding funds deposited with the state by the federal government.[110]

Yet only a few years after its creation the BSSC began to receive criticism, often from the very people who had been the bank's most enthusiastic supporters initially, for not committing more of its resources to the financing of agricultural production in the state. And such criticism continued, varying only in degrees of intensity, throughout the BSSC's existence. Bank defenders usually replied, with considerable justification, that the BSSC was liberal in its extension of agricultural credit, in both the amount and terms of that credit, and that the BSSC was actually forgoing profits by trying up so much of its capital for so long on such a risky venture as staple agriculture. During the Panic of 1837 and its chaotic aftermath, the BSSC was a bedrock of financial stability for the state. In May 1837, the BSSC, which always kept a safe specie-to-paper currency ratio, suspended specie payment only when pressured to do so by state leaders anxious to save private banks from ruin. In 1838, during the middle of the financial crisis, the BSSC sold two million dollars' worth of state guaranteed bonds, mostly to European investors, to help finance the rebuilding of Charleston following the great fire which destroyed much of the city. In 1839, the BSSC maintained specie payments when most of the banks in the state had suspended them, and by the time Franklin Elmore took the helm in 1840, the bank had proven its ability to deal skillfully with hard times, and the conservatively managed institution's record of financial responsibility not only solidified the state's reputation for fiscal prudence but also helped dampen the general anti-bank sentiment which was sweeping the state.[111]

Yet despite its exemplary record, the BSSC had acquired its share of enemies, and these opponents promptly increased their attacks when the politically minded Elmore assumed the presidency. One line of criticism came from financial rivals of the BSSC. Other banks in the state attacked the privileged position of the BSSC and were especially critical of a state law which allowed only the BSSC to issue bills valued at less than five dollars. Leading this assault was Christopher Memminger, a director of the Planters and Mechanics Bank in Charleston, and chairman of the Ways and Means Committee of the state House of Representatives. In 1841, Memminger introduced a bill calling for a reduction in the capital stock of the BSSC and proposing to use the newly freed state funds to retire part of the public debt. Memminger's bill was defeated, but similar assaults on the BSSC by rival financial institutions continued for many years.[112]

The more penetrating criticism of the BSSC, however, was made on political, not financial, grounds. Anti-BSSC leaders raised many of the same objec-

[110]J. Mauldin Lesesne, *The Bank of the State of South Carolina: A General and Political History* (Columbia, S.C.: University of South Carolina Press, 1970), offers a thorough account of the Bank's activities. Hereinafter the Bank of the State of South Carolina will be abbreviated as the BSSC.

[111]Lesesne, *Bank of the State of South Carolina,* especially pp. 35–52.

[112]Henry D. Capers, *The Life and Times of Christopher G. Memminger* (Richmond: Everett Waddey, 1893); Franklin H. Elmore, *Defence of the Bank of the State of South Carolina* (Columbia: *Palmetto State Banner* office, n.d.); Lesesne, *Bank of the State of South Carolina,* pp. 52–70.

tions to the BSSC that Calhoun and the Democrats lodged against Whig proposals for a national bank. The involvement of state government in banking not only created a privileged class of bankers, financiers and politicians, but also corrupted both the government and the banking system. The BSSC's leading opponent, John Felder of Orangeburg, denounced the bank as anti-republican. "One of the greatest curses in our state is the vile concubinage of bank and state," Felder claimed. "Whenever . . . such cohabitation exists, the bank runs into politics and politicians run into the bank and foul disease and corruption ensue . . . Bank first, state second, Bank master, state slave, Bank head, state tail."[113] Other political charges against the Elmore-run BSSC were more specific. The bank, Elmore's critics charged, had created its own political faction in South Carolina, and this "Bank faction" was the primary instrument of Calhoun's influence on state government. The BSSC under Elmore, wrote B. F. Perry, a persistent BSSC critic, "became in a measure, a political machine, and the politicians were freely accommodated with loans by the Board of Directors. The bank controlled the State and Colonel Elmore controlled the bank."[114] John Springs, who owned substantial amounts of stock in several of the BSSC's competitors, insisted that "if the transactions of our Bank [BSSC] from the beginning to the present were thrown open to the Gaze of the *Dear People*" the information would reveal "a black list . . . of Partiality, Favoritism, and Partyism not often equaled."[115] And James Henry Hammond attributed Elmore's political influence to a "set of borrowers and bank men" who were always "ready to combine" against any challenge to the BSSC.[116] Nor was criticism of the "Bank faction" confined to those who often opposed Calhoun. Sampson H. Butler, an Edgefield native and Calhounite, also worried that the "Bank faction" was trying to establish a "spoils party" in the state. In a letter to Hammond, Butler outlined his objection to the "Elmore Regency":

> They are corrupt, selfish, mean, and treacherous. They are degrading the state with their villainy. . . . In fact they now regard it as their province, for the Treasury of the state is at their disposal. Every office is held by them, and no man expects preferment but through them.[117]

Charges that Elmore used the BSSC's economic leverage to influence voters and control state legislators proliferated during the early 1840s, but were never substantiated. Elmore and other pro-Bank spokesmen explicitly denied that they exerted any improper or undue political influence, but these denials were as

[113]John M. Felder to William Gilmore Simms, October 22, 1846, Hammond Papers, LC (microfilm at SCL).

[114]B. F. Perry, *Reminiscences of Public Men*, p. 99.

[115]John Springs to Andrew Baxter Springs, February 6, 1843, Springs Family Papers, SHC.

[116]James Henry Hammond to Francis W. Pickens, December 24, 1839, Francis W. Pickens Papers, DU.

[117]Sampson H. Butler to James Henry Hammond, February 5, 1840, Hammond Papers, LC (microfilm at SCL).

difficult to substantiate as the charges which prompted them. Calhoun was generally silent on the issue. He applauded the BSSC, and its conservative managers, for lending stability to South Carolina's fiscal and financial affairs. He also opposed eliminating or in any way weakening the BSSC because he felt that the resulting economic instability would undermine the state's ability to resist federal usurpation of power. Calhoun did not actively attempt to use the BSSC for his own political ends, nor did he work to silence the Bank's critics.[118]

The charges raised about the BSSC's function as a political, and usually pro-Calhoun, machine were undoubtedly exaggerated. Yet the criticism of the BSSC trapped most of the bank's defenders in an awkward paradox. The BSSC handled the state debt, managed many of its financial affairs, circulated the most widely accepted notes in the state, and helped finance almost every railroad or canal project in the state. As both a bastion of financial stability and an engine for economic development, the BSSC could hardly have served the state better, and no bank without the state's backing could have done nearly as well.[119] At the state level, the BSSC had done exactly what Alexander Hamilton had claimed the First Bank of the United States could do at the national level. Thus South Carolina, a state which had long since renounced Hamiltonianism in national politics, tolerated, and even encouraged, the operation of a powerful, and remarkably successful, Hamiltonian institution at home. Bank critics were well aware of this irony and seldom failed to include it in their polemics. BSSC opponent John Springs chided Calhoun and his loyalists for preaching "separation of the Government from Banks" in Washington and practicing the exact opposite in South Carolina. "How Badly the acts and facts of the case with S.C. politicians correspond with their Professions," Springs remarked. "I would Ask is there any other Government so deeply and intimately connected with a Bank as the State of S.C.?"[120] If Calhoun or his followers found any humor in the irony of their position, they were silent about it.

Moreover, the growing resentment of the pro-BSSC faction, and indirectly of Calhoun, revealed an important new cleavage which was emerging in South Carolina politics during the 1840s. Old divisions, such as that between Nullifiers and Unionists, or Democrats and Whigs, lingered on, but new differences were also developing. No longer were the Calhounites criticized primarily by those who resented South Carolina's relative isolation from the national mainstream and who felt that Calhoun's efforts to maintain an unusual degree of political independence for the state were radical and dangerous. Instead, the Calhounites increasingly began to hear charges that they were too anxious to work with the national Democratic party, too eager to defend South Carolina through political compromises, and too reluctant to take another bold stance of defiance against the federal government. In state politics, these critics charged that Calhoun and

---

[118]John C. Calhoun to Franklin H. Elmore, December 10, 1846, Elmore Papers, LC.
[119]Lesesne, *Bank of the State of South Carolina,* pp. 52–88.
[120]John Springs to Andrew Baxter Springs, February 6, 1843, Springs Family Papers, SHC.

the pro-bank faction had become a political "Establishment" determined to prepetuate its own control of the legislature, to maintain the status quo, even if spoilsmanship, corruption, and timidity were the result of its actions. The voices of B. F. Perry or Joel Poinsett denouncing Calhoun for leading South Carolina away from the Jacksonian majority, or of Petigru, Preston, and Thompson urging South Carolinians to unite with the national Whig party in opposition to Calhoun, were gradually giving way to new voices, usually young, proud, and idealistic in tone, which urged Calhoun to abandon altogether his attempts to work with national parties. The new criticism of Calhoun came, as a rule, from a younger generation of Calhounites who believed that Calhoun was too cautious and conservative, too much the politician and not enough the ideologue.[121]

This younger generation of South Carolina politicians was radical, having been nurtured on nullification and its aftermath but having never known the relative calm of the Monroe years, nor experienced the national perils of the War of 1812. Among the radicals who often criticized Calhoun during the 1840s were William Gilmore Simms, James Henry Hammond, and Robert Barnwell Rhett. Simms, a onetime Unionist newspaper editor who matured into the state's leading literary figure, developed a fast friendship with Hammond, who never forgave Calhoun for failing to support his first gubernatorial bid in 1840. Together, Simms and Hammond plotted a course designed to encourage Southern nationalism and to further their own political ambitions. They were among the most vocal critics of the BSSC and they worked hard to break the hold of the Democratic party on South Carolina. Attacking the Calhounites as "Hunkers," who were too much the creators of the existing order to pave the way for a new one, Hammond and Simms tried to put themselves in the vanguard of a movement that would "reform" South Carolina politics and prepare the state for a radical defense of Southern rights. Rhett, long a member of Calhoun's inner circle and one of his most valuable political operatives, also had his differences with Calhoun during the 1840s. Despite his own close ties to Elmore and the BSSC, Rhett believed that Calhoun's connections with the Charleston financial community, and in particular with the powerful financial *troika* of Ker Boyce, Henry W. Conner, and James Gadsden, gave vested commercial interests too much influence over South Carolina's relations with the federal government. Thus, after first managing Calhoun's unsuccessful presidential campaign, Rhett broke with his own mentor in 1844 and initiated the so-called "Bluffton Move-

---

[121]The strongest criticism of Southern politicians in the 1840s came from a group of Southern intellectuals who felt that the power of ideas and ideals was being overlooked by those who were attempting to fashion a political strategy for defending Southern Rights. Drew Faust, *A Sacred Circle: The Dilemma of the Intellectual in the Old South, 1840–1860* (Baltimore: Johns Hopkins University Press, 1977) offers an insightful analysis of one such group of intellectuals; John McCardell, *The Idea of a Southern Nation: Southern Nationalists and Southern Nationalism, 1830–1860* (New York: W. W. Norton, 1979), provides a thorough survey of the emergence of Southern nationalism and a balanced assessment of its romantic and visionary aspects.

ment," which called for separate state action against the protective tariffs introduced in the previous session of Congress.[122]

None of these radicals posed a serious threat to Calhoun during the 1840s. Simms and Hammond did much of their complaining in private, to a drawing-room constituency. Rhett's Bluffton Movement attracted only a handful of followers outside of his native Beaufort, and Rhett eventually sought to regain favor with Calhoun. Even the more potent anti-BSSC coalition accomplished little while Calhoun was alive. During the middle of the long-running BSSC controversy, Lexington district Democrat Lemuel Boozer told Congressman Armistead Burt that the people of his district "like to hear Calhoun praised very highly."[123] Moreover, in 1846, when a number of Edgefield politicians, including Francis Pickens, attacked Calhoun for his criticism of the Polk Administration's role in triggering the Mexican War, their charges fell largely on deaf ears. "Our people here love Mr. Calhoun as they would love a father," wrote Edgefield newspaper editor Joseph Abney, "and . . . his voice sounds here like a prophet's word.[124]

Yet these rumblings of discontent did cause the Calhounites some problems throughout the 1840s. More important, radical criticism of Calhoun foreshadowed the development of a radical faction in South Carolina politics whose influence would increase once Calhoun was no longer around to contain it. Finally, the "bolt" of former Calhoun lieutenants such as Hammond and Rhett again emphasized the frustration inherent in being an ambitious young politician in Calhoun's South Carolina, and hinted at how vigorous the contest for leadership would be once Calhoun was gone.[125]

---

[122]The political career of Simms has been analyzed by Jon L. Wakelyn, *The Politics of a Literary Man: William Gilmore Simms* (Westport, Conn.: Greenwood Press, 1973); Rhett's career is traced in White, *Rhett,* see especially pp. 68–134. See also Faust, *James Henry Hammond and the Old South,* especially pp. 257–303.

[123]Lemuel Boozer to Armistead Burt, January 2, 1843, Armistead Burt Papers, DU.

[124]Joseph Abney to Armistead Burt, June 6, 1846, Armistead Burt Papers, DU.

[125]White, *Rhett,* pp. 68–84; Wakelyn, *The Politics of a Literary Man,* pp. 158–187.

5

Secession Avoided: The Upcountry during the First Secession Crisis

By the late 1840s, the Jacksonian two-party system, which had brought stability and definition to national politics for at least a decade, strained to contain or ameliorate increasingly explosive sectional antagonisms. South Carolina, though loosely aligned with the Democratic party, remained largely outside the national party system. And John C. Calhoun harbored visions of a new Southern party, which would unite Democrats and Whigs in the region and also would be strong enough to protect the slaveholding interests within the Union. Calhoun maintained conditional ties to the Democrats as a strategy of survival, but he also cultivated Southern unity. After Calhoun crushed the incipient Whig revolt in the early 1840s, no concerted effort was mounted to establish a viable two-party system within South Carolina. Opposition to the dominant Calhoun-Democrats, who generally controlled the state legislature, emerged on an *ad hoc* basis from a variety of quarters, but never coalesced into anything resembling an organized opposition party.[1]

Still, the state's delicately balanced harmony belied important internal divisions on a variety of questions. To be sure, many of these divisions arose over state and local issues which had little to do with slavery. Yet, despite Calhoun's efforts to unify the state, leading South Carolina politicians often disagreed vehemently over how best to defend slavery and Southern society against the growing antislavery movement in the North. There was no significant dissent from the belief that slavery must be defended, even if it meant war and the sacrifice of the Union, but there were violent strategic and tactical disagreements

---

[1]David M. Potter, *The South and the Sectional Conflict* (Baton Rouge: Louisiana State University Press, 1968), pp. 87–150; Michael F. Holt, *The Political Crisis of the 1850s* (New York: John Wiley and Sons, 1978); William J. Cooper, Jr., *The South and the Politics of Slavery, 1828–1856* (Baton Rouge: Louisiana State University Press, 1978), especially pp. 269–321; Charles M. Wiltse, *John C. Calhoun: Sectionalist, 1840–1850* (Indianapolis: Bobbs-Merrill, 1951), pp. 394–473.

over exactly how the defense was to be made. Calhoun held the state's resistance strategy to the middle ground, working with the Democratic party while struggling to build a Southern vanguard which could stand boldly against abolitionists and free-soilers. In South Carolina, Calhoun was criticized, albeit ineffectively, from both sides. One group of conservative, nationally oriented politicians, consisting mainly of old Unionists, continued to berate Calhoun for holding the state out of the national mainstream, where it might fashion its defense of slavery around existing party ties as other Southern states did. From the other extreme, a group of young radicals chastised Calhoun for refusing to support bolder defiance of the federal government, such as the Bluffton movement, and for his continued cooperation with what they perceived as an increasingly unreliable Democratic party. Robert Barnwell Rhett, the state's most outspoken radical, complained loudly that Calhoun allowed his "name and popularity" to be used in support of "submission views" and "against his Old friends . . . the resistance Men of the State." Calhoun's caution, and his insistence that the South act as a whole, the radicals felt, yielded too much time and ground to treacherous opponents.[2]

As long as Calhoun was alive, the Calhounite center easily held against scattered opposition. The only real political contest during Calhoun's lifetime, B. F. Perry once noted, was over "who could get closest to him, and be the first to echo his voice." After Calhoun died, however, the issues surrounding the so-called Compromise of 1850 plunged South Carolina into a new debate over how to defend her rights that very nearly took the state out of the Union. Moreover, the scramble among Calhoun's long-frustrated rivals and eager heirs-apparent only complicated the uncertain political situation in the state.[3] Thus South Carolina entered the 1850s in a state of political turmoil and without the constraint of party fetters to help calm her. This turmoil, the first secession crisis, generated the most vigorous and divisive political campaigns since the nullification crisis and revealed how even strategic and tactical disagreements over Southern rights could nearly tear the state apart.

The catalyst which triggered the first secession crisis was added to the already volatile brew in 1846. That catalyst was the Wilmot Proviso, an amendment offered in the United States House of Representatives by a young Pennsylvania Democrat to President Polk's request for public money to purchase territory from Mexico during possible peace negotiations with that country. The controversial amendment attached a provision to that appropriations bill calling for the prohibition of slavery in any territory gained by the United States as a result of the peace

[2]Robert Barnwell Rhett to Armistead Burt, September 9, 1844, Armistead Burt Papers, DU; Laura A. White, *Robert Barnwell Rhett: Father of Secession* (New York: Century Co., 1931), pp. 68–134; Drew Gilpin Faust, *A Sacred Circle: The Dilemma of the Intellectual in the Old South* (Baltimore: Johns Hopkins University Press, 1977), pp. 132–135; Lillian A. Kibler, *Benjamin F. Perry: South Carolina Unionist* (Durham, N.C.: Duke University Press, 1946), pp. 217–238.

[3]Greenville *Southern Patriot*, February 19, 1852; Drew Gilpin Faust, *James Henry Hammond: A Design for Mastery* (Baton Rouge: Louisiana State University Press, 1982), pp. 296–303.

negotiations. The Wilmot Proviso passed the House easily, but was killed in the Senate. Yet despite the fact that the proviso was never enacted, it became a major issue in national politics. Calhoun called the proviso an "apple of discord" which threatened "to do much to divide the [Democratic] party." The proviso quickly became a focal point in the increasingly heated sectional debate over slavery, not only with regard to territory ceded by Mexico but also with regard to the Oregon territory. Overwhelming majorities of Northern Democrats in the House supported the Wilmot Proviso and similar measures on a number of occasions, and fourteen of the fifteen free state legislatures passed resolutions expressing support of the proviso. The new popularity of such militant antislavery sentiment in the North and the obvious complicity of Northern Democrats in the movement were both noted with alarm in South Carolina, and the state quickly mobilized in opposition.[4]

Oddly enough, South Carolina slaveholders, as a rule, never entertained visions of creating a vast slave empire out of huge chunks of Mexican territory. Newberry Democrat Paul Quattlebaum expressed the dominant sentiment among Upcountry politicians when he observed: "And suppose we acquire the whole of Mexico—then our trouble will have begun in earnest."[5] But when the Wilmot Proviso threw the gauntlet of "free-soil" down before them, Palmetto slaveholders accepted the challenge with both vigor and grim determination. Newspapers from all parts of the state heaped denunciation after denunciation on the proviso. The appearance of the issue, Calhoun argued, "may be made the occasion of successfully asserting our equality and rights, by enabling us to force the issue on the North." Moreover, Calhoun advised the South that it was always best "to meet danger on the frontier, in politics as well as war."[6] Calhoun's old rivals in the state generally agreed with him on this matter. Whig leader Waddy Thompson urged "resistance at all hazards and to every possible extremity to this insulting, degrading and fatal measure" which he believed threatened to reduce the South "into black provinces."[7] Even the devoted Unionist B. F. Perry was vehement in his repudiation of the proviso. Addressing his mountaineer and yeoman constituency in the hill country, Perry denounced the proviso as part of a long-standing abolitionist plot to make the black man "the equal of his master" and "to go with him to the polls and vote, to serve on juries . . . to

[4]Two accounts of South Carolina's first secession crisis written over sixty years ago are still quite useful. See Philip M. Hamer, *The Secession Movement in South Carolina, 1847–1852* (Allentown, Pa.: H. Ray Hass, 1918); and Chauncey Samuel Boucher, "The Secession and Co-operation Movements in South Carolina, 1848–1852," *Washington University Studies* 5 (April, 1918):67–138. More recently an important new monograph on the subject has appeared. See John Barnwell, *Love of Order: South Carolina's First Secession Crisis* (Chapel Hill: University of North Carolina Press, 1982). One shortcoming of Barnwell's monograph is his failure to pay adequate attention to district level politics during the crisis. See also Wiltse, *Calhoun: Sectionalist,* p. 289.

[5]Ernest M. Lander, Jr., *Reluctant Imperialists: Calhoun, the South Carolinians, and the Mexican War* (Baton Rouge: Louisiana State University Press, 1980), pp. 1–24; Paul Quattlebaum to Armistead Burt, February 19, 1848, Armistead Burt Papers, DU.

[6]Calhoun quotation taken from Hamer, *The Secession Movement in South Carolina,* pp. 10–11.

[7]Greenville *Mountaineer,* October 15, 1847.

meet the white man as an equal and visit his family, intermarry with his children and form one society and one family.'' Moreover, Perry not only mobilized opposition to the proviso by playing on the negrophobia of white yeomen but he also issued a stern warning to Northern Democrats who often looked to him as the voice of caution in South Carolina. Passage of the Wilmot Proviso, admonished longtime Unionist Perry, would be "tantamount to the dissolution of the Union."[8]

The people of South Carolina also mobilized in opposition to the Wilmot Proviso. A public meeting in Greenville in the fall of 1847 overwhelmingly endorsed a set of resolutions, drafted by Perry, which emphatically denounced the Wilmot Proviso and pledged the state to resistance ''at all hazards and to the last extremity.''[9] Within a year, organized protest spread to almost every corner of the state. In the lower Piedmont, the citizens of Fairfield district held a public rally on November 6, 1848, which excoriated the Wilmot Proviso as ''a gratuitous insult to the South'' and as the latest in a ''long series of indignities'' heaped upon the Southern people by the abolitionists. The Fairfield rally also protested the ''unjust'' Missouri Compromise, but offered to accept an extension of the 36° 30' line to the Pacific as a final territorial compromise with antislavery forces. After tendering what they considered a conciliatory offer, the citizens of Fairfield also established a permanent committee of correspondence to monitor sectional developments and gave that committee instructions to work for secession if no compromise was reached.[10] Newspapers in Spartanburg and Pendleton urged other districts to approve the Fairfield resolutions, and Congressman Armistead Burt told a wildly anti-Wilmot rally in Abbeville that only a convention of the slaveholding states could save the South from ''ultimate destruction.'' The local newspaper, the Abbeville *Banner,* agreed, calling for resistance to any proposed restriction of slavery in the territories ''if needs be at a sacrifice of the Union.''[11]

A small band of South Carolina Democrats joined an equally small rump of the state's nearly defunct Whig party to support Whig Zachary Taylor's presidential bid in 1848, but most of Calhoun's loyal lieutenants worked to hold an unenthusiastic state for Democrat Lewis Cass, whose past flirtations with free-soilers worried even his most vocal supporters in South Carolina. Calhoun, no doubt disappointed that he had not received serious consideration for the Democratic presidential nomination, remained aloof from the campaign despite anxious pleas from his followers that he state a preference.[12] ''I see much to

[8]Pendleton *Messenger,* December 10 and 17, 1847.

[9]Greenville *Mountaineer,* October 8, 1847.

[10]Columbia *South Carolinian,* November 14, 1848; *Carolina Spartan,* March 6, 1849; Charleston *Mercury,* November 16, 1848.

[11]Abbeville *Banner,* September 9, 1847; Charleston *Mercury,* October 13, 1848.

[12]Henry H. Conner to Armistead Burt, January 20, 1848, A. G. McGrath to Armistead Burt, January 30, 1848, Henry H. Townes to Armistead Burt, March 18, 1848, Henry H. Conner to Armistead Burt, May 25, 1848, Ker Boyce to Armistead Burt, May 31, 1848, Paul Quattlebaum to Armistead Burt, July 11, 1848, Armistead Burt Papers, DU; Richard F. Simpson to James L. Orr,

condemn and little to approve in either candidate," the senator told the editor of the Charleston *Mercury,* while advising friends that they should interpret his position as one of "standing on independent ground."[13] Calhoun's silence, however, was widely interpreted as tacit support for Cass, and most of Calhoun's followers wanted to keep the state in the Democratic column whenever possible. On the whole, the Calhounites accepted Taylor's victory stoically, attributing the triumph largely to the old General's personal popularity. The critical political struggle of the days ahead, they believed, would be waged along sectional rather than party lines.[14]

In the early months of 1849, mass meetings were again being held in almost every district as a show of support for Calhoun's widely circulated "Southern Address," which called for Southerners to unite and "stand up immovably in defense of rights involving your all—your property, prosperity, equality, liberty and safety."[15] On March 6, John Winsmith, a large slaveholder and former Nullifier, chaired a large rally in Spartanburg and advised the people of his home district that the threat from the North "cannot in fact be longer evaded—it must be met and met now." The rally endorsed resolutions declaring that "nothing would be more intolerable than submission to the grievances, injustice, and degradation which we have endured, and with which we are threatened," and established a committee of vigilance to coordinate the district's resistance efforts with those of its neighbors.[16] In neighboring Greenville, a public rally also endorsed Calhoun's address and created a Committee of Vigilance and Safety to protect the people "against all Abolition movements." O. R. Broyles told a crowd in nearby Anderson that "the question of right to our slave property is no longer an open question" and insisted that it was "beneath the dignity of the South to dally with such a subject of paramount consideration."[17] Former Whig J. H. Irby organized a large rally in Laurens, which created a "Committee of Safety" and urged that a state convention be held to map out a coherent strategy of resistance to the "threat of abolition and free-soil."[18]

By the early summer of 1849, every district in the Upcountry and almost every district in the state had endorsed resolves calling for resistance to further

---

March 7, 1848, Orr-Patterson Papers, SHC; John Springs to Andrew Baxter Springs, August 8, 1848, Andrew Baxter Springs to John Springs, August 16, 1848, Richard Austin Springs to John Springs, September 6, 1848, Springs Family Papers, SHC; Jon L. Wakelyn, "Party Issues and Political Strategy of the Charleston Taylor Democrats of 1848," *South Carolina Historical Magazine* 17 (April, 1972):72–86; Faust, *James Henry Hammond and the Old South,* pp. 292–294; John B. Edmunds, Jr., *Francis W. Pickens and the Politics of Destruction* (Chapel Hill: University of North Carolina Press, 1986), pp. 110–112.

[13]Charleston *Mercury,* September 5, 1848.

[14]Wiltse, *Calhoun: Sectionalist,* pp. 369–373.

[15]"Address of the Southern Delegates in Congress," in Richard K. Crallé, ed., *The Works of John C. Calhoun,* 6 vols. (New York: D. Appleton, 1855), vol. 6, pp. 290–313.

[16]*Carolina Spartan,* March 13, 1849.

[17]Speech of O. R. Broyles, [c. 1849], O. R. Broyles Papers, DU.

[18]Laurensville *Herald,* May 11, 1849.

attacks on the institution of slavery. Every district also established a committee of vigilance and safety designed not only to form a network of resistance organizations throughout the state but also to lead an intensified vigil against roving abolitionist incendiaries.[19] Later, after these initially non-partisan committees fell under the control of fire-eaters who favored immediate secession, their activities drew sharp criticism from some Upcountrymen. "What were they [Committees of Vigilance and Safety] organized for," asked the Greenville *Southern Patriot*, "but to over awe and control public opinion; to pry into the secrets of men and families, like the bloody inquisition of Spain, and the all powerful and unknown police of the French Revolution?"[20] When these committees were first organized, however, they enjoyed the whole-hearted support of the entire community.

Occasionally, the diligence of these watchdog committees was rewarded. In April 1849, fifty copies of an abolitionist pamphlet appeared in Spartanburg district, and during the following summer, the Spartanburg Committee of Safety seized an alleged abolitionist incendiary, J. M. Barrett, at Poole's Hotel in the town of Spartanburg. Barrett, posing as a researcher employed by Harwood and Company of New York City to gather data for a gazetteer, was discovered carrying abolitionist pamphlets among his materials. Barrett was arraigned in the informal setting of a town meeting and was then jailed to await trial. Charged with disseminating abolitionist propaganda in portions of the Upcountry, Barrett faced the death penalty. Public sentiment throughout the Upcountry favored that ultimate punishment if the suspect were convicted. Spartanburg authorities, however, deliberately delayed Barrett's trial as a means of prolonging the public's attention to the larger menace of abolition. Ultimately, with the point well made and the passions of the community cooled, Barrett was released on bail and allowed to flee to the North unharmed.[21]

South Carolina's growing hostility toward the North finally came to a head over the question of admitting the California territory to the Union. Even before the war with Mexico had been won, Pendleton Congressman Richard F. Simpson insisted that the South would not go on "sacrificing our lives and property to acquire territory not for the common benefit, but for the exclusive benefit of the non-Slaveholding States."[22] By 1849, former Unionist James Edward Henry emphatically declared, "I am a *disunionist* in preference to submission to the demands of the North."[23] Aware of the darkening public mood, Calhoun renewed his call for a Southern convention. Such a convention, Calhoun believed,

---

[19]Hamer, *The Secession Movement in South Carolina*, pp. 31–37.

[20]Greenville *Southern Patriot*, September 5, 1851.

[21]William Joseph MacArthur, Jr., "Antebellum Politics in an Upcountry County: National, State and Local Issues in Spartanburg County, South Carolina, 1850–1860" (M.A. thesis, University of South Carolina, 1966), pp. 22–23; James Edward Henry to Samuel Finley Patterson, August 8, 1849, Samuel Finley Patterson Papers, DU.

[22]Richard F. Simpson to George F. Townes, December 31, 1846, Townes Family Papers, SCL.

[23]James Edward Henry to Samuel Finley Patterson, March 17, 1849, Samuel Finley Patterson Papers, DU.

would not only help the Southern states agree on a common strategy for defending their rights against the growing antislavery movement in the North but would also present a convincing display of regional solidarity. If the South presented a united front to its opponents, Calhoun maintained, the Union might yet be saved. Still, South Carolina radicals were careful to distance themselves from Mississippi's plan to call for just such a Southern convention because they feared that a close identification of the movement with South Carolina would taint the movement with the suspicion of radicalism. Yet when Mississippi called for a Southern convention to assemble in Nashville in June 1850, South Carolina released her pent-up enthusiasm in favor of the meeting.[24]

Before delegates were selected for the Nashville convention, however, the introduction of Henry Clay's famous "Omnibus Bill," a set of compromises designed to admit California to the Union as a free state under terms somewhat less inimical to Southern interests than those of the Wilmot Proviso, created new turmoil throughout the South. South Carolinians from all quarters lost no time in denouncing Clay's proposals. In Washington, Calhoun, whose health was failing rapidly, prepared a response which called on the North to agree on a permanent sectional truce whose terms would give the slaveholding states control over their own destiny but which would also preserve the Union. A feeble Calhoun appeared in the Senate on March 4 but asked that a young and vigorous James Mason of Virginia be allowed to read the text of what proved to be the great Carolinian's last major speech.[25] If the North insisted on admitting California as a free state, Calhoun argued, it would be clear that the section's real motives were "power and aggrandizement." It was still possible to save the Union, Calhoun maintained, but Clay's plan could not do it. The time had come when the South was forced to demand "a full and final settlement, on the principle of justice, of all questions at issue between the two sections." As far as the preservation of the Union was concerned, Calhoun contended that:

> The North has only to will it to accomplish it—to do justice by conceding the South an equal right in the acquired territory, and to do her duty by causing the stipulation relative to fugitive slaves to be faithfully fulfilled—to cease agitating the slave question, and to provide for the insertion of a provision in the constitution, by an amendment, which will restore to the South, in substance, the power she possessed of protecting herself, before the equilibrium between the sections was destroyed by the action of this Government.

If the Northern people could not accept such a settlement, the South's options would be clearly defined. "If the question is not now settled," Calhoun continued,

> it is uncertain whether it ever can hereafter be; and we . . . should come to a distinct understanding as to our respective views, in order to ascertain whether

[24]Boucher, "The Secession and Cooperation Movements in South Carolina," pp. 86–94.
[25]Wiltse, *Calhoun: Sectionalist*, pp. 406–410; Barnwell, *Love of Order*, pp. 84–85.

the great questions at issue can be settled or not. If you, who represent the stronger portion, cannot agree to settle them on the broad principle of justice and duty, say so; and let the States we both represent agree to part in peace. If you are unwilling we should part in peace, tell us so, and we shall know what to do, when you reduce the question to submission or resistance.[26]

On March 31, 1850, John C. Calhoun died in his Washington quarters. His death was mourned throughout the nation, even in those areas where his principles were deplored. During a momentary hiatus from debate, eulogies were delivered in the United States Senate by Henry Clay and Daniel Webster, by Andrew Pickens Butler, the junior senator from South Carolina, and by Jeremiah Clemens of Alabama, an older cousin of writer Samuel Clemens. Three weeks later, Calhoun's body was returned to South Carolina, where it lay in state at the Charleston City Hall for several days. A burial service was held at St. Phillips Church, and the body was interred in a quiet churchyard across the street. A committee of Calhoun's friends and neighbors from Pendleton went to Charleston prepared to take Calhoun's body back to his beloved Fort Hill so that his final resting place might be in his native Upcountry. The state legislature, however, bowed to the wishes of the people of Charleston and decreed that Calhoun's body should remain in the state's largest and most visited city.[27]

Calhoun's career in public life spanned over forty years. His first speeches in Congress concerned the issues that would eventually lead to the War of 1812 and his last speech dealt with the sectional controversy that was temporarily quieted by the Compromise of 1850. He was truly one of the titans of antebellum American politics, almost a larger-than-life figure, like Jackson, Clay, and possibly Webster, whose persona grew and grew until it became a corporeal institution. Certainly Calhoun was the dominant figure in South Carolina politics throughout most of his lifetime. His prominence undoubtedly focused an unusual amount of national attention on events in South Carolina, and, at the same time, national issues always loomed large in South Carolina politics because of Calhoun's influence.

Calhoun virtually embodied most of the major political themes of Jacksonian America. Nullification, the Bank War, the emergence of the second national party system, the rise of abolitionism, the debate over the sub-treasury, the problems of westward expansion, the controversy over slavery in the territories, and the deepening sectional animosities were foremost among the problems and issues confronting Jacksonian America, and Calhoun was always close to the center stage, always in the thick of the debate, always a figure with whom to be reckoned. Yet if Calhoun was almost the embodiment of Jacksonian politics, he was also something of a pre-Jacksonian politician. If, as some historians claim, the Jacksonian era was the period when vigorous two-party competition joined

---

[26]John C. Calhoun, "Speech on the Slavery Question," March 4, 1850, in Crallé, ed., *Works of Calhoun*, vol. 4, pp. 542–573. Quotation taken from pp. 572–573.

[27]Wiltse, *Calhoun: Sectionalist*, pp. 473–481.

Constitutional democracy as part of the American political gospel, then Calhoun was at least something of an anachronism. Though no stranger to the rigors of political competition, particularly to the hotly contested campaigns of the South Carolina Upcountry, Calhoun never accepted institutionalized competition as a political ideal. Michael Wallace has argued that Van Buren and other New Yorkers eventually saw permanent two-party competition as the great virtue of the democratic political system. It was this competition which not only kept choices before the people but also insured that the will of the majority was heeded, at least to the extent that politicians ever heed the public will. Calhoun, however, was part of an older, and equally legitimate, tradition in American politics, a tradition which had dominated South Carolina since before the American Revolution. That tradition, though democratic in the sense that it was based on white manhood suffrage and insisted on the absolute sovereignty of the people, also emphasized the virtue of political consensus. The truly democratic polity, the one where individual liberty was held most dear, was not the one in which a mere numerical majority held sway, but one in which the government expressed the will of the whole, or at least as much of the whole as possible. Calhoun saw the task of the politician not as simply a matter of forging a majority and then pressing the interests of that majority to fullest advantage, but as a matter of constructing a larger consensus around the majority and using the power of that consensus in defense of liberty and other republican values.[28]

Calhoun, of course, was an astute politician. He did not expect unanimity in South Carolina on any issue, except perhaps opposition to the abolitionists, and, as we have seen, he certainly did not shy away from political competition once a challenge emerged. Yet Calhoun's preference for the "country-republican" consensus ideal always influenced his attitude toward South Carolina politics. He always fought for victory, then sought reconciliation. He never looked only to reward the faithful but also to bring the opposition back into the fold. He never wanted merely to dominate South Carolina politics but rather to unite the state behind his actions. Although Calhoun seldom, if ever, succeeded in actually uniting the whole state behind him, he did frequently have the overwhelming majority of South Carolinians on his side, and he made the unusual cohesion within South Carolina work to give the state a loud and strong voice in national forums. The purpose of the consensus preached by Calhoun, and usually practiced by his followers, was to achieve for South Carolina as a whole a sort of political independence that was essentially the personal independence of the republican freeholder writ large. South Carolina could then, like Calhoun, stand on its "own bottom," beyond the sway of demagogues and above the corrupting influence of spoilsmen. Throughout his life, Calhoun and his followers kept South Carolina half-in and half-out of the Jacksonian mainstream, waging a series of heated grassroots campaigns, literally going field-to-field and door-to-door wooing

---

[28]On the comparison with Van Buren, see Michael Wallace, "Changing Concepts of Party in the United States: New York, 1815–1828," *American Historical Review* 74 (December, 1968):453–491.

voters, but always, even when acting as a tough partisan, standing as a barrier to the development of a permanent two-party system in South Carolina.[29]

In state politics, Calhoun was always the dominant figure, but his dominance was never absolute. Challenges to Calhoun's leadership never succeeded, but they never disappeared either. Calhoun's influence in South Carolina, based as it was upon popular mandate and thorough, though informal, political organization, was often most potent when least overt. Calhoun's presence was felt even when his hand was not visible. Moreover, during the last years of his life, when the hand of Calhoun was visible, it appeared most often as the steadying hand of tradition, of an existing order trying to save both itself and the American experiment in republicanism. With Calhoun no longer at the top, the Calhounite organization was likely to disintegrate into a number of quarreling factions, each vying for dominance. Indeed, at least one reason Calhoun had not retired from public life in the early 1840s was that he feared an unseemly and divisive battle over succession. Several months after Calhoun's death, both Rhett and Hammond, each "contending for the crown," momentarily put their personal ambitions aside and delivered belated eulogies for Calhoun in Charleston. Privately, however, many of Calhoun's former opponents judged his career more harshly. "His death has relieved South Carolina of political despotism," wrote B. F. Perry. "Every man may now breathe more freely as England did after the death of Henry the Eighth. There will be divisions amongst us [and] I am glad of it." Perry's complaint about Calhoun may have been exaggerated, but his prophecy was soon fulfilled. Within a few months of Calhoun's death, South Carolina was divided over the issue of whether or not to secede from the Union.[30]

While South Carolina continued to mourn Calhoun, the debate over slavery in the territories resumed in Washington. Other Palmetto politicians rushed to replace Calhoun as leading Southern critic of Clay's compromise proposals. Back home, the delegation elected to represent South Carolina at the Nashville Convention was moderate as a whole, despite the inclusion of Rhett and a handful of other fire-eaters.[31] Yet even moderates in South Carolina were adamant in their opposition to the admission of California as a free state. James L. Orr, a moderate from Anderson district who was usually quite cautious when speaking on sectional issues, boldly warned the North that the South would not be excluded from all western territory:

> I do not appeal to northern men to do us justice; I hope I never shall be so far
> lost to self-respect as to become a supplicant at the feet of power. We tender you

[29]John C. Calhoun, "A Disquisition on Government and a Discourse on the Constitution and Government of the United States," in Crallé, ed., *The Works of Calhoun*, vol. 1, pp. 1–107; James D. Clarke, "Calhoun and the Concept of 'Reactionary Enlightenment': An Examination of the Disquisition on Government" (Ph.D. dissertation, University of Keele, 1982); Gillis J. Harp, "Taylor, Calhoun, and the Decline of a Theory of Political Disharmony," *Journal of the History of Ideas* 46 (January, 1985):107–120.

[30]Entry of April 28, 1850, Benjamin F. Perry Diary, vol. 2, SHC.

[31]Thelma Jennings, *The Nashville Convention: Southern Movement For Unity, 1848–1850* (Memphis: Memphis State University Press, 1980), pp. 107–111.

this line to the Pacific [the Missouri Compromise line]—you can accept it or reject it; but there is one thing which it is my duty now to say: we do not intend to submit to exclusion from that territory; we will have a fair portion of it, "peacefully if we can—forceably if we must."[32]

John Springs, a still unrepentant Whig who watched some of the Congressional debate from the gallery during the summer of 1850, also concluded that the question had been reduced "to two desperate alternatives, submission or disunion." The Northern majority, Springs reported, "seemed determined to ride roughshod over the minority in perfect disregard of the Constitution and in violation of law and Justice. . . ."[33]

As the various components of the legislative package that would eventually be known as the Compromise of 1850 were steered through a balky and factionalized Congress in the fall, a fledgling secession movement was already underway in South Carolina. The overwhelming majority of South Carolinians saw the various bills passed by Congress not as a compromise but as a series of concessions by the South. "The signs of the times," lamented one Upcountry newspaper editor, "disclose the solemn truth that we must give up the Union or give up slavery."[34] The state's radicals, those men who favored immediate secession, preferably in cooperation with other Southern states but alone if necessary, quickly mobilized a vigorous statewide campaign to rally the people to their cause. New Southern Rights Associations appeared in virtually every district, and many of these Associations quickly fell under radical control, as did many of the remaining Vigilance and Safety committees. Yet almost as quickly as South Carolina began to move toward secession, the other Southern states quietly backed away from it. Fire-eaters such as Yancey in Alabama and Quitman in Mississippi worked hard to radicalize their states, but generally found their constituents willing to acquiesce in the recent compromise. "South Carolina alone is disposed to be dissatisfied and overturn the government," observed the persistent Unionist B. F. Perry. "This she cannot do."[35]

Both the moderate Calhounites and the radical fire-eaters in South Carolina had long feared that the commitment of the rest of the South to the national two-party system would hinder the development of a strong and united resistance movement in the region. In South Carolina, as one Calhounite observed, there were "not two great parties, nearly balanced, waging ever a fierce and dubious warfare upon each other; each watching sleeplessly for advantage over its adversary, making false issues, distorting facts, fabricating motives." Instead, there existed "but one party in South Carolina, and that emphatically the State." As a result, South Carolina was "at liberty to act, on convictions that were common to the whole South, but the force of which was elsewhere obstructed . . . by the jealous rivalry of leaders and the confused strife of parties."[36]

[32]*Congressional Globe,* 31 Congress, 1 Session (June 12, 1850), p. 1189.
[33]John Springs to Andrew Baxter Springs, July 22, 1850, Springs Family Papers, SHC.
[34]Laurensville *Herald,* July 5, 1850.
[35]Entry of December 29, 1850, Benjamin F. Perry Diary, vol. 2, SHC.
[36]Charleston *Mercury,* November 14 and 15, 1849.

South Carolina was not, of course, without its political mavericks and dissi-
dents. Battered remnants of the Whig party still lay scattered around the state,
and their spokesmen, Waddy Thompson, William C. Preston, James L. Petigru
and others were heard from now and then. Certain maverick Democrats who
usually opposed Calhoun, such as Perry and an aging Joel Poinsett, also had
followers. On the whole, however, South Carolina had been a one-party state
since the Calhoun-Democrats overwhelmed the Whigs in the early 1840s, and
Calhoun himself had been the great political impresario at that party's head.
More important, perhaps, was the observation that the interests of the dominant
party were identical to the interests of the state, or, more precisely, that the party
was not, in fact, a party but actually the political arm of the state itself. The
tendency of a party which controls a government so completely, and in the case
of South Carolina controls it with strong popular support, to assume that the
party is, in fact, the government was not unknown in American politics. In the
1790s the Federalists, in their desire to create an Augustan age for the young
Republic, had drifted very far toward that assumption before the rise of the
Jeffersonian opposition destroyed their predominance. The Calhoun-Democrats
of South Carolina during the 1840s would doubtless have found any comparison
to the Federalists odious. The Calhounites believed that the identity between
their loosely organized "party" and the state as a whole insured internal harmony and allowed South Carolina to speak, as Calhoun always desired, with one
voice on national affairs. South Carolina, with the Calhoun-Democrats speaking
on behalf of the state, was free to take the lead in resisting "Northern Aggression" since internal partisan wrangling was minimized by one-party hege-
mony.[37]

Having quickly seized the initiative, Robert Barnwell Rhett and his coterie of
fire-eaters pushed South Carolina far toward secession during 1850–51. Radicals
campaigned hard in the fall of 1850 and won strong representation in the state
legislature in the October elections. When the annual session convened in December, it was soon obvious that radicals favoring the secession of South Carolina controlled both chambers. As a result, the legislature approved much of the
radicals' agenda, though not without lengthy debate. The radicals' first priority
was to have the legislature call for a convention of the state to consider the
question of secession. There were enough legislators who thought that separate
state secession by South Carolina was "impractical" or "impolitic" to prevent
the convention bill from getting the necessary two-thirds' majority in both
houses, but a compromise bill drafted by the radicals passed easily. The compromise bill called for the election of delegates to the proposed state convention and
set February 10 and 11, 1851, as the dates for that election but did not specify a
date for the convention to meet, leaving that task up to the next legislature. The

---

[37]On the Federalists' tendency in this regard, see Gordon S. Wood, *The Creation of the American
Republic, 1776–1787* (Chapel Hill: University of North Carolina Press, 1969), pp. 519–564; and
John D. Howe, *From the Revolution to the Age of Jackson: Innocence and Empire in the Young
Republic* (Englewood Cliffs, N.J.: Prentice Hall, 1973). See also the Charleston *Mercury*, December
1 and 10, 1849.

compromise bill also endorsed the idea that another Southern "Congress or Convention" be held in January 1852, and mandated that South Carolina elect delegates to this regional assembly in October 1851. On other matters, the radicals generally had their way. Rhett was elected to the United States Senate; John Hugh Means, a fire-eater from Fairfield, was elected governor, and an additional $350,000, an amount equal to the total state expenditures for the previous year, was appropriated for military preparedness. To help finance this dramatic military readiness program, the legislature imposed a 50 percent across-the-board tax increase, raising the head tax on slaves from 56¢ to 85¢, and raising the tax rate on real property from 35¢ per $100 of assessed value to 53¢ per $100.[38]

The winter campaign for the election of delegates to the special state convention was an unusually quiet one. The radicals who favored separate state secession by South Carolina pressed their advantage while their opponents floundered. The radicals fielded a slate of candidates in every district and, by most calculations, won more than 120 of the 169 seats in the special convention. The results, however, were anything but conclusive. The turnout for the special mid-winter election was light all across the state. In Charleston there were only 873 votes cast in the special election, compared with 2,743 in the legislative elections of the previous fall. In Richland, Francis Lieber reported that voter turnout fell from 1,400 in October 1850, to about 800 in the special election. In the Upcountry, voter turnout in Spartanburg fell from just over 2,000 in the fall to 1,125 in the special election, while in York district 765 votes were cast in the special election, compared with nearly 2,100 votes in the heated legislative races the previous October.[39] Armistead Burt, the Calhounite and congressman from Abbeville who opposed separate state secession, claimed that he had "heard but very few express opinions in favor of the secession of South Carolina alone," and argued that since "the subject was not discussed before the people," their judgment was "neither exercised nor formed upon it." Moreover, the radicals' victory in February also spurred their loosely organized opposition into concerted action. Indeed, the very term "cooperationist," which the opposition came to use as its party label, first came into common use early in 1851.[40]

In the strictest sense, the term cooperationist referred to those South Carolinians who would support secession if and only if South Carolina seceded along with a number of other Southern states. In actuality, the Cooperationist party was a loose coalition of factions who opposed separate state secession from a variety

[38]Hamer, *The Secession Movement in South Carolina*, pp. 73–83; *Carolina Spartan*, November 21, 1850; Laurensville *Herald*, October 18, 1850; *Acts of the General Assembly of the State of South Carolina, 1850* (Columbia, S.C.: J. C. Morgan, 1850), pp. 1–10; *Reports and Resolutions of the General Assembly of South Carolina, 1851* (Columbia, S.C.: J. C. Morgan, 1851), pp. 1–30.

[39]Charleston *Mercury*, October 17, 1850, and February 12, 1851; Francis Lieber to Daniel Webster, February 13, 1851, quoted in Hamer, *The Secessionist Movement in South Carolina*, p. 86; Laurensville *Herald*, October 18, 1850, and February 14, 1851; Yorkville *Miscellany*, February 15, 1851.

[40]Letter of Armistead Burt to Thomas B. Byrd in *Southern Rights and Cooperation Documents* (Charleston, S.C., 1851), No. 3, pp. 1–16.

of different perspectives. One group of Cooperationists, unofficially headed by strong Southern nationalists such as James Henry Hammond and William Gilmore Simms, saw secession as the only hope for the slave South in the long run, but felt that South Carolina should not act alone. Moreover, they recognized that the South as a whole was not ready for secession and nationhood in 1851. The Southern nationalists' objection to immediate separate state secession was philosophical as well as tactical. Not only would separate action by a single state probably be doomed to failure but advocates of such a policy also ignored the transformation of the Southern mind that would be necessary if a bold policy of Southern resistance was to succeed. It would take more time for the South to prepare itself to accept the saving grace of secession.[41]

Another group of Cooperationists, one which drew considerable support from Upcountry planters, opposed separate state secession for purely tactical reasons. Unlike the Southern nationalists who actually preferred to delay secession, this group of Cooperationists felt that the South had endured enough "humiliation" and "degradation" at the hands of the North, and believed that the terms of the Compromise of 1850 provided sufficient provocation to justify immediate secession, but felt that separate state secession was both foolish and futile. Arch-radical Maxcy Gregg assessed this "section of the [Cooperationist] coalition" as one comprised of men "who, sensible of the degradation and danger of our condition, desire to resist" but who also regarded the cooperation of other Southern states "either as indispensible, or of such paramount importance as not to justify separate action."[42] Perhaps nobody expressed the sentiments of this faction better than did two Cooperationist leaders in York district, planter-lawyer Isaac D. Witherspoon and planter-physician James Rufus Bratton. "One thing I feel confident of," Witherspoon lamented, "is that the abolition movement cannot be stopped; it may be checked for a season . . . but it cannot be reined in." South Carolina, he continued, "has the right to act alone," but the state "should not cut itself off from others" by attempting "to force cooperation by precipitive action." Witherspoon was ready to secede, but he knew that South Carolina's hands were tied by a lack of support from other states. Bratton also campaigned hard against separate state action in 1851, but only did so because he believed the solo course to be foolish, not because he felt secession unnecessary. "In her [South Carolina's] present political connection with the general government," Bratton told his followers, "she has but one choice—a noble and manly defense and self-preservation or slavish submission and self-degradation."[43] This faction agreed with the Southern nationalists that

---

[41]On Hammond, see Faust, *James Henry Hammond and the Old South*, pp. 284–303. On Simms, see Jon L. Wakelyn, *The Politics of a Literary Man: William Gilmore Simms* (Westport, Conn.: Greenwood Press, 1973), pp. 158–187. On budding southern nationalism in South Carolina and the rest of the South, see John M. McCardell, *The Idea of a Southern Nation: Southern Nationalists and Southern Nationalism, 1830–1860* (New York: W. W. Norton, 1979), especially pp. 141–176.

[42]Letter of Maxcy Gregg for Confidential Circulation among Members of the Secession Party, October 24, 1851, Thomas Ellison Keitt Papers, DU.

[43]Yorkville *Miscellany*, June 14 and July 15, 1851; Laurensville *Herald*, August 29 and September 5, 1851; *Carolina Spartan*, September 4 and 11, 1851.

the rest of the South was not ready for secession, but, unlike the Southern nationalists, this group did not see a cultural and intellectual transformation of the South as a necessary prerequisite for a cooperative secession movement. Instead, they waited only for a more politically propitious moment.

Fine shades of meaning distinguished this second faction of Cooperationists from a third faction headed by Anderson Democrat James L. Orr. This so-called "Orr faction" was probably the largest single group of Cooperationists and was certainly the dominant faction in the Upcountry. Orr and most of his followers walked a tightrope. Seeing themselves as loyal Calhounites, the Orr faction wanted to defend slavery and Southern rights within the Union if at all possible. If the choice between slavery and the Union were forced upon them, they would choose slavery, perhaps with some remorse for the Union, but certainly with no reluctance. By 1851, Orr and his supporters believed that the choice was, in fact, being forced upon them. But they were willing to secede if, and only if, a number of the other slaveholding states would join them in a cooperative secession movement. After the Compromise of 1850, Orr predicted that "the dissolution of this Union and the establishment of a Southern and Northern confederacy is an inevitable necessity" unless the federal government was reformed drastically, and, Orr concluded, "I confess I see no hope of it [reform]." Yet Orr was adamantly opposed to separate state secession. He argued that cooperative secession "greatly reduces the prospect of the Federal Government treating secession as revolutionary." "My advice is *patience,*" Orr told the voters, "stand upon your arms until you can give a blow that will finally despatch [sic] your enemy."[44]

Despite his pessimism in 1851, Orr, and many of his followers, had not yet completely given up on the Union. If the Union could be reformed, if, as Calhoun had hoped, a slaveholders' party could be formed to protect Southern rights within that Union, then Orr would work to save it. In 1851, the Orr faction felt that the "redemption" of the federal government was unlikely, but that there were still glimmers of hope. Orr, like Calhoun, believed that the key to the success of the Southern cause, whether in or out of the Union, lay in Southern unity. The Union could not be saved unless Southern politicians presented a united front in Washington, and a secession movement could not succeed without the cooperation of a majority of Southern states. Because the Orr faction maintained some hope, however faint, that the Union could be saved, they were scorned by the radicals as "submissionists," and were suspected in many quarters of being Unionists in disguise. Orr emphatically denied these charges, claiming, "Our people here are not submissionists—nearly all are for resistance . . . to the Clay Compromise." But at the same time the politically adroit Andersonian kept the door open, slightly but noticeably, for national reconciliation. "Let no Carolinian foster the thought of submission," Orr counseled; "let our purpose be unalterably fixed to persevere, if need be, years in

---

[44]On Orr, see Roger P. Leemhuis, *James L. Orr and the Sectional Conflict* (Washington: University Press of America, 1979), pp. 15–27; *Speech of James L. Orr to the Convention of the Southern Rights Association, Held in Charleston, May, 1851* (Charleston, 1851), pp. 1–16.

obtaining redress for past wrongs, either in the Union or by a Southern Confederacy."[45]

During the campaign of 1851, these three Cooperationist factions forged a working alliance with South Carolina's small but vocal band of Unionists. The Unionists were really not "cooperationists" at all, since they opposed secession outright, but they worked closely with the Cooperationist party in opposition to the policy of immediate, separate state secession advocated by the radicals. Throughout the campaign the Unionists sounded the same warnings about the foolhardiness of South Carolina's seceding alone that other Cooperationists trumpeted so widely, but the Unionists also opposed cooperative secession as well as separate state action. Maxcy Gregg, who loathed these Unionists, described them as men who would save the Union "at the expense of whatever submission and degradation may be required." A handful of these men, among whom the eccentric neo-Federalist and Whig James L. Petigru was foremost, were, in fact, unconditional Unionists.[46] They opposed the dissolution of the Union at any time and under any circumstances. The majority of the Unionists, however, including the most popular Unionist leader, B. F. Perry, were conditional Unionists.[47] The conditional Unionists claimed that they would support secession if and when the threat, as they perceived it, to slavery and Southern rights was grave and immediate. In 1851, Perry and other Unionists simply did not think that such danger existed. Perry's sentiments were echoed by his friend and fellow Unionist Richard Yeadon, a Charleston lawyer and journalist:

> If no reasonable compromise can be obtained from our Northern brethren, I am ready for disunion as a dire and hateful alternative and refuge from intolerable insult [and] wrong—but I unhesitatingly prefer Clay's compromise to disunion and will resolutely stand up to that mark.[48]

Perry himself wrote in May 1851, "That we are in favor of the Union, under the Compromise, is most certainly true. . . . We are anxious, therefore, for a Southern Congress, which will secure the rights of the slaveholding States, redress our wrongs, and preserve the Union."[49]

According to one sympathetic observer, only a "very small minority" of South Carolinians were outright Unionists. Like the Union party of the nullifica-

---

[45]Donald H. Breese, "James L. Orr, Calhoun, and the Cooperationist Tradition in South Carolina," *South Carolina Historical Magazine* 80 (October, 1979):273–285; *Speech of James L. Orr to the Convention of Southern Rights Associations,* pp. 1–16.

[46]Letter of Maxcy Gregg for Confidential Circulation among Members of the Secession Party, October 24, 1851, Thomas Ellison Keitt Papers, DU.

[47]Kibler, *Perry,* pp. 239–277; James Petigru Carson, *Life, Letters, and Speeches of James Louis Petigru* (Washington: W. H. Lowdermilk, 1920), pp. 280–294; Lacy Ford, "James Louis Petigru: The Last South Carolina Federalist," in Michael O'Brien and David Moltke-Hansen, eds., *Intellectual Life in Antebellum Charleston* (Knoxville: University of Tennessee Press, 1986), pp. 152–185.

[48]Richard Yeadon to B. F. Perry, June 4, 1850, quoted in Kibler, *Perry,* p. 245; John Calhoun Ellen, "The Public Life of Richard Yeadon" (M.A. thesis, University of South Carolina, 1953).

[49]Greenville *Southern Patriot,* May 16, 1851.

tion era, the Unionists of 1851 were an odd mélange of political outsiders with widely varying viewpoints. Perry and Joel Poinsett were old-line Jacksonian Democrats who believed that nationalism and democracy worked hand-in-hand for the benefit of all Americans. Waddy Thompson was a Nullifier-turned-Whig who was forced into the opposition when he refused to follow Calhoun back into the Democratic fold in the late 1830s. John Belton O'Neall of Newberry was a pious but energetic reformer who thought that radical politics was the enemy of moral uplift and material progress. In the Lowcountry, the aging Petigru, an unconditional Unionist, and the younger Yeadon, a conditional Unionist, were both reform-minded Whigs. Petigru, however, was an unrepentant Federalist who, by 1850, had not only accepted his political isolation and diminishing influence but also viewed his political impotence as a badge of honor. Yeadon still wanted to make a difference, to be in the fray, not above it. Pockets of grassroots Unionist strength were scattered throughout the state. In the Upcountry, Perry, Thompson, and O'Neall were the leaders of the Unionist faction, and by far the largest number of Unionists lived in Perry's native Greenville District, and in the relatively isolated, and yeoman-dominated, northern portions of Greenville's neighboring districts, Pickens and Spartanburg.[50]

Unionists per se, however, comprised only a small fraction of the total Cooperationist strength. Indeed, the very alignment of the Unionists with the Cooperationists left the entire Cooperation movement vulnerable to the charges of "submission" and "cowardice" which were hurled about so recklessly by the radicals. W. W. Boyce, a leading Cooperationist from Fairfield, noted that while there were few outright Unionists in South Carolina, "there are a great many opposed to the secession of South Carolina alone at this time."[51] In this opinion, Boyce pinpointed a crucial aspect of the Cooperationist appeal. Whatever other differences of opinion existed among them, all Cooperationists agreed that "separate secession is no remedy." Factions as diverse as outright Unionists and proselytizing Southern nationalists could agree on that if on nothing else. Thus the strength of the Cooperationists lay, at least in part, in the breadth of their appeal and the ability of their politicians to build a coalition based on shared disapproval of a common enemy—the separate state secessionists.[52]

After the surprising victory of the separate state secessionists in the February election of delegates to an unscheduled state convention, the formerly inchoate opposition coalesced into an active Cooperationist movement which vowed to stop the political momentum of the radicals or "Secessionists." The political unity, the polemical skill, and the ideological homogeneity of the Secessionists had given them the upper hand in February, but the Cooperationists gained momentum during the spring as more and more political leaders and other nota-

[50]Ellen, "Richard Yeadon," pp. 31–40; J. Fred Rippy, *Joel Poinsett: Versatile American* (Durham, N.C.: Duke University Press, 1935), pp. 233–243; Kibler, *Perry*, pp. 255–259; Lacy Ford, "James Louis Petigru: Last South Carolina Federalist," pp. 165–166.

[51]W. W. Boyce to B. F. Perry, March 17, 1851, quoted in Kibler, *Perry*, pp. 262–263.

[52]Yorkville *Miscellany*, July 5, 1851; Pendleton *Messenger*, July 31, 1851; Hamer, *The Secession Movement in South Carolina*, pp. 96–101.

bles spoke out against immediate secession. By May 1851, a number of prominent South Carolinians, including Robert Barnwell, W. J. Grayson, A. P.
Butler, Wade Hampton, John S. Preston, Langdon Cheves, Christopher
Memminger, and many others, joined Orr, Burt, Boyce, and Perry in outspoken
opposition to separate state secession. Yet the radicals had already won control
of the proposed state convention. Unless the Cooperationists could somehow
discredit the radical triumph by demonstrating that the people of South Carolina
did not favor separate state secession, the special convention might take South
Carolina out of the Union in the first months of 1852. Thus the Cooperationists
decided to make the October 1851, election of delegates to the much-discussed
Southern Convention a test of strength between themselves and the separate state
secessionists. Soon, both sides geared up for what proved to be the most vigorous statewide campaign since Calhoun vanquished the Whigs in 1840, and the
most divisive campaign since the nullification era.[53]

The radicals, or "Secessionists," were well organized and had no shortage
of forensic ability and "stumping" talent. In addition to the fiery but loquacious
Rhett, the radical ranks also included Lowcountrymen Whitemarsh Seabrook of
Colleton, James Hopkins Adams and Maxcy Gregg of Richland, and Edward
Bryan of Charleston. In the Upcountry, there was a significant radical faction in
every district, although the bulk of Upcountry notables were Cooperationists of
one stripe or another. The most prominent radicals in the Upcountry were Francis
Pickens of Edgefield, John Hugh Means of Fairfield, and a trio of leading
families, the Gists, the Wallaces, and the Rices, from the radical enclave of
Union district.[54]

The radicals also had clarity of argument on their side. Rhett and his followers argued that South Carolina had endured too much "northern aggression," and maintained that the only way for the state to preserve her liberty was
to leave the Union. The radicals wanted to reduce the argument to a simple
choice between secession or submission, knowing full well that South Carolinians would refuse *en masse* to accept submission. In Laurens district, radical
leader Henry C. Young declared that "no people worthy of the name men would
submit to tyranny . . . our lives, rather than *submission.*" Young's radical ally
in Laurens, planter John Cunningham, agreed, stating that South Carolina "must
secede or sink into submission."[55] Other radicals who ridiculed cooperation as
submission argued that waiting for the cooperation of other Southern states was a
tactical error as well as a sign of weakness.[56] Spartanburg radical John Winsmith

[53]Boucher, "The Secession and Co-operation Movements," pp. 105–129; Barnwell, *Love of Order,* pp. 157–186.

[54]Edmunds, *Francis W. Pickens,* pp. 121–123; Hamer, *The Secession Movement in South Carolina,* pp. 102–126; Unionville *Journal,* June 28, August 23, September 6, and October 18, 1851.

[55]Laurensville *Herald,* October 11, 1850.

[56]Rhett believed that if South Carolina seceded, the state's action would lend new momentum to the faltering secession movements in other Southern states and eventually lead to the formation of a Southern confederacy. Few, if any, Upcountry radicals agreed with Rhett on this point. Even

felt that "separate action is . . . necessary and essential to southern co-operation," while fire-eater William H. Gist of Union declared that separate action by
South Carolina would make "a practical issue" out of cooperation, and that

> the people of the South no longer deluded by the politicians will rush to our
> rescue, and upon the ruins of the old corrupt government will be established a
> Southern Confederacy, uniting a people . . . and commanding the respect and
> admiration of the world.[57]

But even the soaring oratory of Gist could not quite match the emotional
rhetoric of his friend and fellow radical Benjamin Herndon Rice, a wealthy
Union district planter and "capitalist" with substantial mercantile interests in
Charleston. The choice facing South Carolina, Rice insisted, "is a question of
subjugation or redress—of degradation or Resistance." Campaigning hard
throughout Union district, Rice identified abolition as a threat "allowed to loom
over our ancient Republicanism" and argued that separate state secession was
the only means of effecting a "restoration of our lost Liberty and Equality."
Addressing a large rally in his home district, Rice declared that secession was
"our Right" and pleaded that if "anyone here can think of submission let him
think too of his wife in rags and his children in chains."[58] At another campaign
rally in the same district, radical George Peake called on his fellow citizens to
prove themselves deserving heirs of the patriots of 1776. "[T]hey did not wait to
be bound and shorn before they struck," Peake declared. "Is life more dear or
Peace more sweet to us than it was to them—are we Bastards?"[59]

Naturally, the Cooperationists refused to accept the radicals' definition of the
issue as a simple choice between separate state secession and "submission."
Armistead Burt denounced such oversimplification as foolhardy. The secession
of a single state would not, Burt maintained, strengthen slavery in any way. It
would become more difficult, not less, to retrieve fugitive slaves. The protection
of slavery guaranteed by the Constitution would be irretrievably lost. The value
of slave property in the seceding state would fall, and that state's vulnerability to
slave insurrections would increase. Perhaps most important, the right to take
slaves into states further west would also be lost if South Carolina seceded
alone.[60] Other Cooperationist leaders made similar arguments. Separate state
secession was "impractical." It would cut South Carolina off from her natural
political allies in the rest of the South, expose slavery to new dangers, impose

---

Governor John Hugh Means doubted that separate action by South Carolina would unite the South.
"I would not hazard the hopes of so great a cause upon such a desperate adventure," the Fairfield
radical told Rhett in July 1851. See John Hugh Means to Robert Barnwell Rhett, July 20, 1851,
Robert Barnwell Rhett Papers, SHC.

[57]*Carolina Spartan,* September 18, 1851.
[58]Draft of speech of Benjamin Herndon Rice, [c. 1851], Wallace, Rice, Duncan Papers, SCL.
[59]Report of B. H. Rice, [c. 1850–51], Wallace, Rice, Duncan Papers, SCL.
[60]Letter of Armistead Burt to T. B. Byrd, in *Southern Rights and Cooperation Documents,* No.
3, pp. 1–9.

new limitations on the slaveholder, disrupt the state's commerce, place an enormous burden on the state's taxpayers, and invite foreign attack. South Carolina was simply not capable of sustaining nationhood by itself. The hope for the future was to secure the cooperation of the other Southern states. "When the old party lines are once broken down effectively, my life upon it," swore Orr, "the Southern Rights men will sweep the whole South. But do not let us defeat all by moving prematurely."[61]

The Cooperationists also worked hard to prove that cooperation was not simply a euphemism for submission, and that Cooperation leaders were not spineless cowards. The language of the campaign was vintage South Carolina; speakers on both sides of the issue spoke of liberty, courage, pride, manliness, honor, and resistance as precious virtues and decried slavery, cowardice, degradation, weakness, shame, and submission as deadly vices. Even Armistead Burt, one of the most cautious of the Cooperationists, spoke openly about the necessity of upholding the republican code of political ethics:

> Individuals may submit to wrong without the loss of character, or of self-respect, but such submission by nations brings dishonor and degradation. It implies both weakness and pusillanimity, and invites aggression, as well as incites contempt.[62]

In Laurens, fire-eaters abused cooperation as the doctrine of "submission and disgrace." Unionist B. F. Perry countered such charges with claims that it was not the large slaveholder who favored secession but a reckless clique of glory-seeking young hotheads. "The most prominent in this secessionist movement," editorialized Perry, "have been young men, inspired with notions of personal honor to be defended and individual glory to be acquired. They seem to think that a State or a whole people are to be governed by the same punctilious code of honor that would have influenced a hot chevalier in the days of knight errantry."[63]

Indeed, the rhetoric of manliness and honor assumed an unusually literal meaning during one of the campaign's more preposterous but nevertheless revealing incidents. More than the normal amount of mudslinging crept into the debate in York district, where one loose-tongued radical, noting that a prominent but unnamed Cooperationist leader had only one leg, claimed that "no *whole* man" in the district opposed secession. Most Cooperationists allowed the tasteless remark to pass without rebuttal, but a large group of "staunch farmers" from the yeoman-dominated rural community of Bethel met and drafted a reply which was published in the local newspapers. These Bethel farmers invited any radicals who believed that "no *whole* men" supported Cooperation to visit and

---

[61]*Speech of James L. Orr to the Convention of Southern Rights Associations, held in Charleston, May, 1851,* pp. 1–16.

[62]Letter of Armistead Burt to T. B. Byrd, in *Southern Rights and Cooperation Documents,* No. 3, pp. 3–4.

[63]Greenville *Southern Patriot,* reprinted in the Yorkville *Miscellany,* May 3, 1851.

canvass their beat. "I think it ought to convince them," the farmers wrote, "that before York is set down as committed to secession separate, they had better harken unto the voice of her yeomanry."[64]

The brief manifesto drafted by the Bethel yeomanry highlighted a critical aspect of the 1851 campaign: the appeal made by both sides to the yeomanry. This appeal was especially important in the Upcountry, where yeomen constituted a majority and where over 60 percent of all families owned no slaves. In their manifesto, the Bethel yeomen pledged to support resistance even though they opposed separate state action. In Spartanburg district, another yeoman-dominated region where only one out of every 34 households was headed by a planter and where nearly 70 percent of all families owned no slaves, one non-partisan observer declared that "the people of Spartanburg are all, or nineteen-twentieths of them, in favor of resistance, the only difference among them is upon the question of remedy."[65] Clearly both political organizations knew that the yeomanry would stand behind slavery and Southern Rights. Even B. F. Perry acknowledged that yeomen would join planters to "defend the institution of African slavery at all hazards, to the last extremity." Yet Perry, using his Cooperationist newspaper *The Southern Patriot,* took the lead in rallying non-slaveholders in the upper districts against separate state action. Perry warned non-slaveholders that South Carolina risked "civil war and ruinous taxation" if she seceded alone. Moreover, Perry also renewed old Upcountry complaints about "the unfair domination of state government" by the wealthy planters of the Lowcountry parishes. Perry urged non-slaveholders to seek an end to parish domination before supporting the "lords of the lowlands" in a secession movement.[66]

Aware that the Cooperation party was making a strong pitch for the vote of non-slaveholders, the radicals, especially in the Upcountry, tailored many of their arguments specifically for that crucial group of voters. Typical of the Secessionists' appeal to non-slaveholders was that made by a fire-eater writing over the signature of "Candor" in the pro-secession *Carolina Spartan.* "Candor" reminded non-slaveholders of their enormous personal interest in the protection of slavery. If the North prevails in the sectional struggle, "Candor" warned,

> [W]e will be compelled to endure equality with them [Blacks]—we will be forced to allow them the same privileges we enjoy . . . they would insist on a right to vote and send their negro brethren to our State Legislature and to the United States Congress—their children would go to school with your children—they would eat at your *tables,* sleep in your beds and drink out of the same *gourd* that you do; yea, they would do more than this, they would marry your daughters, in despite of everything you could do, and you will be deeply

[64]Yorkville *Miscellany,* May 3, July 5, 12, and 28, 1851.

[65]*Carolina Spartan,* May 1, 1851; see also J. Leander Adams to Andrew Baxter Springs, January 17, 1852, Springs Family Papers, SHC.

[66]Greenville *Southern Patriot,* April 4, June 13 and 20, July 18 and 25, 1851.

humiliated at the thought that your grand-children, those who shall inherit your name and your property, are of *mixed blood*.[67]

Since separate action was the best defense against these calamities, "Candor" advised, non-slaveholders should support the radicals. After all, "Candor" concluded, "If the slaveholder can stand a dismemberment of the Union, the non-slaveholder will not sustain much damage by way of heavy taxes from the State."[68] In Union district, the flamboyant radical B. H. Rice appealed to non-slaveholders with both promises of upward mobility and warnings of impending social degradation. "We have as yet no privileged class. He who has no slaves today may soon—or his children," Rice told yeoman farmers, "[but] if slaves are freed, whites will become menials."[69]

The appeal to the racism, negrophobia, and fear of a racially amalgamated society played on the deepest fears of the non-slaveholders. Yet such appeals were simply part of what was an extremely vigorous, and at times bitter, campaign. Both parties canvassed the state hard, taking their arguments to the usual succession of militia musters, outdoor barbecues, and sales-day meetings. Each party held rallies in every district, and local notables went door to door wooing voters to their cause. Each party also brought in its most prominent leaders and best speakers to address public gatherings. In the Upcountry, where most of the best-known public figures were Cooperationists, the radicals relied heavily on Secessionist speakers from other parts of the state. Rhett, the most famous radical, made a personal tour of the Upcountry late in the summer of 1851, speaking at militia musters in such remote outposts as King's Creek, not far from King's Mountain in northwestern York district, and Ebenezer, a small trading post near the Catawba River on the other side of the same district. Local Cooperationist leaders noted that Rhett was politely received by the backwoodsmen in isolated areas of York, but doubted that he recruited many followers. After leaving York, Rhett was intercepted by radicals in Chester who persuaded the eloquent fire-eater to debate the local Cooperationist leader, Samuel McAiley. Later, one Chester citizen remembered Rhett's zeal on the stump but concluded, "I do not suppose one-half the people believed what he said. They had been warned of him so often as a demagogue."[70]

Finally, on October 13 and 14, 1851, the election of delegates to a Southern Congress was held. Two delegates were to be elected from each congressional district, and each party ran a two-man slate in each district. The Cooperationists easily carried every congressional district which contained a portion of the Upcountry (see Table 5.1). In the Upcountry as a whole, the Secessionists carried only three (Fairfield, Laurens, and Union) of thirteen districts, although the vote was nearly evenly divided in a fourth district, Edgefield. The Cooperationists

[67]*Carolina Spartan,* August 14, 1851.
[68]*Ibid.*
[69]Speech of Benjamin Herndon Rice, [c. 1851], Wallace, Rice, Duncan Papers, SCL.
[70]Yorkville *Miscellany,* September 6, 1851; Chester *Standard,* July 6, 1854.

Table 5.1 Results of Election Held Concerning Question of Secession, 1851

	Secession Ticket	Cooperation Ticket	% Secession	% Cooperation
First District				
Spartanburg	1,181	1,437	45.1	54.9
York	687	1,401	33.0	67.0
Union	988	288	77.4	22.6
Chester	420	926	31.3	68.7
Total	3,276	4,052	44.8	55.2
Second District				
Pickens	152	1,411	9.7	90.3
Anderson	436	1,306	25.0	75.0
Greenville	236	1,499	13.6	86.4
Laurens	973	801	54.8	45.2
Total	1,797	5,017	26.4	73.6
Third District				
Lancaster	279	632	30.6	69.4
Kershaw	231	620	27.1	72.9
Fairfield	706	391	64.4	35.6
Richland	641	697	47.9	52.1
Sumter	661	1,110	37.3	62.7
Total	2,518	3,410	42.2	57.8
Fifth District				
Abbeville	817	977	45.6	54.5
Newberry	536	610	46.7	53.3
Edgefield	938	939	50.0	50.0
Lexington	179	812	18.0	82.0
Total	2,470	3,338	42.5	57.5
Totals				
Lower Piedmont	5,378	4,932	52.2	47.8
Upper Piedmont	2,971	7,686	27.9	72.1
Upcountry	8,349	12,618	39.8	60.2
State	17,471	24,909	41.2	58.8

Sources: Charleston *Mercury,* December 2, 1851; Barnwell, *Love of Order,* pp. 198–199. Since there were two candidates running on each ticket, the ticket strength given in this table is the average of the two candidates' vote totals.

were strongest, as their leaders expected, in the upper Piedmont, where the party won more than two-thirds of the total vote in every district except Spartanburg, where the radicals made a strong showing with 45 percent of the vote. Indeed, in the upper Piedmont as a whole, the Cooperationists received over 72 percent of the vote. By contrast, the election was much closer in the lower Piedmont. The Cooperationists carried Chester easily, but won Abbeville and Newberry only by narrow margins, and carried a hotly contested election in Edgefield by one vote. The Secessionists handily carried Fairfield, the most plantation-dominated district in the Upcountry, and Union, where the personal influence of the powerful and rabidly pro-Secessionist Gist, Wallace, and Rice families was enormous.

They also won a comfortable victory in Laurens. On the strength of the party's strong showing in Union and Fairfield, the Secessionists posted a narrow victory in the lower Piedmont as a whole, winning just over 52 percent of the vote in that portion of the Upcountry.[71]

As a whole, however, the Upcountry went strongly for Cooperation, casting over 60 percent of its total vote in favor of the so-called "wait and watch" party. The Cooperationists ran slightly stronger in the Upcountry than in the state as a whole, but they carried the state easily, polling about 24,900 votes to only 17,471 for the Secessionists. Outside of the Upcountry, the Cooperationists were strong in Charleston, where they carried over 70 percent of the vote, and in the Pee Dee. The Cooperationists also prevailed, usually with ease, in the districts of the lower cotton-belt, carrying Kershaw, Sumter, Clarendon, and Barnwell. The Secessionist strongholds were mainly in the rural Lowcountry parishes, and especially in the rice and sea-island cotton areas. In fact, over 62 percent of the vote in the rural parishes went to the radicals. The Beaufort and Georgetown areas, the homes of many of the foremost fire-eaters, went overwhelmingly for the Secessionists.[72]

Voting patterns, both in the Upcountry and across the state, were not strongly correlated either with the size of the black population or with the voting patterns of the nullification election. There were, however, some discernible trends in the Upcountry returns. As always, the impact of local notables in the various districts was significant. Among those notables, men who had been active in the futile effort to establish an influential Whig opposition to the Calhounites were strong Cooperationists in almost every case. Waddy Thompson and Vardry McBee of Greenville, J. H. Irby of Laurens, and York's John Springs were all Whigs or former Whigs who worked hard for Cooperation in 1851. Also, most Unionists from the nullification era, including Perry, O'Neall, and Joseph Grisham of Pickens, supported the Cooperation party in 1851. Important as the Whigs and old Unionists were, however, the heart of the Cooperation party in the Upcountry was the old rank-and-file Calhoun-Democrats led by men such as Orr, Burt, David Wardlaw, A. P. Butler, Preston Brooks, and many others. The Cooperationists were not able, of course, to hold all the old Calhoun-Democrats; the old Calhounite faction was badly divided on the issue. But by holding at least half of the old Calhounites and adding ex-Whigs and Unionists to that core of support, the Cooperationists built a working majority. The Secessionists drew most of their support from former Nullifiers, even though many former Nullifiers became Cooperationists.[73]

There were also some complicated, and rather curious, geographic and socio-economic trends in the October election returns. The upper Piedmont, the yeo-

---

[71]Boucher, "The Secession and Co-operation Movements," pp. 128–129; Barnwell, *Love of Order,* pp. 198–199; Charleston *Mercury,* December 2, 1851; see Table 5.1.

[72]See Table 5.1.

[73]Greenville *Southern Patriot,* May 16, 1851; Laurensville *Herald,* July 19 and October 11, 1850, January 31, February 14, May 23, and October 17, 1851; Yorkville *Miscellany,* July 19, October 11 and 18, 1851.

man-dominated portion of the Upcountry, voted heavily Cooperationist, with precinct level returns suggesting that in beats where there were few planters, the Secessionist party had virtually no strength. This trend was perhaps most noticeable in Spartanburg district, where the election was hotly contested. The Cooperationists carried the town of Spartanburg and all ten of the polling places in the yeoman-dominated northern half of the district. In the southeastern and south-central portion of the district, where most of the plantations in the district were located, the Secessionists carried seven of eight precincts. In the central portion of the district, the vote was evenly divided. Even though Hugh H. Thomson, Spartanburg's second largest slaveholder, and a few other leading planters favored Cooperation, a large majority of Spartanburg's planters and middling slaveholders supported separate state secession. At the same time, most of the area's leading merchants and entrepreneurs, such as Gabriel Cannon and Simpson Bobo, strongly opposed separate state action. The divisions in Spartanburg were clear-cut. Merchants, manufacturers, and yeomen tended to be Cooperationists; planters and other substantial slaveholders tended to be radicals.[74]

In most other parts of the Upcountry, however, the divisions were far more complicated. Most of York district's largest planters, including John Springs, I. D. Witherspoon, and members of the Bratton family, were Cooperationists, as were most of the large planters in Chester. Yet the bulk of whatever support the radicals had in those districts came from planters and small slaveholders. Yeoman-dominated areas in both districts tended to vote for Cooperation, but there were a few scattered pockets of radicalism in yeoman areas.[75] The situation in Laurens was even more complex. Laurens had always been the home of a surprisingly strong Whig minority. In the secession campaign of 1851, J. H. Irby, the former Whig leader, took the bulk of this persistent Whig minority with him into the ranks of the Cooperationists. But the very strength of the Whig support for Cooperation seemed to push a sizable portion of the natural Democratic majority into the Radical camp. Moreover, unlike their counterparts in Spartanburg, a number of Laurens's most prominent merchants and entrepreneurs, including H. C. Young, Henry Garlington, and John D. Young, all campaigned openly for separate state secession. Of course all of these men had large plantation interests in addition to their mercantile, grist milling, railroad, and manufacturing investments, but they were nevertheless the type of diversified, strongly commercially oriented entrepreneurs, men with Whiggish principles who, in other parts of the Upcountry, tended to support Cooperation.[76]

In the rest of the lower Piedmont, the radicals (Secessionists) were much stronger than they were within the upper Piedmont, due to the higher concentration of planters and other slaveholders in that area. Nearly 12 percent of all household heads in the lower Piedmont were planters and around 55 percent were

[74]MacArthur, "Antebellum Politics in an Upcountry County," pp. 42–46; *Carolina Spartan,* October 16, 1851.

[75]Yorkville *Miscellany,* July 12, October 11, 18, and 25, and November 22, 1851.

[76]Laurensville *Herald,* January 17 and 31, February 14, October 10, 17, and 24, 1851; Zelotus L. Holmes to his Aunt, March 20, 1851, Zelotus L. Holmes Papers, SCL.

slaveholders, while in the upper Piedmont only 3 percent of all household heads were planters and no more than one in three household heads was a slaveholder. Yet while the greater strength of the Secessionists in the lower Piedmont was undoubtedly due in large part to the prevalence of plantation agriculture and the higher incidence of slaveholding in the region, voting patterns did not break down along planter versus yeoman or slaveholder versus non-slaveholder lines. Instead, factional alignments developed gradually as long-standing local cliques cast their lot with one side or the other, building a byzantine network of support for each party. As the plethora of local cliques arranged themselves into ad hoc factional or party organizations, planters found themselves opposing other planters, yeomen opposed other yeomen, and merchants opposed other merchants. As a rule, the Cooperationists clawed their way to narrow victories in areas where the old Calhoun organization still had strong influence; the radicals, however, won handily in areas such as Fairfield and Union, where many of the leading planters had always been essentially independent of Calhoun.[77]

Beneath the byzantine alignments that were so much a part of antebellum South Carolina's political tradition, several broad tendencies were visible. Almost all the former Whigs in the Upcountry, and a majority of the self-proclaimed Calhoun-Democrats who frequently championed Whiggish principles (and there were a good many such men in the Upcountry by 1850) supported Cooperation. Also, yeomen and non-slaveholders, as a group, voted overwhelmingly for Cooperation. Along the northern fringe of the upper Piedmont, where there were almost no plantations, yeoman support of Cooperation was nearly unanimous. The radicals, by contrast, drew most of their support from Democratic planters and lesser slaveholders, and especially from those planters and lesser slaveholders with few non-agricultural investments. The first secession campaign created strange bedfellows. The most commercially oriented of Upcountrymen, the Whig planters, wealthy merchants, industrialists, and other entrepreneurs, strongly opposed separate state action, and so did the least commercially oriented of Upcountrymen, the yeoman farmers and backwoodsmen of the upper Piedmont.[78]

While seemingly odd at first glance, the alliance of Whiggish entrepreneurs and yeomen was actually quite logical in the peculiar circumstances of the first secession crisis. Separate state secession posed an enormous threat to commercial stability. Secession under any circumstances promised to disrupt existing financial arrangements and other commercial networks, and might possibly plunge the nation into civil war—hardly any businessman's dream. Yet the

[77]Thomas H. Pope, *The History of Newberry County, South Carolina, 1749–1860* (Columbia, S.C.: University of South Carolina Press, 1973), pp. 201–212; Unionville *Journal,* October 18, 1851; Columbia *Daily South Carolinian,* April 11, 1851; Abbeville *Banner,* April 19 and 26, May 10 and 17, July 9 and 16, 1848; Edgefield *Advertiser,* January 9, February 13, June 19 and 26, July 10, August 7, September 4, October 16 and 23, 1851; Thomas P. Magrath to Benjamin C. Yancey, October 18, 1851, Benjamin C. Yancey Papers, SHC.

[78]Samples of this sentiment can be found in the Greenville *Southern Patriot,* May 16, 1851; Yorkville *Miscellany,* June 14 and October 11, 1851; *Carolina Spartan,* March 27, 1851.

prospect that South Carolina would secede alone presented even greater dangers to commercial stability. South Carolina could easily find herself cut off from the rest of the world, isolated from major capital markets, and crushed by the burden of the heavy taxes levied for the state's defense. The "staid, prudent, intelligent, wealthy and meritorious part of the community will not consent to split off and form an independent little nation of the Palmetto state," explained John Springs. The York district planter-entrepreneur acknowledged that "politicians in their bursts of patriotism will tell you dollars and cents are not taken into the calculation," but he also believed that in practice, considerations of financial "loss and gain" were ultimately decisive in the minds of most voters, especially among members of the business and financial elite. Men with diverse and far-flung commercial interests had a strong, vested interest in stability, and therefore indirectly in nationhood, regardless of whether the nation was the existing Union or a new Southern Confederacy. They had little to gain and much to lose from separate state secession.[79]

Yeoman farmers were only marginally concerned about commercial stability, but they were nevertheless adamantly opposed to separate state secession. The prospect of dramatically higher taxes, the fear that the state could not police its large slave majority alone, and their relative isolation from national political affairs combined to solidify yeoman opposition to unilateral action by South Carolina. Throughout the campaign, the yeomen reiterated their desire to protect the South's peculiar institution and their willingness to resist "Northern aggression," but in 1851, the remedy proposed by the radicals seemed worse than the disease.[80]

In the final analysis, the Cooperationists prevailed because a majority of South Carolinians simply did not think it was wise to leave the Union without any prospect of cooperation from other Southern states. The influential Cooperationist John Springs probably explained the rejection of the radicals as well as anyone. During the hard-fought campaign, Springs maintained a cautious Cooperationist stance in public, but he admitted privately that, despite a genuine affection for the Union, his "mind" was "made up for a Southern secession." Springs's annual trips through parts of the North left him convinced that "the great mass of People in all the free states are Free soilers" and thus that the dissolution of the Union was inevitable.[81] Yet Springs's painful conclusions about the future of the Republic did not translate into support for separate state secession, which he ridiculed as "rash, precipitate and suicidal." South Carolina "may rush headlong out of the Union," Springs observed, "but she can not ever crawl in again without degradation and disgrace—it is humiliating to think of it." Springs opposed individual action by South Carolina largely because he

[79]John Springs to Andrew Baxter Springs, August 22, 1851, Springs Family Papers, SHC.

[80]Yorkville *Miscellany*, June 28, 1851; Laurensville *Herald*, November 14, 1851; Greenville *Southern Patriot*, May 2 and 9, 1851; J. Leander Adams to Andrew Baxter Springs, January 17, 1852, Springs Family Papers, SHC.

[81]John Springs to Andrew Baxter Springs, August 22, 1851, John Springs to Andrew Baxter Springs, September 6, 1850, Springs Family Papers, SHC.

believed that the government in Washington would use force to keep the state in the Union and that South Carolina could not defend her independence against federal might. "[I]f I understand anything about the meaning of the terms, secession and Revolution are synonomous terms," Springs reasoned, "I believe it . . . very likely that it [secession] could not be affected without a civil war and that of the worst kind."[82] South Carolina, Springs insisted, would find itself "isolated" in any military struggle because secession was still not a popular idea in other Southern states even though those states "suffer equally with her [South Carolina] in any degradation." A civil war, Springs predicted, "would be one of the most unnatural bloody struggles almost ever heard of, it would be brother against brother, the father arraigned against the Son and the son against the Father." Springs also recognized that the danger of slave insurrection would increase dramatically once armed conflict began. "And suppose," Springs hypothesized, "armies marched into the Southern states and free flags set up, freedom and protection offered to all who choose to come in and accept liberty on such easy and flattering terms."[83] He blanched at the thought. In Springs's view, South Carolina, standing alone, lacked the manpower, the money, and the morale needed to prevail against the combined force of federal armies, a small but pesky Unionist militia, and a large and potentially rebellious slave population. If secession was to succeed, it would have to be a cooperative effort.

Springs's analysis, and the strength of the Cooperation vote, suggest that a healthy number of South Carolinians had learned the practical lesson of the nullification crisis well. South Carolina could not go it alone. The future of Southern rights, as even Calhoun had argued during his last years, lay in cooperative efforts with other Southern states. Former Nullifier Robert Barnwell, a prominent Lowcountry planter and son of a Revolutionary veteran, freely admitted that he had seen too much brinksmanship during the nullification crisis to desire any more of it. "If anything surprises me," Barnwell told Cooperation leader James L. Orr, "it is to witness the bitter forgetfulness into which men have fallen with subject to our experience at that time [nullification]." The precedent of the Force bill, Barnwell argued, was one "which the Jackson Democrats never rejected and which the Whigs openly and at all times boast of as the true course for the government to pursue." Pointing to William Yancey's lack of success in Alabama, Barnwell concluded that no other state would join South Carolina in secession and equated separate action with "ruin."[84] Springs and Barnwell, both ardent Nullifiers in 1832, were prudent Cooperationists in 1851. To some extent at least, the political course of these prominent planters was representative of that of the state as a whole. South Carolina was no less

[82]John Springs to Andrew Baxter Springs, August 22, 1851, Springs Family Papers, SHC.

[83]John Springs to Richard Austin Springs, September 5, 1851, John Springs to Andrew Baxter Springs, September 6, 1850, Springs Family Papers, SHC.

[84]Robert W. Barnwell to James L. Orr, August 26, 1851, Orr-Patterson Papers, SHC. The arguments of both John Springs and Robert Barnwell suggest that, in 1851, as was the case in 1832, those South Carolinians most concerned over the threat of slave insurrection tended to take the conservative side.

jealous of her liberty in 1851 than she had been two decades earlier, but the strategic innovation of the nullification era had given way to the strategic caution of cooperation.

The defeat of the Secessionists in the October elections almost literally stopped the radical movement in its tracks. In December, the legislature called for the special state convention to be held in the spring of 1852, with the delegates elected in the radical-dominated elections of the previous February to be seated. Yet even though the radicals would have numerical control of the convention, only a few diehards refused to admit that separate state action was impossible after the Cooperationist victory in October. Radicals hoped that the convention might devise other strategies of resistance to the Northern aggression and recognized the value of the convention as a pulpit from which to emphasize the state's commitment to Southern rights. When the convention met in April 1852, an overwhelming majority of Secessionists and Cooperationists agreed to endorse a resolution which not only affirmed the right of secession but which also stated that "the frequent violations of the Constitution of the United States by the Federal Government, and its encroachments on the reserved rights of the sovereign States . . . especially in relation to slavery, amply justify this State . . . in dissolving at once all political connection with her co-States." South Carolina, according to the convention, declined to exercise this right "from considerations of expediency only." This resolution was approved by the convention by a vote of 136 to 19. The nineteen who voted against the resolution came from a handful of outright Unionists, headed by B. F. Perry, on the one hand, and a handful of unrelenting fire-eaters, led by Maxcy Gregg, on the other.[85]

On the day after the special convention closed, Robert Barnwell Rhett resigned his seat in the United States Senate so that he would not have to defend the state's course of "absolute submission" in Washington. What appeared to be "absolute submission" to the radical Rhett translated into "comfortable quietude" in the language of Lowcountry Unionist William John Grayson.[86] Neither man's words proved prophetic. The Cooperationists' triumph at the polls in October 1851 saved the Union, but it was not, contrary to B. F. Perry's claims, a victory for Unionism in South Carolina. It was simply a repudiation, and not an especially strong repudiation at that, of the rash and precipitate course of action advocated by Rhett and the radicals.

There remained in South Carolina politics a huge middle ground lying somewhere between the strong Unionism of Perry or Petigru, and the radical pro-secession stance of Rhett and Gregg. Moreover, the middle ground was heavily populated. Certainly a majority of Upcountrymen made their political home there. They would defend the independence and honor of the South, and fight to protect slavery, "to the last extremity." Yet there was still considerable uncer-

---

[85]*Journal of the State Convention of South Carolina* (Columbia, S.C.: Johnson and Davis, 1852), pp. 16–24.

[86]William John Grayson to B. F. Perry, July 30, 1852, quoted in Kibler, *Perry*, p. 277.

tainty in their minds over the proper means to these ends. Some favored the
creation of a new southern Confederacy; others still hoped that the united action
of the slaveholding states within the Union might succeed. By 1851, the majority
of Upcountrymen were clearly committed to "resistance," even though they did
not necessarily equate resistance with secession.[87] Perhaps the public mood was
best summarized by the comments of J. J. Atwood, the Laurens farmer and
onetime sheriff, on the whole crisis of 1851:

> Last fall in the election for delegates to the Southern Convention, the
> Separate Secessionists, or fire-eaters, tried to make a flourish, but we met them
> at the ballot box and left them several thousand behind. Politics have not been
> mentioned since, though we are all Southern Rights men and would be in favor
> of separation with the other Southern States with us if we can't go to California
> with our slaves.[88]

Much to the chagrin of the radicals, the election revealed that the people of
South Carolina agreed, albeit somewhat reluctantly, to acquiesce in the decision
of the other slaveholding states to remain in the Union for at least a while longer.
No other state had gone nearly as far toward secession in 1851, and, ultimately,
South Carolina decided to pull back rather than go it alone. Grayson was right in
portraying the period immediately following as one of unusual political quietude,
at least as far as the state's relationship with the federal government was concerned. B. F. Perry was also right when he observed, in the aftermath of the
Cooperationist victory, that the "people of South Carolina desire repose, and
must have it."[89] The emotional fervor of the previous year's campaign left even
so politically hot-blooded a state as South Carolina in need of a respite. A spirit
of reconciliation was in the air throughout the Upcountry. After a public meeting
in Greenville in July 1852, Perry commented that "secessionists and cooperationists, Union men and disunion men, whigs and democrats" all shared a
common desire to heal old political wounds. In Laurens district, according to J.
J. Atwood, "All old parties, Nullifiers, Union, Whig and Democrat have become the same."[90]

A period of such political calm could not, of course, last long. As soon as the
state began to recover from its political exhaustion, new controversies and new
political divisions began to emerge. Indeed, even as B. F. Perry applauded the
political unity of the Upcountry in the summer of 1852, a decision made by
James L. Orr and a number of other Cooperationists to support Franklin Pierce,

[87]Greenville *Southern Patriot,* November 6, 1851; Pendleton *Messenger,* July 31, 1851.

[88]J. J. Atwood to Joseph H. and Menoah Atwood, April 4, 1852, reprinted in the Laurens
Advertiser, June 10, 1970; on this point, see also Zelotus L. Holmes to his Aunt, June 15, 1852,
Zelotus L. Holmes Papers, SCL.

[89]Greenville *Southern Patriot,* November 6, 1851.

[90]Greenville *Southern Patriot,* July 15, 1852; J. J. Atwood to Joseph H. and Menoah Atwood,
April 4, 1852, reprinted in the Laurens *Advertiser,* June 10, 1970.

the national Democratic candidate, for President sparked a new political flap in the Palmetto State. The radical Charleston *Mercury* blasted Orr for attempting to involve South Carolina in the "undignified contentions and intrigues" of national politics, while others charged that South Carolina could not "mingle actively in the canvass without dishonor."[91] Orr's decision to work more closely with the national Democratic party in an effort to return control of that party to the slaveholding states triggered a reemergence of factionalism in South Carolina politics which persisted for the rest of the decade.

Between 1852 and 1860, South Carolina was divided, for practical purposes, into two very loosely organized political factions, both of which were devoted to a carefully conceived strategy for the defense of slavery and Southern rights, both of which claimed to be the true heirs of the Calhoun tradition, and both of which were inordinately suspicious of the other. One of these factions, the so-called National Democrats, with James L. Orr as its leading spokesman, sought to build a pro-slavery coalition within the national Democratic party. Orr hoped that the coalition would be strong enough to control the Democratic party and to use its control of the party to prevent any further erosion of the South's position within the Union. The other faction, whose members quickly assumed the label of Southern Rights Democrats or sometimes simply the Southern Rights party, wanted South Carolina to retain its nominal attachment to the national Democratic party, but urged the state's politicians to remain aloof from the party and outside its official machinery, such as the party caucuses. Since separate state action had been renounced, the Southern Rights faction looked not to Southern control of the Democratic party but to the creation of a new Southern party, one which would express the consensus position of the slaveholding states, as the best mechanism for guaranteeing Southern rights.[92]

Both factions could lay legitimate claim to the Calhoun tradition. Despite his independent posture, Calhoun had worked in cooperation with the Democratic party from the time of his return to the party fold in 1837 until his death, just as the National Democrats urged South Carolinians to do during the 1850s. Moreover, Calhoun's lifelong commitment to preserve the Union if possible but to defend Southern rights at any cost also closely resembled the proclaimed intentions of the National Democrats. Yet Calhoun had also worked long and hard to build harmony among the slaveholding states, and for the creation of a single Southern party to represent the interests of the slaveholding section. In Calhoun's last years, a new tone of urgency entered his plea for a single Southern party, and his political treatises, published posthumously, called for concerted Southern action and a constitutional amendment to "give the South a negative [veto] on the action of government." These arguments clearly presaged those of the South

[91]Charleston *Mercury*, June 11, 18, and 26, 1852.

[92]Harold S. Schultz, *Nationalism and Sectionalism in South Carolina, 1852–1860* (Durham, N.C.: Duke University Press, 1950), pp. 26–57; Chauncey S. Boucher, "South Carolina and the South on the Eve of Secession, 1852 to 1860," *Washington University Studies* 5 (April, 1919):81–144; Leemhuis, *James L. Orr*, pp. 29–68.

Carolina Southern Rights faction of the 1850s, and helped place that faction within the broad boundaries of the Calhoun tradition.[93]

The National Democrats drew much of their strength from the Upcountry, where large numbers of Cooperationists followed Orr into the new faction. Yet not all segments of the Cooperation party joined the National Democrats. Many Cooperationists who had favored the creation of a Southern Confederacy, such as W. W. Boyce of Fairfield, allied with Southern Rights Democrats and vowed to remain at arm's length from the national party. The National Democrats attracted little support from the radical-dominated parishes, while in the Upcountry almost all of the Secessionist leaders from the 1851 campaign flocked to the Southern Rights banner. Old-line Unionist Democrats, most of whom had been Cooperationists in 1851, eagerly joined their leader, B. F. Perry, in open support of the new National Democratic faction, but Unionist Whigs such as Petigru and Waddy Thompson found themselves pushed deeper into the backwater of political isolation. Aside from the small groups of Unionist-Whig political misfits, most South Carolinians eventually found themselves drawn either to the conciliatory National Democrats or to the militant Southern Rights faction. But one clique of important South Carolinians deliberately chose isolation over affiliation with either faction. James Henry Hammond, James Chesnut, William H. Trescot, William P. Miles, and a number of other men of some political prominence preferred to remain independent. This clique of non-aligned notables distrusted both the National Democratic party, which it believed to be infected with virulent and deadly free-soilism, and the Rhett-led radicals, whom clique leaders believed were still looking for a pretext that would justify secession. As a whole, the members of this non-aligned clique looked favorably on the idea of a Southern Confederacy, but they also knew that the prominence of Rhett and his followers in any such movement would do it more harm than good. By maintaining their independence, this group of politicians assumed the posture of "disinterested statesmen," and attempted to establish credentials as honest brokers.[94]

Thus an exhausted South Carolina emerged from the first secession crisis only to face renewed factional competition. The party of reconciliation, the National Democrats, confronted a party of intransigence, the militant Southern Rights Democrats, while a clique of non-aligned political leaders walked the fence between factions.

[93]Wiltse, *Calhoun: Sectionalist,* pp. 411–427.

[94]The best analysis of this clique of would-be political managers is Robert Nicholas Olsberg, "A Government of Class and Race: William Henry Trescot and the South Carolina Chivalry, 1860–1865" (Ph.D. dissertation, University of South Carolina, 1972), especially pp. 204–304.

III

THE BOOM

Seldom has the economic outlook of a state changed so rapidly for the better as did that of South Carolina between 1848 and 1860. The 1840s were the decade of the agricultural jeremiad in South Carolina. A wide range of observers, including planters, politicians, scientists, and even Edmund Ruffin, the special outside consultant called in to study the situation, pointed to obvious and perhaps insurmountable problems. Excessive specialization in cotton and careless and wasteful methods of cultivation were identified as the root cause of an economic malady whose symptoms—soil erosion and exhaustion, the declining profitability of Palmetto soils compared to those of the still fertile Southwest, and the emigration of the population—were ugly and unmistakable. The substance of the agricultural jeremiad was repeated in speech after speech. The decline of agriculture in the Upcountry was often singled out for special criticism. Over and over again, Upcountry farmers were admonished to diversify their crops, to learn and practice improved farming techniques, and, above all, to become self-sufficient in foodstuffs. Upcountry entrepreneurs were lectured about the necessity of developing stronger commercial and industrial sectors within the region's primarily agricultural economy, and the familiar warnings about the dangers inherent in building an economy around one staple crop were sounded from all quarters.[1]

In the late 1840s, however, the economy of the cotton South began to pull out of the prolonged slump of the previous decade, and the jeremiads quickly began to lose their ring of urgency. Cotton prices rose to reasonable levels as early as

[1] For an analysis of agricultural rhetoric in South Carolina, see Drew Gilpin Faust, "The Rhetoric and Ritual of Agriculture in Antebellum South Carolina," *Journal of Southern History* 45 (November, 1979):541–568; and for a sampling of the jeremiads see *The Proceedings of the Agricultural Convention and of the State Agricultural Society of South Carolina from 1839–1845* (Columbia, S.C.: Summer and Carroll, 1846). The overall story of soil exhaustion and erosion in the region is best told in Arthur R. Hall, *The Story of Soil Conservation in the South Carolina Piedmont, 1800–1860* (U.S. Department of Agriculture, Miscellaneous Publication, No. 407: Washington, 1940). See also Oscar M. Lieber, *Report on the Survey of South Carolina: The Fourth Annual Report to the General Assembly of South Carolina, 1859* (Columbia, S.C.: R. W. Gibbes, 1860), pp. 123–124.

1847, despite that year's bumper crop. Prices fell again in 1848 when the largest cotton crop in the South's history to that date glutted a European market disrupted by the rumble of revolution. Once stability was restored in Europe, cotton prices rebounded, and by 1850 it was clear that the grip of a long agricultural depression was finally broken. In South Carolina, cotton growers produced more of the staple in 1848 and 1849 than ever before, raising over 300,000 bales in each year, after producing only 130,000 bales in 1840, 118,000 in 1843, and 168,000 in 1845.[2] Moreover, despite the increase in cotton production which occurred after 1847, world demand grew rapidly enough to keep prices high. With prices high and output expanding, cotton profits began to flow into the hands of South Carolina farmers. By 1849, the cancellation, in many parts of the state, of the regularly scheduled "sheriff's sale" of property on which taxes were unpaid, spoke "more loudly than words could do the prosperous condition of our people."[3] During the early 1850s, cotton prices and grower profits remained generally high; and by the end of the decade boasts, like that of James Henry Hammond, that the world would pay tribute to King Cotton, replaced the jeremiad as the dominant motif in the state's agricultural rhetoric. South Carolina, in other words, spent most of what was perhaps the pivotal decade in her history flush with the prosperity of the last of the great short-staple cotton booms.[4]

The long-awaited recovery, however, meant more to the South Carolina economy, and especially to the Upcountry, than simply the resurgence of cotton profits, although without those profits little else would have been possible. In fact, the Upcountry economy went through a remarkable evolution during the 1850s. During that decade, rudimentary railroad and banking systems were developed, and towns whose leisurely commercial pace had been dictated by their role as local trading centers became important staple markets with close ties to large commercial centers and the world cotton market. Moreover, many of the same economic promoters and entrepreneurs who pushed their long-frustrated plans for banks and internal improvements through to completion during the 1850s also used the decade of prosperity to mount an escalating campaign for industrial development. To be sure, the economic evolution of the 1850s did not alter the fundamental fact that the Upcountry economy was overwhelmingly agricultural. Nor did it substantially reduce the region's vulnerability to fluctuations in the world cotton market. Indeed, by intensifying the region's commercial

[2]Alfred G. Smith, Jr., *Economic Readjustment of an Old Cotton State: South Carolina, 1820–1860* (Columbia, S.C.: University of South Carolina Press, 1958), pp. 53–61; Julian J. Petty, *The Growth and Distribution of Population in South Carolina* (Columbia, S.C.: State Council for Defense, 1943), Appendix G, p. 231.

[3]Columbia *Daily Telegraph*, August 2, 1849.

[4]James Henry Hammond, "Speech on the Admission of Kansas," in Clyde N. Wilson, ed., *Selections From the Letters and Speeches of James H. Hammond* (Spartanburg, S.C.: The Reprint Company, 1978), pp. 301–322; Gavin Wright, *The Political Economy of the Cotton South: Households, Markets, and Wealth in the Nineteenth Century* (New York: W. W. Norton, 1978), pp. 89–157.

involvement and strengthening the ties of Upcountry merchants to the world economy, the changes of the 1850s actually increased the region's dependence on the strength of world demand for cotton. During the 1850s, however, the Upcountry experienced a dramatic boom, one tied not only to the renewed cotton prosperity but also to major changes in the transporting and marketing of cotton and other commodities. This commercial quickening was facilitated by the development of railroads and the creation of banks, as well as by increased income from cotton. Thus rapid economic growth helped finance the creation of a new economic infrastructure, which reduced the Upcountry's isolation, intensified its commercial orientation, and laid the foundation for further commercial intensification and future development in the region.

6

Transportation and Commerce

Upcountry entrepreneurs, including both planters looking for easier methods of transporting their staple to market and village merchants eager to increase the commercial traffic in their locales, had long been interested in internal improvements. The canal system constructed during the 1820s had proven both expensive and ineffective. By the late 1830s, when railroad technology became generally available to South Carolina boosters, the state was locked in the grip of a deep recession. Between 1837 and 1848, general economic stagnation dried up local sources of private capital and stymied the efforts of promoters to begin a rail system in the Upcountry.[1]

Since the principal obstacle to railroad development was the lack of investment capital, Upcountry promoters were encouraged in 1845 when Governor William Aiken suggested in his message to the legislature that the state's surplus revenue fund of $1,051,000, money received by South Carolina when the federal government decided to distribute the surplus in the federal treasury to the states in 1836, be used as a revolving fund to supply capital to private railroad companies. Also, Aiken proposed that the legislature pledge itself to take subscriptions for at least two-fifths of the stock of any railroad company chartered by the state.[2] Unwilling to commit itself to such an ambitious spending program during an economic slump, the legislature ignored the governor's recommendations in 1845 only to hear Aiken reiterate his suggestions the following year. Railroads and other internal improvements were necessary, Aiken maintained, "To unlock resources . . . to awaken the energy and enterprise of our citizens, and to secure to them the opportunity of competing with other portions of our own country, and with foreign nations."[3] Aiken's successor, Governor David Johnson, also believed that railroad development was essential if South Carolina was to avoid becoming a wasteland depopulated by the flow of its people to the Southwest.

---

[1]Alfred G. Smith, Jr., *Economic Readjustment of an Old Cotton State: South Carolina, 1820–1860* (Columbia, S.C.: University of South Carolina Press, 1958), pp. 167–175.

[2]*Journal of the Senate of South Carolina, 1845* (Columbia, S.C.: Summer and Carroll, 1845), pp. 8–22; Columbia *Daily Telegraph*, December 14, 1847; *Debow's Review* 2 (1846):416–417.

[3]*Senate Journal*, 1846, p. 12.

Moreover, Johnson told the legislature that "the state is relied upon to contribute, in some form or other, towards the completion of these enterprises [railroads]; and that without it [state aid] some or all of them must fail."[4]

Finally, in 1847, when the state's economy began to improve, the legislature approved an innovative plan, similar to that recommended by Aiken, for providing state aid to seven newly chartered railroad companies. The plan called for the establishment of a revolving fund, consisting of the stock owned by the state in the South Carolina Railroad Company and in that company's financial arm, the Southwestern Railroad Bank.[5] Whenever the state made a subscription to a new railroad, that subscription would be paid from the revolving fund in the form of stock from the South Carolina Railroad or the Southwestern Bank. The state would receive in return an equivalent amount of stock in the new railroad. The stock of both the SC Railroad and the Southwestern Bank sold for cash at par during the late 1840s, so the new railroad companies could easily turn these stocks into liquid capital. As a result, the legislature's plan allowed the state to make an effective subscription to the new railroads, one entirely satisfactory to the companies, without increasing either its current spending or its total indebtedness.[6]

Railroad building, Upcountry planter Richard Austin Springs reported approvingly, had become "the ruling Mania of the day."[7] In Newberry, a local

[4]Columbia *Daily Telegraph,* December 1, 1847.

[5]The South Carolina Railroad Company was the corporate descendant of the South Carolina Canal and Railroad Company, chartered by the legislature in 1827. Originally, the SCCR was a private company authorized to raise $700,000 in capital. In 1833, the railroad from Charleston to Hamburg, designed to divert the Savannah River valley trade away from Augusta and Savannah, was completed. Then, in 1835, the legislature chartered the Louisville, Cincinnati and Charleston Railroad Company and authorized that company to raise money for a railroad stretching from Charleston through the Blue Ridge Mountains to Cincinnati. In 1836, the legislature granted the LCC banking privileges by creating the Southwestern Railroad Bank as its financial arm. Moreover, the legislature agreed that the state would purchase up to $1,000,000 in the stock of the bank and railroad, using funds from the surplus revenue to be deposited with the states by the federal government. According to the provisions of the charter, however, the bank could not begin operations until $8,000,000 in railroad stock subscriptions had been taken, and by early 1837, over $2,000,000 was still needed to bring subscriptions in the LCC up to that level. This additional capital was raised through a complicated, and unusual, transaction. The LCC agreed to purchase 20,000 shares of the existing SCCR, par $100, at $120 per share, on the condition that for each share of the SCCR purchased, the stockholders would buy a share in the LCC. The LCC project fell victim to the depression which followed the panic of 1837 despite a $600,000 advance on state subscriptions approved by the legislature in 1839. As the company began to retrench, plans for building the transmontane road were abandoned, and finally in 1842, the LCC and the SCCR were united into one organization, the South Carolina Railroad Company, which pushed the construction of a branch line to Columbia through to completion. This new company and the Southwestern Railroad Bank continued to operate throughout the antebellum period, and the stock owned by the state in these companies, worth in excess of $2,000,000, served to help finance most railroad projects in the state after 1847. See Samuel M. Derrick, *Centennial History of the South Carolina Railroad* (Columbia, S.C.: The State Company, 1930), especially pp. 152–191; and Ulrich B. Phillips, *A History of Transportation in the Eastern Cotton Belt to 1860* (New York: Columbia University Press, 1908), pp. 132–220.

[6]Smith, *Economic Readjustment of an Old Cotton State,* pp. 170–188.

[7]Richard Austin Springs to John Springs, December 18, 1846, Springs Family Papers, SHC.

minister observed that "most of the people appear much in the spirit" of building railroads while only a few "doubt the expediency of it."[8] As soon as the
legislature approved the idea of the revolving fund, the seven new railroad
companies chartered by the legislature in 1846 and 1847 began their organizational and money-raising efforts. The flurry of railroad building which began
during this period and continued through much of the next decade created a new,
far-reaching, and modern transportation system in South Carolina. In 1848, there
was only one railroad, the South Carolina Railroad, operating in the state. This
road, which used 248 miles of track, ran from Charleston to Hamburg with
branches to Columbia and Camden and represented a total investment of about
$6,500,000. By 1860, there were eleven railroads operating in the state, using
nearly 1000 miles of track and representing a total investment of well over
$22,000,000. Many of the new railroads served areas of the state, such as the
Upcountry and the Pee Dee, which had previously been without rail connections
to major markets. In fact, in the Upcountry alone, over 400 miles of railroad
track were built between 1848 and 1860, establishing rail connections between
every district in the region, except Lancaster, and the major commercial centers
of Columbia and Charleston.[9] Of the six railroads built in the Upcountry during
this era, two were major arteries, one connecting Columbia with Greenville, an
important local trading center for the foothills, and the other linking Columbia
with Charlotte, an important commercial center in North Carolina whose hinterland included a large portion of the grain-rich North Carolina Piedmont. The
other four new railroads were short feeder lines tying small villages and
courthouse towns, such as Yorkville, Spartanburg, Union, Laurensville, and
Pendleton, to the two main rail lines, thus establishing rail connections between
these towns and villages and a major fall-line market. The cost of building these
Upcountry railroads ultimately ran to more than $9 million, and although both of
the major lines were in full operation by 1853, the last of the feeder lines was not
completed until the spring of 1859.[10]

Both of the major lines traversing the Upcountry had little trouble raising
capital, but both were plagued by bickering over route selection. At one of the
conventions called to organize the Charlotte and South Carolina Railroad, York
district entrepreneur John Springs tried to persuade his fellow investors that
Camden rather than Columbia should be the southern terminus of the new road.
Springs, who had been elected to chair the convention, was supported by his son
Leroy, a prominent Charlotte merchant, and his son-in-law, Adam Brevard
Davidson, a wealthy planter from the "Rural Hill" section of Mecklenburg
County. Proponents of a Charlotte-to-Columbia route charged that Springs want-
ed the road for Camden because he owned over $20,000 worth of stock in the

[8]Entry of January 19, 1846, John McLees Diary, SCL.

[9]*Eighth Census of the United States,* IV, p. 328; Phillips, *History of Transportation,* pp. 335–
380; Smith, *Economic Readjustment of an Old Cotton State,* pp. 170–192.

[10]*Carolina Spartan,* December 1, 1859; Laurensville *Herald,* September 1, 1854; John Gettys
Smith, "A Sketch of the Town of Yorkville, 1850–1859" (unpublished manuscript), available at the
SCL.

Bank of Camden. Springs denied that personal considerations shaped his preference for Camden as a terminus, and pointed out that his banking investments in Columbia were nearly equal to his Camden interests and that a railroad to Columbia would actually run nearer to his Catawba River plantation than would a road bound for Camden. The advantage of building the railroad to Camden instead of Columbia, Springs argued, was simply that the route would be shorter and, as a result, the cost of construction less expensive. Columbia merchants and wealthy planters from Fairfield and Chester lobbied hard for Columbia as the southern terminus, and eventually, because their financial resources exceeded that of Camden merchants and Lancaster planters, won the battle of subscriptions and insured that the new railroad would run from Charlotte to Columbia.[11]

But even the decision to locate the southern terminus of the C and SC in Columbia did not end the squabbling over the route of the road. In an effort to prevent the C and SC from bypassing Yorkville, the courthouse town of York district, a group of prominent citizens from the Yorkville area petitioned the stockholders of the C and SC to allow the new railroad to veer through Yorkville on its way from Chester to Charlotte. The petitioners promised a subscription of over $100,000 from the Yorkville area on the condition that the road pass through the town. After some debate, the C and SC stockholders rejected the Yorkville offer, largely because the route which bypassed Yorkville was ten miles shorter and bisected "one of the richest and most prosperous sections" of the Upcountry.[12]

Construction of the C and SC railroad began in 1849, and by the end of 1852 the road was in full operation. The completed road was 110 miles long and cost slightly more than $1.7 million to build. Of that amount, $1.1 million was raised through stock subscriptions and the other $600,000 through loans and bond sales. Sixty percent of the stock subscriptions were made by private investors, while the rest came from state and municipal aid.[13] The C and SC received solid financial backing from planters and merchants residing along its route. Promoters in Fairfield and Chester raised over $200,000 in private subscriptions from each district. Fairfield planters Edward Palmer, J. B. McCants, and Theodore S. Dubose, invested $5500, $2000, and $7000 respectively in the project. Thomas

[11]Thomas J. Withers to John Springs, October 20, 1845, Henry W. Conner to John Springs, November 2, 1846, James M. Osborne to John Springs, November 24, 1846, Thomas J. Withers to John Springs, April 14, 1847, Henry W. Conner to John Springs, April 16, 1847, John Springs to James W. Osborne, May 18, 1847, C. J. Shannon to John Springs, July 13, 1847, William R. Myers to John Springs, September 11, 1847, Franklin H. Elmore to John Springs, September 13, 1847, Edward G. Palmer to John Springs, October 29, 1847, Cadwallader Jones to John Springs, January 20, 1848, Springs Family Papers, SHC; Inventory and Will of John Springs [c. 1853], Davidson Family Papers, SHC.

[12]*Proceedings of the Charlotte and South Carolina Railroad Company at Chesterville, October 11, 1848; Proceedings of the Convention of Stockholders of the Charlotte and South Carolina Railroad,* January 13, and 14, 1848, pp. 16–19.

[13]*Proceedings of the Stockholders' Meeting of the Charlotte and South Carolina Railroad Company at Chesterville,* November 17 and 18, 1852; Smith, *Economic Readjustment of an Old Cotton State,* p. 183.

McLure, a planter from Chester took $10,000 worth of stock, and Chester merchant Hiram C. Brawley invested $1500. Both the Charlotte and the Columbia areas raised over $100,000 each in private subscriptions. In the Charlotte area, Leroy Springs and A. Brevard Davidson both invested $7000. Richland district planter B. F. Taylor subscribed to $2700 worth of stock, and James Gadsden, a commission merchant with houses in Columbia and Charleston, pledged $5000. Only $24,000 in private subscriptions was received from York district, however, and the bulk of that amount came from stock purchases by John Springs and other members of his family.[14] Still, despite strong backing for the C and SC from private investors, the railroad could not have been built without state and municipal support. The C and SC received $270,000 in aid from the state's revolving fund between 1848 and 1852, and during those same years received $100,000 in municipal subscriptions from both Charlotte and Columbia, as well as a $15,000 subscription from Charleston. Private investors were acutely aware of the importance of state and municipal assistance. James Hemphill, a Chester planter-lawyer who purchased $2000 worth of C and SC stock and worked very hard behind the scenes encouraging others to invest in the project, acknowledged that "reasonable ground for hope that the enterprise may succeed" appeared only "after the assistance granted by the Legislature" was received.[15]

The C and SC railroad operated successfully from the time of its completion until the outbreak of the Civil War. The road's revenues exceeded its operating costs and paid reasonable dividends to stockholders in most years. In the mid-1850s, the road embarked on an expensive program of laying new and better track and financed the program largely through loans and bond sales. These improvements increased the company's total indebtedness and cast doubt on its ability to meet its long-term obligations despite its short-run earnings.[16]

Traffic over the southern section of the C and SC increased when the Kings Mountain Railroad, a feeder line linking Yorkville with the C and SC near the town of Chester, was completed late in 1852. The Kings Mountain Railroad was organized by the same group of planters, lawyers, and merchants from the Yorkville area whose earlier efforts to lure the C and SC through that village had been rebuffed. This group of local investors was headed by Isaac D. Witherspoon and William C. Beatty, two successful lawyers with extensive planting interests, and Robert G. McCaw, a wealthy planter. Spanning a distance of twenty-two miles at a cost of $225,000, the Kings Mountain road tied the western portion of York district into the emerging Upcountry rail system. All of the capital for the road was raised from private investors with the exception of a

[14]*Proceedings of the Fourth Annual Meeting of the Stockholders of the Charlotte and South Carolina Railroad at Chesterville,* November 19, 1851; Inventory of A. B. Davidson's property, June 16, 1879, Davidson Family Papers, SHC.

[15]James Hemphill to W. R. Hemphill, December 16, 1848, Hemphill Family Papers, DU.

[16]*Proceedings of the Stockholders' Meeting of the Charlotte and South Carolina Railroad,* February 3, 1858, pp. 3–13.

$50,000 stock purchase by the state from its revolving fund.[17] With the C and SC and the Kings Mountain railroads both in full operation by the end of 1852, the eastern section of the Upcountry enjoyed relatively easy access to a number of important commercial centers. "I am now ready to say *Huzzah* for the Columbia and Charlotte Road," delighted investor John Springs told his son, "I expect in the future you will not only go to Charlotte by RR but to Yorkville. Is it not a great change in the condition of the Country?"[18]

The process of opening the central and western portions of the Upcountry, those large and diverse areas lying between the Broad and Savannah Rivers, to railroad traffic proved difficult, expensive, and acrimonious. Much of the controversy stemmed from competition among various towns and districts anxious to influence the route of the proposed railroad running from Columbia to Greenville. The original charter of the Greenville and Columbia Railroad company, granted by the legislature in 1845, specified that the road was to run from Columbia through Newberry and Laurens to Greenville, and allowed a branch line to be constructed from the main line west to the town of Abbeville. Leading citizens of Anderson and Abbeville districts, however, began a money-raising campaign designed to entice the road through their area, and in 1847 the legislature amended the Greenville and Columbia charter to allow consideration of several different routes. Almost immediately competition began between Laurens district on the one hand, and Anderson and Abbeville districts on the other. Greenville promoters and investors generally favored the shorter Laurens route, which was only 109 miles long, over the rival "Saluda River route" through Abbeville and Anderson, which was 158 miles in length. Merchants in Columbia and Newberry, however, were eager to tap the rich cotton trade of the upper Savannah River valley and thus tended to favor the longer route through Abbeville and Anderson.[19]

The issue was debated at a stockholders' meeting in Newberry on November 19, 1847, with investors along both prospective routes fully represented. The argument grew heated. Greenville stockholders made impassioned pleas for the selection of the shortest and cheapest route. Their opponents from Anderson and Abbeville countered by reminding other stockholders of the agricultural riches produced in their districts. Since the route question was to be decided by a vote of the stockholders, the amount of stock taken by investors in the various districts was critical. The citizens of Laurens district pledged nearly $140,000 in support of the direct route, but Abbeville citizens raised over $180,000 in subscriptions and Anderson raised more than $200,000 to support the winding route through the upper Savannah region.[20] When the vote was finally taken, Anderson and Abbeville stockholders, with strong support from Columbia and some support

[17]For a complete history of the Kings Mountain Railroad, see Yorkville *Enquirer*, February 27, 1889; see also Yorkville *Miscellany*, September 25, 1852.

[18]John Springs to Andrew Baxter Springs, August 31, 1852, Springs Family Papers, SHC.

[19]Greenville *Mountaineer*, January 23, 1846; Lillian Kibler, *Benjamin F. Perry: South Carolina Unionist* (Durham, N.C.: Duke University Press, 1946), pp. 209–216.

[20]Greenville *Mountaineer*, November 26, 1847.

from Newberry, outvoted the Laurens and Greenville stockholders and the longer route was chosen. Laurens stockholders immediately withdrew from the company in disgust, and Greenville investors also walked out of the meeting, demanding a refund of the installments paid on their stock subscriptions and a release from the company. The directors of the G and C denied these requests on the grounds that the Greenville subscriptions were unconditional.[21]

For a time it appeared that the future of the Greenville and Columbia Railroad was in jeopardy. Entrepreneurs from Laurens and Greenville discussed the possibility of forming a separate company and investment in the G and C from the Greenville area dwindled to nothing. John Belton O'Neall of Newberry, the president of the G and C and himself a former advocate of the direct route from Newberry to Greenville, chastised Greenville because "her stockholders have stood aloof from the enterprise [the G and C]," and warned that the town of Greenville would suffer every bit as much as the railroad company if Anderson remained the western terminus of the road.[22] Eventually, O'Neall, along with two of Greenville's most influential men, B. F. Perry and Waddy Thompson, organized a public meeting in Greenville to discuss the future of that town's involvement with the project. At the meeting, Greenville stockholders decided to offer the G and C directors a compromise. Greenville promised to fulfill its financial obligations and even increase its subscriptions if the railroad directors agreed to allow the road to veer east of the town of Anderson on its way on the Greenville. Under this proposal, the town of Anderson was to be connected to the road by a short branch line. At the urging of O'Neall and Perry, the stockholders of the G and C accepted the compromise offered by Greenville despite vociferous protests from the Anderson delegation. Once the compromise was accepted, Vardry McBee, a wealthy Greenville industrialist, raised his personal stock subscription from $12,000 to $50,000.[23]

By the end of 1853, the G and C was in full operation between Columbia and Greenville, with spurs running to the towns of Abbeville and Anderson. The road was over 160 miles long and cost over $2,000,000 to build.[24] Just over $1.1 million was raised from stock subscriptions and slightly over half of those subscriptions were made either by the state or by various municipalities. The state authorized a $200,000 subscription from the revolving fund in 1848 and increased that subscription to $350,000 by the mid-1850s. The town of Columbia, eager to improve its connections with the interior, took $250,000 worth of stock

[21]*Proceedings of the Greenville and Columbia Railroad Company*, May 1 and 2, 1848; Greenville *Mountaineer*, May 5, 1848.

[22]*Proceedings of the Stockholders of the Greenville and Columbia Railroad Company*, Meeting in Columbia, December 1 and 2, 1848, especially pp. 12–13; Greenville *Mountaineer*, August 11, 1848.

[23]Greenville *Mountaineer*, September 14 and 21, 1848; Entries of September 29, 1848, November 21, 1849, Benjamin F. Perry Diary, vol. 2, SHC.

[24]Thomas H. Pope, *The History of Newberry County, South Carolina, 1799–1860* (Columbia, S.C.: University of South Carolina Press, 1973), pp. 40–146; John Belton O'Neall, *Annals of Newberry* (Charleston: S. G. Courtenay, 1859), pp. 392–398; *Proceedings of the Annual Stockholders' Meeting of the Greenville and Columbia Railroad*, held at Abbeville, July 11, 1855.

in 1849, and Charleston pledged $100,000 in stock subscriptions in 1850. Even with these public subscriptions, the G and C was unable to raise enough money from private investors to cover the expenses of construction and was forced to sell over $750,000 in 6 percent coupon bonds in order to complete the road. Late in the 1850s, the burden of heavy indebtedness placed the G and C in a financial bind, and the road's directors asked the state to endorse $900,000 worth of its bonds. In 1860, with talk of secession on every tongue, the state agreed to the G and C's request.[25] Over half a million dollars in private capital for the G and C was raised in the Upcountry. According to local legend, eleven prominent Andersonians invested $5000 each to help lure the G and C to their town, and, in Greenville, Vardry McBee's personal subscription was half as large as that taken by the city of Charleston.[26] Still, the successful completion of the G and C Railroad depended heavily on state and municipal aid and guarantees, demonstrating once again that successful railroad entrepreneurs had to be not only men of financial means and local influence but also skillful politicians and lobbyists.

Despite its circuitous route, the G and C quickly emerged as the major commercial artery in the western portion of the state. As a result, sections of the Upcountry which had been bypassed by the G and C rapidly grew interested in establishing connections with the road. By 1860, three feeder lines had been constructed, each delivering cargo to the G and C at various points along its route and together connecting every district west of the Broad River to the major road. The first feeder line completed was the Laurens Railroad, a comparatively short line running from the town of Laurens to Newberry, where it intersected with the G and C. After the compromise between Greenville investors and the G and C directors quashed Laurens's hopes for a direct line from Greenville to Newberry, Laurens promoters pushed forward with plans for a feeder line. At an organizational meeting held at Laurens courthouse in September 1849, James H. Irby, a prominent Laurens attorney and one-time Whig candidate for Congress, was elected president of the Laurens Railroad, and twelve local notables were elected as a board of directors. Irby, whose personal fortune exceeded $500,000, promoted the project vigorously, and by 1850 the company had raised more than $110,000 in private subscriptions and had received a $50,000 subscription from the state. Newberry merchants and planters invested heavily in the road, as did their counterparts in Laurens, but neither Columbia nor Charleston was willing to offer municipal aid to a road likely to add little to its commerce. As the early enthusiasm for the road waned, financial woes began to plague the project. In 1853, the Laurensville newspaper complained that the energy of the railroad promoters was flagging and that weeds were growing up around the Laurensville depot. Ultimately, however, the G and C came to the rescue of the Laurens railroad when G and C directors approved a plan calling for their road to buy

[25]*South Carolina Statutes at Large* (hereinafter SCSAL), vol. 12, pp. 885–887; Smith, *Economic Readjustment of an Old Cotton State,* pp. 179–183.

[26]Louise Ayer Vandiver, *A History of Anderson County* (Atlanta: Ruralist Press, 1928), p. 180; Appraisal of Vardry McBee, Sr.'s estate, February 1, 1864, McBee Papers, SHC.

stock in the Laurens Railroad. With this boost, the Laurens Railroad, which ran for thirty-two miles and cost just over $540,000 to build, was completed on April 26, 1854, and served as an effective feeder line for the G and C for the rest of the decade.[27]

A second, and equally important, feeder line for the G and C, the Spartanburg and Union Railroad, which ran from Spartanburg courthouse through Union to intersect with the G and C at Alston, was not completed until 1859. The S and U obtained a charter in 1849 but was plagued by financial difficulties for most of the next decade. Planters and merchants in both Spartanburg and Union invested heavily in the project, but the cost of building the road over long stretches of rugged hill-country terrain was much higher than originally estimated.[28] In 1855, S and U President Daniel Wallace, a Jonesville resident with far-flung business and political connections launched a new campaign to increase private investment. Wallace hailed the S and U as "an indispensable link in the great chain of social and commercial connection and progress."[29] Wallace also pleaded with the state, which had taken $150,000 in S and U stock in 1854, for additional financial support. Wallace told legislators that all "schemes of internal improvement . . . are calculated to elevate the standard of her [the state's] civilization and confer lasting benefit to the community."[30] The legislature responded to Wallace's plea with an additional $100,000, but by 1857 the S and U again found itself on the brink of insolvency when that year's sharp recession left many private investors unable to meet their obligations.[31]

Again, the directors of the S and U appealed to the state for help, asking the legislature to endorse $450,000 worth of S and U bonds. The state agreed and the road survived the Panic of 1857. During 1858, operations began on that portion of the S and U running from Alston depot on the G and C to the town of Unionville, but the directors announced that at least another $100,000 was needed to complete the road to Spartanburg. A group of Spartanburg stockholders, led by wealthy merchant and manufacturer Gabriel Cannon, increased their subscriptions and insured the road's completion. The arrival of the first S

[27]Pope, *History of Newberry*, pp. 144–146; Laurensville *Herald*, September 14, 1849, and October 25, 1850; *Cyclopedia of Eminent and Representative Men of the Carolinas of the Nineteenth Century*, 2 vols. (Madison: Brant and Fuller, 1892), vol. 1, pp. 219–220; Laurensville *Herald*, September 1 and 15, 1854; Zelotus L. Holmes to his Aunt, August 19, 1853, Zelotus L. Holmes Papers, SCL.

[28]*Carolina Spartan*, July 7 and August 4, 1853; Franklin H. Elmore to Hosea J. Dean, October 11, 1849, Simpson, Young, Dean, and Coleman Papers, SCL; John Springs to Andrew Baxter Springs, January 15, 1852, Springs Family Papers, SHC.

[29]*Carolina Spartan*, June 21, 1855. Born in Laurens, Daniel Wallace moved to Union district in 1833 at age 32. Wallace was admitted to the bar and practiced law in both Unionville and Jonesville. Within a few years, Wallace purchased a plantation in the Jonesville area. He was also a partner in several profitable mercantile firms. Wallace served two terms in the state legislature before being elected to Congress in 1848. In 1853, Wallace retired from politics and assumed the presidency of the S and U RR. He died in 1859. See the *Biographical Directory of the American Congress, 1774–1944* (Washington, D.C.: Government Printing Office, 1950), p. 1968.

[30]*Carolina Spartan*, August 23, 1855.

[31]*Carolina Spartan*, August 20, 1857.

and U train in Spartanburg in November 1859 was celebrated with a massive public barbecue and festival. The celebration attracted over 8000 people into a small courthouse town with a population of less than 1200 and was marked by self-congratulatory speeches by railroad promoters who praised the road as a symbol of progress and civic virtue.[32]

The third feeder line of the G and C built during the 1850s was the short segment of the Blue Ridge Railroad which ran from the town of Anderson northward through Pendleton village to the tiny settlement of Walhalla in the western section of Pickens district. Chartered in 1852, the Blue Ridge Railroad was designed to be anything but a short feeder line. Instead, the original plan for the Blue Ridge Railroad represented a revival of South Carolina's long-standing desire to build a transmontane railroad linking the port of Charleston with the great commercial cities of the old Northwest. Plans for such a trunk line had lain dormant since the collapse of the old Louisville, Charleston, and Cincinnati Railroad Company due to serious financial problems and rancorous political disputes over route selection in 1839. Most of the renewed interest in a transmontane railroad came from Charleston, and much of the financial support for the Blue Ridge Railroad was generated by that city, which hoped to divert a significant portion of the commerce from the rich Ohio River valley to its wharves on the Atlantic coast.[33]

Like its predecessor, the Blue Ridge Railroad company was plagued by a variety of political, financial, and technological problems. The proposed route of the line, which was to branch off of the G and C at Anderson, tunnel through Stump House Mountain and into Rabun Gap before winding through the valley of the Little Tennessee River to Knoxville and beyond, covered some of the most rugged terrain in the southeast and was certainly the most difficult and ambitious railroad project ever undertaken by South Carolina. Moreover, few private investors outside of Charleston were willing to risk capital in a road whose principal beneficiary would be the port city. In 1854, the legislature rescued the project by authorizing state purchases of Blue Ridge Railroad stock totalling one million dollars, and agreeing to endorse another $1,250,000 in Blue Ridge Railroad bonds if the company raised at least one million in matching subscriptions. Since the city of Charleston had earlier subscribed to $1,100,000 in Blue Ridge stock, the conditions of the state's contingent allocation were satisfied immediately, and the Blue Ridge Railroad received a massive infusion of capital in 1855 despite the continued indifference of private investors toward the project. Indeed, by the end of 1855, only $53,000 in private subscriptions had been taken in

[32]Carolina *Spartan*, February 4 and September 2, 1858, January 27 and December 7, 1859; Writers Program, Works Progress Administration, *A History of Spartanburg County* (Spartanburg, S.C.: Band and White, 1940), pp. 114–116.

[33]See George Dewitt Brown, "A History of the Blue Ridge Railroad, 1852–1874" (M.A. thesis, University of South Carolina, 1967); Derrick, *Centennial History of the South Carolina Railroad*, pp. 190–219; and Smith, *Economic Readjustment of an Old Cotton State*, pp. 15–190.

Charleston, and private subscriptions received from outside of Charleston were negligible.[34]

But even the generosity of the state did not solve the financial problems of the Blue Ridge Railroad. The company had raised over $5,500,000 in capital by the end of 1856, but the estimated cost of building the road was $7,500,000. Unable to raise the money from private sources, the company spent the rest of the decade seeking more aid from the state legislature. The railroad's seemingly endless appetite for state funds alarmed many politicians and vigorous and outspoken opposition to further state appropriations to the Blue Ridge Railroad emerged. Without state aid, the Blue Ridge project first sputtered and then stalled altogether in 1859. The primary obstacle to the successful completion of the South Carolina portion of the railroad was the expense and difficulty of building a one-mile tunnel through the solid granite base of Stump House Mountain. Work began on the tunnel in 1856 and continued for the better part of three years. The construction effort, marred by the death of ten workers, cost over $1,000,000 and was still one thousand feet short of completion when the work was abandoned due to the company's financial problems. By the time all construction along the Blue Ridge line was halted, over $2,500,000 had been expended to build thirty-three miles of track, running from Anderson to Walhalla, and coming to a dead end there with, as one local historian observed, "the old tunnel at Walhalla" standing as "a mute witness to the blasted hopes of its promoters." Conceived as a grandiose transmontane trunk line siphoning the freight of Tennessee, Kentucky, and perhaps even part of Ohio away to Charleston, the short spur of the Blue Ridge Railroad which was actually completed served as a small feeder line, built at enormous expense, which hauled the cotton crops of Pendleton area planters to the junction with the G and C at Anderson courthouse.[35]

Despite the failure of the Blue Ridge Railroad company to build a major trunk line to the Midwest, the Upcountry, by 1860, possessed a substantial, though somewhat skeletal, railroad network which tied the region more tightly than ever before to the larger world economy. Most planters were delighted. Yeoman farmers generally greeted the arrival of the railroads with a mixture of awe, amazement, and approval. Washington Cowan, a small slaveholder from the Nation's Ford section of York district, noted as early as 1849 that "the railroad from Columbia to Sharlot [sic] is going on very fast." The C and SC route passed within three miles of Cowan's farm, and he expected it to expedite the marketing of his substantial cotton crops.[36] In Spartanburg district, small farmer David Harris made a special trip in the summer of 1859 to view the

[34]Brown, "Blue Ridge Railroad," pp. 24–56; *Annual Report of the President and Chief Engineer to the Stockholders of the Blue Ridge Rail Road Company, July 11, 1854.*

[35]Brown, "Blue Ridge Railroad," pp. 24–56; Vandiver, *History of Anderson County*, p. 146; Joseph Norton to Miles Norton, February 6, 1860, Joseph J. Norton Papers, SCL; Speech of William D. Simpson, [c. 1855], Simpson, Young, Dean, and Coleman Papers, SCL.

[36]Washington Cowan to John Cowan, March 4, 1849, Nancy Cowan Papers, SHC.

progress of the S and U railroad. "I was determined to go have a peep at the RR," Harris wrote; after seeing the road, Harris pronounced himself "pleased" with the impact it was having on his section of the Upcountry.[37] When the S and U was finally completed in November 1859, Spartanburg yeoman James F. Sloan took three children to the huge "Railroad barbecue." An excited Sloan and one of his daughters rode the train with "such another collection of people I never saw at one time before." Sloan's only complaint about the road was that on his way home from the celebration the train was so crowded that it stalled repeatedly until an additional engine was added.[38]

This transportation revolution was financed largely by private enterprise. Of the more than $9,000,000 in capital raised to build Upcountry railroads, over $5,000,000 was raised in the private sector, while the other $4,000,000 came from state or municipal stock purchases and bond endorsements. Moreover, if the ill-fated Blue Ridge Railroad, which was always a pet project of Charleston and a clique of state legislators, is excluded from consideration, the cost of building the Upcountry rail network would total just over $6,000,000, of which only $1,800,000 came from state or municipal stock subscriptions.[39] Yet even though well over half of all capital invested in Upcountry railroads came from private sources, the financing of the roads was a cooperative effort, requiring strong support from the state as well as considerable private initiative. The state was generally supportive, but it was also cautious and circumspect in granting assistance to most fledgling railroad companies. With the exception of its spendthrift attitude toward the Blue Ridge Railroad, the state never raised taxes nor increased its total indebtedness in order to offer economic assistance to an Upcountry railroad. The legislature was able to avoid the political controversy and financial risks that necessarily would have arisen from tax levies or increased indebtedness through the use of the revolving fund, which made state investments in risky and uncertain new projects by selling state-owned stocks in established and profitable enterprises, and by funding existing debt service with profits earned by the Bank of the State of South Carolina.[40]

This unique system of financing internal improvements at a minimum of risk to the state and with little or no added burden to the taxpayers helped the state develop its economic infrastructure while maintaining its solid financial reputation. Still, the long-term financial outlook of the new railroads was uncertain

[37]Entry of July 23, 1859, David G. Harris Farm Journals, SHC.

[38]Entry of November 25, 1859, James F. Sloan Journal, SCL.

[39]For an overview of railroad building in South Carolina, see Frederick B. Collins, "Charleston and the Railroads: A Geographic Study of a South Atlantic Port and Its Strategies for Developing a Railroad System, 1820–1860" (M.A. thesis, University of South Carolina, 1977). Figures on the sources of capital raised for Upcountry railroads were derived from the "Reports of the Comptroller General" in *Reports and Resolutions of the General Assembly*, 1850–1859, from Smith, *Economic Readjustment of an Old Cotton State*, pp. 179–190, and from the proceedings of stockholders' meetings of the various companies cited in previous footnotes.

[40]J. Mauldin Lesesne, *The Bank of the State of South Carolina: A General and Political History* (Columbia, S.C.: University of South Carolina Press, 1970), especially pp. 106–109, 157, and 162; and from the "Reports of the Comptroller General" in *Reports and Resolutions*, 1848–1860.

enough to arouse considerable concern among the state's official financial stewards. First in 1855 and again in 1857, the office of the Comptroller General warned the legislature that "none of the Roads in our State are [sic] setting aside a fund to meet their indebtedness at maturity."[41] The state's financial officers feared that unless the railroad companies began to set aside a percentage of each year's profit, by forgoing dividend payments if necessary, there was a real danger that "the bondholders of the several Companies will hereafter become owners of the Railroads at the expense of the present stockholders, or drive the State into purchase of the Roads . . . to save her own Stock." The Civil War intervened before most of the railroad obligations became due, but the comptroller's fears were eventually realized during Reconstruction, when much of the state's bankrupt rail system fell into receivership.[42]

Much of the credit for raising the more than $3,000,000 in private capital that was invested in Upcountry railroads, and for cajoling investors into making their installment payments on time, belonged to the men chosen as directors of the various railroad companies. These directors were almost always men who had invested heavily in the railroad, and they supplied most of the entrepreneurial talent and promotional drive needed to complete the difficult task of building a railroad network in the Upcountry. A prosopographical analysis of the individuals who served on boards of directors of Upcountry railroad companies during the 1850s reveals that all the directors identified resided in South Carolina with the exception of the four men who represented Charlotte on the board of the C and SC. Over 75 percent of all directors were either from one of the Upcountry districts or from Columbia. The directors who did not hail from Columbia or the Upcountry were all from Charleston. Yet of the nineteen Charlestonians who served as directors of Upcountry railroads, twelve were directors of the Blue Ridge Railroad, a project which always attracted most of its support from Charleston. If the directors of the Blue Ridge are excluded from the analysis, then nearly 90 percent of all railroad directors lived north and west of the fall line.[43]

<hr/>

[41]"Report of the Comptroller General" in *Reports and Resolutions of the General Assembly of the State of South Carolina* (Columbia, S.C.: E. H. Britton, 1855), pp. 10–21.

[42]"Report of the Comptroller General" in *Reports and Resolutions* (1857), pp. 5–17; Willie Frank Putnam, "An Analysis of Public Aid to Railroads in South Carolina, 1865–1906" (M.A. thesis, University of South Carolina, 1957).

[43]The analysis of directors of Upcountry railroad companies included all the individuals who served as directors from the time the companies were formed until 1860. Since I was unable to find complete and reliable lists of the directors of the Kings Mountain Railroad, the short line between Yorkville and Chester, I have excluded that road from the analysis. Of the 89 men who served on boards of directors of Upcountry railroads during the 1850s, I was able to identify 79, or almost 89 percent. Of the ten unidentified directors, four were North Carolinians who served as directors of the C and SC. Possible identification was made on the remaining six directors, but ambiguities arising from the presence of more than one individual with the same name in certain districts prevented positive identification. As a result of this problem, I have not included this handful of men in my analysis. The principal sources used in identifying railroad directors were the *Cyclopedia of Eminent Men*, vols. 1 and 2; John Belton O'Neall, *Biographical Sketches of the Bench and Bar of South Carolina* (Charleston: S. G. Courtenay, 1859), vols. 1 and 2; Chalmers Gaston Davidson, *The Last*

For the most part, railroad directors were men with business connections, and often political connections as well, which reached well beyond the borders of their home district. If the directors of the Blue Ridge Railroad are omitted from the analysis, almost 30 percent of all railroad directors were planters, and another 9 percent were planter-lawyers. The business concerns of the typical Upcountry planter involved him not only with other leading planters of his district but also with factors and other merchants and bankers in Columbia and Charleston. Moreover, planter-lawyers, men who devoted most of their daily energies to the practice of law but who also supervised the operation of a plantation, had legal as well as business connections with lawyers and commercial leaders throughout the state. Twenty-one percent of all railroad directors were lawyers pure and simple. These attorneys, though not directly involved with plantation agriculture or mercantile activity, nevertheless toured the various judicial circuits frequently, arguing cases and meeting local notables. As a result, these attorneys played an especially important role in securing the cooperation of entrepreneurs and politicians scattered across the state. Upcountry merchants filled about 10 percent of the directors' seats. These merchants hoped that improved transportation would increase commerce in their locale. Just over 7 percent of all directors were prominent Charleston cotton factors, commission merchants, and wholesalers who were eager to establish better connections with the rich cotton areas of the Upcountry even at the risk of creating a new breed of competitors among merchants in Upcountry railroad towns. The remaining dozen or so directors came from a variety of different backgrounds, including farming, medicine, banking, the ministry, and the newspaper business. There were also three important industrialists who served as railroad directors.[44]

Naturally, railroad directors were men of considerable means as well as influence. Solid financial backing and the availability of investment capital were essential to the success of any railroad project, and the directors played a crucial role in establishing and maintaining a firm economic foundation for the roads, frequently drawing heavily on their own resources to do so. As a young Lancaster attorney interested in the fate of the C and SC told John Springs late in 1847, "In Railroad matters it is not the argument of small fry like myself that carries weight . . . But it is men of wealth and capital who have the wherewithal to back their judgment. These are the kind of men who carry weight and influence with them, and one word from men like these are worth more than 40,000 speeches."[45] Yet while most railroad directors were either wealthy or well-

Foray: The South Carolina Planters of 1860, A Sociological Study (Columbia, S.C.: University of South Carolina Press, 1971); John Amasa May and Joan Reynolds Faunt, *South Carolina Secedes* (Columbia, S.C.: University of South Carolina Press, 1960); Emily B. Reynolds and Joan Reynolds Faunt, *Biographical Directory of the Senate of South Carolina, 1776–1964* (Columbia, S.C.: South Carolina Archives Department, 1964); *Charleston City Directory* for various years; and the manuscript census returns for 1850 and 1860. Also, a variety of other county and local histories, newspapers, and manuscript collections were used.

44See Table 6.1.

45John Williams to John Springs, October 14, 1847, Springs Family Papers, SHC.

Table 6.1 Occupations of Railroad Directors

	All Upcountry Railroads		Excluding Blue Ridge Railroad	
	No.	Percentage	No.	Percentage
Planters	20	25.3%	19	28.3%
Lawyers	15	19.0	14	20.9
Charleston Merchants	9	11.4	5	7.4
Upcountry Merchants	7	8.9	7	10.4
Planter-Lawyers	7	8.9	6	9.0
Physicians	3	3.8	3	4.4
Bankers	3	3.8	1	1.5
Industrialists	3	3.8	3	4.4
Farmers	3	3.8	3	4.4
Planter-Merchants	2	2.6	2	3.0
Planter-Bankers	2	2.6	0	0
Editors	1	1.3	1	1.5
Clergy	1	1.3	1	1.5
Officeholders	2	2.6	1	1.5
Occupation Unknown	2	2.6	1	1.5
Total	79	100.0	67	100.0

Source: See footnote 52.

fixed, by Upcountry standards at least, their interest in promoting and financing railroad development grew out of a larger entrepreneurial outlook. Upcountry capitalists, whether planters or merchants, had learned all too well about the region's economic vulnerability during the long slump of the 1840s. They accepted, at least in part, the basic Victorian faith that progress was possible whenever men of talent and resources committed themselves to the effort, and they demonstrated that faith by investing heavily in an economic infrastructure which they believed to be essential to long-term economic growth, development, and prosperity in their region.[46]

The entrepreneurial ethos, rooted firmly in the early Victorian view of progress, manifested itself in a variety of ambiguous motives which spurred men to invest in Upcountry railroads. These motives ranged from a simple eye for the main chance to grand dynastic ambitions. To be sure, many investors desired to profit either directly from the operation of the railroad or indirectly from its residual benefits to the region. Upcountry planters, for example, invested in railroads to improve their connections with coastal and fall-line factors and to expedite all aspects of the cotton trade. Yet while railroads provided certain valuable conveniences to Upcountry planters, many planter-investors possessed

[46]For discussions of the prevailing entrepreneurial ethos in the United States during the early Victorian period, see Daniel Walker Howe, "American Victorianism as a Culture," *American Quarterly* 27 (December, 1975):507–532; Richard D. Brown, "Modernization: A Victorian Climax," *American Quarterly* 27 (December, 1975):533–548. See also Howe's *The Political Culture of the American Whigs* (Chicago: University of Chicago Press, 1979).

enough wealth to live comfortable through several lifetimes even without the benefits of a railroad. John D. Williams of Laurens, a planter who owned 225 slaves in 1860 and whose total worth in that year was estimated at $500,000, invested heavily in the Laurens Railroad at age fifty-six. Williams, a wealthy man long before there was even any talk of bringing a railroad to Laurens, supported the road more because he believed it essential to the economic future of the Laurens area than for the prospect of personal gain.[47]

Commitment to local economic development, of course, was not altruism. The impulse behind railroad investment was essentially entrepreneurial in the largest sense. Rich planters wanted to diversify their portfolios, transferring some of their resources out of agriculture and into commerce, as a hedge against future agricultural depressions. Many of them also wanted to lay a firm foundation for long-term economic growth in the region to insure the economic well-being of their children. Moreover, many promoters saw railroad development as a matter of sectional pride and necessity, an essential prerequisite if the South was to avoid falling behind the developing North.[48] John Springs probably diversified his investments more than any other Upcountry planter, and he continued to invest in railroads as he passed the age of sixty. When he died in 1853, Springs owned over $100,000 worth of railroad stocks and bonds. Springs used his fortune to establish his several sons and sons-in-law as men of wealth in their own right. Before his death Springs started two sons in the mercantile business and turned over three plantations to sons or sons-in-law. Clearly an important part of Springs's ambition was the creation of an economic empire which could be bequeathed to his children and fragmented among them and still remain an empire.[49]

Upcountry merchants who invested heavily in railroads usually expected more direct and immediate benefits from their investment than did planters. On the whole, these merchants, though men of some means, were far from wealthy, and usually they were rather young. Hiram Brawley, a merchant in the town of Chester, was still in his thirties and worth only about $7000 when he invested in the C and SC railroad. In Unionville, William J. Keenan was a young merchant still in his twenties and worth less than $5000 when he invested in the S and U railroad. Within ten years, Brawley was worth nearly $50,000, with extensive holdings in land and slaves as well as in his profitable mercantile business. By 1860, Keenan's assets were valued at $30,000, and Keenan had become a director of the S and U, a bank agent, and the most prosperous merchant in Union district.[50] Although Upcountry merchants such as Brawley and Keenan

[47]May and Faunt, *South Carolina Secedes*, p. 226; Laurensville *Herald*, October 25, 1850.

[48]For example, see Edward G. Palmer, *Address to the People of Richland, Fairfield, Chester, and York Districts on the Subject of the Charlotte and South Carolina Railroad* (Columbia, S.C.: Office of the *South Carolinian*, 1847).

[49]Katherine Wooten Springs, *The Squires of Springfield* (Charlotte, N.C.: William Lofton, 1965), pp. 54–148; Inventory and Will of John Springs, January 1, 1853, Davidson Family Papers, SHC.

[50]R. G. Dun and Company, Credit Ledgers, South Carolina, IX, 144, 148, XIV, 94, 98, Baker.

expected to profit directly from the faster commercial pace which the railroads would bring to Upcountry towns, these ambitious merchants, like their planter counterparts, were true entrepreneurs. They were men willing to bet on the future, men eager to seize opportunities for personal gain by investing their capital in ventures which promised to breed new opportunities and foster long-term prosperity as well as return a healthy profit on investment.

It was this same entrepreneurial spirit, writ large, that possessed Upcountry towns during the 1850s. In almost every town, a group of merchants, lawyers, and other town boosters threw much of its energy and capital behind various railroad projects in hopes of accelerating the tempo of local commercial activity. Indeed, the entire promotional campaign waged in support of railroads was filled with bold and even hyperbolic claims regarding the benefits which the railroads would bring to the local economy. In a public letter promoting the C and SC project, John Springs claimed that the railroad was of "paramount importance to this [York district] and the surrounding country" because "it [the C and SC] would give a new stimulus to industry, economy and enterprise, and create a market for innumerable articles now wasted and lost."[51] In 1848, industrialist Simpson Bobo urged the residents of Union and Spartanburg to invest in a railroad connecting their districts with the fall line. Transportation improvements, Bobo argued, would double iron production in the region, increase the amount of flour and corn meal exported, and give Upcountry textile mills access to larger markets. A railroad, Bobo predicted, "would stimulate labor and industry, cause the farmers to improve their lands [and] draw an increased amount of capital and labor in[to] the Country."[52] That same year, the editors of the Laurensville *Herald,* still hoping that the G and C line would come through their town, told their readers that "if we build a railroad, instead of never-ending cotton fields, grain and orchards will appear, as well as manufacturing" and that "bustling villages will spring up . . . and with the proper use of the material for advancement that is so thickly strewn around us, we will soon be in a state of prosperity and independence."[53] To the citizens of Newberry, G and C promoter John B. O'Neall made an even more melodramatic appeal:

> The railroad is *to you a matter of life and death.* Without it you might as well abandon your homes and seek new residences. . . . At least one third of the entire area of the Districts of Lexington, Newberry, Laurens, and Greenville is not cultivated. The effect of a Railroad will be to place part of this immense wasteland in cultivation, and to cover it and the other parts of the Districts with a dense population.[54]

Although the arguments in these calls for public support of railroads were intentionally overstated, the completion of railroads, combined with the pros-

[51]Letter of John Springs on C and SC Railroad, May 7, 1847, Springs Family Papers, SHC.
[52]Simpson Bobo to J. H. Saye, November 22, 1848, J. H. Saye Papers, DU.
[53]Laurensville *Herald,* November 3, 1848.
[54]Columbia *South Carolinian,* August 3, 1847.

perity arising from high cotton prices and bumper crops, had a striking impact on the Upcountry economy, and especially on the commercial life of Upcountry towns. Undoubtedly, a good portion of the economic boom which occurred in these towns can be attributed to the resurgence of cotton profits, but the arrival of railroads in Upcountry towns also contributed to the rise of a new dynamism there during the 1850s. As a rule, Upcountry towns began to grow as soon as plans for railroad construction in the area were announced. Men with an eye for the main chance opened new stores both to make a fast buck from the business generated by railroad construction and in anticipation of the increase in commercial activity that would follow the completion of the road. The number of stores doing business in Yorkville increased from ten in 1850 to twenty-five in 1852 when the Kings Mountain Railroad was completed, and the number of stores operating in Laurensville increased from six in 1848 to twenty-five in 1855 as work on the Laurens Railroad was completed. In the town of Anderson, the number of firms doing business increased from eight in 1848 to thirty-five by 1857, after the G and C railroad had been in full operation for several years.[55]

In addition to triggering growth in existing towns, railroads also created new towns and villages along their path. One new town, Rock Hill, sprang up out of cotton fields and grazing land when the C and SC railroad passed through eastern York in 1851. Alexander T. Black, a large landowner who lived between the settlement of Ebenezer and the proposed rail line, hired John Roddy, a respected surveyor, to lay out a town on a tract of Black's land that would be bisected by the C and SC. By 1860, Rock Hill was a thriving village of ten stores, a school, two churches, and a handful of grog shops.[56] In Anderson district, a new town, named Belton in honor of John Belton O'Neall, appeared at the intersection of the G and C and its branch line into the town of Anderson. At the same time that old towns were growing and new towns appearing along Upcountry rail lines, villages which were bypassed by the railroads were not faring nearly as well. The town of Pickens, located fifteen miles west of Greenville and nearly thirty miles east of Walhalla, had four stores operating in 1850 and only six stores doing business a decade later.[57]

The boom of the 1850s and the expansion of railroads into the Upcountry did more than attract new firms into business; it also increased dramatically the volume of business transacted in Upcountry towns. In 1848, before any Upcountry railroads were under construction and long before the cotton boom hit full stride, the value of merchandise held in Upcountry stores when inventory was taken for tax purposes was just over $725,000. In 1852, with several railroads operating on a limited basis, the value of Upcountry inventories was estimated at $1,124,195, an increase of 77 percent in just five years. Moreover, in some

[55]Figures on the numbers of firms in these towns calculated from a year by year survey of the R. G. Dun and Company, Credit Ledgers, South Carolina, I, II, IX–XIV, Baker.

[56]Douglas Summers Brown, *A City Without Cobwebs: A History of Rock Hill, South Carolina* (Columbia, S.C.: University of South Carolina Press, 1953), especially pp. 73–91.

[57]Pope, *History of Newberry County*, p. 143; R. G. Dun and Company, Credit Ledgers, South Carolina, XII, Baker.

areas, the increase was even more spectacular. In Chester district, where the town of Chester was the major commercial center, the value of year-end inventories increased from $88,950 in 1848, before construction began on the C and SC, to more than $137,880 in 1852, when the road was completed.[58] In Newberry, along the G and C line, the value of consumer goods on hand increased from $54,000 in 1848 to $115,250 in 1852. Moreover, the volume of commerce transacted in Upcountry towns continued to increase dramatically throughout the 1850s. In 1853, the value of goods sold in the Upcountry was $2,717,776, but by 1859 over $4,020,000 in goods were sold there. In the upper Piedmont, an area which was rather isolated prior to the arrival of the railroads during the fifties, the value of goods sold increased by more than 100 percent, from $729,586 to $1,477,300, between 1853 and 1859. In York district, where the towns of Yorkville, on the Kings Mountain Railroad, and Rock Hill on the C and SC, became bustling trading centers during the decade, the value of goods sold increased from $175,505 in 1853 to $314,000 in 1859, while in Greenville, the terminus of the G and C, the value of goods sold increased from $177,800 in 1853 to $396,690 in 1860.[59]

The dramatic increase in the volume of commerce transacted in Upcountry towns helped trigger an equally dramatic rise in the value of town property in the region. The assessed value of town property in the Upcountry quadrupled between 1848 and 1859. The increase in property values was especially pronounced in towns located along railroad lines. Town property values in Anderson increased from $70,295 in 1848 to $145,420 in 1853, when the G and C depot

---

[58]"Report of the Comptroller General," *Reports and Resolutions* (1848), exhibit No. 7, and (1852), exhibit No. 10.

[59]From 1822 through the state fiscal year ending on October 1, 1852, merchandise in South Carolina was taxed through the use of an inventory tax. The inventory tax levied a certain charge (in 1852 it was 60 cents per every $100 worth of goods) on "all the articles of trade, sale, barter or exchange" which were in the possession of the merchant on January 1 of that year. Beginning with the fiscal year ending on October 1, 1853, however, the inventory tax was abandoned in favor of a sales tax. The new law levied a tax on "the amount of sales of goods, wares, and merchandise . . . which any person shall have made" during the previous year. Merchants were allowed to deduct the value of the inventory on hand as of January 1 from the amount of total sales before the tax was charged. In 1853, the sales tax was set at 15 cents per $100 of goods sold. Because of this change in the tax laws, direct comparisons between the late 1840s and the late 1850s are not possible. Relying on the inventory tax as an indicator of the level of commercial activity between 1848 and 1852 presents a few problems. Inventories may, in some cases, have been higher not because business was brisk and the merchants needed the goods on hand, but because business was slack and the firms were overstocked. The preponderance of the evidence, however, both from the R. G. Dun collection and from other sources, indicates that business in the Upcountry was, in fact, growing between 1848 and 1852. Moreover, the very nature of the inventory tax prompted merchants to hold the amount of goods on hand as of January 1 to a minimum. Therefore, inventories on that date were likely to have been no larger than was necessary to keep the merchant adequately stocked during the first weeks of January. Thus larger inventories likely reflected greater demand. After 1852, of course, the sales tax offers an excellent index to the pace and volume of commercial activity in the Upcountry. *Acts of the General Assembly of the State of South Carolina*, 1851, pp. 74–75; *Acts of S.C.*, 1852, pp. 139–140; Alexander S. Salley, "The Methods of Raising Taxes in South Carolina Prior to 1868," *Bulletin of the Historical Commission of South Carolina* 7 (1925):1–13.

opened there, and rose to $372,300 by 1859. The C and SC railroad helped boost town property values in Chester from $97,140 in 1848 to $175,975 in 1852. Also, the sustained cotton boom of the 1850s boosted the value of town property to some extent even in towns which lacked the benefit of rail connections. The value of town lots in Spartanburg rose from $44,475 in 1848 to $68,995 in 1852 due to a surge in business linked to improved cotton profits. In the late 1850s, however, as the S and U railroad first approached and then actually reached the town of Spartanburg, the value of town property there rose to $156,925. By contrast, the value of town property in Edgefield district, where the only new railroad track laid in the district between 1848 and 1860 was a short stretch of the G and C which skirted the district's northern boundary and did not pass through a single important town, increased by only $8000 between 1848 and 1859. Of course the actual market value of agricultural property also increased markedly during the 1850s, and the value of prime cotton land probably at least doubled during the decade, but the even larger increase in town property values is both remarkable and noteworthy. During the 1850s, small and rather isolated Upcountry towns and villages were being transformed from sleepy trading centers and courthouse settlements, where the commercial tempo ebbed and flowed with the seasonal country trade and periodic flurries of legal activity, into bustling market towns.[60]

Most local observers attributed the commercial boom in Upcountry towns during the 1850s to the influence of the railroads. "Our town is growing some under the influence of the RR, building and to be built through this region," noted James Hemphill of Chester as work on the C and SC progressed. Several years later, after the Kings Mountain railroad was completed, Hemphill traveled north to Yorkville on a special excursion train to survey the railroad's impact. "Yorkville is improving greatly," Hemphill concluded.[61] In the spring of 1851, Presbyterian minister John McLees reported that the arrival of the G and C railroad had "produced considerable improvement in Newberry."[62] In Jonesville, a small trading center in Union district, a credit reporter outlined the impact of the railroad on that place in clear terms during January 1860. "The S and U RR having reached this neighborhood during the past year has improved the chances of success of the merchants at that point," the reporter observed, "by inducing farmers to bring their produce to that place [Jonesville] in exchange for goods."[63]

[60]For an excellent study of the rise of inland towns throughout the South during the 1850s, see Harold D. Woodman, *King Cotton and His Retainers: Financing and Marketing the Cotton Crops of the South, 1800–1925* (Lexington: University of Kentucky Press, 1968). Data on town property values cited in this paragraph were compiled and calculated from the annual reports made by the state comptroller general to the legislature. My survey of these reports covered the period from 1837 to 1861. These reports were published annually in the *Reports and Resolutions of the South Carolina General Assembly.*

[61]James Hemphill to W. R. Hemphill, December 16, 1848, and James Hemphill to W. R. Hemphill, March 18, 1853, Hemphill Family Papers, DU.

[62]Entry of May 5, 1851, John McLees Diary, SCL.

[63]R. G. Dun and Company, Credit Ledgers, South Carolina, XIV, 88, Baker.

The commercial boom of the 1850s created important qualitative as well as quantitative changes in the role played by Upcountry towns in the region's economy. The volume of goods traded in Upcountry towns expanded enormously during the decade, but the very nature of commerce in the Upcountry also changed dramatically during these same years. Foremost among these qualitative changes was the emergence of Upcountry towns as important centers for the cotton trade. After the new rail lines penetrated the Upcountry, large quantities of cotton were bought and sold in the region's towns. The railroads gave Upcountry merchants direct and reliable quick connections with major coastal cotton markets, and many interior merchants quickly began to buy and sell substantial amounts of cotton on their own accounts.

While some planters and a few small farmers continued to market their cotton through distant factors, many planters and most yeomen began to sell their cotton to Upcountry merchants as soon as a railroad reached their area. Laurens planter Mabra Madden, who had previously sold most of his cotton in Hamburg, sold his cotton to any of three mercantile firms in the town of Laurens after the completion of the Laurens Railroad in 1854. Spartanburg planter-merchant Elihu P. Smith terminated his own mercantile operations in the southern section of his district early in the 1850s and began to sell his cotton to firms operated by Thomas Pitts in the town of Clinton on the Laurens Railroad. Spartanburg yeoman James F. Sloan also sold some of his cotton in Clinton once rail connections with Columbia and Charleston were available there.[64]

By the late 1850s, the cotton buyer had become as familiar a figure in most Upcountry towns as the local hardware merchant, grocer, or blacksmith. In fact, many hardware merchants, grocers, and general storekeepers were themselves cotton buyers, and by the end of the 1850s, most of the strongest mercantile firms in the Upcountry were actively involved in the cotton trade. John Roddy, the surveyor, opened a general store in Rock Hill, and by 1857 his firm, Roddy and Company, was buying cotton and doing "all the business in Rock Hill." In nearby Yorkville, Carroll, Clarke and Co., a respected dry goods and grocery house, bought and sold around $10,000 worth of cotton annually during the 1850s, and maintained their reputation as a "solvent and frugal" firm despite the risks involved in cotton trading. Hiram Brawley, one of Chester's leading merchants, also traded heavily in cotton in the 1850s and lost heavily when the Charleston factorage house of Rice Dulin failed in 1854, but rebounded to make huge profits later in the decade. Along the S and U railroad, the firm of Keenan and Norris, which did over one-half of all the business in Unionville, bought and sold significant amounts of cotton, and the general store of Johnson and Rogers,

[64]Receipt, October 13, 1846, Receipt, October 23, 1848, Receipt, March 12, 1855, Receipt, December 19, 1855, Receipt, October 31, 1856, Receipt, January 7, 1859, Mabra Madden Papers, SCL; Receipt from J. N. Lyle, March 5, 1849, Receipt of "Walker and Glenn," December 15, 1853, Receipts of November 9 and December 18, 1855, Receipt of "Pitts and Langston," October 2, 1858, Elihu P. Smith Papers, SCL; Entries of March 27, 1857, February 20, 1858, James F. Sloan Journal, SCL.

doing business at the S and U depot of Santuc in southeastern Union district, was also involved in the cotton trade.[65]

The potential profit from the Upcountry cotton trade was so attractive that a number of businessmen from outside the region moved in to take advantage of the new opportunity. Once the G and C railroad was in operation, a number of merchants descended on the town of Anderson from other parts of South Carolina and Georgia. The Athens, Georgia, mercantile firm of Pitner and England opened a branch in Anderson and dispatched one of its most promising clerks, Sylvester Bleckley, to run the new store. By 1860, England, Bleckley and Co. had become one of Anderson's leading mercantile houses, and after the Civil War Bleckley became one of the largest cotton buyers in the Upcountry.[66] Fisher and Agnew, a leading commission house in Columbia, opened two branch stores in the Upcountry, one in Laurensville and one in Chester, during the 1850s, and these branch stores immediately became heavily involved in the cotton trade and remained so until the parent firm in Columbia was destroyed by Sherman in 1865. Another Columbia cotton merchant, Amos Estes, sent his brother, S. A. Estes, to Yorkville to establish a cotton buying and grocery firm which quickly developed a "more than average business" there. Cotton buyers and commission merchants from major markets other than Columbia were also eager to gain a foothold in Upcountry railroad towns. John McKie, a cotton merchant from Hamburg who had made over $100,000 in the cotton trade there, opened a store in Chester which became heavily involved in the buying and selling of cotton once construction on the C and SC railroad began. The elder McKie, who spent most of his winters in Charleston, sold his Chester store to his son, John McKie, Jr., in 1854, and the younger McKie ran the store successfully for the rest of the decade.[67]

While many of the new group of Upcountry cotton buyers were among the most respected and successful merchants in the region, the lucrative cotton trade also attracted more than its share of reckless speculators. Of course all merchants who bought and sold cotton on their own accounts wanted to buy low and sell high, but a number of Upcountry cotton buyers ran businesses backed by little capital and took but little interest in the actual marketing process. In Yorkville, Samuel McConnell, a grocer known as the "most extravagant man in the District," entered the cotton business in 1852 and during the next year "bought more cotton than anyone in Yorkville" at high prices, leading the local credit

[65]R. G. Dun and Company, Credit Ledgers, South Carolina, XIV, 138, 163, 98 and 78, IX, 144, 148, Baker.

[66]R. G. Dun and Company, Credit Ledgers, South Carolina, II, 58, 72F, Baker; *Cyclopedia of Eminent Men,* vol. 1, p. 625. I am indebted to David L. Carlton for sharing his notes on firms in Anderson district from the R. G. Dun and Company records with me. For a more detailed account of commercial development in Anderson, see David L. Carlton, "The 'Town People' of Anderson, South Carolina: A Case Study in Modernization" (paper presented at the annual convention of the American Historical Association, December, 1980).

[67]R. G. Dun and Company, Credit Ledgers, South Carolina, XI, 124, IX, 144G, XIV, 142, IX, 109, Baker.

reporter to label him "a speculator, a braggart, and a coward." By the end of 1853, when McConnell died suddenly, his losses in cotton were so heavy that he left his once substantial estate virtually insolvent.[68] In Chester, two firms, Graham and Son and Thomas S. Mills, earned reputations for reckless speculation in cotton. Graham and Son lost $2000 on cotton in 1854 and were forced to mortgage their business to bankers who ultimately liquidated it. Thomas S. Mills speculated heavily in cotton in 1855 and lost nearly $5000. In 1856, the Charleston commission house of Wardlaw, Walker, and Burnsides sought judgment against Mills for bad debts and Mills closed his business.[69] In the central Upcountry, Joe Crews of Laurensville earned a reputation as perhaps the most notorious cotton speculator in the Upcountry. Crews, formerly a clerk for the respected mercantile firm of Hastie and Nicols, moved out on his own as a cotton buyer in the 1850s. When the cotton market temporarily collapsed in 1854, Crews "lost much money" and was stuck with large quantities of cotton which he was unable to sell. Crews, always accused of being "close to meanness" by local notables, was hounded by creditors throughout 1855 before declaring bankruptcy and settling his old debts at thirty-three cents on the dollar. In 1856, however, Crews was back in business as a cotton buyer, acting as agent for his father-in-law, Lewis Dial.[70] In the upper Savannah River valley, Anderson druggist Isham Taylor alarmed his friends and creditors with his speculation in cotton, and J. J. Brown, son of one of Anderson's leading merchants, Daniel Brown, developed a dubious reputation as a "regular helter-skelter cotton-buyer." "J.J." one observer noted with alarm, "pays high for cotton, is very excitable, and gets drunk."[71]

Risky and dangerous speculation in cotton was not the only seamy aspect of the commercial boom of the 1850s. The cotton boom of that decade also revived another profitable, if disreputable, type of commerce, the slave trade. As cotton profits soared, the steady demand from the Southwest for slaves persisted. Most Upcountrymen accepted the slave trade as a necessary evil in a mature slave society so heavily dependent on the expansion of staple agriculture. Nevertheless, local leaders tended to frown upon slave trading as a vocation and viewed those men who earned a living chiefly through slave trading with considerable suspicion. At least part of Joe Crews's reputation as a local blackguard doubtless grew from his activity as a slave trader as well as a cotton-speculator. Cadwallader Pride of Rock Hill and J. C. Lipford of Chester also maintained "slave-pens" in their respective towns to accommodate local planters and slave-buyers from the deep South. Rumors that these slave traders captured runaways and sold them illegally and that living conditions in the slave-pens were horrible

[68]R. G. Dun and Company, Credit Ledgers, South Carolina, XIV, 135, Baker.

[69]R. G. Dun and Company, Credit Ledgers, South Carolina, IX, 155, 177, Baker.

[70]R. G. Dun and Company, Credit Ledgers, South Carolina, XI, 109–124, Baker; Legal document of April 14, 1855, and Barrie and Co. to Young, Simpson, and Simpson, May 25, 1855, William D. Simpson Papers, DU.

[71]R. G. Dun and Company, Credit Ledgers, South Carolina, II, 58, 68, 70, 72D, 72G, Baker.

even by prevailing antebellum standards flourished during the 1850s, and a number of slave traders made substantial profits throughout the decade.[72]

The sharp increase in commercial activity during the 1850s was supported and enhanced by an expansion of banking activity in the Upcountry. Prior to 1850, there were no banks in the Upcountry and the region's merchants and planters had to rely on notes from Charleston and fall-line banks as the major source of negotiable paper. During the 1850s, however, three banks were established in railroad towns of the lower Piedmont and a number of bank agencies were created throughout the Upcountry, largely to help provide the paper currency needed to sustain the new local cotton trade. The Bank of Chester, the Bank of Newberry, and the Planters' Bank of Fairfield were each organized in 1852. Each was originally capitalized at $300,000, with the bulk of the stock subscription made by local merchants and planters. Stockholders of the Bank of Chester elected James Hemphill as president and twelve "local men of property" as directors. In 1857, when a number of other banks suspended specie payment, the Bank of Chester refused to suspend and was said to be "as safe as any Bank."[73]

Not to be outdone by private banks in the effort to supply banking services to the Upcountry, the BSSC established agencies at Newberry, Laurens, Clinton, Yorkville, and Abbeville during the 1850s. Private banks in the Upcountry and in Charleston also expanded their service area through the use of agents. The Bank of Chester employed S. A. Brown, the treasurer of the Kings Mountain railroad, as its agent in Yorkville, and W. J. Keenan, the prosperous merchant, as its agent in Union. Unionville's wealthiest merchant, John S. Young, served as that town's agent for the Bank of Newberry. In Greenville, Thomas Cox, a partner in the Upcountry's leading carriage-making firm, was the agent for the Bank of Newberry, while Hamlin Beattie, a lawyer and scion of a leading Upcountry merchant, was the Greenville agent of the Bank of Charleston, the state's most prosperous private bank.[74]

Although planter capital played a large role in the creation of Upcountry banks, these banks devoted a larger percentage of their resources to the support of commercial activity than to the provision of long-term agricultural credit. A stable and plentiful supply of paper currency was essential to the continued expansion of commercial activity in the Upcountry, and particularly to the rise of railroad towns as important cotton markets. Bank agents and agencies, of course, could circulate bank notes and endorse personal notes, thereby keeping a supply of negotiable paper in circulation and providing the liquidity necessary to finance the local cotton trade. Unlike banks, however, agents and agencies could not offer a full range of banking services. Since agents and agencies did not attract deposits, they could not serve as institutions of capital formation and therefore

[72]R. G. Dun and Company, Credit Ledgers, South Carolina, IX, 181, XI, 111–124, Baker.

[73]Lesesne, *Bank of the State of South Carolina*, pp. 117–152; Washington A. Clark, *The History of the Banking Institutions Organized in South Carolina* (Columbia, S.C.: The State Company, 1922), pp. 160–214; R. G. Dun and Company, Credit Ledgers, South Carolina, IX, 160, Baker.

[74]R. G. Dun and Company, Credit Ledgers, South Carolina, XIV, 149, 98, 78, X, 40, 167, I, 187, Baker.

did not stimulate the creation of any new local enterprises requiring a large pool of investment capital. The creation of banks and bank agencies in the 1850s, however, did help alleviate the chronic shortage of paper currency which had plagued the Upcountry through much of the antebellum period. Still, the dificulty of procuring long-term agricultural loans, the pronounced seasonal fluctuations in the quantity of floating paper currency, and the tendency of banks to invest in economic activity outside the region, continued to frustrate and aggravate Upcountry planters and farmers, who frequently held the banking system responsible for any number of their economic problems.[75]

Unquestionably, major transportation improvements and steady profits from the cotton boom sparked an important commercial quickening in Upcountry towns during the 1850s. This quickening was highlighted by the emergence of these Upcountry towns as important cotton markets and the development of the banking facilities needed to sustain the new local cotton trade. Though certainly generously aided by the state and by the Charleston financial and mercantile community, inland railroad and banking development received crucial support from Upcountry capital. Wealthy planters and, to a lesser extent, merchants and aspiring industrialists, invested heavily in the economic future of their region. As the South Carolina Piedmont found it increasingly difficult to compete with the fresh cotton lands in other parts of the South, the Upcountry's "men of large capital" put at least a portion of their accumulated resources to work in an effort to reverse that trend.[76] Upcountry entrepreneurs bet part of their fortunes that infrastructural improvements could guarantee future prosperity in an area where the soil alone was no longer up to the task. During the 1850s, it seemed like a reasonable wager.

[75]Lesesne, *Bank of the State of South Carolina*, pp. 117–135; *Carolina Spartan*, October 1, 1857; Pope, *History of Newberry County*, pp. 147–152; J. J. Blackwood to Andrew Baxter Springs, February 7, 1856, Springs Family Papers, SHC.

[76]The phrase "men of large capital" was used by a relative of Benjamin C. Yancey to describe wealthy Upcountry cotton planters who looked to broaden their entrepreneurial scope. See William G. Beene to Benjamin C. Yancey, August 6, 1846, Benjamin C. Yancey Papers, SHC.

7

Agriculture and Industry

The 1850s was the most profitable decade in history for growing cotton. Prices paid for the fleecy staple failed to reach the lofty heights attained during earlier booms, but they hovered at or above the ten cents per pound mark for much of the decade, and the world market absorbed ever-increasing quantities of cotton without any corresponding decline in prices. Accompanied by the expansion of railroads and the emergence of active cotton markets in towns above the fall line, this last antebellum cotton boom generated unprecedented prosperity in the South Carolina Upcountry and inspired a degree of economic optimism unknown in the region since the heady days of the first cotton boom a half-century earlier. With the advantage of hindsight, historians and economists now know that the boom of the 1850s was merely a brief flurry of prosperity preceding a long period of relative economic stagnation in the American South. After the boom of the 1850s, cotton, the raw material which supplied the world's first industrial revolution, would never again bring sustained prosperity and rapid economic growth to the South. In the post-Civil War era, growth in world demand for cotton slowed dramatically, and sluggish growth in demand for cotton severely hindered economic growth and development in the South. Thus the long-term costs of the South's dependence on cotton were staggering in terms of both economic backwardness and human suffering. But the bleak economic future of the cotton South was unknown to those Southerners who enjoyed the fruits of the boom of the 1850s; they could see only the flush times surging around them. In the autumn of his glory, King Cotton delivered one final round of prosperity to his subjects, and they were thankful.[1]

In the South Carolina Upcountry, cotton production expanded significantly during the 1850s. The average quantity of cotton produced on Upcountry farms

[1]Gavin Wright, *Old South, New South: Revolutions in the Southern Economy since the Civil War* (New York: Basic Books, 1986), pp. 124–129; Alfred G. Smith, Jr., *Economic Readjustment of an Old Cotton State: South Carolina, 1820–1860* (Columbia, S.C.: University of South Carolina Press, 1958), pp. 45–111; Gavin Wright, "Cotton Competition and the Post-bellum Recovery of the American South," *Journal of Economic History* 34 (September, 1974):610–635; William N. Parker, "The South in the National Economy, 1865–1970," *Southern Economic Journal* 46 (April, 1980):1019–1048: Gavin Wright, *The Political Economy of the Cotton South: Households, Markets, and Wealth in the Nineteenth Century* (New York: W. W. Norton, 1978), pp. 89–127.

Table 7.1 Agricultural Output per Farm—1850

	Improved Acreage per Farm	Cotton (lbs.) per Farm	Corn (Bushels) per Farm	Swine per Farm
Lower Piedmont				
Abbeville	117.2	5996.0	581.1	36.7
Chester	228.4	8440.7	679.0	35.0
Edgefield	129.7	5040.4	569.2	36.3
Fairfield	180.1	10,738.9	784.4	34.2
Laurens	113.8	3953.1	558.5	34.5
Newberry	175.0	7614.9	635.5	36.4
Union	187.3	6515.9	753.8	36.0
Upper Piedmont				
Anderson	89.9	1343.4	413.2	21.8
Greenville	122.4	918.4	597.2	34.1
Lancaster	173.6	5973.1	607.3	36.2
Pickens	75.7	440.9	515.0	30.7
Spartanburg	133.5	1716.0	561.2	33.4
York	106.7	3190.4	551.5	28.6
Totals				
Lower Piedmont	148.5	6256.6	622.3	35.8
Upper Piedmont	110.0	1866.4	522.5	29.5
Upcountry	130.7	4221.7	576.0	32.9

Source: Seventh Census of the United States, 1850 (Washington: Robert Armstrong, 1853), pp. 345–348; J.D.B. DeBow, *A Statistical View of the United States: A Compendium of the Seventh Census* (Washington: Beverly Tucker, 1854), pp. 304–307.

increased by 21.8 percent between 1850 and 1860. Per farm output increased most dramatically in the rich cotton-growing areas of the lower Piedmont, where it rose by 31.2 percent. In the hilly upper Piedmont, the mean cotton output during the 1850s increased by nearly 15 percent, from 1,866 pounds per farm to 2,143 even though cheap commercial fertilizers were still not generally available in the region.[2] Moreover, these statistics, which were calculated from decennial

[2]Calculated from the *Seventh Census of the United States, 1850* (Washington: Robert Armstrong, 1853), p. 348; and the *Eighth Census of the United States, Agriculture, 1860* (Washington, D.C.: Government Printing Office, 1864), p. 129. The bale weights used in making these calculations are 400 lbs. per bale for 1850 and 445 lbs. per bale for 1860. These are the approximate bale weights for those years suggested by the *Abstract of the Eleventh Census* (Washington, D.C.: U.S. Census Office, 1894), p. 59. The use of these bale weights is ably defended by Robert McGuire and Robert Higgs, ''Cotton, Corn, and Risk in the Nineteenth Century: Another View,'' *Explorations in Economic History* 14 (April, 1977):167–182. For reports of contemporary observers confirming that average bale weights in South Carolina increased by forty to fifty pounds between 1850 and 1860, see Harry Hammond, *South Carolina: Resources and Population, Institutions and Industries* (Charleston, S.C.: Walker, Evans and Cogswell, 1883), pp. 11–12; on use of commercial fertilizers in the Upcountry, see Rosser W. Taylor, ''Commercial Fertilizers in South Carolina,'' *South Atlantic Quarterly* 29 (April, 1930):179–189. The Upcountry as a whole produced 8 percent more cotton in 1859 than it had in 1849. The average increase per farm was substantially larger than the overall increase because there were fewer farms in the region in 1859 than in 1849. The decline in the total number of farms is discussed later in this chapter.

Table 7.2 Agricultural Output per Farm—1860

	Improved Acreage per Farm	Cotton (lbs.) per Farm	Corn (Bushels) per Farm	Swine per Farm
Lower Piedmont				
Abbeville	193.1	7931.7	539.9	30.4
Chester	231.5	9274.7	537.1	28.4
Edgefield	183.2	7136.0	559.6	37.0
Fairfield	341.0	12,862.0	763.5	34.3
Laurens	235.9	5567.2	482.7	24.3
Newberry	172.5	9247.1	537.7	31.0
Union	157.7	8987.2	631.9	30.7
Upper Piedmont				
Anderson	92.4	1546.1	402.0	18.1
Greenville	90.3	1083.0	565.6	28.7
Lancaster	103.5	5930.2	453.5	19.5
Pickens	85.3	316.3	511.3	23.2
Spartanburg	97.9	1747.4	500.9	37.0
York	153.3	3860.5	514.8	24.0
Totals				
Lower Piedmont	169.0	8207.8	564.8	31.1
Upper Piedmont	105.4	2143.2	489.7	25.7
Upcountry	136.9	5143.2	526.8	28.4

Source: Eighth Census of the United States, 1860: Agriculture (Washington: Government Printing Office, 1864), pp. 128–131, 214.

census data, probably understate the increase in cotton production which actually occurred in the region during the 1850s. Throughout most of the cotton South 1859 was a year of bumper cotton crops, but in the South Carolina Upcountry, as in other cotton-growing areas of the Southeast, 1859 was not a particularly good year for cotton. Indeed, contemporary observers remarked that cotton crops were down by at least one-fourth in most Upcountry districts.[3] Other evidence also suggests that census figures understate the expansion of cotton production during the 1850s. The production records of a number of planters, middling slaveholders, and yeoman farmers show steady and substantial increases in cotton production throughout the decade.[4] Railroad freight reports also suggest that

[3]Donald F. Schaefer, "The Effect of the 1859 Crop Year upon Relative Productivity in the Antebellum Cotton South," *Journal of Economic History* 43 (December, 1983):851–865, shows that while 1859 was an excellent year for cotton in the South Central states, it was a relatively poor year for cotton and other crops in the South Atlantic cotton belt. I have surveyed the district by district reports on growing conditions available in the Manuscript Census of South Carolina, 1850, Schedule VI (Social Statistics), and the Manuscript Census of South Carolina, 1860, Schedule VI (Social Statistics) and found that 1859 was, in fact, a sub-par year for cotton as well as other crops in the South Carolina Piedmont.

[4]For evidence on this point, see the following collections: John D. Ashmore Plantation Journal, SHC; Jones, Watts, Davis Papers, SCL; Zelotus L. Holmes Papers, SCL; Mabra Madden Papers, SCL; W. W. Renwick Papers, SCL; Elihu Penquite Smith Papers, SCL; James F. Sloan Papers, SCL.

cotton production in the Upcountry increased more dramatically than census records indicate. The quantity of cotton shipped to market on the C and SC railroad increased from 45,000 bales in 1852 to 70,000 bales in 1855. The number of bales shipped from Chester, the most active cotton depot on the C and SC line, rose from 24,363 in 1852 to 33,306 in 1855, and from Winnsboro, another busy depot, cotton shipments increased from 3,172 bales in 1852 to 9,259 in 1855. At Fort Mill, a small depot in the upper Piedmont, increases in the amount of cotton shipped were equally dramatic, rising from 1,190 bales in 1852 to 2,235 in 1855.[5] These increases in the amount of cotton shipped on the C and SC depended partially on market conditions during particular years and partially on the growers' decisions regarding the mode of transportation used in marketing their staple, but these freight figures nevertheless suggest an even more substantial expansion of cotton production in the Upcountry during the 1850s than that documented by decennial census figures.

The trend toward expanded cotton production included yeoman farmers as well as large slaveholders. In the Upcountry as a whole, cotton output on farms operated by slaveless yeomen increased by 18.4 percent between 1849 and 1859. Yeomen owning five or fewer slaves produced 9 percent more cotton per farm in 1859 than they had a decade earlier. In the upper Piedmont district in Anderson, non-slaveholding farmers increased their per farm cotton production by more than 7 percent during the 1850s, while the average cotton production of small slaveholders in the district rose by nearly 10 percent. In the lower Piedmont district of Abbeville, an area where yeoman farmers were deeply involved in the cotton economy long before the 1850s, slaveless yeomen increased their per farm cotton output only slightly, but slaveholding yeomen produced 22 percent more cotton per farm in 1859 than they had in 1849. Moreover, not only did the amount of cotton produced by yeoman farmers increase significantly during the 1850s but the percentage of yeomen growing cotton also rose substantially during the decade. In 1849, just over 70 percent of all nonslaveholding yeomen in the Upcountry raised cotton, but by 1859 over 80 percent of all slaveless farmers grew cotton. During the same decade, the percentage of small slaveholders growing cotton increased from 81.6 to 87.4. Increased participation among non-slaveholders was most pronounced in the upper Piedmont. In Anderson district, the proportion of non-slaveholding yeomen raising cotton rose from 66 percent in 1849 to 80 percent in 1859. At the eastern edge of the upper Piedmont, participation in the cotton economy among slaveless yeomen in York district increased from 58 percent in 1849 to 74 percent in 1859. Also, the proportion of hill-country farmers working fewer than fifty improved acres but also growing cotton rose from roughly 60 percent in 1849 to nearly 80 percent in 1859.[6]

Additionally, while the absolute level of cotton production rose during the 1850s, the level of specialization in cotton also increased significantly. In every

[5]Figures taken from a survey of freight reports in the *Proceedings of the Annual Stockholders' Meetings of the Charlotte and South Carolina Railroad, 1852–1855.* Copies of these privately published reports can be found in the SCL.

[6]See Tables 7.3 and 7.4.

Table 7.3   Production and Value on Upcountry Farms, 1860

	Type of Farm Operator				
	Non-slaveholding Yeomen (0 slaves)	Slaveholding Yeomen (1–5 slaves)	Middling Slaveholders (6–19 slaves)	Planters (20 or more slaves)	Tenants
Mean Output					
Cotton (lbs.)	1373.0	1917.2	4504.6	16,066.7	764.2
Corn	228.9	308.7	511.8	1,320.4	112.5
Swine	11.9	16.5	26.1	52.8	6.9
Mean Value					
Improved Acres	62.6	93.9	168.3	433.7	NA
Cash Value of Farms	$1161.7	$2274.7	$3956.9	$11,169.8	NA
% Growing					
Cotton	81.4	87.4	90.9	86.4	60.2
% Self-Sufficient					
Grain	53.4	63.9	68.3	76.9	28.6
Meat	46.6	36.1	30.0	23.1	13.3
Cotton-Corn Ratio	6.0	6.2	8.8	12.2	6.8

Source: Manuscript Census of South Carolina, 1860, Abbeville, Anderson, and York Districts, Schedules I, II, and IV.

district sampled, cotton accounted for a larger share of total farm output in 1859 than it had in 1849. In the upper Piedmont, cotton's share of total farm output among yeoman farmers who owned no slaves rose substantially during the decade in both Anderson and York districts. Among slaveholding yeomen in York district, cotton's share of total farm output rose during the 1850s, increasing from 21.8 percent in 1850 to 28.5 percent by 1860. In the lower Piedmont, where yeoman farmers were already heavily involved with the cotton economy at the outset of the decade, the level of specialization in cotton also increased considerably during the 1850s. Cotton's share of total farm output among non-slaveholding farmers in Abbeville district grew from 34.5 percent in 1850 to 40.7 percent in 1860; among Abbeville's small slaveholders, cotton's share of total output leaped from 32.7 percent in 1850 to 43.2 percent a decade later. Even in 1860, yeoman farmers in the hill country remained markedly less specialized in cotton than yeomen in the black belt, but throughout the Upcountry, yeoman farmers were more deeply involved in the cotton economy, and more likely to produce cotton at the expense of other crops, than they had been a decade earlier.[7]

[7]See Table 7.5; the value of cotton produced on Upcountry farms as a share of total agricultural output on those farms was calculated using the methods and values outlined in Roger L. Ransom and Richard Sutch, *One Kind of Freedom: The Economic Consequences of Emancipation* (Cambridge: Cambridge University Press, 1977), pp. 203–210.

Table 7.4 Yeoman Farmers in the Upper and Lower Piedmont, 1860

	Non-slaveholding Yeomen		Slaveholding Yeomen	
	Mean Value	Share of Total	Mean Value	Share of Total
Anderson District				
Cotton (lbs.)	954.1	29.4%	1018.2	17.1%
Corn (bushels)	256.9	31.1	306.2	19.5
Swine	10.9	29.2	14.4	21.3
Improved acres	57.4	29.5	62.6	17.3
Cash Value of Farms	$1449.4	18.8	$1988.8	23.5
Abbeville District				
Cotton (lbs.)	1343.9	3.5%	2945.9	6.4%
Corn (bushels)	124.0	4.8	230.5	7.0
Swine	9.1	6.9	17.8	10.8
Improved acres	56.7	5.3	79.3	6.7
Cash Value of Farms	$1463.5	5.3	$2239.7	7.9

Source: Manuscript Census of South Carolina, 1850, Abbeville and Anderson Districts, Schedules I, II, and IV.

Rising cotton-corn ratios and cotton's growing share of total agricultural output on virtually all types of farms in nearly every section of the Upcountry certainly reflected an expansion of the cotton economy in the region during the 1850s. But at least part of the apparent increase in the level of specialization in cotton can be attributed to a striking decline in the production of subsistence crops during the decade. The absolute level of corn production in the Upcountry fell by 18.4 percent, from 9,535,338 bushels to 7,776,713 bushels, between 1850 and 1860. In 1850, the Upcountry had produced 58.6 percent of all corn grown in South Carolina, but by 1860, its percentage of the state's total corn production fell to 51.6 percent. Average corn production in the Upcountry fell from 576 bushels per farm in 1850 to only 526 bushels per farm in 1860. The decline in corn production was more pronounced in the lower Piedmont than in

Table 7.5 Cotton's Share of Total Agricultural Output, 1850 and 1860 (in percent)

	Type of Farm (by slaveholdings)				
District (Year)	0	1–5	6–9	10–19	20 or more
Anderson (1850)	15.9	15.0	14.5	11.7	8.0
Anderson (1860)	20.5	19.8	19.3	18.9	18.5
York (1850)	18.5	21.8	23.8	35.5	36.4
York (1860)	22.2	28.5	32.3	41.8	40.6
Abbeville (1850)	34.5	32.7	35.7	39.0	45.6
Abbeville (1860)	40.7	43.2	43.0	40.6	48.6

Source: Manuscript Census of South Carolina, 1850 and 1860, Abbeville, Anderson, and York Districts, Schedules I, II, and IV.

Table 7.6   Agricultural Production—1850

	Number of Farms	Improved Acreage	Cotton (lbs.)	Corn (bushels)	Swine	Cotton/Corn Ratio
Lower Piedmont						
Abbeville	1814	212,628	10,876,800	1,054,233	66,548	10.3
Chester	844	192,801	7,124,000	573,070	29,579	12.4
Edgefield	2030	263,374	10,352,000	1,155,489	73,742	9.0
Fairfield	675	121,593	7,248,800	529,461	23,080	13.6
Laurens	1603	182,525	6,336,800	895,291	55,288	9.8
Newberry	1045	182,952	7,957,600	664,058	38,033	12.0
Union	869	162,787	5,662,400	655,078	31,262	8.6
Upper Piedmont						
Anderson	1986	178,455	2,668,000	820,544	43,242	3.3
Greenville	1068	130,727	980,800	637,784	36,555	1.7
Lancaster	580	100,728	3,464,400	352,218	20,997	11.8
Pickens	1231	93,206	542,800	634,011	37,786	0.9
Spartanburg	1555	207,666	2,668,400	873,654	51,921	3.0
York	1252	133,596	3,994,400	·690,447	35,797	5.8
Totals						
Lower Piedmont	8880	1,318,666	55,558,400	5,526,680	317,532	10.1
Upper Piedmont	7276	844,378	14,318,800	4,008,658	226,298	3.6
Upcountry	16,552	2,163,044	69,877,200	9,535,338	543,830	7.3

Source: Same as Table 7.1. The cotton-corn ratio is calculated by dividing pounds of cotton by bushels of corn.

the upper Piedmont. In the lower Piedmont, corn production fell by more than 1,400,000 bushels, or 25.3 percent, between 1850 and 1860, while in the upper Piedmont, corn production fell by 350,000 bushels, or nearly 10 percent, during the same period. Per farm corn output declined by nearly fifty bushels in the lower Piedmont and by about thirty bushels in the upper Piedmont during the 1850s.[8]

The decline in subsistence production occurred on all types and sizes of Upcountry farms. On the average, non-slaveholding yeomen in the region raised nearly 326 bushels of corn per farm in 1849, but a decade later they grew only 229 bushels per farm. Yeoman farmers owning five or fewer slaves raised 389 bushels of corn per farm in 1849, but in 1859 these small slaveholders produced only 309 bushels of corn per farm. Between 1849 and 1859, the average level of corn production on farms operated by farmers who owned more than five but less than twenty slaves declined by nearly 26 percent, and average corn production by Upcountry planters fell by just over 12 percent. Upcountry tenants raised nearly 22 percent less corn per farm in 1859 than they had in 1849. Corn production also declined sharply on Upcountry farms of 100 or fewer improved acres. In York district, farms with less than fifty improved acres had produced 292 bushels of corn per farm in 1849, but in 1859 average corn output on York district farms

[8]See Tables 7.6 and 7.7.

Table 7.7   Agricultural Production—1860

	Number of Farms	Improved Acreage	Cotton (lbs.)	Corn (bushels)	Swine	Cotton/Corn Ratio
Lower Piedmont						
Abbeville	1233	238,039	9,779,765	665,698	37,541	14.6
Chester	791	183,106	7,336,270	424,815	22,489	17.2
Edgefield	1696	310,786	12,102,665	949,117	62,760	12.8
Fairfield	684	233,295	8,797,650	522,200	23,460	16.8
Laurens	1271	299,862	7,075,945	613,486	30,939	11.5
Newberry	841	145,085	7,776,820	452,191	26,048	17.2
Union	786	123,986	7,063,930	496,713	24,102	14.2
Upper Piedmont						
Anderson	1442	133,249	2,229,450	579,682	26,058	3.8
Greenville	1102	99,589	1,193,490	623,288	31,677	1.9
Lancaster	797	82,525	4,726,345	361,421	15,511	13.0
Pickens	1321	112,736	417,855	675,407	30,701	0.6
Spartanburg	1599	156,534	2,794,155	800,960	59,147	3.5
York	1198	183,704	4,624,885	616,735	28,768	7.5
Totals						
Lower Piedmont	7302	1,234,297	59,933,045	4,124,220	227,339	14.5
Upper Piedmont	7459	786,339	15,986,180	3,652,493	191,880	4.4
Upcountry	14,761	2,020,636	75,919,225	7,776,713	419,219	9.7

Source: Same as Table 7.2.

of fifty acres or less fell to 212 bushels. In the same district, farms with at least fifty but less than 100 improved acres produced an average of 318 bushels of corn in 1859, a decline of 150 bushels from the mean output of farms in the same size category a decade earlier. In another upper Piedmont district, Anderson, corn production on farms of less than 100 improved acres fell by more than 100 bushels per farm between 1849 and 1859. Small farms in the black belt produced considerably less corn per farm than did small farms in the hillcountry in 1849, but average corn production on small farms in the lower Piedmont nevertheless fell sharply during the 1850s. In 1849, farms in Abbeville district with fewer than fifty acres produced an average of 156 bushels of corn, but by 1859 farms in that same size range produced only 122 bushels of corn, a decline of over 21 percent. On lower Piedmont farms with at least fifty but fewer than 100 acres, corn production fell from 409 bushels per farm in 1849 to only 264 bushels in 1859, a decline of over 35 percent.[9]

In addition to the sharp decrease in corn output, the production of pork also declined sharply in the Upcountry during the 1850s. The number of swine in the region decreased by more than 100,000 between 1850 and 1860. This decline in the size of the hog population was most dramatic along the route of the G and C

[9]See Tables 7.3 and 7.4; calculations based on a sample of farms from the Manuscript Census of South Carolina, 1850, Abbeville, Anderson, and York Districts, Schedules I, II, and IV.

railroad through the upper Savannah River valley. The number of swine in Abbeville district fell from 66,598 in 1850 to 37,541 in 1860, and in Anderson district the total number of hogs fell from 43,242 in 1850 to 26,058 in 1860. But the upper Savannah valley was not the only part of the Upcountry to see the size of its swine herds shrink. In Lancaster, the average number of swine per farm fell from 36.2 in 1850 to 19.5 in 1860. In the high hill country, the mean size of swine herds in Greenville fell from 34.2 in 1850 to 28.7 in 1860, and in Pickens the mean herd size fell from 30.7 to 23.2 during the same period. Thus, even in those parts of the Upcountry which were the least specialized in staple agriculture, the number of hogs being raised, and therefore the amount of pork available, declined during the 1850s.[10]

The decrease in pork production on small farms in the Upcountry was especially striking. The average number of hogs owned by slaveless farmers in the Upcountry declined from 20.2 in 1850 to 11.9 in 1860. Among small slaveholders in the Upcountry, the average size of swine herds fell from 21.5 to 16.5 during the 1850s. The "typical" tenant farmer in the Upcountry owned eleven hogs in 1850 but only seven in 1860. Both hill country and black belt were effected by the trend. In the white majority district of Anderson, the average size of the non-slaveholder's swine herd dropped from 17.3 in 1850 to 10.9 in 1860, while the average small slaveholder's herd shrank from 20.8 to 14.4 during the same decade. In the black-belt district of Abbeville, non-slaveholders owned an average of 16.3 hogs in 1850 but only 9.1 in 1860, and slaveholding yeomen saw the average size of their herds shrink from 25.9 to 17.8 during the decade. The size of the hog population of farms of less than 100 improved acres declined sharply in both upper and lower Piedmont during the 1850s. In 1850, the average number of swine owned by farmers who worked fewer than fifty acres was 12.8, but by 1860 that figure had fallen to 9.5. Anderson farmers with at least fifty but less than 100 improved acres owned an average of 26.7 hogs in 1850 but only 17.9 hogs in 1860. In the lower Piedmont, the mean size of swine herds on farms of less than fifty acres fell from 14.1 in 1850 to 8.7 by 1860, and the average herd size of farms with more than forty-nine but less than 100 acres declined from 27.3 to 18.0 during the same ten years.[11]

With production of both corn and pork down substantially during the 1850s, the percentage of Upcountry farms which achieved self-sufficiency also declined significantly. In 1860, a majority of Upcountry farms with fifty or more improved acres were still self-sufficient in grain, but a much smaller percentage of these farms met their own subsistence needs than had been the case a decade earlier, and only a minority of farms were self-sufficient in meat. By 1860, only 42.1 percent of all farms with less than fifty acres were self-sufficient in grain compared to 53.6 in 1850. The percentage of Upcountry planters and middling

---

[10]See Tables 7.1, 7.2, 7.6, and 7.7.

[11]See Tables 7.3 and 7.4; data on farms of less than 100 improved acres calculated from sample of Upcountry farms cited in footnote 9.

slaveholders who were self-sufficient was decidedly lower in 1860 than in 1850, but the decline of self-sufficiency was most noticeable among yeoman farmers. In 1850, 66 percent of all slaveless yeomen in the Upcountry were self-sufficient in grain and 64 percent were self-sufficient in meat; by 1860, 53 percent of all non-slaveholders were self-sufficient in grain and only 47 percent were self-sufficient in meat. The percentage of slaveholding yeomen who achieved self-sufficiency in grain fell from 79.4 in 1850 to 63.9 in 1860, and the percentage of these small slaveholders who were self-sufficient in meat declined from 66.3 in 1850 to 36.1 in 1860. The trend away from self-sufficiency effected both the upper and the lower Piedmont, but was far more pronounced in the latter. In the black-belt district of Abbeville, the proportion of slaveless farmers achieving self-sufficiency in grain fell from 51 percent in 1850 to only 21 percent in 1860, and during that same period the percentage of Abbeville's small slaveholders who were self-sufficient in subsistence crops dropped from 68.0 to 47.1. Self-sufficiency also declined, though less drastically, in the hill country. In 1850, nearly 69 percent of all non-slaveholders in Anderson were self-sufficient in grain, but by 1860 only 60 percent of all slaveless yeomen in the district raised enough grain to meet the needs of their own households. Sixty-five percent of Anderson's small slaveholders achieved self-sufficiency in 1860, but nearly 80 percent had been self-sufficient in 1850. The percentage of small farmers achieving self-sufficiency remained significantly higher in the upper Piedmont than in the lower Piedmont, and the proportion of small farmers who failed to achieve self-sufficiency was growing more rapidly in the lower Piedmont than in the upper, but yeoman farmers in both black belt and hill country were less likely to be self-sufficient in 1860 than in 1850.[12]

In retrospect, the trends in agricultural production in the Upcountry during the 1850s appear clear. Cotton production was expanding significantly, and concentration on cash crops was intensifying considerably even among yeoman farmers. At the same time, production of basic foodstuffs was declining sharply. As a result, a much lower percentage of Upcountry farmers were self-sufficient in 1860 than in 1850. Part of the decline in self-sufficiency might be explained by one-time crop shortfalls. Across the Upcountry, crop yields were below average in 1859, and not just in cotton but also in important subsistence crops such as corn and wheat. But one-time crop shortages can hardly explain the dramatic decline in pork production in the region during the 1850s, since swine herds fed largely off the open range. Moreover, the concept of "safety-first" agriculture, one which was widely implemented by small farmers in the Upcountry prior to the 1850s, rests on the experienced farmer's ability to estimate how much acreage he must allot to subsistence crops in order to maintain self-sufficiency even when his crop yields fall well below normal. If at all possible, the

[12]See Tables 7.3, 7.4, 7.8, and 7.9. Contrast these figures with those of Tables 2.1, 2.3, and 2.5. The test for self-sufficiency used in these calculations was that developed by Robert Gallman, "Self-Sufficiency in the Cotton Economy of the Antebellum South," *Agricultural History* 44 (January, 1970):5–23.

Table 7.8 Self-Sufficiency on Upcountry Farms, 1860

Percentage Achieving Self-Sufficiency	Farm Size (Improved Acres)			
	1–49	50–99	100–199	200 or more
Grain	42.1	64.0	66.3	72.5
Meat	24.4	50.3	41.6	33.8
Total farms: 861				

Source: Manuscript Census of South Carolina, 1860, Abbeville, Anderson, and York Districts, Schedules I, II, IV.

farmer seeking self-sufficiency must base his calculations on worst-case scenarios and allow himself a "margin of safety" sufficient to cover any reasonable fluctuation in subsistence crop yields. The kind of sub-par, or below average, yields which occurred in 1859 were common enough in the Upcountry (there were worse years earlier in the 1850s), and the region's farmers were well aware of such possibilities. Additionally, the fact that cotton production was up measurably in an "off year" while subsistence production was down sharply indicates that most yeomen could have allocated more resources to subsistence crops and thus allowed themselves a larger "margin of safety" if they had wanted to do so. Instead, more and more yeoman farmers were becoming dependent on the marketplace for corn and pork.[13]

Once again, these trends in Upcountry agriculture, toward increased cotton production and away from self-sufficiency, are best explained by high cotton prices and an improved transportation system. Because returns were high, farmers planted more land in cotton, and, at the same time, the new Upcountry railroads brought substantial quantities of imported grain and pork into the region at reasonable prices. The traffic in food products in Upcountry railroad towns was brisk. J. J. Atwood, a yeoman farmer and onetime sheriff from Laurens district, explained the impact of the new railroad connections in some detail in a letter to relatives in Jonesborough, Alabama. "By the aid of our railroad," Atwood wrote, "we can get as much [corn] as we want at $1.05 per bushel. Everything else is plenty and cheap enough. Sugar, coffee, salt, molasses, etc. are here in abundance." The availability of a wide range of goods at lower prices, Atwood claimed, prompted changes in the pattern of production on Upcountry farms. "We have quit trying to see who can tend the most acres of land," the Laurens farmer maintained. "Twenty acres of land will now do as

---

[13]Lacy K. Ford, "Yeoman Farmers in the South Carolina Upcountry: Changing Production Patterns in the Late Antebellum Period," *Agricultural History* 60 (Fall, 1986):17–37; Gavin Wright, *The Political Economy of the Cotton South,* pp. 62–74, 164–176; Remarks, 1856, John D. Ashmore Plantation Journal, SHC; John Springs to Andrew Baxter Springs, August 22, 1851, and John Springs to Andrew Baxter Springs, January 22, 1852, Springs Family Papers, SHC.

Table 7.9 Cotton and Self-Sufficiency in the Upper and
Lower Piedmont, 1860

	Non-slaveholding Yeomen	Slaveholding Yeomen
Anderson District		
% Growing Cotton	80.3	80.3
% Self-Sufficient (Grain)	60.0	65.2
Cotton-Corn Ratio	3.7	3.3
Abbeville District		
% Growing Cotton	87.0	94.1
% Self-Sufficient (Grain)	21.0	47.1
Cotton-Corn Ratio	10.8	12.8

Source: Manuscript Census of South Carolina, 1860, Abbeville and Anderson Districts, Schedules I, II, and IV.

well as eighty used to. Flour and wheat is plenty at $6.50 per barrel and $1.00 per bushel.''[14]

Yet while the new railroads encouraged the expansion of cotton production and a growing dependence on the market for food among yeoman farmers, they also reduced the small farmer's vulnerability to subsistence crop shortages. Prior to the coming of the railroads, when an Upcountry yeoman failed to achieve self-sufficiency because of poor crop yields, it was highly probable that many of his neighbors would suffer from similar shortfalls. Growing seasons that were too dry or too wet, too hot or too cool, killing frosts that came too late or too early, and infestations of destructive insects all tended to affect whole neighborhoods or even entire districts rather than a few isolated farms. Any shortage of corn was likely to be a general neighborhood shortage, or possibly even one that affected much of the Upcountry. Thus market corn usually fetched a high price because it had to be imported from outside the region over a poor transportation system. Before the development of rail connections to outside markets, the price of corn and other grain in local markets depended heavily on local supply. Thus, during local subsistence crop shortages, when market grain was most needed, the price of grain in local markets was ordinarily quite high. One farmer's failure to achieve self-sufficiency, when repeated by most of his neighbors, as it probably would be during a year of either drought or excessive rainfall, usually proved expensive indeed because of the high price of grain in the local market. During the 1850s, however, the expansion of railroads into the Upcountry changed the small farmer's crop-mix calculus considerably. Once the railroads were in operation, it became much easier to import grain and other food when it was needed.

[14]J. J. Atwood to Joseph H. and Menoah Atwood, April 4, 1852, reprinted in the Laurens *Advertiser,* June 10, 1970; Atwood was referring to the Laurens Railroad which originated in Laurensville and connected with the G and C Railroad near Newberry.

The price of grain and other food commodities in Upcountry markets no longer depended so heavily on local supplies, and thus the likelihood of wild fluctuations in the market price of food diminished. As the range of market prices for corn and other foodstuffs became more and more predictable due to improved transportation, small farmers in the Upcountry could afford to operate with a smaller "margin of safety" in food production because they knew that local shortages did not necessarily mean prohibitive increases in local prices.[15]

Thus the yeoman farmers' gradual drift away from self-sufficiency was based largely on their own changing calculations. With the help of the railroads, the constraints which had made the logic of self-sufficiency so compelling were loosened, and Upcountry yeomen eased that much deeper into the market economy. But the deepening market involvement of Upcountry yeomen did not mean that these small farmers had surrendered their traditional notions of independence. The economic base of the yeoman farmer's independence, his ownership of productive property, remained intact, even though high cotton prices made the expansion of staple production more attractive at the very time when transportation improvements lowered the risks involved in the reduction of subsistence production. Most yeomen were still as averse to risks that threatened their status as property owners as they had ever been, but by the middle of the 1850s, a sustained cotton boom and more predictable market prices for corn and pork reduced the importance of self-sufficiency in foodstuffs as part of an overall strategy of risk-averse production. In time, many Upcountry yeomen discovered that their increased market involvement could have unhappy, and perhaps even disastrous, consequences. But these yeomen were not prescient; they could not foresee all possible outcomes, and as long as cotton prices were high and the market price of food cheap their increased market involvement seemed to enhance rather than endanger their independence, that most cherished of traditional values.

Despite their increased cotton production, yeoman farmers in the Upcountry produced a slightly smaller share of the region's total output of the staple in 1859 than they had a decade earlier. In 1849, Upcountry yeomen produced 21.9 percent of all cotton produced in the region, but ten years later their share declined to 19.5 percent. By contrast, planters, who raised 45 percent of the region's cotton in 1849, produced over 50 percent of all cotton grown in the Upcountry in 1859. Yeoman farmers also controlled a smaller share of improved acres and total farm value at the end of the decade than they had at the beginning. In 1850, Upcountry yeomen owned nearly 40 percent of the improved acreage and controlled just over 30 percent of all farm wealth (as measured by cash value of farms) in the region. By 1860, yeomen controlled only 28 percent of the improved acres and only 25 percent of the total farm wealth in the Upcountry.

[15]Ford, "Yeoman Farmers in the South Carolina Upcountry," pp. 34–36; Remarks, 1857, John D. Ashmore Plantation Journal, SHC; Edward Lipscomb to Smith Lipscomb, December 13, 1851, Smith Lipscomb to Joshua Lipscomb, March 30, 1853, and J. H. Lipscomb to Smith Lipscomb, January 29, 1854, Lipscomb Family Papers, SHC; Thomas Robertson to Andrew Baxter Springs, April 21, 1858, Springs Family Papers, SHC.

Table 7.10 Distribution of Production and Wealth on Upcountry Farms, 1860 (in percent)

	Type of Farm Operator				
	Non-slaveholding Yeomen (0 slaves)	Slaveholding Yeomen (1–5 slaves)	Middling Slaveholders (6–19 slaves)	Planters (20 or more slaves)	Tenants
Farms	28.7	21.6	25.6	12.9	11.4
Slaves	0	7.0	29.3	62.8	0.1
Cotton	9.5	10.0	27.8	50.2	2.1
Corn	14.6	14.8	29.0	37.8	2.8
Swine	15.9	16.8	31.3	31.9	3.7
Improved Acreage	13.0	14.7	31.2	40.5	NA
Cash Value	10.1	14.9	30.6	43.7	NA

Total Farms: 861

Source: Manuscript Census of South Carolina, 1860, South Carolina, Abbeville, Anderson, and York Districts, Schedules I, II, and IV.

The planters' share of both improved acreage and farm value increased during the 1850s. At the beginning of the decade, Upcountry planters owned 31.3 percent of the region's improved acres and controlled almost 40 percent of its total farm value. Ten years later, planters owned 40.5 percent of all improved acres in the Upcountry, and their share of the region's total farm value had risen modestly to 43.7 percent.[16]

One reason that the yeoman farmers' share of total farm output and wealth declined between 1850 and 1860 was that yeomen comprised a smaller percentage of all farm operators in the latter year than they had in the former. In 1850, nearly 54 percent of all farms in the Upcountry were operated by yeoman farmers, but by 1860 that percentage had fallen slightly to 50.3. During the same period, the proportion of farm operators who were either middling slaveholders or planters increased modestly. Of all farm operators in the Upcountry in 1850, 23.6 percent were slaveholders who owned more than five but less than twenty slaves; by 1860, this group of slaveholding farmers comprised 25.6 percent of all farm operators in the region. In 1850, only 9.6 percent of all Upcountry farm operators were planters, but ten years later almost 13 percent of Upcountry farms were owned and operated by planters. These gains by planters and middling slaveholders during the 1850s were modest and hardly reflect any wholesale displacement of yeomen by large slaveholders. The growing proportion of planters and substantial slaveholders in the total farm population does reflect, however, the success of those slaveholders who lived in the Upcountry in both 1850 and 1860 and who rose in status largely through the natural increase among their slaves.[17]

[16]See Table 7.10. Compare with Table 2.2.
[17]*Ibid.*

Overall, Upcountry farms were larger in 1860 than in 1850, but there were fewer of them. The total number of farms in the region dropped from 16,552 in 1850 to 14,761 in 1860, a decline of nearly 11 percent. Practically all of the decrease occurred in the lower Piedmont, where there were 1600 fewer farms in 1860 than in 1850. A large percentage of the decline in the lower Piedmont came in the Savannah valley districts of Edgefield and Abbeville. In 1850, there were 2,030 farms in Edgefield and 1,814 farms in Abbeville, but by 1860 there were only 1,696 farms in Edgefield and 1,233 farms in Abbeville. By contrast, the number of farms in the upper Piedmont remained essentially constant over the last antebellum decade. The decline in the number of working farms in the Upcountry resulted from a combination of factors, including the lure of richer soil in the Southwest, the problem of soil exhaustion in the lower Piedmont, and the incentives to emigrate offered to small farmers by large cotton growers eager to·expand their acreage.[18]

As the exodus to the Southwest continued, however, the remaining Upcountry farms expanded a bit. The average improved acreage of an Upcountry farm increased from 130.7 in 1850 to 136.9 in 1860. This expansion was confined to the lower Piedmont, where average improved acreage rose from 148.5 in 1850 to 169.0 in 1860, essentially to facilitate expanded cotton production in that black-belt area. In the upper Piedmont, where the cotton orientation was less pronounced, average farm size actually decreased slightly, from 110.0 acres to 105.4 acres, between 1850 and 1860. Despite the growth in the average size of Upcountry farms during the 1850s, there is little evidence that small farmers were being forced to emigrate due to pressure from their wealthy planter neighbors. The total number of improved acres in the Upcountry actually declined, from 2,164,044 to 2,020,636, between 1850 and 1860. This fact suggests that farmers left the area out of a desire to leave worn-out and unproductive land behind rather than because there was no farm land available.[19]

The principal obstacle to the fulfillment of the landless white's ambition of becoming a landowner was not a general shortage of land, but the fact that most land was either nearly exhausted or relatively expensive. As early as 1850, John Springs advised his son against buying much, if any, of the large quantity of land up for sale in York district. The elder Springs described the available tracts as "much cut down, worn, and washed in gullies and have not the timber to put them in repair and keep them up" and maintained that "anyone with much means would not likely want to settle on such places." Springs frowned on land speculation in general because he believed that "the interest absorbs the profit" and that bank and railroad stock afforded a better return on investment.[20] Yet enough Upcountry farmers were less selective than John Springs to keep the price of land, including land of rather poor quality, quite high during the 1850s.

---

[18]See Tables 7.6 and 7.7; Tommy W. Rogers, "The Great Population Exodus from South Carolina: 1850–1860," *South Carolina Historical Magazine* 68 (January, 1967):14–22.

[19]See Tables 7.6 and 7.7.

[20]John Springs to Andrew Baxter Springs, August 14, 1850, Springs Family Papers, SHC.

According to census data, the total value of real property in the Upcountry rose by more than 100 percent, from $38,471,409 to $78,211,287, between 1850 and 1860. In York district, for example, the estimated value of real property jumped from $2,665,649 in 1850 to $5,227,473 in 1860, an increase of 96 percent.[21] This remarkable appreciation in real estate values reflected the combined impact of railroad development and the cotton boom on Upcountry land prices. J. J. Atwood, the Laurens farmer, described the rise in land prices prompted by the arrival of the railroad in his district to his brother in Alabama. "Land that was when you were here worth $3.00 per acre is now worth ten, and I think cheaper at ten now than it was at $3 then," Atwood explained. "Though you may think mine strange doctrine, I will cite you a few places that you know . . . I have been offered $8.00 per acre but I would refuse $12 if it was offered." Despite the high prices, however, Atwood reported that "there is plenty of land for sale and as much trading in land as ever."[22]

If the cotton boom acted in combination with transportation improvements to drive Piedmont land values upward dramatically during the 1850s, the cotton boom alone was enough to trigger an enormous increase in the value of slave property. Unlike land values, which depended heavily on a variety of decidedly local factors, such as the quality of available transportation, the value of slave property was determined by a larger regional market which encompassed the entire South. During a sustained cotton boom like that of the 1850s, demand for slave labor increased and the value of slave property rose throughout the South. In the South Carolina Upcountry, the total value of personal property, the bulk of which was slave property, vaulted from $64,572,381 in 1850 to $185,106,478 in 1860. This appreciation in value produced what amounted to huge, and untaxed, "capital gains" for Upcountry slaveholders.[23] The increase in slave values was, of course, a problem and not a blessing to those Upcountrymen hoping to buy slaves. Prime field hands sold from two to three times as much in the mid-1850s as they had a decade earlier. James F. Sloan, a slaveless yeoman from Spartanburg who prospered during the 1850s, was unable, despite his success, to purchase slaves and had to content himself with renting a female slave for four dollars a month in 1859.[24] As the price of acquiring slaves became nearly prohibitive, a vocal minority of South Carolina politicians tried to counter the high prices by calling for a reopening of the slave trade. But the crusade to reopen the foreign slave trade never attracted broad-based support. Ultimately, the effort succumbed to a confluence of objections, including negrophobia, the desire of slaveholders to protect the value of their property, and even an ethical

[21]See Table 7.11. Data on wealth taken from the Manuscript Census of South Carolina, 1850, Schedule VI (Social Statistics); and the *Eighth Census of the United States, 1860: Miscellaneous Statistics* (Washington, D.C.: Government Printing Office, 1866), p. 312.

[22]J. J. Atwood to Joseph H. and Menoah Atwood, April 4, 1852, reprinted in Laurens *Advertiser*, June 10, 1970.

[23]See Table 7.11; on the "capital gain" enjoyed by slaveholders, see Gavin Wright, *Political Economy of the Cotton South*, pp. 139–142.

[24]Entries of January 26 and 27, and December 30, 1859, James F. Sloan Journal, SCL.

Table 7.11 Wealth in the Upcountry—1850 and 1860

	1850				1860			
	Value of Real Property	Value of Personal Property	Total Wealth	Per Capita Wealth (Free Pop.)	Value of Real Property	Value of Personal Property	Total Wealth	Per Capita Wealth (Free Pop.)
Lower Piedmont								
Abbeville	$5,154,501	$8,939,590	$14,094,151	$1079.5	$8,076,782	$23,103,725	$31,180,507	$2623.9
Chester	3,166,581	4,699,970	7,866,551	965.1	4,860,010	12,494,995	17,360,005	2393.2
Edgefield	5,977,450	10,507,629	16,485,079	996.9	11,025,269	27,492,589	38,467,858	2430.5
Fairfield	2,117,000	5,870,000	7,987,000	1115.8	7,121,969	19,245,392	26,367,361	4009.0
Laurens	2,616,120	4,500,000	7,110,120	620.8	6,152,900	15,288,629	21,441,569	2011.8
Newberry	2,577,785	6,001,551	8,579,336	1150.8	6,595,162	18,485,219	25,080,381	3491.1
Union	3,130,829	4,333,698	7,464,520	789.1	5,293,770	10,983,169	16,277,468	1842.6
Upper Piedmont								
Anderson	2,650,080	3,709,437	6,359,517	455.5	5,486,428	12,103,507	17,589,935	1217.5
Greenville	2,000,128	3,168,923	5,169,051	383.9	5,951,018	11,821,289	17,772,307	1197.4
Lancaster	1,959,035	2,283,272	4,242,307	710.1	2,420,946	5,750,096	8,171,042	1329.3
Pickens	1,555,315	1,971,213	2,926,528	221.3	3,998,502	6,147,722	10,146,224	657.0
Spartanburg	2,900,938	4,585,643	7,486,581	407.7	6,001,056	10,375,887	16,376,943	876.8
York	2,665,649	4,001,455	6,667,104	583.5	5,227,473	11,859,459	17,085,902	1483.4
Totals								
Lower Piedmont	24,740,264	44,852,438	69,586,757	949.7	49,125,864	127,049,518	176,195,129	2582.9
Upper Piedmont	13,731,145	19,719,943	32,851,088	429.9	29,085,423	58,056,960	87,142,353	1075.2
Upcountry	38,471,409	64,572,381	102,437,845	684.3	78,211,287	185,106,478	263,337,462	1469.0

Source: See footnote 21.

dislike for the slave trade. Yet the mere fact that a reopening of the slave trade was broached by politicians in search of a hobby reveals that at least some South Carolinians were aware of the growing difficulty of becoming a slaveholder.[25]

Together, the increases in land and slave values reflected the general prosperity flowing from the last short-staple cotton boom. The per capita wealth of the free population of the Upcountry grew from $684 in 1850 to $1,469 in 1860, an increase of nearly 115 percent. Levels of per capita wealth were higher in the lower Piedmont than in the upper Piedmont in both years, and the increase in wealth was also more dramatic in the black belt. Between 1850 and 1860, per capita wealth in the lower Piedmont rose by 172 percent, from $950 to $2,583. The per capita wealth of the free population of the hill country also rose sharply during the 1850s. In the upper Piedmont, per capita wealth increased by 150 percent, from $430 to $1,075, between 1850 and 1860, even though the absolute level of wealth remained considerably lower in the hill country than in the black belt. The largest part of this spectacular increase in per capita wealth can be attributed to the rising value of slave property. During the 1850s, slave values in the Upcountry increased at an average annual rate of over 11 percent. But land values, which rose at an average annual rate of almost 8 percent during the same decade, also played an important, if secondary, role in boosting the level of per capita wealth in the Upcountry.[26]

To varying degrees, the rising value of farm property benefited nearly all landholding farmers in the Upcountry. Among planters, average farm wealth, as measured by the cash value of farms, increased by 24 percent during the 1850s, while the average cash value of farms operated by slaveholders who owned more than five but less than twenty slaves increased by more than 45 percent. The average farm wealth of yeoman also increased substantially during the decade. The mean cash value of farms owned by nonslaveholders rose by more than 20 percent, from $963 to $1,162, between 1850 and 1860, and the average farm wealth of small slaveholders increased by 47 percent, from $1,542 to $2,275, during the same years. Yeoman farmers in both upper and lower Piedmont saw the value of their farm assets rise sharply. In the upper Piedmont, the average value of farms owned by non-slaveholders rose by roughly 25 percent, while mean value of farms owned by small slaveholders increased by a striking 52 percent. In the lower Piedmont, the farms of slaveless yeomen rose in value by an average of 66 percent, and the cash value of farms owned by slaveholding yeomen increased by 39 percent. In the Upcountry, the flush times of the 1850s were enjoyed by planter and yeoman alike.[27]

[25]Barton J. Bernstein, "Southern Politics and Attempts to Reopen the African Slave Trade," *Journal of Negro History* 51 (January, 1966):16–35; Ronald Takaki, "The Movement to Reopen the African Slave Trade in South Carolina," *South Carolina Historical Magazine* 66 (January, 1965):38–54; Steven A. Channing, *Crisis of Fear: Secession in South Carolina* (New York: Simon and Schuster, 1970), pp. 149–152; Wright, *Political Economy of the Cotton South*, pp. 150–154.

[26]Calculation made from data on wealth found in sources cited in footnote 21 above and from data on population found in Julian J. Petty, *The Growth and Distribution of Population in South Carolina* (Columbia, S.C.: State Council for Defense, 1943), pp. 226–227.

[27]See Tables 7.3, 7.4, and 7.5; compare with Tables 2.3, 2.4, and 2.5.

Yet the same economic boom that more than doubled per capita wealth in the Upcountry also fostered growing inequalities of wealth in the region. In 1860, the distribution of both real and personal property among Upcountry households was more uneven than it had been ten years earlier. For real property, the Gini coefficient of inequality rose from .703 in 1850 to .771 in 1860. The Gini for total wealth, including real and personal property, increased from .740 to .790 during the same decade. Even among farm households, the distribution of productive property was growing more uneven, especially in the lower Piedmont. In Abbeville district in 1850, the wealthiest 10 percent of all farmers controlled 35.8 percent of the improved acreage, while the poorest 50 percent controlled 15 percent. By 1860, the share of the wealthiest 10 percent had grown to 40.1 percent, while the share of the poorest 50 percent had diminished to 12.3 percent.[28]

On the whole the cotton boom of the 1850s, aided by railroad development, bestowed great material favors upon the Upcountry, but it bestowed them unevenly. The rich not only got richer but they also controlled a larger share of the riches than they had a decade earlier. With the value of slave property rising faster than the value of other assets, the slaveholder's wealth was growing more rapidly than that of the non-slaveholder, and with the price of slaves soaring, chances for non-slaveholders to enter the slaveholding ranks were disappearing, at least temporarily. During the 1850s, the economic gap between slaveholder and non-slaveholder widened. Still, despite its tendency to enhance exisiting inequalities, the boom of the 1850s was, in the fullest sense, a "rising tide that lifted all boats," increasing the wealth of yeoman farmers as well as planters and middling slaveholders. The rich got richer during the 1850s, but the plain folks got richer too.

With cotton prices, land values, and slave values all high, Upcountry planters were clearly at the height of their economic power during the 1850s. Profits were again flowing into their pockets from the cotton trade, and, largely with their own energy and capital, planters had built a railroad network which quickened the pace of commerce in the Upcountry and had begun to revolutionize the process of cotton marketing. Yet even in 1860, planters were just a small, though highly visible and successful, minority in the Upcountry. In 1860, only 7.3 percent of all free heads of household owned twenty or more slaves. In the lower Piedmont, about one in 10 household heads was a planter, while in the upper Piedmont, fewer than one in 30 household heads was a planter. In absolute numbers, there were just over 2,000 planters in the entire Upcountry, and nearly 29,000 free heads of household. In the upper Piedmont, fewer than 500 of the more than 15,000 heads of household were planters. Of all Upcountry planters, only about one in five owned 50 or more slaves, and only one in 33 owned as

---

[28]Gini coefficient calculated from a sample of all households drawn from the Manuscript Census of South Carolina, 1860, Laurens, Spartanburg, and York Districts, Schedules I, II, and IV. The sample for 1850 was described in chapter 2, footnote 51. Statistics on the changing distribution of agricultural wealth calculated from a sample of farms in the districts mentioned. Samples are described in my appendix on Statistical Methods and Samples.

many as 100 slaves. Indeed, there were as many planters who owned 100 or more slaves in the single coastal district of Beaufort as there were in the entire Upcountry, and fourteen times as many planters owning 100 or more slaves in the rice district of Georgetown than there were in the six districts of the upper Piedmont. The "typical" Upcountryman was not a planter, and neither were most of his neighbors. Moreover, the differences between the Upcountry, including the plantation-belt of the lower Piedmont, and the rich rice and sea-island cotton districts of the Lowcountry, such as Beaufort, Colleton, and Georgetown, where more than one in five heads of household was a planter, were striking. Doubtless, planters wielded considerable economic power and, in most cases, enjoyed a measure of social prestige. Yet even in 1860, planters were hopelessly outnumbered by slaveholders with fewer than twenty slaves and by non-slaveholders, most of whom shared, albeit unevenly, in the fruits of the great economic boom of the 1850s.[29]

The one signal shortcoming of the Upcountry economy during the 1850s was its failure to generate a dynamic industrial sector. Indeed, in some respects, the pace of industrial development in the region actually slowed during the decade despite a vigorous, though largely uncoordinated, promotional campaign waged by political leaders, newspaper editors, local manufacturers, and other capitalists.[30] But the failure of the Upcountry to industrialize rapidly during this era of great agricultural and commercial prosperity is more a telling irony than a puzzling contradiction. Industrial progress in the Upcountry slowed during the 1850s at least partially because of the spectacular boom in other sectors rather than in spite of it. As Gavin Wright has perceptively noted, the general prosperity of the 1850s affected Southern industry largely through its impact on the labor market, where the agricultural boom drove the cost of labor dramatically higher, thus cutting profits and discouraging investment. Of course the boom also raised the price of raw material for the South's fledgling textile industry and diverted capital that might otherwise have flowed into industry into land and slaves, but it was primarily by raising the price of both slave and free labor that the agricultural prosperity of the 1850s hindered industrial development in the Old South. As a result, it was those industries, such as textiles and iron, which depended on a relatively large and reliable labor force which suffered the most.[31]

By 1850, the fear of industrialization voiced by some members of the South Carolina elite during the 1830s had largely dissipated. The objection to manufacturing raised during the 1830s had been more political than economic. Some Nullifiers, including Calhoun, feared that infant industries in South Carolina, especially iron and textiles, could not survive without tariff protection, and that these industries would quickly create in South Carolina a large pro-tariff political

[29]*Eighth Census of the United States, 1860: Agriculture* (Washington, D.C.: Government Printing Office, 1864), p. 237.

[30]Chauncey S. Boucher, "The Antebellum Attitude of South Carolina Towards Manufacturing and Agriculture," *Washington University Studies* 3 (April, 1916):243–270.

[31]Wright, *Old South, New South*, pp. 10–13, 124–129; James C. Cobb, "Making Sense of Southern Economic History," *Georgia Historical Quarterly* 71 (Spring, 1987):53–74.

constituency ready to join the clamor for protective duties. Yet most Nullifiers were hardly systematic opponents of manufacturing; instead, they were liberal optimists who believed that technological progress would eventually enable American industry to meet foreign competition without the artificial protection offered by tariff barriers. For the South, Nullifiers generally envisioned the gradual development of an industrial sector as an adjunct to, rather than as a rival of, the dominant agricultural sector, thus freeing the region from its dependence on Great Britain and the North for finished goods. A number of prominent Nullifiers, including George McDuffie, John Springs, William H. Gist, and Calhoun himself lent tangible support to their views by investing in a variety of manufacturing or mining enterprises during the 1830s.[32]

The agricultural depression which followed the Panic of 1837 prompted a chorus of calls for industrial development, but the general lack of liquid capital available during the slump, particularly among planters, hampered the Upcountry's ability to heed those calls. Still, a few industrial projects, especially in textiles, were successfully launched between 1845 and 1850. James Bivings, a textile entrepreneur from New England who had established the Bivingsville Cotton Manufacturing Company in Spartanburg district in 1837, sold his interest in that operation after a dispute with other stockholders and opened another small cotton mill in the same district in 1847.[33] Also in Spartanburg district, prosperous merchant Gabriel Cannon joined farmer and grist-mill operator Joseph Finger in organizing the Pacolet Manufacturing Company in 1848. Within a year, the aggressive Cannon was offering "an excellent article of cotton yarn" at "the lowest prices" to Upcountry planters and merchants.[34] Also, by 1850, prominent Union district planter Joseph Starke Sims had opened a small, two-hundred-spindle, yarn manufacturing and wool carding mill on his property at Grindal Shoals.[35] But none of these small mills compared, in size or significance, to William Gregg's giant textile factory at Graniteville in Edgefield dis-

[32]On the attitudes of Calhoun and other Nullifiers toward manufacturing, see the introduction by editor Clyde N. Wilson in *The Papers of John C. Calhoun* (Columbia, S.C.: University of South Carolina Press, 1980), vol. 13, xvii–xviii; and Theodore R. Marmar, "Anti-industrialism and the Old South: The Agrarian Perspective of John C. Calhoun," *Comparative Studies in Society and History* 9 (1967):377–406; Robert A. Garson, "Proslavery as Political Theory: The Examples of John C. Calhoun and George Fitzhugh," *South Atlantic Quarterly* 84 (Spring, 1985):197–212; James D. Clarke, "Calhoun and the Concept of 'Reactionary Enlightenment': An Examination of the Disquisition on Government" (Ph.D. dissertation, University of Keele, 1982); and Lacy K. Ford, "Republican Ideology in a Slave Society: The Political Economy of John C. Calhoun," *Journal of Southern History* (forthcoming).

[33]J. B. O. Landrum, *A History of Spartanburg County* (Atlanta: Franklin Printing, 1900), p. 163; Ernest McPherson Lander, Jr., *The Textile Industry in Antebellum South Carolina* (Baton Rouge: Louisiana State University Press, 1969), pp. 66–67; Charleston *Courier*, October 22, 1847.

[34]Lander, *The Textile Industry*, p. 67; Landrum, *History of Spartanburg County*, pp. 437–439; Gabriel Cannon to Elihu P. Smith, June 5, 1849, Elihu P. Smith Papers, SCL.

[35]Edwin Thomas Sims, "Joseph Starke Sims: A Nineteenth Century Upcountry Planter, Politician and Business Entrepreneur of South Carolina" (M.A. thesis, University of South Carolina, 1983), pp. 53–69; J. D. Bailey, *History of Grindal Shoals and Some Early Adjacent Families* (Gaffney, S.C., 1927).

trict. The large Graniteville project was the brainchild of Gregg, a Charleston jeweler who earned a fortune in the import-export business before he was forty. Gregg and Abbeville planter Joel Smith received a charter for the Graniteville Company in 1845, and with the support of Charleston merchant-banker Ker Boyce, Hamburg banker Hiram Hutchinson, and Upcountry planter John Springs, Gregg and Smith raised $300,000 in capital.[36] Within a year after the charter was granted, construction was in full swing, and by late 1847 both the mill and the village were taking shape. After viewing the progress at Graniteville, J. J. Blackwood, cashier at the Bank of Hamburg, reported that one needed "but little imagination to hear the music of 10,000 spindles, and see the sylph-like forms of the 500 spinsters that are to hold them." The capitalists' "fancy," Blackwood confessed, "would need to stretch a little more to see the *dividends on the investment.*"[37] In March 1849, Gregg informed the stockholders that production would begin the following June. John Springs attended the March stockholders' meeting, toured the entire area, and pronounced himself pleased with the facilities. The town, Springs observed, was "one of the handsomest little places in the State" because many of the buildings sported the "most modern style of architecture." The factory, Springs judged, held "every prospect of success and probably profit to the owners."[38] By July 1849, Graniteville was in full operation, producing over 1200 yards of shirting and sheeting daily. The mill ran more or less successfully throughout the 1850s, and by the end of the decade it produced over a quarter of a million dollars' worth of cotton goods annually.[39]

Upcountry boosters missed few chances to tout industrial development through a discussion of Gregg's success at Graniteville. One Upcountry entrepreneur used the columns of the *Carolina Spartan* to applaud Gregg's efforts at Graniteville, where company stockholders were allegedly earning 18 percent profit on their investment in 1854. "We know a small cotton factory in our district," the promoter continued, "which . . . pays better than Graniteville itself." The editors of the *Spartan* also congratulated Gregg on his success, praised the "happy condition" of the operatives, and urged others to follow Gregg's lead into manufacturing.[40] In Chester, planter-lawyer James Hemphill prodded local merchants, who were flush with new-found profits from the cotton trade, to become active in industrial development. "Some people have an idea that a Railroad will do everything," Hemphill observed, "[but] there must be something else to enlarge and enrich towns—There is need of manufactures."[41]

[36]Lander, *The Textile Industry*, pp. 50–62; Broadus Mitchell, *William Gregg: Factory Master of the Old South* (Chapel Hill: University of North Carolina Press, 1928); Thomas P. Martin, "The Advent of William Gregg and the Graniteville Company," *Journal of Southern History* 11 (August, 1945):389–423; Hiram Hutchinson to John Springs, December 19, 1845, January 8, 1846, January 20, 1846, October 20, 1846, Springs Family Papers, SHC.

[37]J. J. Blackwood to John Springs, November 8, 1847, Springs Family Papers, SHC.

[38]John Springs to Andrew Baxter Springs, March 22, 1849, Springs Family Papers, SHC.

[39]Lander, *The Textile Industry*, pp. 50–62, 101–104.

[40]Carolina *Spartan*, May 10 and 17, 1855.

[41]James Hemphill to Robert W. Hemphill, March 18, 1853, Hemphill Family Papers, DU.

Despite the promise it showed during the 1840s, and despite Hemphill's admonition and dozens of others like it, the Upcountry textile industry showed little or no growth during the 1850s. The number of factories producing cotton goods rose from 14 in 1850 to 20 in 1860, and the total capital invested in Upcountry textiles grew from $612,700 to $733,795 during the decade, but almost all of the increased capitalization came from the expansion of the Graniteville and Vaucluse mills in Edgefield, and the dollar value of textile goods produced in the region actually fell from $677,260 in 1850 to $568,514 in 1860. Yet even though the textile industry in the Upcountry barely held its own during the decade, Upcountry mills generally fared better in the 1850s than did mills in other parts of the state. In South Carolina as a whole, the number of mills producing cotton goods declined during the period, and the capital invested in the textile industry fell from $902,600 in 1850 to $801,800 in 1860. The value of cotton goods manufactured in South Carolina declined by almost 40 percent during the same decade.[42] Much of the decline was the result of the closing of a number of textile mills in the lower and middle districts of the state. These black-belt mills used mostly slave labor, and with slave values skyrocketing and agricultural profits high, the use of slaves in cotton mills became prohibitively expensive during the 1850s. According to Ernest M. Lander, the number of slaves employed by the South Carolina textile industry declined from more than 200 in 1850 to less than 50 a decade later. Upcountry mills survived the decade more easily because they had never relied as heavily on slave labor as did their counterparts in the lower and middle districts.[43]

Still, in 1860, the Upcountry textile industry was little more than a number of small mills, concentrated in the upper Piedmont and capitalized at much less than $100,000, which produced a relatively small quantity of cotton goods for sale in local markets. The exception to this characterization was Gregg's operation at Graniteville. Almost one-half of all the capital invested in Upcountry mills in 1860 was invested in Graniteville, and over half of all cotton goods produced in the Upcountry in 1860 were manufactured at Graniteville. Moreover, Graniteville was four times larger, in terms of capital investment, than the second largest textile mill in the Upcountry. Without Graniteville, the Upcountry textile industry, that favorite hobby of the area's industrial boosters, would have been

[42]Figures for manufacturing in the Upcountry in 1850 were calculated from the Manuscript Census of South Carolina, 1850, Schedule V (Manufacturing). The figures for 1860 were taken from the *Eighth Census of the United States, 1860: Manufacturing* (Washington: Government Printing Office, 1865), pp. 552–558 and cross-checked against the manuscript census returns for that year and corrected where necessary. The published census returns on manufacturing in 1850 are available in *Abstract of the Statistics of Manufacturers, Returns of the Seventh Census*, Senate Documents, 2nd Session, 35th Congress, Ex. Doc. 39. The published returns for 1850 do not provide information from the district level and are generally unreliable. For a brief discussion of the unreliability of the returns of the manufacturing census during the late antebellum era, see Ernest M. Lander, Jr., "Charleston: Manufacturing Center of the Old South," *Journal of Southern History* 26 (August, 1960):330–351.

[43]Ernest M. Lander, "Slave Labor in South Carolina Cotton Mills," *Journal of Negro History* 38 (April, 1953):161–173; Allen H. Stokes, Jr., "Black and White Labor and the Development of the Southern Textile Industry" (Ph.D. dissertation, University of South Carolina, 1977), pp. 98–132.

smaller, at least in terms of capitalization, than the region's struggling iron industry.[44]

A number of small iron foundries, such as those of William Hill on the Catawba River in York district and Adam Carruth on the Reedy River in Greenville, supplied local markets with nails and munitions in the early nineteenth century, but by the late antebellum era only three chartered iron companies, the South Carolina Manufacturing Company, the Nesbitt Manufacturing Company, and the Kings Mountain Iron Company, all located in the upper Broad River valley, were in operation in the Upcountry. Chartered in 1826, the South Carolina Manufacturing Company ran furnaces, forges, and rolling mills at Cowpens and Hurricane Shoals in Spartanburg district. Skillfully managed by Simpson Bobo and backed by $100,000 of capital, the company operated without interruption into the 1860s. The Nesbitt Company, located in the northern tip of Union district on the west bank of the Broad River, was chartered in 1835. Though headed by politically powerful investors such as Franklin Elmore, Wade Hampton II, and Pierce Butler, the Nesbitt Company was plagued by financial difficulties from its inception and tottered on the brink of bankruptcy during most of the 1840s. In 1850, the company was sold to a group of Swedish investors for $114,000 even though Nesbitt stockholders had over $200,000 invested in land, slaves, and machinery. The new investors, who changed the name of the company to the Swedish Iron Company, also had trouble making a profit and closed down half of the works by 1856. Located near the mouth of Kings Creek in western York district, the Kings Mountain Iron Company operated from 1837 to 1867. Capitalized at $97,000 in 1860, the Kings Mountain Iron Company was probably the most successful of the Upcountry iron companies. In 1856, the company paid a 7 percent dividend, and its largest stockholder declared that the "company now is in very good condition" with its assets far outstripping its debts.[45]

The list of investors in these iron companies reads like a Who's Who of South Carolina planters and capitalists. Franklin H. Elmore, Benjamin T. Elmore, Wade Hampton II, Pierce Butler, Judge Baylis Earle, and former Spartanburg Congressman Wilson Nesbitt all invested in the Nesbitt Manufacturing Company and all shared in its financial embarrassment. Greenville mill owner Vardry McBee, textile entrepreneur Simpson Bobo, and Spartanburg merchant Gabriel Cannon all invested heavily in the South Carolina Manufacturing Company, while William H. Gist, George McDuffie, and John Bryce were the largest stockholders in the Kings Mountain Iron Company.[46]

[44]*Eighth Census of the United States, 1860: Manufacturing,* pp. 552–558.

[45]Ernest M. Lander, Jr., "The Iron Industry in Antebellum South Carolina," *Journal of Southern History* 20 (August, 1954):337–355; William H. Gist to Armistead Burt, August 24, 1856, Armistead Burt Papers, DU.

[46]J. Mauldin Lesesne, *The Bank of the State of South Carolina: A General and Political History* (Columbia, S.C.: University of South Carolina Press, 1970), pp. 89–100; Lander, "The Iron Industry in Antebellum South Carolina," pp. 344–348; Landrum, *History of Spartanburg County,* pp. 156–166; Minute Books of the Kings Mountain Iron Company, 1837–1867, Records of York County, S.C., SCDAH; John Bryce to George McDuffie, [c. 1836], George McDuffie Papers, DU.

Buoyed by sales of iron to companies building the Upcountry railroads, the Kings Mountain Iron Company and the South Carolina Manufacturing Company flourished briefly during the late 1840s and early 1850s, but by the end of the latter decade these companies struggled to hold their own. The problems of the Upcountry iron industry during the late 1850s were three-fold. All three companies relied heavily on slave labor, often hiring slaves from nearby planters on a part-time basis, and used whites only as supervisors or in a few skilled positions. Thus both the rising cost of hiring slaves and the growing opportunity costs of holding slaves out of agricultural labor hurt the iron companies immensely. Second, the very railroads whose construction had given the industry a temporary boost ultimately hurt the Upcountry iron companies by bringing cheaper iron from Northern anthracite furnaces into markets previously protected by geographic isolation. Finally, and perhaps less important, the Kings Mountain Iron and South Carolina Manufacturing companies found it difficult to raise capital because of the well-publicized financial woes of the Nesbitt Company. In 1856, William H. Gist, who owned over $30,000 worth of Kings Mountain Iron Company stock, complained that "owing to the almost universal failure of joint stock companies in the state" stock in the Kings Mountain works was selling at only fifty cents on the dollar even though the company was making a profit and paying dividends.[47]

Yet the stagnation of the Upcountry textile and iron industry in the 1850s was not indicative of the fate of all types of manufacturing in the region during the decade. On the whole, manufacturing in the Upcountry grew slowly but significantly during the 1850s. Capital invested in Upcountry industries rose by 19.9 percent, from $2,425,102 to $2,908,810, between 1850 and 1860, and the value of industrial goods produced in the Upcountry increased by 31.4 percent, from $2,604,924 to $3,422,171, during the same period.[48] Manufacturing, however, as defined by the census takers in 1850 and 1860, included a wide range of endeavors, such as blacksmithing, tanning, and wagon-making, which were usually performed by local artisans in small, family-run shops rather than in factories or large workshops where a capitalist employed a number of workers to mass produce certain commodities. A significant portion of the Upcountry's "industrial" output was the product of artisans who performed specialized services for the region's large agricultural community. Blacksmiths, wheelwrights, coopers, tinsmiths, carpenters, saddle and harness makers, wagonmakers, and tanners all produced goods which were essential to the local agricultural economy in almost every Upcountry district. As a rule, these artisans prospered when local farmers prospered and struggled when local farmers struggled. Also, a handful of Upcountry artisans, mostly tailors and boot and shoemakers, pro-

[47]Minute Books of the Kings Mountain Iron Company, 1837–1867, Records of York County, S.C., SCDAH; Yorkville *Enquirer*, February 24, 1859; Lander, "The Iron Industry in Antebellum South Carolina," pp. 353–355; William H. Gist to Armistead Burt, August 24, 1856, Armistead Burt Papers, DU.
[48]See Table 7.12.

Table 7.12 Manufactures—1850 and 1860

	1850			1860		
	Capital	No. of Hands Employed	Value of Annual Product	Capital	No. of Hands Employed	Value of Annual Product
Lower Piedmont						
Abbeville	$268,920	403	$257,183	$224,195	248	$223,528
Chester	104,370	162	101,360	114,950	122	147,729
Edgefield	724,435	1064	635,096	989,175	739	761,155
Fairfield		[omitted]			[no report]	
Laurens	184,475	250	419,715	137,600	165	312,535
Newberry	71,810	116	151,145	10,500	16	11,000
Union	286,518	227	194,793	54,800	30	117,320
Upper Piedmont						
Anderson	$134,445	233	$289,105	185,480	173	246,491
Greenville	176,850	290	213,510	471,705	576	701,376
Lancaster	36,400	35	46,100	46,225	43	131,608
Pickens	27,923	59	41,192	100,460	40	36,085
Spartanburg	265,350	363	173,820	369,370	309	408,007
York	143,606	136	81,905	204,350	231	325,387
Totals						
Lower Piedmont	1,640,528	2222	1,759,292	1,531,220	1320	1,573,267
Upper Piedmont	784,574	1116	845,632	1,377,590	1372	1,848,904
Upcountry	2,425,102	3338	2,604,924	2,908,810	2692	3,422,171

Source: See footnote 41.

duced a small range of consumer goods which were generally absorbed by the local market. The increased availability of shoes and clothes imported from outside the region threatened tailors and shoemakers once the railroads arrived during the 1850s, but those artisans producing items essential to local agriculture generally flourished during the cotton boom.[49]

Industries which processed agricultural commodities also thrived during the 1850s, accounting for almost half of the region's total industrial output in 1860. Indeed, grist milling, the grinding of corn and wheat into corn meal and flour, was the largest single industry in the Upcountry in both 1850 and 1860, outstripping textiles in total value of product by $150,000 in 1850 and by over $750,000 in 1860, when the value of the product of Upcountry grinding mills was two and one-half times larger than the value of the product of Upcountry textile mills. Moreover, the grist milling industry flourished during the 1850s as the value of the flour and meal produced at these mills increased from just over $800,000 in 1850 to almost $1,400,000 by 1860. Yet during these years of prosperity, the

[49]Manuscript Census of South Carolina, 1850, Schedule V (Manufacturing); Manuscript Census of South Carolina, 1860, Schedule V (Manufacturing); *Eighth Census of the United States, 1860: Manufacturing*, pp. 552–558.

nature of grist milling in the Upcountry was being radically transformed by the transportation revolution. In 1850, prior to the coming of the railroads, most of the grinding mills in the Upcountry served small local markets and enjoyed protection from non-local competition due to poor transportation and the general isolation of the area. As the Upcountry railroads were completed during the 1850s, the markets of Upcountry grist mills were no longer protected by geography and the scope of operation of most mills changed dramatically, as did the distribution of grinding mills within the region. In 1850, there were about 185 grinding mills in the lower Piedmont with an average value of product of $3,326, and fewer than 100 grinding mills in the upper Piedmont with an average value of product of $2,388. The transportation revolution of the 1850s drove a number of the small mills in the lower Piedmont out of business, but allowed those that survived to secure a larger share of the market and perhaps even to ship some of their product out of the region. By 1860, there were only 75 grist mills still operating in the lower Piedmont, but the average output of these mills was $6,906 worth of flour and meal. In the upper Piedmont, where water power to run mills was abundant, the coming of the railroads gave grist mills easy access to outside markets for the first time. Existing mills expanded their production and a large number of new mills began operations. Flour from upper Piedmont mills began to flow into the lower Piedmont, to Charleston, and to other parts of the state. By 1860, there were 147 grist mills in the upper Piedmont and the average value of output of these mills was over $6,000, more than doubling the average value of output in 1850. The absolute increase in the total value of output of upper Piedmont grinding mills during the 1850s was truly remarkable. While the value of output of mills in the lower Piedmont was declining from $612,133 in 1850 to $517,955 in 1860, the value of output of upper Piedmont mills was increasing from just over $200,000 to more than $575,000.[50]

The dollar value of corn mean and flour and other grist mill products in the upper Piedmont was over four times greater than the dollar value of the sub-region's textile products, but, with a few exceptions, the capital investment necessary to establish a grinding mill was rather small. The average capital investment in Upcountry grist mills in both 1850 and 1860 was around $3,000, and even the largest grinding mills in the region, such as Vardry McBee's operation in Greenville, required capital investments of no more than $12,000 to $15,000. Since only comparatively small investments were required, most grist mills were sole proprietorships rather than cooperative ventures, and these mills generally employed no more than a handful of workers. McBee's mill, probably the most successful in the Upcountry, employed only ten workers in 1850, and John Garlington's large grist mill in Laurens employed only seven. Thus, as transportation improvements drew more and more Upcountry grist mills into competition for non-local markets, the expansion of output was achieved with a

---

[50]Calculations made from sources cited in footnote 49.

minimum of capital investment and without a dramatic increase in the number of operatives employed by millowners.[51]

The prosperity of the 1850s did, however, trigger a significant expansion in one industry, carriage-making, which required larger capital outlays than grist milling and where the typical production unit was a workshop with five or more employees. Carriage-making had long been a minor industry of some significance in the Upcountry, especially in areas such as Edgefield and Abbeville where earlier cotton booms generated demand for certain luxury items among local planters. But the agricultural depression of the 1840s sent the carriage industry into a prolonged slump which prompted moneylenders to give the industry a poor credit rating. Indeed, one credit reporter went so far as to suggest that "a prejudice existed . . . against all men" in the carriage business. Then the cotton boom of the 1850s revived the carriage industry by creating "a more than ordinary demand for carriages" and made it one of the most successful industries in the Upcountry by 1860. The value of the carriage industry's output increased from just over $100,000 in 1850 to over $180,000 in 1860, and the amount of capital invested in carriage workshops increased from less than $100,000 to over $275,000 during the same period. Moreover, by 1860, carriage shops employed an average of 7.6 workers compared to the average of 1.4 hands employed in Upcountry grist mills or the average 2.4 workers employed at Upcountry saw mills. Of course even in prosperous times there was a limit to the demand for carriages, though most of the carriages produced in the Upcountry were plain and utilitarian rather than fancy showpieces.[52]

In the final analysis, whether they produced goods used in the agricultural economy, processed agricultural commodities, or simply depended on demand generated by agricultural profits, those Upcountry industries whose success was closely tied to agricultural prosperity generally flourished during the 1850s. As a rule, those industries consisted of a large number of rather small firms, usually wholly owned by a single proprietor. These firms ordinarily required relatively small capital outlays to establish and maintain and they normally employed no more than a handful of workers. But during those same years, industries, such as iron and textiles, whose success depended upon high levels of capitalization, the cooperation of a large number of investors, the successful management of factory production, and the availability of a reliable supply of relatively cheap labor either declined or struggled to hold their own.

In light of the promising strides made by the South Carolina textile industry during the late 1840s, and, perhaps more importantly, in view of the emergence of a strong textile industry in the Southern Piedmont in the late nineteenth century, the problems of the textile industry during the 1850s have long posed

[51]Calculations made from sources cited in footnote 49; see also *DeBow's Review* 8 (September, 1852):314–318; Alfred Taylor Letterbooks, SHC.

[52]Calculations made from sources cited in footnote 49; quotation is from R. G. Dun and Company, Credit Ledgers, South Carolina, IX, 173, Baker.

vexing questions for historians. Unquestionably, the lack of managerial and technical expertise among South Carolina owners and investors, the difficulty of hiring and retaining experienced textile men from other parts of the country, and the reluctance of many owners to devote their full attention to the acquisition of such experience and expertise plagued the textile industry in antebellum South Carolina. As early as 1838, John Bauskett, the co-owner and manager of the Vaucluse mill in Edgefield's Horse Creek Valley, observed that a textile mill was a "very active business requiring constant attention." But Bauskett was also a successful planter, an active lawyer, and a sometime politician who seldom gave Vaucluse his full attention. During the 1850s, Joseph Starke Sims was in almost constant need of technical assistance at his Grindal Shoals mill, and Sims's repeated efforts to secure an experienced manager for the operation always ended in failure. Moreover, and again with the exception of Graniteville, most of the Upcountry mills marketed their products primarily in naturally protected local markets. After the coming of the railroads, the competitive advantage of local products in local markets diminished.[53]

Yet for all these engineering and marketing difficulties, the problem which most perplexed Upcountry textile managers was that of labor.[54] Bauskett moved slaves back and forth between Vaucluse and his Edgefield plantation, always trying to employ them where their labor would earn the most profit. While the Graniteville mill was under construction, stockholder Hiram Hutchinson worried that the huge mill could not be staffed initially with white operatives. Whites, Hutchinson believed, would be reluctant to leave the countryside and their agricultural pursuits for village life and mill work, and even if whites were attracted to Graniteville, the Hamburg banker anticipated difficulty in "disciplining" a cracker proletariat.[55] Despite loud public claims by William Gregg and James Henry Hammond that the Southern backcountry was teeming with poor whites eager for work in cotton mills, Hutchinson's more sober judgment proved at least partially correct. Gregg originally hoped to pattern his operation after successful New England examples, like that of the mills in Waltham, Massachusetts, where large numbers of young female operatives worked in the mill and lived in well-kept, tightly supervised boarding-houses. As the Graniteville factory neared completion, Gregg advertised for four hundred young female workers, preferably over the age of fourteen, plus thirty matrons. He also offered a limited number of separate dwellings to families that could furnish at least four workers.

---

[53]Lander, *The Textile Industry,* pp. 99–111; John Bauskett to Ann Waddlington, September 25, 1838, and John Bauskett to Thomas Bauskett, April 19, 1839, Thomas Ellison Keitt Papers, DU; Sims, "Joseph Starke Sims," pp. 62–69; George McDuffie to John Bauskett, February 3, 1838, George McDuffie Papers, SCL; Stephen J. Goldfarb, "A Note on Limits to Growth of the Cotton-Textile Industry in the Old South," *Journal of Southern History* 48 (November, 1982):545–558.

[54]Gavin Wright, *Old South, New South,* pp. 125–129; Lander, "Slave Labor in South Carolina Cotton Mills," pp. 161–173; Richard W. Griffin, "Poor White Laborers in Southern Cotton Factories, 1789–1865," *South Carolina Historical Magazine* 41 (January, 1960):26–40.

[55]John Bauskett to Thomas Bauskett, April 19, 1839, Thomas Ellison Keitt Papers, DU; Hiram Hutchinson to John Springs, April 22, 1846, Springs Family Papers, SHC.

The family dwellings filled up quickly, but few young women found the prospect of leaving their rural homes and families for mill work and life in a boarding house attractive. The dormitories remained unfilled, and Gregg moved quickly to recruit more families to his village. In a predominantly rural economy, where the household had long been the primary unit of production as well as consumption, Gregg found it easier to attract whole households to his village than to pry young women away from their families.[56]

Yet even the family recruitment strategy was not without its pitfalls. There were few jobs for adult men in the factory, and thus men were forced to seek other employment, usually in the form of odd jobs in the village or to hire themselves out as farm laborers in the surrounding countryside. Some males found this frustrating. Nor did everyone, whether male or female, adjust readily to factory discipline. Late in 1851, Benjamin C. Yancey, a former Edgefield attorney who had recently moved to Alabama, inquired about placing a hard-pressed white family from his new neighborhood at Graniteville. James Montgomery, treasurer of the Graniteville Manufacturing Company, replied that he did not think it "advisable for the whole family to move at once." Montgomery, still seeking young female labor, suggested that the two "oldest girls come [and] go to a boarding house until they learn the business." As soon as the two young women "became acquainted with the practical working of factory life," they could then judge whether or not the rest of the family should come. "There are many who come to the factories who do not succeed—[who] do not like the work nor the regulations," Montgomery cautioned. The vast horde of poor whites which Gregg thought eager for cotton mill work proved less amenable to factory discipline than he had anticipated. Graniteville managers soon learned what Hiram Hutchinson had known all along. South Carolina whites, if they were to accept factory discipline at all, could be trained "to the Harness best by degrees."[57]

In a provocative analysis of the labor problems faced by textile entrepreneurs in the antebellum South, Gavin Wright has challenged the long-standing belief that labor costs were lower in the Old South than in New England. The boasts of textile promoters concerning the endless supply of cheap labor available in the Southern countryside were exaggerations. White labor was actually comparatively scarce in the South because the free population of the region was smaller and more widely scattered than in the North. Since free labor markets in the antebellum era were decidedly local in nature, good supplies of cheap labor might exist in some areas, but if a factory was established in one of those areas

[56]James Henry Hammond, *Anniversary Oration of the State Agricultural Society of South Carolina* (Columbia, S.C., 1841), pp. 3–26; William Gregg to James Henry Hammond, November 3, 1841, James Henry Hammond Papers, SCL; Charleston *Courier*, November 6, 11, 1845; Laurensville *Herald*, April 14, 1848; J. H. Taylor, "Manufactures in South Carolina," *DeBow's Review* 8 (January, 1850):26–28; Charleston *Courier*, September 8, 1849; Lander, *The Textile Industry*, pp. 60–61; Wright, *Old South, New South*, p. 138.

[57]James Montgomery to Benjamin C. Yancey, October 14, 1851, Benjamin Cudworth Yancey Papers, SHC; Hiram Hutchinson to John Springs, April 22, 1846, Springs Family Papers, SHC.

the local labor supply might soon be exhausted and would seldom be replenished by in-migration. The relative scarcity of labor would then drive up wage rates. Of course Southern entrepreneurs could always turn to slave labor, but, unlike the free labor market, the slave labor market was a regional one. Demand for slave labor anywhere in the slaveholding South could increase the price of slave labor in every corner of the region. During the 1850s, the cotton boom drove slave prices and hiring rates quite high, so textile employers were forced to rely almost exclusively on free labor. But in the South Carolina Upcountry, the increased profits in agriculture, the growing demand for artisanal services, and the new opportunities in commerce also made free labor increasingly scarce and expensive. Thus, more than anything else, rising labor costs stalled the expansion of the textile industry during the 1850s.[58] And, perhaps more important in the long run, the cotton boom of the 1850s made slaves employed in agriculture so valuable that most masters withdrew their slaves from the mills and returned them to farm work. This meant that the overwhelming majority of textile operatives in the late antebellum era, experienced workers who would be available to train "green" hands in the post-Civil War era, were white. In the postbellum era, the determination of these experienced white workers not to train or work alongside black operatives and the political delicacy of integrating white-dominated work forces helped keep the Southern textile industry largely, though certainly not exclusively, a white preserve until well into the twentieth century.[59]

The rising labor costs of the 1850s slowed the growth of textiles and other industries which required sizable labor forces, but agricultural prosperity and the related appreciation of real and personal property values also contributed to the sluggishness of industrial development in the late antebellum era. Returns on capital invested in agriculture were unusually high during the 1850s, and the capital gains enjoyed by those holding land and slaves, as we have seen earlier, were considerable. Thus the returns on capital invested in manufacturing had to be especially lucrative to attract planter-investors.[60] Moreover, the regional mar-

[58]Gavin Wright, "Cheap Labor and Southern Textiles before 1880," *Journal of Economic History* 39 (September, 1979):655–680; see also Gary Saxonhouse and Gavin Wright, "Two Forms of Cheap Labor in Textile History," in Saxonhouse and Wright, eds., *Technique, Spirit and Form in the Making of the Modern Economies: Essays in Honor of William N. Parker* (Greenwich, Conn.: JAI Press, 1984), pp. 3–32; Claudia Goldin and Kenneth Sokoloff, "The Relative Productivity Hypothesis of Industrialism: The American Case, 1820–1850," *Quarterly Journal of Economics* 44 (August, 1984):461–487; Heywood Flesig, "Slavery, the Supply of Agricultural Labor, and the Industrialization of the South," *Journal of Economic History* 36 (September, 1976):572–597; for a study emphasizing the availability of labor in the Graniteville area, see Tom E. Terrill, "Eager Hands: Labor for Southern Textiles, 1850–1860," *Journal of Economic History* 36 (March, 1976):84–99.

[59]On this point, see especially David L. Carlton, *Mill and Town in South Carolina, 1880–1920* (Baton Rouge: Louisiana State University Press, 1982), pp. 75–76, 112–115, 158–160, 244–247; Gavin Wright, "Cheap Labor and Southern Textiles, 1880–1930," *Quarterly Journal of Economics* 96 (November, 1981):605–629; and Stokes, "Black and White Labor," pp. 98–132.

[60]Wright, *Political Economy of the Cotton South*, pp. 89–127; Wright, *Old South, New South*, especially pp. 17–50; Stanley Engerman, "Some Considerations Relating to Property Rights in Man," *Journal of Economic History* 33 (March, 1983):43–65.

ket in slaves, for all its ups and downs, was a far less volatile market than the informal, and highly uncertain, market for industrial stocks such as those of Graniteville and the Upcountry iron companies. Even if rates of return in manufacturing were higher than those in agriculture, as a recent study by Bateman and Weiss suggests, the risk involved in such investment doubtless deterred many planters whose earnings from land and slaves seemed more than acceptable.[61] Banker Hiram Hutchinson, though quite an entrepreneur in his own right, thought that only men "who mix with the world" should invest in railroads because of the risk involved in holding such stocks, and railroad stocks were generally considered far safer investments than stock in manufacturing companies.[62] Thus it was not an ideological aversion to industry or devotion to some grand seigneurial design which prompted Upcountry planters and other investors to hold their assets in the form of land and slaves, but rather a structural characteristic, even a peculiarity, of the slave economy itself. Upcountry planter-investors could earn enormous profits and substantial capital gains without investing heavily in intensive local development simply by putting their money in the regional slave market. Such investment may have supported essentially speculative, rather than productive, endeavors, but during the cotton boom it steadily increased the wealth of the investor.[63]

By encouraging the deployment of some capital in a speculative rather than an entrepreneurial manner, the idiosyncrasies of the slave economy helped slow industrial development during the agricultural boom of the 1850s, but it was a systemic hindrance whose effects could diminish significantly when the cotton boom ended. Certainly both planters and merchants in the Upcountry had long shown a willingness to invest in manufacturing when the economic rewards made it desirable to do so, as demonstrated by long-standing planter investments in such risky ventures as iron works and textile mills. With the railroad system in place, and with a dynamic new class of merchants developing in towns along the railroads, the Upcountry in 1860 may have been poised on the edge of a new era of industrial development, an era which could be ushered in by something as inevitable as the next secular decline in cotton prices.

Overall, the economic changes which occurred in the Upcountry in the 1850s were the most significant to affect the region since the first short-staple cotton boom a half-century earlier. To be sure, the changes were, in large part, predicated on the cyclical upswing of cotton prices, but at the same time the economic expansion of the 1850s was also marked by significant structural shifts in pat-

---

[61]For estimated rates of return on investment in manufacturing, and a different view from my own, see Fred Bateman and Thomas Weiss, *A Deplorable Scarcity: The Failure of Industrialization in the Slave Economy* (Chapel Hill: University of North Carolina Press, 1981), especially pp. 99–156. Bateman and Weiss admit that the profitability of manufacturing in South Carolina was declining during the 1850s, but argue that the Palmetto state was an exception to the general trend.

[62]Hiram Hutchinson to John Springs, May 11, 1848, Springs Family Papers, SHC.

[63]For an excellent analysis of this point, see Gavin Wright, *Political Economy of the Cotton South*, pp. 128–157.

terns of production, exchange, and marketing, as well as in the extent of market orientation, which would long outlive the cotton boom. Despite the agricultural prosperity, and the unprecedented appreciation of land and slave values during the decade, the economic boom of the 1850s was not an example of growth without development. Instead, buoyed by high cotton prices and capital gains in land and slaves, Upcountry entrepreneurs, with planter-investors taking the lead, used the period of renewed prosperity to finance major infrastructural improvements in the region's economy. These improvements not only served the existing agricultural economy but also facilitated the emergence of dynamic new elements in an economy which had not seen much structural change for several decades. The completion of railroads brought new commercial vigor to the flagging economy of Upcountry towns, and together with new banks and new bank agencies, supported the development of an active local cotton trade handled by a new and enterprising group of indigenous cotton traders. Transportation improvements also destroyed the natural protection of small local markets for some commodities in parts of the Upcountry while enhancing the commercial orientation of other producers. The railroad network and embryonic banking system established an economic base in transportation, marketing, and finance that could serve as a foundation for future industrial development in the region. Moreover, to residents of the Upcountry during the 1850s, the transforming power of the infrastructural improvements, and especially of the railroads, was dramatic and unmistakable. "There is nothing like a railroad running through a county," Laurens farmer J. J. Atwood told his brothers in Alabama, "I have $200 in stock in the road and if I never receive a cent of dividend, I will be the better of it than not to have the road. You speak of going to Arkansas or some other new country and advise me to leave this old place—in reply I would advise you to return to this country. It has become an entirely new place."[64]

In many ways, Atwood was right. But what sort of "new place" was the Upcountry in 1860? The answer was certainly not clear to Atwood's contemporaries, and the question has generated a good deal of confusion among historians in more recent times.[65] On the one hand, the flush times of the 1850s, and the concomitant changes in the Upcountry economy, had a distinctly Southern flavor, one seasoned heavily by the peculiarities of a slave economy. The cotton boom itself was generated by forces largely extrinsic to the region. The South was simply a commodity-producing region enjoying great benefit from the world need for its staple. The cotton boom fueled spectacular, and partially speculative, increases in the value of the slave property held by the region's slaveholding minority and thus encouraged continued investment in slavery and pushed slaveholders toward an even more intransigent defense of their peculiar institu-

---

[64]J. J. Atwood to Joseph H. and Menoah Atwood, April 4, 1852, reprinted in the Laurens *Advertiser,* June 10, 1970.

[65]A number of recent interpretations are thoughtfully evaluated in Harold Woodman, "Global and Local Perspectives on Power, Politics, and Ideology," *Civil War History* 25 (December, 1979):339–351; and James Oakes, "The Politics of Economic Development in the Antebellum South," *Journal of Interdisciplinary History* 15 (August, 1984):305–316.

tion. The boom also accentuated certain trends which were seemingly inherent in the South's reliance on slavery and staple agriculture. It widened the absolute economic gap between slaveholders and non-slaveholders, and lured more and more Upcountry farmers into deeper involvement with commercial agriculture.

On the other hand, a number of the changes in the Upcountry economy during the 1850s had clear "Yankee" overtones. Upcountrymen frequently referred to business acumen, dedication to the intensification of commerce, and interest in manufacturing as "Yankee" characteristics and successful Upcountry merchants were often labeled as "close Yankee merchants" or "shrewd Yankee traders" even if they were native sons of the South. The building of the railroads, the creation of bustling railroad towns, the appearance of a new coterie of town merchants, the intensified commercial orientation, especially among small farmers, and the talk of industrialization all clearly carried "Yankee" connotations, despite the fact that many of these changes were sponsored by Southern planters. Despite the continued reliance on slave labor, the Upcountry economy was feeling the first twinges of modernization during the 1850s, as it participated rather vigorously, though in a fashion shaped by slavery, in the "Age of Capital."[66]

Certain political anxieties accompanied each aspect of this economic expansion. Confidence in the cotton economy and the economic stake in slavery were probably at an all-time high during the 1850s, just as external threats to the South's peculiar system were also growing increasingly potent. The desire of Upcountrymen to defend a prosperous economy and a stable labor system against outside interference was a central theme in the politics of the 1850s. It was, however, generally a theme which served as a unifying force despite the potential frustration among non-slaveholders at the growing difficulty of acquiring slaves. The anxieties which grew out of heightened commercial involvement and increased vulnerability to commercial fluctuations, and the distrust of a state government growing more and more active in its sponsorship of economic improvements, however, were tensions which could divide as well as unify, and tensions which did, in fact, divide South Carolinians on questions such as regulation of banks, growth in government spending, and the use of tax money to finance railroad development during the 1850s. Together, when added to South Carolina's already volatile political culture, these anxieties helped produce a decade of political agitation and turmoil which ended in revolution.

[66]Survey of R. G. Dun and Company, Credit Ledgers, South Carolina, I, II, IX–XIV, Baker; Eric Hobsbawn, *The Age of Capital, 1848–1875* (London: Weidenfeld and Nicolson, 1975).

IV

THE CRISIS

The political crisis of the 1850s involved turmoil over state and local issues as well as the heightened agitation of the increasingly explosive sectional controversy. Historians have long acknowledged that the collapse of the Jacksonian party system had a profound impact on politics in those states where party competition had been the warp and woof of political life for the better part of two decades. In the South, outside of South Carolina, Jacksonian party competition served as a method of focusing and expressing political differences over state and local issues. Its role in giving institutionalized expression to internal divisions was every bit as important as its role in bringing coherence to national political dialogue. Internal divisions in the South did not disappear simply because the party system which had given them formal expression disintegrated. Indeed, as Michael F. Holt has observed, "Local and state politics were just as crucial as national developments in shaping the political crisis of the 1850s."[1]

Moreover, most of the explosive state and local issues which generated so much controversy during the 1850s had, at best, only a tangential relationship to the looming sectional crisis. To be sure, Southern politicians and their constituents often disagreed with each other over how best to defend slavery and Southern society against the centralizing tendencies of the federal government and the increasing political potence of the antislavery movement. Yet these disagreements over national issues, though crucial and often extremely bitter, were essentially tactical and strategic rather than fundamental or philosophical. Few Southern leaders doubted that their region had peculiar and vulnerable interests, and few denied that some sort of defensive strategy was mandated by the politicization of antislavery sentiment in the North. At the same time, however, Southern states were being ravaged internally by a series of state and local controversies which would have made the 1850s the most disputatious decade in the region's history even if the issues growing out of the sectional crisis had been ignored. Most of these important and divisive state and local issues fell into one

---

[1]Michael F. Holt, *The Political Crisis of the 1850s* (New York: John Wiley and Sons, 1978), p. 4; see also Joel H. Silbey, *The Partisan Imperative: The Dynamics of American Politics Before the Civil War* (New York: Oxford University Press, 1985), especially pp. 33–68.

of two major categories. One set of issues, including disagreements over legislative apportionment, representation, and basic tax structure, revealed dissatisfaction with the existing distribution of political power. In addition to these disputes, which can be grouped together as "who shall rule at home" issues, a second group of questions, generally rooted in the tensions growing out of the economic development taking place in the South during the 1850s, also stirred up considerable political controversy at the grassroots level. These economic issues, which included disputes over state and local aid to railroads, the relationship between state government and the banks, and laws regarding usury and homestead exemptions, usually centered around fundamental disagreements over what role state and local governments should play in sponsoring or sanctioning economic development.[2]

South Carolina, like most other Southern states, experienced a good deal of controversy over both the "who shall rule at home" and the economic development issues during the 1850s. Indeed, a veritable torrent of disruptive state and local issues threatened the state's remarkable and long-cultivated internal harmony at the very time when growing external threats made that special harmony seem all the more precious. To complicate matters even further, many of these divisive issues surfaced just as the death of Calhoun robbed South Carolina of the leader to whom she had turned, in times both of protest and of reconciliation, for at least a quarter-century.

[2]See J. Mills Thornton III, *Politics and Power in a Slave Society: Alabama, 1800–1860* (Baton Rouge: Louisiana State University Press, 1978), pp. 269–342; Michael P. Johnson, *Toward a Patriarchal Republic: The Secession of Georgia* (Baton Rouge: Louisiana State University Press, 1977); and Alison Goodyear Freehling, *Drift toward Dissolution: The Virginia Slavery Debate of 1831–1832* (Baton Rouge: Louisiana State University Press, 1982), pp. 129–163; Marc W. Kruman, *Parties and Politics in North Carolina, 1836–1865* (Baton Rouge: Louisiana State University Press, 1983), pp. 29–103; Thomas E. Jeffrey, "National Issues, Local Interests, and the Transformation of Antebellum North Carolina Politics," *Journal of Southern History* 50 (February, 1984):43–74.

8

"The Beautiful Harmony in the Body Politic": The Concurrent Majority and the Controversy over Who Shall Rule at Home

Despite the concessions made by the parishes in 1808, the Upcountry never gained the whip hand in South Carolina politics. As the years passed, the famous Compromise of 1808 was more and more frequently portrayed by Lowcountry politicians and a few of their prominent Upcountry allies as a sacred and inviolable bargain struck between the two sections. The bargain guaranteed the parishes effective control of the state senate while conceding a nominal majority in the house to the districts of the upper division. The intent of the agreement was to give the Lowcountry, narrowly defined as simply the state's twenty-one parishes, all of which had black majorities as early as 1790, and the Upcountry, broadly defined to include not only those districts above the fall line but also the state's middle and Pee Dee districts, an equal voice in state government. Obviously such a balance could be achieved only by limiting the power of the white majority of the Upcountry. To accomplish this, representation in the state legislature was not apportioned on the basis of white population. In the senate, each unit of local government, whether district or parish, was given one senator. In the house, representation was apportioned on the twin bases of white population and taxable property. As a result, the Lowcountry dominated the senate, while the wealthy parishes were over-represented in the house because property as well as white population was a factor in apportionment. Nevertheless the inland districts did hold a clear majority in the lower chamber.[1]

---

[1]Chauncey Samuel Boucher, "Sectionalism, Representation, and the Electoral Question in Antebellum South Carolina," *Washington University Studies* 4 (October, 1916):3–62; William A. Schaper, "Sectionalism and Representation in South Carolina: A Sociological Study," in the *Annual Report of the American Historical Association for the Year 1900* (Washington: Government Printing Office, 1901), vol. 1, pp. 237–464.

The arrangement established in 1808 was remarkably successful in achieving its original goal. In practice as well as in theory, Upcountry and Lowcountry each held veto power in the legislature over the other's actions. Moreover, the interests of property, and especially slave property, were strongly represented in Columbia. Thus South Carolina had stumbled into the practice of government by "concurrent majority" long before Calhoun ever presented his systematic formulation of that theory. During the late antebellum era, however, some Upcountry politicians, no longer satisfied with the terms of the bargain, demanded renegotiation. An equal voice in state government and practical veto power over parish-supported proposals in the legislature were no longer enough to appease many Upcountry politicians. They chafed under what they perceived as "parish domination" of the state legislature and at the wildly disproportionate power that could be wielded by just a few score whites in certain parishes. Lowcountry parishes making up the districts of Beaufort and Georgetown sent ten men to the house to represent less than 11,000 whites, while the Upcountry districts of Greenville and Spartanburg sent nine men to the house to represent over 32,000 whites. Such over-representation of the parishes produced charges from the Upcountry that state government was "anti-democratic" and that the Upcountry majority was subjugated by "masters of overgrown plantations" or "barons of the low country."[2]

Such Upcountry protests against the status quo established by the Compromise of 1808 arose as early as the nullification era. Benjamin F. Perry and other Unionists agitated the issue of "parish domination" during the nullification era in a calculated effort to weaken the Nullifiers in the Upcountry, but pro-nullification forces responded quickly and effectively. Under the pseudonym "Upper Country," a leading Nullifier defended the "solemn agreement and compromise by which each section of the State acquires a perfect security for its peculiar interests." The Compromise of 1808, "Upper Country" insisted, was regarded by "the upper and middle districts" as "a most just and wise adjustment" to which the people of the interior were bound "by every principle of honor and patriotism."[3] Since the Nullifiers carried the Upcountry handily, there is little evidence that Perry's efforts to fan the flames of sectional rivalry within the state enhanced the appeal of Unionism among Upcountrymen to any significant degree. If anything, it appears that Perry's gambit, which entangled the apportionment issue with South Carolina's stance on major national questions, actually played into the hands of his opponents and worked to the long-term disadvantage of those who favored reapportionment. Perry's identification of reapportionment with Unionism in 1832 helped solidify the tenuous alliance between unabashed defenders of the status quo and those Nullifiers who were at least nominally sympathetic to calls for a reapportionment along lines more favorable to the

[2]Boucher, "Sectionalism, Representation, and the Electoral Question," pp. 39–41; Greenville *Southern Patriot,* May 9 and July 25, 1851.
[3]Columbia *Telescope,* October 2, 1832.

Upcountry but who felt that the apportionment issue was secondary to the need for South Carolina to stand firm against the expansion of federal power.[4]

Moreover, Perry's insistence upon mixing questions concerning the distribution of power within the state with the issue of South Carolina's relationship with the national government allowed defenders of the existing system to couch their defense in terms which extolled the strategic virtues of maintaining the existing peace between the various portions of the state so that South Carolina might present a bold and united front to the federal government. As early as 1838, Calhoun advised his supporters in South Carolina against trying to change the balance of power in state government. "The tendency of our State Govern- [ment], as it now stands," Calhoun maintained, "is to union among ourselves, as experience amply proves." This unity, Calhoun continued, "results from our peculiar political institutions, which from the admirable adjustment of the conflicting political elements of the State, prevents any one from gaining the ascendancy and oppressing the other, and thus preserves [the] harmony . . . which so strongly characterizes our State, and gives it that disperportional [sic] weight in the Union compared to its population and wealth."[5] Many Upcountrymen, perhaps even a majority, agreed with Calhoun's estimation that, as a small state, South Carolina's influence in national affairs depended on internal harmony. Thus Perry's attempts to use the "parish domination" issue as a political hobby against Calhoun in the Upcountry not only failed; they backfired, diluting otherwise strong grassroots support for proposals which called for the democratization of state government by associating those potentially popular proposals with the generally unpopular idea that South Carolina should temper its radical opposition to what it perceived as the usurpation of power by the federal government.

Most Upcountry politicians considered the terms of the Compromise of 1808 as onerous yet binding. The terms were clearly unfair to the Upcountry, and gave the parishes a degree of influence over state affairs that galled ordinary Upcountrymen. Yet short of open rebellion, the Upcountry had little choice except to live with the arrangement. Any alteration of the existing system required amendment of the state constitution, and the provision for amending that aged but august document required that all amendments receive the support of a two-thirds' majority of two successive General Assemblies. In other words, the parishes would have to preside over their own demise, willingly stripping themselves of the power to block all state legislation they considered inimical to their interests. Recognizing that the parishes' ability to block all constitutional amendments rendered the reapportionment of the state legislature virtually impossible,

---

[4]On Perry's efforts, see Lillian A. Kibler, *Benjamin F. Perry: South Carolina Unionist* (Durham, N.C.: Duke University Press, 1946), pp. 225–238, and 260–278; James Wylie Gettys, "Mobilization for Secession in Greenville District" (M.A. thesis, University of South Carolina, 1967), pp. 67–89.

[5]John C. Calhoun to Alton H. Pemberton, November 19, 1838, and John C. Calhoun to Armistead Burt, December 24, 1838, in Clyde N. Wilson, ed., *The Papers of John C. Calhoun* (Columbia, S.C.: University of South Carolina Press, 1981), vol. 14, pp. 459–461, 498–499.

Upcountry political leaders resigned themselves to living with the terms of the Compromise. Doubtless, Upcountrymen chafed under the restrictive political yoke of malapportionment, but they accepted their responsibility to the compromise dutifully, if grudgingly.[6]

But if legislative reapportionment seemed beyond the reach of Upcountry leaders, reforms in related aspects of the state's political system lurked within the realm of the possible. Upcountry political leaders sourly conceded that undue parish influence in the state legislature, arising from the seemingly sacrosanct system of apportionment, was an unpleasant but unalterable fact of political life in South Carolina. But Upcountry leaders were not, on the whole, reconciled to the dominance of state politics by the state legislature. In South Carolina, the legislature not only elected a number of local office-holders but also elected both the governor of the state and the presidential electors, long after every other state had turned these elections over to the people. Not only did the legislature's continued control of these elections defy the momentum of Jacksonian democracy and act as a barrier to the creation of a permanent two-party system in the state but it also allowed the parish minority disproportionate influence in the selection of the governor and the presidential electors because of its exaggerated representation in the legislature.[7] Pressures of *realpolitik* in South Carolina dictated that there would be no serious reapportionment of the legislature, but some Upcountry political leaders were nevertheless determined to chip away at the Lowcountry's political clout by divesting the legislature of a small, but symbolically important, portion of its enormous power.

The bit of legislative prerogative most vulnerable to attack was the legislature's control of the election of the governor and presidential electors. A number of influential Upcountry politicians, including many who supported Calhoun on most matters, as well as a few of his perennial opponents, wanted to give the election of those officials to the people. Popular election of the governor and presidential electors would, in effect, give the Upcountry control over those offices unless the region's voters were badly divided. This increase in the Upcountry's political clout, especially on national issues, would serve to counterbalance the disproportionate power of the Lowcountry in the state legislature. Since the governor had very little power other than that of a propagandist, the only real concession required of the Lowcountry was a diminution of its influence over the state's position in national politics. By and large, the Lowcountry could have acquiesced in giving the election of the governor and the presidential electors to the people without seriously compromising its position in state politics, and, at the same time, have done something to mollify the Upcountry. The

---

[6]Greenville *Mountaineer*, June 11, 1830, and October 6, 1832; Charleston *Mercury*, November 1, 1834; Charleston *Southern Patriot*, August 19, 1836; John C. Calhoun to James Henry Hammond, February 18, 1837, in Wilson, ed., *The Papers of John C. Calhoun*, vol. 13, pp. 442–444; Francis W. Pickens to Armistead Burt, December 11, 1844, Armistead Burt Papers, DU.

[7]For an introduction to Calhoun's ideas of this subject, see Charles M. Wiltse, *John C. Calhoun, Sectionalist, 1840–1850* (Indianapolis: Bobbs-Merrill, 1951), pp. 289–291.

Lowcountry, however, refused to surrender any of its power voluntarily, even as a conciliatory gesture designed to placate an increasingly restless Upcountry.[8]

In the face of Lowcountry intransigence, Upcountry politicians looked for an opportunity to press for democratic elections of presidential electors. Opportunity presented itself in 1846, when Congress passed a bill fixing a uniform day for holding presidential elections. Customarily, the South Carolina legislature did not convene until three weeks after the day fixed by Congress, so, in order to comply with the new federal law, South Carolina was either forced to call a special session of the legislature every four years, or, as many Upcountry leaders hoped, alter her method of choosing presidential electors. Upcountry politicians, led by B. F. Perry, seized the opening to campaign vigorously for popular election of the state's presidential electors. Debate over the issue filled the important newspapers throughout the fall of 1846, and in most districts candidates for the state legislature were required to take a stand on the issue, which promised to loom large when the new legislature met in late November. In mid-November, however, one week after the election of legislators and just two weeks before the legislative session was scheduled to begin, the hopes of Upcountry reformers were dealt a devastating blow when Calhoun reaffirmed his opposition to the popular election of presidential electors in a public letter to members of the Pendleton legislative delegation.[9]

Calhoun had actually composed his defense of the existing system nearly a month earlier, after James L. Orr and a number of other important Upcountry politicians asked for his views on the issue, but he delayed publication of his opinion to avoid the appearance of trying to influence hotly contested legislative elections. Calhoun's argument against changing the method of electing presidential electors was elaborate and multi-faceted, but it rested on one fundamental principle—that the unique conception of republican government implemented through the peculiar political structure of South Carolina and nurtured by several generations of Palmetto politicians must be preserved. To save its unusually harmonious political system, Calhoun argued, the state must remain true to the principles of the Compromise of 1808, which placed both Upcountry and Lowcountry "on grounds of perfect political equality." The two regions, Calhoun contended, constituted "not only the two great geographical, but also the two great political divisions of the State, on which its political fabric rests." The homogenizing effect of more than fifty years of statehood had failed to eliminate the great distinctions, one demographic and one ethnocultural, which set the Upcountry and Lowcountry apart. The demographic difference between the regions was simply "the great excess of the slave population of the one [Low-

---

[8]Boucher, "Sectionalism, Representation, and the Electoral Question," pp. 19–32; Kibler, *Perry,* pp. 225–230; Pendleton *Messenger,* November 29, 1844; Greenville *Mountaineer,* January 10, 1845; Charleston *Mercury,* August 26, September 10 and 28, 1846; The Charleston *Courier,* October 7, 1846.

[9]Calhoun's letter was printed in the Pendleton *Messenger,* November 13, 1846. The letter has also been printed in Richard K. Crallé, ed., *The Works of John C. Calhoun* (New York: D. Appleton, 1855), vol. 6, pp. 254–272.

country], compared with the other," while the lingering ethnocultural distinctions harkened back to the original differences between the largely Anglican Englishmen, joined by a generous sprinkling of Huguenots, who settled the parishes and the hordes of Celtic, most often Scotch-Irish, backwoodsmen, who poured into the Piedmont from the North, bringing all manner of dissenting religious beliefs with them. That Calhoun, whose own father sallied forth from his farm in Long Canes as the champion of his fellow Scotch-Irish back-countrymen against the political power structure of the parishes, would remain sensitive to the persistent differences between Upcountry and Lowcountry, is hardly surprising. Yet for Calhoun, a son of the backcountry, the desire to transcend those recognized differences was paramount. He guarded the terms of the truce, as embodied in the Compromise of 1808, as jealously as his father had worked to achieve parity for the Upcountry a generation earlier.[10]

Taking the election of presidential electors away from the legislature and giving it to the people would, Calhoun warned, violate the spirit, if not the letter, of the binding accommodation between the regions. By Calhoun's calculations, about 55 percent of the state's voting population lived north and west of the fall line, giving the Upcountry the ability to control popular statewide elections even without the support of voters in those areas, such as the Pee Dee, which lay below the fall line but which did not ordinarily side with the black-majority parishes on state issues. Thus a united Upcountry could exercise unilateral control over the selection of presidential electors if their election were given to the people. Calhoun viewed such a change as a violation of the sacred compromise. "That a mode of appointing which would lead to such a result," Calhoun argued, "would be neither fair nor just towards the lower division, no one, who has any regard to equity or justice, will deny." Moreover, Calhoun continued:

> If I do not greatly mistake, the upper country has too deep a sense of both [equity and justice] to wish it, even if it had the power; and if it had, and should attempt to exercise it, the lower has too much spirit to acquiesce in it. But, thanks to the justice and wisdom of our State Constitution, neither of the divisions has the power to encroach on the just rights of the other. It has secured to each the power to protect itself; so that neither can oppress or injure the other, should it desire it.[11]

Half of Calhoun's objection to the popular election of presidential electors, therefore, grew out of his desire to maintain a balance of power between two very different subregions within his state by preserving a truce negotiated by "sensible and patriotic men" on both sides nearly forty years earlier. For Calhoun, the moral obligation to uphold the terms of that political bargain was reason enough to oppose any change in the system of choosing presidential electors, but it was not his only, or even his most important, reason for doing so.

[10]See Crallé, *Works of Calhoun*, vol. 6, especially pp. 259–264.
[11]*Ibid.*, p. 261.

Calhoun also feared that popular election of electors would prove to be the vanguard of a false or illusory democratic revolution in state politics which would destroy the state's delicate experiment with true republicanism, an experiment over which Calhoun had been chief custodian for much of his political life. Popular election of presidential electors, Calhoun maintained, would not give "power to the people," but "would be the most effectual way that could be devised of divesting them of it, and transferring it to party managers and cliques." In South Carolina, Calhoun estimated, there were about 50,000 voters scattered over an area of approximately 30,000 square miles. In such a situation, any general election did not constitute a true election but instead "a mere delusion, undeserving the name." The reason that general elections provided only the illusion of democracy, Calhoun argued, was that "it is impossible for the great body of voters to be guided by their individual knowledge in selecting the candidates, either from personal acquaintance or reputation, which is indispensable to that exercise of judgment in making a selection necessary to constitute an election." Moreover, not only would the "great mass of voters" be unable to exercise judgment based on knowledge or reputation of the candidates running in a statewide race but "even the most intelligent and best informed would be at a loss to do it." Calhoun was not complaining that ordinary South Carolinians were ill-equipped to exercise the franchise, but simply that national or statewide elections were ill-suited to rural republics.[12]

What worried Calhoun most, however, was not the natural and inevitable limitations on the voters' knowledge, but the political forces which rushed in to fill the vacuum created by voter uncertainty. Statewide elections would eventually generate "two parties, with all the usual party machinery of caucus, conventions, cliques, and managers" in an effort to woo voters and win the race. Calhoun believed that once parties were created, they "would not be slow" in extending their jurisdiction far beyond the election of presidential electors to "the nomination of the Governor, Lieutenant-Governor, Senators in Congress, Judges, and all others elected by the Legislature." Soon the party system, with "all its train of party divisions and party managers," and with all its "cliques and machinery," would control state politics. Burgeoning patronage systems and widespread corruption would not be far behind. For Calhoun, however, the evils of sustained party politics went far beyond the increased coarseness or vulgarity of political discourse, and even beyond the likelihood of spreading corruption. Party competition would eventually lead, he reasoned, to the "taking of the sense of the State" through "the mere numerical majority." Of all forms of power in a popular government, Calhoun argued, the power of the majority was "by far the most absorbing in its character, and [the most] difficult to counteract." The power of the numerical majority was "indeed but the absolute and despotic form of popular government, just as much as the absolute and despotic form of one man or a few is of the monarchical and aristocratical." It was, after all, liberty, not democracy, which must be preserved. The power of the many,

[12]*Ibid.*, pp. 255–259.

just like that of the one or the few, was the natural enemy of liberty and had to be checked.[13]

It was this sensitivity to the dangers of the tyranny of the majority that set Calhoun, and many of his more attentive followers, apart from typical Jacksonian politicians outside South Carolina. Good Jacksonians everywhere feared unchecked power just as much as Calhoun did. Moreover, good Jacksonians feared the unchecked power of government every bit as much as, if not more than, they feared the power of a monster bank, a huge standing army, corporate privilege, or concentrated wealth. Yet outside South Carolina, Jacksonians increasingly viewed partisan politics as an effective method of containing governmental power. In the proper hands, the powers of government could be actively used in a negative fashion, protecting the liberty of the people by checking dangerous concentrations of power, especially in the form of corporate wealth and privilege, which were forming outside government. At the same time, Jacksonians believed, popular control of the government guaranteed that the government itself would not become an instrument of oppression. Thus, to a certain extent, the Jacksonians were drifting away from the complex code of republican political ethics inherited from the Revolutionary era and toward a more modern formulation of republicanism which emphasized the role of political democracy, and of the machinery of democratic politics, in checking or controlling the power at the expense, at least up to a point, of constitutional guarantees. The broad ideological ends of Jacksonian democracy were still those of the received republican tradition—to protect the independence of the people from its dreaded and tireless enemy, unchecked power. But the preferred means of achieving those ends were being gradually modified even if most Jacksonians failed to recognize the modifications. The political success of early Jacksonian popular crusades against special privilege, corporate wealth, and "aristocratic" cliques, along with the continued expansion of democracy through constitutional reforms at the state and local level, created a growing faith in the beneficent impact of democracy itself, rather than in the institutional mechanisms and constitutional system of checks and balances in which the Founding Fathers had vested their hopes for the future of the Republic.[14]

Calhoun was quick to recognize ideological heresy when he saw it, even when it was wrapped in so winsome a disguise as that of democracy or majority rule. Calhoun, of course, had seen the earlier schism between South Carolina on the one hand and Jacksonians in the rest of the South on the other over the issue

[13]*Ibid.*, especially pp. 265–272.

[14]The literature on the role of republicanism in American politics during the first half of the nineteenth century is vast and growing. The best recent survey of this literature is Sean Wilentz, "On Class and Politics in Jacksonian America," in Stanley I. Kutler and Stanley N. Katz, eds., *The Promise of American History: Progress and Prospects* (Baltimore: Johns Hopkins University Press, 1982), pp. 45–63. The best state study of these issues is Thornton, *Politics and Power in a Slave Society: Alabama, 1800–1860* (Baton Rouge: Louisiana State University Press, 1978), and the best local study is Harry L. Watson, *Jacksonian Politics and Community Conflict: The Emergence of the Second Party System in Cumberland County, North Carolina* (Chapel Hill: University of North Carolina Press, 1982).

of nullification as essentially a conflict between the logic of the republican political tradition expressed in the innovative concept of state interposition and the growing popular belief that democracy itself could protect republican citizens against the steady encroachments of governmental power. Outside South Carolina, Southern Jacksonians felt that high tariffs and all future oppressive measures could best be resisted by controlling the democratic process and keeping the reins of government in safe hands. Calhoun, on the other hand, saw the need for some constitutional mechanisms which provided a meaningful check on all forms of governmental power, including those arising from policies enjoying the approval of a majority. Calhoun's position had changed little by 1846. The distinguished South Carolinian still drew upon an older, and to his mind purer, brand of republicanism than did most other Jacksonians. Whatever the virtues of democracy, and in Calhoun's eyes they were many, it was nevertheless not without its attendant vices. Popular elections and the democratic political process were crucial to the health and safety of republics, but true republicanism allowed no more license to a majority than to an oligarchy or an autocrat. American republicanism was not majoritarianism or populism. Its aim was not merely to insure majority rule or to guarantee that the popular will would be done. Its aim was to serve a higher purpose: the defense of the liberty and political rights of all citizens.[15]

It was on these grounds that Calhoun justified his concept of the concurrent majority and his opposition to popular election of presidential electors. Calhoun rejected what he referred to as "the final and radical assumption" of those who favored popular election of electors, "that the majority has the natural, inherent and indefeasible right of governing." Calhoun branded this assumption as "unfounded" and "of the most dangerous character." Instead, Calhoun argued:

> All natural rights are individual rights, and belong to them as such. They appertain neither to majorities nor minorities. On the contrary, all political rights are conventional. Neither majorities nor minorities can rightfully exercise any such, but by compact or agreement, expressed or implied. . . . Some of the States of the Union, it would seem, have based their Constitution on the assumption that the mere numerical majority has the right to govern. . . . But such is not our case. Our State is organized on the far broader, and more solid and durable, foundation of the concurrent majority, to the entire exclusion of the numerical.[16]

Government by concurrent majority prevented any "mere numerical majority" from seizing the reins of government and expanding its power at the expense of the independence of the individual citizen. Fundamentally, government by con-

[15]See John C. Calhoun, "A Disquisition on Government," in Crallé, ed., *The Works of Calhoun*, vol. 1, pp. 1–107; Robert E. Shalhope, "Republicanism and Early American Historiography," *William and Mary Quarterly* 39 (April, 1982):334–356; Lance Banning, "Jeffersonian Ideology Revisited: Liberal and Classical Ideas in the New American Republic," *William and Mary Quarterly*, 43 (January, 1986):3–19.

[16]Crallé, *Works of Calhoun*, vol. 6, pp. 269–270.

current majority was government through consensus rather than through party competition. Drawing on his experience in South Carolina, Calhoun again fashioned an innovative, and indeed novel, mechanism for saving an old and respected, but increasingly archaic, set of republican ideals. The original republican prescription for governance, as Calhoun interpreted it, called for checking the power of those elected to rule so as to preserve the maximum possible latitude for individual autonomy. Liberty, or personal independence, was essentially a static quality, a condition in which the citizen was free, or as nearly free as is possible, from the manipulation of external forces other than those emanating from God or nature. Thus individual liberty could be best guaranteed by minimizing external interference and severely restricting the government's power to place any except the most fundamental sanctions on individual freedom of action. Embracing this old but familiar set of republican ideals, Calhoun eschewed the new and popular strain of republicanism which was emerging as American politics adopted an increasingly democratic style during the Jacksonian era. A transfusion of the raw power of Jacksonian democracy into the brittle arteries of republicanism not only invigorated that ideology but also transformed it in important ways. Party competition, not slow consensus building, emerged as the dominant theme of Jacksonian politics, and with the rise of party competition came more than a whiff of the majoritarian sentiment, *vox populi, vox dei,* which was so feared by republican theorists like Calhoun. A well-organized majority, especially when held tightly in line with party discipline, might trample roughshod over individual liberties in pursuit of programmatic party goals. Few Jacksonian Democrats pushed their advantages so hard, and Whigs seldom had the chance, but Calhoun nevertheless feared such possibilities.[17]

The results of government by concurrent majority in South Carolina, Calhoun contended, were sanguine. The state was "blessed with a unanimity of sentiment and freedom from parties altogether without example in any other member of the Union." In Calhoun's view, the last thing the state needed was the emergence of intense party competition over the popular election of the governor and the presidential electors. Calhoun characterized such a development as "an entire and disastrous political revolution" which would replace rule by the concurrent majority with rule by the numerical majority. The triumph of the numerical majority would necessarily transform South Carolina from "a beautiful and well-adjusted Republick, protecting the interests of all, and uttering the voice of the whole community" into "a wild factious and despotick democracy under the control of the dominant interest."[18]

[17]*Ibid.,* pp. 254–272. On the various strains of republican thought flourishing in early nineteenth-century America, see Daniel Walker Howe, "European Sources of Political Ideas in Jeffersonian America," in Kutler and Katz, eds., *The Promise of American History,* pp. 28–44. The standard overview of the Jacksonian party system is still Richard P. McCormick, *The Second American Party System: Party Formation in the Jacksonian Era* (Chapel Hill: University of North Carolina Press, 1966).

[18]Pendleton *Messenger,* November 13, 1846; John C. Calhoun to Alton H. Pemberton, November 19, 1838, in Wilson, ed., *The Papers of John C. Calhoun,* vol. 14, pp. 459–461.

Calhoun's public opposition to the popular election of presidential electors, though hardly unexpected, dealt the movement a severe setback, but Perry and a handful of other Upcountry leaders continued to push for the measure. When the legislature convened in late November, the issue was debated vigorously for ten days, but the senate killed the measure by a vote of 26 to 15 and the house took no action on the moot bill. In the senate vote, all of the senators representing Lowcountry parishes voted against any change in the mode of electing electors. By contrast, the Upcountry was far from unanimous in its support of the change. Senators from Edgefield, Abbeville, Union, and Fairfield voted with the parishes, and the senators from Chester and Laurens did not vote. Without solid Upcountry support, the bill was doomed.[19]

In 1847, however, some Upcountry leaders again pushed for the popular election of presidential electors, but chose to make their fight first in the house, where the Upcountry enjoyed a majority, before trying to guide the measure through the parish-dominated senate. In December 1847, the house approved a bill giving the election of the presidential electors to the people by a margin of 64 to 54. The vote was essentially a straight sectional division. All Lowcountry representatives, except the solitary member from the white-majority district of Horry, voted against the bill, while the Upcountry cast only five votes against the bill, with four of those five votes coming from the delegation representing Fairfield, which had the lowest proportion of whites in the region. The bill was again killed easily in the senate, with senators from Abbeville, Union, and Fairfield joining the Lowcountry in opposing the change.[20] The indefatigable B. F. Perry introduced the measure in the senate again in 1848, hoping the new senate elected in the fall would respond to voter preferences and approve the measure. In 1848, Perry's bill picked up two votes from the parishes, but was nevertheless defeated in the senate on a close vote, 23 to 21. Eleven of the thirteen Upcountry senators joined a united Pee Dee in favor of the bill, but the two crucial swing votes, belonging to William H. Gist of Union and John Buchanan of Fairfield, were cast against the change.[21]

Defeat of the measure in 1848 ended agitation of the issue for several years, as South Carolinians united to defend their right to carry slaves into western territories. Perry raised the issue again during the secession campaign of 1851 in an effort to rally Upcountrymen behind Cooperation or even outright Unionism by linking separate state secession to Lowcountry dominance of state politics. Many of Perry's Cooperationist allies doubted the wisdom of his strategy, since

[19]*Journal of the Senate of the State of South Carolina, 1846* (Columbia, S.C.: Summer and Carroll, 1846), p. 113; Charleston *Courier*, December 14, 15 and 16, 1846; John T. Seibels to his father, December 25, 1846, Seibels Family Papers, SCL.

[20]*Journal of the House of Representatives of the State of South Carolina, 1847* (Columbia, S.C.: A. G. Summer, 1847), pp. 145–151; *Journal of the Senate of the State of South Carolina, 1847* (Columbia, S.C.: A. G. Summer, 1847), pp. 88 and 130; Charleston *Courier*, December 9, 1847; Henry H. Conner to Armistead Burt, January 20, 1848, Armistead Burt Papers, DU.

[21]*Journal of the Senate of the State of South Carolina, 1848* (Columbia, S.C.: A. S. Johnston, 1848), pp. 115–117. For maps of all these votes, see Boucher, "Sectionalism, Representation, and the Electoral Question," pp. 31, 33, and 39.

it not only aggravated existing tensions between the regions at the very time when Cooperationists were attempting to cultivate Lowcountry support in the fight against the Secessionists but also diverted grassroots attention from the real crisis involving the state's relationship with the federal government, a relationship which even Cooperationists believed to be deteriorating. Still, despite objections from those preoccupied with larger strategic concerns, the legislature resumed debate of "who shall rule at home" issues well before the first secession crisis dissipated.[22]

In 1851, the discussion shifted from the question of popular election of presidential electors to that of giving the Upcountry additional representation in the state senate by dividing the large and populous electoral district of Pendleton, which was already divided into two judicial districts, into two election districts. An amendment to the state constitution proposing to divide Pendleton was introduced in the house and passed with the necessary two-thirds' majority. The senate, however, failed to give the amendment the necessary two-thirds' approval, with twenty-two senators voting in favor of the bill and eighteen voting against it. The Upcountry voted as a bloc in favor of the division, while all eighteen nays came from the Lowcountry. The senate might have been willing to accept the division of Pendleton, a move which would give the Upcountry only one extra vote in the senate, but feared establishing a precedent which would invite other large districts in the Upcountry to seek a similar division. The Charleston *Mercury* interpreted the Upcountry's strident and acrimonious response to the defeat of the Pendleton bill as a threat "to declare a war of extermination against the parishes."[23] But Arthur Simkins, a prominent Upcountry planter and editor of the Edgefield *Advertiser* who was an outspoken radical during the first secession crisis, warned his friends and allies among the parish elite that the defeat of the proposal to divide Pendleton openly invited increased strife between Upcountry and Lowcountry. The intransigence of the Lowcountry, Simkins predicted, would give the "various demagogues of the upcountry a hobby on which to ride" in their efforts to "ride down the existing Compromise between the two sections of our state." Most Upcountrymen, Simkins insisted, were willing "to suffer that Compromise to stand intact as long as it works as well as it heretofore has done," but the Edgefield editor also cautioned his "low country brethren" that this "conservative feeling" might change dramatically if the Lowcountry refused to show any flexibility on the Pendleton question.[24]

To the surprise of many political observers in the state, an important segment of the Lowcountry elite heeded this solemn warning and others like it. In December 1852, the house again passed the amendment dividing Pendleton by an

[22]Greenville *Southern Patriot*, April 4 and May 9, 1851; Laurensville *Herald*, September 26 and October 10, 1851.

[23]*Journal of the House of Representatives of the State of South Carolina, 1851* (Columbia, S.C.: I. C. Morgan, 1851), pp. 184–186; *Journal of the Senate of the State of South Carolina, 1851* (Columbia, S.C.: I. C. Morgan, 1851); Charleston *Mercury,* December 30, 1851.

[24]Edgefield *Advertiser,* December 25, 1851.

overwhelming vote, 91 to 25, but this time the senate also gave the amendment the needed two-thirds' approval, passing it by a vote of 31 to 12. The rural parishes still tended to oppose the amendment, but the politically influential Charleston *Mercury,* representing a still potent rump of the old Calhounite "junto" in the Lowcountry convinced several Lowcountry senators to support the bill. The *Mercury* supported the bill as a gesture of respect and conciliation toward the Upcountry with the hope that it would remove "a constant theme for carping against the parish representation." In 1854, the bill again received two-thirds' approval of both houses of the legislature and, as a result, became part of the state constitution. The creation of an additional senate seat for the Upcountry was a small concession for the Lowcountry to make, and it still left the parishes only a few votes shy of a controlling majority in the upper house. A handful of Upcountry politicians, led by the volatile George D. Tillman of Edgefield, warned that the Upcountry would not be pacified by such a meager concession, and voted to continue the fight against "parish rule."[25]

Even antebellum South Carolina produced few politicians as colorful or as obstreperous as George Dionysius Tillman. Born in Edgefield district in 1826, George Tillman was the son of Benjamin Ryan Tillman, Sr., a successful planter who owned fifty slaves and 1800 acres of land when he died in 1848, and the much older brother of Benjamin R. Tillman, Jr., the fiery leader of agrarian revolt in postbellum South Carolina who served as governor of the state from 1890 to 1894 before winning election to the United States Senate. George Tillman received his early education at rural academies in South Carolina and Georgia, attended Harvard for one year, and then returned to Edgefield to read law under the respected Francis H. Wardlaw, a political ally of Calhoun. Tillman was admitted to the bar in 1848 and settled in Edgefield village, where he enjoyed an active law practice. After the death of their father, George Tillman served as something of a "second father" to young Ben, who was twenty-one years his junior. The younger Tillman may have learned part of his flamboyant and caustic speaking style and his irreverent stump manner from his older brother, but "Pitchfork Ben" also displayed organizational skills, political savvy, and interest in policy details that George Tillman seldom demonstrated. Still, George Tillman's early career doubtless served as something of a political school for Ben, even if the pupil actually learned more than the teacher taught. Even George Tillman's opponents credited him with "a keen vivacious intellect," but he was also a hot-tempered young scion of the South Carolina chivalry described by his father as a man "not of a disposition to submit to imposition or insult." Tillman fought three duels before reaching the age of forty-five, and his temper temporarily derailed his political ambitions when he killed an Edgefield mechanic during a quarrel over a faro game in 1856. Facing murder charges, Tillman

---

[25]*Journal of the House of Representatives of the State of South Carolina, 1852* (Columbia, S.C.: R. W. Gibbes, 1852), pp. 105–113; *Journal of the Senate of the State of South Carolina, 1852* (Columbia, S.C.: R. W. Gibbes, 1852), pp. 127–128; Charleston *Mercury,* December 11, 1852 and December 4, 1854.

fled the country. He sought refuge in Nicaragua, where he joined William Walker on the latter's famous "filibuster." When Walker was captured by the United States Navy in 1857, Tillman was also taken prisoner and deported to the United States. Upon his arrival in South Carolina, Tillman, still a fugitive, hid in his mother's house until his family convinced him to surrender to the local authorities. Tillman was tried and convicted of manslaughter. He was sentenced to two years in the Edgefield jail and fined $500. While serving his sentence (1858–60), Tillman apparently resumed his law practice, but he refused a pardon offered by Edgefield native Francis Pickens when Pickens became governor in 1860.[26]

During the early 1850s, however, George Tillman's personal tribulations lay in the future. In 1851, Tillman was a loquacious radical who gave full-throated support to separate state secession, but as soon as that crisis passed he proved equally energetic and outspoken in his opposition to "parish domination" of South Carolina politics. Tillman's own family certainly belonged to the planter elite of the Upcountry. In 1860, the Tillmans were worth over $100,000 and were one of only 100 or so of Edgefield's nearly 3000 white families who owned as many as fifty slaves. Yet despite this relative wealth, the Tillmans were not as rich as the Butlers, the Pickens, the Simkins, or the Brooks families, and the Tillman genealogical chart listed fewer names of distinguished and influential South Carolinians than did those of the so-called "first families" of Edgefield. This comparative lack of distinction and social prestige appears to have made a strong impression on the ambitious George Tillman, who, despite his family's wealth, entered politics as the self-styled champion of the Upcountry's white majority and an unstinting critic of the powerful Lowcountry gentry. Of course, even though he occasionally turned his savage oratory on the Upcountry gentry as well, Tillman's fundamental complaints were based on sectional rather than class grievances, and most of his proposed reforms would have opened new opportunities for members of Edgefield's own gentry while diluting the influence of the parish elite.[27]

In 1853, while the constitutional amendment dividing Pendleton into two election districts was still awaiting ratification, Tillman suggested a similar division for Edgefield, and possibly Spartanburg as well. Each division would have given the Upcountry an additional seat in the state senate and, in all likelihood,

---

[26]N. Louise Bailey, Mary L. Morgan, and Carolyn R. Taylor, eds., *Biographical Directory of the South Carolina Senate, 1776–1985* (Columbia, S.C.: University of South Carolina Press, 1986), vol. 3, pp. 1613–1615; Francis Butler Simkins, *Pitchfork Ben Tillman* (Baton Rouge: Louisiana State University Press, 1944), pp. 23–56; Orville Vernon Burton, *In My Father's House Are Many Mansions: Family and Community in Edgefield, South Carolina* (Chapel Hill: University of North Carolina Press, 1985), especially pp. 51–77, 91–106; Charleston *Daily South Carolinian,* December 19, 1865; Benjamin Ryan Tillman, Sr. to Iveson Brookes, August 6, 1844, Iveson Brookes Papers, SCL; Robert E. May, *The Southern Dream of a Caribbean Empire* (Baton Rouge: Louisiana State University Press, 1973), pp. 77–113.

[27]Burton, *In My Father's House,* pp. 135–136; J. William Harris, *Plain Folk and Gentry in a Slave Society: White Liberty and Black Slavery in Augusta's Hinterland* (Middleton, Conn.: Wesleyan University Press, 1985), pp. 108–109, 129–130.

improved George Tillman's chances of winning and holding a seat in the state legislature. Edgefield was a large (fifth in the state in square miles) and diverse district with a high turnover rate among state legislators. Representatives from Edgefield occupied six seats in the South Carolina house throughout the 1850s, but never did more than one incumbent win reelection in the biennial balloting. And no incumbent was reelected to the state senate from Edgefield during the 1850s.[28] The Edgefield *Advertiser* attributed the high rate of turnover among legislators to the rigors of democracy in the district. Electioneering was "carried on to an almost unparalled excess," the newspaper complained, ". . . it has come to such a pass that a man, however deserving and capable, asks in vain the privilege of representing Edgefield, unless he can make up his mind to ransack every nook and corner of the District and court the favor of every man who lives at a cross-roads and keeps a dram shop."[29] George Tillman agreed that fierce competition made it difficult for politicians to win and hold offices, but he saw the disadvantage of such a vigorous democracy not in the reluctance of some local patricians to subject themselves to such a gruelling canvass but in Edgefield's inability to keep an experienced delegation in Columbia. At every election, Tillman explained, there were so many candidates for Edgefield's seats in the legislature that the contests became so "protracted" and "severe" and "the road to a seat in the Legislature from our District so long and difficult" that "almost invariably before a member has been in the Legislature long enough to fit himself for the discharge of his duties, some demagogue mounts a hobby and ousts him." The result, Tillman argued, was that "for many years" Edgefield had "not wielded that influence in the General Assembly" it had "a right to expect" from its large delegation.[30]

Having recently conceded the creation of a new senate seat in the Upcountry, the Lowcountry was hardly in the mood to do more of the same, but in the 1854 elections, George Tillman mounted the hobby of dividing Edgefield and won election to the state house of representatives, ousting several incumbents in the process. Once elected, Tillman's voice was heard in support of a variety of democratic reforms in state government for the duration of his two-year term.[31]

In Columbia, the broader fight to give the election of presidential electors to the people had reached new levels of intensity. B. F. Perry and other advocates of the change realized that Calhoun's death had silenced the most important voice opposing the change in the Upcountry. Perry and other legislative point men working for popular election of electors felt that few, if any, Upcountry legislators would oppose the change since Calhoun's stern objection was no longer a factor. This proved to be a serious miscalculation on the part of sponsors

[28]Walter B. Edgar, ed., *Biographical Directory of the South Carolina House of Representatives* (Columbia, S.C.: University of South Carolina Press, 1974), vol. 1, pp. 362–381; Bailey et al., eds., *Biographical Directory of the South Carolina Senate,* vol. 3, pp. 1874–1885.

[29]Edgefield *Advertiser,* September 1, 1852.

[30]Edgefield *Advertiser,* September 21, 1853.

[31]Thomas McGrath to Benjamin C. Yancey, October 20, 1853, Benjamin C. Yancey Papers, SHC; Edgefield *Advertiser,* September 9, 1856.

of the legislation, but it nevertheless triggered a dramatic series of confrontations over the issue in the state legislature. A bill to give the election of electors to the people was introduced in the house by Perry during December 1851, but even the house would not approve the measure during the middle of a secession crisis, voting the bill down 66 to 48. Moreover, a substantial number of Upcountry representatives voted against the change, reversing the usual pattern of virtual unanimity in favor of the change among house members from the Upcountry. The entire six-man delegation from Edgefield, six of seven from Pendleton, two of three from Fairfield, and single representatives from Abbeville, Laurens, Union, Spartanburg, and York voted against the popular election of presidential electors in 1851, because they deemed it "inexpedient" to "distract" the state over such a matter during a major crisis.[32]

Perry and his allies were not chastened by their failure. Indeed, Perry took up the cudgels for popular election of presidential electors, and for popular election of the governor, with a regularity that bordered on monotony. The legislature again defeated bills proposing popular election of electors in 1852 and 1853, turning back the Upcountry's challenge in almost desultory fashion. Despite the importance of the issue, and the growing resentment among Upcountry politicians of the almost cavalier treatment it received at the hands of Lowcountry legislators, the effort to turn the election of presidential electors to the people had become an utterly predictable legislative sideshow. The melodrama opened yearly soon after the legislature convened, usually with B. F. Perry introducing the bill calling for a change in the method of electing electors. Next the venomous charges and countercharges would fly back and forth, Upcountry legislators denouncing the Lowcountry aristocracy as "unrepublican," and Lowcountry politicians charging that Upcountrymen wanted to breach sacred obligations sealed with the blessing of Calhoun. Ultimately the bill would be defeated on an essentially sectional vote, with enough Upcountrymen defecting to the Lowcountry side to prove that Calhoun's argument still carried weight in the western portion of the state.[33]

In 1854, Upcountry champions of the issue waged a campaign to defeat all legislators from their region who habitually voted with the Lowcountry to prevent popular election of electors. The issue was hotly debated on the stump in almost every district in the Upcountry. Supporters of the change hoped the campaign would mobilize widespread popular support for their cause and purge dissenting Upcountrymen from the legislative rolls. Always in the forefront of the campaign to democratize South Carolina politics, B. F. Perry charged that the state was ruled by "an Anti-republican spirit, [an] oligarchic regime, which distrusts the people. . . ." During the campaign, the Chester *Standard* forcibly echoed Perry's charges, claiming that South Carolina leaders asserted "in theory

[32]*House Journal, 1851*, p. 70; Greenville *Southern Patriot*, January 8, 1852.

[33]Greenville *Southern Patriot*, May 2, 9, and July 11, 19, and 25, 1851; Boucher, "Sectionalism, Representation, and the Electoral Question," pp. 3–61; Yorkville *Miscellany*, August 28, 1852; Charleston *Southern Standard*, June 29, 1852; Charleston *Mercury*, November 13, 16, and 29, 1852; John Springs to Andrew Baxter Springs, September 19, 1852, Springs Family Papers, SHC.

the doctrines of true republicanism'' but, in practice, upheld ''the policy of an unguarded and, in fact, irresponsible aristocracy.'' South Carolina, the Upcountry newspaper argued, had always ''battled in favor of the States Rights doctrine and against Consolidated power,'' yet in the management of her own state politics she had allowed an intriguing clique of legislators, most of whom hailed from the Lowcountry, to acquire an enormous amount of power which they used to rule the state conservatively but high-handedly during brief yearly sojourns in Columbia. This anomalous state of affairs left South Carolina in the awkward posture of ''demanding from others the acknowledgement of a principle which she sternly repudiates at home. . . .'' Earlier, the Yorkville *Miscellany* had pronounced a similar judgment on the refusal of the legislature to allow popular election of electors. ''Our present system,'' the editors concluded, ''when closely examined, is nothing less than pure despotism.''[34]

Carefully orchestrated by supporters of popular election of presidential electors, the political debate raged on throughout the summer and fall of 1854. Small groups of voters in every district wrote to nearby newspapers demanding that all candidates for the state legislature state their views of the issue publicly. Most candidates accepted the challenge gracefully and discussed the issue freely both on the stump and in public letters to local newspapers. Sensing the public mood, a substantial majority of the legislative candidates came out in favor of popular election. In Chester, all candidates favored giving the election of electors to the people, as did eight of the eleven legislative candidates in Laurens. Yet in Spartanburg, a heavily populated district with a large white majority, four of ten candidates opposed any change in the existing system. One of the opponents of the change, B. F. Kilgore, a prominent planter-physician, labeled popular election of electors ''unrepublican'' and ''unpredictable.'' ''I do not sanction it [popular election of electors],'' explained Kilgore, ''because it recognizes the assumption that a mere numerical majority should always govern instead of a concurrent majority.''[35]

Oddly, despite considerable bruiting about, the question of how to choose presidential electors did not become a critical test issue around which clear, if temporary, factional lines could be drawn. Even the vigorously pro-change Chester *Standard* admitted that although the ''politicians were out in force'' at a battalion militia muster in the late summer, they seemed ''lamentably in want of a hobby.'' Moreover, one observer of the political situation in Laurens reported that ''the people seem to be in great measure indifferent to the issue [popular election of electors].''[36] Instead of a referendum on one issue, the legislative

[34]*Carolina Spartan*, September 14 and 21, 1854; Laurensville *Herald*, April 7, September 22, 1854; Greenville *Southern Patriot*, December 2, 1854; Chester *Standard*, June 29 and August 17, 1854; Yorkville *Miscellany*, August 28, 1852; James Henry Hammond to James L. Orr, June 19, 1854, Orr-Patterson Papers, SHC.

[35]Chester *Standard*, June 29, 1854; Laurensville *Herald*, September 22 and 29, October 13, 1854; *Carolina Spartan*, September 14 and 21, 1854.

[36]Chester *Standard*, June 29 and August 3, 1854; Laurensville *Herald*, April 7, 14, 21, and 28, 1854.

elections of 1854 ended up as politics-as-usual, with the same local cliques and same local notables rallying their usual "friends and neighbors" networks in support of this or that candidate. In Perry's home district of Greenville, all of the winners supported popular election, but in other districts, the results were mixed. In Laurens, three of the four successful house candidates supported giving the vote to the people, but J. H. Irby, who was easily elected to the senate, was a vehement opponent of popular election. In Spartanburg, a stronghold of anti-Lowcountry sentiment, the election results were even more curious. Four of the five victorious house candidates favored letting the people vote for presidential electors, but the most outspoken opponent of popular election, B. F. Kilgore, led the ticket, polling over 75 percent of all possible votes. Moreover, Gabriel Cannon, also a longtime opponent of changing the method of choosing electors, was reelected to the state senate without opposition, polling large vote totals in areas allegedly most resentful of Lowcountry intrigue in the legislature.[37]

Clearly, the effort to purge Upcountry legislative delegations of men who sided with the Lowcountry in the fight against introducing statewide popular elections in South Carolina had failed. And even if the campaign had succeeded in guaranteeing absolute unanimity among Upcountry legislators on the issue, it would have done no more than insure that the measure would pass the house, provided that the delegations from the white-majority districts of the Pee Dee remained firmly aligned with the Upcountry. The Lowcountry could still have blocked the measure in the senate. When the newly elected legislature met late in 1854, supporters of popular election of electors found that their failure to elect solid pro-election slates in every Upcountry district had weakened their cause considerably. The handful of Lowcountry leaders who had previously felt it expedient to yield to Upcountry demands for popular election of electors retreated into staunch defense of the status quo when it became evident that popular passions in the Upcountry could be controlled. James Chesnut, Jr., a wealthy Camden area planter, backed away from an earlier stance in favor of popular elections, and the Charleston *Southern Standard,* which had once suggested that the Lowcountry accept popular election of electors in order to placate the Upcountry, now insisted that no change was necessary. After the usual discussion of the issue in 1854, both houses of the legislature postponed further debate on the matter until the next year, setting the stage for a premeditated donnybrook during the 1855 session.[38]

The rhetorical fireworks began soon after the legislature convened in late November 1855, when B. F. Perry again introduced a bill in the state House of Representatives giving the election of presidential electors to the people. A number of Upcountry legislators spoke eloquently in favor of the bill. J. Wofford Tucker of Spartanburg attacked the existing system of legislative dominance as "a practical repudiation of our theory of self-government as established by republican institutions." To deny the people the right to vote directly for presi-

---

[37]Laurensville *Herald,* October 13, 1854; *Carolina Spartan,* October 12, 1854.
[38]Charleston *Mercury,* October 2, 1854; Charleston *Southern Standard,* April 1, 1854.

dential electors, Tucker maintained, was to say "that they are incapable of self-government" and "to go to an aristocracy or some other form of government than republican."[39] Even more impressive, however, was the appeal for popular election made by a former opponent of the change, Edward Noble of Abbeville, a friend and supporter of John C. Calhoun. Noble admitted that it had seemed "a palpable absurdity in agitating for this change" during the secession crisis of 1850 through 1852, but now that secession was no longer a live issue, the Upcountry's complaints should be given a serious hearing. "Is there any political justice in . . . giving to the minority the rights of the majority?" Noble complained:

> Though it may have been wisely enacted that in reference to all matters pertaining exclusively to the state there should be a great inequality in representation, much to the advantage of one section, it does not follow that in federal matters the same principle of inequality prevails. . . . To my mind, it is plain, the compromises of the state constitution have no reference to the federal might each section should have in federal elections, but were entirely confined to the distribution of power in reference to State affairs.[40]

Moreover, Noble contended, there was no danger that the state would be corrupted or destroyed by an excess of democracy, or by the temptations of partisan politics. "We, in the South," Noble continued, "should not dread popular elections. Slavery with us is a powerful element of conservatism, sufficient of itself to keep in check all dangerous tendencies among us toward expansive and explosive radicalism. The citizen with us belongs to a privileged order in society—to a privileged class."[41] Slavery for blacks, according to Noble, elevated all whites to membership in a single, "privileged" class, defined almost exclusively by racial lines, thereby minimizing the likelihood of overt class conflict in Southern politics.

The case made by Upcountry representatives did not go unchallenged, as Lowcountry legislators replied with equal eloquence. Edward B. Bryan of St. John-Colleton equated Noble's ideas with the truly radical "red republicanism" emanating from Europe in 1848 and, repeating arguments often used by Calhoun, claimed that once South Carolina allowed popular election of presidential electors the partisan spoils system of the Jacksonian era would also invade and debase the state. John Izard Middleton of Prince George Winyah offered a somewhat less strident defense of the status quo. "I represent a constituency," he stated, "who have a particular interest in preventing a radical change from taking place on the subject not because we have power, or because we have an oligarchical spirit, but for the reason that we are somewhat conservative, and do not think change is necessarily progress." Despite Middleton's denial of the preeminence of self-interest among the motives of Lowcountry representatives

[39]*Legislative Times* (Columbia, S.C.: E. H. Britton, 1855), p. 85.
[40]*Ibid.*, pp. 84–85.
[41]*Ibid.*

who opposed popular election, most Upcountrymen simply believed that the parishes possessed disproportionate and undue power over the selection of electors which they refused to yield. A few Upcountrymen spoke against changing a system which had served the state well. William Simpson of Laurens expressed his reluctance to permit popular election of electors for fear of weakening the state's influence on national affairs by creating internal party divisions.[42]

The strongest rhetoric of the entire debate, however, came from the fire-eating Upcountryman, George Tillman of Edgefield. A maverick even when riding a popular hobby, Tillman lived up to his reputation for bombast and invective during the House debate over Perry's bill. As he had during his election campaign, Tillman again explained how the sparse white population of the parishes actually enhanced their already disproportionate influence in the legislature. "The parish representatives, having but small constituencies, can easily be returned again and again, like the members for the boroughs in Parliament," Tillman argued, "and no matter who represents a parish, he knows that his people would as soon part with property . . . as give up their political power which rightly belongs to the upcountry." By contrast, Tillman continued, Upcountry representatives "have generally large constituencies, so turbulent, so hard to manage, so full of ambition, so conflicting in local interests, that but few members are reelected." This "constant rotation in up-country representation," Tillman concluded, "virtually leaves the parishes in possession of most of the experience and tact of the legislature." Thus, in Tillman's view, since the parishes dominated the legislature, and the legislature controlled the election of presidential electors, the parishes also controlled the presidential ballots of the state even though the parishes contained a small minority of the state's eligible voters.[43]

Tillman addressed Calhoun's traditional opposition to changing the method of electing electors with a rare display of respect and decorum. "There is no man whose memory I reverance [sic] more than I do Mr. Calhoun," the Edgefield representative assured the legislature. Calhoun, Tillman argued, had tried "to keep South Carolina united while he carried on his gigantic warfare . . . with the federal government." Under the circumstances it was not "wrong" for "a wise statesman" to concentrate on "staying the hand of discord" at home. But despite his respect for the departed Calhoun, Tillman could not stay his own resentment of parish domination of state politics. "Talk of the people of South Carolina ruling the state!" Tillman exclaimed, "They have nothing to do with it, but [power rests with] an odious, cunning, tyrannical, intriguing oligarchy. Yes, sir, an oligarchy, for I will not disgrace the English language by calling it an aristocracy, which I can, at least, respect in a proper way."

Tillman's colorful language denied legitimacy to the wealthy parish elite which wielded so much power in South Carolina's malapportioned legislature. Yet once again Tillman's scathing denunciation of the state's ruling "oligarchy"

---

[42]*Ibid.*, pp. 86–87.
[43]*Ibid.*, pp. 97–101.

was more an expression of sectional grievance than an attack on any particular class. The "oligarchy" which controlled the state legislature was comprised of wealthy slaveholders, most of whom were planters, but it was also a Lowcountry organization which defended its legislative prerogative against Upcountry challenges. "To change, alter, amend, or modify anything in South Carolina, the parishes say, would bring ruin to us," Tillman concluded sarcastically.[44]

Although Tillman's barbs may have drawn blood from his opponents, his speeches changed few votes. After prolonged debate, an effort to kill Perry's bill in the house by tabling it failed by a vote of 42 to 65, indicating that a majority of house members wanted to act on the bill, one way or the other. Then, in a very close vote, the house approved popular election of presidential electors 54 to 53. All representatives from the rural parishes voted against the bill, but nearly half of the large Charleston delegation voted in favor of it. Upcountry support for the bill, however, was far from solid. Only the Greenville, York, Lancaster, and Newberry delegations were unanimously in favor of the bill, while the Fairfield delegation was solidly against it. Abbeville and Edgefield representatives were evenly split on the issue, and negative votes were cast by individual members from Pendleton, Laurens, Spartanburg, and Chester. The bill's narrow victory in the house did nothing to rally support for it in the senate, which killed the bill 24 to 17, with a number of Upcountry senators voting against popular election.[45]

Despite the defeat of Perry's proposal, a number of Upcountry leaders who opposed popular election of presidential electors felt compelled to defend their position publicly once the legislature adjourned.[46] One such leader was Edgefield representative William C. Moragne, who had voted against the measure in December 1855 and defended his vote in February 1856 in a speech delivered at Edgefield courthouse.[47] Moragne, a well-read lawyer and former newspaper editor, laced his speech thoroughly with historical references to Greece, Rome, Carthage, and Great Britain as he answered Tillman's charges that the existing method of choosing presidential electors was "anti-republican and an usurpation on the rights of the people." Moragne claimed that it was impossible for the

---

[44]Ibid.

[45]Journal of the House of Representatives of the State of South Carolina, 1855 (Columbia, S.C.: E. H. Britton, 1855), pp. 173–177; Journal of the Senate of the State of South Carolina, 1855 (Columbia, S.C.: E. H. Britton, 1855), p. 150; Boucher, "Sectionalism, Representation, and the Electoral Question," pp. 58–62.

[46]Paul Johnston to William W. Renwick, September 17, 1856, William W. Renwick Papers, SCL; Job Johnston to Joseph Starke Sims, June 14, 1856, Joseph Starke Sims Papers, DU.

[47]William Moragne, the son of a prominent Abbeville planter, graduated from South Carolina College in 1837, taught school for three years, and then resumed his education abroad at Heidelberg and Berlin. He was admitted to the South Carolina Bar in 1844 and set up a law practice in Edgefield. He married a woman from the Butler family in the early 1850s and died during the Civil War. See Delle M. Craven, ed., The Neglected Thread: A Journal from the Calhoun Community, 1836–1842 (Columbia, S.C.: University of South Carolina Press, 1951), xxiii; John A. Chapman, History of Edgefield County (Newberry, S.C.: Elbert H. Aull, 1897), pp. 270–271. The works by Burton and Harris cited earlier in this chapter identify Moragne as the state senator from Edgefield. In fact, Moragne never served in the state senate, but he represented Edgefield in the state house of representatives in 1851 and again in 1854–1855. See the biographical directories cited in footnote 28.

legislature, which was itself elected by the people, to usurp power from the people. "Were this a Government legally recognizing distinct castes or privileged orders, as in a monarchy or aristocracy, the justice of such a charge might sometimes be allowed," Moragne argued, "but we live in a Republic, where the people are the legitimate source of all power—in which only one class is known to the law—where all are politically free and equal, enjoying the same rights and privileges."[48]

After denying the charge of legislative usurpation, Moragne countered the charge that the existing system was "unrepublican." Republics, Moragne reminded his audience, were not mere democracies where numerical majorities ruled without consideration of the rights of voting minorities. Proponents of giving the election of electors directly to the people, Moragne charged, "seem, in this fast age, to be forgetting the plain, old-fashioned doctrines taught by our fathers of the Republican school, and to have now about as much relish for pure *Republicanism* as for an old garment quite out of fashion." Moragne then contrasted the "wild spirit of mobcracy" that prevailed in states where "broken-down politicians and aspiring demagogues" excited "constant factious excitement" over presidential elections with the relative calm that prevailed in South Carolina during presidential contests. The South Carolina system, Moragne admitted, "may appear somewhat irregular and unequal in its exterior," but, in practice, "it . . . contains, in an eminent degree, the blessings of practical equality." Moreover, Moragne, an Upcountryman, insisted that it was not only expedient but also right for the less heavily populated Lowcountry to enjoy an equal voice with the Upcountry on both state and federal questions. The balance of power in the legislature, Moragne explained, "hampers and controls the will of the majority" and granted the minority "an active substantial power." This "happy inspiration of Legislative genius" secured "equal rights, equal laws to each and every part of the State." The liberty of all South Carolinians, Moragne concluded, was best guaranteed if this "just balance of power between the various sections of the state" and "the beautiful harmony in the body politic" were left undisturbed.[49]

By 1856, it was clear that the effort to unite the Upcountry behind the cause of popular election of presidential electors had failed. Without unanimity among Upcountry legislators on the issue, there was no chance of pushing the change through a reluctant, if not intransigent, legislature. After the session of 1855, the issue was only occasionally debated by the legislature, and there were no further concerted efforts to secure reform. During the late 1850s, other matters, including the growing crisis over slavery, pushed reform of the state's peculiar political system into the background, but not without leaving a sizable contingent of

[48]William C. Moragne, *To the People of Edgefield District: The Electoral Question* (Edgefield: Advertiser Office, 1859), pp. 1–19. This pamphlet is a reprint of a speech given by Moragne in February, 1856. The speech was originally published in a series of issues of the Edgefield *Advertiser* during February, 1856.

[49]Moragne, *To the People of Edgefield District*, pp. 1–19.

Upcountry voters with a gnawing suspicion that their liberty was subject to the whims of a power-hungry oligarchy.[50]

As the reform campaigns receded into the background, South Carolina remained, as it had been since the eighteenth century, a legislative state. Not only did the legislature retain its control over the election of the governor and the presidential electors, but it also continued to elect a broad range of other state and local officers from attorney general to poll manager. To be sure, the legislature's steadfast refusal to turn the election of the governor and the presidential electors over to the people hindered the development of coherent statewide parties in South Carolina, but since the governorship was largely a ceremonial office, a popularly elected governor would have wielded only a modest amount of power. The governor could not personally introduce legislation; he lacked veto power, and he made few appointments. As a result, the primary importance of the gubernatorial election lay in its political symbolism. Ordinarily, the governor's chair was handed out after several rounds of elaborate wheeling and dealing among various legislative cliques and cabals. The legislature often used the office to reward an individual for distinguished service to the state or to groom a promising young politician for future service. During Calhoun's lifetime, the governorship was on two or three occasions used as a means of reconciling warring factions within the state.[51]

Yet while the governor lacked institutional authority, his ceremonial functions gradually acquired considerable importance because of the significance of public theater in South Carolina's informal but dynamic political culture. As governor, an astute politician, especially a skilled orator with a winning public manner, could use his office as a roving political pulpit from which he could attempt to influence the state's congregation of voters. First of all, the governor's annual message to the legislature, given at the beginning of each session, tended to set the tone for that year's General Assembly. The governor often either raised new issues in his address or singled out certain old ones for special attention. The address was generally reprinted in full, and accompanied by discussion and editorial comment, in weekly newspapers throughout the state. This frequently aroused considerable public interest in the legislature's activity, particularly if the governor's recommendations were at all controversial, as they sometimes were. The governor's most effective forum, however, grew out of his duties as commander-in-chief of the state militia. According to law, the governor was supposed to review personally all militia units in the state once a year, and in years marked by hot political contests or important debates over public issues, governors seldom neglected this obligation. The late summer militia musters were always alive with political talk in election years, and most politicians did

[50]Edward Noble to Francis W. Pickens, August 10, 1859, Francis W. Pickens Papers, DU.

[51]Columbus Andrews, *Administrative County Government in South Carolina* (Chapel Hill: University of North Carolina Press, 1933); John Peyre Thomas, *The Formation of Judicial and Political Subdivisions in South Carolina* (Columbia, S.C.: Bryan Printing, 1890), pp. 1–26.

much of their necessary canvassing there. The Nullifiers were the first organized faction to recognize and take full advantage of the possibilities for grassroots mobilization which the muster system offered. A few years later, Waddy Thompson saved his congressional seat with enthusiastic and effective "stumping" at militia musters, and by the 1840s militia fields were prime battlegrounds during every campaign. Musters were especially festive occasions when the governor attended, usually dressed in full regalia and accompanied by a large entourage. More important than the ceremonial review of troops, however, was the commander-in-chief's speech to the assembled throng, and his informal mingling with troops and visitors. A number of governors used these reviews as traveling political rallies, carrying a hobby from one muster to the next, and riding it for all it was worth. In efforts to mobilize grassroots support behind a cause, the governor, as titular head of the state militia, could do much to enhance, or cripple, a political movement.[52]

The governor's influence, then, depended largely on his ability to use the prestige of the office skillfully. Real political leverage in the state lay with the legislature, which elected not only the United States senators, the governor, judges and chancellors, and all the state officers but also the board of directors of the Bank of the State of South Carolina, trustees of South Carolina College, election officials and poll managers, and members of some of the numerous district commissions which handled the affairs of local government. Naturally, the legislature's control of all judgeships, both common law and equity, and especially of positions on the state's supreme court, left the South Carolina bench open to political influence. The legislature also elected important constitutional officers, such as the comptroller general and attorney general, who played an important role in managing the state's business. The legislature's control of appointments to the boards of the BSSC, the Lunatic Asylum, South Carolina College, the military academies, and of state proxies to private banks and railroads also drew much criticism. In his long tirade against "parish rule" in South Carolina, George Tillman charged that these appointive offices constituted "a *third*, and the most powerful branch of our legislature." Perhaps Tillman's charge was an overstatement, but clearly the legislature's control of these appointments put critical patronage at its disposal.[53]

The legislature also had a hand in local government in South Carolina. Since the abolition of the county court system in 1799, districts and parishes had been governed by a casual, but seemingly effective, system of local commissions, most of which were chosen by the legislature. In most districts, there were four local commissions of some importance: the Commission of Roads and Bridges, the Commission of the Poor, the Commission of the Free Schools, and the Commission of Public Buildings. At the beginning of the nineteenth century all

---

[52]For examples, see *Carolina Spartan,* December 6, 1855, and July 30, 1857; Chester *Standard,* August 3, 1854.

[53]James M. Banner, "The Problem of South Carolina," in Stanley Elkins and Eric McKitrick, eds., *The Hofstadter Aegis: A Memorial* (New York: Alfred A. Knopf, 1974), pp. 60–93; *Legislative Times,* p. 99.

of these commissions were elected by the legislature, as were the local sheriffs, tax collectors, and clerks of court. During the 1830s, democratic reforms gave the election of the sheriffs, tax collectors, clerks of court, and commissioners of the poor to the people of the districts. Every local commission except the Commission of Free Schools had the power to levy taxes, in the form of a pro rata share of the state tax, on citizens in their district. Popular election of sheriffs, tax collectors, clerks of court, and commissioners of the poor gave the electorate direct control of some important local offices and stripped away some of the legislature's centralized control over local affairs. Still, the legislature's role in choosing the members of the other commissions gave politicians at the State House in Columbia a great deal of influence over local government.[54]

Few politicians from the parishes or from the Pee Dee cared who sat on the various commissions in the Upcountry districts. Nor did Upcountry legislators ordinarily take interest in the election of commissioners in districts other than their own. As a result, an informal system developed which allowed the legislative delegation from each district virtually unchallenged control of the election of commission members in that district. The involvement of the district legislative delegation in choosing important officers in local government not only added an intensely local aspect to the election of state legislators, thus raising the stakes considerably in races for the legislature, but also created an informal two-way patronage network which could be nicely manipulated by local politicians and their cliques of followers. Local notables desiring a seat on one of the commissions courted the favor of certain candidates for the legislative, who, if elected, would be in a position to award positions to a few of their friends and allies. The courting of favor, however, worked both ways. Candidates for the legislature needed the support of local notables and the votes of local cliques in order to win election. The potential patronage at the disposal of a successful candidate for the legislature was crucial to that candidate's ability to ally himself with enough notables and local cliques to build a winning coalition. Thus the legislature's control of several important commissions not only helped legitimate the existing influence of local notables and their cliques but actually provided that informal system with institutional support and authority. All of this helped reinforce the highly personal, clannish, "friends-and-neighbors" style of grassroots politics in South Carolina. Moreover, it helped guarantee that whenever grassroots mobilization was attempted for ideological or well-organized partisan purposes, as happened from time to time, that mobilization would necessarily occur through, and with assistance of, local notables and their cliques.[55]

[54]Andrews, *Administrative County Government,* pp. 30–70.

[55]On the highly personal style of South Carolina politics in the antebellum era, see the reminiscences of William Henry Trescot in *An Oration Delivered before the Alumni of the College of Charleston, June 25, 1889* (Charleston: Walker, Evans, Cogswell, 1889), pp. 1–17; and William Gilmore Simms to James Lawson, February 28, 1860, in Mary C. Simms Oliphant, Alfred Taylor Odell, T. C. Duncan Eaves, eds., *The Letters of William Gilmore Simms,* 5 vols. (Columbia, S.C.: University of South Carolina Press, 1952–1956), vol. 4, pp. 201–203.

The various commissions usually met quarterly around festive boards, hold-ing each meeting in a different section of the district, to dispose of pressing business. Once a year, those commissions with the power to levy taxes estimated the revenue their duties would require for the next twelve months and added a surcharge to each citizen's state tax liability. The amount of these surcharges varied widely from year to year. This was especially true of the taxes levied by the Commissioners for Roads and Bridges since their revenue needs fluctuated according to the amount of damage done by storms, freshets, gully-washers, and droughts during the previous year. In rare cases, road commissioners would levy surcharges as high as 80 to 100 percent of the state tax bill, although usually the road and bridge surcharge ran from 15 to 40 percent. Commissioners of the poor were prohibited by state law from attaching a pro rata charge of more than 37.5 percent for poor relief, and in most districts, commissioners seldom levied the maximum. Lacking the power to tax, free-school commissioners were simply charged with the responsibility of distributing the district's share of the state free-school appropriation fairly among the needy children of the locale.[56]

Sometimes local notables viewed serving on these commissions as more of a chore than a privilege. More than a few of these notables used their political influence to keep themselves off these boards rather than to secure a seat on one. Nevertheless, few politically active notables were willing to see these positions fall into the hands of a local rival or an opposing faction. At their best, the commissions tried both to do their jobs and to keep the level of tax surcharges low. As long as the commissions were relatively unobtrusive, the voters seemed to care little whether commissioners were chosen by the legislature or elected by popular vote. Moreover, the same can be said for those local officials, such as sheriffs, who were popularly elected. As James Louis Petigru noted in a learned discourse on equity jurisprudence, sheriffs who pounded the gavel often, selling slaves or land attached for bad debts or back taxes, usually found themselves surrendering the small wooden hammer to someone else after the next election. William Henry Trescot, a Lowcountry planter who thought a slave society might be better served by stronger local government, observed that local government in South Carolina was so informal and unobtrusive that "a stranger might live among us for years and see no traces of government." To most South Caroli-nians, Trescot's observation was not an indictment but a tribute. Upcountrymen seemed resentful of all contact with government at any level. That local govern-ment was best which kept taxes low and remained nearly invisible.[57]

It was more difficult for the state government to remain nearly invisible, but it tried. For all its considerable powers, from the election of presidential electors

[56]See, for examples, Commissioners of Roads, Bridges, and Ferries Records, 1852–1858, Lan-caster District, Commissioners of Roads, Bridges, and Ferries, 1830–1868, Pickens District, Com-missioners of the Poor Records, 1796–1827, Spartanburg District, Commissioners of Roads, Bridges and Ferries Records, 1825–1868, Spartanburg District, Commissioners of Roads, Bridges and Fer-ries, 1806–1852, York District, and Commissioners of Free Schools, York District, SCL.

[57]James Louis Petigru, "Court of Chancery," *Southern Review* 3 (1829):63–77; William Henry Trescot, "Bench and Bar," *Russell's Magazine* 6 (1859–1860):289–297, especially p. 296.

to the appointment of free school commissioners, the South Carolina legislature usually seemed determined to govern according to the old folk maxim that "if it ain't broke, don't fix it." This ruling precept was given less colloquial expression by John I. Middleton in 1855. "We believe that in great political questions," the Lowcountry representative explained, "those who call for a change must point out the difficulty, and show us, before we make a change, that there are evils to be remedied."[58] The legislature normally met once each year, convening during the last week in November and adjourning *sine die* in time for members to spend Christmas at home. The single most important task which faced the legislature each year was the drafting of the state appropriation and supply bills, which determined the level of state spending and taxes. These bills ordinarily commanded more of the legislature's time and attention than any other measures, but, during the antebellum era, the legislature also spent a good deal of time debating resolutions which addressed major national issues. These "sense of the state" resolutions played an important role in defining South Carolina's position on matters under discussion in Washington. Despite the brevity of the session, and the numerous responsibilities which the legislature allocated to itself, legislators always found time to enjoy the various dinners, grand balls, and other festive moments offered by Columbia society. Dutiful legislators complained from time to time that the bulk of all legislative work had to be done early in the day because "John Barleycorn" would hold the floor in the afternoon. On the whole, however, such depictions of the legislature's activity were caricatures. Most legislators faced a demanding schedule which began with committee meetings at 9 a.m. in the morning. The full legislature convened at 11 a.m., adjourned at 4 p.m. for dinner, reconvened at 6 p.m., and remained in session until around 9 p.m. Most legislators then ate late suppers and retired to their rooms where many worked until well past midnight drafting bills and committee reports. In general, the legislature was a diligent body which usually handled its business with dignity and dispatch, produced more than its share of eloquent oratory, and made few changes in the status quo.[59]

[58]*Legislative Times*, pp. 96–99.

[59]For two interesting accounts of legislative activity, and the surrounding festivities, see Robert Nicholas Olsberg, "A Government of Class and Race: William Henry Trescot and the South Carolina Chivalry, 1860–1865" (Ph.D. dissertation, University of South Carolina, 1972), pp. 74–97; and Benjamin Yancey to his wife, December 8, 1849, Benjamin C. Yancey Papers, SHC.

9

"Resist . . . King or Capital":
The Economic Tensions of the
1850s

Prior to 1850, the South Carolina legislature generally cultivated a reputation for stinginess, but occasionally savaged that reputation with extravagant spending, such as the canal building mania of the 1820s, support for the Louisville, Cincinnati and Charleston Railroad in the 1830s, and aid given to rebuild Charleston after the disastrous fire there in 1837. Internal improvement expenditures were usually financed through bond sales, and interest payments were made with BSSC profits, so that no tax increases were necessary. Proposals for even small increases in state spending often triggered loud cries of protest from legislators. In 1828, public outrage over a $10,000 appropriation made to help relieve the indebtedness of Thomas Jefferson's daughter enabled Alexander Speer, a representative from Edgefield and a tight-budget crusader, to cut the next year's spending by 20 percent. In 1846, the ordinarily pragmatic Upcountryman James L. Orr worked hard to defeat a modest $30,000 appropriation earmarked to buy food for those districts ravaged by the severe drought of the previous year, even though his native Anderson was one of the hardest hit areas. Successful in his efforts to kill the measure, Orr publicly deplored "the dangerous consequences which may result from adopting the principle of going to the public crib to supply sufferers from any and every calamity."[1]

Thus, with a few noteworthy exceptions, the South Carolina legislature prided itself on its fiscal restraint. Indeed, prior to 1850, the legislature always held actual annual expenditures under $350,000, with over a third of that money going for salaries in the executive, legislative, and judicial branches of the state government and roughly 10 percent going to maintain the state's militia system and military arsenals. The overwhelming proportion of the money spent by the

---

[1]William W. Freehling, *Prelude to Civil War: The Nullification Controversy in South Carolina, 1816–1836* (New York: Harper & Row, 1965), pp. 120–121; Anderson *Gazette,* September 5 and December 19, 1845.

Table 9.1 Tax Revenues in Antebellum South Carolina, 1840–1860

	Percentage of Total Tax Revenues Generated by Each Item					
	Tax on Land	Tax on Slaves	Tax on Merchandise	Tax on Town Lots	Tax on Professions	Other Taxes
1840	10.2	59.7	10.8	14.8	2.3	2.2
1841	9.9	60.1	9.4	15.0	2.3	3.3
1842	9.8	60.7	9.1	15.2	2.1	3.1
1843	10.6	61.4	7.5	14.8	2.1	3.6
1844	10.5	62.1	7.9	13.9	2.4	3.2
1845	10.2	61.4	8.8	14.0	2.3	3.3
1846	10.2	61.4	8.7	14.0	2.3	3.7
1847	9.8	61.6	7.9	14.2	2.2	4.3
1848	10.2	61.4	9.0	12.5	1.8	5.1
1849	10.2	62.3	7.8	15.2	2.2	2.3
1850	10.7	61.8	8.9	14.2	2.3	2.1
1851	10.6	60.8	9.3	14.3	2.5	2.5
1852	10.4	59.6	10.5	15.4	2.3	1.8
1853	11.3	62.7	5.6	15.9	2.5	2.0
1854	11.9	53.3	11.9	14.6	2.3	6.0
1855	12.9	57.8	6.3	13.6	2.4	7.0
1856	11.6	54.5	11.0	13.8	2.0	7.1
1857	13.3	59.0	8.1	8.0	2.0	9.6
1858	13.2	58.8	8.1	8.0	1.9	10.0
1859	13.0	58.8	7.9	8.2	2.2	9.9
1860	13.0	58.0	7.5	8.4	2.1	11.0

Source: Calculated from data in "Reports of the Comptroller General," in Reports and Resolutions of the South Carolina General Assembly, 1840–1860.

state was raised through the general tax bill. Again, prior to 1850, the legislature never raised more than $307,000 through taxes. Of that total, just over 60 percent was raised from a head tax on slaves. Around 10 percent was raised from an *ad valorem* tax on land, while about 14 percent was raised from a tax on town lots and about 8 percent from an inventory tax on merchandise. The legal upper division of the state, which included not only the Upcountry but also the middle portion of the state, generated about one-half of the state's tax revenue, while the parishes generated the other half. Moreover, the tax on land, slaves, town lots, and merchandise in Charleston itself generated about one-fourth of the state's total tax revenue through most of the antebellum period. Of the tax revenue actually taken from the Upcountry prior to 1850, over 75 percent was raised from the tax on slaves. The real estate tax raised about 10 percent of the Upcountry's tax burden, and the inventory tax raised between 5 and 6 percent.[2]

---

[2]These calculations were made from data obtained from the examination of the "Report of the Comptroller General," in *Reports and Resolutions of the South Carolina General Assembly* for the years 1840 through 1860, and from a study of the "Acts for Raising Supplies," in the *Acts of the General Assembly* for the same years. See Table 9.1.

The tax structure of antebellum South Carolina placed the heaviest burden on large land and slave owners, town merchants, and professionals. The roughly 50 percent of the state's families which owned no slaves escaped the burden of the slave tax altogether and paid only the low thirty cents per $100 *ad valorem* land tax. Moreover, land values in South Carolina were never reassessed after 1815, when the multiple classification system adopted during the 1780s was refined somewhat. This classification system divided the state's land into ten different categories, mostly by geographical region, and assigned all land in each category a specific taxable value, ranging from $26 per acre in the tidal swamps of the Lowcountry to 30 cents per acre for land in the foothills of Pendleton and 20 cents per acre for land in the state's vast pine barrens. The bulk of all land in the Upcountry, including much of the best short-staple cotton growing land, fell into categories assessed at $4 per acre or less. Thus a substantial non-slaveholding farmer in the Upcountry might own and work a hundred acres of good Upcountry soil and pay only $1.20 in state taxes, and probably no more than $2 in state *and* local taxes. If that farmer owned ten slaves, however, his state tax bill would have been raised considerably to about $7.20, and when local surcharges were added on, to around $12 or $13. Clearly the tax structure placed a heavier burden on slaveholders than on non-slaveholders, and the unchanging land classification system rewarded the Upcountry at the expense of the Lowcountry. To be sure, land was generally undervalued in both regions, but the undervaluation was most pronounced in the Upcountry, which had scarcely begun its involvement with large-scale commercial agriculture when the assessments were made. Thus the tax policy of South Carolina, while not progressive in any systematic or calculated way, spared the non-slaveholder at the expense of the slaveholder, the Upcountryman at the expense of the Lowcountryman, and the hardscrabble farmer at the expense of the planter. Indeed, estimates based on the distribution of real and slave property and the state's tax structure suggest that the wealthiest one-fifth of the population paid 80 to 85 percent of the taxes. Of course, the tax burden was hardly onerous for any segment of the population, since the absolute level of taxation was kept low, as were state expenditures.[3]

In the 1850s, however, the legislature drifted away from its practice of tight-fisted fiscal conservatism and minimal state spending. Between 1841 and 1850, actual state expenditures rose by just over 22 percent from $278,806 to $340,595, and the actual tax burden imposed on the people of the state increased even less noticably, by only 11 percent for the decade. During the 1850s, however, the legislature abandoned its traditional caution, and increased state spending dramatically in a variety of areas. State spending nearly trebled during the decade, rising from $340,595 in 1850 to a peak of $1,036,924 in 1858 before

[3]On the classification and valuation of land for tax purposes, see *The Statutes at Large of South Carolina* (Columbia, S.C.: A. S. Johnston, 1839), vol. 6, pp. 7–10. Tax estimates were made using land values from this source and tax rates from the yearly supply acts approved by the legislature. See also J. Mills Thornton III, "Fiscal Policy and the Failure of Radical Reconstruction in the Lower South," in J. Morgan Kousser and James M. McPherson, eds., *Region, Race, and Reconstruction: Essays in Honor of C. Vann Woodward* (New York: Oxford University Press, 1982), pp. 349–394.

Table 9.2 Revenues and Expenditures in Antebellum
South Carolina, 1840–1860

	Total State Expenditures	Total Tax Revenue	Total Revenue	Cash Balance
1840	$349,722	$305,119	$412,000	$62,426
1841	278,806	309,832	364,634	85,827
1842	301,714	312.072	391,477	89,763
1843	277,834	288,207	388,960	111,126
1844	347,904	291,429	417,957	70,253
1845	288,702	301,135	398,395	109,685
1846	322,400	306,186	427,277	104,827
1847	333,465	310,480	434,465	101,071
1848	324,484	299,123	389,638	65,144
1849	333,724	299,155	401,613	62,889
1850	340,595	329,908	410,023	69,428
1851	395,913	515,679	603,457	207,544
1852	463,022	349,931	739,696	276,674
1853	482,975	361,776	658,103	175,131
1854	533,123	429,976	638,898	105,775
1855	484,884	399,740	621,593	136,810
1856	591,146	532,744	730,772	139,626
1857	608,295	463,195	731,776	123,481
1858	1,036,924	465,518	1,137,897	100,973
1859	908,698	635,525	1,059,280	150,582
1860	967,968	632,434	1,204,121	236,152

Source: Same as Table 9.1.

falling back slightly, to $967,968, by 1860. The huge increase in state spending reflected significant increases in expenditures for salaries, which rose by 50 percent during the decade, and for free schools, where spending doubled, and modest increases in spending for poor relief, the state Lunatic Asylum, and a handful of similar items. The enormous railroad expansion of the decade, which received considerable support from the state's revolving fund, cost the taxpayers next to nothing. The bulk of the dramatic increase in state spending went toward construction of new public buildings, particularly the impressive and expensive new state capitol. Most of the money needed for the new capitol was raised through the sale of short-term state bonds, though a smaller portion was taken from current operating revenues. Nevertheless, the interest payments on these bonds, which, unlike railroad bonds, were sold to finance a non-revenue generating project, had to be made with tax money. By the end of the decade, these interest payments were considerable, and the new capital building, plagued by large cost overruns, remained unfinished.[4]

[4]See Table 9.2; see also Barbara Bellows, "'Insanity is the Disease of Civilization': The Founding of the South Carolina Lunatic Asylum," *South Carolina Historical Magazine* 82 (July, 1981):263–272; Laylon Wayne Jordan, "Education for Community: C. G. Memminger and the Organization of Common Schools in Antebellum Charleston," *South Carolina Historical Magazine* 83 (April, 1982):99–115; Kibler, *Perry,* pp. 302–313.

Table 9.3   Tax Rates in Antebellum South Carolina, 1840–1860 (in cents)

	Tax on Land (per $100 of assessed value)	Tax on Slaves (per capita)	Tax on Town Lots (per $100 of assessed value)	Tax on Professions (per $100 of income)	Tax on Merchandise (per $100 of stock on hand)	Tax on Stocks (per $100 of par value)
1840	30	60	30	60	60	—
1841	30	60	30	60	60	—
1842	30	60	30	60	60	—
1843	30	55	20	60	55	—
1844	30	55	25	60	55	—
1845	30	55	25	60	55	—
1846	30	55	25	60	55	—
1847	30	55	25	60	55	—
1848	30	52	25	60	55	—
1849	30	52	25	60	55	—
1850	35	56	25	60	60	—
1851	53	85	37½	90	90	—
1852	35	56	25	60	60	—
1853	40	60	25	60	10*	—
1854	50	60	25	60	15	—
1855	50	60	20	60	10	30
1856	60	75	25	60	25	40
1857	60	70	12½	50	15	25
1858	60	70	12½	50	15	25
1859	81	95	17	68	21	35
1860	81	95	17	68	18	35

Source: Data compiled from survey of *Statutes at Large for the State of South Carolina, 1840–1860.*
*Beginning with the 1853 fiscal year, South Carolina shifted its tax on merchandise from a tax on stock on hand (inventory) to a tax on every $100 worth of goods sold by merchants (a sales tax). For more details, see Chapter 6, footnote 59.

Tax revenues did not increase apace with state spending, but they increased dramatically nonetheless, rising from $299,155 in 1849 to $635,525 a decade later. The increased tax revenue was generated largely by substantial, but uneven, increases in tax rates. The huge tax increase passed in 1851 to finance military preparedness for secession proved to be a one-time measure, as tax rates for 1852 fell back close to normal levels. Beginning in 1853, however, tax rates rose due to increased state spending, and these tax hikes continued intermittently for the rest of the decade. These tax increases not only raised more revenue but they also shifted, albeit modestly, some of the tax burden off slaveholders and town property owners and onto landowners and citizens holding stock in banking, insurance, or gas-light corporations. The capitation tax on slaves rose from 52 cents in 1849 to 60 cents in 1853, then to 75 cents in 1856, and finally to 95 cents in 1859. The *ad valorem* tax on real property, however, increased more rapidly, rising from 30 cents in 1849 to 60 cents in 1856 and finally to 81 cents in 1859. As a result, the percentage of total tax revenue raised from real property taxes rose slightly, from 10.2 percent in 1849 to over 13 percent by 1860. Owners of town property also profited from the redistribution of the tax burden which occurred during the 1850s. In 1849, over 15 percent of all tax money came from the tax on town lots. A decade later, only 8.2 percent of all tax revenue came from this tax, despite the fact that the value of town property in the state had increased dramatically. The legislature provided this relief to town property holders by slashing the *ad valorem* rate in half in 1857. Merchants and warehouse owners shouldered about the same proportion of the total tax burden in 1859 as they had a decade earlier, paying 7.8 percent of the total in 1849 and 7.9 percent ten years later. New tax monies, however, were generated by a series of new taxes on banks, insurance, and gas-light corporation stock, plus a new tax on insurance premiums. These taxes, which did not exist in 1849, accounted for 5 to 6 percent of the state's tax revenue a decade later.[5]

Whatever the proportion of the total tax revenue paid by a specific group, the absolute tax burden of all citizens increased significantly during the 1850s, doubling the taxes paid by most citizens in less than ten years. In January 1856, just after the legislature raised the head tax on slaves from sixty to seventy-five cents and the real property tax from fifty cents per $100 of assessed value to sixty cents per $100, David Gavin, a slaveholding farmer from the Lowcountry and a frequent critic of state government, complained that although legislators pretended "to be much opposed to the abolition of slavery" they were actually "burdening it with taxes" while letting "other property" pay little or no tax.[6] In fact, the total tax burden in 1859 was probably less than 5 percent of the income generated by the sale of the state's short-staple cotton crop of that year, and a much lower percentage of the state's total income which included the sale of rice, sea-island cotton, grain, slaves, lumber products, and manufactured goods. Nevertheless, while the levels of state taxation and state spending remained low, they were rising dramatically, and the state's voters found themselves paying higher taxes to finance a state government that was increasingly generous, at least by South Carolina standards, in its expenditures. Though hardly extravagant in its support of education, poor relief, and care for the sick and deranged, the state was growing more active in those areas and assuming a sense of *noblesse oblige* which had previously been the province of private benefactors. In some cases, the legislature did a great deal less than it was being urged to do by reform leaders, but it was gradually establishing a larger role for state government in the lives of its citizens. The low-profile government of the 1840s was no longer nearly invisible, but was instead becoming a larger and larger presence.[7]

Not only were state expenditures increasing rapidly during the 1850s but the state was also becoming much more active in its efforts to promote and regulate economic growth and development. The state, of course, had a long history of

[5]See Tables 9.2 and 9.3.

[6]Entry of January 27, 1856, David Gavin Diary, SHC.

[7]See Table 9.2; on similar developments in other Southern states, see Thornton, "Fiscal Policy," especially pp. 349–377; Peter Wallenstein, *From Slave South to New South: Public Policy in Nineteenth Century Georgia* (Chapel Hill: University of North Carolina Press, 1987); Peter Wallenstein, "From Slave South to New South: Taxes and Spending in Georgia From 1850 Through Reconstruction," *Journal of Economic History* 36 (March, 1976):287–290; Peter Wallenstein,

Whiggish attitudes toward economic development, but the Whiggish leanings were always thoroughly leavened by lingering Jeffersonian misgivings about expanding commercial involvement, and especially about using the state government as an instrument to promote economic development. The conflict between the growing Whiggish faith in material progress and the persistent Jeffersonian suspicion of both commerce and an active government produced a mixed legislative record on crucial economic questions. On the one hand, the state had maintained and operated a heavily capitalized state bank since 1813, helped finance an extensive program of internal improvements, including both canals and railroads, and granted valuable corporate charters to banks and would-be manufacturers. On the other hand, the state steadfastly maintained strict usury laws which slowed the influx of capital into the state, passed legislation imposing stiff penalties on banks which suspended specie payments or otherwise violated their charters, and repeatedly declined to create a general statute of incorporation. Indeed, the Panic of 1837 and the suspension of specie payments by most banks fueled the submerged Jeffersonian-Jacksonian resentment of the special privileges conferred by corporate charters and soured the attitude of the state toward corporations for several years. In his legislative message of 1839, Governor Patrick Noble, a close friend of Calhoun, denounced corporate charters with pure Jacksonian venom as instruments which "confer exclusive privileges on certain persons" and "intrench [sic] upon the equal rights of the rest of the Community." Several years later industrialist William Gregg complained that the state seemed "to entertain apprehensions of harming the public weal" by granting charters.[8]

The state, it seemed, was of two minds about economic development. The divided mind of the legislature, however, merely reflected the divided mind of the people. The Whiggish faith that the government could use its power to enlarge the economic foundations of independence tried to conquer the lingering "country-republican" fear that a government powerful enough to foster eco-

"'More Unequally Taxed than Any People in the Civilized World': The Origin of Georgia's Ad Valorem Tax System," *Georgia Historical Quarterly* 69 (Winter, 1985):459–487; Donald C. Butts, "The 'Irrepressible Conflict': Slave Taxation and North Carolina's Gubernatorial Election of 1860," *North Carolina Historical Review* 58 (Winter, 1981):44–66; Donald C. Butts, "A Challenge to Planter Rule: The Controversy over the Ad Valorem Taxation of Slaves in North Carolina, 1858–1862" (Ph.D. dissertation, Duke University, 1978); Marc W. Kruman, *Parties and Politics in North Carolina, 1836–1865* (Baton Rouge: Louisiana State University Press, 1983), especially pp. 180–221.

[8]J. Mauldin Lesesne, *The Bank of the State of South Carolina: A General and Political History* (Columbia, S.C.: University of South Carolina Press, 1970), pp. 35–51; Alfred G. Smith, Jr., *Economic Readjustment of an Old Cotton State: South Carolina, 1820–1860* (Columbia, S.C.: University of South Carolina Press, 1958), pp. 113–126; *Speech of William Gregg, of Edgefield, on a Bill to Amend an Act Entitled "An Act to Authorize Aid to the Blue Ridge Railroad Company in South Carolina" In the House of Representatives, December 8, 1857* (Columbia, S.C.: R. W. Gibbes, 1857); and [William Gregg] *An Enquiry into the Propriety of Granting Charters of Incorporation for Manufacturing and Other Purposes in South Carolina* (Charleston: Walker and Burke, 1845), pp. 6–13; *Southern Chronicle,* March 19, 1845.

nomic development was powerful enough to infringe on the liberties of the people. By the late 1840s, the Whiggish view gained new ascendancy in South Carolina. As memories of the Panic of 1837 faded, the legislature again granted charters liberally. The centerpiece of the state's new role in supporting economic development was the use of capital from the state's revolving fund to finance the dramatic expansion of railroads into the Upcountry and Pee Dee sections of the state and to attempt the construction of a transmontane railroad to the Midwest, but the state also continued to operate the most powerful financial institution in the state, the BSSC, and granted charters readily to new banking corporations as well as new manufacturing enterprises. All of this vigorous new state activity, fed by the prosperity, boosterism, and growing confidence in material progress that were characteristic of the 1850s, was met almost immediately with a new backlash of anti-government hostility, an opposition which endangered the success of some of the state's pet projects from the outset and eventually claimed a few victims.

One obvious target for critics of the state's increasingly active role in promoting economic development was the plethora of railroad projects which enjoyed state subsidies during the early 1850s. Naturally the porkbarrel effects of these projects and the influence of the local entrepreneurs who lent financial and political support to railroad construction not only diluted much of the potential opposition to such projects but also generated a good deal of popular support for them. As a result, as long as the state's investment came from the revolving fund and required no new tax revenues, the railroad projects encountered little legislative opposition, but when the Blue Ridge Railroad asked the legislature for a capital subsidy that would eventually increase the state's total indebtedness by more than 30 percent, political opposition to the request quickly mobilized. Just a few weeks before his death in 1853, John Springs, one of the Upcountry's foremost railroad promoters, expressed alarm at the Blue Ridge Railroad's appetite for state funds and the willingness of at least some legislators to provide the subsidy. "Our State," Springs warned, "seems running wild about . . . RR's— they will run a good thing *into* the ground."[9]

But the most adamant opposition to the Blue Ridge Railroad's request for aid originated in those sections of the state which stood to gain little from the project. Spartanburg politicians, who wanted the transmontane road to head westward through the French Broad River valley in their area rather than through the Rabun Gap in Pendleton led the fight against state aid to the Blue Ridge Railroad. In 1854, all legislative candidates in the district vehemently opposed further state aid to the road.[10] The financially troubled company appealed to the legislature for aid again in 1856, 1858, and 1859. With each appeal, the road encountered

[9]For a survey of the battle over the Blue Ridge Railroad, see George DeWitt Brown, "A History of the Blue Ridge Railroad, 1852–1874" (M.A. thesis, University of South Carolina, 1967), especially pp. 24–49; quotation is from John Springs to Andrew Baxter Springs, September 27, 1853, Springs Family Papers, SHC.

[10]*Carolina Spartan,* September 7 and 14, 1854.

increased opposition. In Fairfield district, Edward G. Palmer, onetime president of the rival C and SC Railroad, condemned the expensive Blue Ridge project as "a gigantic scheme of wanton extravagance." In Laurens, taxpayers complained to the local newspaper that the state stood to gain but little from the transmontane road and charged that the project was a "conspiracy" in which the powerful BSSC was "trying to influence the people's legislature to spend the people's money" for a useless railroad. "When the capital of a joint stock company is composed chiefly of individual subscriptions the state as a stockholder may rely upon the vigilance of the individual subscriber for the proper expenditure of funds," Laurens Representative William D. Simpson told his supporters, "but where the reverse is the fact and the state Treasury is the principle source of revenue a wild and reckless extravagance generally prevails." Simpson maintained that the Blue Ridge Railroad could be built cheaper by "private capitalists" and that the government should "protect individuals in the enjoyment of their natural and inalienable rights—the rights of personal security and personal liberty" and leave the building of railroads to private investors.[11] Chester Representative C. D. Melton told his constituents, "The more I learn of the matter [Blue Ridge Railroad], the more gratified am I that I persisted in my views of opposition to it." Melton reported that the total cost of the Blue Ridge road might run as much as ten million dollars over budget and branded the entire project as "a stupendous fraud." The entire Spartanburg delegation, led by state Senator Gabriel Cannon, a director of the S and U Railroad, worked tirelessly to prohibit further state aid to the Blue Ridge.[12]

Despite its financial and technical problems, the Blue Ridge was not without powerful supporters in the legislature. Christopher Memminger led the united and influential Charleston delegation which supported the road, and B. F. Perry worked hard to rally Upcountry support. Moreover, districts along the route of the road scrambled to defend the company. The *Keowee Courier,* published at Pickens Courthouse, praised the progress made on the road as late as 1857, and in 1858, the newspaper noted approvingly that all legislative candidates from Pickens favored more state aid to the company. Newberry area promoters, arguing that the increased railroad traffic through their town would trigger another boom in the local economy, also campaigned in favor of the road's requests for more state aid. Moreover, the Newberry *Rising Sun* sharply criticized opponents of more state aid to the Blue Ridge for raising the cry of "Yankee, Yankee" against all state-aided internal improvement projects. This attempt to identify state support for economic improvement with crass Northern materialism or scheming Yankee capitalists, according to the *Rising Sun,* was not only the cheapest sort of demagoguery, but was also short-sighted. It slighted the real benefits which railroad development had brought to Newberry and ignored the

---

[11]Laurensville *Herald,* September 23, 1859; Speech of William D. Simpson [c. 1854], Simpson, Young, Dean, and Coleman Papers. SCL.

[12]Chester *Standard,* December 9, 1856; *Carolina Spartan,* July 29, 1859.

pressing need for the South to keep pace with the North economically in order to maintain equality between the sections.[13]

The strenuous efforts of Blue Ridge supporters secured legislative approval of a relatively modest amount of state aid for the company in 1856 on a very close vote. One proponent of the new aid package, Representative William P. McBee of Greenville, admitted to his wife, "I did not like to vote for it [state aid] simply for the reason that I had my doubts about the ability to build it [Blue Ridge Railroad]." Finally, when the Panic of 1857 put the Blue Ridge Railroad Company in yet another financial bind and actual work on the road lagged badly behind schedule, the legislature yielded to growing pressure from critics of the road and refused requests by the company for major transfusions of capital from the state in 1858 and 1859. Instead, the legislature granted the company an additional $300,000 to insure the completion of the line between Anderson and Walhalla, and washed its hands of the project. By 1859, the state had invested over $1,300,000 in Blue Ridge Railroad stock and endorsed over $1,000,000 in company bonds in order to build a thirty-three-mile spur line along the Georgia border. Longtime opponents of the project had a political field day with the company's failure, turning the project into one of the state's legendary boondoggles. Friends of the road, including B. F. Perry and Charleston's Christopher Memminger, lamented the reluctance of the state to see the project through to completion.[14]

The battle of selfish interests which surrounded the controversial Blue Ridge Railroad hardly reflected large-scale public disenchantment with economic development. Only a small part of the opposition to the Blue Ridge project came from people who feared that the expansion of the state's railroad network would lure more and more of the Upcountry's sturdy yeomen into the market economy and thus tighten the grip of commerce and commercial agriculture on the region. Instead, most of the opposition to the Blue Ridge Railroad was animated by the familiar republican fear of higher taxes and growing government indebtedness. Critics of the Blue Ridge project focused their attack on the role that the railroad's developers wanted the state to play in financing and insuring the project rather than on the efficacy of railroad development in general. Like William D. Simpson of Laurens, most critics of state aid to the Blue Ridge Railroad Company were willing to accept the building of the road if it could be financed with private capital. Moreover, the politicians who manipulated the electorate's fear of active government sponsorship of private corporations most vigorously and articulated the public's resentment most clearly were, in many cases, politicians whose own personal or local interests ran contrary to those of the Blue Ridge Railroad. Spartanburg, for example, vehemently opposed state aid for the Blue

[13]*Keowee Courier*, May 23, 1857, and April 3 and 24, 1858; Newberry *Rising Sun*, December 15 and 22, 1858; Greenville *Patriot and Mountaineer*, September 3, 1857; Greenville *Southern Enterprise*, April 8, 1858.

[14]William P. McBee to Harriet McBee [c. 1856], William P. McBee Papers, SCL; Smith, *Economic Readjustment*, pp. 188–190.

Ridge even as it begged for more state aid for the completion of the S and U Railroad, and S and U directors made no secret of their desire to see their railroad extended into North Carolina to become part of a transmontane hook-up. Clearly the Blue Ridge controversy never devolved into a clear choice between supporting or opposing railroad development, or even into a clear debate over the desirability of continued state funding of internal improvements. The Blue Ridge controversy did suggest, however, that the state's actively Whiggish policies of the 1850s were generating a significant political backlash which tied injured or ignored special interests to a general discontent over the state government's growing activism and the intensification of commercial dependencies.[15]

Projects designed to promote economic development met rooted indifference more often than orchestrated hostility. The Blue Ridge Railroad Company was hindered throughout its existence by a general indifference to the project outside of the Charleston commercial community. As a rule, Upcountry planters, even in districts along the route, declined to invest in the project, since the rudimentary railroad network connecting Upcountry towns to major fall-line and coastal markets was nearing completion. Occasionally, however, public criticism of railroads was more pointed. In 1857 a court in Laurens returned a verdict against the Laurens Railroad which required the company to pay $3600 in damages to local citizens whose property was destroyed in a minor accident. "It is a lamentable fact that strong prejudice against railroads exists among the people," complained the Laurensville *Herald,* "Why it is, we can not imagine." The editors attributed the anti-railroad prejudice to a general fear of change and a preference for the tried and true traditional ways of life. "Away with such old fogyism!" the newspaper demanded, "The idea of going back to road wagons and tobacco rolling is behind the spirit of the age." Attachment to old customs and traditional practices was also evident in Lancaster, the only Upcountry district which did not have a railroad by 1860. The Lancaster *Ledger* criticized the district's phlegmatic citizens in no uncertain terms. "There is an old customer in our country called 'Old Fogyism,' " wrote the paper; "his business is to snarl at and find objections to all new improvements and say 'it won't do.' " Moreover, the *Ledger* warned, Old Fogyism "has a pretty strong hold" on Lancaster, and "he will always keep us standing still or retrograding."[16]

To the extent that "Old Fogyism" represented opposition to railroad construction, or to economic development in general, it was a rather vague reluctance to give up old habits and practices, though no less intractable for its lack of definition. Seldom, if ever, did "Old Fogyism" present any systematic indictment of progress or any bill of particulars about the horrors which might lie ahead. To expect such a coherent and specific argument from "Old Fogyism," however, is to expect the impossible. Fear of the unknown, and of the unknowable, was the very essence of "Old Fogyism," and an indictment of the future is necessarily vague and general. The desire to cling stubbornly to tradition did not

[15]*Carolina Spartan,* November 15, 1855, August 14, 1856, and July 21, 1859.
[16]Laurensville *Herald,* April 24, 1857; Lancaster *Ledger,* August 21, 1859.

require prescient criticism of the evils of intensified commercial involvement. It required only an instinctive distrust of anything new or different. Thus "Old Fogyism," born largely of habit, indifference, and fear of the unknown, was an obstacle to economic development in the Upcountry, but, for the most part, it provided only passive and unfocused opposition.

When continued railroad development required increased taxation, however, more focused, and much more belligerent, opposition quickly emerged. Throughout the late 1850s, directors of the S and U Railroad and other commercial leaders from the Spartanburg area pushed for the extension of the S and U to Asheville, North Carolina, and eventually to Knoxville, Tennessee. In 1859, after work on the rival Blue Ridge Railroad was halted, Spartanburg Senator Gabriel Cannon cajoled the legislature into authorizing the road commissioners in Spartanburg District to subscribe to the stock of the Greenville and French Broad Railroad, a company chartered to build a line from somewhere in South Carolina to Greenville, Tennessee. Since the stock subscription would be paid with local tax revenues, it had to be approved by Spartanburg voters in a special referendum. The bulk of Spartanburg's entrepreneurial talent threw its weight behind the railroad project. Senator Gabriel Cannon and Representative James Farrow stumped the district trying to convince voters to support the subscription, and the two local newspapers both used their editorial columns to hail the virtues of railroad development. The *Carolina Spartan* suggested that the district should purchase at least $100,000 of railroad stock, which would have required raising local road taxes from $18,000 to $25,000 a year. Opposition to the tax-financed subscription surfaced quickly, and John Winsmith, a planter-physician from the southeastern section of Spartanburg, emerged as the leading spokesman for opponents of the tax. Winsmith stood alone against the rest of the delegation on the stump in the spring of 1860. Winsmith charged that the "free-citizens" of Spartanburg would be taxed to support a railroad which would benefit only merchants in the town of Spartanburg. Moreover, local farmers might actually be hurt by the cheap grain imported on the road from the West. Winsmith's main objection to the tax, however, was simply his opposition to public subsidies for internal improvements.[17]

Farrow retorted with the usual praise of the railroad's salutary impact on local commerce and property values. Still, rising public opposition forced supporters of the road to try a new tack. The road commissioners decided that only taxpayers, not all citizens, would be allowed to vote in the referendum. Secondly, the commissioners decided that all railroad tax levies totaling less than five dollars would be refunded by allowing the taxpayers to use tax receipts for under five dollars as cash. This latter ploy would have insured that 1300 of the poorest taxpayers in the district would be spared any tax increase. Farrow applauded the commission's action on both matters. Since only the taxpaying citizens would be

[17]MacArthur, "Antebellum, Politics in an Upcountry County: National, State, and Local Issues in Spartanburg County, South Carolina, 1850–1860" (M.A. thesis, Univ. of South Carolina, 1966), pp. 58–61; *Carolina Spartan,* January 4, February 2 and 4, and April 12, 1860.

directly affected by the results of the referendum, Farrow argued, it was perfectly fair, in this one case only, to limit the vote to taxpayers only. Moreover, the five-dollar tax credit given to the poorest 1300 taxpayers would defuse charges that a railroad for rich entrepreneurs was going to be built with the poor man's tax dollars.[18]

Winsmith, however, saw in the actions of the road commissioners a political hobby that he could ride to victory. He denounced the five-dollar tax credit as an attempt by railroad supporters to purchase the acquiescence of the district's hardscrabble farmers, and branded the ploy as a crass form of bribery which would undoubtedly "boomerang and backfire." Winsmith also appealed to the cherished tradition of political equality among whites by claiming that "the man who pays no tax should be equally entitled [with] the taxpayers to vote his vote."[19] Winsmith's rhetoric, and the long-standing opposition to tax increases, rallied rural Spartanburg against the tax subsidy for the railroad. When the day for the special referendum arrived, the eligible voters trooped to the polls to defeat the tax increase handily, 766 to 431, even though over half the district's voters were denied the right to cast their ballot. Farmer David Harris noted that there were "very few for taxation" at the polling place in Woodruff. "This [the tax measure] is an unpopular thing," Harris observed, "and will be lost by a large majority."[20] Harris was right; the Woodruff box tallied 39 votes against the tax and only two in favor of it. In the district as a whole, the tax-financed subsidy was defeated at 28 out of 36 polling places. The only strong support for the measure came from the town of Spartanburg and other small villages and crossroads along the proposed route of the road. Outside of the town of Spartanburg, over 70 percent of all voters opposed the measure. The defeat of the tax subsidy effectively killed the Greenville and French Broad Railroad. It also opened a permanent rift between the Winsmith faction and the Cannon-Farrow faction in Spartanburg politics and sparked a blood feud between Winsmith and Farrow which nearly ended on the dueling ground. Indeed, as the likelihood of secession dominated South Carolina politics in the fall of 1860, the hotly contested legislative races in Spartanburg hinged around the Winsmith-Farrow feud and continuing recriminations from the fight over the railroad tax.[21]

In addition to the various political battles waged over railroad expansion, South Carolina was divided internally around a series of issues related to the growing importance of credit, currency, and finance in an increasingly commercial society. When the degree of market orientation and the number and frequency of commercial transactions increased, as happened in South Carolina during the 1850s, the importance of reliable lines of credit, a stable and plentiful currency,

[18]*Carolina Spartan,* April 12 and 19, 1860.

[19]*Carolina Spartan,* April 19 and 26, May 3, 1860.

[20]Entry of May 12, 1860, David G. Harris Journals, SHC.

[21]*Carolina Spartan,* May 17, September 13, October 18, 1860; see also entries of May 14 and 16, 1860, James F. Sloan Diary, SCL; and Joseph Norton to Miles Norton, February 6, 1860, Joseph Jeptha Norton Papers, SCL.

and access to concentrations of capital was also magnified. The cotton boom and the commercial expansion of the 1850s lured more and more Upcountrymen into hot pursuit of the main chance, and, as a result, prompted a marked increase in the demand for credit. At first, both private capital and the state responded to this demand in the expected manner; banks were organized privately and chartered by the legislature, while existing banks established new agencies and expanded their operations. At the same time, however, the supply of credit available in the state was sharply limited by a long-standing usury law which placed a 7 percent ceiling on interest rates. To be sure, individual lenders often ignored the law in private transactions, knowing that the equity courts would allow them to recover principal plus legal interest even if the loan agreement was tainted with usury. Banks circumvented the law with "inland bills of exchange" which were allowed to bring whatever interest the market would bear.[22]

Skirting the law, however, was not a satisfactory means of procuring credit and capital. Once the boom of the 1850s began, Upcountry entrepreneurs began calling for the repeal of all usury laws, or at the very least, for allowing the legal rate of interest to rise to 10 or 12 percent. The general prosperity of the 1850s was interrupted momentarily by a panic in the winter of 1854 when a rapid contraction in the supply of currency drove cotton prices sharply downward. The brief, but painful, palpitation in the cotton market sparked new interest in ways of guaranteeing a liberal and stable flow of credit and currency into South Carolina. Meeting in December 1854, the legislature refused to repeal the existing usury laws despite the scarcity of credit. The *Carolina Spartan* criticized the legislature's caution and declared, "[T]he whole political philosophy of usury laws is becoming obsolete." The newspaper then recommended that the legislature allow the maximum legal interest to rise by 1 percent a year until it reached 12 percent.[23] The Chester *Standard* also called for the repeal of all usury laws. "The Legislature should not set the 'price' of money," declared the editors, "since . . . commerce has its own laws."[24] The next year, Governor James Hopkins Adams, a rich planter from lower Richland, called for the repeal of the usury laws in his annual message to the legislature. "The trade in money," Adams recommended, "should be as free as the trade in any other commodity . . . and the price should be left to the regulation of supply and demand." The governor went even further to suggest that, until private money lenders could receive as much return on personal loans as they could from investment in railroads and other corporations, short-term loans would be hard to obtain. Thus there should be no artificial restrictions placed on interest rates. "Competition in money," Adams declared, "as in everything else, must operate beneficially to the public at large."[25]

[22]Lesesne, *Bank of the State of South Carolina*, pp. 117–152; Thompson v. Nesbit, 2 Rich 73 (1845); Planters Bank of Fairfield v. Bivingsville Cotton Manufacturing Co., 11 Rich 677 (1857).
[23]*Carolina Spartan*, January 11, 1855.
[24]Chester *Standard*, December 21, 1854.
[25]Quoted in the *Carolina Spartan*, December 6, 1855.

Although the agricultural interests of the state suffered due to the scarcity of credit, agriculturalists generally opposed the repeal of usury laws. As a result, the legislature defeated bills calling for the repeal of usury laws handily in both 1855 and 1856. Then the Panic of 1857, and the severe contraction of currency and credit which accompanied it, reopened the debate over usury laws. In his message to the legislature, Governor Robert F. W. Allston, the fabulously wealthy Georgetown rice planter, asked for the repeal of all usury laws. "Money is entitled to the benefit of a market as well as every other commodity," Allston told the General Assembly.[26] The *Keowee Courier,* published in Pickens district, and the Edgefield *Advertiser* also urged the legislature to eliminate the manmade ceiling on interest rates. "Money," wrote the Edgefield *Advertiser,* "should be placed on the same basis as other commodities."[27]

During the Panic, however, hostility toward banks, financiers, and moneylenders was unusually intense, and defenders of the usury laws rode the popular hobby ably. John Douglass, a Chester area planter who headed the Fishing Creek Agricultural Society, presented an essay defending usury laws to his fellow members during the heat of the crisis. According to Douglass, repeal of the usury law was unlikely to make credit more readily available to the agriculturalist, since higher returns could still be earned elsewhere. Instead, it would simply make the credit that was already available more expensive, and farmers or planters who were forced to pay 10 or 12 percent interest would soon be broke. Repeal of usury laws was simply a windfall for moneylenders. "There may be gentlemen urging the repeal from honest, patriotic, but mistaken motives," Douglass announced, "but in my own experience and observation, they are generally of that class with money to loan."[28] Moreover, the *Carolina Spartan,* which had favored repeal two years earlier, backtracked and opposed repeal in 1857, when it urged the legislature not to create any further chaos by changing economic customs. The house voted 57 to 32 against repeal in mid-December, but the debate was renewed again the following year. "It will be a sad day," the Newberry Agricultural Society predicted, "when the capital of South Carolina is turned loose by law to depredate upon the property and industry of our people."[29] Yet banks in Chester, Fairfield, and Newberry joined other commercial interests in the state in a continued clamor for repeal. Aware of the anti-capitalist, anti-financier sentiment fostered by the sudden hard times, the legislature killed every attempt at repeal, thus refusing to free capital from yet another set of traditional fetters.

Indeed, if anything, politicians seemed inclined to give debtors more protection during the rapid commercial expansion of the 1850s than it had previously. In 1851 the legislature passed the so-called Homestead Act which allowed every property owner to exempt up to fifty acres of real estate as well as $500 of personal property from levy and sale. J. Wofford Tucker of Spartanburg, the

---

[26]*Carolina Spartan,* December 18, 1856, and December 3, 1857.

[27]*Keowee Courier,* December 5, 1857; Edgefield *Advertiser,* quoted in the Chester *Standard,* March 19, 1857.

[28]Chester *Standard,* September 24, 1857.

[29]*Carolina Spartan,* December 10 and 17, 1857; Newberry *Rising Sun,* July 28, 1858.

leading sponsor of the homestead bill, claimed the homestead exemption would stem the disturbing flow of small farmers from the Upcountry to fresh lands further west. "With a home and a small farm guaranteed to him," Tucker declared, "the desire to go in search of a new home and fresh lands will be greatly diminished, and the homestead would be cherished to an extent we know nothing of in this section."[30] By ensuring that a small farmer's homestead could not be attached or sold to satisfy creditors, the new law protected the homestead but made it more difficult for small farmers to secure credit. Still, farmers seemed to appreciate the benefits of the law.

Upcountry merchants, however, protested loud and long about the exemption's harmful impact on their business. In Union district, one observer criticized the new law as excessive "government interference in private affairs" and claimed that it destroyed the credit of the small farmer and worked an undue "hardship on merchants."[31] In York district, planter-entrepreneur John Springs predicted that "the Homestead bill . . . will encourage and produce fraud and corruption" and "increase drunkenness, extravagance, and reckless idleness" because every property owner could "console himself that let things come to the worst he has a living that can't be touched by his creditors." Springs insisted that "there is no strictly honest man who does not pay his debts and when need require a high-minded honorable man would deliver his effects to the last cent to his creditors."[32] The criticisms of the homestead law did not go unanswered. "As we anticipated," observed the Greenville *Mountaineer*, "we find many of the usurers, merchants, and money-changers hereabouts clamorous against this wise and humane law. It is the howl of the wolf for the lamb—the scream of the vulture for his prey."[33] Supporters of the homestead exemption argued that merchants extended credit to tenant farmers who owned less than $500 worth of any kind of property but refused to lend to landowning yeomen of modest means. Merchants mounted a serious effort to have the Homestead Act repealed in 1852, but were rebuffed by a legislative committee.[34] The extreme shrinkage of credit lines accompanying the Panic of 1857, however, forced the legislature to rethink its position on the homestead exemption. Farmers and planters alike were unable to sell much of that year's cotton crop. Strapped for cash and unable to pay old debts, agriculturalists needed credit desperately in the winter of 1857–58 in order to plant the next year's crop. Thus the same exemption which protected the homestead of small farmers also threatened to prevent them from planting a crop in 1858. The legislature, yielding to pressure from both small farmers and supply merchants, repealed the six-year-old Homestead Act in December 1857.[35]

[30]Manning v. Dove, 10 Rich 395 (1857); Yorkville *Miscellany,* December 7, 1851.

[31]Unionville *Journal,* March 19, 1852.

[32]John Springs to Andrew Baxter Springs, September 7, 1852, Springs Family Papers, SHC.

[33]Quoted in Yorkville *Miscellany,* January 17, 1852.

[34]Yorkville *Miscellany,* December 23, 1852.

[35]J. A. Compton to William W. Renwick, November 25, 1857, James Rogers to William W. Renwick, December 16, 1857, William W. Renwick Papers, SCL; entry of May 27, 1856, David Gavin Diary, SHC; Mary Milling to James S. Milling, December 5, 1857, James S. Milling Papers, SHC; *In re* Sarah Kennedy, 2 South Carolina 216 (1870).

The curious history of South Carolina's usury and homestead laws during the 1850s reflected the state's general confusion over how best to protect the independent producer from the vicissitudes of commerce without condemning him to the poverty of a hermetic economy. Despite pressure from merchants, bankers, and other entrepreneurs, the state refused to roll back ancient usury laws to create a free market for capital in South Carolina. At the same time, however, farmers and planters used credit far more liberally than ever before as they expanded operations and plunged deeper into commercial involvement. Never reluctant to find fault in others, forty-five-year-old David Gavin observed that when he was a boy "people worked for a living," but "now many live on credit, or by some other swindling process."[36] Moreover, as the economic boom began, the legislature moved to protect small farmers from the ravages of fickle commerce by putting their homesteads beyond the reach of creditors. Yet during the Panic of 1857, when bankruptcies multiplied and debtors were hard-pressed, the legislature quickly removed the protection of the homestead law in order to make more credit available to hardscrabble farmers. The overwhelming majority of planters and farmers operated on credit, and a good portion of them could not have operated at all without it. Nevertheless, the dependencies engendered by constant indebtedness still weighed heavily on the minds of a people who prized personal independence above all else. Commerce was a treacherous but indispensable handmaiden of civic virtue. Credit was a necessary evil.

Doubtless the most controversial part of South Carolina's economic infrastructure were the banks. The state-controlled BSSC had a long and exemplary record as a sound and conservatively managed institution which had done much to bring financial stability to the state. Despite its nearly impeccable financial record, however, the BSSC was repeatedly assailed for becoming excessively political and abusing its considerable power. When they were not taking pot shots at the powerful BSSC, private banks in South Carolina often found themselves under attack, usually for sending too much of their capital out of state rather than aiding capital-starved South Carolinians. On the whole, the record of private banks in South Carolina was remarkably good. Only two banks in the state collapsed prior to the Civil War, and private banks generally avoided the reckless speculation and wild inflationary policies so often characteristic of banks in other Southern states. The public, however, never forgave the banks for what it perceived as their shoddy and irresponsible performance during the depression of the late 1830s. Responsible, reform-minded politicians, led by Calhoun, had turned the anti-bank fury of those years into a useful push for tighter regulation of banking practices in South Carolina. In 1840, the legislature passed a rigorous set of new banking regulations which imposed a substantial fine (5 percent per annum on all circulating notes) on all banks which suspended specie payment for any reason, and required all banks to make a monthly report to the comptroller general, who was to study these reports and then publish them in state newspapers. A number

---

[36]Entry of May 27, 1856, David Gavin Diary, SHC.

of banks refused to submit to these new regulations on the grounds that the new laws violated rights granted by their charters. The state responded by initiating legal action against those banks which refused to comply with the new regulations. State Circuit Judge Andrew Pickens Butler decided the first two test cases, both involving Charleston banks, in favor of the banks. Butler argued that the legislature could not revoke a bank's charter except for violation of conditions stipulated in the original charter. Both cases were appealed to the Court of Errors, the highest court in the state at the time, which overturned Butler's ruling in one case but upheld him on a technicality in the other. With the constitutionality of its new banking laws still very much in doubt, the state dropped its efforts to revoke the charters of existing banks but persuaded all banks to comply voluntarily with the new regulations.[37]

As the state recovered from the agricultural depression which followed the Panic of 1837, the anti-bank hysteria subsided, but the old Jeffersonian contention that the government and the banks should be separated remained a popular political hobby. This variety of anti-bank sentiment was aimed almost exclusively at the BSSC. During the late 1840s, anti-BSSC politicians renewed their campaign against the institution. According to its critics, the BSSC, especially when under the leadership of the politically astute Franklin H. Elmore, used its influence to create and support a powerful and corrupt "Court" faction, which dominated state politics in a manner reminiscent of the way the wicked Walpolean system controlled Great Britain a century earlier. Emphasizing a fundamental principle of old republicanism, anti-BSSC spokesman B. F. Perry declared that the preservation of free and uncorrupted institutions required the separation of the banks from the government. "[I]t is absolutely necessary," Perry claimed, "that the public funds should be under the control of the government and this renders the government incapable of banking with wisdom and success."[38] Charleston radical John Cunningham echoed Perry's sentiments in even more colorful language. Cunningham yearned for the day "when South Carolina will stand neither as a supplicant debtor nor frowning creditor; when she is no longer a speculator and stockjobber, with skirts polluted in the shambles of the market, and when in accordance with her high mission and duty, she in unsullied robes of sovereignty, simply receives and distributes her revenue, in administering, in republican dignity and simplicity, her Government for the happiness, protection and prosperity of her people."[39]

Emboldened by the apparent popularity of James Henry Hammond's widely circulated "Anti-Debt" essays attacking the BSSC, anti-BSSC forces decided to fight the state-owned bank in the legislature in 1848. Hiram Hutchinson, presi-

[37]Lesesne, *Bank of the State of South Carolina*, pp. 35–61; Smith, *Economic Readjustment*, especially p. 194; *The Bank Case: A Report of the Proceedings in the Cases of the Bank of South Carolina and the Bank of Charleston . . .* (Charleston, 1844).

[38]See entry of December 25, 1850, James Henry Hammond Diary, SCL; B. F. Perry to Franklin H. Elmore, November 22, 1849, Franklin H. Elmore Papers, LC.

[39]John Cunningham, *Speech on the Bill to Provide for the Approaching Expiration of the Bank Charter, Delivered in the House of Representatives* (Charleston, 1850).

dent of the Bank Hamburg and a friend of Hammond, helped orchestrate the anti-BSSC campaign in the Upcountry, while Christopher Memminger, a Charlestonian with strong ties to a private bank in that city, served as point man for the anti-BSSC forces in the legislature. Anti-BSSC leaders wanted the legislature to announce that the BSSC's charter, which was to expire in 1856, would not be renewed and to force the bank to begin liquidation of its assets in preparation for the end of its corporate existence.[40] Pro-BSSC forces, led by the eloquent Benjamin C. Yancey of Edgefield, fought back. Yancey argued that the BSSC had not only reduced the state debt, guaranteed the loan needed to rebuild Charleston after the 1837 fire, and helped finance railroad development in the state but that it had also accommodated planters and farmers "on longer paper than the short discounts and regular reductions . . . so universally adopted for commercial accomodation" at a sacrifice of profits. The Edgefield representative dismissed the attacks on the BSSC as "idle gossip" circulated by "political demagogues."[41] After heated debate, the anti-BSSC forces succeeded in getting both houses of the legislature to endorse, on very close votes, a set of resolutions deeming it "unwise and inexpedient for a State to engage in Banking" but failed in their efforts to force more dramatic or conclusive action.[42]

Despite the mixed results of the 1848 legislative session, anti-BSSC leaders continued their political war against the state's bank for the next four years. Upcountry entrepreneurs John Springs and William Gist, and J. Foster Marshall, a state senator from Abbeville, joined Perry, Memminger, Hammond and others in active opposition to the BSSC. The legislature of 1849 passed another joint resolution insisting that the BSSC prepare to end its operations when its charter expired in 1856. But in 1850 and 1851, legislators paid less attention to charges against the BSSC because of their preoccupation with the first secession crisis. Anti-BSSC leader John Felder, state senator from Orangeburg, kept the fight alive in the legislature but confided to Hammond that most legislators considered the anti-bank campaign "unpatriotic" during a period of sectional crisis. Moreover, the appointment of controversial BSSC President Elmore to fill the United States Senate seat vacated when Calhoun died in 1850 helped defuse the anti-BSSC campaign. Elmore, who was constantly criticized for using the power of the BSSC to aid his own political cause, was replaced as president by Charles M. Furman, the cashier of the BSSC since 1832. Furman, though well-connected around the state, possessed more financial than political expertise and was expected by most observers to function as more of a technician and less of a

[40][James Henry Hammond], *The Railroad Mania and Review of the Bank of the State of South Carolina: A Series of Essays by Anti-Debt* (Charleston, 1848); Lesesne, *Bank of the State of South Carolina*, pp. 71–79; Hiram Hutchinson to John Springs, April 14, 1848, Springs Family Papers, SHC; James Edward Henry to Samuel Finley Patterson, December 28, 1848, Samuel Finley Patterson Papers, DU.

[41]*Speech of Benjamin C. Yancey of Edgefield, in Relation to the Bank of the State of South Carolina, Delivered in Committee of the Whole House, December Session of the Legislature, 1848* (Hamburg, 1849), pp. 1–24.

[42]Lesesne, *Bank of the State of South Carolina*, p. 78.

politician than his predecessor.[43] Nor were pro-BSSC forces without their resources. In 1850, a pro-BSSC planter from Edgefield, R. O. Griffin, urged the
popular attorney Benjamin Yancey, planter-industrialist John Bauskett, mil-
lionaire gold miner William "Billy" Dorn, and Frank Burt, the younger brother
of Congressman Armistead Burt, all of whom supported the BSSC, to "take the
Stump . . . and attack the private Banks, Capitalists, etc" and defend the BSSC.
The spectacle of Bauskett, long the principal owner of the Vaucluse textile mill,
and Billy Dorn, who once pledged $150,000 to an unsuccessful railroad project,
taking to the hustings to attack "Capitalists" must have been an odd one indeed,
and none were elected to office in 1850, but the support of these men and others
like them gave the BSSC a degree of staying power that it sorely needed.[44]

In the aftermath of the first secession crisis, the anti-BSSC crusade lost its
momentum entirely. Longtime BSSC opponent John Felder died in 1851, and
Christopher Memminger decided not to seek election to the House in 1852. The
BSSC had strengthened its position by depositing $200,000 in the state treasury
to help finance the state's greatly increased military appropriations during the
crisis of 1850 and 1851, and new governor John Hugh Means of Fairfield
supported the BSSC. In 1852, with a strong endorsement from Means and a
glowing annual report from President Furman, the BSSC persuaded the legislature to reverse its earlier position and extend the BSSC's charter until 1871. The
statute extending the bank's charter, however, explicitly prohibited the BSSC
from buying stock in railroad companies without the expressed consent of the
legislature and required the bank to pay off as much of the state's debt each year
as its profits allowed.[45] Critics of the BSSC were disgusted. John Springs criticized his son Andrew Baxter Springs, a legislator from York district, for not
pressing his opposition to the bank more aggressively. "The People," the elder
Springs told his son, "would have sustained you against the Political intrigues of
a monied Aristocracy, against the hireling dupes of the Political Monster which
now controls the State." John Springs admitted that in the folly of his youth (and
before he became a major stockholder in a number of private banks) he had
supported the BSSC, but claimed that "experience" had "since convinced" him
that the old Radical William Smith was right in characterizing the BSSC as "a
demoralizing, corrupting institution and . . . a ruinous one to the Purity and
welfare of the State." South Carolinians, Springs claimed, were "louder and
more clamorous" in favor of a "divorce of the Governments from Banks" than
any other people, yet the state was "the last to give it [banking] up in practice"

[43]Christopher G. Memminger to James Henry Hammond, December 27, 1848, and John M.
Felder to James Henry Hammond, December 16, 1850, James Henry Hammond Papers, LC (on
microfilm at SCL); Charleston *Courier*, November 30, 1849; *Daily South Carolinian*, April 1, 1850;
Lesesne, *Bank of the State of South Carolina*, pp. 79–103.

[44]R. O. Griffin to Benjamin C. Yancey, February 15 and June 4, 1850, John Bauskett to
Benjamin C. Yancey, August 17, 1850, A. Y. Teague to Benjamin C. Yancey, August 20, 1850,
Thomas McGrath to Benjamin C. Yancey, October 20, 1853, Benjamin C. Yancey Papers, SHC.

[45]Lesesne, *Bank of the State of South Carolina*, pp. 104–105; Charleston *Courier*, November 24,
1852; Greenville *Southern Patriot*, December 16, 1852.

and had a bank "which now has got the ascendency" in state politics. "It has now become dangerous to run counter to the Banking Party," Springs warned. "It [the BSSC] supports and is the meat and drink of a number of broken-down disappointed Politicans and idlers that is [sic] too lazy to go to work for their bread, men selected not for their integrity and capacity but for their noisy Political zeal and influence, and now let one attack their hive and they swarm out like so many yellow-jackets that . . . bite and sting both at the same time."[46]

Despite the fact that the BSSC enjoyed the best of financial health during the early 1850s, the key to its political survival was the increased demand for banking services. As railroads penetrated new areas of the state, towns and villages along the rail lines wanted banks to provide the liquid capital needed to finance the growing volume of local trade. Thus politicians from locales in need of banking services dropped or diluted their opposition to the BSSC in return for support from pro-BSSC legislators for the creation of new banks and banking agencies, especially in interior towns. In 1851, the legislature granted a bank charter for the first time since 1836, and during the next five years granted a total of eleven new bank charters and approved the establishment of a number of new banking agencies. Also, the total dollar value of the notes in circulation from South Carolina banks increased from a maximum of $6,472,716 during the stagnant 1840s to over $11,000,000 during the boom years of the early 1850s.[47]

Yet despite the crucial role played by banks in facilitating the new commercial vitality of the 1850s, the banks found themselves the objects of considerable popular animosity on several occasions during the decade. Triggered by the short but dramatic currency contraction of 1854 and fueled by the traumatic Panic of 1857, a resurgence of anti-bank feeling in the Upcountry produced not merely a call for separation of the banks and the government but also more radical calls for the elimination of all banks, the revocation of existing bank charters, and for stringent state regulation of banks. Indeed, during the late 1850s, critics unleashed a barrage of political fire against banks in South Carolina which matched, and possibly surpassed, the spectacular Jacksonian anti-bank crusade of two decades earlier, and much of this new anti-bank venom was aimed at the new banks and banking agencies which set up shop in the Upcountry only a few years earlier.[48]

At first the new banks and banking agencies in the Upcountry were generally hailed as yet another sign of the progress and prosperity which railroad development, along with rebounding cotton prices, brought to the region. A few signs of

[46]John Springs to Andrew Baxter Springs, September 7 and 19, 1852, Springs Family Papers, SHC.

[47]Lesesne, *Bank of the State of South Carolina*, pp. 101–106; *Hunt's Merchants Magazine* 28 (1853):221.

[48]On the severity of financial problems in 1854 and again in 1857, see J. H. Lipscomb to Smith Lipscomb, January 29, 1854, Lipscomb Family Papers, SHC; J. J. Blackwood to Andrew Baxter Springs, January 4, 1855, Springs Family Papers, SHC; J. A. Compton to William W. Renwick, April 20, 1858, William W. Renwick Papers, SCL; John Cothran to James S. Cothran, December 11, 1857, Thomas C. Perrin Papers, DU.

discord, however, appeared during the mild Panic of 1854. Most Upcountry cotton growers blamed the low cotton prices of that year on a drastic shrinkage in the amount of circulating currency. As banks called in notes, low cotton prices left planters and farmers alike unable to pay. Banks and other creditors, themselves hard-pressed by their capital sources, often went to court to recover their capital. Since most sales of agricultural supplies in the Upcountry were made on a credit basis, the monetary crisis resulted in an unprecedented number of debt actions. In 1854, there were 275 such suits in Chester district and over 500 in York district, representing a ten- to twenty-fold increase over the normal number of such cases. Banks blamed the problem on the usury laws, while optimists predicted that "a full cotton crop, with good prices, will pay it [debt] off in a flash."[49]

The recovery in 1855, however, did not pay all agricultural debts off in a flash, nor did it drive the memory of the banks' performance during the crisis out of the farmers' minds. Charges were made, with considerable accuracy, that the banks were investing much of their capital out of state and that they were speculating in inland or foreign bills of exchange, which were exempt from usury statutes, rather than using their resources to finance the planting and selling of cotton and other crops in South Carolina. Bank defenders blamed the shortage of currency on the tax on bank stock levied by the legislature in 1852. Prior to that tax, bank corporations paid a sizable fee to the state treasury to obtain charters. The new tax, complained the *Carolina Spartan,* hurt the Upcountry by slowing the creation of banks in a region long plagued by a shortage of circulating currency.[50] In April 1856, Chester farmer Jonathan Newland renewed the attack on the growing power of banks. Banks, Newland charged, create "a monied aristocracy" and have "a tendency to make the rich richer and the poor poorer." Such actions, Newland protested, were "partial and unjust, and antagonistic to the republican institutions of our country."[51] Once Newland began the attack, others quickly joined the fray. Another Chester citizen claimed that banks were a curse rather than a blessing to area planters and farmers. When granted charters, this citizen noted, the banks promised to lend "easy" money to farmers so they could expand staple production, but once a bank was formed it tied up most of its money in thirty- or sixty-day loans, mainly to merchants. The writer blamed the Bank of Chester, organized in 1852, for driving private moneylenders, a traditional source of credit for small farmers, out of the market. "The truth is," the citizen continued, "this whole banking business is a fraud practiced upon the interest of the honest and industrious farmer . . . and the people are pronouncing [the Bank of Chester] an unmitigated curse."[52]

The Bank of Chester, however, was not without its champions. One Chester native maintained that the bank actually did farmers a service by discouraging the

[49]Chester *Standard,* March 22, 1855.
[50]*Carolina Spartan,* December 18, 1855.
[51]Chester *Standard,* April 24, 1856.
[52]Chester *Standard,* May 1, 1856.

use of credit, while praising the bank for improving local commerce by discounting over $1 million in notes in 1855. Another defender, writing under the pseudonym "Adam," acknowledged that banks worked hardships on some people, but pleaded that the overall benefits of banks outweighed the injustices. "Some fifteen years ago, when railroads began to develop themselves," "Adam" recalled, "how often we heard wagoners, stage contractors, and drivers damn the infernal Railroad for taking the bread out of honest people's mouths. Did the community stop building railroads on account of these?"[53] Such arguments failed to mollify Chester farmers. "When the Railroad made Chester a market, almost a seaport town, was it not necessary to have a Bank and afford proper mercantile facilities[?]" questioned one farmer. "We answer emphatically No!" he replied to his own query.[54] Farmers could have relied on the traditional sources of credit in Charleston and Columbia. The Bank of Chester, this citizen alleged, was nothing more than a "monied aristocracy" given legal recognition by its charter. "Banks," lamented Chester lawyer and House member C. D. Melton in December 1856, "occupy in the popular mind much the same place as did the Jews in former times."[55]

When the Panic of 1857 hit, the already considerable anti-bank sentiment in the Upcountry spewed forth with a vengeance. Although there was some tightness of credit throughout the year, business went on essentially as usual in 1857 until the cotton crop began to reach the market in the early fall. Suddenly, New York and London banks called in their debts, and panic quickly spread out from the metropolises to satellite areas such as Columbia and Charleston. The crisis caught South Carolina banks grossly overextended and with woefully inadequate specie reserves. On October 1, 1857, banks in the state had deposits of nearly $3,000,000 and notes in circulation of over $7,000,000 and yet held just under $1,000,000 in specie. The BSSC alone had $1,750,000 in deposits and currency to redeem while holding only $20,000 in specie. To meet the crisis, the BSSC board of directors voted on October 10 to suspend specie payments indefinitely, and ten other banks immediately followed suit.[56] J. J. Blackwood, the new president of the Bank of Hamburg, admitted that "these are trying times" and defended the suspension of specie payment as an effort "to keep the 'old Ship' above the waves and finally make a safe harbor."[57]

Public outrage against the banks quickly erupted. On October 22, planter T. W. Moore told the Fishing Creek Agricultural Society that the banks were responsible for the crisis because they maintained inadequate specie reserves. But Moore's attack on banks went beyond the causes of the current crisis. The rapid creation of so many new banks during the decade, Moore asserted, had tied "the entire surplus capital in the country" up in bank stock, thus fostering

[53]Chester *Standard*, May 23, 1856.

[54]Chester *Standard*, May 19, 1856.

[55]Chester *Standard*, December 16, 1856.

[56]*Reports and Resolutions of the South Carolina General Assembly, 1857* (Columbia, S.C.: R. W. Gibbes, 1857), pp. 11–79.

[57]J. J. Blackwood to Andrew Baxter Springs, November 5, 1857, Springs Family Papers, SHC.

speculation and driving men out of agriculture because "all the aids to enter-prise" were placed "utterly beyond their reach" by the banks.[58] The *Carolina Spartan,* previously a supporter of banks, complained that Upcountry banks sent too much capital out of the state "seeking large profits" when they should have provided a "home supply of money" by circulating notes locally. "Banks are chartered for the benefit of the people," the *Spartan* announced angrily, "not for the exclusive advantage of the stockholders."[59] Within a matter of weeks, hostile citizens were attacking banks on all fronts. A grand jury in Fairfield reported banks, and in particular the Planters' Bank of Fairfield, to be "evils" and "public nuisances" and was later joined by grand juries in Spartanburg, Abbeville, Newberry, and Chester.[60]

Banks did what they could to calm increasingly savage public opinion. In October 1857, cotton buyers in Chester created "a little excitement" when they charged that the Bank of Chester had refused to advance money for cotton purchases because it was on the verge of bankruptcy. The bank's president, George S. Cameron, countered that the cotton buyers who made the charges had been unable to provide the bank with the security it required. Cameron's re-sponse, however, failed to calm the public's nerves, and by early November the twelve directors of the Bank of Chester made a dramatic move to allay fears about the bank's condition. Even though the bank had not suspended specie payment, all twelve directors publicly pledged their personal fortunes to the solvency of the bank. Included among those taking this pledge were a number of the area's wealthiest men, such as Thomas McLure, James Hemphill, George Cameron, Samuel McAliley, Nathaniel Eaves, and A. B. Springs. The directors obviously hoped that their dramatic pledge would allow the Bank of Chester to remain open without exposing itself to the danger of a run by depositors. To suspend specie payments, the directors knew, destroyed public confidence in a bank, but to continue payments during a panic could bring it to the brink of failure. The Bank of Chester hoped to avoid either calamity.[61] In Spartanburg, all the prominent merchants in the district publicly promised that they would continue to accept all bills from all banks in South Carolina and Georgia, re-gardless of whether a bank had suspended specie payments or not. Indeed, these merchants applauded suspension of specie payments as the best way for banks to avoid a potentially disastrous run on banks by a panic-stricken public. Merchants in other parts of the state followed the example of those in Spartanburg and continued to accept notes from banks which had suspended specie payments. One observer even went so far as to contend that even during the worst moments of the crisis, bank bills "circulate and answer all our purposes as well as gold." The merchants' decision to continue accepting bank bills helped them collect a portion of their debts from planters and farmers, but until the banks could again

[58]Chester *Standard,* October 22, 1857.

[59]*Carolina Spartan,* October 1, 1857.

[60]Presentments of the Grand Jury, Fall and Spring, 1857, Fall and Spring, 1858, SCA.

[61]George S. Cameron to Andrew Baxter Springs, October 10, 1857, Jonathan A. Bradley to Andrew Baxter Springs, December 10, 1857, Springs Family Papers, SHC.

make large loans to cotton buyers, these same planters and farmers had no market for their staple. As a result, the merchants' action did little to soothe an irate public. "One bank is evil," the *Carolina Spartan* railed in late October; "two is a curse."[62]

When the legislature met in late November, it quickly turned its attention to the banking crisis. In general, public opinion demanded that the General Assembly not only punish the banks for suspending specie payments but also adopt new and stricter regulations concerning out-of-state speculation. David Gavin observed the mercurial nature of public attitudes toward the banks with some amusement. "The people are making a great fuss and talk about the suspension of [specie payments by] the banks," he noted, "when five or six years ago they were incorporating little banks all over the State for shaving shops and speculating on credit they never thought of paying."[63] The banks, instead of pleading for mercy, demanded that the legislature repeal the 5 percent penalty for suspension imposed by the Banking Act of 1840 as a precondition for the banks' releasing future loans to staple buyers. A spate of proposals calling for reforms in the state banking structure, ranging from William Gregg's recommendation to establish a mandatory 3-to-1 specie-reserve ratio and to raise the legal limit on interest rates to 8 percent, to Governor R. F. W. Allston's plan to require a one-to-one reserve ratio and reduce the number of banks in the state to six, were bandied about the legislature.[64] The Bank of Hamburg's J. J. Blackwood worried that the "subject of banking" was poorly understood by most legislators and thus any legislation would only "make matters worse," but Jonathan Bradley, an officer with the Bank of Chester, saw "little danger" of "any inconsiderate legislation" precisely because the General Assembly knew that it would "only make matters worse by unskillful tampering with the delicate subject of the Banks and money."[65] Ultimately, the big fight of the legislative session centered around the rather narrow issue of whether the 5 percent suspension penalty required by the existing statute should, or could, be enforced. The banks lobbied hard for a stay on the penalty, while House Ways and Means Chairman Christopher Memminger, buoyed by vehemently anti-bank public opinion, fought for strict enforcement.[66]

After long and bitter debate, the legislature ultimately passed a complex compromise measure. The 5 percent penalty against banks suspending specie payments was postponed until January 1, 1859, but the banks were prohibited from seeking judgments against debtors for the same period. The banks were

[62]*Letter of William Gregg to Thornton Coleman, June 8, 1858* (Charleston: Walker, Evans, 1858), pp. 1–15; *Carolina Spartan,* October 29 and November 5, 1857.

[63]Entry of October 18, 1857, David Gavin Diary, SHC.

[64]Lesesne, *Bank of the State of South Carolina,* pp. 110–112.

[65]J. J. Blackwood to Andrew Baxter Springs, December 10, 1857, Jonathan A. Bradley to Andrew Baxter Springs, December 10, 1857, Springs Family Papers, SHC.

[66]*Speech of C. G. Memminger in the House of Representatives of South Carolina upon the Bill and Resolutions Relating to Bank Issue and Suspensions, December, 1857* (Charleston, 1858); *Carolina Spartan,* December 3, 1857.

allowed to charge the debtor 7 percent interest during the one-year stay. More-over, beginning on January 1, 1860, all banks were to circulate no more than $300 in currency for each $100 of specie held in reserve, and were prohibited from issuing any notes for less than ten dollars. Also, banks were required to make weekly, rather than quarterly, financial reports to the state comptroller general. On the whole, the new banking regulations mandated more conservative banking policies and practices from banks in South Carolina while trying to ease the pain inflicted on both banks and debtors by the Panic of 1857 through stays on debt repayment and the suspension penalty. According to one observer, the legislature agreed with the banks' contention "that merchants should be supplied with funds in order to purchase the crop of cotton coming to market," but that they could not make these funds available if forced to pay "the intolerable tax" imposed by the penalty.[67]

The legislature's decision to stay both the suspension penalty and debt judg-ments probably saved many South Carolinians from hardship. If it had enforced the penalty, the banks would have undoubtedly called in loans and contracted their note circulation. These moves would have left many debtors unable to pay and produced an unprecedented number of lawsuits and property judgments. The outraged public, however, was still so angry with the banks that they were unimpressed with the legislature's wisdom and magnanimity. Newspapers throughout the Upcountry denounced the legislature for lifting the 5 percent penalty from the banks and for allowing the banks to charge interest over the period that specie payments were suspended. The Laurensville *Herald* charged that the new regulations left the people "at the mercy of soul-less banks," while the *Carolina Spartan* predicted that allowing the banks to charge interest during the stay "would cause many people to lose their property." A. C. Garlington, a wealthy Laurens planter and grist mill owner, charged that "banks feel they are superior to people," and suggested that the penalty should be imposed unless banks reduced the amount of capital invested outside of the state.[68]

In the spring of 1858, Upcountry grand juries again complained about the activities of banks in their locales. Particularly virulent were the charges leveled against the Bank of Newberry by the grand jury of that district. The grand jury presented the Bank of Newberry as a public nuisance which not only sent most of its capital out of state but also attempted "to manipulate the price of cotton by dictating who one should or should not ship cotton to." The Newberry grand jury also openly accused Bank of Newberry president B. D. Boyd with conspiring to control the price of cotton in the local market. Boyd, the jury reported, sent circulars to local cotton buyers threatening not to supply the buyers with loans if they paid more than a certain price for cotton. Initially, Boyd flatly denied that he had issued such circulars, but he retreated when cotton buyers in both Laurens

[67]Lesesne, *Bank of the State of South Carolina*, pp. 111–116; *Letter of William Gregg*, pp. 7–8; *Carolina Spartan*, December 17 and 31, 1857.

[68]Laurensville *Herald*, January 22 and February 19, 1858; *Carolina Spartan*, December 31, 1857; Chester *Standard*, December 17, 1857; *Keowee Courier*, December 5, 1857; Newberry *Rising Sun*, April 7, 1858.

and Clinton produced copies of the circulars carrying Boyd's name. Boyd's next tack was to threaten the local newspaper, the Newberry *Rising Sun,* with libel action if it printed any further communications damaging to his character. The *Rising Sun* rebuked Boyd for his heavy-handed attempt to gag the press denouncing it "as hostile and at war with the principles of Republican liberty."[69]

Local dissatisfaction with Boyd's stewardship of the Bank of Newberry actually pre-dated the crisis of 1857. Other Upcountry bankers recognized that the Bank of Newberry did a very active business in the mid-1850s but noted that it was "very unpopular in its own neighborhood."[70] A number of Newberry area planters, including Job and Silas Johnston, who together owned roughly a quarter of the Bank's stock, complained that Boyd disdained the long-term loans needed by the Newberry agricultural community while advancing large sums in the form of ninety-day notes to merchants and cotton buyers. Boyd dismissed these complaints about his management as the work of a "one-horse party" more interested in "popular business" than in the sound financial performance of the bank.[71] In fact, defenders of Boyd and the Bank of Newberry were not entirely without ammunition. They leveled the familiar charge that bank critics were simply trying to drum up a hobby which would serve them well if they chose to run for the state legislature. That charge, of course, was true. Candidates for office always looked for the issue that might carry them to victory and then tried to work that issue to their best advantage, but no issue could become a successful hobby unless the voters thought it important. If they had not, the issue would have died quickly. Bank defenders also revealed that Whitfield Walker, foreman of the accusatory grand jury, had a personal grievance against the bank. Walker, a former planter who had moved to the town of Newberry to set up shop as a cotton merchant, had owed the Bank of Newberry $35,000 since April 1857. During the next fall and winter the Bank refused to loan any more money to Walker. Moreover, Walker believed, perhaps rightly, that Boyd deliberately steered business away from him that season. Walker's business, like many others in the state, teetered on the brink of failure in early 1858, and collapsed later that year. Walker, bank champions argued, was simply trying to make Boyd and his bank the scapegoat for his own failure.[72]

If Walker was motivated by personal pique, most who rallied behind him were not. The grassroots resentment directed at the Bank of Newberry was not easily defused. In the spring and summer of 1858, voters began to push candidates for the legislature who were sharply critical of the banks. "Bush River" suggested prominent militia leader H. H. Kinard because he was "no friend to that Madagascar Bat, the Newberry Bank, which is sucking away the life blood of the people, in the shape of usurious exchange."[73] Also, local farmer Randall

---

[69]Newberry *Rising Sun,* April 28 and May 19, 1858; Laurensville *Herald,* May 21, 1858; Keowee *Courier,* June 19, 1858.

[70]J. J. Blackwood to Andrew Baxter Springs, February 7, 1856, Springs Family Papers, SHC.

[71]B. D. Boyd to Andrew Baxter Springs, November 24, 1855, Springs Family Papers, SHC.

[72]Newberry *Rising Sun,* June 9, 1858.

[73]Newberry *Rising Sun,* April 14 and June 2, 1858.

Croft, whose name was also broached as a possible candidate for the legislature, claimed that banks "are an incubus to any agricultural community." Drawing heavily on the rhetoric of Andrew Jackson, Croft unleashed an unvarnished attack on banks that would have done any hard-money Jacksonian proud. "I have never seen a bank erected in any town or village," Croft observed, "that it did not ruin after a while . . . though the people be thrifty, and out of debt, whenever banks are in their midst, they become indebted to the bank—their property mortgaged or sold, and the many laboring for the few. And after they have acquired strength by holding mortgages and liens on the people generally, are they not the lords and masters of these people?"[74]

The banks in South Carolina all resumed specie payments by early June 1858; the credit supply loosened a bit, and cotton prices began to rebound. The crisis was over, and the immediacy faded from the public's crusade against the banks. But popular resentment of banks lingered on. In Newberry, as well as in most other Upcountry districts, all successful candidates for the legislature pledged to work for tighter regulation of banks in the state. The new legislature did discuss new and more severe restrictions on banks, but ultimately failed to pass any significant new regulations. After John Brown's raid on Harper's Ferry in 1859 and the ensuing alarm which spread through South Carolina, the banking issue fell from prominence in state politics. Yet even as the controversy fell out of sight, public opinion of banks in South Carolina remained sour. Anti-bank charges such as those made by Randall Croft still weighed on the voters' minds. The citizens did not want the banks or any other institution or individual serving as their "lords and masters."[75]

The whole bank controversy, for all the vitriol it generated, did little to wean the people from their dependence on banks. It was too late for that. "Who is it," William Gregg asked knowingly, "that can say he is not a debtor to the banks?"[76] But the banking controversy did illustrate, as did the squabbles over state aid for internal improvements, usury laws, and homestead exemption, that South Carolinians could be easily divided over how best to reconcile their desire for material progress with the cherished principles of republican political economy. The latter ethic hailed the virtues of the independent producer and his contribution to economic growth, but frowned, at least in theory, on the myriad of dependencies fostered by the very market which rewarded the producer for his efforts, for the free and full productive efforts of himself and his property. Material progress and increasing wealth strengthened the economic basis of personal independence on the one hand but undermined it with all sorts of commercial dependencies on the other. For most Upcountrymen, personal resolution of this conflict was easy enough. Unbridled pursuit of the main chance, aided, if necessary, by a state-supported economic infrastructure, enabled the

[74]Newberry *Rising Sun*, June 30, 1958.

[75]Lesesne, *Bank of the State of South Carolina*, pp. 113–116; Newberry *Rising Sun*, December 8, 1858.

[76]*Letter of William Gregg*, p. 8.

good republican citizen to enjoy the full fruits of both his property and his labor and to create an ever-larger material foundation for his independence. That citizen's neighbors in the next district, however, were generally urged to live lives of simple republican asceticism to prevent the growth of corrupting dependencies. Such hypocrisy was, of course, not usually self-conscious and was seldom even recognized. Acceptable contradictions for individuals, however, present dilemmas to societies.

The society as a whole struggled to reconcile its internal contradictions. The legislature instinctively groped for, and to a remarkable extent found, some middle way between profligate state spending and unfettered capitalism on the one hand, and the futility of languid Spartan hermeticism on the other. It sought the best of both worlds. Upcountrymen did the same. They embraced the profits and prosperity brought by the commercial boom of the 1850s, but they protested vehemently against banks' suspensions, debt judgments, and low prices that came with each downturn, and saw rising taxes and the emergence of powerful railroad and banking corporations as threats to their republican liberty. As market orientation and market activity increased during the 1850s, Upcountrymen saw the two faces of commerce in bold relief. They praised commerce as dame fortune when they prospered and cursed her as bitch goddess when they faltered, but they could not put the winsome maiden out of their lives.

As the sectional crisis worsened in 1859, Upcountrymen were angry, frightened, and divided among themselves over a number of issues which had little to do with slavery. The general prosperity of the 1850s left them basically confident about the economic future of the cotton economy and the slave society which it supported. Yet the commercial expansion of the 1850s also exposed Upcountrymen to new dangers and left them anxious about their ability to maintain their personal independence. Growing corporate power, currency shortages, indebtedness, bank suspensions, higher taxes, and a more active government all suggested that the new South Carolina being created by continued commercial expansion and economic development might well be a treacherous place in which to nurture republican values. Thus it is easy to understand why Union district planter Benjamin Herndon Rice might draw wild applause from Upcountry audiences when he concluded his public speeches with a simple yet eloquent and rousing statement which not only evoked the proud Revolutionary heritage of the cherished republican ethic but also invoked that ethic in defiance of more modern tyrannies. "Our duty is based upon a high Independent Manhood," Rice declared, "[one] that dares resist encroachments upon our Rights and Liberties whether made by King or Capital, or corporation, or monopolies."[77]

In the shadow of these doubts over whether South Carolina was still a safe haven for the independent republican citizen, the people of the state were also forced to confront an older, but no less dangerous, enemy, an external enemy: the growing political power and broadening ideological appeal of the antislavery movement in the North. Yet the internal tensions and turmoil of the 1850s

[77]Scrapbook of Benjamin H. Rice, [c. 1860], Wallace, Rice, Duncan Papers, SCL.

profoundly affected the way many South Carolinians responded to the external threat. During the secession crisis of 1850–51, an odd coalition comprised of South Carolina's most cosmopolitan and most actively commercial and entrepreneurial elite and the state's least commercial citizens—the yeoman farmers and other common whites of the upper Piedmont—defeated a well-organized secession movement orchestrated by the parish gentry and the cotton planters of the inland black belt. The commercial elite, which provided most of the leadership for the successful Cooperation movement, had been, as a whole, opposed primarily to the particular form of secession—separate state action—that was proposed by the radicals. They feared not only turmoil and upheaval but also commercial and financial isolation. A Southern Confederacy that proferred safety in numbers plus commercial and financial networks of its own would be inherently more appealing to these businessmen and entrepreneurs than a small republic composed of a single, and small, former state. The yeoman farmers and other common whites, who supplied most of the Cooperation movement's strength at the ballot box, had been no less devoted to republican ideals than were the radicals who used those ideals to justify their calls for secession. But for most of the common whites in the Upcountry, the threats to their liberty seemed remote, intangible, and even hypothetical in 1850 and 1851. To be denied the right to take one's slaves to California might be a slight to one's sense of honor and equality, but for someone who neither owned slaves nor planned to move to California, such a restriction, however galling, was a rather abstract form of oppression. During the first secession crisis, many yeomen, and especially those in the upper Piedmont, simply felt that the present dangers did not justify a response as radical as secession. But by 1860, the expanding sphere of commerce and corporation had penetrated even the previously isolated enclaves of the upper Piedmont in very tangible ways. The common white of the Upcountry could now hear locomotives roaring in the distance and experience the bustle of trade firsthand in the towns he visited. If he remained nonplussed by those developments, he also knew that his own yearly taxes were getting higher and had doubtless heard several local politicians complain about the seemingly inexorable growth of corporate power and about those reckless spenders down in Columbia who had taken such a fancy to railroad subsidies, free schools, and insane asylums. And, on top of everything, the legislature had even spent millions of dollars on a palace to house its own shenanigans. By 1860, the threat of concentrated and unchecked power, and of active governments with their own agendas for progress, loomed larger in the minds of Upcountry whites than ever before because the changes of the 1850s had ushered such forces, in easily identifiable forms, into Upcountry communities. With tangible threats to their liberty close at hand, Upcountrymen were more easily convinced that drastic measures were required if their independence was to be saved.

10

"A Desperate Remedy": Politics, Ideology, and Secession

During the summer of 1850, as South Carolina actively contemplated leaving the Union in response to the perceived affronts to Southern rights and honor emanating from the famous compromise of that year, J. E. Broome, a local political leader in Tallahassee, Florida, wrote to his friend Iveson Brookes of Edgefield comparing the political situation in his state to that in South Carolina. "Our condition in this state is somewhat different from yours," Broome reported. "We are tied down to a great extent by party fetters and the Whig party for the most part [is] afraid to move a finger." Worse still, Broome noted, "everything looking to strong measures is caught up [and] the cry of disunion stamped upon it." Broome was a radical by Florida standards, a strong Southern Rights advocate who supported Calhoun's old idea of a united Southern party and who feared that the South was rapidly loosing its political rights within the Union. "The character of the [European] immigration to the free states warrants the presumption that they will be overwhelmed in a few years with all kinds of fanaticism," Broome predicted. "Socialism will doubtless prevail there in less than twenty years, will control their legislatures, and will then enter the National legislature as abolition has." The only alternative to "submission" to all manner of political insults and threats to property rights, Broome concluded, was the creation of an aggressive Southern Rights party which could maintain political equality for the region within the Union or, failing that, lead the South out of the Union. The creation of a single Southern party, however, was no easy task in Florida. Before such a party could unite Florida under its banner, Southern Rights advocates would have to break the shackles of the existing party organizations, and that, Broome admitted, could be done only if Southern Rights activists entered the ranks of one of the parties, seized control of its machinery, and drove the other party off the field with success at the polls.[1]

As Iveson Brookes, a Methodist minister and author of several pro-slavery tracts, knew, the situation in South Carolina was quite different. The Palmetto

[1] J. E. Broome to Iveson Brookes, July 2, 1850, Iveson Brookes Papers, SHC.

State had always worn party fetters lightly when it wore them at all. Party organization in the Palmetto State consisted of little more than the periodic rallying of like-minded local cliques behind the party banner. Moreover, by the early 1850s, virtually all traces of the national party system had been purged from the state. The battered rump of the Whig party in South Carolina, which had been badly thrashed by the Calhounites in 1840, was hopelessly fragmented by disagreements over secession in 1851. In that year, Upcountry Whigs vigorously endorsed cooperation, while most Lowcountry Whigs remained outright Unionists. With no Whig opposition to annoy them, the Democrats continued to quarrel peevishly among themselves. After the state decided not to secede in 1851, most disputes over national issues were carried on between two groups which owed varying degrees of allegiance to both the Democratic party and the political tradition of John C. Calhoun. One group, led by James L. Orr, advocated close cooperation with the national Democratic party as the best mechanism for maintaining an effective pro-slavery political front in Washington. The other group, with Robert Barnwell Rhett as its most visible if not its most effective spokesman, accepted, at least temporarily, the necessity of maintaining some loose affiliation with the national Democratic party, but advocated the formation of a radical Southern Rights party as the South's best hope of defending her peculiar way of life.[2] Since the basic political divisions in South Carolina were temporary factional splits rather than long-term party rivalries, politicians hoping to establish a vigorous Southern Rights movement in the state faced a far more open field, one lined with far fewer obstacles, than did their counterparts in other Southern states.

The absence of binding party ties in South Carolina was to some extent the product of the unusual political harmony on which the state prided itself, and of the state's unique demographic and socioeconomic characteristics which made such harmony possible. Yet to a considerable degree, the "no-party" situation in South Carolina was created by purely political forces arising from the state's peculiar political tradition. First, the nullification crisis created a bitter and long-lasting factionalism in the state which had no parallel in other Southern states and which hindered the emergence of the second American party system in South Carolina. Then, when a significant Whig party did begin to coalesce in the state, Calhoun unleashed all of his considerable political influence and energy to crush it. Initially, Calhoun found his quarry elusive, but by 1842 the Whigs had been routed and scattered. Yet for all of his hostility to the Whigs, whom he saw as the party of consolidation, Calhoun maintained only a conditional alliance with the Democratic party, always imploring the Southern states to unite and act in harmony in defense of Southern interests. But even Calhoun's conditional affiliation with the Democrats was more than some radical South Carolinians could

[2]Harold S. Schultz, *Nationalism and Sectionalism in South Carolina, 1852–1860* (Durham, N.C.: Duke University Press, 1950), pp. 26–57; Chauncey S. Boucher, "South Carolina and the South on the Eve of Secession, 1852–1860," *Washington University Studies* 6 (April, 1919):79–144.

bear. Robert Barnwell Rhett's abortive Bluffton movement grew out of growing dissatisfaction with the nominal Calhounite allegiance to the Democratic party, and Calhoun's cooperation with other Democrats led idealistic Southern nationalists such as Simms and Hammond to denounce Calhoun and his followers as corrupt, opportunistic "Hunkers." Throughout all the storms of his political career, however, Calhoun urged South Carolina to maintain a stance of political independence. As an independent bulwark of republican values, the state could enter the party fold when strategic considerations so dictated, as they ordinarily did, but should never sacrifice its republican principles or entirely relinquish the defense of those values to a party.[3]

Though certainly orchestrated by the skillful hand of Calhoun, South Carolina's political independence was not the result of personal dictation. Indeed, the state's long tradition of independence dated back to the Revolution, and was as much a part of the state's cherished political lore as the "country-republican" ideology which prescribed it. The widespread popularity of the state's independent political course not only gave Calhoun the free hand which he needed in national affairs during his lifetime, but also insured that many South Carolina politicians would seek to maintain an independent course after Calhoun departed. The strategy of independence, of course, was not without its critics. B. F. Perry, a Democrat, and James L. Petigru, a Whig, both denounced Calhoun's strategy as one of radical "isolation" rather than noble independence. After Calhoun died, politicians who claimed that South Carolina's efforts to remain outside the mainstream of national party politics reduced the state to ineffectual isolation and left it without a voice in national affairs gained strength. Thus, despite the weakness of party ties in South Carolina and the fluidity of political alliances within the state, the Southern Rights movement, or at least the radical pro-secession wing of the movement led by Rhett and other fire-eaters, failed to gain ascendancy in the state during the crisis of 1851, and struggled to maintain its credibility in the aftermath of the sweeping Cooperationist victory of that year. Doubtless the Southern Rights movement probably enjoyed more support in South Carolina during the 1850s than it did in most other Southern states, but for most of the early and middle years of the decade the fire-eaters struggled under the burden of public disfavor.[4]

As the radicals of 1851 retired to salve their wounds and rethink their strategy, their problem, unlike that of their counterparts in other Southern states, was not how to break down the existing party structure. Instead, the difficulty confronting South Carolina radicals was the possibility that prominent Cooperation leaders would forge strong ties with the Democratic party following their victory at the polls and thus create a formidable partisan influence in South Carolina. In

[3]Robert M. Weir, "The South Carolinian as Extremist," *South Atlantic Quarterly* 74 (December, 1975):86–103.

[4]Charles M. Wiltse, *John C. Calhoun, Sectionalist, 1840–1850* (Indianapolis: Bobbs-Merrill, 1951), pp. 394–410; Laura A. White, "The National Democrats in South Carolina, 1852 to 1860," *South Atlantic Quarterly* 28 (October, 1929):370–389; Boucher, "South Carolina and the South," pp. 105–127.

particular, radicals feared that James L. Orr, encouraged by other Upcountry Cooperationists, would fashion a close working relationship with the national Democratic party. Arch Southern Rights men quickly put their pens and presses to work discouraging such an alliance. "The method by which national partyism has obtained in the South for the last twenty years has been by yielding her rights," charged the Charleston *Mercury*. "The North aggresses; the North persists; the South yields."[5] The radical Laurensville *Herald* claimed that vigilance could only be effected "by keeping aloof from the trammels of party, of Conventions and caucuses, by maintaining the same glorious independence, which, under the great leadership of Mr. Calhoun, prompted us to act with the Democratic party only when it was consistent with the dictates of a pure patriotism." A close alliance with the national party, the *Herald* warned, might involve the state in the extensive spoils system, and "rock [South Carolina] to sleep in the arms of National Democracy."[6] The Edgefield *Advertiser* was also sharply critical of those "who perhaps style themselves *National* Democrats" and who believed "that the conservative element of Southern safety is the friendly disposition of the bulk of our Northern brethren." Instead, the *Advertiser* asserted, the best way to protect the South "is to rally the Southern people, in defense of Southern interests and institutions, under a Southern banner."[7]

South Carolina's so-called "National Democrats" viewed things differently. In 1853, the realignment of the state's congressional districts by the legislature threw two incumbents, the moderate Cooperationist James L. Orr and the radical Southern Rights leader Daniel Wallace of Union, into the same district. In the new district, which included Pendleton, Greenville, Spartanburg, and Union, Orr trounced Wallace and affirmed the supremacy of the moderate Democrats in the northwest corner of the state. In Washington, Orr became a leading candidate for Speaker of the House but lost when the rest of the South Carolina delegation absented themselves from the Democratic caucus.[8] This incident did much to establish the terms of debate between National and Southern Rights Democrats in South Carolina for the rest of the decade. "When will our state see the folly and absurdity of this transcendental isolation[?]," an angry Orr demanded, while B. F. Perry praised the Andersonian for "throwing off that terrapin notion of living within one's own shell, which has been so popular in South Carolina."[9] Yet, while Orr and other National Democrats believed that their state's "idiosyncracy" was costing her influence in Washington, radicals claimed that "Orrism" amounted to little more than the shameless pursuit of party spoils, such as the Speakership. Of Orr's unsuccessful candidacy for that influential post, the Charleston *Mercury* observed, "We thought it inconsistent with the position of a

[5]Charleston *Mercury*, July 7, 1855.

[6]Laurensville *Herald*, October 23, 1857.

[7]Edgefield *Advertiser*, September 28, 1854.

[8]Roger P. Leemhuis, *James L. Orr and the Sectional Conflict* (Washington, D.C.: University Presses of America, 1979), pp. 32–33; Charleston *Courier*, December 9, 1853.

[9]James L. Orr to B. F. Perry, December 9, 1853, quoted in Leemhuis, *James L. Orr*, p. 34; Greenville *Southern Patriot*, March 3 and 10, 1853.

Resistance man of 1850 to be a candidate for an office which necessarily fettered him by a pledge of Unionism," and Edgefield's Francis W. Pickens predicted that Orr's "national reputation will be his ruin at home."[10] Hamburg banker J. J. Blackwood offered a more balanced assessment that probably captured the mixed emotions of many Upcountrymen. "We all regret that Mr. Orr failed [to get] the Speakership," Blackwood wrote, "but I think he was too eager to court the favor of the Democracy."[11]

Despite the factional polarization between National Democrats and Southern Rights men during the 1850s, there was a shifting and uncertain middle ground between the two groups which was home for a talented coterie of noted South Carolina politicians. Most of these men were strong Southern nationalists of one stripe or another who felt that the Southern people were not yet ready for secession and a Southern Confederacy but who also felt that it was their obligation as political stewards of the region to help prepare the people for that eventuality. Notable among this group of independent politicians were William Gilmore Simms, James Henry Hammond, William Henry Trescot, William P. Miles, William W. Boyce, and Armistead Burt. Simms hoped to cultivate a cohesive Southern nationalism and then to use the persistent abolitionist attack on Southern society to precipitate the cooperative secession of a united South, but he lacked a strong political base from which to wage his crusade. As a result, his energies were channeled into propaganda and advice to influential men.[12] James Henry Hammond, a Simms confidante, had been forced into political exile by his feud with the Hampton family and did not regain political viability until Wade Hampton II died in 1857. Trescot, like Simms and Hammond, was a romantic Southern nationalist, but at the same time he was also a hard-headed politician. Having seen the state retreat from secession in 1851, Trescot was reluctant to see South Carolina at the forefront of any future secession movement. Instead, he preferred that his native state wait until the rest of the South was ready to lead a radical movement.[13] In the Upcountry, W. W. Boyce of Fairfield tried to walk the tightrope between the National Democrats and the Southern Rights group. "I wish the South to pursue a prudent, wise course," Boyce explained, "so as, if possible, by acting in concert with the conservative section of the North, to protect the interests of the South."[14] Yet even the moderate Boyce opposed Orr's plan of close cooperation with the National Democrats and advocated secession if the "conservative section" of the North

[10]Charleston *Mercury,* December 7, 1853; Francis W. Pickens to Milledge Bonham, December 11, 1857, Milledge Bonham Papers, SCL.

[11]J. J. Blackwood to Andrew Baxter Springs, February 7, 1856, Springs Family Papers, SHC.

[12]Jon L. Wakelyn, *The Politics of a Literary Man: William Gilmore Simms* (Westport, Conn.: Greenwood Press, 1973), pp. 158–252.

[13]Drew Gilpin Faust, *James Henry Hammond and the Old South: A Design for Mastery* (Baton Rouge: Louisiana State University Press, 1982), pp. 241–245, and 338–358; Robert Nicholas Olsberg, "A Government of Class and Race: William Henry Trescot and the South Carolina Chivalry, 1860–1865" (Ph.D. dissertation, University of South Carolina, 1972), pp. 204–253.

[14]Autobiographical sketch of W. W. Boyce [c. 1856], W. W. Boyce Papers, SCL.

refused to recognize the rights of slaveholders within the Union. Boyce, a former Cooperationist, was joined on the middle ground by former radicals, such as Thomas O. P. Vernon of Spartanburg, who moderated their stance after their defeat in 1851. "We are thoroughly convinced that there can be no peace for the South in the Union," editorialized Vernon, "but we oppose sectional organiza tion on grounds that the people are not ready for it."[15] This statement again revealed the perils which Southern nationalists in South Carolina faced during the 1850s. South Carolina's reputation as a hotspur state prompted other Southern states to view the Palmetto State with suspicion and distrust. Yet the defeat of separate state action in 1851 seemed to indicate that even in South Carolina the great mass of citizens were wary of radical action. South Carolina was cursed abroad for excessive radicalism, while fire-eaters within the state worried about the state's timidity. Having been in the vanguard of one aborted secession movement, the state strained to regain credibility with her sister states.

During the mid-1850s, crucial incidents brought continued sectional hostility home to South Carolina over and over again. When Stephen Douglas of Illinois introduced the Kansas-Nebraska bill in Congress in 1854, the South Carolina delegation seized the opportunity to renew their plea that the Missouri Compromise was unconstitutional because Congress had no power to prevent citizens from carrying their slave property into the territories. Almost to a man, the delegation doubted that either Kansas or Nebraska would ever become a slave state, but the opportunity to recover the constitutional right of taking slaves anywhere in the territories proffered a major victory on principle. Senator A. P. Butler, an Edgefield native, announced:

> I am willing to take this bill as it is. I am willing to take it, even upon the assumption that no slaves will go into Nebraska or Kansas. I am willing to take it upon the ground that, if you adopt it, it will take a festering thorn from the side of the South. I am willing to take it upon the ground that by it sentiments of honor are regarded.[16]

In the House, W. W. Boyce, Preston Brooks, and James L. Orr echoed Butler's opinion of the bill. Despite these declarations of support, the South Carolina delegation was hardly enthusiastic over the bill since it raised a new controversy over the concept of "squatter sovereignty." The South Carolina delegation unanimously denied Stephen Douglas's contention that a territorial legislature could exclude slavery from a territory. The people of the territory could decide to prohibit slavery only at the time that they began drafting a state constitution in preparation for admission to the Union.[17]

The passage of the Kansas-Nebraska Act, although supported by the entire South Carolina delegation, gave the state only a Pyrrhic victory. Neither South

[15]*Carolina Spartan*, August 9, 1855.

[16]*Congressional Globe*, 33 Congress, 1 Session, Appendix, pp. 232–240.

[17]Josiah J. Evans to James H. Hammond, December 7, 1857, James Henry Hammond Papers, LC; Lancaster *Ledger*, March 29, 1854; Edgefield *Advertiser*, February 22, 1854.

Carolina nor the South received any practical gain from the measure, since it was unlikely that a slaveholding state would ever be formed out of any portion of the territory. The act, warned the Edgefield *Advertiser*, "will not benefit the slaveholding portion of the Confederacy one iota. It is not expected . . . that our institution will ever be introduced upon any part of the broad expanse of territory now under legislation."[18] Moreover, the passage of the bill precipitated a new wave of antislavery agitation in the North and helped produce a resounding defeat for Northern Democrats at the polls in November 1854. This combination of renewed abolitionist fervor and the obvious weakening of the Democratic party in the North alarmed South Carolinians. "Compromising politicians have cried peace, but there is no peace," lamented the Laurensville *Herald*. "The North is pressing her purposes now more than ever."[19] With the benefit of hindsight, a number of influential South Carolinians criticized the state's congressional delegation for inadvertently reopening the sectional controversy through their support of the Kansas-Nebraska bill. "When the Kansas-Nebraska bill was under discussion," William Porcher Miles noted, "Southern man after Southern man declared in his seat in Congress that all the South wanted was a practical, legislative acknowledgement of her equality—that slavery by the laws of climate could never take foot-hold in Kansas—but that a just deference to the sensitive honor of the Southern people demanded that there should be at least a distinct theoretical recognition of her constitutional rights, etc. This was a bad way certainly of preparing the Southern mind for a war to the knife on the question of making Kansas a slave state."[20]

A "war to the knife" over Kansas was not what South Carolina expected, but it was essentially what she got. As soon as antislavery groups in the North mobilized to send cadres of antislavery immigrants to Kansas, South Carolina joined the effort to send Southern volunteers to the new territory. Every district in the Upcountry raised money to equip and send a band of volunteers to Kansas. By the spring of 1855, Abbeville had organized a corps of 300 volunteers, while Edgefield had prepared fifty men to emigrate and raised $3000 to support them.[21] Other districts continued to support the emigration effort well into 1856. The citizens of York district raised money to support emigrants, claiming that such action was the only way to support "our republican edifice" from "the corruption and utter demoralization of Northern sentiment." Admitting that winning Kansas for slavery had become a political hobby for his paper, the editor of the Yorkville *Enquirer*, Jonathan S. Miller, declared that the "Kansas battle is worth our steele." Kansas, Miller urged, should be the place where the people of the South "meet the Yankee Abolitionists, as Southerns should meet them, with sword in hand."[22] In the summer of 1856, York's neighbor Chester sent a score

[18]Edgefield *Advertiser*, March 8, 1854.

[19]Laurensville *Herald*, June 17, 1855.

[20]William Porcher Miles to James Henry Hammond, November 8, 1858, James Henry Hammond Papers, SCL.

[21]Abbeville *Banner*, September 18, 1856; *Carolina Spartan*, April 12, 1855.

[22]Yorkville *Enquirer*, July 17, 1856; Jonathan S. Miller to Andrew Baxter Springs, January 25, 1856, Springs Family Papers, SHC.

of settlers to Kansas with funds raised from local sources. The problem with this orchestrated emigration was that while Upcountry slaveholders gave money willingly to encourage others to settle in Kansas, few were willing to risk their own slave property in an embattled territory. On the whole, only the down-and-out, drifters, and a few score hardy adventurers found Kansas at all alluring even though their resettlement there would be heavily subsidized. Unionist Robert W. Hemphill of Chester privately referred to the Kansas emigrants from his district as "Loafers" and "the very scum of creation" and predicted that most of the men were so ignorant that they were "as likely to vote the Free-Soil ticket as any other" once they got to Kansas. B. F. Perry also spoke of the Kansas emigrants as men of low or mean character, but the outspoken Greenville Unionist was sternly rebuked by the Upcountry press for defaming these "patriotic" South Carolinians. Thus, by 1856, South Carolina was engaged in active, albeit bizarre, competition with free-soilers for control of western territory. The uneasy sectional truce which followed the Compromise of 1850 was broken, and compelling national issues again moved to the forefront of South Carolina politics.[23]

As the crisis in Kansas worsened, James L. Orr began a concerted effort to convince South Carolina Democrats to send a delegation to the party's national convention in 1856. Calhoun, as part of his strategy of maintaining independence for the state, held the state out of national conventions, and that practice continued after the powerful senator's death. By 1856, the state had not participated in a national party convention for more than a decade. After a tour of the Northeast in the winter of 1855–56, Orr returned convinced that President Franklin Pierce was a friend of the South and that many Northern Democrats were sympathetic to Southern principles. South Carolina's presence at the Democratic national convention would not only nurture persistent Northern sympathy for the South but also help secure Pierce's renomination. "Isolation will give neither security nor concert," counseled Orr. Orr's efforts quickly won support from the expected quarters. B. F. Perry and other Upcountry Unionists loudly applauded Orr, as did most, but not all, former Cooperationists in the Upcountry. Among other members of the state's congressional delegation, however, only Congressman Preston S. Brooks of Edgefield, a moderate National Democrat, gave Orr whole-hearted support. "For one, I have had enough of Bluffton stupidity and am disposed to take things as we find them," Brooks, a confirmed moderate on sectional matters despite his quick temper, told Orr late in 1855.[24]

Beginning in January 1856, pro-convention Democrats were at work throughout the Upcountry trying to convince voters that South Carolina should send delegates to the national Democratic convention in Cincinnati the following summer. If nothing else, Orr's convention movement revealed the unusual fluidity and informality which characterized South Carolina politics in the absence of

[23]R. W. Hemphill to W. R. Hemphill, August 11, 1856, Hemphill Family Papers, DU; Abbeville *Banner*, September 18, 1856.

[24]Orr quoted in Schultz, *Nationalism and Sectionalism*, p. 92; Leemhuis, *James L. Orr*, pp. 50–53; Greenville *Patriot and Mountaineer*, February 7, 1856; Robert Neil Mathis, "Preston Smith Brooks: The Man and His Image," *South Carolina Historical Magazine* 79 (December, 1978):196–210; Preston Brooks to James L. Orr, November 10, 1855, Orr-Patterson Papers, SHC.

permanent party machinery. Since no formal beat or district organizations existed to hold regular party caucuses or conventions, Orr and his followers created their own organization, called for public meetings in courthouse towns on sales day or during court week, and wrested a concerted pro-convention movement out of the raw material present at these meetings. In York district, a public meeting was held on March 6. Cooperationist leader I. D. Witherspoon was elected chair. After hearing a number of speeches, the informal assembly elected a slate of delegates to the state convention to be held in Columbia in May. Although all the York delegates favored sending representatives to the national convention in Cincinnati, the minority anti-convention faction in York held no counter-rallies and accepted the legitimacy of the decision made at the March 6 meeting without question.[25]

Virtually the same practice was followed in Chester, where a well-attended public meeting was held at the end of sales day in early March. The sentiment of the gathering was strongly in favor of participation in the national Democratic convention, and the people of Chester elected delegates pledged to support this position to the state convention. In Spartanburg, where the local *Carolina Spartan* gave surprisingly enthusiastic support to Orr's movement, a public meeting overwhelmingly endorsed the idea of sending delegates to the national convention and elected a slate of delegates, including both radicals and moderates, pledged to support Orr at the state convention. Again, dissenters accepted the decision of the public meeting and the pro-convention forces faced no serious opposition in Spartanburg. In nearby Laurens, however, Orr's convention movement was initially defeated at a public rally. The separate state secessionists carried Laurens in 1851, and a number of local notables and the local newspaper were strong Southern Rights advocates. Upon hearing of the defeat in Laurens, Preston Brooks, whose congressional district included Laurens, penned a letter expressing his regret that his constituents were not united in support of the convention movement.[26]

As the popularity of the convention movement in the Upcountry grew, vacillating politicians decided to throw their support behind it. Senator A. P. Butler, initially cool to the idea, concluded that the people of the state wanted representation at the national convention. Yielding to the "tide of events and the current of popular opinion," Butler reluctantly endorsed the convention movement in March, but pleaded that "in anything that is likely to be done, do not let us de-Carolinaize ourselves."[27] Butler's colleague, Senator Josiah Evans from Darlington, followed suit. As more and more prominent men endorsed the convention movement, more and more districts elected delegates to the state Democratic convention in Columbia. By late spring, every district in the Upcountry except Newberry and Lancaster had elected delegates to the Columbia convention. In the rest of the state, Kershaw and Orangeburg districts chose not to be

[25]Yorkville *Enquirer,* February 28 and March 6, 1856.

[26]Chester *Standard,* March 5, 1856; *Carolina Spartan,* March 6, 1856; Lancaster *Ledger,* April 16, 1856; Charleston *Mercury,* March 11, 1856.

[27]Columbia *Carolina Times,* March 7, 1856; *Carolina Spartan,* March 13, 1856; Andrew Pickens Butler to Waddy Thompson, August 20, 1856, Waddy Thompson Papers, SCL.

represented, but, more important, all of the rural Lowcountry parishes boycotted the Columbia convention.[28]

The convention movement had attracted its share of opponents from its very inception. The radical Charleston *Mercury* ridiculed the idea, and one anonymous writer from Newberry charged that Orr and his followers were mere spoilsmen. "Our great object," he wrote, "should be to unite the Southern States in opposition to Northern aggression and this will be impossible so long as our leaders at the South shall engage in the strife for Federal offices and honors." The spoils system, this Upcountry radical continued, was responsible for the timidity of the South's response to repeated Northern aggression:

> Ours has been the only State that has been prepared to resist encroachments upon our rights. Why has this been so? Because we have kept out of these conventions, whose object is the spoils. We have refused to engage in the corrupting scramble for the Federal patronage. The other Southern states have pursued a different course. Their politicians have been more concerned for the success of national parties than for Southern honor and rights.[29]

From the state's congressional delegation, Lawrence Keitt, John McQueen, and W. W. Boyce opposed the convention movement. Although Keitt believed that "the Democratic party is, to-day, purer and truer to the Constitution than it has been for years," he refused "to wear a party collar" and argued that South Carolina should maintain its traditional independence from the national party apparatus. More troubling to pro-convention forces, however, was the opposition of the influential Upcountry moderate, W. W. Boyce of Fairfield. Congressman Boyce feared that allowing "the Federal government on the stage, with her tons of gold and national distinctions," would weaken "the exclusive devotion to South Carolina," which was the genius of the political posture designed by Calhoun and passed down to the new generation of politicians coming to power during the 1850s.[30]

Though not without weight, the objections of the moderate Boyce did no more to slow the convention movement than did the expected opposition of the more radical Southern Rights faction. When the state Democratic convention met in Columbia on May 5 and 6, it elected a prominent National Democrat, Francis W. Pickens, to the chair and, after hearing an explanatory speech from Orr, elected sixteen delegates, two from each of the six congressional districts and four at-large representatives, to the National Democratic convention in Cincinnati. Orr's National Democratic faction clearly held the upper hand in state politics in the late spring of 1856, even though there was considerable hostility to the movement in the rural parishes of the Lowcountry. When the state's delegation reached the national convention in Cincinnati, it unanimously supported the

---

[28]Boucher, "South Carolina and the South," pp. 111–113.

[29]Charleston *Mercury,* April 5, 1856; Columbia *Carolina Times,* January 16, 1856.

[30]Elmer Don Herd, "Chapters from the Life of a Southern Chevalier: Laurence Massillon Keitt's Congressional Years, 1853–1860" (M.A. thesis, University of South Carolina, 1958), pp. 53–69; Sumter *Watchman,* November 14, 1855.

incumbent Pierce through fourteen ballots, then boldly threw its weight behind
Stephen Douglas for two ballots. Finally, when Douglas's name was withdrawn,
the delegation shifted its support to James Buchanan, who won the nomination
on the seventeenth ballot.[31]

Before the National Democrats could enjoy their ascendancy in South Carolina, however, events created new issues which gave the fiery rhetoric of
Southern Rights leaders a new ring of realism. Throughout 1856, the situation in
"Bleeding Kansas" worsened. "If abolitionism be successful in Kansas,"
warned the *Carolina Spartan*, "we believe the battlefield of Southern rights will
be brought to our own doors in less years than the life of a man."[32] In the middle
of the raging, and sometimes violent, controversy came an incident which raised
sectional passions to new levels of intensity. Senator Charles Sumner of Massachusetts, speaking in Congress on the alleged "Crime against Kansas," suggested that Senator A. P. Butler had "Chosen a mistress to whom he has made
his vows, and who, though ugly to others, is always lovely to him; though
polluted in the sight of the world, is chaste in his sight—I mean the harlot,
slavery."[33] Preston Brooks, a National Democrat and a cousin of the aging
Butler, took it upon himself to avenge this verbal insult of his kinsman, and
eventually caned Sumner on the floor of the United States Senate. One week
after the caning, Lawrence Keitt reported from Washington that:

> The feeling is pretty much sectional. If the northern men had stood up, the city
> would now float with blood. The fact is the feeling is wild and fierce. . . .
> Everyone here feels as if we are upon a volcano.[34]

In South Carolina, Brooks was a hero, and people begged for fragments of his
cane as "*sacred relics*." Moreover, the *Carolina Spartan* reported that no one
could oppose Brooks and still "hope political life." The new round of sectional
tension triggered by the Brooks-Sumner incident united the state once again
against the North. "We have an abiding conviction that it is impossible for the
Union to last," claimed the Charleston *Mercury*. "The South has the simple
alternative of separating herself from the Union or being destroyed by it."[35]

By the late 1850s, South Carolinians clearly believed that they were living in a
society under siege. Beneath the many tactical disputes and strategic disagreements lay general agreement that the South's right to exist as a slave society was
in jeopardy. For more than two decades, the abolitionists had waged their psy-

[31]Schultz, *Nationalism and Sectionalism*, pp. 102–133; John Boyd Edmunds, Jr., *Francis W. Pickens and the Politics of Destruction* (Chapel Hill: University of North Carolina Press, 1986), pp. 126–134; Francis W. Pickens to Armistead Burt, August 8, 1856, Armistead Burt Papers, DU.

[32]*Carolina Spartan*, June 19, 1856.

[33]*Congressional Globe*, 34 Congress, 1 Session, Appendix, pp. 529–530; Mathis, "Preston Brooks," pp. 297–298.

[34]Lawrence Keitt to Sue Sparks, May 29, 1856, Lawrence M. Keitt Papers, DU.

[35]Preston Brooks to J. H. Brooks, May 23, 1856, quoted in Boucher, "South Carolina and the South," p. 115; *Carolina Spartan*, July 24, 1856; Charleston *Mercury*, June 19, 1856.

chological war on the region, encouraged insurrection, and convinced even conservative Southerners such as Beaufort planter William Elliott, a lifelong Unionist, that what the North wanted for the South was "an agricultural prosperity like that of Jamaica" and "such security as is found in St. Domingo." South Carolina slaveholders, and non-slaveholders for that matter, were not about to surrender their proud society, one wrested by their forefathers from wilderness and disease and Indians, to what they perceived as the "mawkish sentimentality" of Northern abolitionists. Yet although the fundamental right of the South to exist as a slave society always lay beneath the region's response to the abolitionists' attack and at the heart of the sectional conflict, the South's growing dissatisfaction with the Union was more than a primitive struggle for survival. Also at issue were other equally fundamental rights, rights stemming from the right of survival but also transcending and ennobling that right, which South Carolinians believed to be threatened by the increasingly militant antislavery and free-soil movements in the North.[36]

As always, South Carolinians perceived threats through the lens of their gripping republican ideology and with a stubborn refusal to yield rights they believed to be guaranteed by the Constitution. From within this well-fortified frame of reference, the question of slavery in the territories involved a number of fundamental republican rights. First of all, South Carolinians believed that while Congress had the right to control the territories, Congress had no right to prevent slaveholders from taking slaves into the territories, since the slaveholder's property rights must be considered the equal of other citizens' property rights, as guaranteed by the Constitution. As early as 1852, Laurens's Zelotus Holmes told his Northern relatives that their "new and prevailing doctrine" of "no more slave territory" was "so different from that which the old States originally set out under the Constitution" and constituted "such bad faith in carrying out the original understanding" that the South was justified in its complaints about Northern tyranny and aggression. Southerners, Holmes argued, might accept *de facto* restrictions on the expansion of slavery arising from "natural causes" or "moral influences," but the Southern people were determined not to be "legislated out of the possible chances" to take their slaves into the territories.[37] Moreover, if Congress did not have the power to exclude slavery from the territories, it certainly had no right to delegate such authority to territorial legislatures. Thus territories could only prohibit slavery when they drafted a constitution and applied for statehood. This position, though subject to considerable legal dispute throughout the antebellum period, was essentially that taken by the Supreme Court in the Dred Scott decision of 1857.[38]

[36]William Elliott, *Anniversary Address of the State Agricultural Society of South Carolina, November 30, 1848* (Charleston: Miller and Browne, 1848), pp. 44–46.

[37]Zelotus Holmes to his Aunt, June 15, 1852, Zelotus Holmes Papers, SCL.

[38]For an overview of the 1850s, see David M. Potter, *The Impending Crisis, 1848–1861* (New York: Harper and Row, 1976); Joel H. Silbey, *The Transformation of American Politics, 1840–1860* (Englewood Cliffs, N.J.: Prentice Hall, 1967). On the Dred Scott case, see Don E. Fehrenbacher, *The Dred Scott Case: Its Significance in American Law and Politics* (New York: Harper and Row, 1978).

Yet more than mere legalism was involved in the controversy. If slaveholders were prohibited from taking their slave property into the territories, they were denied their full rights as citizens. Southerners were especially sensitive to what they regarded as the necessity of equality among republican citizens. If the slaveholder's rights were in any way circumscribed, he lost his equality within the Union. Such a reduction in status lowered the slaveholder to a position of shame and degradation, and forfeited his honor and independence. Moreover, as the number of free states continued to increase while the number of slave states remained constant, the slave South found itself in the same minority position in the Senate that it had long occupied in the House of Representatives. As a minority, Southern politicians were zealous in defense of the South's right to "equality" within the Union.[39] Francis W. Pickens summed up the position of most South Carolinians well in a speech on the crisis in Kansas at Anderson courthouse in 1855. "I trust in God that the watchword will always be, *Equality forever or Independence,*" Pickens declared, "and that it will ring over a thousand hills and start from their scabbards the swords of a hundred thousand freemen."[40] But Iveson Brookes, the Edgefield minister, perhaps stated the South's position even more clearly:

The South desires not to encroach upon any right of the North, and intends not to set foot in the spirit of hostile invasion upon an inch of the North's territorial provinces. She has no disposition to retaliate for the wrongs of which we so justly complain. Nor does the South ask at the hands of the North to make the least sacrifice of their just and constitutional rights. . . . For we have simply asked them to let us remain in the Union with them under the original intentions of the Constitution upon the equality of brotherhood. If then the North have no fellowship with us, and refuse to allow us the standing of political equality with them, we shall have exhausted the argument by presenting in respectful terms our request that they will allow us to depart in peace—a request based upon the great principle that two cannot walk together except they be agreed.[41]

By the middle of the 1850s, most South Carolinians were convinced that almost every aspect of the sectional conflict involved significant ideological disagreements between North and South. This ideological component of sectional conflict had been evident for a number of years, and was often painted in

[39]On the importance of equal rights for all citizens, see J. Mills Thornton III, *Politics and Power in a Slave Society: Alabama, 1800–1860* (Baton Rouge: Louisiana State University Press, 1978), pp. 220–222; and William J. Cooper, Jr., *Liberty and Slavery: Southern Politics to 1860* (New York: Alfred A. Knopf, 1983), especially pp. 213–281. On the typical white Southerner's sense of honor and sensitivity to shame and degradation, see Bertram Wyatt-Brown, *Southern Honor: Ethics and Behavior in the Old South* (New York: Oxford University Press, 1982), especially pp. 25–114; and Edward L. Ayers, *Vengeance and Justice: Crime and Punishment in the Nineteenth Century American South* (New York: Oxford University Press, 1984), pp. 9–33.

[40]*Carolina Spartan,* August 23, 1855.

[41]Iveson L. Brookes, *A Defence of Southern Slavery* (Hamburg, S.C.: Robinson and Carlisle, 1851), p. 41.

bold relief by Calhoun's relentless insistence that the South defend its moral and ideological values as well as its narrow political and economic interests. Moreover, as Southerners responded to incessant abolitionist attacks with an increasingly sophisticated defense of slavery, the region's moral and ideological commitment to slavery became both stronger and more visible. Yet despite the ideological overtones which were evident throughout the period of sectional conflict, the presence of pervasive, and perhaps fundamental, ideological antagonism did not become obvious until free-labor ideology gained widespread popularity in the North during the 1850s. To be sure, politicians and ideologues in both North and South used the inherited republican tradition as a prism through which to refract their respective visions of the good society, sometimes badly distorting republicanism itself in the process. But, as Eric Foner has demonstrated, the emergence of the Republican party in the North during the 1850s marked the triumph of an ideology devoted to the principles of "free soil, free labor, and free men." This Northern free-labor ideology was a dynamic version of republicanism adjusted to the peculiarities of nineteenth-century commercial capitalism. According to free-labor ideology, the good society was one dominated by independent, property-holding, petty producers, free to attain self-sufficiency and pursue the main chance in an expanding market economy. The ideal-typical North of free labor enthusiasts was a veritable republican utopia of "family farms, small shops, and village artisans," a competitive society of petty capitalists, where labor knew neither the oppression of alienation from capital nor the degradation of competition with slavery.[42]

South Carolinians, as well as other Southerners, shared a republican heritage that was not, at first glance, very different from that of the North. For Southerners, the good society was also one dominated by independent, property-holding producers who sought both to maintain their autonomy and to enjoy the benefits of material accumulation. By the 1850s, however, many South Carolinians were convinced that the community of independent producers which provided the foundation for republican government could, ironically, only survive in a slave society. "[N]o social state, without slavery as its basis," asserted Iveson Brookes, "can permanently maintain a republican form of government."[43] To Southerners, the marriage of republicanism and capitalism which seemed so natural at one time now threatened to pervert republicanism beyond recognition.

[42]Eric Foner, *Free Soil, Free Labor, Free Men: The Ideology of the Republican Party before the Civil War* (New York: Oxford University Press, 1970), especially pp. 11–72, and *Politics and Ideology in the Age of Civil War* (New York: Oxford University Press, 1980), especially pp. 34–56; Lacy Ford, "Labor and Ideology in the South Carolina Upcountry: The Transition to Free-Labor Agriculture," in Walter J. Fraser, Jr., and Winfred B. Moore, Jr., eds., *The Southern Enigma: Essays on Race, Class, and Folk Culture* (Westport, Conn.: Greenwood Press, 1982), pp. 25–42; William E. Gienapp, *The Origins of the Republican Party, 1852–1856* (New York: Oxford University Press, 1987), pp. 347–373; Kenneth M. Stampp, "Race, Slavery, and the Republican Party of the 1850s," in his *The Imperiled Union: Essays on the Background of the Civil War* (New York: Oxford University Press, 1980), pp. 105–135.

[43]Iveson L. Brookes, *A Defence of Southern Slavery* (Hamburg, S.C.: Robinson and Carlisle, 1851), pp. 45–47.

The good republican citizen had to maintain his personal independence, and it was crucial that that personal independence rest on a proper economic base. Since ownership of productive property was considered the best economic guarantee of personal independence, republican values were easily corrupted and destroyed in a society whose population included hordes of propertyless, and therefore dependent, citizens. Thus, as the process of industrialization slowly began to transform an economy of independent proprietorships into one of capitalists and laborers, the economic foundation of republican values was threatened by invidious new dependencies and class distinctions. In a slave economy, however, the propertyless, dependent, laboring class was defined out of the body politic where it would remain forever beyond the reach of dangerous radicals, aspiring dictators, and scheming demagogues.[44]

Throughout the sectional conflict, South Carolina leaders argued that the Southern experiment in slave-labor republicanism had better prospects for long-term success than did its Northern free-labor counterpart. As early as the writing of the *Exposition and Protest,* Calhoun argued that only slavery stood to prevent the conflict between labor and capital from destroying the Republic. "After we are exhausted," Calhoun observed, "the contest will be between the capitalists and operatives; for into these two classes it must, ultimately, divide society."[45] A few years later, Calhoun again suggested that slavery could preserve republicanism in the South long after class struggle had destroyed it in the North:

> There is and always has been in an advanced stage of wealth and civilization, a conflict between labor and capital. The condition of society in the South exempts us from the disorders and dangers resulting from this conflict. . . . The experience of the next generation will fully test how vastly more favorable our condition of society is to that of other sections for free and stable institutions. . . .[46]

After Calhoun's death, these arguments were picked up by the prominent Beaufort planter William H. Trescot. In an eloquent defense of slave-labor republicanism, Trescot summarized the danger that strife between labor and capital posed to republican liberty:

> There is one relation, lying at the basis of all social and political life, the shifting character of which fairly indicates the national progress in wealth and

[44]Howard Temperly, "Capitalism, Slavery, and Ideology," *Past and Present* 75 (May, 1977):94–118; David Brion Davis, "Slavery and the Idea of Progress," *The Bulletin of the Center for the Study of Southern Culture and Religion* 3 (June, 1979):1–9; Alan Dawley and Paul Faler, "Working-Class Culture and Politics in the Industrial Revolution: Sources of Loyalism and Rebellion," *Journal of Social History* 9 (Winter, 1976):466–480.

[45]Clyde N. Wilson, ed., *The Papers of John C. Calhoun* (Columbia, S.C.: University of South Carolina Press, 1977), vol. 10, pp. 480–482.

[46]John C. Calhoun, "Remarks on Receiving Abolition Petitions," February 6, 1837, in Clyde N. Wilson, ed., *The Papers of John C. Calhoun* (Columbia, S.C.: University of South Carolina Press, 1980), vol. 13, pp. 396–397.

civilization—the relation of labor to capital. . . . The history of all that is great in achievement . . . proves that the best interests of humanity require, first, that labour should be subordinate to, and controlled by capital; and second, that the interests of the two should by that very dependence be as closely as possible identified. It may be safely asserted . . . that the interest of labour and capital can never be permanently or properly reconciled, except under the institution of slavery; for it stands to reason, that wherever the political theory of government recognizes the equality of capital and labor, while the great reality of society shews the one in hopeless and heartless dependence on the other, there will exist between the two a constant jealousy and a bitter strife, the weaker demanding its rights with impotent cursing, or enforcing them with revolutionary fierceness.[47]

Slavery, based on racial differences, Trescot contended, prevented such problems from arising in the South:

At the North, the relation of labour and capital is voluntary service; at the South, it is involuntary slavery. At the North, labour and capital are equal; at the South, labour is inferior to capital. At the North, labour and capital strive; the one, to get all it can; the other, to give as little as it may—they are enemies. At the South, labour is dependent on capital, and having ceased to be rivals, they have ceased to be enemies. Can a more violent contrast be imagined?[48]

Although antislavery leaders dismissed the Southern critique of Northern society as merely a *tu quoque* response to their attacks on slavery, what emerged during the 1850s was not only a scathing indictment of "wage-slavery" but also a thorough-going defense of slave-labor republicanism. As it existed in South Carolina, chattel slavery enhanced republican liberty in a number of important ways. First, it allowed the economy to expand beyond the subsistence level without the creation of a vast proletariat which was economically dependent but politically dangerous. Since slaves were not citizens, the dependent laboring population in the South posed no challenge to the political rule of independent producers. Second, according to South Carolinians, slavery dampened the conflict between labor and capital not only by rendering labor politically impotent but also by introducing a "moral" dimension into capital's control of labor. In a slave society, labor (slaves) was dependent on capital, yet capital (the masters) was placed in a position where its responsibilities went far beyond mere contractual obligation. Instead, masters were charged with the entire physical and moral stewardship of their chattels. Finally, and most important, South Carolinians argued that slavery strengthened republican values by enhancing the "independence" of whites and creating a pervasive sense of equality among all whites, since all whites could claim membership in a privileged class simply on the basis of race. But black slavery did more for common whites in the South than simply allow them to enjoy whatever psychological satisfaction grew from a sense of belonging to a superior caste defined solely by race. By providing the labor

[47]William Henry Trescot, *The Position and Course of the South* (Charleston: Walker and James, 1850), pp. 9–10.
[48]*Ibid.*, pp. 10–11.

necessary for large-scale commercial agriculture like that of Southern plantations, the so-called "factories in the fields," slavery insulated Southern yeomen
from that which they feared most: the danger that they would one day be forced
to become a laboring class dependent on capitalists for their livelihood. Though
deeply rooted in the traditional ideal of personal independence, by the late 1850s,
the yeomanry's fear of being proletarianized was fed by the growing power of
capital and commerce in the region. Thus, while some planters doubtless saw the
profoundly conservative implications of a pro-slavery republicanism which minimized class conflict by literally enslaving the working class, yeoman farmers and
other whites saw that same ideology as profoundly egalitarian. Slavery liberated
the yeoman from his own potential dependency; slavery for blacks guaranteed
the freedom of common whites.[49]

Republican theorists had long argued that republics could not survive if the
great mass of citizens were cut off from control of productive property and forced
into economic dependency. In the late antebellum period, the Southern critique
of free-labor ideology focused on this issue. Southern thinkers argued that the
North was not headed toward a free-labor millennium of prosperous producers,
but rather toward an unfettered capitalism of rapacious robber barons, belligerent
wage-laborers, and corrupt political leaders. In free-labor societies, propertyless
citizens were forced to sell their labor in the marketplace, where it was necessarily placed under the control of capital. "If money is power," noted Chester
slaveholder Jonathan Newland in 1856, "money must ultimately succeed in
bringing all the laboring classes into subjection to itself."[50] As a result, the
independence of the laborer was sacrificed for profits for the capitalists and
living wages for the laborers. "The capitalist sits alone in his easy chair, and
learns to regard labor in the aggregate," noted the *Carolina Spartan*, "[and] the
individuality of the laborer is lost sight of."[51] Having lost their independence,
free laborers were no longer fit citizens for a republic, and, in fact, were reduced
to a form of subjugation that Southerners called "wage-slavery." The man
"who has to put out his labour in the market and take the best he can get for it; in
short, your whole hireling class of manual laborers and 'operatives,'" James
Henry Hammond told Northern senators, ". . . are essentially slaves." The
North, according to Hammond, had not done away with slavery, it had merely
eliminated the "*name,* but not the *thing.*"[52] Several years earlier, Louisa Mc-

---

[49]Ford, "Labor and Ideology in the South Carolina Upcountry," pp. 25–27; for a thorough
survey of the literature on white society in the antebellum South and an interpretation slightly
different from my own, see Drew Gilpin Faust, "The Peculiar South Revisited: White Society,
Culture, and Politics in the Antebellum Period, 1800–1860," in John B. Boles and Evelyn Thomas
Nolen, eds., *Interpreting Southern History: Historiographical Essays in Honor of Sanford W. Higginbotham* (Baton Rouge: Louisiana State University Press, 1987), pp. 78–119.

[50]Chester *Standard,* May 8, 1856.

[51]*Carolina Spartan,* September 22, 1853.

[52]James Henry Hammond, "Speech on the Admission of Kansas Under the Lecompton Constitution," in *Selections from the Letters and Speeches of the Hon. James H. Hammond,* with an
introduction by Clyde N. Wilson (Spartanburg: The Reprint Company, 1978), pp. 301–322, especially p. 319.

Cord, daughter of Langdon Cheves, declared in a reply to abolitionist criticisms:

> He who has not the right to dispose of his own labour becomes consequently
> and necessarily, to a greater or lesser extent . . . the serf or bondsman of the
> individual or government, thus shackling or limiting his exchanges.[53]

Moreover, a number of South Carolinians argued, the "wage-slavery" of the North was more cruel and oppressive than the chattel slavery of the South. "Starvation is not an *approach* towards slavery," McCord declared, "The Southern slave is . . . well clothed, well fed, well treated, in every way comfortable beyond the labouring class of any country, and, although not enjoying the luxuries of life, is as far from starvation as his master."[54] Indeed, many educated Southerners chided the North for the plight of its workers. "We see want filling the streets of their [Northern] cities with beggars and their gaols with criminals," observed Greenville planter-lawyer William K. Easley. "We see their workshops crowded with withered forms and haggard faces; amid the din of looms and the roar of spindles and wheels in their giant factories we hear the smothered cough of consumptive and starving operatives."[55] Anderson district planter O. Reed Broyles told Northern reformers that "if their philanthropy required . . . constant and vigorous exercise in warring against the miseries of mankind," they should "set forth about the good work of emancipating their own slaves—Slaves that wear their own color, now everywhere reduced by the progress of their manufacturing systems to a condition of toil and abject submission to their Master's will even more debasing than that of the Southern slave."[56]

Supposedly, slavery saved the South from all these evils of free-labor capitalism. According to Edgefield's Iveson Brookes, slavery was "a main pillar to the peace and safety of a republic." The South's peculiar institution, Brookes argued, "unites labor and capital, and prevents the alienation of feeling and strife of opposing interests experienced where labor and capital stand in antagonistic relation to each other."[57] Jonathan Newland of Chester advanced a similar argument, claiming that slavery was "destroying the antagonism which exists in other states of society, between labor and capital." Newland maintained that slavery "interposes a barrier between the oppression of the rich and the rough turbulence of the poor." Moreover, he continued,

> where slavery exists there can be no considerable antagonism between capital
> and labor. Men own their own laborers, and where this is not the case, every

[53]Louisa S. McCord, "Carey on the Slave Trade," *Southern Quarterly Review* 9 (January, 1854):115–184.

[54]*Ibid.*, p. 143.

[55]Speech of William King Easley, [c. 1850], William King Easley Papers, SCL.

[56]Address of O. Reed Broyles, [c. 1849], O. R. Broyles Papers, DU.

[57]Brookes, *A Defence of Southern Slavery*, pp. 45–46.

man in the peculiar institutions of his country is secured in the possession of all
that his labor produces. Labor cannot to any large extent be an article of trade.[58]

Whitemarsh Seabrook, onetime governor of the state and a wealthy sea-island
cotton planter, also explained the superiority of slave-labor republicanism to the
free-labor variety in the same manner. "In one section," Seabrook declared,
"capital and labor are theoretically equal, but from influence perhaps incapable
of controlment [sic], they are practically antagonistic; in the other, capital is
superior to labor, and the relation between them is a moral one."[59] B. H. Rice, a
planter from Union district, summed up the critique of free-labor republicanism
at a public meeting in his home town. "[A]t the South, labour and capital are
friendly," Rice explained, "they mutually support and sustain each other . . . at
the North, this Harmony is antagonism. Capital grinds and seeks to impoverish
labor, it does degrade it socially and politically."[60]

In antebellum America, North and South, the standard unit of production was
not the factory or the workshop but the household. Households whose members
enjoyed control of productive property enjoyed the economic independence that
formed the bedrock of republican values. In a free-labor society, however, there
were fundamental constraints on the ability of a household to expand its productive capacity. The most important of these constraints, of course, was the absolute limit on the household supply of labor. To expand production beyond a
certain point, the household had to procure its labor in the marketplace. Once
employees were hired in any significant number, the household was transformed
into a workshop and the labor discipline of the marketplace replaced that of the
family. Ultimately, as the shop and factory replaced the household as the standard unit of production, the relationship between capital and labor became that of
employer and worker instead of that between the head of the household and his
familial dependents.[61]

In the South, however, chattel slavery allowed the household head (master)
to expand production almost indefinitely without abandoning the household as
the principal unit of production simply by expanding his definition of the household to include his extended "family" in the slave quarters. Doubtless the
metaphors of the plantation as a vastly extended household and of the slaves as
part of a much extended family were in part intellectual constructs designed to

[58]Chester *Standard*, May 16, 1856.

[59]Laurensville *Herald*, November 29, 1850.

[60]Draft copy of speech by B. H. Rice [c. 1860], Wallace, Rice, Duncan Papers, SCL.

[61]Gavin Wright, *The Political Economy of the Cotton South: Households, Markets, and Wealth
in the Nineteenth Century* (New York: W. W. Norton, 1978), pp. 43–88; Heywood Flesig, "Slav-
ery, the Supply of Agricultural Labor, and the Industrialization of the South," *Journal of Economic
History* 36 (September, 1976):572–597; Christopher Clark, "The Household Economy, Market
Exchange, and the Rise of Capitalism in the Connecticut Valley, 1800–1860," *Journal of Social
History* 13 (Winter, 1979):169–190; Thomas Dublin, "Women and Outwork in a Nineteenth-
Century New England Town: Fitzwilliam, New Hampshire, 1830–1850," in Steven Hahn and
Jonathan Prude, eds., *The Countryside in the Age of Capitalist Transformation: Essays in the Social
History of Rural America* (Chapel Hill: University of North Carolina Press, 1985), pp. 51–69.

blunt the impact of the abolitionists' portrayal of the harsh relationship between master and slave. But it was a metaphor which grew logically from the nature of the master-slave relationship and which contained a great deal of meaning for Southern slaveholders. As the influence of evangelical Christianity expanded in the slave South during the nineteenth century, slaveholders increasingly came to view their responsibilities as moral as well as economic. The slave did not enjoy even the limited freedom of the labor market and, with a few exceptions, enjoyed little protection from the law. The power of the master over the slave, at least in theory, was nearly absolute. Yet the very scope of the master's responsibility for the slave, the completeness of his stewardship over his bondsmen, introduced a moral element into the relationship that was absent in the relations of capitalists and laborers in a free-labor society.[62]

One of the very first Southerners to argue openly that slaves belonged to the master's extended family was South Carolinian Richard Furman, the unifier of the state's Baptists. "A bond-servant," Furman wrote in 1823, "may be treated with justice and humanity as a servant; and a master may, in an important sense, be the guardian and even father of his slaves." The plantation or large farm, in Furman's view, was not only an extended household but a private benevolent institution, with the master serving as benevolent patriarch. Slaves, Furman wrote, "become a part of his [the master's] family, the whole forming under him a little community, and the care of ordering it, and providing for its welfare, devolves on him." As a result of the slaveholder's stewardship, Furman argued, "what is effected, and often at great public expense, in a free community, by taxes, benevolent institutions, better houses, and penitentiaries, lies here on the master."[63] Years later, John C. Calhoun also emphasized the crucial role of the slaveholder, as patriarch, in freeing the South from the irrepressible conflict between labor and capital. "Every plantation is a little community," Calhoun explained, "with the master at its head, who concentrates in himself the unified interests of capital and labor, of which he is common representative."[64] In 1850, Iveson Brookes again emphasized the salutary impact that the slaveholder's personal interest in his slaves had on Southern society as a whole. "The master's ownership in his slave brings a powerful personal interest into active exercise in behalf of that slave as his property," Brookes noted, "Add to this the exercise of

---

[62]On pro-slavery thought, see William Sumner Jenkins, *Pro-slavery Thought in the Old South* (1935, reprinted ed., Gloucester, Mass.: Peter Smith, 1960); David Donald, "The Proslavery Argument Reconsidered," *Journal of Southern History* 37 (February, 1971):3–18; and the introduction by Drew Faust in Drew Gilpin Faust, ed., *The Ideology of Slavery: Proslavery Thought in the Antebellum South, 1830–1860* (Baton Rouge: Louisiana State University Press, 1981), pp. 1–20; for a strikingly different view of the pro-slavery argument, see Kenneth S. Greenberg, *Masters and Statesmen: The Political Culture of American Slavery* (Baltimore: Johns Hopkins University Press, 1985), pp. 85–103.

[63]Richard Furman, *Exposition of the Views of the Baptists Relative to the Colored Population of the United States in Communication to the Governor of South Carolina* (Charleston, 1823).

[64]John C. Calhoun, "Further Remarks in Debate on His Fifth Resolution," January 10, 1838, in Clyde N. Wilson, ed., *The Papers of John C. Calhoun* (Columbia, S.C.: University of South Carolina Press, 1981), vol. 14, pp. 84–85.

the common principle of humanity towards the disobedient . . . with the public
guarantee of law in behalf of slaves, and the slave's condition is rendered
enviable to those who in any nonslaveholding country have to fill the slave's
place."[65] Slavery, William Trescot boasted, "has solved for us in the wisest
manner, that most dangerous of social questions, the relation of labor to capital,
by making that relation a moral one."[66]

The problem, of course, with the "moral" or familial relationship between
master and slave was that it placed the slave at the mercy of his master. There
was nothing to prevent a master from selling, whipping, overworking, or otherwise mistreating slaves except his own enlightened self-interest and sense of
moral responsibility. In a raw and racially divided society like that of antebellum
South Carolina, these internal constraints offered little comfort to the slaves.[67]
From an ideological standpoint, however, the idea that slavery created a moral
relation between labor and capital, between master and slave, and that that
relationship bestowed upon the slaveholder certain familial or patriarchal responsibilities for his slaves was crucial to the development of a coherent attack by
South Carolinians on the increasingly popular free-labor dogma of the North. In
emphasizing the moral relationship between master and slave, and the patriarchal
responsibilities of the slaveholder as the head of an extended household or "little
community," pro-slavery ideologues were asserting the compatibility of non-
market forms of labor control with the continued experiment in republican
government.[68]

The slaveholder's role as chief steward of his extended household established
his credentials as a "paternalist," even if paternalism was a model relationship
between master and slave which seldom if ever actually existed. As D. K.
Roberts has shown in a study of Great Britain, paternalism was gaining acceptance in all parts of the transatlantic world as a method of softening the harsher
aspects of free-market capitalism and slowing the erosion of traditional values
during commercial and industrial revolutions. In Great Britain, traditional
sources of authority such as the Crown, the nobility, and the Church of England
attempted to shore up their position in a market society by actively shouldering
more and more social responsibility.[69] Paternalism appeared in the antebellum
North when capitalists in the first industrial areas moved to promote community
harmony and tranquility by accepting responsibility for preserving social order in
the industrial community. Thus the rhetoric of paternalism and the idea that

[65]Brookes, *A Defence of Southern Slavery*, pp. 46–47.

[66]Trescot, *The Position and Course of the South*, p. 60; for more on the slaveholders' views on
these questions, see Lawrence Shore, *Southern Capitalists: The Ideological Leadership of an Elite,
1832–1885* (Chapel Hill: The University of North Carolina Press, 1986), pp. 3–78.

[67]For a survey of the recent literature, see Charles B. Dew, "The Slavery Experience," in Boles
and Nolen, eds., *Interpreting Southern History*, pp. 120–161.

[68]On patriarchy as a system of labor control, see Michael P. Johnson, "Planters and Patriarchy:
Charleston, 1800–1860," *Journal of Southern History* 46 (February, 1980):45–72.

[69]For an excellent account of these developments in Great Britain, see David K. Roberts,
Paternalism in Early Victorian England (New Brunswick, N.J.: Rutgers University Press, 1979).

capitalists as well as more traditional figures of authority had to take an active role in the moral, spiritual, and physical uplift of their society flourished in free-labor societies as well as in the slave South.[70] In both free and slave societies, paternalism was an idiom of social responsibility and moral uplift adopted with more or less sincerity by those who enjoyed economic and political power. By maintaining that masters were paternalistic in their control of slaves, South Carolinians adopted an idiom of enlightened social control which placed them clearly within the mainstream of the early Victorian intellectual world, yet they adapted that idiom to justify the persistence of a slave society in a world increasingly dominated by free labor.[71]

To the extent that paternalism gained acceptance in South Carolina, it did so as a model for the relationships between a master class, which was, with a few exceptions, white, and slaves who were always black or colored. No one in South Carolina argued that paternalism did or should serve as a model for relations among whites. Indeed, the racial aspect of Southern slavery was crucial to the acceptance of slavery as the proper foundation for republican government. "I am sure no one would deny that if the slave had been of the same race as his master, slavery would have been long ago extinguished and forgotten," William Henry Trescot asserted.[72] Indeed, slavery was seen as a buttress to republican liberty because it supplied dependent laborers to a growing economy without creating invidious class distinctions among whites. "In every community," observed Whitemarsh Seabrook, "where the institution of slavery is interwoven with its social system, the public tranquility and safety demand the toleration of only two classes, white men and colored slaves."[73] James Henry Hammond claimed that any society must have its "mud-sill" class "requiring but a low order of intellect and but little skill." Fortunately for the South, Hammond continued, "she found a race adapted to that purpose to her hand. A race inferior to her own, but eminently qualified in temper, in vigor, in docility, in capacity to stand the climate, to answer all her purposes." Prodding Northern senators about

---

[70]On paternalism in the antebellum North, see Clifford S. Griffin, *Their Brothers Keepers: Moral Stewardship in the United States, 1800–1865* (New Brunswick, N.J.: Rutgers University Press, 1960); Allen Dawley, *Class and Community: The Industrial Revolution in Lynn* (Cambridge, Mass.: Harvard University Press, 1976); Paul E. Johnson, *A Shopkeeper's Millennium: Society and Revivals in Rochester, New York 1815–1837* (New York: Hill and Wang, 1978); Anthony F. C. Wallace, *Rockdale: The Growth of an American Village in the Early Industrial Revolution* (New York: Alfred A. Knopf, 1978).

[71]On the concept of paternalism and the relationship between master and slave in the antebellum South, see Eugene Genovese, *Roll, Jordan, Roll: The World the Slaves Made* (New York: Pantheon, 1974); Drew Gilpin Faust, *A Sacred Circle: The Dilemma of the Intellectual in the Old South* (Baltimore: Johns Hopkins University Press, 1977), and "A Southern Stewardship: The Intellectual and the Pro-slavery Argument," *American Quarterly* 31 (Spring, 1979):63–80; Jack P. Maddex, Jr., "Proslavery Millennialism: Social Eschatology in Antebellum Southern Calvinism," *American Quarterly* 3 (Spring, 1979):46–62.

[72]William Henry Trescot, *Oration Delivered before the Alumni of the College of Charleston, June 25, 1889* (Charleston: Walker, Evans, Cogswell, 1889), pp. 1–17.

[73]Laurensville *Herald,* November 29, 1860.

the condition of wage-laborers in their region, Hammond explained the South's defense of slavery:

> We do not think that whites should be slaves either by law or necessity. Our slaves are black, of another and inferior race. The status we have placed them in is an elevation. . . . Yours are white, of your own race; you are brothers of one blood. They are your equals in natural endowment of intellect and they feel galled by the degradation.[74]

William Henry Trescot stated the racial justification for slavery more succinctly. The South, he claimed, was "a country peopled by two races—one superior, the other inferior; one white, the other black; one master, the other slave."[75]

Black slavery, therefore, was portrayed as a bulwark of republican liberty for whites. It brought racial and class lines in antebellum South Carolina into close identification. One group was independent, enfranchised, white, and free, the other was dependent, politically impotent, black, and enslaved. With black slavery serving as a foundation for white liberty, the sentiments of kinship and democracy among whites were intensified. "In a country like the South, those invidious distinctions which prevail in all free-soil States must be to a very considerable extent unknown," claimed Chester's Jonathan Newland.[76] W. L. Hudgen of Laurens believed "African slavery to be of Heaven appointment" and that the South's peculiar civilization was "of all others the best adapted to the freedom and equality of the white."[77] No South Carolinian was more aware of the identity of race and class lines in the South than Trescot, who noted that political democracy for whites in his state produced a thoroughly republican "government of class and race." Slavery, Trescot wrote, "draws a broad line between the class who merely labor and the white population of the State who are thus created a governing, privileged class." For South Carolina, Trescot observed, slavery "has realized the dream of political philosophers; it has been the great leveller, not by dragging down, but by raising up; it has made a society of equals, by elevating all citizens of the State to the condition of a privileged class."[78] Clearly, the appeal of slave-labor republicanism extended well beyond the planter class. Yeomen, as well as planters, aspired to fulfill the "country-republican" ideal of the independent producer. Indeed, to many South Carolinians, the prosperous planter simply represented the virtues of the independent

---

[74]Hammond, "Speech on Kansas," pp. 318–321.

[75]William Henry Trescot, "Oration before the South Carolina Historical Society, 1859," *Russell's Magazine* 3 (July, 1859):289–307; see also George M. Fredrickson, "Masters and Mudsills: The Role of Race in the Planter Ideology of South Carolina," *South Atlantic Urban Studies*, 2 (1978):34–48. On the larger implications of racism as a product of ideology, see Barbara J. Fields, "Ideology and Race in American History," in J. Morgan Kousser and James M. McPherson, eds, *Region, Race, and Reconstruction: Essays in Honor of C. Vann Woodward* (New York: Oxford University Press, 1982), pp. 143–177.

[76]Chester *Standard*, May 16, 1856.

[77]Laurensville *Herald*, June 25, 1858.

[78]Trescot, "Oration before the South Carolina Historical Society," pp. 298–305.

yeoman writ large. Waxing eloquent at an Agricultural Society meeting in 1855, Edgefield planter Arthur Simkins elaborated on the common zeal for independence shared by planters and yeomen alike:

> The commonest cottager, on his hundred acres of pine land, looks upon his little possession around him as his own without reservation, in the enjoyment of which he is safe from intrusion so long as he discharges his obligation to the community in which he lives; while many a Southern planter, as he surveys his broad acres and passes in review his hundreds of slaves, feels all the pride of a baron of the olden time. . . . Each man is master within his own domain and has no rival there . . . [and] is in most instances literally lord of all he surveys. . . . Alone and unfettered, he directs his household. prepares his land . . . he jostles no one and no one jostles him.[79]

Moreover, Union's B. H. Rice contended that the common people of South Carolina were the most determined enemies of the free-soil movement. "They understand," Rice maintained, "that . . . where Capital rules, where there are no black slaves, there must be white ones." According to Rice, "no Southern born [white] man would brush the boots and carry out the stink pots of his extortionate Master," and "no industrious, energetic white man in the South ever fails to get full remuneration for his respectable services." Rice also warned yeomen that if the Republican party triumphed the federal government would move quickly to make them "serfs of the Manufacturers like the coolies of India or the Peons of Mexico," a fate which Rice described as "worse than negro slavery."[80]

In a slave society the white man's zeal for personal independence and his fear of dependence and consequent degradation often developed some peculiar manifestations. The ideal of independence required individual autonomy but also prized mastery over others considered unfit for citizenship. Mastery, defined by James Henry Hammond as simply the desire "to control and scorn to be controlled," gained acceptance in South Carolina as an elaborate form of republican independence, an overt expression of individual liberty. Yet the psychological

[79]Arthur Simkins, *Address before the State Agricultural Society of South Carolina* (Edgefield: Advertiser Office, 1855), pp. 1–2.

[80]Draft copy of a speech by B. H. Rice [c. 1860], Wallace, Rice, Duncan Papers, SCL.

[81]James Henry Hammond, "Anniversary Oration of the State Agricultural Society of South Carolina, 25 November, 1841," in *Proceedings of the Agricultural Convention of the State Agricultural Society of South Carolina from 1831 to 1845* (Columbia: Summer and Carroll, 1846), p. 183. Sociologist Pierre L. van den Berghe found that in societies which are "democratic for the master race but tyrannical for subordinate groups," the subjugation of one race actually reinforces democratic and egalitarian sentiments among members of the dominant race. Van den Berghe's concept of *herrenvolk* democracy has been applied to the American South by George Fredrickson and Kenneth Vickery. See Pierre van den Berghe, *Race and Racism: A Comparative Perspective* (New York, 1967), pp. 17–18; George M. Fredrickson, *The Black Image in the White Mind: The Debate on Afro-American Character and Destiny* (New York: Harper and Row, 1971), pp. 61–68; Kenneth Vickery, "*Herrenvolk* Democracy and Egalitarianism in South Africa and the United States South," *Comparative Studies in Society and History* 16 (January, 1974):309–328.

appeal of mastery, like that of independence, reached yeomen as well as planters. The presence of black slaves allowed an entire race of would-be masters without slaves to enjoy certain caste privileges and to flaunt a certain instinctive sense of natural mastery.[81] "The right to command an inferior is a guarantee of respect to an equal," Trescot noted in 1859, "and the tone in which you speak to a slave of necessity changes when you address a freeman." Indeed, Trescot, surely as proud and refined a planter as South Carolina produced, thought the principal product of his state's slave society was "a striking individuality" which at times seemed "subject to no authority." This "absolute independence," observed Trescot, "created naturally a great tenacity of rights, and a watchful and resentful jealousy of any outside interference."[82] The fierce independence and "striking individuality" which Trescot so admired in his fellow South Carolinians also inspired a protean zeal for republican equality and an acute and prickly sensitivity to any suggestion that class distinctions among whites were either desirable or permissible. Equality of wealth and talent was not expected, or even desired, but every white man was entitled to his independence, and in that independence stood as the equal as man and citizen with his wealthiest and most powerful neighbor. "Wealth must ever have its influence, it is puerile to think otherwise," admitted the Yorkville *Enquirer,* "but when it aspires to rule the world and bend genius and intelligence to its will, it becomes a dangerous element, especially dangerous to a democratic government."[83] Insistence on republican equality, based on common independence, for all white men produced a rather elaborate, and carefully observed, code of republican etiquette which dominated public life and discourse in South Carolina. In a society where the degradation of slavery was so visible, white men demonstrated a jealousy of their own independence and equality that bordered on obsession. "The habit of command, where you have a right to obedience," explained Trescot, "develops necessarily the habit of considerate courtesy where there is no right to command; and the very existence of a large body of inferiors made men both jealous and cautious as to the manner which was to indicate their relations to each other."[84]

South Carolina's defense of its way of life, its slave-labor republicanism, was obviously one which struck deep emotional chords among Southern whites, slaveholders and non-slaveholders alike. It not only provided a rebuttal to Northern antislavery attacks but also based that defense of slavery on the strongest possible ground, the society's interest in preserving white independence and equality. In the North, the free-labor movement had broadened its appeal by shifting the theme of its attack on slavery away from the moral criticisms leveled by abolitionists to an emphasis on the threat which slave labor posed to the economic opportunity and political equality of the mass of Northern whites. In the South, however, slavery was seen as a buttress of white equality and independence, not as a threat to it. Both regions were zealous in their pursuit of re-

[82]Trescot, "Oration before the South Carolina Historical Society," pp. 298–300.
[83]Yorkville *Enquirer,* June 18, 1857.
[84]Trescot, "Oration before the South Carolina Historical Society," pp. 298–300.

publican ideals, but by the 1850s, each region's prescription for living up to those ideals was seemingly inimical to that of the other, and each region believed that its own particular experiment in republican government had the best chance for continued success.[85]

For all its coherence, however, the argument for slave-labor republicanism was not without its loose ends. Most Southern agriculturalists, regardless of the size of their holdings, could easily identify themselves as independent producers. Even tenant farmers, who controlled productive property but did not own it, were essentially independent producers for the length of their tenure. White sharecroppers and day-laborers lacked such independence, but in South Carolina at least, white sharecropping was very uncommon before the Civil War, and white day-laborers were usually young adult males who either still lived as dependents in their father's household or who had just started a household of their own. Moreover, in the loose, informal setting of rural South Carolina, where the overwhelming majority of white males did control productive property, white skin was ordinarily enough to entitle the small minority of propertyless and economically marginal whites to recognition as independent citizens. Outside of the agricultural sector, however, the status of white workers presented more of a problem to "country-republican" ideologues. Artisans, mechanics, and skilled tradesmen, most of whom owned at least the tools and equipment of their trade, were readily accepted as independent producers, and as long as the number of laborers who worked as apprentices or in workshops was comparatively small, their dependent status, which was usually viewed as temporary, caused little concern. White artisans, mechanics, and tradesmen, however, feared the competition of slave labor, and occasionally used their political power to demand protection from it. Moreover, the question of how a large class of white factory workers could be accepted into the community of independent producers prompted considerable disagreement among South Carolinians.[86]

B. F. Perry, frequently out of step with the dominant trends in South Carolina political thought, vehemently objected to any effort to deny the free laborer republican citizenship. Perry claimed that this idea was "as degrading and insulting to labor and laboring classes as it is false to liberty and republicanism." Labor, Perry believed, had fallen into disrepute in the South because it was identified with black slaves. As a result, an "indolent, self-satisfied, and inert prodigal spirit" had taken over the South and slowed its economic development. "[I]t is contended," Perry noted, "that slavery is necessary to republicanism, in order to afford the laboring classes, who ought to be excluded from republicanism, and who are unfit to exercise the rights which belong to a republican citizen." Perry, however, countered this argument with the claim that "in the Northern States, where slavery does not exist, they have as much re-

[85]Foner, *Free Soil, Free Labor, Free Men*, pp. 301–317; Fredrickson, *The Black Image in the White Mind*, pp. 130–164; Thornton, *Politics and Power in a Slave Society*, especially pp. 130–164; Ford, "Labor and Ideology in the South Carolina Upcountry," pp. 25–27.

[86]For more on this subject, see Shore, *Southern Capitalists*, pp. 42–78.

publicanism as we have in South Carolina . . . and they show that labor is not antagonistic to education and republicanism.''[87] Perry wanted the South to develop manufacturers and mechanics as well as planters and cotton merchants. National Democrat James L. Orr agreed with the Unionist Perry, at least with regard to the region's need for artisans and mechanics in its towns and cities. ''We want manufactories and machine shops—they coexist together,'' declared Orr. ''We want enterprising, intelligent, inventive mechanics.'' Moreover, Orr saw no reason why artisans and mechanics, as long as they were white, could ''not stand up and exact recognition of [their] perfect equality with the most favored and exalted class of [their] fellow-men.'' Orr's confidence in artisans and mechanics, however, did not weaken his belief that slavery was essential to republicanism. He denounced the view ''that slavery is a political evil . . . and that it is incompatible with the personal and mental development of the white man'' as the ''most palpable error.'' Instead, he argued, slavery encouraged ''the highest development and civilization of the master race.''[88]

Other South Carolinians were not as confident as Perry and Orr about the value of mechanics and artisans to a slave society. Christopher Memminger of Charleston worried that white artisans, mechanics, and operatives would eventually grow frustrated with slave competition and rebel. Memminger outlined his views in a letter to James H. Hammond:

> I find an opinion gaining ground that slaves ought to be excluded from mechanical pursuits and everything but agriculture, so as to have their places filled with whites; and ere long we will have a formidable party on this subject. The planters generally do not perceive how it affects their interest, and very frequently chime in with this cry. I think our friend Gregg of Graniteville, with those who are agog about manufacturers, without knowing it are lending aid to this party which is in truth the only party from which danger to our institutions is to be apprehended among us. Drive out negro mechanics and all sorts of [Negro] operatives from our cities, and who must take their places. The same men who make the cry in the Northern cities against the tyranny of Capital— and there as here would drive before them all who interfere with them—and would soon raise here the cry against the Negro, and be hot Abolitionists. And every one of these men would have a vote.[89]

The Upcountry Yorkville *Enquirer* also feared the creation of an indigenous white proletariat which might form ''that most dangerous viper,'' an ''organized, determined free-labor party, whose bond of union will be hatred of slave competition'' and whose ''final aim will be total emancipation.''[90] In the short term, however, artisans and mechanics simply demanded that slave competition

[87]*Carolina Spartan*, January 26, 1854.

[88]James L. Orr, ''Address Delivered before the South Carolina Institute,'' *DeBow's Review* 19 (1855):1–22.

[89]Christopher G. Memminger to James H. Hammond, April 28, 1849, James Henry Hammond Papers, SCL (microfilm).

[90]Yorkville *Enquirer*, October 8, 1857.

be minimized and that the prevailing code of republican etiquette for whites be observed. South Carolina politicians eagerly obliged. In 1860, white artisans and mechanics in Charleston complained about the nearly 300 slaves who did similar work while hiring on their own time, and the mayor responded to the pressure by campaigning against the practice. "The line of demarcation between the castes should be clear and distinct," asserted an angry Charleston grand jury in that same year.[91]

Despite its unresolved inconsistencies, slave-labor republicanism, as an ideology, gained broad acceptance in South Carolina during the 1850s. The voice of B. F. Perry urging Southerners to "take lessons from the Yankees in industry, wisdom, and economy" became increasingly isolated. More frequently heard were warnings like that issued by Perry's neighbor and longtime rival in Greenville politics, William K. Easley, against that "insatiable thirst for advancement and amelioration," which always seemed to emanate from the North. "For all intents and purposes," Easley observed, "they [North and South] are two peoples, two separate and distinct nationalities differing in genius and spirit."[92] By the late 1850s, independent South Carolinians were besieged. At home, growing commercial dependencies, the increasing power of banks and other corporations, and a new profligacy in state spending seemed to threaten their prized autonomy. From outside the state, a dangerous enemy, armed with an alien and aggressive ideology, threatened the South's proud republican society with the loss of its equality within the Union and perhaps with all the horrors associated with emancipation. With threats to their independence visible on all sides, freemen in South Carolina searched desperately for relief from the siege.

In 1857, the delicate factional balance between National Democrats and Southern Rights men was tested. A. P. Butler's death left a United States Senate seat vacant. Neither Robert Barnwell Rhett, the radicals' choice, nor Francis Pickens, the leading candidate of the National Democrats, could muster the needed majority in the state legislature. On the third ballot, James Henry Hammond, whose forced retirement from politics ended with the death of Wade Hampton II earlier in the year, was elected as a compromise choice. Hammond was loyal to neither of the two major factions in the state, and his long hiatus from politics left many questions in the public mind about Hammond's stance on pressing national issues. In 1858, another senatorial election produced yet another compromise choice. After much jockeying, James Chesnut, a moderate not committed to either faction, was elected on the ninth ballot. Again, the chief complaint heard around the state over Chesnut's election was that few people knew where he stood on the issues.[93] Throughout 1857 and 1858, radical Southern Rights lead-

[91]Charleston *Daily Courier*, August 9, 1860; Michael P. Johnson and James L. Roark, *Black Masters: A Free Family of Color in the Old South* (New York: W. W. Norton, 1984) pp. 153–194.

[92]Greenville *Southern Patriot*, May 11, 1854; Draft copy of speech by William K. Easley, December, 1860, William King Easley Papers, SCL.

[93]Schultz, *Nationalism and Sectionalism*, pp. 135–177; Frank Sexton to Andrew Baxter Springs, October 10, 1858, Springs Family Papers, SHC.

ers continued their campaign for a Southern Confederacy. At a cavalry muster in Lancaster in September 1857, militia general States Rights Gist, a fire-eater from Union district, told his troops that there existed "a terrible antagonism between North and South," and warned that "Black Republicanism is a fungus which will continue to grow and ultimately elect a President." When that happened, Gist argued, the South would have no choice but secession. Orr and the National Democrats feared the new Republican party nearly as much as the radicals did, but in 1857, they did not see an eventual Republican triumph as inevitable. Samuel Melton, a National Democrat from York district, rebutted Gist's argument, claiming that he "saw little danger ahead in politics as long as the South worked closely with the Democratic party."[94] Moreover, the moderate Fairfield *Register* warned that the alarmist outlook of the Southern Rights men was itself dangerous to the public safety. "Next to the sentinel who sleeps on duty," wrote the paper, "is he who is constantly attempting to arouse the garrison unnecessarily."[95]

By 1858, however, it was clear that both National Democrats and Southern Rights men, as well as the clique of independents led by Hammond and Chesnut, felt that the election of a "Black Republican" President would be the death knell of the Union. In June 1858, J. Perkins Hoyt, a cautious National Democrat from Laurens, told voters in his native district:

> I shall never attempt to become a leader in disunion while it is a question, but . . . the South has borne her full share of hardship and oppression at the hands of the Federal Government and should, as one man, come to a stand point, where must be fought the battle of equal rights. This point should be the election of a Black Republican President in 1860. If that foul, God-defying party should succeed in the next election . . . and the South remains in the Union, she will deserve nothing better than to become a slave, and remain so.[96]

This emotional attack on the Republican party came from one of the state's calmest politicians. Hoyt had opposed the radicals in 1851 and encouraged reconciliation with the North during the rest of the decade. If Hoyt was ready to secede when the Republicans won the presidency, those less moderate would certainly do the same. Southern Rights leaders John McQueen, L. M. Keitt, Milledge L. Bonham, and W. W. Boyce all announced as early as 1858 that South Carolina should leave the Union if a Republican were elected President, and the radical Charleston *Mercury* predicted that the "steady progress and fatal purposes of the powerful Black Republican faction" would eventually drive "all true men in South Carolina" to support secession. Among leading South Carolina politicians, only die-hard Unionist B. F. Perry thought that the Union could survive a Republican victory in 1860.[97]

[94]*Carolina Spartan,* September 10, 1857.
[95]Quoted in Charleston *Mercury,* July 6, 1857.
[96]Laurensville *Herald,* June 25, 1858.
[97]Newberry *Rising Sun,* September 1, 1858; *Keowee Courier,* September 18, 1858; Lancaster *Ledger,* September 22, 1858; Edgefield *Advertiser,* October 27, 1858; Charleston *Mercury,*

Southern Rights advocates in South Carolina received unexpected help in October 1859, when John Brown's well-planned but ill-fated raid on the arsenal at Harper's Ferry, and the exposure of Brown's plan to incite major slave insurrections throughout the South, reminded white South Carolinians that some abolitionists were willing to resort to terrorism to achieve their goals. Moreover, the subsequent revelation that Brown's efforts were financed by the so-called "Secret Six" of Boston alarmed members of the South Carolina gentry who had long pinned their hopes for the nation's future on the desire of conservative Northern businessmen to restrain the most radical antislavery forces in their region. As soon as the first reports of Brown's raid reached South Carolina, a brief panic swept the state. Almost immediately, vigilance committees were formed in nearly every beat in the Upcountry. For most of the next year, all strangers were suspected of being abolitionists, any hint of slave revolt met with a strong show of force, and the siege mentality in the state capital grew so intense that William Campbell Preston described Columbia as "a focus of slave traders, disunionists and lynching societies." Beat-level vigilance committees were officially organized "for the purpose of protecting our homes, families, and property, and for the general welfare of the community," but were also important in mobilizing the white population politically. "Vigilance is everywhere needed," noted the Yorkville *Enquirer*. "The roving mendicant, the tobacco-wagoner, the whisky peddler, the sample trader may be honest and reliable, but in such like disguise abolitionists have prowled about elsewhere and may do so here."[98]

The general alarm that followed Harper's Ferry led to the harassment of suspicious whites, uncovered a few abolitionists and abolition sympathizers, and led to closer supervision of slaves in many parts of the state, but it also brought new urgency to calls for a more lasting remedy to the South's problems. Entering the critical election year of 1860, the grip of fear on the state was still tight, and the radicals had just the sort of emotional issue they needed to win popular support for secession. According to Senator Hammond, "999 in every 1000 of the voters and 49 in every 50 of the substantial and influential men of the South" would go "for the Union until it pinches them and then for dissolving it."[99] John Brown's raid was just the "pinch" needed to create a successful secession movement, and radical politicians worked hard for secession throughout 1860. National Democrats from South Carolina worked equally hard to save the national party, but few of them could accept Douglas as the party nominee. Edward

---

November 19, 1858. In addition to the works by Foner and Gienapp on the rise of the Republican party already cited, see Michael F. Holt's provocative case study, *Forging a Majority: The Formation of the Republican Party in Pittsburgh, 1848–1860* (New Haven: Yale University Press, 1969); and Stephen E. Maizlish, *The Triumph of Sectionalism: The Transformation of Ohio Politics, 1844–1856* (Kent, Ohio: Kent State University Press, 1983).

[98]For an excellent account of the impact of the Harper's Ferry incident on South Carolina politics, see Steven A. Channing, *Crisis of Fear: Secession in South Carolina* (New York: Simon and Schuster, 1970), especially pp. 17–57; William C. Preston to Waddy Thompson, January 27, 1860, William Campbell Preston Papers, SCL; Yorkville *Enquirer*, September 20, 1860.

[99]James Henry Hammond to William P. Miles, November 28, 1858, William Porcher Miles Papers, SHC.

Noble of Abbeville predicted that the nomination of Douglas would "divide the state badly" and eventually lead to the triumph of Southern Rights radicalism. As the elections of 1860 grew closer, it became increasingly clear that a Republican victory would provoke secession in South Carolina.[100] In February 1860, Frank Sexton, a native of York district, explained his reluctant radicalism to his old friend Andrew Baxter Springs. "I fear the south has already forborne too long for her own best interests," Sexton observed. "Clearly there is *now* no alternative left her but submission or resistance." Sexton's own recommendation was for the South to "assert her own independence in the event of the election of a Bl[ac]k Republican President."[101] That same month, Charleston's Christopher Memminger described the Republicans as a "sectional party" determined to make the Union "an instrument of tyranny."[102]

Throughout the secession campaign, Upcountry leaders insisted that they were defending republican values, and that secession was not the radical, but rather the conservative, course of action. "We are upholding the great principles which our fathers bequeathed us," maintained the Presbyterian theologian James Henley Thornwell. "We shall perpetuate and diffuse the very liberty for which Washington bled, and which the heroes of the Revolution achieved."[103] In York district, radical Jonathan L. Miller claimed that Lincoln's election would leave South Carolina with a clear choice. "We must be content with the mere shadow of a Republic, with every feature of republicanism completely obliterated," Miller asserted, "or we must reaffirm and re-establish the fundamental principles of our government in building up a Southern Confederacy."[104] The Yorkville *Enquirer* claimed that the South only wanted to preserve "simple republicanism." The question of secession was the major issue in the fall campaigns for the state legislature, and politicians found public opinion strongly in favor of secession if Lincoln were elected. Candidates such as Unionist A. S. Wallace of York, who advocated "patriotic forbearance" if Lincoln won, were, as a rule, soundly defeated. When news of Lincoln's victory finally reached the state on November 7, the legislature immediately called for a special convention to meet on December 17. Minutemen chapters quickly formed in every Upcountry district, and public meetings were called to select delegates to the secession convention.[105]

[100]Edward Noble to Francis W. Pickens, August 10, 1859, Francis W. Pickens Papers, DU.

[101]Frank Sexton to Andrew Baxter Springs, February 15, 1860, Springs Family Papers, SHC.

[102]Christopher G. Memminger to Governor William H. Gist, February 13, 1860, Christopher G. Memminger Papers, SHC.

[103]Draft of Thornwell's speech, "Our Danger and Our Duty," in James Henley Thornwell Papers, SCL; the best account of Thornwell's life is James Oscar Farmer, Jr., *The Metaphysical Confederacy: James Henley Thornwell and the Synthesis of Southern Values* (Macon, Ga.: Mercer University Press, 1986), especially pp. 175–283.

[104]Yorkville *Enquirer*, October 4, 1860.

[105]Yorkville *Enquirer*, October 11, 1860; *Carolina Spartan*, December 6 and 13, 1860; Schultz, *Nationalism and Sectionalism*, pp. 225–230; A. S. Wallace to Andrew Baxter Springs, September 21, 1859, Springs Family Papers, SHC.

Reluctant and eager secessionists alike agreed that unity was essential to a successful secession movement. As a result, secession propaganda emphasized that planter and yeoman, slaveholder and non-slaveholder, debtor and creditor all had much to lose from submission to rule by a "Black Republican" President. National Democrat John D. Ashmore of Pendleton, congressman from the yeoman-dominated western district of South Carolina, told his constituents that they had much to lose from the triumph of the Republican party. "The hardy farmer or mountaineer, who has been accustomed to the use of the axe, the hoe, the plow, and more important still, the rifle, grasps it more firmly in his hand when he is told that it is the object of the North to turn loose a hungry horde of free negroes upon him, whom [sic] he well knows, without the guardianship of a master are too lazy to work, but not too proud to steal," Ashmore maintained. "But more than all, he [the mountaineer] knows the honor of his wife and daughter would hardly be safe an hour if these slaves, totally unfit for self-government, were turned loose upon his community."[106] Greenville fire-eater William K. Easley told the yeomen in his district that "the loss of slave property would not be the only loss" under Republican rule. "[W]e will lose every right and every liberty which belongs to the name of freemen," warned Easley, "when slaves are emancipated and made our equals . . . those who will not resist are slaves and cowards." In Union district, B. H. Rice found that "the common people" were "the most resolute" opponents of "Northern aggression."[107]

Once the secession convention was called, a special effort to rally popular support behind secession was launched in many Upcountry districts. In Greenville, where Unionist B. F. Perry had always been influential, other local notables worked to win yeoman support for secession. On November 22, prominent Baptist minister James C. Furman and a number of other political and religious notables published an open letter to the citizens of Greenville:

> Men of Greenville, show yourselves men. . . . Self-respect, honor, and the safety of our wives, our children, and our slaves themselves . . . all conspire to urge you to sustain the state. . . . The negro is not your equal, unless the Bible is untrue, or you prove yourselves unworthy of the name free men.[108]

On election day, Greenville elected a solid slate of secessionists, headed by Easley and Furman. The secessionists all polled over 1300 votes, while Perry led the Union ticket with 225 votes. It was the first time Perry had ever lost an election in Greenville.[109] In neighboring Spartanburg district, there were scarce-

---

[106]*Carolina Spartan*, March 22, 1860.

[107]Speech of William K. Easley [c. 1860], William King Easley Papers, SCL; Speech of B. H. Rice [c. 1860], Wallace, Rice, and Duncan Papers, SCL.

[108]*Carolina Spartan*, November 22, 1860; Harvey Toliver Cook, *The Life Work of James Clement Furman* (Greenville, S.C.: Alester G. Furman, 1926), pp. 194–201.

[109]Greenville *Southern Enterprise*, December 13, 1860.

ly any Unionists left to make a fight. Industrialist Simpson Bobo, a Unionist in both 1832 and 1851, supported secession in 1860. "We have no Union now," Bobo lamented after Lincoln's election, "and with the forces arrayed against us, it is folly to hope for its restoration." Spartanburg farmer David G. Harris reported that everyone "was in a fever heat to secede . . . almost without a dissenting voice" at a public meeting in Spartanburg on November 24.[110] When the election was finally held on December 6, Spartanburg elected a solid slate of secessionists in a landslide. The Greenville and Spartanburg story was repeated in district after district throughout the Upcountry. Indeed, virtually no opposition to secession surfaced in most districts. Upcountry delegates to the secession convention were unanimous in the support of secession, and on December 20, 1860, the convention, meeting in Charleston after a smallpox epidemic forced the members to flee Columbia, adopted the ordinance of secession by a vote of 170 to 0.[111] Lowcountryman David Gavin, a half-hearted secessionist, worried that South Carolina's pro-secession politicians had not made their case honestly. "Men call secession a constitutional remedy or act, and yet say we are in the midst of a revolution," a perplexed Gavin complained, "how a legal or constitutional act can be revolutionary I cannot imagine, but they [secessionists] must humbug the democracy or people."[112] But Upcountry Presbyterian Zelotus Holmes viewed the situation differently. Secession, Holmes insisted, was not the work of demagogues or short-sighted politicians but of the "oldest, gravest, soundest men that the state affords."[113]

A few voices of protest were heard, but not heeded. Perry, who agreed to support his state if it seceded, opposed secession to the bitter end. "Fellow citizens," Perry pleaded, "the honor of the patriot and statesmen is not the honor of a duellist . . . the duellist may go and sacrifice his own life and society is but little injured by it, [but it is] not so with those who stir up revolutions and civil wars."[114] In Charleston, Perry's longtime friend James L. Petigru, who remained loyal to the Union even after South Carolina seceded, did not actively oppose secession. Petigru summarized his feelings of helplessness in a long letter to Perry:

> If all our countrymen were as lost to respect for the difference between Right and Wrong as South Carolina, it would be time for Hell to enlarge its borders. . . . The truth is, my friend, I have contracted a disinclination to write or speak when truth is in question. For I look upon my countrymen with the despair of old Fontenelle who said that if he had the truth in his closed hand he

[110]*Carolina Spartan,* November 22, 1860; Entry of November 24, 1860, David G. Harris Journal, SHC.

[111]*Carolina Spartan,* December 13, 1860.

[112]Entry of December 6, 1860, David Gavin Diary, SHC.

[113]Zelotus L. Holmes to his aunt, January 6, 1861, Zelotus L. Holmes Papers, SCL.

[114]Anderson *Intelligencer,* October 18, 1860.

would not open it. And why should one put himself to the pains of speaking to
the insane if he has not the power of commanding a strait jacket for them?[115]

Petigru, however, reportedly broke his self-imposed vow of silence long enough
to warn an assemblage of secessionists that "South Carolina is too small for a
republic, but too large for an insane asylum."[116]

It was easy to ignore cautionary voices in the winter of 1860. Secession
feeling was high. Men of all ages sported the blue cockade of resistance proudly.
As military companies were organized, the state found itself flooded with more
volunteers than it could use. Wade Hampton III, the wealthy Richland planter,
outfitted an entire legion out of his personal fortune. Others made similar sacrifices. To be sure, this enthusiasm for sacrifice and harmony among all citizens
did not last long once the fighting actually began, but in December 1860, most
Upcountrymen agreed with the sentiments of David Harris. "She [South Car-
olina] has taken a bold and noble stand, she must and will maintain it let it cost as
much blood and money as it may," the Spartanburg farmer confided to his
journal. "I for one am glad she has committed herself, and do not fear the
consequences."[117]

For more than a decade before secession, a cadre of radical leaders, self-styled
Southern Rights men, had argued that the South could not maintain independence and equality within the Union. The free-labor section was bound to dominate the slaveholding section, they argued; separate nationhood was the solution.
These radicals, in many ways, were the idealists, the visionaries, among their
people. They attributed to secession, or at least to Southern nationalism, a
regenerative power. Outside the Union, the South would no longer have to
grapple with the problems of living in a republic that was half slave and half free.
Instead, the region could become a proud, slaveholding republic which could, as
one Upcountry radical put it, "command the respect of her enemies, and the
admiration and envy of the world."[118] But how did this radical vision, this
search for the ideal slaveholding republic, which had long gleamed in the eyes of
the few, come to triumph in a society whose members were ordinarily so reluctant to be driven toward visions? The answer is that it did not, at least, not
entirely. South Carolina seceded not because her citizens were looking for a
more perfect confederacy, but because they believed they no longer had any
choice. The only alternative appeared to be submission to Black Republican rule
and the sacrifice of republican independence and equality. "Secession is a des-

[115]James L. Petigru to B. F. Perry, December 8, 1860, quoted in Julius Griffin Campbell,
"James Louis Petigru: A Rhetorical Study" (Ph.D. dissertation, University of South Carolina,
1960), p. 146.

[116]Sally Edwards, *The Man Who Said No* (New York: Coward-McCann, 1970), p. 65.

[117]Entry of December 30, 1860, David G. Harris Journal, SHC.

[118]Laurensville *Herald,* November 20, 1857. These are the words of the newspaper's retiring
editor, radical W. L. Hudgens.

perate remedy," acknowledged David Harris, "but of the two evils I do think it is the lesser."[119]

Late in the 1850s, the bloody struggle in Kansas and the suggestive horror of John Brown's raid on the arsenal at Harper's Ferry made the political warfare with the Republicans and abolitionists seem like a struggle to the death. Enemies willing to incite insurrection and wage campaigns of terror were enemies real and dangerous enough to curdle the blood of the bravest Upcountryman. Moreover, these external threats appeared at a time when most Upcountrymen were increasingly uneasy about their own experiment in republicanism. The sweeping commercial revolution of the 1850s, an increasingly active and spendthrift state government, the growing power of bank and railroad corporations, and the vicissitudes of staple agriculture all posed serious threats to the fictive republican elysium which most South Carolinians believed that they had inherited from their forefathers. The triumph of an avowedly antislavery President pushed an already anxious citizenry to rebellion. Yeoman joined planter to make a revolution.

Almost literally, Upcountrymen saw secession as the required defense of basic republican values. The republican citizen's most cherished possession, his own independence and that of his household, was threatened by powerful external forces. One set of those forces threatened to force him into slavery and degradation through the loss of his economic independence. The other set of forces threatened to free the entire black slave population to violate his home and family. Secession offered the independent citizen a chance to meet this challenge at the threshold, to defend the autonomy of his household by literally throwing himself across the doorway in defiance. This was the secessionist appeal that reached not just planters and slaveholders but all whites who considered themselves entitled to liberty and personal independence.[120]

In the final analysis, a unified South Carolina could secede because the dominant ideal in her society was not the planter ideal or the slaveholding ideal, but the old "country-republican" ideal of personal independence, given peculiar fortification by the use of black slaves as a mud-sill class. Yeoman rose with planter to defend this ideal because it was not merely the planter's ideal, but his as well. To be sure, the yeoman did not share equally in the riches and rewards of the slave economy, but he could enjoy an equal share of independence and accept what William Henry Trescot called "an adequate adjustment of inequalities" in other areas.[121] Perhaps no single incident reveals the extent to which the "adequate adjustment of inequalities" and a sense of personal independence placed the common white in delicate equipose with rich planters in an essentially democratic society than an episode recounted by Mary Boykin Chesnut. Mary

[119]Entry of November 19, 1860, David G. Harris Journal, SHC.

[120]The three best surveys of the recent literature on the coming of the Civil War are: Eric Foner, "The Causes of the American Civil War: Recent Interpretations and New Directions," *Civil War History* 20 (September, 1974):197–214; Kenneth M. Stampp, "The Irrepressible Conflict," in his *The Imperiled Union*, pp. 191–245; and Don E. Fehrenbacher, "The New Political History and the Coming of the Civil War," *Pacific Historical Review* 54 (May, 1985):117–142.

[121]William H. Trescot, *Oration before the Alumni of the College of Charleston*, pp. 1–5.

Chesnut, with her husband James Chesnut, a former United States senator and wealthy Camden planter, and her cousin Louisa McCaa Haile, attended a dinner party at the home of her uncle, Alexander Hamilton Boykin, a state legislator and planter, in Kershaw district. Mary Chesnut offered the following account of the proceedings:

> We had been at one of Uncle Hamilton's splendid dinners—plate glass, Sevres china, and everything that was nice to eat. In the piazza, when the gentlemen were smoking after dinner, in the midst of them sat Squire Mac-Donald, the well-digger. . . . Apparently he was most at his ease of all. He had his clay pipe in his mouth. He was cooler than the rest, being in his shirtsleeves, and leaned back luxuriously in his chair tilted back on its two hind legs, with his naked feet upon the bannister. Said Louisa McCaa, "Look the mud from the well is sticking up through his toes."
> "Uncle H is going for the country *strong*."
> "No—he is a free white man, and he is a near relation, descendent, or something, of Jasper MacDonald, who nailed up our colors at Fort Moultrie, etc., etc."
> "See how solemnly polite and attentive Mr. Chesnut is to him."
> "Oh! that is his way. The raggeder and more squalid the creature, the more polite and softer Mr. Chesnut grows, etc, etc."[122]

Unknowingly, the refined and ambitious Mary Chesnut has captured the essence of the antebellum Southern social order in a single vignette. Two of South Carolina's wealthiest men spent a warm fall evening on the porch of a big plantation house currying the favor of a well-digger who still had mud from his day's work oozing from between his toes. Neither Boykin, a planter of Federalist lineage, nor Chesnut, who would ultimately serve the Confederacy on Jefferson Davis's personal staff, provided the controlling presence on the Boykin piazza. Instead, the man at the center of attention, the man who seemed most satisfied and at ease with his situation, was the common white, Squire McDonald. Even though the sophisticated Mary Chesnut found him ragged and uncouth, her husband, a politician, knew McDonald's importance. "Country-republican" etiquette demanded that the well-digger be recognized as an equal, and Chesnut and Boykin readily obliged. After all, the Squire was "a free white man," and if Chesnut and Boykin were members of old and prominent South Carolina families, McDonald also had blood ties to heroism and the proud Revolutionary heritage. Mary Chesnut was undoubtedly right. Squire McDonald, the well-digger, was "the most at ease of all." The rich and supposedly powerful were mesmerized by his presence and respectful of his heritage. They were supplicants for his favor, almost captive to his will. How could he doubt that he had a stake in the liberty purchased with the blood of his family and in a society where he was so much the center of attention?

---

[122]C. Vann Woodward, ed., *Mary Chesnut's Civil War* (New Haven: Yale University Press, 1981), pp. 204–205. The Jaspar MacDonald mentioned in the passage was actually Sergeant William Jasper, a hero in the defense of Charleston against the British in 1776.

Appendix

Statistical Methods and Samples

The statistical data on occupations, wealth, land ownership, slave ownership, size of slaveholdings, farm size and value, livestock, and agricultural production used in this study was, in many cases, derived from information available in the Federal Manuscript Census for 1850 and 1860. Since a variety of different questions were being asked of this data, several different samples were used. Questions about the general population of the Upcountry were addressed using the Upcountry Population Sample. Originally compiled for use in my dissertation, "Social Origins of a New South Carolina: The Upcountry in the Nineteenth Century," the Population Sample included one of every ten households in the Upcountry districts of Laurens, Spartanburg, and York. Thus the sample sizes were as follows:

	Size of Sample	
Area	*1850*	*1860*
Laurens	214	214
Spartanburg	320	340
York	220	230
Upcountry	754	774

Though not representative of the Upcountry in any statistically verifiable way, the three districts chosen included one lower Piedmont district (Laurens), one upper Piedmont district (Spartanburg), and a third district (York), which lay in the upper Piedmont but contained a substantial number of plantations and large farms. In compiling the population sample, I began by recording information on households from Schedule I (Population) of the manuscript census. When that task was completed, I then searched Schedules II (Slave) and IV (Agriculture) for further information on the households included in the sample.

A second sample, the Upcountry Farm Sample, provided much of the statistical evidence for my arguments about agriculture. The Farm Sample was compiled by gathering data on a specific fraction of all farms in three districts, Abbeville, Anderson, and York. The sample sizes used were:

375

Area	1850		1860	
	Size	Fraction	Size	Fraction
Abbeville	267	$1/7$	298	$1/4$
Anderson	288	$1/7$	360	$1/4$
York	196	$1/7$	294	$1/4$
Upcountry	752	—	952	—

Again, the districts included in the farm sample were not "typical" in a statistical sense, but they included one lower Piedmont district (Abbeville), one upper Piedmont district (Anderson), and the upper Piedmont district (York), where production patterns seemed to fall between the two extremes. Moreover, the use of two upper Piedmont districts and only one lower Piedmont district tended to bias the sample against a strong market orientation (and thus against the general thrust of my argument). In compiling the Farm Sample, I began by recording the information on farms from Schedule IV (Agriculture) of the Manuscript Census, and then I searched Schedules I and II for more information about the farm operator's household and slave holdings.

In many cases, I examined production patterns or farm mix in one particular district. The samples used for such analysis were simply subsets of the larger Farm Sample outlined above. For example, my analysis of agricultural wealth and production in the lower Piedmont district of Abbeville in 1850 is based on the 267 Abbeville farms included in the Sample of Upcountry Farms for 1850. There is one exception to this pattern. My analysis of York district in 1850 is based on a sample of 1 out of every 5 farms in the district (N = 277) rather than merely on the 196 farms included in the Upcountry Farm Sample. The supplementary sample was compiled in order to increase the absolute number of York district farms analyzed to more than 250. At the 90 percent confidence level, samples with 250 observations have a margin of error of plus or minus 5.2 percent.[1]

Samples drawn from the manuscript census have been widely used by historians for more than a decade, and the pitfalls involved in using them are now well known. The original census takers doubtless missed some households or farms, and at times they used estimates of farm size and crop output. In other cases, respondents seem to have supplied the census takers with erroneous or incomplete information. Still, there is no evidence of widespread abuse or lassitude by census takers, and the imperfect records they left behind are still the best evidence we have about the lives of the plain folk of the Old South.[2]

Finally, a few words of explanation are in order about other statistics used in this study. The cotton-corn ratio, which I calculated by dividing the number of pounds of

[1]Charles M. Dollar and Richard J. Jensen, *Historian's Guide to Statistics: Quantitative Analysis and Historical Research* (New York: Holt, Rinehart and Winston, 1971), pp. 11–14; see also Roderick Floud, *An Introduction to Quantitative Methods for Historians* (Princeton, N.J.: Princeton University Press, 1973), pp. 161–175.

[2]For good brief introduction to the subject, see Gavin Wright, "Note on the Manuscript Census Samples," *Agricultural History* 44 (January, 1970):95–99; see also Mark D. Schmitz and Donald F. Schaefer, "Using Manuscript Census Samples to Interpret Antebellum Southern Agriculture," *Journal of Interdisciplinary History* 17 (Autumn, 1986):399–414 for a thorough discussion of the shortcomings of manuscript census data and a careful defense of the continuing usefulness of such samples.

cotton grown by the number of bushels of corn raised, is a rough measure of emphasis on staple production as opposed to subsistence output. The Gini coefficient is a measure of inequality which compares real distribution against a hypothetical distribution of perfect equality. For example, if each household controlled exactly the same share of the total wealth in a region, then the Gini coefficient would be 0; but if one household controlled all the wealth, the Gini would be 1.0.[3]

[3]Dollar and Jensen, *Historian's Guide to Statistics*, pp. 121–126.

Select Bibliography

This is a select bibliography listing the most important primary and secondary sources used in this study. Not included in this select bibliography are the legal cases, official journals of the South Carolina Senate and House of Representatives, official collections of legislative reports and resolutions, acts and statutes of the State of South Carolina, and samples taken from the federal manuscript census used in the study. Full citations to these sources are given in the appropriate footnotes throughout the text. Readers are asked to refer to those notes for bibliographic information on sources not listed in this bibliography.

Primary Sources

Manuscripts

Manuscripts Department, Baker Library, Graduate School of Business Administration, Harvard University, Cambridge, Massachusetts
    R.G. Dun and Company Collection

Manuscripts Department, Perkins Library, Duke University, Durham, North Carolina

Richard Bibb Papers	Stephen D. Miller Papers
William Blanding Journal	James L. Orr Papers
Iveson Brookes Papers	Samuel Finley Patterson Papers
Oze Reed Broyles Papers	Thomas C. Perrin Papers
Armistead Burt Papers	Francis W. Pickens Papers
Nancy Cowan Papers	William Moultrie Reid Papers
John Douglas Papers	William W. Renwick Papers
John Fox Papers	Robert Barnwell Rhett Papers
Frederick Fraser Papers	Robert Y. Russell Papers
Robert N. Gourdin Papers	James H. Saye Papers
Wade Hampton Papers	John Simpson Papers
Hemphill Family Papers	William Dunlap Simpson Papers
John Hollingsworth Papers	Joseph Starke Sims Papers
Alfred Huger Papers	William Sims Papers
Thomas Ellison Keitt Papers	Whiteford Smith Papers
Kirby Family Papers	George M. Witherspoon Papers
Job Johnston Papers	John Wesley Young Papers
George McDuffie Papers	

Manuscripts Division, Library of Congress, Washington, D.C.
    Franklin H. Elmore Papers   Pickens-Bonham Papers
    James Henry Hammond Papers   Waddy Thompson Papers
    James Louis Petigru Papers   William Henry Trescot Papers

South Carolina Historical Society, Charleston, S.C.
    Miller-Chesnut-Manning Papers

Manuscripts Division, South Caroliniana Library, University of South Carolina, Columbia, South Carolina
    David Wyatt Aiken Papers   Samuel W. Melton Papers
    William W. Boyce Papers   Noble Family Papers
    Bratton Family Papers   Joseph J. Norton Papers
    Iveson Brookes Papers   B.F. Perry Papers
    Mary Davis Brown Diary   James Louis Petigru Papers
    James Edward Calhoun Papers   William C. Preston Papers
    Childs Family Papers   William Renwick Papers
    William King Easley Papers   William Dunlap Simpson Papers
    John Fox Papers   Seibels Family Papers
    James Henry Hammond Papers and   Sims Family Papers
        Diary   James F. Sloan Papers and Diaries
    Hampton Family Papers   Elihu P. Smith Papers
    Harrison Family Papers   Spratt Family Papers
    Zelotus L. Holmes Papers   John Springs Papers
    Izard Family Papers   Thomas Sumter Papers
    Samuel C. Jackson Papers   Waddy Thompson Papers
    Jones, Watts, Davis Papers   Thomson-Jones Papers
    Kincaid-Anderson Papers   James Henley Thornwell Papers
    Hugh Swinton Legaré Papers   Townes Family Papers
    George McDuffie Papers   Wallace, Duncan, Rice Papers
    John McLees Papers   David Rogerson Williams Papers
    Mabra Madden Papers   John Winsmith Papers
    William Pinckney McBee Papers   Witherspoon Family Papers
    Means, English, Doby Papers

Southern Historical Collection, University of North Carolina at Chapel Hill
    John D. Ashmore Plantation Journal William P. Hill Diary
    Iveson L. Brookes Papers   Samuel Cram Jackson Diary
    Chapin-Tunnell Papers   Latta Family Papers
    John Ewing Colhoun Papers   Lipscomb Family Papers
    Robert Cunningham Papers   McBee Family Papers
    Davidson Family Papers   Christopher G. Memminger Papers
    William R. Davie Papers   William Porcher Miles Papers
    James Dawkins Papers   James S. Milling Papers
    James M. Gage Papers   Orr-Patterson Family Papers
    William Gaston Papers   Perrin Family Papers
    David Gavin Diary   Benjamin F. Perry Diaries
    James Hamilton Papers   William Ravenel Papers
    David G. Harris Books   Robert Barnwell Rhett Papers

William Dunlap Simpson Papers
Springs Family Papers
Alfred Taylor Books

William D. Valentine Diaries
Witherspoon-McDowall Papers
Benjamin Cudworth Yancey Papers

Government Documents

Compendium of the Enumeration of the Inhabitants and Statistics of the United States, At the Department of State from the Returns of the Sixth Census. Washington, D.C.: Thomas Allen, 1841.

United States Bureau of the Census. *The Seventh Census of the United States: 1850.* Washington, D.C.: Robert Armstrong, 1853.

United States Bureau of the Census. *The Eighth Census of the United States: Population, Agriculture, Manufactures, Mortality, and Miscellaneous Statistics, 1860.* Washington, D.C.: Government Printing Office, 1864.

Published Letters, Speeches, Pamphlets, and Miscellaneous Documents

Allen, J.D. *The Banking System: A Speech.* Columbia, S.C.: R.W. Gibbes, 1857.

Benedict, David. *A General History of the Baptist Denomination in America.* 2 vols. Boston, 1813.

Brookes, Iveson L. *A Defense of Southern Slavery.* Hamburg, S.C.: Robinson and Carlisle, 1851.

Charlotte and South Carolina Railroad. "Proceedings of the Convention of Stockholders." Chesterville: Jan. 13 and 14, 1848, pp. 16–19.

———. "Proceedings of the Stockholders." Chesterville: Nov. 19, 1851.

Charlotte and South Carolina Railroad Company. "Proceedings." Chesterville: Oct. 11, 1848, pp. 1–23.

———. "Proceedings of the Stockholders' Meeting." Chesterville: Nov. 17 and 18, 1852.

Clarke, Elmer T., ed. *The Journal and Letters of Francis Asbury.* Nashville: Abingdon Press, 1958.

Crallé, Richard K., ed. *The Works of John C. Calhoun.* 6 vols. New York: D. Appleton, 1853–57.

Cunningham, John. *Speech on the Bill to Provide for the Approaching Expiration of the Bank Charter, Delivered in the House of Representatives.* Charleston, 1850.

———. *Suggestions on the Causes of the Present Scarcity of Money.* Charleston: James, Williams and Gitsinger, 1854.

DeBow, J.D.B. *Statistical View of the United States . . . Being a Compendium of the Seventh Census.* Washington: Beverly Tucker, 1854.

"The Diary of Edward Hooker, 1805–1808." *American Historical Association Annual Report. 1896.* Washington, D.C.: Government Printing Office, 1897.

Dickson, Dr. S.H. "An Address to the Charleston Horticultural Society, 1832." *Southern Agriculturalist* 5 (1832):449–56.

Drayton, John. *A View of South Carolina.* Charleston, S.C.: W.P. Young, 1802.

Elliott, William. *Carolina Sports, by Land and Water; Including Incidents of Devil-Fishing, etc.* Charleston: Burges and James, 1846.

Furman, Richard. *Exposition of the Views of the Baptists Relative to the Colored Population of the United States in Communication to the Governor of South Carolina.* Charleston, 1823.

Greenville and Columbia Railroad Company. "Proceedings of the Stockholders Meeting." Columbia, S.C.: May 1 and 2, 1848, pp. 1–30.

Greenville and Columbia Railroad. "Proceedings of the Annual Stockholders Meeting." Abbeville: July 11, 1848.

[Gregg, William]. *An Enquiry into the Propriety of Granting Charters of Incorporation for Manufacturing and Other Purposes in South Carolina.* Charleston: Walker and Burke, 1845.

――――. *Essays on Domestic Industry.* Charleston: Burges and James, 1845.

[――――]. *Speech of William Gregg, of Edgefield, on a Bill to Amend an Act Entitled "An Act to Authorize Aid to the Blue Ridge Railroad Company in South Carolina" in the House of Representatives December 8, 1857.* Columbia, S.C.: R.W. Gibbes, 1857.

――――. *Letters of William Gregg to Thornton Coleman.* Charleston: Walker, Evans, 1858.

Grimké, Thomas Smith. *Argument Delivered in the Court of Appeals in the State of South Carolina, 2 and 3 April 1834.* Charleston, S.C.: J.S. Burger, 1834.

Hammond, James Henry. "Speech on the Admission of Kansas, under the Lecompton Constitution." In Clyde N. Wilson, introduction, *Selections from the Letters and Speeches of the Hon. James H. Hammond.* Columbia, S.C.: Southern Studies Program, 1978.

――――. "Anniversary Oration of the State Agricultural Society, November 25, 1841." In *The Proceedings of the Agricultural Convention of the State of South Carolina.* Columbia, S.C.: Summer and Carroll, 1846.

Harper, Robert Goodloe [Appius]. "An Address to the People of South Carolina." Charleston, 1794.

Hayne, Robert Y. *A Defense of the South.* Charleston, S.C.: A.E. Miller, 1830.

――――. *An Oration Delivered in the Presbyterian in Columbia on July 4, 1831.* Columbia, S.C., 1831.

Heilman, Grace E., and Bernard S. Levin, eds. *Calendar of Joel R. Poinsett Papers.* Philadelphia: Gilpin Library of the Historical Society of Pennsylvania, 1941.

Jameson, J. Franklin, ed. *Letters of John C. Calhoun.* Washington: American Historical Association Annual Report, 1899.

Jenkins, James. *Experiences, Labours and Sufferings of the Rev. James Jenkins of the South Carolina Conference.* Columbia, S.C.: State Printing, 1842.

Jenkins, Joseph E. "Address Delivered before the Agricultural Society of St. Johns Colleton." *Southern Agriculturist* 11 (Aug. 1838):393–410.

Journal of the State Convention of South Carolina. Columbia: S.C.: Johnson and Davis, 1852.

Lee, Jesse. *A Short History of the Methodists in the United States of America.* Baltimore, 1810.

The Letters of William Gilmore Simms. Edited by Mary C. Simms Oliphant, Alfred Taylor Odell, T.C. Duncan Eaves. 5 vols. Columbia: Univ. of South Carolina Press, 1950.

Legislative Times. Columbia, S.C.: E.H. Britton, 1855.

Lieber, Oscar M. *South Carolina: Mineralogical, Geological, and Agricultural Survey: Report on the Survey of South Carolina, 1856.* Columbia, S.C.: R.W. Gibbes, 1856–60.

――――. *Report on the Survey of South Carolina: The Fourth Annual Report to the General Assembly of South Carolina, 1859.* Columbia, S.C.: R.W. Gibbes, 1860.

McCord, Louisa S. "Carey on the Slave Trade." *Southern Quarterly Review* 9 (Jan. 1854):115–84.

McDuffie, George. "Anniversary Oration of the State Agricultural Society of South Carolina, 26 November, 1840." In *The Proceedings of the Agricultural Convention of the State Agricultural Society of South Carolina*, p. 98. Columbia: Summer and Carroll, 1846.

Meats, Stephen, and Edwin T. Arnold, eds., *The Writings of Benjamin F. Perry: Essays, Public Letters and Speeches*. 3 vols. Spartanburg, S.C.: The Reprint Company, 1980.

[Memminger, C.G.]. *Speech of C.G. Memminger in the House of Representatives of South Carolina upon the Bill and Resolutions Relating to Bank Issues and Suspensions, December, 1857*. Charleston: Walker, Evans, 1858.

Meriwether, Robert L., et al., eds. *The Papers of John C. Calhoun*. 13 vols. to date. Columbia: Univ. of South Carolina Press, 1959–81.

Mills, Robert. *Atlas of the State of South Carolina*. Baltimore: F. Lucas, Jr., 1825.

————. *Statistics of South Carolina*. Charleston, S.C.: Hurlbut and Lloyd, 1826.

Minutes of the Annual Conferences of the Methodist Episcopal Church for the Years 1773–1828. New York: 1840.

Minutes of the Bethel Baptist Association, 1793.

Minutes of the Saluda Baptist Association, 1807.

Nichols, George Ward. *The Story of the Great March*. New York: Harper and Brothers, 1865.

O'Neall, John Belton. "An Address Delivered before the State Agricultural Society, at Their Meeting in Greenville, 11 September, 1844." In *The Proceedings of the Agricultural Convention of the State Agricultural Society of South Carolina*, p. 219. Columbia: Summer and Carroll, 1846.

————. *The Annals of Newberry*. Charleston, S.C.: S.G. Courtenay, 1859.

————. *Biographical Sketches of the Bench and Bar of South Carolina*. 2 vols. Charleston, S.C.: S.G. Courtenay, 1859.

Orr, James L. *Speech to the Convention of Southern Rights Associations, held in Charleston, May, 1851*. Charleston, S.C.: n.p., 1851.

————. "Address Delivered before the South Carolina Institute," *Debow's Review* 19 (1855):1–22.

Palmer, Edward G. *Address to the People of Richland, Fairfield, Chester, and York Districts on the Subject of the Charlotte and South Carolina Railroad*. Columbia, S.C.: Office of the South Carolinian, 1847.

Perry, Benjamin F. *Reminiscences of Public Men*. Philadelphia: John D. Avil, 1883.

Petigru, James Louis. "Court of Chancery." *Southern Review* 3 (1829):63–77.

Pinckney, Henry Laurens. *An Oration Delivered in Charleston on July the Fourth . . .* Charleston: A.E. Miller, 1833.

————. *An Address to the Electors of Charleston District*. Charleston: Burger and Honour, 1836.

The Proceedings of the Agricultural Convention and of the State Agricultural Society of South Carolina from 1839–1845. Columbia, S.C.: Summer and Carroll, 1846.

"Reminiscences of Major Benjamin Sloan, President of South Carolina College, of His Early Years in Pendleton." In C. L. Newman and J.C. Stribling, eds., *Pendleton Farmers' Society*. Atlanta: Foote and Davies, 1908.

"Report of the Fishing Creek Agricultural Society." *Southern Agriculturalist* 3 (1842):420–25.

Ruffin, Edmund. *Report of the Commencement and Progress of the Agricultural Survey of South Carolina for 1843*. Columbia: A.H. Pemberton, 1843.

Seabrook, Whitemarsh B. *A Memoir on the Origin, Cultivation, and Use of Cotton.* Charleston, 1844.

Simkins, Arthur. *Address before the State Agricultural Society of South Carolina*. Edgefield: Advertiser Office, 1855.

Simons, James. *A Rallying Point for All True Friends to Their Country*. Charleston, 1800.

Trescot, William Henry. *The Position and Course of the South*. Charleston: Walker and James, 1850.

———. "Oration before the South Carolina Historical Society, 1859." *Russell's Magazine* 3 (July 1859):289–307.

———. "Bench and Bar." *Russell's Magazine* 6 (1859–1860):289–97.

———. *Oration Delivered before the Alumni of the College of Charleston, June 25, 1889*. Charleston, S.C.: Walker, Evans and Cogswell, 1889.

Turnbull, Robert J. *The Crisis*. Charleston: A.E. Miller, 1827.

Wightman, William M. *Life of William Capers*. Nashville: Southern Methodist Publishing House, 1858.

Wilson, Clyde N., ed. *Selections from the Letters and Speeches of James H. Hammond*. Spartanburg, S.C.: The Reprint Company, 1978.

Newspapers

Abbeville *Banner*

Anderson *Gazette*

Anderson *Intelligencer*

Charleston *Courier*

Charleston *Mercury*

Charleston *Southern Standard*

Chester *Standard*

Columbia *Daily Telegraph*

Columbia *South Carolinian*

Columbia *Southern Chronicle*

Columbia *Telescope*

Edgefield *Advertiser*

Greenville *Mountaineer*

Greenville *Patriot and Mountaineer*

Greenville *Southern Patriot*

Lancaster *Ledger*

Laurensville *Herald*

Newberry *Rising Sun*

Pendleton *Messenger*

Spartanburg *Carolina Spartan*

Unionville *Journal*

Walhalla *Keowee Courier*

Yorkville *Enquirer*

Yorkville *Miscellany*

Secondary Sources

Books

Abernathy, Thomas P. *The South in the New Nation, 1789–1819*. Baton Rouge: Louisiana State Univ. Press, 1961.

Andrews, Columbus. *Administrative County Government in South Carolina*. Chapel Hill: Univ. of North Carolina Press, 1983.

Appleby, Joyce O. *Capitalism and a New Social Order: The Republican Vision of the 1790s*. New York: New York Univ. Press, 1984.

Atherton, Lewis E. *The Southern Country Store, 1800–1860*. Baton Rouge: Louisiana State Univ. Press, 1949.

Ayers, Edward L. *Vengeance and Justice: Crime and Punishment in the Nineteenth Century American South.* New York: Oxford Univ. Press, 1984.

Bailey, J.D. *History of Grindal Shoals and Some Early Adjacent Families.* Gaffney, S. C., 1927.

Bailey, N. Louise, ed. *Biographical Directory of the South Carolina House of Representatives.* Columbia, S.C.: Univ. of South Carolina Press, 1984.

Bailey, N. Louise, Mary L. Morgan, and Carolyn R. Taylor. *Biographical Directory of the South Carolina Senate, 1776–1985.* Columbia, S.C.: Univ. of South Carolina Press, 1985.

Ball, William Watts. *The State That Forgot: South Carolina's Surrender to Democracy.* Indianapolis: Bobbs-Merrill, 1932.

Banning, Lance. *The Jeffersonian Persuasion: Evolution of a Party Ideology.* Ithaca, N.Y.: Cornell Univ. Press, 1978.

Barney, William L. *The Secessionist Impulse: Alabama and Mississippi in 1860.* Princeton: Princeton Univ. Press, 1974.

Barnwell, John. *Love of Order: South Carolina's First Secession Crisis.* Chapel Hill: Univ. of North Carolina Press, 1982.

Bateman, Fred, and Thomas Weiss. *A Deplorable Scarcity: The Failure of Industrialization in the Slave Economy.* Chapel Hill: Univ. of North Carolina Press, 1981.

Benson, Lee. *The Concept of Jacksonian Democracy: New York as a Test Case.* Princeton: Princeton Univ. Press, 1961.

Betts, Albert D. *History of South Carolina Methodism.* Columbia, S.C.: Advocate Press, 1952.

Bleser, Carol R. *The Hammonds of Redcliffe.* New York: Oxford Univ. Press, 1981.

Boeke, J.H. *Economics and Economic Policy of Dual Societies.* New York: Institute of Pacific Relations, 1953.

Boles, John B. *The Great Revival, 1787–1805.* Lexington: Univ. Press of Kentucky, 1972.

Boles, John B., and Evelyn Thomas Nolen. *Interpreting Southern History: Historiographical Essays in Honor of Sanford W. Higginbotham.* Baton Rouge: Louisiana State Univ. Press, 1987.

Bolton, S. Charles. *Southern Anglicanism: The Church of England in Colonial South Carolina.* Westport, Conn.: Greenwood Press, 1982.

Boucher, Chauncey. *The Nullification Controversy in South Carolina.* Chicago: Univ. of Chicago Press, 1916.

Broussard, James. *The Southern Federalists, 1800–1816.* Baton Rouge: Louisiana State Univ. Press, 1978.

Bruce, Dickson D., Jr. *And They All Sang Hallelujah: Plain-Folk Camp-Meeting Religion, 1800–1845.* Knoxville: Univ. of Tennessee Press, 1974.

Burton, Orville Vernon. *In My Father's House Are Many Mansions: Family and Community in Edgefield, South Carolina.* Chapel Hill: Univ. of North Carolina Press, 1985.

Burton, Orville V., and Robert C. McMath. *Class, Conflict, and Consensus: Antebellum Southern Community Studies.* Westport, Conn.: Greenwood Press, 1982.

Campbell, Randolph, and Richard Lowe. *Wealth and Power in Antebellum Texas.* College Station: Texas A & M Press, 1977.

Caper, Henry D. *The Life and Times of Christopher G. Memminger.* Richmond: Everett Waddey, 1893.

Carlton, David L. *Mill and Town in South Carolina, 1880–1920*. Baton Rouge: Louisiana State Univ. Press, 1982.

Carson, James Petigru. *Life, Letters and Speeches of James Louis Petigru: The Union Man of South Carolina*. Washington, D.C.: W.H. Lowdermilk, 1920.

Carwile, John B. *Reminiscences of Newberry County*. Charleston, S.C.: Walker, Evans and Cogswell, 1890.

Channing, Steven A. *Crisis of Fear: Secession in South Carolina*. New York: Simon and Schuster, 1970.

Chapman, John A. *History of Edgefield County*. Newberry, S.C.: Elbert H. Aull, 1897.

Chreitzberg, Abel M. *Early Methodism in the Carolinas*. Nashville: Publishing House of the Methodist Episcopal Church, South, 1897.

Clark, Blanche Henry. *The Tennessee Yeomen*. Nashville: Vanderbilt Univ. Press, 1942.

Clark, W.A. *The History of the Banking Institutions Organized in South Carolina Prior to 1860*. Columbia, S.C.: The State Company, 1922.

Cleveland, Catherine. *The Great Revival in the West, 1797–1805*. Chicago: Univ. of Chicago Press, 1916.

Coclanis, Peter A. *The Shadow of a Dream: Economic Life and Death in the South Carolina Low County, 1670–1920*. New York: Oxford Univ. Press, forthcoming.

Coit, Margaret L. *John C. Calhoun: American Portrait*. Boston: Houghton Mifflin, 1950.

Cole, Arthur C. *The Whig Party in the South*. Washington, D.C.: American Historical Association, 1913.

Cook, Harvey T. *The Life and Legacy of David Rogerson Williams*. New York, 1916.

———. *The Life Work of James Clement Furman*. Greenville, S.C.: Alester G. Furman, 1926.

Cooper, William J. *The Conservative Regime: South Carolina, 1877–1890*. Baltimore: Johns Hopkins Univ. Press, 1968.

———. *The South and the Politics of Slavery, 1828–1856*. Baton Rouge: Louisiana State Univ. Press, 1978.

———. *Liberty and Slavery: Southern Politics to 1860*. New York: Alfred A. Knopf, 1983.

Craven, Delle M. *The Neglected Thread: A Journal from the Calhoun Community, 1836–1842*. Columbia, S.C.: Univ. of South Carolina Press, 1951.

Davidson, Chalmers G. *The Last Foray: The South Carolina Planters of 1860*. Columbia: Univ. of South Carolina Press, 1971.

Davis, David Brion. *The Problem of Slavery in the Age of Revolution, 1770–1823*. Ithaca: Cornell Univ. Press, 1965.

Dawley, Allen. *Class and Community: The Industrial Revolution in Lynn*. Cambridge, Mass.: Harvard Univ. Press, 1976.

Derrick, Samuel M. *Centennial History of the South Carolina Railroad*. Columbia, S.C.: The State Company, 1930.

DeVries, Jan. *The Dutch Rural Economy in the Golden Age, 1500–1700*. New Haven: Yale Univ. Press, 1974.

Dickson, Peter G. *The Financial Revolution in England, 1688–1756*. London: St. Martin's Press, 1967.

Dollar, Charles M., and Richard J. Jensen. *Historian's Guide to Statistics: Quantitative Analysis and Historical Research*. New York: Holt, Rinehart, and Winston, 1971.

Dundas, F. de Sales. *The Calhoun Settlement, District of Abbeville, South Carolina*. Staunton, Va., 1949.

Edmunds, John B. *Francis W. Pickens and the Politics of Destruction.* Chapel Hill: Univ. of North Carolina Press, 1986.

Ellis, Richard. *Union At Risk: Jacksonian Democracy, States' Rights, and the Nullification Crisis.* New York: Oxford Univ. Press, 1987.

Essig, James D. *The Bonds of Wickedness: American Evangelicals against Slavery, 1770–1808.* Philadelphia: Temple Univ. Press, 1982.

Farmer, James Oscar, Jr. *The Metaphysical Confederacy: James Henley Thornwell and the Synthesis of Southern Values.* Macon, Ga.: Mercer Univ. Press, 1986.

Faust, Drew Gilpin. *A Sacred Circle: The Dilemma of the Intellectual in the Old South, 1840–1860.* Baltimore and London: Johns Hopkins Univ. Press, 1977.

————. *James Henry Hammond and the Old South: A Design for Mastery.* Baton Rouge: Louisiana State Univ. Press, 1982.

Fehrenbacher, Don E. *The Dred Scott Case: Its Significance in American Law and Politics.* New York: Harper and Row, 1978.

Fishlow, Albert. *American Railroads and the Transformation of the Antebellum Economy.* Cambridge, Mass.: Harvard Univ. Press, 1965.

Floud, Roderick. *An Introduction to Quantitative Methods for Historians.* Princeton: Princeton Univ. Press, 1973.

Foner, Eric. *Free Soil, Free Labor, and Free Men: The Ideology of the Republican Party Before the Civil War.* New York: Oxford Univ. Press, 1971.

Fox-Genovese, Elizabeth and Eugene D. Genovese. *Fruits of Merchant Capital: Slavery and Bourgeois Property in the Rise and Expansion of Capitalism.* New York: Oxford Univ. Press, 1983.

Fraser, Walter J., and Winfred B. Moore. *The Southern Enigma: Essays on Race, Class, and Folk Culture.* Westport, Conn.: Greenwood Press, 1983.

Fredrickson, George M. *The Black Image in the White Mind: The Debate on Afro-American Character and Destiny.* New York: Harper and Row, 1971.

Freehling, Alison Goodyear. *Drift toward Dissolution: The Virginia Slavery Debate of 1831–1832.* Baton Rouge: Louisiana State Univ. Press, 1982.

Freehling, William W. *Prelude to Civil War: The Nullification Controversy in South Carolina, 1816–1836.* New York: Harper and Row, 1965.

Garrett, T.J. *A History of the Saluda Baptist Association.* Richmond: B.F. Johnson Publishing, 1896.

Genovese, Eugene D. *The Political Economy of Slavery.* New York: Pantheon, 1965.

————. *The World the Slaveholders Made.* New York: Pantheon, 1969.

————. *Roll, Jordan, Roll: The World the Slaves Made.* New York: Pantheon, 1974.

————. *"Slavery Ordained of God": The Southern Slaveholders' View of Biblical History and Modern Politics.* Gettysburg, Pa.: Gettysburg College, 1985.

Gienapp, William E. *The Origins of the Republican Party, 1852–1856.* New York: Oxford Univ. Press, 1987.

Gray, Lewis C. *History of Agriculture in the Southern United States to 1860.* Gloucester, Mass.: Peter Smith, 1933.

Green, Edwin L. *George McDuffie.* Columbia, S.C.: The State Company, 1936.

Green, Fletcher M. *Constitutional Development in the South Atlantic States 1776–1860: A Study in the Evolution of Democracy.* Chapel Hill: Univ. of North Carolina Press, 1930.

Greenberg, Kenneth S. *Masters and Statesmen: The Political Culture of American Slavery.* Baltimore: Johns Hopkins Univ. Press, 1985.

Gregorie, Anna King. *Thomas Sumter*. Columbia, S.C.: R.L. Bryan, 1931.

Griffin, Clifford S. *Their Brothers Keepers: Moral Stewardship in the United States, 1800–1865*. New Brunswick, N.J.: Rutgers Univ. Press, 1960.

Hahn, Steven. *The Roots of Southern Populism: Yeoman Farmers and the Transformation of the Georgia Upcountry, 1850–1890*. New York: Oxford Univ. Press, 1983.

Hahn, Steven, and Jonathan Prude, eds. *The Countryside in the Age of Capitalist Transformation: Essays in the Social History of Rural America*. Chapel Hill: Univ. of North Carolina Press, 1985.

Hall, Arthur R. *The Story of Soil Conservation in the South Carolina Piedmont, 1800–1860*. Washington, D.C.: U.S. Department of Agriculture, 1940.

Hamer, Philip M. *The Secession Movement in South Carolina, 1847–1852*. Allentown, Pa.: H. Ray Haas, 1918.

Hammond, Bray. *Banks and Politics in America: From the Revolution to the Civil War*. Princeton: Princeton Univ. Press, 1957.

Hammond, Harry. *South Carolina: Resources and Population, Institutions and Industries*. Charleston: Walker, Evans and Cogswell, 1883.

Harris, J. William. *Plain Folk and Gentry in a Slave Society: White Liberty and Black Slavery in Augusta's Hinterlands*. Middletown, Conn.: Wesleyan Univ. Press, 1985.

Hilliard, Sam Bowers. *Hog Meat and Hoecake: Food Supply in the Old South, 1840–1860*. Carbondale: Southern Illinois Univ. Press, 1972.

Hirschman, Albert O. *The Strategy of Economic Development*. New Haven: Yale Univ. Press, 1957.

Hobsbawm, Eric J. *The Age of Revolution 1789–1848*. London: Weidenfeld and Nicholson, 1962.

——. *The Age of Capital, 1848–1875*. London: Weidenfeld and Nicolson, 1975.

Hollis, Daniel Walker. *South Carolina College*. Columbia, S.C.: Univ. of South Carolina Press, 1951.

Holt, Michael F. *Forging a Majority: The Formation of the Republican Party in Pittsburgh, 1848–1860*. New Haven: Yale Univ. Press, 1969.

——. *The Political Crisis of the 1850s*. New York: John Wiley and Sons, 1978.

Hooker, Richard J., ed. *The Carolina Backcountry on the Eve of the Revolution: The Journal and Other Writings of Charles Woodmason, Anglican Itinerant*. Chapel Hill: Univ. of North Carolina Press, 1953.

Howe, Daniel Walker. *The Political Culture of the American Whigs*. Chicago: Univ. of Chicago Press, 1979.

Howe, George. *History of the Presbyterian Church in South Carolina*. 2 vols. Charleston, S.C.: Walker, Evans and Cogswell, 1883.

Howe, John C. *From the Revolution to the Age of Jackson: Innocence and Empire in the Young Republic*. Englewood Cliffs, N.J.: Prentice Hall, 1973.

Huff, Archie Vernon. *Langdon Cheves of South Carolina*. Columbia: Univ. of South Carolina Press, 1977.

Jenkins, William Sumner, *Pro-slavery Thought in the Old South*. Reprinted edition. Gloucester, Mass.: Peter Smith, 1960.

Jennings, Thelma. *The Nashville Convention: Southern Movement for Unity, 1848–1850*. Memphis: Memphis State Univ. Press, 1980.

Jervey, Theodore D. *Robert Y. Hayne and His Times*. New York: Macmillan, 1909.

Johnson, Michael P. *Towards a Patriarchal Republic: The Secession of Georgia*. Baton Rouge: Louisiana State Univ. Press, 1977.

Johnson, Michael P., and Roark, James L. *Black Masters: A Free Family of Color in the Old South*. New York: W.W. Norton, 1984.

Johnson, Paul E. *A Shopkeeper's Millennium: Society and Revivals in Rochester, New York, 1815–1837*. New York: Hill and Wang, 1978.

Jones, Alice Hanson. *Wealth of a Nation to Be: The American Colonies on the Eve of the Revolution*. New York: Columbia Univ. Press, 1980.

Jones, Lewis P. *Stormy Petrel: N.G. Gonzalez and His State*. Columbia, S.C.: Univ. of South Carolina Press, 1973.

Jordan, Winthrop D. *White over Black: American Attitudes toward the Negro, 1550–1812*. Chapel Hill: Univ. of North Carolina Press, 1968.

Kelley, Robert. *The Transatlantic Persuasion: The Liberal-Democratic Mind in the Age of Gladstone*. New York: Alfred A. Knopf, 1969.

Kerber, Linda K. *Federalists in Dissent: Imagery and Ideology in Jeffersonian America*. Ithaca: Cornell Univ. Press, 1970.

Kibler, Lillian A. *Benjamin F. Perry: South Carolina Unionist*. Durham: Duke Univ. Press, 1946.

Kohn, David., ed. *Internal Improvements in South Carolina, 1817–1828*. Washington, D.C., 1938.

Kousser, J. Morgan, and James M. McPherson. *Region, Race, and Reconstruction: Essays in Honor of C. Vann Woodward*. New York: Oxford Univ. Press, 1982.

Kruman, Marc W. *Parties and Politics in North Carolina, 1836–1865*. Baton Rouge: Louisiana State Univ. Press, 1983.

Lander, Ernest M., Jr. *The Textile Industry in Antebellum South Carolina*. Baton Rouge: Louisiana State Univ. Press, 1969.

———. *Reluctant Imperialists: Calhoun, the South Carolinians, and the Mexican War*. Baton Rouge: Louisiana State Univ. Press, 1980.

———. *The Calhoun Family and Thomas Green Clemson: The Decline of a Southern Patriarchy*. Columbia, S.C.: Univ. of South Carolina Press, 1983.

Landrum, J.B.O. *A History of Spartanburg County*. Atlanta: Franklin Printing, 1900.

Latner, Richard B. *The Presidency of Andrew Jackson: White House Politics, 1829–1837*. Athens: Univ. of Georgia Press, 1979.

Leemhuis, Roger P. *James L. Orr and the Sectional Conflict*. Washington: Univ. Press of America, 1979.

Lesesne, J. Mauldin. *The Bank of the State of South Carolina: A General and Political History*. Columbia, S.C.: Univ. of South Carolina Press, 1970.

Lofton, John. *Insurrection in South Carolina: The Turbulent World of Denmark Vesey*. Yellow Springs, Ohio: Antioch Press, 1964.

Loveland, Anne C. *Southern Evangelicals and the Social Order, 1800–1860*. Baton Rouge: Louisiana State Univ. Press, 1980.

Luraghi, Raimondo. *The Rise and Fall of the Plantation South*. New York: New Viewpoints, 1978.

Maizlish, Stephen. *The Triumph of Sectionalism: The Transformation of Ohio Politics, 1844–1856*. Kent: Kent State Univ. Press, 1983.

Malone, Dumas. *The Public Life of Thomas Cooper*. New Haven: Yale Univ. Press, 1926.

Mathews, Donald G. *Slavery and Methodism: A Chapter in American Morality, 1780–1845*. Princeton: Princeton Univ. Press, 1965.

———. *Religion in the Old South*. Chicago: Univ. of Chicago Press, 1977.

May, John Amasa, and Joan Reynolds Faunt. *South Carolina Secedes*. Columbia, S.C.: Univ. of South Carolina Press, 1960.

May, Robert E. *The Southern Dream of a Caribbean Empire*. Baton Rouge: Louisiana State Univ. Press, 1973.

McCardell, John. *The Idea of a Southern Nation: Southern Nationalists and Southern Nationalism, 1830–1860*. New York: W.W. Norton, 1979.

McCormick, Richard P. *The Second American Party System: Party Formation in the Jacksonian Era*. Chapel Hill: Univ. of North Carolina Press, 1966.

McCoy, Drew R. *The Elusive Republic: Political Economy in Jeffersonian America*. Chapel Hill: Univ. of North Carolina Press, 1980.

McMaster, Fitz Hugh. *History of Fairfield County, South Carolina*. Columbia, S.C.: State Commercial Printing, 1946.

Meriwether, Robert L. *The Expansion of South Carolina, 1729–1765*. Kingsport, Tenn.: Southern Publishers, 1940.

Meyers, Marvin. *The Jacksonian Persuasion: Politics and Belief*. Stanford: Stanford Univ. Press, 1957.

Miles, Edwin A. *Jacksonian Democracy in Mississippi*. Chapel Hill: Univ. of North Carolina Press, 1960.

Mitchell, Broadus. *William Gregg: Factory Maker of the Old South*. Chapel Hill: Univ. of North Carolina Press, 1928.

Mooney, Chase C. *William H. Crawford, 1772–1834*. Lexington: Univ. of Kentucky Press, 1974.

Morgan, Donald G. *Justice William Johnson: The First Dissenter*. Columbia, S.C.: Univ. of South Carolina Press, 1954.

Morgan, Edmund. *American Slavery, American Freedom: The Ordeal of Colonial Virginia*. New York: Norton, 1975.

Oakes, James. *The Ruling Race: A History of American Slaveholders*. New York: Alfred A. Knopf, 1982.

O'Brien, Michael. *A Character of Hugh Legare*. Knoxville: Univ. of Tennessee Press, 1985.

O'Brien, Michael, and David Moltke-Hansen. *Intellectual Life in Antebellum Charleston*. Knoxville: Univ. of Tennessee Press, 1986.

Owsley, Frank L. *Plain Folk of the Old South*. Baton Rouge: Louisiana State Univ. Press, 1949.

Parker, William N., and Eric L. Jones. *European Peasants and Their Markets: Essays in Agrarian Economy History*. Princeton: Princeton Univ. Press, 1975.

Peterson, Merrill D. *Olive Branch and Sword: The Compromise of 1833*. Baton Rouge: Louisiana State Univ. Press, 1982.

Petty, Julian J. *The Growth and Distribution of Population in South Carolina*. Columbia, S.C.: State Council for Defense, 1943.

Phillips, Ulrich Bonnell. *A History of Transportation in the Eastern Cotton Belt to 1860*. New York: Columbia Univ. Press, 1908.

———. *Life and Labor in the Old South*. Boston: Little, Brown, 1929.

Pope, Thomas H. *The History of Newberry County, South Carolina: 1749–1860*. Columbia: Univ. of South Carolina Press, 1973.

Potter, David M. *The South and Sectional Conflict*. Baton Rouge: Louisiana State Univ. Press, 1968.

———. *The Impending Crisis, 1848–1861*. New York: Harper and Row, 1976.

Ramsay, David. *The History of South Carolina*. 2 vols. Charleston, S.C., 1809.

Ransom, Roger L., and Sutch, Richard. *One Kind of Freedom: The Economic Consequences of Emancipation*. Cambridge: Cambridge Univ. Press, 1977.

Remini, Robert V. *Andrew Jackson and the Course of American Democracy, 1833–1845*. New York: Harper and Row, 1984.

Reynolds, Emily B., and Joan Reynolds Faunt. *Biographical Directory of the Senate of South Carolina, 1776–1964*. Columbia, S.C.: South Carolina Archives Department, 1964.

Rhea, Linda. *Hugh Swinton Legare: A Charleston Intellectual*. Chapel Hill: Univ. of North Carolina Press, 1934.

Rippy, J. Fred. *Joel R. Poinsett: Versatile American*. Durham, N.C.: Duke Univ. Press, 1946.

Risjord, Norman K. *The Old Republicans: Southern Conservatives in the Age of Jefferson*. New York: Columbia Univ. Press, 1965.

Rogers, George C., Jr. *Evolution of a Federalist: William Loughton Smith of Charleston*. Columbia, S.C.: Univ. of South Carolina Press, 1962.

――――. *Charleston in the Age of the Pinckneys*. Norman: Univ. of Oklahoma Press, 1966.

――――. *A History of Georgetown County, South Carolina*. Columbia, S.C.: Univ. of South Carolina Press, 1970.

Rogers, James A. *Richard Furman: Life and Legacy*. Macon, Ga.: Mercer Univ. Press, 1985.

Rostow, Walt W. *The Stages of Economic Growth: A Non-Communist Manifesto*. Cambridge: Cambridge Univ. Press, 1962.

Saxonhouse, Gary, and Gavin Wright. *Technique, Spirit and Form in the Making of the Modern Economies: Essays in Honor of William N. Parker*, Greenwich: JAI Press, 1984.

Schultz, Harold S. *Nationalism and Sectionalism in South Carolina, 1852–1860*. Durham, N.C.: Duke Univ. Press, 1950.

Sexton, Irvin, and Sexton, Kathryn. *Samuel A. Maverick*. San Antonio: Naylor, 1964.

Shade, William G. *Banks or No Banks*. Detroit: Wayne State Univ. Press, 1972.

Shalhope, Robert. *John Taylor of Caroline: Pastoral Republican*. Columbia: Univ. of South Carolina Press, 1980.

Sharp, James Roger. *The Jacksonians versus the Banks: Politics in the States after the Panic of 1837*. New York: Columbia Univ. Press, 1970.

Sherrill, William L. *Annals of Lincoln County, North Carolina*. Baltimore: Regional Publishing, 1972.

Shipps, Albert M. *The History of Methodism in South Carolina*. Nashville: Southern Methodist Publishing House, 1883.

Shore, Laurence. *Southern Capitalists: The Ideological Leadership of an Elite, 1832–1885*. Chapel Hill: Univ. of North Carolina Press, 1986.

Silbey, Joel H. *The Transformation of American Politics, 1840–1860*. Englewood Cliffs, N.J.: Prentice Hall, 1967.

――――. *The Partisan Imperative: The Dynamics of American Politics before the Civil War*. New York: Oxford Univ. Press, 1985.

Simkins, Francis Butler. *Pitchfork Ben Tillman*. Baton Rouge: Louisiana State Univ. Press, 1944.

Simpson, Richard W. *History of Old Pendleton District*. Anderson, S.C.: Oulla Printing and Publishing, 1913.

Smith, Alfred Glaze. *Economic Readjustment of an Old Cotton State: South Carolina, 1820–1860*. Columbia: Univ. of South Carolina Press, 1958.

Springs, Katherine Wooten. *The Squires of Springfield*. Charlotte, N.C.: William Lofton, 1965.

Stampp, Kenneth. *The Imperiled Union: Essays on the Background of the Civil War*. New York: Oxford Univ. Press, 1980.

Sweet, William Warren. *Religion in the Development of American Culture, 1765–1840*. New York: Scribner, 1952.

Sydnor, Charles S. *The Development of Southern Sectionalism, 1819–1848*. Baton Rouge: Louisiana State Univ. Press, 1948.

Temin, Peter. *The Jacksonian Economy*. New York: W.W. Norton, 1969.

Thomas, John Peyre. *The Formation of Judicial and Political Subdivisions in South Carolina*. Columbia, S.C.: Bryan Printing, 1890.

Thompson, Henry T. *General Waddy Thompson*. Columbia, S.C., 1929.

Thornton, J. Mills, III. *Politics and Power in a Slave Society: Alabama, 1800–1860*. Baton Rouge: Louisiana State Univ. Press, 1978.

Tindall, George B. *The Emergence of the New South, 1913–1945*. Baton Rouge: Louisiana State Univ. Press, 1967.

Townsend, Leah. *South Carolina Baptists*. Florence, S.C.: Florence Printing, 1935.

Tyron, Rolla Milton. *Household Manufactures in the United States, 1640–1860: A Study in Industrial History*. Chicago: Univ. of Chicago Press, 1917.

Van den Berghe, Pierre. *Race and Racism: A Comparative Perspective*. New York: Wiley, 1967.

Vandiver, Louise Ayer. *Traditions and History of Anderson County*. Atlanta: Revivalist Press, 1928.

Wakelyn, Jon L. *The Politics of a Literary Man: William Gilmore Simms*. Westport, Conn.: Greenwood Press, 1973.

Wallace, Anthony F.C. *Rockdale: The Growth of an American Village in the Early Industrial Revolution*. New York: Alfred A. Knopf, 1978.

Wallace, David Duncan. *South Carolina: A Short History, 1520–1948*. Chapel Hill: Univ. of North Carolina Press, 1951.

Wallenstein, Peter. *From Slave South to New South: Public Policy in Nineteenth Century Georgia*. Chapel Hill: Univ. of North Carolina Press, 1987.

Ward, John William. *Andrew Jackson: Symbol for an Age*. New York: Oxford Univ. Press, 1955.

Watkins, J.L. *King Cotton*. New York: J.L. Watkins, 1908.

Watson, Ellen Batson. *A History of the Bethel Baptist Association*. Spartanburg, S.C.: B. F. Long Printing, 1967.

Watson, Harry L. *Jacksonian Politics and Community Conflict: The Emergence of the Second American Party System in Cumberland County, North Carolina*. Baton Rouge: Louisiana State Univ. Press, 1981.

Watson, Margaret. *Greenwood County Sketches*. Greenwood, S.C.: Attic Press, 1970.

Wayne, Michael. *The Reshaping of Plantation Society: The Natchez District, 1860–1880*. Baton Rouge: Louisiana State Univ. Press, 1983.

Weaver, Herbert. *Mississippi Farmers, 1850–1860*. Nashville: Vanderbilt Univ. Press, 1945.

Weir, Robert M. *Colonial South Carolina: A History*. Millwood, N.Y.: KTO Press, 1983.

White, Laura A. *Robert Barnwell Rhett: Father of Secession*. New York: Century Co., 1931.

Wiltse, Charles M. *John C. Calhoun, Nationalist 1782–1828*. Indianapolis: Bobbs-Merrill, 1944.

―――. *John C. Calhoun, Nullifier*. Indianapolis: Bobbs-Merrill, 1949.

―――. *John C. Calhoun, Sectionalist*. Indianapolis: Bobbs-Merrill, 1951.

Wilson, Major L. *Space, Time, and Freedom: The Quest for Nationality and the Irrepressible Conflict, 1815–1861*. Newport, Conn.: Greenwood Press, 1974.

Wood, Gordon S. *The Creation of the American Republic, 1776–1787*. Chapel Hill: Univ. of North Carolina Press, 1969.

Woodman, Harold D. *King Cotton and His Retainers: Financing and Marketing the Cotton Crop of the South, 1800–1925*. Lexington: Univ. of Kentucky Press, 1968.

Woodward, C. Vann, ed. *Mary Chesnut's Civil War*. New Haven: Yale Univ. Press, 1981.

Wooster, Ralph A. *The People in Power: Courthouse and Statehouse in the Lower South, 1850–1860*. Knoxville: Univ. of Tennessee Press, 1969.

Wolfe, John Harold. *Jeffersonian Democracy in South Carolina*. Chapel Hill: Univ. of North Carolina Press, 1940.

Wright, Gavin. *The Political Economy of the Cotton South: Households, Markets, and Wealth in the Nineteenth Century*. New York: W.W. Norton, 1978.

―――. *Old South, New South: Revolutions in the Southern Economy since the Civil War*. New York: Basic Books, 1986.

Wyatt-Brown, Bertram. *Southern Honor: Ethics and Behavior in the Old South*. New York: Oxford Univ. Press, 1984.

Articles and Essays

Anderson, Ralph V., and Robert E. Gallman. "Slaves as Fixed Capital: Slave Labor and Southern Economic Development." *Journal of American History* 64 (June 1978):47–66.

Appleby, Joyce O. "The Social Origins of American Revolutionary Ideology." *Journal of American History* 64 (March 1978):935–58.

―――. "What Is Still American in the Political Philosophy of Thomas Jefferson?" *William and Mary Quarterly (WMQ)* 39 (April 1982):287–309.

―――. "Republicanism in Old and New Contexts." *WMQ* 43 (Jan. 1986):20–34.

Applewhaite, J.D. "Some Aspects of Society in Rural South Carolina in 1850." *North Carolina Historical Review* 29 (Jan. 1952):39–63.

Banner, James. "The Problem of South Carolina." In Stanley Elkins and Eric McKitrick, eds., *The Hofstader Aegis: A Memorial*. New York: Alfred A. Knopf, 1974.

Banning, Lance. "Jeffersonian Ideology Revisited: Liberal and Classical Ideas in the New American Republic." *WMQ* 43 (Jan. 1986):3–19.

Battalio, Raymond C., and John Kagel. "The Structure of Antebellum Southern Agriculture: South Carolina, A Case Study." *Agricultural History* 44 (Jan. 1970): 25–38.

Bellows, Barbara. "'Insanity Is the Disease of Civilization': The Founding of the South Carolina Lunatic Asylum." *South Carolina Historical Magazine (SCHM)* 82 (July 1981):263–72.

Bergeron, Paul H. "The Nullification Controversy Revisited." *Tennessee Historical Quarterly* 35 (Fall 1976), 263–75.

―――. "Tennessee's Response to the Nullification Crisis." *Journal of Southern History (JSH)* 39 (Feb. 1973):23–44.

Berlin, Ira. "White Majority: A Review Essay." *Social History* 5 (May 1977):653–60.

Bernstein, Barton. "Southern Politics and Attempts to Reopen the African Slave Trade." *Journal of Negro History* 51 (Jan. 1966):16–35.

Blanks, W.D. "Corrective Church Discipline in the Presbyterian Churches of the Nineteenth Century South." *Journal of Presbyterian History* 44 (June 1966):89–105.

Bode, Frederick A., and Donald E. Ginter. "A Critique of Landholding Variables in the 1860 Census and the Parker-Gallman Sample." *Journal of Interdisciplinary History* 15 (Autumn 1984):277–95.

Bonner, James C. "Profile of a Late Antebellum Community." *American Historical Review* 49 (July 1948):663–80.

Boucher, Chauncey S. "The Antebellum Attitude of South Carolina Towards Manufacturing and Agriculture." *Washington University Studies (WUS)* 3 (April 1916):243–70.

———. "Sectionalism, Representation, and the Electoral Question in Antebellum South Carolina." *WUS* 4 (Oct. 1916):3–62.

———. "The Secession and Cooperation Movements in South Carolina, 1848–1852," *WUS* 5 (April 1918):67–138.

———. "South Carolina and the South on the Eve of Secession, 1852 to 1860." *WUS* 6 (April 1919):81–144.

———. "The Annexation of Texas and the Bluffton Movement in South Carolina." *Mississippi Valley Historical Review* 6 (June 1919):3–33.

Breese, Donald H. "James L. Orr, Calhoun, and the Cooperationist Tradition in South Carolina." *SCHM* 80 (Oct. 1979):273–85.

Bridgeforth, Lucie Robertson. "Mississippi's Response to Nullification, 1833." *Journal of Mississippi History* 45 (Feb. 1983):1–22.

Brown, Richard D. "Modernization: A Victorian Climax." *American Quarterly* 27 (Dec. 1975):533–48.

Brown, Richard H. "The Missouri Crisis, Slavery, and the Politics of Jacksonianism." *South Atlantic Quarterly* 65 (Winter 1966):55–72.

Brown, Thomas. "Southern Whigs and the Politics of Statesmanship, 1833–1841." *JSH* 46 (Aug. 1980):361–80.

———. "The Southern Whigs and Economic Development." *Southern Studies* 20 (Spring 1981):20–38.

Butts, Donald C. "The 'Irrepressible Conflict': Slave Taxation and North Carolina's Gubernatorial Election of 1860." *North Carolina Historical Review* 58 (Winter 1981):44–66.

Campbell, Randolph B. "Planters and Plain Folk: Harrison County, Texas, as a Test Case, 1850–1860." *JSH* 40 (Aug. 1974):369–98.

Clark, Christopher. "The Household Economy, Market Exchange, and the Rise of Capitalism in the Connecticut Valley, 1800–1860." *Journal of Social History* 13 (Winter 1979):169–90.

Cobb, James C. "Making Sense of Southern Economic History." *Georgia Historical Quarterly* 71 (Spring 1987):53–74.

Coclanis, Peter A. "Rice Prices in the 1720s and the Evolution of the South Carolina Economy." *JSH* 48 (Nov. 1982):531–44.

———. "The Rise and Fall of the South Carolina Low Country: An Essay in Economic Interpretation." *Southern Studies* 24 (Summer 1985):143–66.

Coulter, E. Merton. "The Nullification Movement in Georgia." *Georgia Historical Quarterly* 5 (March 1921):4–39.

Davis, Mary Katherine. "The Featherbed Aristocracy: Abbeville District in the 1790s." *SCHM* 80 (April 1979):136–55.

Dawley, Allen, and Paul Faber. "Working-Class Culture and Politics in the Industrial Revolution: Sources of Loyalism and Rebellion." *Journal of Social History* 9 (Winter 1976):466–80.

DesChamps, Margaret B. "Antislavery Presbyterians in the Carolina Piedmont." *Proceedings of the South Carolina Historical Association* (1954):6–13.

Donald, David. "The Proslavery Argument Reconsidered." *JSH* 37 (Feb. 1971):3–18.

Easterlin, Richard A. "Regional Income Trends, 1840–1950." In Seymour Harris, ed., *American Economic History*. New York: McGraw-Hill, 1961.

Ellsworth, P.T. "The Dual Economy: A New Approach." *Economic Development and Cultural Change* 10 (July 1962):434–38.

Engerman, Stanley. "The Effects of Slavery upon the Southern Economy: A Review of the Recent Debate." *Explorations in Entrepreneurial History* 4 (Winter 1967):71–97.

———. "The Antebellum South: What Probably Was and What Should Have Been." *Agricultural History* 44 (Jan. 1970):127–42.

———. "Some Economic Factors in Southern Backwardness in the Nineteenth Century." In John F. Kain and John R. Meyer, eds., *Essays in Regional Economics*. Cambridge: Harvard Univ. Press, 1971.

———. "Some Considerations Relating to Property Rights in Man." *Journal of Economic History* 33 (March 1973):43–65.

Epting, Carl. "Inland Navigation in South Carolina and Traffic on the Columbia Canal." *Proceedings of the South Carolina Historical Association* (1936):18–23.

Faust, Drew. "A Southern Stewardship: The Intellectual and the Pro-slavery Argument." *American Quarterly* 3 (Spring 1979):63–80.

———. "The Rhetoric and Ritual of Agriculture in Antebellum South Carolina." *JSH* 45 (Nov. 1979):541–68.

Fehrenbacher, Don E. "The New Political History and the Coming of the Civil War." *Pacific Historical Review* 54 (May 1985):117–42.

Fishlow, Albert. "Antebellum Interregional Trade Reconsidered." *American Economic Review (AER)* 54 (May 1964):352–64.

Flesig, Haywood. "Slavery, the Supply of Agricultural Labor, and the Industrialization of the South." *Journal of Economic History* 36 (Sept. 1976):572–97.

Fogel, Robert. "Discussion." *AER* 54 (May 1969):377–89.

Fogel, Robert W., and Stanley L. Engerman. "Explaining the Relative Efficiency of Slave Agriculture in the Antebellum South." *AER* 67 (June 1977):275–96.

———. "Explaining the Relative Efficiency of Slave Agriculture in the Antebellum South: A Reply." *AER* 70 (Sept. 1980):672–90.

Folsom, Burton W. "Party Formation and Development in Jacksonian America: The Old South." *Journal of American Studies* 7 (Dec. 1973):217–29.

Foner, Eric. "Politics, Ideology, and the Origins of the American Civil War." In George M. Frederickson, ed., *A Nation Divided: Essays on the Civil War and Reconstruction*. Minneapolis: Burgess Publishing, 1975.

Ford, Lacy K. "Rednecks and Merchants: Economic Development and Social Tensions in the South Carolina Upcountry, 1865–1900." *Journal of American History* 71 (Sept. 1984):294–318.

———. "Republican Ideology in a Slave Society: The Political Economy of John C. Calhoun." *JSH* (forthcoming).

————. "Self-Sufficiency, Cotton, and Economic Development in the South Carolina Upcountry, 1800–1860." *Journal of Economic History* 45 (June 1985):261–67.

————. "Yeoman Farmers in the South Carolina Upcountry: Changing Production Patterns in the Late Antebellum Period." *Agricultural History* 60 (Fall 1986):17–37.

Formisano, Ronald P. "Deferential-Participant Politics: The Early Republic's Political Culture, 1789–1840." *American Political Science Review* 68 (June 1974): 473–87.

————. "Toward a Reorientation of Jacksonian Politics: A Review of the Literature, 1959–1975." *Journal of American History* 63 (June 1976):42–65.

Fox-Genovese, Elizabeth. "Antebellum Southern Households: A New Perspective on a Familiar Question." *Review* 7 (Fall 1983):215–53.

Frank, Andre Gunder. "Economic Dependence, Class Structure, and Underdevelopment Policy." In James Cockroft, Andre Gunder Frank, and Dale L. Johnson, eds., *Dependence and Underdevelopment: Latin America's Political Economy.* New York: Doubleday, 1972.

Fredrickson, George M. "Masters and Mudsills: The Role of Race in the Planter Ideology of South Carolina." *South Atlantic Urban Studies* 2 (1978):34–48.

Friedman, Harriet. "Household Production and the National Economy: Concepts for the Analysis of Agrarian Functions." *Journal of Peasant Studies* 7 (Jan. 1980): 158–64.

Gallman, Robert E. "Gross National Product in the United States, 1834–1909." In *Studies in Income and Wealth.* Vol. 30. New York: Columbia Univ. Press, 1966.

————. "Self Sufficiency in the Cotton Economy of the Antebellum South." *Agricultural History* 44 (Jan. 1970):5–23.

————. "Slavery and Southern Economic Growth." *Southern Economic Journal* 14 (April 1979):1007–22.

Garson, Robert A. "Proslavery as Political Theory: The Examples of John C. Calhoun and George Fitzhugh." *South Atlantic Quarterly* 84 (Spring 1985):197–212.

Genovese, Eugene D. "Livestock in the Slave Economy of the Old South—A Revised View." *Agricultural History* 36 (July 1962):143–149.

————. "Yeoman Farmers in a Slaveholders' Democracy." *Agricultural History* 49 (April 1975):331–42.

Genovese, Eugene D., and Elizabeth Fox-Genovese. "The Slave Economies in Political Perspective." *Journal of American History* 66 (June 1979):7–23.

————. "The Religious Ideals of Southern Slave Society." *Georgia Historical Quarterly* 70 (Spring 1986):1–16.

Goldfarb, Stephen J. "A Note on Limits to Growth of the Cotton-Textile Industry in the Old South." *JSH* 48 (Nov. 1982):545–58.

Goldin, Claudia, and Kenneth Sokoloff. "The Relative Productivity Hypothesis of Industrialism: The American Case, 1820–1850." *Quarterly Journal of Economics* 94 (Aug. 1984):461–87.

Graham, Richard. "Slavery and Economic Development: Brazil and the United States South in the Nineteenth Century." *Comparative Studies in Society and History* 23 (Oct. 1981):620–55.

Green, Fletcher M. "Cycles of American Democracy." *Mississippi Valley Historical Review* 48 (June 1961):3–23.

Greene, Jack P. "Changing Interpretations of Early American Politics." In Allen Billington, ed., *The Reinterpretation of Early American History: Essays in Honor of John E. Pomfret.* San Marino, Calif.: Huntington Library, 1966.

————. "'Slavery or Independence': Some Reflections on the Relationship among Liberty, Black Bondage, and Equality in Revolutionary South Carolina." *SCHM* 80 (July 1979):193–214.

Greenberg, Kenneth S. "Representation and the Isolation of South Carolina, 1776–1860." *Journal of American History* 64 (Dec. 1977):723–43.

Griffin, Richard W. "Poor White Laborers in Southern Cotton Factories, 1789–1865." *SCHM* 41 (Jan. 1960):26–40.

Grinde, Donald A., Jr. "Building the South Carolina Railroad." *SCHM* 77 (April 1976):84–96.

Gunderson, Gerald. "Southern Antebellum Income Reconsidered." *Explorations in Economic History* 10 (Winter 1973):151–76.

Harp, Gillis J. "Taylor, Calhoun, and the Decline of a Theory of Political Disharmony." *Journal of the History of Ideas* 46 (Jan. 1985):107–20.

Harris, J. William. "Last of the Classical Republicans: An Interpretation of John C. Calhoun." *Civil War History* 30 (Sep. 1984):255–67.

Henretta, James. "Families and Farms: *Mentalité* in Pre-industrial America." *WMQ*, Third Series, 35 (Jan. 1978):3–33.

Higgins, Benjamin. "The 'Dualistic Theory' of Underdeveloped Areas." *Economic Development and Cultural Change* 4 (Jan. 1956):99–115.

Hollis, Daniel W. "James H. Thornwell and the South Carolina College." *Proceedings of the South Carolina Historical Association* (1953):17–36.

————. "Costly Delusion: Inland Navigation in the South Carolina Piedmont." *Proceedings of the South Carolina Historical Association* (1968):29–44.

Houekek, John T., and Charles F. Heller, Jr. "Searching for Nineteenth Century Farm Tenants: An Evaluation of Methods." *Historical Methods* 19 (Spring 1986): 55–61.

Howe, Daniel Walker. "American Victorianism as a Culture." *American Quarterly* 27 (Dec. 1975):507–32.

————. "European Sources of Political Ideas in Jeffersonian America." In Stanley I. Kutler and Stanley N. Katz, eds., *The Promise of American History: Progress and Prospects.* Baltimore: Johns Hopkins Univ. Press, 1982.

Hymer, Stephen, and Stephen Resnick. "A Model of an Agrarian Economy with Non-agricultural Activities." *American Historical Review* 59 (Sep. 1969):493–506.

Inscoe, John C. "Mountain Masters: Slaveholding in Western North Carolina." *North Carolina Historical Review* 61 (April 1984):143–73.

Jeffrey, Thomas E. "National Issues, Local Interests, and the Transformation of Antebellum North Carolina Politics." *JSH* 50 (Feb. 1984):43–74.

Johnson, Michael P. "Planters and Patriarchy: Charleston, 1800–1860." *JSH* 46 (Feb. 1980):45–72.

Jones, Lewis, P. "William Elliott: South Carolina Non-conformist." *JSH* 17 (Aug. 1951):361–81.

Jordan, Laylon Wayne. "Education for Community: C.G. Memminger and the Organization of Common Schools in Antebellum Charleston." *SCHM* 83 (April 1982):99–115.

Jorgenson, Dale W. "The Development of Dual Economy." *Economic Journal* 71 (June, 1961):309–34.

King, J. Crawford. "The Closing of the Southern Range: An Exploratory Study." *JSH* 48 (Feb. 1982):53–70.

Klein, Rachel. "Ordering the Backcountry: The South Carolina Regulation." *WMQ* 38 (Oct. 1981):661–80.

Kunreuther, Howard, and Gavin Wright. "Safety-First, Gambling, and the Subsistence Farmer." In James A. Roumasset et al., eds., *Risk, Uncertainty, and Agricultural Development*. New York: Agricultural Development Council, 1979), 213–30.

Lander, Ernest M. "Slave Labor in South Carolina Cotton Mills." *Journal of Negro History* 38 (April 1953):161–73.

———. "The Iron Industry in Antebellum South Carolina." *JSH* 20 (Aug. 1954): 337–55.

———. "The Calhoun-Preston Feud, 1836–1842." *SCHM* 59 (Jan. 1958):24–37.

———. "Charleston: Manufacturing Center of the Old South." *JSH* 26 (Aug. 1960):330–51.

Latner, Richard B. "The Nullification Crisis and Republican Subversion." *JSH* 43 (Feb. 1977):19–38.

Linden, Fabian. "Economic Democracy in the Slave South: An Appraisal of Some Recent Views." *Journal of Negro History* 31 (April 1846):140–89.

Lindstrom, Diane. "Southern Dependence upon Interregional Grain Supplies: A Review of the Trade Flows, 1840–1860." *Agricultural History* 44 (Jan. 1970):101–13.

Lord, C.W. "Young Louis Wigfall." *SCHM* 59 (1958):96–112.

Maddex, Jack P., Jr. "Proslavery Millennialism: Social Eschatology in Antebellum Southern Calvinism." *American Quarterly* 3 (Spring 1979):46–62.

Maier, Pauline. "The Road Not Taken: Nullification, John C. Calhoun, and the Revolutionary Tradition in South Carolina." *SCHM* 82 (Jan. 1981):1–19.

Marmar, Theodore R. "Anti-industrialism and the Old South: The Agrarian Perspective of John C. Calhoun." *Comparative Studies in Society and History* 9 (1967):377–406.

Marshall, Lynn L. "The Strange Still-birth of the Whig Party." *American Historical Review* 72 (Jan. 1967):445–68.

Martin, Thomas P. "The Advent of William Gregg and the Graniteville Company." *JSH* 11 (Aug. 1945):389–423.

Mathews, Donald G. "The Second Great Awakening as an Organizing Process, 1780–1830." *American Quarterly* 21 (Spring 1969):23–43.

Mathis, Robert Neil. "Preston Smith Brooks: The Man and His Image." *SCHM* 17 (Dec. 1978):196–210.

McCormick, Richard P. "New Perspectives on Jacksonian Politics." *American Historical Review* 65 (Jan. 1960):288–301.

McDonald, Forrest, and Grady McWhiney. "The Antebellum Southern Herdsman: A Reinterpretation." *JSH* 41 (May 1975):147–66.

McElligott, Caroll Ainsworth. "Maverick South Carolinian." *Carologue* (May-June 1986):1–9.

McGuire, Robert, and Robert Higgs. "Cotton, Corn, and Risk in the Nineteenth Century: A Reply." *Explorations in Economic History* 14 (April 1977):183–85.

Mendenhall, Marjorie S. "The Rise of Southern Tenancy." *Yale Review* 27 (Sep. 1937):110–29.

Menius, Arthur C., III. "James Bennitt: Portrait of an Antebellum Yeoman." *North Carolina Historical Review* 58 (Autumn 1981):305–26.

Merrill, Michael. "Cash Is Good to Eat: Self-Sufficiency and Exchange in the Rural Economy of the United States." *Radical History Review* 3 (Winter 1977):42–71.

Mohl, Raymond A. "'The Grand Fabric of Republicanism': A Scotsman Describes South Carolina." *SCHM* 71 (July 1970):170–88.

Morgan, David T., Jr. "The Great Awakening in South Carolina." *South Atlantic Quarterly* 70 (Autumn 1971):595–606.

Mulkey, Floyd. "Reverend Philip Mulkey, Pioneer Baptist Preacher in Upper South Carolina." *Proceedings of the South Carolina Historical Association* (1945): 3–12.

Oakes, James. "The Politics of Economic Development in the Antebellum South." *Journal of Interdisciplinary History* 15 (Aug. 1984):305–16.

———. "From Republicanism to Liberalism: Ideological Change and the Crisis of the Old South." *American Quarterly* 37 (Fall 1985):551–71.

Ochenkowski, J.P. "The Origins of Nullification in South Carolina." *SCHM* 83 (April 1982):121–53.

Otto, John Solomon. "Slaveholding General Farmers in a 'Cotton' County," *Agricultural History* 55 (April 1981):167–78.

Owsley, Frank L., and Harriet C. Owsley. "The Economic Basis of Society in the Late Ante-bellum South." *JSH* 6 (Feb. 1940):24–45.

Parker, William. "The South in the National Economy, 1865–1970." *Southern Economic Journal* 46 (April 1980):1019–48.

Patton, James Welch. "John Belton O'Neall." *The Proceedings of the South Carolina Historical Association* (1934):3–13.

Pease, Jane H., and Pease, William. "The Economics and Politics of Charleston's Nullification Crisis." *JSH* 47 (Nov. 1981):335–62.

Pessen, Edward. "How Different from Each Other Were the Antebellum North and South?" *American Historical Review* 85 (Dec. 1980):1119–49.

Phifer, Edward. "Slavery in Microcosm: Burke County, North Carolina." *JSH* 28 (May 1962):137–65.

Phillips, U.B. "The Origins and Growth of the Southern Black Belts." *American Historical Review* 11 (July 1906):798–816.

———. "The South Carolina Federalists. Part I and Part II." *American Historical Review* 14 (April and July 1909):529–43, 731–790.

Pocock, J.G.A. "Machiavelli, Harrington, and English Political Ideologies in the Eighteenth Century." *WMQ* 26 (October 1965):549–83.

———. "Virtue and Commerce in the Eighteenth Century." *Journal of Interdisciplinary History* 3 (Summer 1972):119–34.

Pruitt, Bettye Hobbs. "Self-Sufficiency and the Agricultural Economy of the Eighteenth Century Massachusetts." *WMQ* 41 (July 1984):333–64.

Reid, Joseph O. "Antebellum Share Rental Contracts." *Explorations in Economic History* 13 (Jan. 1976):69–84.

Richards, Miles S. "Pierce Mason Butler: The South Carolina Years, 1830–1841." *SCHM* 87 (Jan. 1986):14–29.

Rogers, George C., Jr. "South Carolina Federalists and the Origins of the Nullification Movement." *SCHM* 71 (Jan. 1970):17–32.

———. "Henry Laurens Pinckney—Thoughts on His Career." In James B. Meriwether, ed., *South Carolina Journals and Journalists*. Spartanburg: The Reprint Company, 1975.

Rogers, Tommy W. "The Great Population Exodus from South Carolina, 1850–1860." *SCHM* 68 (Jan. 1967):14–22.

Rothenberg, Winifred. "The Market and Massachusetts Farmers, 1750–1855." *Journal of Economic History* 41 (June 1981):283–314.

————. "The Market and Massachusetts Farmers: A Reply." *Journal of Economic History* 43 (June 1983):479–80.

Rothstein, Morton. "The Antebellum South as a Dual Economy: A Tentative Hypothesis." *Agricultural History* 41 (Oct. 1967):373–82.

Rubin, Julius. "Urban Growth and Regional Development." In David T. Gilchrist, ed., *The Growth of Seaport Cities*. Charlottesville: Univ. Press of Virginia, 1967.

————. "The Limits of Agricultural Progress in the Nineteenth Century South." *Agricultural History* 49 (April 1975):362–73.

Rumble, John W. "A Carolina Country Squire in the Old South and the New: The Papers of James F. Sloan." *South Atlantic Quarterly* 81 (Summer 1982):323–37.

Schaefer, Donald F. "Yeoman Farmers and Economic Democracy: A Study of Wealth and Economic Mobility in the Western Tobacco Region, 1850–1860." *Explorations in Economic History* 15 (Oct. 1978):421–37.

————. "The Effect of the 1859 Crop Year upon Relative Productivity in the Antebellum Cotton South." *Journal of Economic History* 43 (Dec. 1983):851–65.

Schaper, William A. "Sectionalism and Representation in South Carolina." In the *Annual Report of the American Historical Association for the Year 1900*. Washington: Government Printing Office, 1901.

Sellers, Charles G., Jr. "Who Were the Southern Whigs?" *American Historical Review* 59 (Jan. 1954):335–46.

Shalhope, Robert E. "Toward a Republican Synthesis." *WMQ* 29 (Jan. 1972):49–80.

————. "Thomas Jefferson's Republicanism and Antebellum Southern Thought." *JSH* 12 (Nov. 1976):529–57.

————. "Republicanism and Early American Historiography." *WMQ* 39 (April 1982):334–56.

Sharp, James Roger. *The Jacksonians versus the Banks: Politics in the States after the Panic of 1837*. New York: Columbia Univ. Press, 1970.

Sharrar, G. Terry. "The Indigo Bonanza in South Carolina, 1740–1790." *Technology and Culture* 12 (July 1971):447–55.

Siegel, Fred. "The Paternalist Thesis: Virginia as a Test Case." *Civil War History* 25 (Sep. 1979):246–61.

Skeen, C. Edward. "Calhoun, Crawford, and the Politics of Retrenchment." *SCHM* 73 (July 1972):141–55.

Stampp, Kenneth M. "The Concept of a Perpetual Union." *Journal of American History* 65 (June 1978):5–33.

Stewart, James Brewer. "'A Great Talking and Eating Machine': Patriarchy, Mobilization and the Dynamics of Nullification in South Carolina." *Civil War History* 37 (Sep. 1981):197–220.

Stokes, Durwood T. "The Presbyterian Clergy in South Carolina and the American Revolution." *SCHM* 71 (Oct. 1970):270–82.

————. "The Baptist and Methodist Clergy in South Carolina and the American Revolution." *SCHM* 73 (April 1973):87–96.

Stoney, Samuel Gaillard, ed. "The Poinsett-Campbell Correspondence." *SCHM* 42 (Oct. 1941):149–68.

————., ed. "Memoirs of Frederick A. Porcher." *SCHM* 46 (July 1945):141–42.

Takaki, Ronald. "The Movement to Reopen the African Slave Trade in South Carolina." *SCHM* 66 (Jan. 1965):38–54.

Taylor, R.W. "Commercial Fertilizers in South Carolina." *South Atlantic Quarterly* 29 (April 1930):179–89.

Temin, Peter. "The Causes of Cotton Price Fluctuations in the 1830's." *Review of Economics and Statistics* 49 (Nov. 1967):463–70.

Temperly, Howard. "Capitalism, Slavery, and Ideology." *Past and Present* 75 (May 1977):94–118.

Terrill, Tom E. "Eager Hands: Labor for Southern Textiles, 1850–1860." *Journal of Economic History* 36 (March 1976):84–99.

Vickery, Kenneth. "*Herrenvolk* Democracy and Egalitarianism in South Africa and the United States South." *Comparative Studies in Society and History* 16 (Jan. 1974):309–28.

Wakelyn, Jon L. "Party Issues and Political Strategy of the Charleston Taylor Democrats of 1848." *SCHM* 17 (April 1972):72–86.

Wallace, Michael. "Changing Concepts of Party in the United States: New York, 1815–1828." *American Historical Review* 74 (Dec. 1968):453–91.

Wallenstein, Peter. "From Slave South to New South: Taxes and Spending in Georgia from 1850 through Reconstruction." *Journal of Economic History* 36 (March 1976):287–90.

———. "'More Unequally Taxed than Any People in the Civilized World': The Origins of Georgia's Ad Valorem Tax System." *Georgia Historical Quarterly* 69 (Winter 1985):459–87.

Wallerstein, Immanuel. "The Rise and Future Demise of the World Capitalist System: Concepts for Comparative Analysis." *Comparative Studies in Science and History* 16 (Sep. 1974):387–415.

———. "American Slavery and the Capitalist World Economy." *American Journal of Sociology* 81 (March 1976):1119–1213.

Watson, Harry L. "Conflict and Collaboration: Yeomen, Slaveholders, and Politics in the Antebellum South." *Social History* 10 (Oct. 1985):273–98.

Wehmann, Howard H. "Noise, Novelties, and Nullifiers: A U.S. Navy Officer's Impressions of the Nullification Controversy." *SCHM* 76 (Jan. 1975):21–24.

Weir, Robert M. "'The Harmony We Were Famous For': An Interpretation of Pre-Revolutionary South Carolina Politics." *WMQ* 26 (Oct. 1969):473–501.

———. "The South Carolinian as Extremist." *South Atlantic Quarterly* (Dec. 1975):86–103.

Weiss, Rona S. "The Market and Massachusetts Farmers, 1750–1850: Comment." *Journal of Economic History* 43 (June 1983):475–78.

White, Laura A. "The National Democrats in South Carolina, 1852 to 1860." *South Atlantic Quarterly* 28 (Oct. 1929):370–89.

Wilentz, Sean. "On Class and Politics in Jacksonian America." In Stanley I. Kutler and Stanley N. Katz, eds., *The Promise of American History: Progress and Prospects*. Baltimore: Johns Hopkins Univ. Press, 1982, pp. 45–63.

Wiltse, Charles M. "John C. Calhoun: An Interpretation." *Proceedings of the South Carolina Historical Association* (1948):26–39.

Wilson, Major L. "'Liberty and Union': An Analysis of Three Concepts Involved in the Nullification Controversy." *JSH* 33 (Aug. 1967):331–55.

Woodman, Harold D. "Economic History and Economic Theory: The New Economic

History in America." *Journal of Interdisciplinary History* 3 (Autumn 1972): 323–50.

————. "New Perspectives on Southern Economic Development: A Comment." *Agricultural History* (April 1975):374–80.

————. "Global and Local Perspectives on Power, Politics, and Ideology." *Civil War History* 25 (Dec. 1979):339–51.

Wright, Gavin. "'Economic Democracy' and the Concentration of Agricultural Wealth in the Cotton South, 1850–1860." *Agricultural History* 44 (Jan. 1970):63–94.

————. "An Economic Study of Cotton Production and Trade, 1830–1860." *Review of Economics and Statistics* 53 (May 1971):111–20.

————. "Cotton Competition and the Post-bellum Recovery of the American South." *Journal of Economic History* (Sep. 1974):610–35.

————. "Cheap Labor and Southern Textiles, 1880–1930." *Quarterly Journal of Economics* 96 (Nov. 1981):605–29.

————. "The Efficiency of Slavery: Another Interpretation." *AER* 69 (March 1979):219–26.

Wright, Gavin, and Howard Kunreuther. "Cotton, Corn, and Risk in the Nineteenth Century." *Journal of Economic History* 35 (Sep. 1975):526–55.

————. "Cotton, Corn, and Risk in the Nineteenth Century: A Reply." *Explorations in Economic History* 14 (April 1977):183–85.

Theses and Dissertations

Allman, John Mitchell. "Yeoman Regions in the Antebellum Deep South: Settlement and Economy in Northern Alabama, 1815–1860." Ph.D. diss., Univ. of Maryland, 1979.

Bass, Robert D., ed. "The Autobiography of William J. Grayson." Ph.D. diss., Univ. of South Carolina, 1933.

Bell, Daniel J. "Interpretive Booklets for Local Historical Sites: Rose Hill State Park, Union, South Carolina as a Model." M.A. thesis, Univ. of South Carolina, 1983.

Brady, Patrick. "Political and Civil Life in South Carolina, 1787–1833." Ph.D. diss., Univ. of California at Santa Barbara, 1971.

Bridwell, Ronald Edward. "The South's Wealthiest Planter: Wade Hampton I of South Carolina, 1754–1833." Ph.D. diss., Univ. of South Carolina, 1980.

Brown, George Dewitt. "A History of the Blue Ridge Railroad, 1852–1874." M.A. thesis, Univ. of South Carolina, 1967.

Butts, Donald C. "A Challenge to Planter Rule: The Controversy over the Ad Valorem Taxation of Slaves in North Carolina, 1858–1862." Ph.D. diss., Duke Univ., 1978.

Clarke, James D. "Calhoun and the Concept of 'Reactionary Enlightenment': An Examination of the Disquisition on Government." Ph.D. diss., Univ. of Keele, 1982.

Collins, Frederick B. "Charleston and the Railroads: A Geographic Study of a South Atlantic Port and Its Strategies for Developing a Railroad System, 1820–1860." M.A. thesis, Univ. of South Carolina, 1977.

Coon, David L. "The Development of Market Agriculture in South Carolina, 1670–1785." Ph.D. diss., Univ. of Illinois, 1972.

Coussons, John Stanford. "Thirty Years with Calhoun, Rhett, and the Charleston Mercury: A Chapter in South Carolina Politics." Ph.D. diss., Louisiana State Univ., 1971.

Culler, Justin Bond. "John Taylor: Neglected South Carolinian." M.A. thesis, Univ. of South Carolina, 1970.

Cutler, E. Wayne. "William H. Crawford: A Contextual Biography." Ph.D. diss., Univ. of Texas, 1971.

Draughton, Ralph Brown, Jr. "The Political Transformation of William Lowndes Yancey." M.A. thesis, Univ. of North Carolina at Chapel Hill, 1963.

Edmunds, John Boyd, Jr. "Francis W. Pickens: A Political Biography." Ph.D. diss., Univ. of South Carolina, 1968.

Ellen, John Calhoun. "The Public Life of Richard Yeadon." M.A. thesis, Univ. of South Carolina, 1953.

Fletcher, Ralph Henry. "George McDuffie: Orator and Politician." M.A. thesis, Univ. of South Carolina, 1986.

Foust, James D. "The Yeoman Farmer in the Westward Expansion of U.S. Cotton Production." Ph.D. diss., Univ. of North Carolina at Chapel Hill, 1967.

Gettys, James Wylie. "Mobilization for Secession in Greenville District." M.A. thesis, Univ. of South Carolina, 1967.

Glenn, Virginia Louise. "James Hamilton, Jr., of South Carolina: A Biography." Ph.D. diss., Univ. of North Carolina at Chapel Hill, 1964.

Greenberg, Kenneth S. "The Second American Revolution: South Carolina Politics, Society, and Secession, 1776–1860." Ph.D. diss., Univ. of Wisconsin, 1976.

Herd, Elmer Don. "Chapters from the Life of a Southern Chevalier: Laurence Massilon Keitt's Congressional Years, 1853–1860." M.A. thesis, Univ. of South Carolina, 1958.

Kaplanoff, Mark D. "Making the South Solid: Politics and the Structure of Society in South Carolina, 1790–1815." Ph.D. diss., Univ. of Cambridge, 1979.

Kell, Carl Lewis. "A Rhetorical History of James Hamilton, Jr.: The Nullification Era in South Carolina." Ph.D. diss., Univ. of Kansas, 1971.

Klein, Rachel. "The Rise of the Planters in the South Carolina Backcountry, 1765–1808." Ph.D. diss., Yale Univ., 1979.

MacArthur, William Joseph. "Antebellum Politics in an Upcountry County: National, State, and Local Issues in Spartanburg County, South Carolina, 1850–1860." M.A. thesis, Univ. of South Carolina, 1966.

Mendenhall, Marjorie S. "A History of Agriculture in South Carolina 1790–1860: An Economic and Social Study." Ph.D. diss., Univ. of North Carolina, 1940.

Olsberg, Robert Nicholas. "A Government of Class and Race: William Henry Trescot and the South Carolina Chivalry, 1860–1865." Ph.D. diss., Univ. of South Carolina, 1972.

Putnam, Willie Frank. "An Analysis of Public Aid to Railroads in South Carolina, 1865–1906." M.A. thesis, Univ. of South Carolina, 1957.

Scafidel, Beverly R. "The Letters of William Elliott." Ph.D. diss., Univ. of South Carolina, 1978.

Sims, Edwin Thomas. "Joseph Starke Sims: A Nineteenth Century Upcountry Planter, Politician and Business Entrepreneur of South Carolina." M.A. thesis, Univ. of South Carolina, 1983.

Stokes, Allen H., Jr. "Black and White Labor and the Development of the Southern Textile Industry." Ph.D. diss., Univ. of South Carolina, 1977.

Strickland, John Scott. "Across Space and Time: Conversion, Community, and Cultural Change among South Carolina Slaves." Ph.D. diss., Univ. of North Carolina at Chapel Hill, 1985.

Tucker, Robert C. "James Henry Hammond: South Carolinian." Ph.D. diss., Univ. of North Carolina at Chapel Hill, 1958.

Weiman, David F. "Petty Commodity Production in the Cotton South: Upcountry Farmers in the Georgia Cotton Economy." Ph.D. diss., Stanford Univ., 1984.

Wild, Philip T. "South Carolina Politics, 1816–1833." Ph.D. diss., Univ. of Pennsylvania, 1949.

Index